MARKETING MANAGEMENT

MARKETING MANAGEMENT

SECOND EDITION

EDITORS

S MARX
A VAN DER WALT

AUTHORS

G J DE J CRONJE
H J DEKKER
C J JOOSTE
C L KOEKEMOER
M LEIBOLD
S MARX
A VAN DER WALT
D C VAN ROOYEN

CONTRIBUTORS

J W STRYDOM
J A R BOTHA

JUTA & CO, LTD

CAPE TOWN   WETTON   JOHANNESBURG

First published 1989
Reprinted 1990
Second Edition 1993

© Juta & Co, Ltd., 1989

Box 14373, Kenwyn 7790

ISBN 0 7021 2879 1

Printed on 70 g/m^2 Chambrill

Set, printed and bound in the Republic of South Africa by
Creda Press, Solan Road, Cape Town

PREFACE

This is the second edition of *Marketing Management*. The first edition was received particularly well by students, lecturers and marketing practitioners. In the light of the feedback received and other developments in the South African community, the following important changes were made in the second edition:

- The Market Environment (Chapter 3) was rewritten entirely, approached and illustrated on a regional basis.
- Every chapter was updated by the inclusion of the latest information and schools of thought.
- A chapter on Retail Marketing (Chapter 21) was added.
- One or more of the following was inserted at the end of every chapter:
    — Relevant practice-orientated questions and tasks
    — Brief case studies
    — Additional illustration of the chapter content with business reports and articles from newspapers, magazines and other sources.

The reason for the above was to lend force to the approach that marketing management can probably best be studied and practised by **useful** and **relevant** study material being made available — study material that can be **taught**, **studied** and **examined** and that is **scientifically based** and **practice-orientated**.

With a view to this, the content of the new edition was again compiled as succinctly and systematically as possible. The reader can become acquainted with *Marketing Management* quickly and without unnecessary effort.

Marketing Management's target market is still students and other persons who are formally studying marketing management for the first time. The book is aimed primarily at the under- and postgraduate training of students in marketing management. Practising marketers and experienced, well-trained marketing experts will also, however, find the book of use in their profession.

The structure of the book was left largely unchanged and consists of 21 chapters divided into four sections. Section 1 deals with the **bases of marketing**, in other words marketing in perspective. Section 2 discusses the **marketing environment**, emphasising environmental variables, the market environment, market segmentation, target market selection and product positioning, marketing information and research, and market gauging and forecasting.

Section 3 looks in detail at **marketing strategy** in terms of four decision-taking aspects: **product**, **distribution**, **marketing communication** and **price**. The theme of section 4 is **integrated marketing strategy**; the product life cycle, strategic marketing and specialised marketing areas are given attention. A chapter is also devoted to retail marketing.

The new edition of *Marketing Management* is again based on the extensive expertise of students and numerous colleagues in marketing. The following authors are gratefully acknowledged for their contributions and inputs:

Prof. Gerhard Cronje, University of South Africa (Chapter 2);

Dr Hennie Dekker, former professor at the University of Pretoria (Chapters 16 and 17);

Prof. Chris Jooste, Rand Afrikaans University (Chapters 15 and 20);

Prof. Ludi Koekemoer, Rand Afrikaans University (Chapters 12 and 13);

Prof. Marius Leibold, University of Stellenbosch (Chapters 5 and 6);

Prof. Sieg Marx, University of Pretoria (Chapters 7, 8 and 9 and parts of chapter 1);

Prof. Annamarie van der Walt, University of South Africa (Chapters 3, 4, 14, 18, 19 and 21 and parts of chapter 1);

Prof. Dirk van Rooyen, University of Pretoria (Chapters 10 and 11);

A special word of thanks to our co-workers Dr Johan Strydom and Johan Botha of the University of South Africa.

Profs S Marx
A van der Walt
PRETORIA
July 1992

CONTENTS

CHAPTER 3 *The market environment*

CHAPTER 6   *Market measurement and market forecasting*

PART 3

MARKETING STRATEGY: DECISION MAKING AREAS

CHAPTER 7   *The product*

CHAPTER 11 *Distribution management*

CHAPTER 12 *The marketing communication process*

CHAPTER 13 *Advertising*

CHAPTER 14 *Personal selling*

CHAPTER 15   *Sales promotion methods and publicity*

CHAPTER 16   *Price and price determination*

PART 4

INTEGRATED MARKETING

CHAPTER 18 *The product life cycle*

CHAPTER 19 *Strategic marketing*

CHAPTER 20   *Application areas of marketing*

CHAPTER 21   *Retail marketing*

CHAPTER 1

PERSPECTIVES ON MARKETING

1.1 INTRODUCTION

The objectives of this chapter are to provide an overview of marketing and to indicate how the marketing process developed from an initially simple bartering transaction between two people to a complicated process which must be carefully planned, organised, co-ordinated and controlled under the leadership of the marketing management team.

Throughout Chapter 1 references are made to topics which are more fully developed in other chapters of the book. Chapter 1 therefore serves as an introduction to topics which are later discussed in much more detail.

In the penultimate section of the chapter a definition of marketing management is given. This definition describes the marketing process and the nature of the strategic approach to marketing management on which this book is based.

ORGANISATION OF THE CHAPTER

The nature of marketing: How marketing originated, the gap theory, marketing activities, middlemen in the marketing process, product specialisation in marketing, macro and micro approaches to marketing.

The marketing function: The place of marketing in the enterprise, the marketing process.

Evolution of marketing thought: The phases in the development process, the marketing concept as managerial philosophy, the principles of the marketing concept, the value of the marketing concept.

The marketing management process: Definition of marketing, key words in the definition.

The model for the book: The contents of the different chapters and parts.

1.2 THE NATURE OF MARKETING

1.2.1 How marketing originated

Bartering between two people in direct contact with one another can be regarded as the simplest form of marketing. In this type of exchange the satisfaction of both parties can be ensured.

In primitive times people initially bartered basic necessities (especially food). This process later progressed to include other products, perhaps even manufactured items. One can just picture a man searching for something to offer in exchange for a handy tool (such as a sharpened stone), or a woman accepting a pretty sea shell necklace in exchange for a piece of meat. Perhaps even services were bartered. An old woman might have offered her services as a baby-sitter in exchange for food and shelter to keep her alive. It is important to realise that the exchange took place only if both parties were satisfied that the items they exchanged were more or less equal in value. Even today this principle guides the marketing process. The consumer desiring a specific product or service must be willing to offer something of more or less equal value in exchange.

The need for a universally acceptable medium of exchange arose as the bartering process became more complicated. A gap — created by differences in place, time, space and knowledge — developed between those who had things to barter and those who needed them. This gap could only be bridged by someone supplying additional services, such as information or transport. These additional services were supplied by 'middlemen' who had to be paid for their services in a medium acceptable to all parties. The middlemen were hawkers who used camels and donkeys to transport products for bartering. Hence such media of exchange as sea shells, gold coins, banknotes and the modern 'plastic money' (credit cards) served throughout the ages as methods of payment for intangible services delivered. The services offered by middlemen became increasingly important. Today wholesalers, retailers and agents act as middlemen between sellers and buyers to provide services to facilitate bartering in a sophisticated, highly developed economy.

The middleman plays a very important role in the development of the economy of a region or country, and also the evolution of society. In areas where primitive men are not inclined to barter products and services, and exist only to provide for their own basic needs and to ensure survival, there is no economic development and growth, and therefore little need for the services of middlemen. In modern society marketing plays a crucial role in economic development. One cannot imagine life without stores, products and services. We owe our pleasant life style and relatively high standard of living to marketing efforts, a fact which is often overlooked by critics of marketing.

Nobody is compelled to exchange his money for anything. Thus marketing does not force products on anybody; a consumer can decide for himself which products to purchase. The five conditions set by Kotler[1] for an exchange show clearly that there is no vestige of compulsion. These five conditions are as follows:

- At least two participants are always involved in the potential exchange transaction.

- Each participant owns something desired by the other participant.
- Participants must be able to conclude the transaction and to deliver.
- Participants are free to accept the offer or to reject it.
- Participants are eager to negotiate.

In modern society man's natural desire for new and pretty things plays a crucial role in economic development. Without this desire, stagnation and decline are inevitable. Successful trading usually results in economic development and growth in a country or area.

While it is true that marketing activities can provide a stimulus to economic growth, it is also an unfortunate fact that uncontrollable events can put a sudden end to it. This is exactly what happened in AD 79 in Pompeii. In one day a volcanic eruption ended all economic activity as well as the apparently sophisticated and pleasant life style enjoyed by Pompeians. Natural disasters aside, there are many other environmental factors which cannot be controlled but which can detrimentally influence the marketing process and which may even lead to the demise of enterprises. The negative (and sometimes positive) effects of environmental variables on the marketing process are discussed in Chapters 2 and 3.

From the preceding discussion it is clear that marketing originated in primitive times in the form of bartering transactions and that it eventually developed into a sophisticated exchange process, which is the driving force behind economic growth.

It is clear from these prerequisites that participants must be willing and even eager to conclude the transaction and that there is no evidence of force or coercion being applied.

The so-called gap between participants in the bartering transacion is subsequently described in more detail.

1.2.2 The gap theory

According to McInnis[2] a gap opened up between potential participants in a bartering transaction, brought about by differences, inter alia, in space, time and knowledge. For example, the participants may not be in direct contact with one another; one perhaps does not know of the existence of the other; or the products to be exchanged may not be ready for delivery when needed. A closer look at the different gap categories clearly indicates the marketing activities needed to bridge the gap between participants in the marketing process. In bartering one participant is usually the *producer* delivering need-satisfying products to potential consumers.

The five gap categories are as follows:

- **Space gap.** South African Breweries produces Castle beer mainly in the Transvaal but consumers are spread throughout South Africa.
- **Time gap.** Mealies are harvested in the Transvaal in winter while consumers want their mealie meal porridge throughout the year.

- **Information gap.** Consumers do not always know who the producer is and may not even be aware of certain need-satisfying products being offered. The producer may also not be fully aware of potential consumers or their needs.
- **Ownership gap.** When a new automobile is purchased the consumer becomes the owner only when it is registered in his name.
- **Value gap.** Sometimes one participant may find it easy to put an objective value on his offer (money) but the other may not be able to quantify exactly the value of the bartered item. If a consumer says the new automobile is 'expensive' he means that the need-satisfying properties of the product are less than those of the money he must tender in exchange. Before this gap can be closed the two participants must agree on an acceptable 'exchange rate'.

The activities needed to bridge the gaps on various levels are inter alia transportation (to bridge the space gap) and storage (to bridge the time gap). These activities are discussed in more detail in the following section.

1.2.3 Marketing activities

1.2.3.1 Different types of activities

Marx & Dekker[3] discuss the activities depicted in Figure 1.1.

FIGURE 1.1   Marketing activities

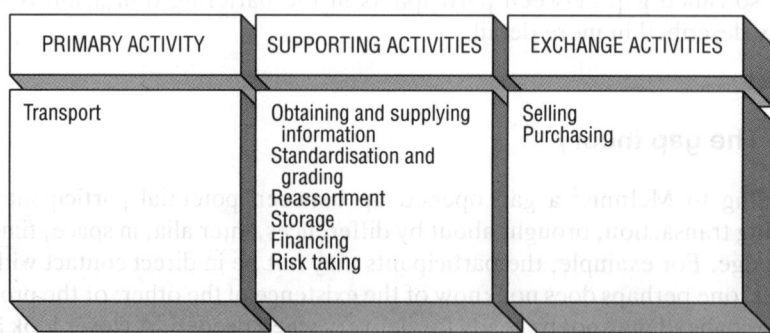

PRIMARY ACTIVITY	SUPPORTING ACTIVITIES	EXCHANGE ACTIVITIES
Transport	Obtaining and supplying information Standardisation and grading Reassortment Storage Financing Risk taking	Selling Purchasing

1.2.3.2 Transport

Transport is the primary activity in the transfer of products from the producer to the consumer. The buyer and the marketer are often geographically separated from one another, and place utility is then created by transporting the product. Virtually all transactions require some form of transport. A housewife, for example, is responsible for transporting her purchases from the store to her home.

The earliest methods of transport used in ancient bartering transactions were probably donkeys or camels. Today there are many different types of transport methods, such as rail, air and water transport as well as pipelines. The merits of the different methods of transport are discussed as an aspect of physical distribution in Chapter 11.

1.2.3.3 *The auxiliary activities*

Six activities, namely the obtaining and supplying of information, standardisation, reassortment, storage, financing and the carrying of risk, are regarded as auxiliary activities in the transfer of products from the producer to the consumer. These activities are auxiliary in the sense that not all of them need to be performed in the marketing of all products. However, when a particular auxiliary activity is applicable, it facilitates the transfer of products from the producer to the consumer.

Obtaining and supplying information

Before products can be transported from the producer to the consumer, it is necessary for the producer to possess information concerning the consumer and to inform the consumer of the availability of the product.

The producer has to know, inter alia:

- how many consumers there are for his product;
- what products the consumers need;
- where the consumers want to buy the products;
- when the consumers want to buy the products;
- why the consumers want to buy the products;
- how the consumers want to buy the products;
- who will be buying the products; and
- what the available income of the consumers is.

Marketing research (see Chapter 5) is usually undertaken to supply answers to these and other questions for marketing decision-making.

Furthermore, the marketer has to inform the consumer about the available products. This information can be supplied to the consumer via television and radio commercials, and advertisements in periodicals, newspapers and brochures. Information can also be supplied by sales representatives. The provision of information to the consumer by means of advertising and sales representatives is discussed in greater detail later.

Standardisation and grading

Standardisation pertains to the determination or acceptance, by a group of enterprises or by the authorities, of specific dimensions or norms (standards) to which products have to conform or according to which they are assessed. Standardisation of manufactured products is discussed in Chapter 7. In this section only the standardisation of agricultural products is considered.

The quality of a particular agricultural product can vary from farmer to farmer, from time to time and from region to region. It is also possible that a farmer can produce varying qualities of the same agricultural product during one harvest. A uniform product is, however, needed by processors for their production requirements and demanded by final consumers.

Standardisation of agricultural products is the establishment of specifications, usually a highest or a lowest standard, of the quality and/or other attributes with which a product has to comply in order to qualify for a specific grade. *Grading is the activity whereby products are sorted into grades according to particular specifications (standards).*

Standardisation and grading are both examples of methods which can be used to bridge the *value gap* between two participants in a transaction.

Grading of meat

The housewife knows the difference between SUPER beef and Grade 3. She expects SUPER beef to be of better quality and is therefore prepared to pay more per kilogram for it.

Reassortment

Reassortment or rearrangement of products is necessary because the product quantities and varieties offered by producers differ from those required by consumers. The product quantities and kinds (the assortment) have to be reassorted in a way that will satisfy consumers' specific needs.

Two types of reassortment can be distinguished, namely accumulative reassortment and distributive reassortment. The general wholesaler (a wholesaler typically markets only to retailers and not directly to final consumers) accumulates a wide selection of products in different quantities from a variety of producers. The wholesaler perhaps also distributes other assortments to many other retailers. The producer is usually only involved in distributing the product(s) which he markets. The consumer normally accumulates products and is not concerned with their distribution.

In reassortment emphasis can be placed either on accumulation or distribution or both.

- **Accumulative reassortment** takes place when a large number of producers, manufacturing on a small scale, supply a small number of big buyers.
- **Distributive reassortment** occurs when a product is supplied by one or a small number of producers and is then bought by a large number of buyers.
- Both **accumulative and distributive reassortment** take place if a large number of producers and a large number of purchasers of a product exist.

Storage

In transferring products from the producer to the consumer it is often necessary to store the products temporarily. Storage is that marketing activity which more than any other serves to bridge the **time gap** and so to provide the consumer with time utility.

The following are reasons for storage:

- First, the demand for some products and the production of others are **unstable.** If this is the case then storage facilitates a smooth flow of production. For example, the demand for jewellery is higher at Christmas than during the rest of the year; the production of jewellery, however, takes place throughout the course of the year. The demand for agricultural products is usually steady during the year, but production is largely seasonal. In both examples the demand for and the supply of products are better correlated because of the advantages offered by storage. The equilibrium of supply and demand also contributes to more equable prices.
- Secondly, factories store raw materials to **protect** themselves against inter alia acts of God and strikes that can disrupt the supply of raw materials.
- Thirdly, factories that are situated far from the consumer market have to store products in the form of **safety stocks.** Various factors can cause delays in the delivery of stocks.
- Fourthly, some products — such as tobacco, wine and certain kinds of meat — are often stored to improve their **quality.** Storage of this kind, however, is more a production than a marketing activity.

Financing

The process of transferring the goods from the producer to the consumer has to be **financed.**

Example of financing a retail transaction

Suppose a retailer borrows R1 000 from his bank at 15 per cent per annum interest on 1 September to pay for products bought from a wholesaler. The retailer sells the products on 30 September for R1 200 and on the same day pays back the loan plus interest of R12,50 to the bank. The bank financed the retailer with R1 000 for one month and thus the retailer's financing cost is R12,50.

The retailer could have financed his purchase himself, but the financing costs would then have been equal to the interest he could have earned on an investment elsewhere — the so-called **opportunity cost.**

Obviously all the parties involved in transferring products attempt to keep financing costs as low as possible.

Risk taking

In all the stages of transferring products the owner is exposed to risk of loss due to the following risk sources:

- **Economic risks** originate from changes in the demand for or supply of a certain product. These changes in demand and supply usually influence the price of the product and the sales volume.
- **Physical risks** are brought about by natural causes, such as fire, earthquakes, lightning, storms, rodent and locust plagues.
- **Human risks** have their origin in the dishonesty or negligence of man, such as theft, indifference or absent-mindedness.

The enterprise can transfer certain physical and human risks, but not economic risks, at a price (premium) to others (insurance companies). Good management can probably reduce the economic risks, but they cannot be entirely eliminated or transferred to others.

1.2.3.4 *Exchange activities*

After the auxiliary activities have been performed the product must be placed in the possession of the consumer to bridge the **ownership gap**. Possession utility is obtained by the conclusion of a sales transaction by the marketer and a buying transaction by the buyer. These exchange activities are now discussed.

Selling

The selling activity of the marketer consists of product planning, negotiation and the drawing up of a contractual agreement.

- **Product planning** means that the marketer consciously plans to offer a product to satisfy the consumer's needs. This product has to be available in the right quantities, at the right place and time, and at the right price. The product is the focal point of all marketing activities.
- **Negotiations** have to be entered into by the marketer and the buyer to reach agreement on quantities, quality, price, delivery dates, methods of transport, risks and the form of payment for the product.
- The **contractual agreement** concludes the sales transaction and brings about the transfer of title to the buyer who obtains possession utility.

Buying

From the buyer's viewpoint the buying activity is the mirror image of the selling activity and also includes product planning, negotiation and the contractual agreement.

The consumer's product planning centres on the assortment of products he requires for need satisfaction, while the assortment dealers offer for resale must provide their customers with need satisfaction.

1.2.3.5 *Summary*

The most important characteristics of the marketing activities thus far discussed are that they:

- must be performed;
- can be divided; and
- can be shifted.

These activities are performed by intermediaries such as wholesalers and retailers. Most of the marketing activities can be divided between these institutions. The producer, for example, transports the finished product from the factory to the wholesaler, while the wholesaler arranges transport to the retailer. The responsibility for many of the marketing activities can be shifted from one institution to another. Whatever the situation, the main thing to keep in mind is that somebody must take the responsibility for and perform these marketing activities.

1.2.4 Intermediaries in the marketing process

The transfer of title to products from the seller to the buyer is facilitated by a variety of intermediaries carrying out some or all of the marketing activities necessary to bridge the gap between buyer and seller.

Three groups of intermediaries can be identified, namely middlemen, sales intermediaries and auxiliary enterprises.

- **Middlemen** are enterprises directly involved in the transfer of title from the producer to the consumer. These middlemen take title to products and are thus concerned with buying and selling. Wholesalers and retailers are probably the most important groups of middlemen.
- **Sales intermediaries** are enterprises which are also directly involved in the transfer of title from the producer to the consumer. These sales intermediaries, however, do not take title to the products themselves and do not sell on their own account. The best-known examples of sales intermediaries are manufacturer's agents, sales agents and brokers.
- **Auxiliary enterprises** are those which contribute to the transfer of title from the producer to the consumer, but which are not actively engaged in this transfer of title. Examples are private hauliers, advertising practitioners, public warehouses, commercial banks and insurance companies.

A discussion of all such enterprises found in the Republic of South Africa would be tantamount to a discussion of South Africa's economic system. Attention will therefore be given only to middlemen and sales intermediaries. In this text the word 'intermediaries' refers to middlemen and sales intermediaries, and excludes auxiliary enterprises.

Because intermediaries are concerned mainly with distribution tasks, the different kinds of intermediaries are discussed in Chapter 10 on distribution channel decisions.

Intermediaries create a distribution channel between the producer and the consumer. A typical, simple distribution channel for consumer products appears in Figure 1.2.

FIGURE 1.2   A typical distribution channel for consumer products

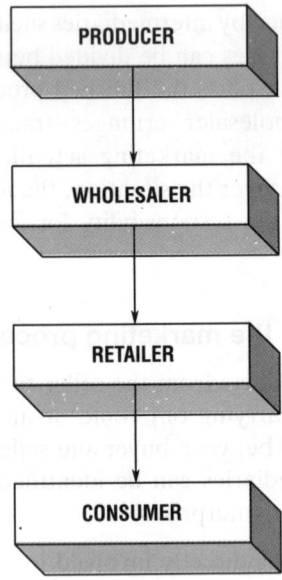

It is of course possible for a producer to bypass the wholesaler and the retailer and to sell directly to the consumer. In such a situation the producer will obviously be solely responsible for all the marketing activities.

1.2.5 Product specialisation in marketing

It has now become clear that there are many different products and different ways of marketing them. Marketing activities and the involvement of specialist intermediaries are determined by, and differ as a result of the nature of a specific product.

Examples of product specialisation

Irwin & Johnson specialises in the handling of frozen perishable food products. The marketing of these products obviously differs drastically from marketing preserved tinned food and even more drastically from marketing iron products from Iscor.

There are four main types of products, namely:

- mining products
- agricultural products
- consumer products
- industrial products.

In this book the emphasis is on the marketing of consumer products (services included). The marketing theory pertaining to consumer products also applies to a greater or lesser extent to the marketing of other products. In Chapter 20 the attributes of agricultural products and industrial products and the unique marketing methods used in marketing these products are discussed in some detail.

1.2.6 The macro and micro approaches to marketing

Up to this point a **macro approach to marketing** has been adopted. The attention has been focused mainly on marketing as a social and economic process whereby consumer needs are satisfied by means of an exchange between the producer and the consumer. The activities involved in bridging the gap between participants (the producer on one side and the consumer on the other) have been explained. It has become apparent that different intermediaries are responsible for performing different marketing activities and that different products need to be marketed in different ways. The marketing activities facilitating the flow of products, services, money and information between producers and consumers have been reviewed at national level from a mainly macro viewpoint. When intermediaries perform the marketing activities in a satisfactory way the gap between producer and consumer is bridged to the advantage of all parties concerned. In contrast to the macro approach at national level, the individual enterprise is the focal point of the micro approach.

In this book the emphasis falls on the **micro approach to marketing** in which marketing is regarded as the task of the individual enterprise striving to attain profit maximisation in a free-market system. Providing consumer satisfaction is a prerequisite for attaining profit maximisation. The macro approach is, however, still relevant. Even though the marketing function is viewed from another vantage point the marketing activities must still be performed and the enterprise must still work with other institutions to direct the flow of products from the producer to the consumer.

FIGURE 1.3   Approaches to marketing

Macro approach. Refers to the marketing activities which must be performed and the intermediaries concerned with the transfer of many types of products and services to a country-wide dispersion of consumers.

Micro approach. Refers to the management of marketing tasks and decisions which must be taken (in a profit-seeking enterprise) to ensure profitable marketing of the enterprise's products.

1.3 THE MARKETING FUNCTION IN THE ENTERPRISE

1.3.1 The place of marketing management

It is important to place the marketing function in the profit-seeking enterprise in the correct perspective. Marketing can be regarded as one of the key functions because of its inputs for top management decision making and its crucial contribution to maximising profitability.

Seven functional departments can usually be distinguished in a large enterprise. The managers heading these departments must work together as a team to ensure the success of the enterprise in the market. The typical functional organisational structure is depicted in Figure 1.4.

FIGURE 1.4   A functional organisational structure

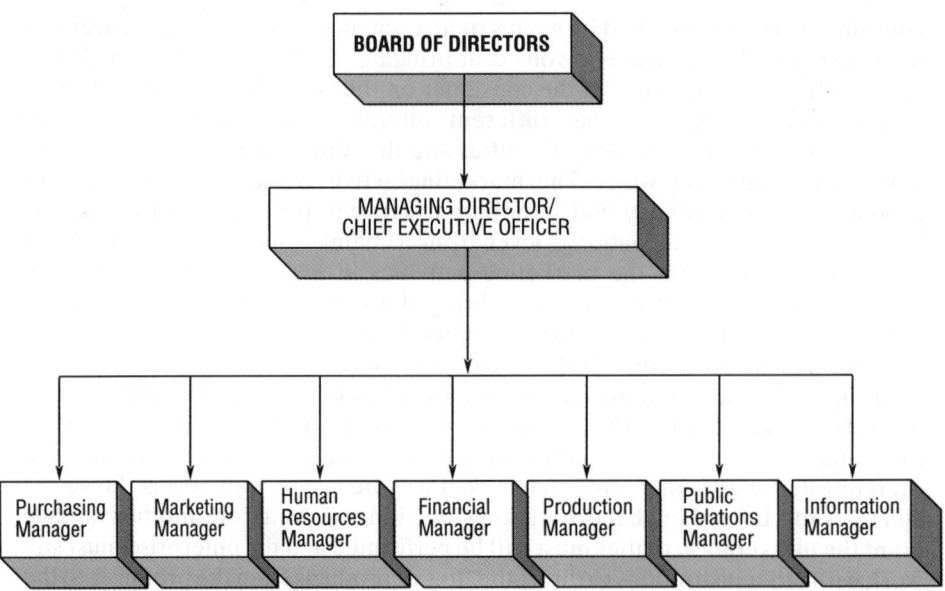

Marx & Dekker[4] *describe these functions as follows:*

- The **production function** comprises the physical exploitation of raw materials and their conversion into manufactured materials and finished products.
- The **personnel function** (human resources management) pertains to the acquisition, training, utilisation and retaining of a sufficient number of competent personnel.
- The **financial function** includes the acquisition, utilisation and control of the funds necessary for running the enterprise. The main activities here are the acquisition and application of funds for the profitability, liquidity, solvency and continuity of the enterprise.

- The **purchasing function** ensures that the materials necessary for production are bought at the right places, at the right times, in the right quantities and at the right prices.
- The **public relations function** maintains and cultivates a favourable and objective image of the enterprise among those whose opinion is important to the achievement of the business objectives.
- The **information function** makes available internal information for planning and control.
- The **marketing function** generates income from sales and is responsible for managing the marketing process.
- **General management** includes the activities of persons in managerial positions. These persons in top, middle and lower management have to plan for, organise, co-ordinate and control the enterprise as a whole as well as its individual functions.

In practice there are also other functions and structures, and indeed other names may be used. Marx & Dekker, for example, also distinguish an administrative function.

In this book the tasks of marketing management are dealt with. The following brief summary lists the reponsibilities of the marketing department:

- markets the enterprise's products and/or services, thus generating the main source of income, namely sales;
- links the enterprise to its market;
- scans the environment in which the marketing task is to be performed;
- identifies opportunities and threats in the environment;
- considers the enterprise's resources and abilities in terms of consumers' demands, needs and preferences;
- makes realistic sales forecasts in uncertain circumstances, thereby facilitating planning;
- takes marketing decisions; and finally
- controls costs (especially marketing costs) in order positively to influence the profit position.

It is therefore correct to say that the activities of an enterprise 'begin with and revolve around the marketing function'[5]. The marketing process is the next topic under discussion.

1.3.2 The marketing process

The marketing process, which has been described as a simple bartering transaction between at least two participants (namely the producer and the consumer), is managed by the marketing department. The product involved in this bartering transaction is more than a mere physical object — it can better be described as a market offering.

Example of a market offering

The automobile bought by a businessman has, besides its utility as a vehicle, other need-satisfying properties. The well-known brand name (BMW), the leather upholstery, the electronic controls, the glossy magazine advertisement, the warranty, the after-sales service and even the high price all contribute to the utility the product affords its owner.

Marketing management has four marketing instruments at its disposal with which to create a market offering. The four marketing instruments are:

- The **product** consisting of a physical object plus other properties inherent in the product, such as the name, supportive services and the guarantee.
- The places where the product is offered for sale — or, in other words, the **distribution** thereof.
- The **marketing communication media and message** used to inform consumers of the marketing offering and to persuade them that it is worth the 'sacrifice' that they must make (money to be paid).
- The **price** of the product, which usually reflects the worth or value the product will afford the consumer.

Marketing management comprises a team of managers each responsible for certain well-defined tasks. The team takes decisions regarding the four marketing instruments and co-ordinates its decisions in a marketing strategy.

Who is the consumer at whom the market offering is directed? The answer is that the term seldom refers to a single person, but rather to a group of individuals with more or less homogeneous need patterns. Such a group of individuals is known as a market segment or a target market. The target market is in fact a particular market segment which has been chosen by the marketing management of a specific enterprise and at which the market offering is directed.

A target market for BMW

BMW (SA) identified executives in the higher income bracket as one of the tarket markets at which its market offering is directed.

Different market segments can be defined according to various characteristics such as age, sex, or personality. Children, for example, comprise a market segment for the marketer of candy or toys. Teenagers, pretty young girls, newlyweds and adventurous men are further examples of market segments for specific market offerings.

Because marketing management needs information about the needs, demands and preferences of consumers in different market segments, *marketing research* is conducted to determine what consumers want before any decision regarding the marketing strategy can be taken. Marketing research supplies, on a continuous basis, the necessary information and feedback to marketing management.

Marketing also takes place in a certain *environment*, which influences the relationship between the marketer and the consumer. Political unrest, inflation and legislation are some environmental influences to which marketers must of necessity adapt. Furthermore, competition with other marketers of similar products invariably complicates the marketing process.

As explained previously the marketing process in its simplest form can be regarded as a bartering transaction between at least two parties. A more detailed analysis of the marketing process shows just how involved it can be and how many influencing variables there are to complicate it even further.

The marketing process is depicted in Figure 1.5. The main objective of marketing management is indicated as long-term profit maximisation, while the objective of consumers in the target market is to obtain total need-satisfaction. In practice the realisation of these objectives is difficult, if not impossible; however, striving for this realisation of objectives by both parties is characteristic of the marketing process.

Thus far marketing has been viewed as a simple bartering transaction which eventually developed into a complicated process. This development has given rise to various approaches to marketing, as will be shown in the following discussion.

1.4 EVOLUTION OF MARKETING THOUGHT

1.4.1 Phases in the development process

The important contribution of marketing management to the overall management of a business enterprise cannot be denied. However, it often happens that top management fails to realise this fact and still maintain that a good product will sell itself to consumers. Over the years different phases in management thought on this issue can be identified. At first management was production oriented, but this approach gradually changed to the present-day strategic marketing orientation.

Production-oriented management

The era of production-oriented management began in the time of the Industrial Revolution. Before the technological developments of the era which made mass production possible, households were largely **self-sufficient**. Families were compelled to produce their own food and simple consumer articles as needed. There were families that gradually developed certain skills and tended to **specialise**, producing specific products on order and for bartering purposes. Products not specifically demanded were not made. After the Industrial Revolution the new machinery which made mass production in production plants possible gave many technological problems. No wonder management became production oriented and concentrated mainly on solving production problems.

The consumers in those days were relatively poor and unsophisticated. They were eager to obtain the wonderful, new mass-produced products. There was no need actively to market these products. However, a surplus started building up as soon as the main technological problems were solved. Management now came to realise that demand had to be stimulated and this led to a change in management thought.

FIGURE 1.5 The marketing process

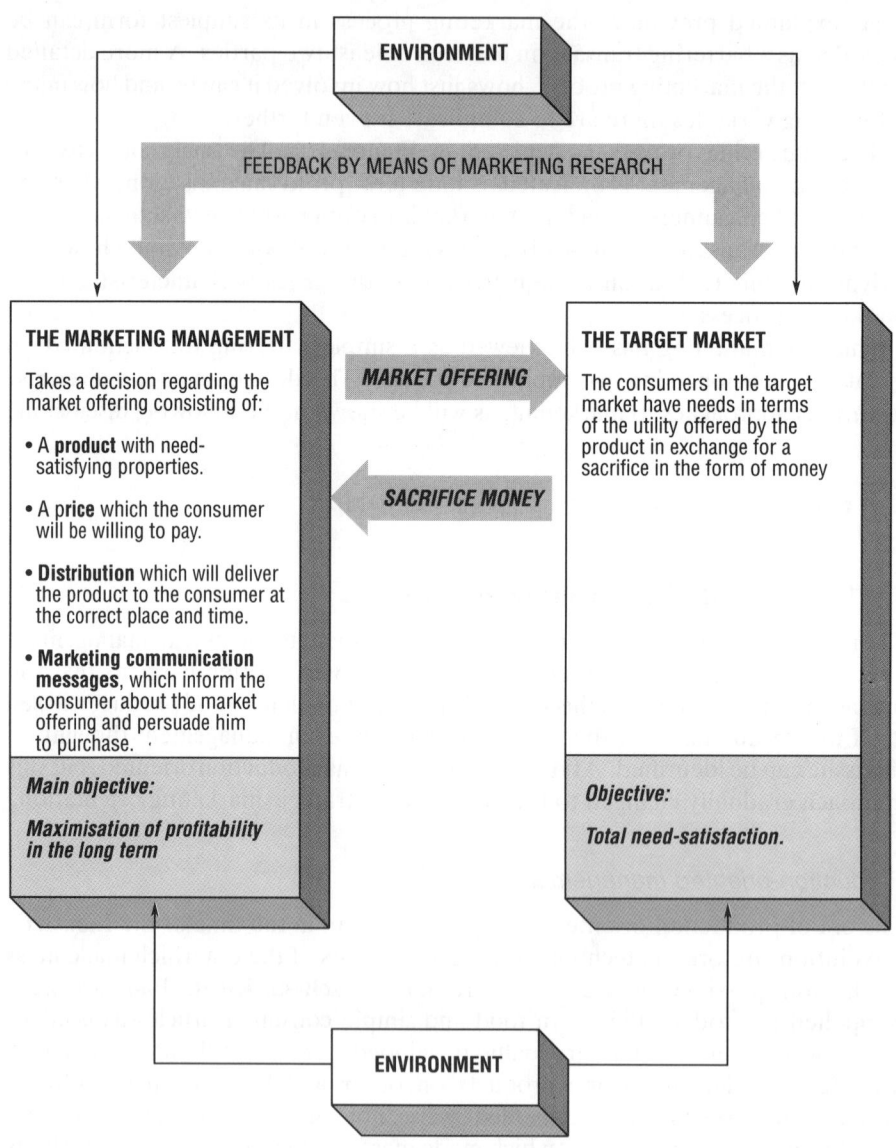

Source: Adapted from Cronjé, GJ de J. et al (eds). 1987. *Introduction to business management* Pretoria. Southern Book Publishers, p 133.

Sales-oriented management

The sellers' market of the Industrial Revolution in due course changed to a buyers' market where the supply exceeded the demand. In order to encourage consumers to buy as much as possible and to get rid of surplus stocks, unethical sales practices and misleading advertising were often used. This state of affairs led to a consumer backlash heralding the beginning of consumerism in 1900 in the United States of America.[6] Consumerism is discussed in more detail in Chapter 3.

Marketing-oriented management

After the Second World War demand once again exceeded supply. The production plants producing war material could now be used to satisfy the demand for all sorts of consumer products. Because of the widening gap between the producer and the consumer, management needed reliable information on how best to satisfy consumer needs. A change from sales-oriented management to marketing-oriented management resulted in an emphasis not only on the sales message and the price but also on the quality of products, the packaging thereof, the methods of distribution and the necessity to provide information by means of advertising. Consumers also developed more sophisticated needs and were financially in a better position to satisfy these needs. There was a large array of competing products from which they could choose. This led management to realise the importance of the marketing function. Production could begin only after management obtained market information on what the consumer wanted, how much he would be willing to pay and how he could best be reached by means of persuasive marketing communication.

Strategic approach to marketing management

The strategic approach is the most recent development in marketing thought, according to Murphy & Enis.[7] Until around 1970 marketing management played a relatively unimportant role in the strategic planning process of top management.

Two important reasons for the new, more strategic approach to marketing are the following:

- An ever-changing marketing environment necessitates long-term planning and continuous environmental scanning in order to enable the enterprise to survive and grow.
- Utilisation of opportunities in a dynamic environment requires input by marketing management in the planning process. Strategic threats cannot be overcome without the input provided by marketing management, which is in direct contact with the consumer market and closely involved with competitors.

Recent changes in the marketing environment

- The unexpected stock exchange crash in October 1987.
- High inflation rate.
- Changes in the tax structure.
- Restrictive legislation.
- Increase in the income of Black consumers.
- Changing composition of the consumer market.
- Recession and unemployment.
- Increasing consumerism.
- New technology.
- Increasing competition in the consumer market.
- Increasing prices of raw materials.
- Declining value of the rand compared to other international currencies.
- A lower gold price.

**Inputs of marketing management to
strategic marketing planning**

- Information on consumer needs, demands and preferences.
- Information on competitors and potential competitors.
- Evaluation of product/market opportunities.
- Development and testing of new products.
- Decision making on diversification and extension of the product range.
- Positioning the enterprise's products in the market.
- Information on the nature and size of market segments.
- Target market selection.
- Identifying environmental threats.
- Identifying inherent strengths and weaknesses of the enterprise.
- Development of a marketing strategy.

Strategic marketing management therefore means a continuous scanning of the marketing environment in order to identify possible **opportunities** which can be exploited and also **threats** which must be countered. It furthermore entails an indepth knowledge of the enterprise's inherent **strengths** and **weaknesses** in terms of skills and resources. This knowledge is a prerequisite in deciding on the best way to meet threats and to utilise opportunities to the enterprise's best advantage.

The strategic approach to marketing management is clearly reflected in the marketing concept, the philosophy guiding marketing management's actions.

1.4.2 The marketing concept

1.4.2.1 *The marketing concept as a managerial philosophy*

The marketing concept can be regarded as an ethical code or philosophy according to which the marketing task is performed. There are indeed few marketing textbooks that do not emphasise the marketing concept in the initial chapter. Figure 1.6 indicates that many writers agree that the marketing concept serves as a guideline for marketing decision-making.

FIGURE 1.6   Writers' view of the marketing concept

Marx & Dekker[8] view the marketing concept as the basis for the enterprise's survival.

Cronje et al (eds)[9] identify the four principles of the marketing concept that reflect changes in marketing thought over the years.

Lucas (ed)[10] lists the fundamental principles according to which marketing activities are planned, implemented and controlled.

Busch & Houston[11] say that the marketing concept is a philosophy consistent with modern marketing management.

Pride & Ferrell[12] view the marketing concept as '. . . a way of thinking . . . about an organisation's entire activities'.

Schoell[13] records the principles of the marketing concept which emerged in 1950 as a managerial philosophy.

McDaniel & Darden[14] view the marketing concept as a philosophy of doing business which must be '. . . accepted and believed in by all members of the organisation'.

Kotler & Armstrong[15] note that most successful large enterprises in the consumer market apply the marketing concept and that some even emphasise their adherence to it in advertising messages.

The three basic principles of the marketing concept, which emerged as early as 1950, are long-term maximisation of profitability, a consumer orientation, and the integration of all business activities directed at profitability and at satisfying consumer needs, demands and preferences.

The strategic approach to marketing management saw the emergence of a fourth principle, namely social responsibility, identified first by Kotler in 1972. The so-called 'pure marketing concept' — consisting of the aforementioned three basic principles — was severely criticised as being short-sighted. The pure marketing concept disregarded environmental changes and problems and focused more on short-term consumer satisfaction rather than on the long-term well-being of society. Involvement with and concern for the environment and the society in which the marketing task is to be performed are typical characteristics of a strategic approach to marketing management.

In the next section the four principles of the marketing concept, which form the foundation for all marketing decisions and activities, are discussed.

1.4.2.2 *The principles of the marketing concept*

Consumer orientation

In marketing literature consumer orientation is discussed as the first principle of the marketing concept, indicating that all marketing actions should be aimed at satisfying consumer needs, demands and preferences.

The consumer is king.

In section 1.3.2 it was pointed out that the consumer's objective is to achieve total need-satisfaction. This, however, does not mean that marketing management must also provide for unrealistic consumer needs. The enterprise can provide need-satisfaction only in so far as its resources enable it to do so. Achieving the profitability objective must also be taken into account in the endeavour to provide for consumer needs. However, failure to appreciate what the consumer wants creates opportunities for competitors and can adversely affect profits.

Profit orientation

In a free market system achieving profitability is of crucial importance. Maximising profitability is the primary objective of a profit-seeking enterprise and can be achieved only with due consideration of consumer needs. This overriding objective is usually expressed in quantitative terms. The enterprise can, for example, strive to attain a **rate of return** of 25 per cent on investment, and regards this figure as the maximum profitability which could be achieved in a specific time and under specific conditions. The financial model for this calculation is well known.

The rate of return on total assets

- Income (sales) − Costs = Profit
- $\dfrac{\text{Net profit after tax}}{\text{Total assets}}$ %
  = Rate of return on total assets.

Profit-seeking enterprises attempt to achieve a specific rate of return in the long term rather than to obtain unduly high returns in the short term, as a short-term approach can endanger its survival. The long-term nature of the profitability objective distinguishes **marketing** from a mere **bartering transaction** from which it originally developed. Various secondary objectives can also be set to facilitate long-term achievement of the primary objective.

Non-profit-seeking organisations focus on effective and efficient utilisation of resources and cost reduction rather than on profits. In an economic decline a profit-seeking enterprise too can concentrate on efficiency and effectiveness rather than profits in order to protect its position until economic conditions improve and profits can once again be made.

Secondary objectives are set in order to contribute directly or even indirectly to the achievement of the main objective.

Secondary objectives

A secondary objective can, for example, be to enhance the corporate image of the enterprise in the eyes of the public. Achievement of this objective can contribute indirectly to profitability.

A secondary objective of increasing sales can influence the profit figure directly by increasing the income of the enterprise.

A secondary objective of promoting awareness of costs in the marketing department can have a direct influence on profit by encouraging cost reduction.

A systems orientation

A system is an integrated whole — a group of unrelated units that work together to achieve a joint objective. This principle of the marketing concept is also known as organisational integration. All departments in the enterprise work together eventually to achieve the successful marketing of the enterprise's market offering. All the sections in the marketing department also direct their activities and decisions towards achieving a specific objective. The four marketing instruments should complement and reinforce one another in such a way that the target market will prefer the enterprise's market offering to that of competitors.

Social orientation

As explained in section 1.4.2.1, the principle of responsibility towards the society in which the marking task is to be performed originated because of questions about the validity of the 'pure marketing concept', which is regarded by some as short-sighted.

The objection against the pure marketing concept

Kotler & Armstrong[16] clearly state the following objection against the pure marketing concept:

'It asks if the firm that senses, serves and satisfies individual wants is always doing what is best for consumers and society in the long run. The pure marketing concept ignores possible conflicts between short-run consumer wants and long-run consumer welfare.'

Enterprises often demonstrate social responsibility by spending large sums of money on projects contributing to the well-being of the public at large instead of focusing only on the enterprise's target markets. Marketing management, which is in close contact with the target market as well as the broader public, can easily identify and evaluate the merits of such projects.

Examples of social responsibility projects

Some enterprises sponsor projects that have a direct relationship to the nature of their market offering. KWV, for example, allocates funds for the rehabilitation of members of their work force who are alcoholics.[17] Other enterprises sponsor projects which have no connection with their own line of business.

In 1988 Checkers allocated part of their advertising budget to the relief of the victims of the floods.

Premier Milling sponsors the Kaizer Chiefs soccer team.

Volkswagen (SA) spent more than R6,3 million in 1984 on technical training programmes.[18]

Spending money on social responsibility projects often comes in for a lot of criticism. Some are of the opinion that a profit-seeking enterprise is responsible only for profits for its shareholders, since deliberate profit-seeking will ultimately benefit society as a whole in any case. Dividends accruing to shareholders are regarded as 'wasted' on projects aimed at the well-being of society.

Three good arguments can be levelled at this view point:

- A project aimed at social well-being can have marketing advantages. By sponsoring Kaizer Chiefs, Premier Milling succeeded in establishing brand loyalty for its products (such as Iwisa mealie meal) in the Black community.
- An imaginative and unusual social responsibility programme can result in favourable publicity because it is regarded as newsworthy by the mass media such as newspapers, magazines and radio.

- By demonstrating social responsibility the enterprise can earn the goodwill of the public. This has a long-term dimension which can in the future favourably influence the profit position.

Social responsibility does not only involve external groups such as the authorities, consumers and public. The enterprise also has a social responsibility towards the welfare of its own employees. A corporate image of social responsibility cannot be created if employees are uninvolved and even excluded. Social responsibility programmes for employees include housing and health programmes. Care centres for toddlers and babies can perhaps be offered to working mothers in order to create an atmosphere in which they can give their full attention and best efforts. Dissatisfaction and disloyalty are reflected in negative attitudes towards clients and consumers and eventually affect the corporate image.

Social responsibility also means that the enterprise will abstain from any action in conflict with current norms or moral or ethical standards. Contravention of the norms of society can result in loss of goodwill and result in consumer resistance.

The enterprise must furthermore show responsibility in its adherence to formal rules, regulations and legislation. In Chapter 2 South African legislation to which the enterprise must adapt is discussed.

But responsibility towards an enterprise's own employees goes much further than mere welfare programmes. All employees must be made to realise the importance of marketing. Here reference is made to internal marketing programmes[17] where employees must be informed about marketing objectives, the nature of environmental threats, success which has been achieved and even the nature of marketing communication messages. Everybody must work together well and enthusiastically to achieve success in the market. Even the tea lady can contribute to this if she treats clients with the respect they deserve. The success or failure of the marketing effort is also reflected in the tea lady's own renumeration and further prospects.

1.4.2.3 *The merits of the marketing concept*

Adherence to the principles of the marketing concept does not guarantee success. However, if these principles are ignored success can be achieved only in the short term. Sooner or later problems will be encountered and these may even lead to the demise of the enterprise. An enterprise that ignores the principles of the marketing concept and its ethical code of conduct is not really engaged in marketing at all, but rather in a short-term bartering situation.

Social responsibility

Social responsibility programmes are contentious issues between management and trade unions. Many trade unionists believe that such programmes are patronising and paternalistic, while management sees them as vital in ensuring a worthwhile future for South Africa.

Workers believe that companies are not sincere in their attempts to help the underprivileged, and are merely looking for favourable publicity. Conversely management cannot understand why its good intentions are not appreciated.

Corporations usually look at four major areas in which to invest funds: education, health, housing and employment. The objectives of investments in such areas are seen as setting up an economic, social and politically stable environment, optimising profits and creating a positive image among employees and consumers.

Unions are adamant that they should have a say in the way in which profits are spent. They argue that workers play a large part in generating profits but management is not always eager to consider sharing the responsibility to make these decisions.

Source: Adapted from Chalmers, R. Agonising issue of social responsibility. Sunday Times, *Business Times*, 26 March 1989.

SACCOLA code

Social responsibility programmes are often launched with a deliberate lack of publicity. Spending on such programmes is determined by a code which was put forward in 1977 by the Urban Foundation. The requirements of this code — the SACCOLA code — are not enforced but determine that, *inter alia*, employers should strive to:

- discontinue discrimination in development and promotion programmes for all employees;
- ensure non-discrimination in training programmes and facilities aimed at improving productivity in technical, administrative and management positions.

Source: Cronjé, GJ de J *et al* (eds). 1987. *Introduction to management*. Pretoria: Southern Book Publishers, p 374.

Large enterprises are often unwilling to supply details of their budgets for social development programmes. They are sensitive to the criticism that they are merely looking for publicity. The selection of certain programmes furthermore invariably leads to disappointment if requests are declined. This had led in the past to boycott actions and even demonstrations by organisations which have applied unsuccessfully for sponsorships or financial aid. In the final instance social responsibility is not merely charity — these programmes should provide a certain and specific advantage to a business enterprise.

Barlow Rand regards the R7,5 million budgeted for social responsibility programmes in 1989 as an investment in the development of a social infrastructure in South Africa.

Source: Venter DJ. 1989. *South Africa: Sanctions and the multi-nations*. Chichester: Corden Publishers, p 117.

What marketing is not

The milk culture fiasco is a good example of a non-marketing project. The 'entrepreneur' strove to make as much profit as possible. The product itself had no use or utility and there was no consumer demand for it. No marketing research was conducted and buyers were not informed about the real nature or uses of the market offering. There was no question of social responsibility. In fact, society was exploited and robbed.

The principles of the marketing concept argue against the criticism levelled at marketing. This criticism mainly applies to sales-oriented management where consumers are misled and exploited.

The advantageous influence of the marketing concept on the marketing process can be summarised as follows. Adherence to the principles of the marketing concept emphasises:

- the continual development of new products to satisfy consumer needs;
- market segmentation and the grouping of consumers with more or less homogeneous characteristics;
- marketing communication messages which inform, remind and persuade consumers, but which do not mislead them;
- the choice of appropriate marketing communication media aimed at specific market segments;
- the distribution function which places products conveniently near to most consumers in a specific target market;
- marketing research to obtain first-hand knowledge of consumer needs;
- environmental scanning in order to identify opportunities and threats in time to do something about them;
- long-term planning and the formulation of strategies that will ensure the enterprise's survival and growth; and
- the creation of a positive image of the enterprise.

From the previous discussion it is quite clear that the marketing process is indeed complicated. It cannot be approached in a haphazard way but must be properly managed according to the principles of the marketing concept.

1.5 THE MANAGEMENT TASKS OF MARKETING

The management tasks consist of a continuous process of **planning**, **organising**, **co-ordinating**, **leading** and **controlling** marketing activities. Marketing management is responsible for the following:

- Identifies opportunities and threats in the marketing environment.
- Identifies those opportunities which can be utilised in terms of internal strengths and weaknesses.
- Compiles marketing data.
- Chooses a specific target market.
- Decides on the products to be produced in order to satisfy consumer needs.
- Decides on the selling price of the product in order to attain the profitability objective.
- Decides on specific distribution channels.
- Decides on marketing communication methods whereby consumers can be informed, reminded and persuaded.
- Decides on selection, training, renumeration and motivation of marketing personnel.
- Organises the activities of the marketing department.
- Co-ordinates marketing activities.
- Controls the marketing process.

These responsibilities are part of the five management tasks which are summarised in Figure 1.7.

Planning by marketing management entails the examination of and the choice between various ways of utilising marketing opportunities, countering marketing threats, and achieving marketing objectives. Marketing decisions thus begin with the identification and evaluation of marketing opportunities and threats, and internal strengths and weaknesses.

Organising calls for the creation of an organisational structure best suited to the implementation of the marketing decisions in order to achieve marketing objectives. Marketing activities are grouped rationally and individual divisions and managers are tasked with carrying them out. Finally, the levels of authority, areas of responsibility, lines of communication and methods of co-ordination between the divisions and individuals are determined.

Co-ordinating is often regarded as part of the organising function since it entails facilitating co-operation between the various divisions and individuals. Co-operation is achieved by intergrating the interests of divisions, individuals, consumers, investors, suppliers, entrepreneurs and the community as a whole. Figure 1.8 shows a typical organisation chart for a marketing department, with the marketing manager at the head.

Leading involves a wide range of tasks, such as staffing, communicating, and motivating. From a marketing viewpoint leading embraces all the marketing decisions for putting preparation (planning, organising, co-ordinating, controlling) into practice. Briefly, once the marketing strategy has been formulated, people have to be found to perform the required marketing activities (staffing), they have to be instructed as to what they should do and told how well they are doing (communicating), and a positive attitude towards work and the enterprise must be carefully cultivated and maintained (motivating). Leading is therefore of paramount importance in the effective performance of the other management tasks.

Controlling or evaluation is the regulatory task of marketing management, and its purpose is to align actual performance with marketing plans. In order to exercise control it is first essential to set standards, which requires determination of what has to be controlled and where marketing control is necessary. Secondly, actual marketing performance has to be measured and compared with these standards. Thirdly, the differences between actual performance and standards have to be evaluated. Finally, if necessary, corrective measures should be taken to ensure that future performance is in line with marketing plans.

FIGURE 1.7   The management tasks of marketing management

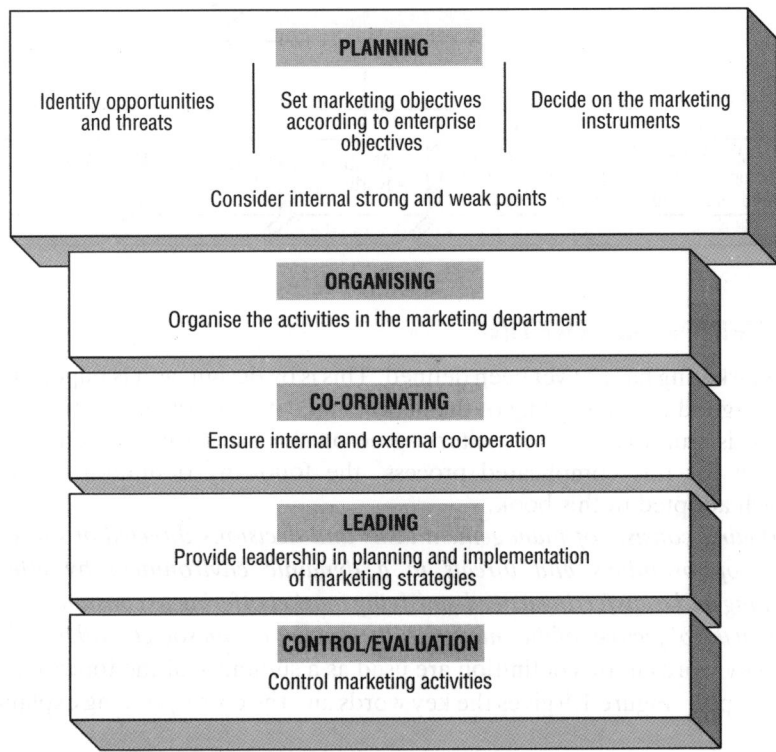

Source: Adapted from Marx, S and Dekker, HJ. 1983. *Marketing Management: Principles and Decisions*. Pretoria, HAUM, p 21.

If marketing does not perform the management tasks properly:

- purchasing management will not know which raw materials and components to purchase;
- public relations management will not know how to perform or improve its liaison function;
- financial management will not know how much funding is required;
- human resources management will not know how many people to employ; and
- production management will not know which products and how much to produce.

FIGURE 1.8   Functional marketing organisation

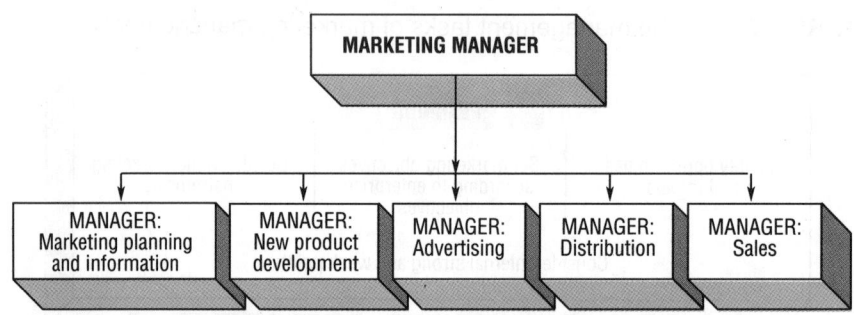

1.6 DEFINING MARKETING

So far marketing has not yet been defined. This is by design, as it is imperative first to have a good understanding of the nature and extent of the marketing process. Whilst it is true that no two writers agree on the exact formulation of a good definition for this complicated process, the following definition reflects the approach adopted in this book.

Marketing consists of management tasks and decisions directed at successfully meeting opportunities and threats in a dynamic environment by effectively developing and transferring a need-satisfying market offering to consumers, in such a way that the objectives of the enterprise, the consumer and society will be achieved.

The key words in this definition are used as a summary of the topics discussed in this chapter. Figure 1.9 gives the key words and the corresponding explanation.

1.7 CLASSIFICATION OF CHAPTER TOPICS

Figure 1.10 serves as a model on which this book is based. This model consists of the main components of the marketing task of an enterprise operating in a specific marketing environment. The topics of the four parts of the book are reflected in the model.

FIGURE 1.9   Key words in the definition of marketing management

MANAGEMENT TASKS	Planning, organising, co-ordinating, leading, controling.
DECISIONS	Regarding the product, distribution, marketing communication methods, and price
OPPORTUNITIES	Favourable circumstances in the marketing environment which must be utilised by marketing management
THREATS	Unfavourable conditions which marketing management must endeavour to change into opportunities
DYNAMIC ENVIRONMENT	Continualy changing environmental variables which necessitate appropriate reaction from marketing management
DEVELOPMENT	Creating a need-satisfying product or service
TRANSFERRING	Effectively bridging the gap between the producer and consumer
NEED-SATISFYING	Properties of a product based on what the consumer wants
MARKET OFFERING	Product, price, distribution, marketing communication
ATTAINMENT OF OBJECTIVES	
• the enterprise	Maximisation of profitability in the long term
• the consumer	Need-satisfaction within the resources and abilities of the enterprise
• society	Ensuring the well-being of society in the longer term

Part 1 places marketing in perspective and gives a broad overview of the components of the marketing strategy. Part 2 consists of five chapters in which the variables in the marketing environment, market segmentation, target marketing and marketing information, measurement and forecasting are discussed. The first block of the model in Figure 1.10 refers to these two parts of the book.

Part 3 deals with the four marketing instruments and the decisions that have to be taken by marketing management in developing a marketing strategy. The marketing strategy is aimed at a specific target market and, to be successful, must bridge the gap between the stated objectives and reality. In Chapters 7, 8 and 9 product decisions are discussed; Chapters 10 and 11 deal with distribution decisions; marketing communication decisions receive attention in Chapters 12,

FIGURE 1.10 Marketing Management

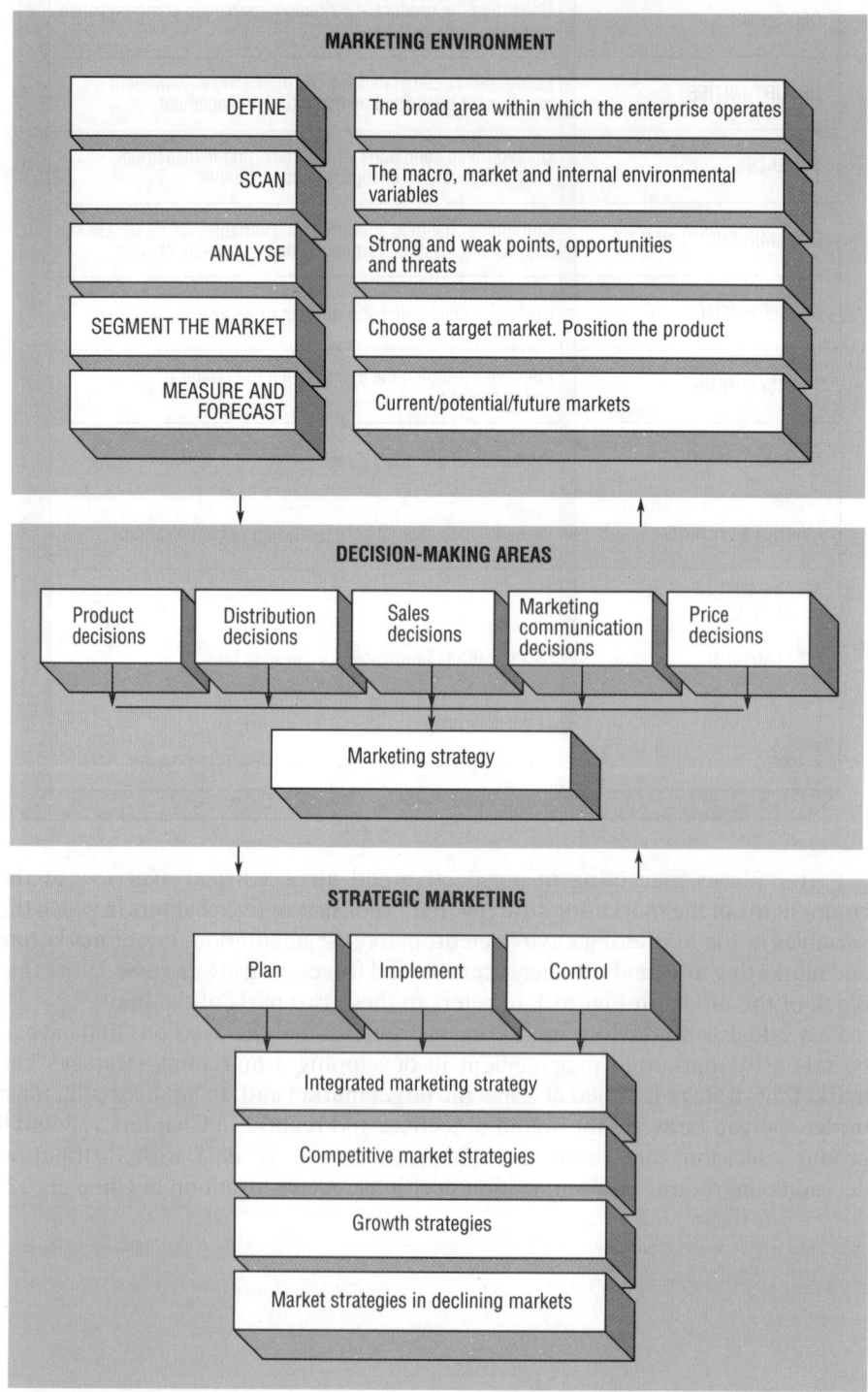

13, 14 and 15; and price decisions are dealt with in Chapters 16 and 17. The changes in the integrated marketing strategy over the life cycle of the product, including marketing warfare, are discussed in Chapter 18. The second block in Figure 1.10 comprises these topics.

In Part 4 planning, implementation and control of the integrated marketing strategy are discussed. All four marketing instruments once again receive attention in the discussion of market strategies aimed at competition, growth and survival. The market strategies of large multi-product enterprises consisting of independent strategic business units receive attention in Chapter 19. The feedback arrows in the model in Figure 1.10 suggest that control leads to continual attention being given to environmental scanning, marketing decisions and the integrated marketing strategy. This section on planning, implementation and evaluation comprises the third block in the model. The book concludes with a discussion of strategic marketing in specialised areas, inter alia industrial, agricultural, services, non-profit and retail marketing.

1.8 SUMMARY

This chapter particularly emphasises the marketing concept, the managerial philosophy according to which the marketing task is to be performed. Attention is focused on the marketing process and the marketing concept. A definition of marketing management is given. Scanning the marketing environment can be regarded as the point of departure for the performance of the marketing task. The marketing environment is discussed in Chapters 2 and 3.

REFERENCES

1. Kotler, P. 1984. *Marketing Management: Analysis, Planning and Control.* Englewood Cliffs, NJ: Prentice-Hall, p 8.
2. Busch, PS and Houston, MJ. 1985. *Marketing: Strategic Foundations.* Homewood, Illinois: Richard D Irwin, p 15.
3. Marx, S & Dekker, HJ. 1982. *Marketing Management: Principles and Decisions.* Pretoria: HAUM, pp 2–11.
4. Ibid pp 18–19.
5. Cronjé, GJ de J et al (eds). 1987. *Introduction to Business Management.* Pretoria: Southern Book Publishers, p 127.
6. Schoell, WF. 1985. *Marketing: Contemporary Concepts and Practices.* Boston: Allyn & Bacon Inc, p 15.
7. Murphy, PE & Enis, BM. 1987. *Marketing.* Glenview, Illinois: Scott, Foresman & Co, p 40.
8. Marx & Dekker op cit, p 25.
9. Cronjé et al, op cit, pp 138–41.
10. Lucas, GHG (ed). 1983. *The Task of Marketing Management.* Pretoria: Van Schaik, p 21.
11. Busch & Houston op cit, p 34.
12. Pride, WM & Ferrell, OC. 1985. *Marketing: Basic Concepts and Decisions.* Dallas: Houghton Mifflin Co, p 13.

13. Schoell op cit, p 16.
14. McDaniel, C and Darden, WR. 1987. *Marketing*. Boston: Allyn & Bacon Inc, p 19.
15. Kotler, P and Armstrong, G. 1987. *Marketing: An Introduction*. Englewood Cliffs, NJ: Prentice-Hall, p 15.
16. Ibid p 17.
17. Richardson, BA & Robertson CG. 1986. 'The Impact of Internal Marketing on Customer Service in a Retail Bank'. *International Journal of Bank Marketing*, p 12.
18. Cronjé et al (eds). op cit, p 409.
19. Ibid p 408.

CASE STUDY

THE BEGINNING OF THE SOUTH AFRICAN ECONOMY

On 6 April 1652 Van Riebeeck dropped anchor in Table Bay with a list of instructions issued by the Dutch East India Company (DEIC), *inter alia* to establish a refreshment station at the Cape, to build a fort with hospital facilities for sick seamen, and to establish a garden to provide fresh produce to combat the curse of scurvy caused by a lack of vitamin C (which cost the DEIC a great deal of money in lost time). From these prime motives of ensuring the safety and productivity of the Dutch fleet a new settlement was to arise, which would grow into a colony and a country. In this process marketing activities were to play a big role.

The indigenous people of the Cape at that time were a few nomadic tribes of Khoikhoi (Hottentots), who visited the Cape Peninsula with their livestock at times, and the San (Bushman clans Van Riebeeck called "strandlopers"), who lived mainly off the products of the sea and the veld. The Khoikhoi regarded their livestock as wealth. The first trading between visiting ships, the first Dutch settlers, and the Khoikhoi took the form of barter: copper, beads, tobacco, blankets, brandy and various trinkets being offered in exchange for livestock. The San used beads made of the shells of ostrich eggs and the Zulus of the east coast used assegai blades, picks made of iron and bracelets of brass and copper as a medium of exchange and in barter but this was never a factor at the Cape.

The common coins in those days were the guilder and the stiver. There were 20 stivers to a guilder. It was also usual to accept gold and silver coins of various other countries, like the Spanish dollar (which later became the daalder), the rupee from Java and the ducats from Italy.

The coin at the Cape was indeed a strange mixture of currencies and must have caused many a petty-cash nightmare. The wide variety does not, however, mean that there was a surplus of coins; the Cape, in fact, always suffered a shortage of coins, which led to much barter in the transactions allowed by the DEIC. The first paper money at the Cape — the rix-dollar — was printed only in 1722.

Generally, the burghers were prosperous. The Capetonians, true to a trading instinct no laws or regulations could extinguish, kept an eye open for the money of the strangers calling there. Each private home was practically a shop where many a clandestine transaction was concluded, some of them illegal, for, like the officials, the burghers were not averse to denting the monopoly of the DEIC, and so the buying and selling of foreign products were not limited to the DEIC store. This retail trade put money into the pockets of the Capetonians, but its adverse results could not be avoided. Precisely because it had to take place on a small scale and largely in secret, it could hardly generate broad and sound economic concepts in those who practised it. This trade flourished particularly when the large fleets were in the bay. More than 2 000 seamen and other visitors would then come ashore and Capetonians could make a good profit.

A conversion to rands and cents of the various monetary units current at the Cape in the time of the DEIC would be arbitrary and misleading. A few examples of the buying power of some of these old coins would perhaps give one a better idea of their value. Van Riebeeck's journal and contemporary travel journals contain some interesting examples.

A gold ducat (78 stivers) bought a sheep. A sailor received 8 guilders as his salary. A soldier was paid 9 guilders, besides his allowance of meat and rice. The hangman received 24 guilders for each execution.

In Van Riebeeck's time consumables and household goods had fixed prices. The price of meat per pound (454 g) was 3 stivers for mutton, 2 stivers for beef and 4 stivers for pork. Butter cost 1 guilder a pound, tobacco 6 guilders a pound, milk 1 stiver for half a litre.

Source: Summarised from Engelbrecht, C L. 1987. *Money in South Africa*. Cape Town: Tafelberg Publishers, pp 14-17.

QUESTIONS

1. Give examples of bartering in modern trade, locally and internationally.

2. Explain the fact that one still find areas in South Africa where small stores are opened in private homes.

3. Which regulations and circumstances limited the growth of the South African economy in the early days?

4. What were the advantages and disadvantages of maintaining fixed prices? Is it still possible today to maintain fixed prices? Explain.

5. Discuss bartering between the burghers and the Khoikhoi in terms of the marketing process as illustrated in figure 1.5. Use your imagination.

Note: You will only be able to answer these questions properly after you have studied the chapters on distribution and pricing decisions.

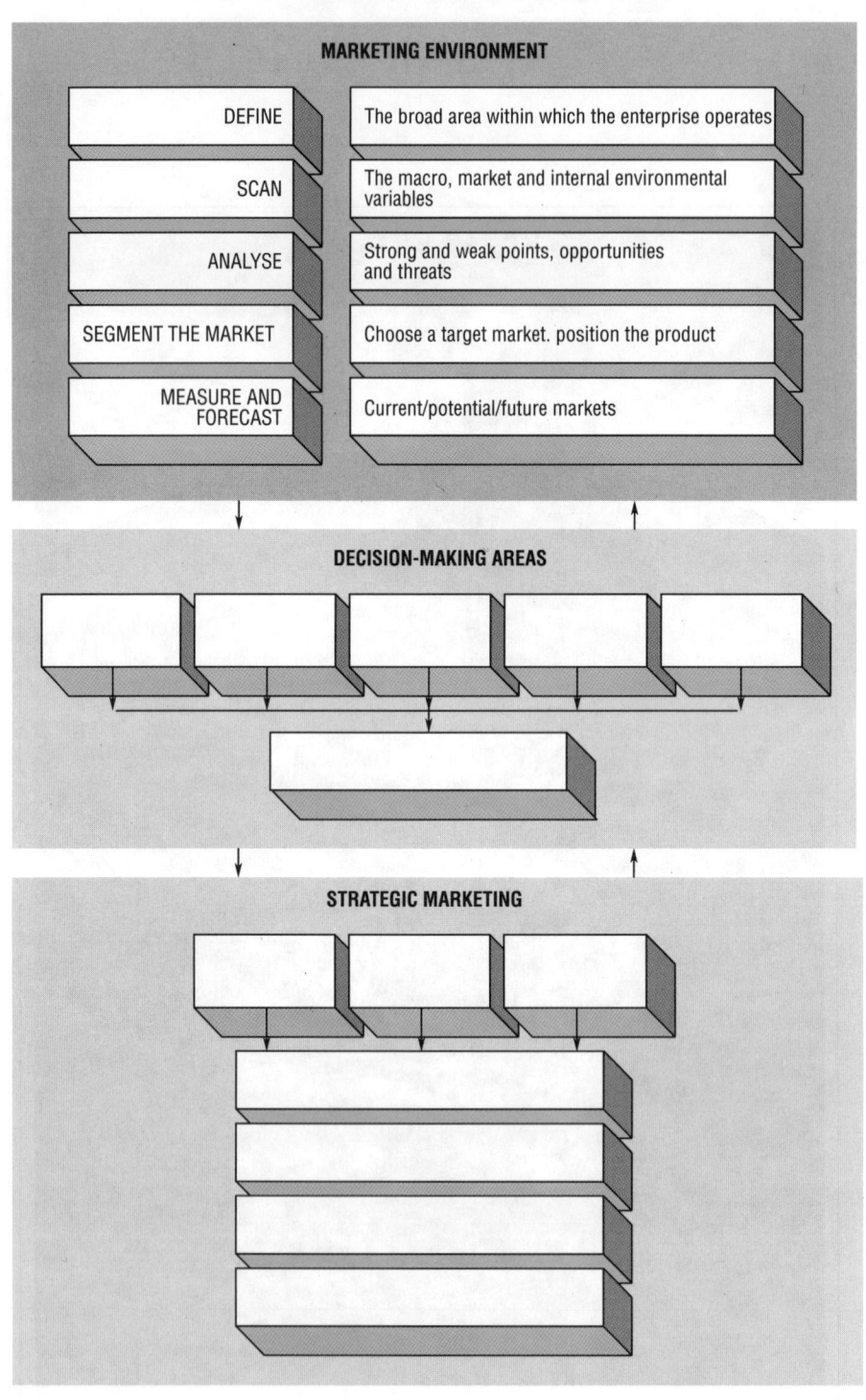

CHAPTER 2

ENVIRONMENTAL VARIABLES

2.1 INTRODUCTION

In the introductory chapter the marketing function was depicted as a process by which the enterprise markets its product. As such it involves a variety of activities in the enterprise which are prescribed by top management and must be performed in collaboration with other departments. The prescribed activities refer more specifically to the mission, objectives and broad strategies which are formulated by top management and which must be implemented, strived for and supported by all the functional departments, including the marketing department. Marketing management must work in close co-operation with other departments to implement the marketing plan.

The performance of marketing activities also implies contact with the market and the environment outside of the enterprise. And in no small measure is the success of an enterprise's marketing efforts dependent on certain variables in the environment. The position of consumers and competitors in the market, relations with suppliers, economic, social and political trends and various other events which occur in the environment from time to time, will threaten the successful functioning of the enterprise. These factors may alternatively create a favourable environment which presents numerous marketing opportunities.

The many variables and forces inside as well as outside the enterprise which influence marketing management's decisions constitute the **marketing environment**, which can be defined as the sum total of the factors or variables that potentially affect the marketing of an enterprises' product or service.

The successful management of marketing activities calls for an awareness by marketing management of the internal and external variables which can affect their marketing effort. It requires constant monitoring of the environment; internal surveillance to ascertain the enterprise's strengths and weaknesses as well as internal developments which may affect marketing management; and external scanning to search for opportunities and threats. The aim is to deploy the enterprise's strengths and resources in the market in such a way that it can fully utilise the opportunities and ward off any possible threats. Timeous and continuous scanning of the total environment in which marketing management must operate, internal as well as external to the enterprise, will enable marketing management to adapt to a changing environment and to adjust their marketing strategies to such a degree that their products will be successfully marketed.

Against the background of these introductory remarks regarding the environment in which marketing management operates, the following aspects will be discussed in this chapter:

ORGANISATION OF THE CHAPTER

The marketing environment concept: Definition of the marketing environment and the interdependence between the enterprise and its environment.

The interfaces between marketing management and the environment: The role of marketing management in the environment, change and marketing management, opportunities and threats in the environment.

The composition of the marketing environment: The micro-, market and macro-environments, variables in the environment and their implications for marketing management.

Methods of environmental scanning.

2.2 MARKETING MANAGEMENT AND THE MARKETING ENVIRONMENT

2.2.1 The enterprise and the environment

The contemporary enterprise in the free-market system of the Western world does not exist in isolation. In fact, in a free-market system the business enterprise originates from the community with the purpose of serving the community. The organisation utilises the community's resources in the form of labour, capital, raw materials and entrepreneurship to produce products and services for the community. The community is to a large extent dependent on the business organisation for satisfying its needs regarding products, services and job opportunities; the community thus constitutes the market for the products of the organisation. The enterprise and its community, or the environment in which it operates, are not closed systems, but are interdependent upon each other for survival. At the same time the one influences the other, and this interaction results in a complex relationship between the enterprise and its environment, where the latter can be described as *the sum total of the factors or variables which influence the long-term profitable existence of the enterprise*. It mainly involves the set of external variables which affect the enterprise and its profitable existence. The decisions taken by marketing management influence the environment, but these decisions are in turn affected by the numerous variables in the environment. In the long term this mutual influence brings about a changed environment; it results in new challenges and creates new opportunities to which the enterprise must adapt. It must meet the challenges and utilise the opportunities.

Mutual influence

As a result of the disinvestment campaign against South Africa (an uncontrollable variable in the environment) Barclays Bank was sold by the British parent company to local shareholders. During this period the bank changed its name to First National Bank and a series of unfortunate events contributed to a negative public image. To counter the 'influences from the environment', First National Bank in turn influenced the environment by striving to become the 'rugby bank'. The bank created for itself a positive image by financing Ellis Park which was bought back by the Transvaal Rugby Union, as well as by sponsoring Northern Transvaal's half-centenary celebration to the tune of R1 million.

Source: Advertising supplement to *Financial Mail*. 21 August 1987, p 49.

2.2.2 Management and environmental change

Since the business enterprise and the environment in which it operates are not closed systems but influence each other reciprocally, it follows that the organisation cannot exist successfully if it is out of pace with its environment. The fact that the enterprise may at a particular point in time be in equilibrium with its environment, ie in a situation where its resources are deployed in such a way that the opportunities offered by the environment are fully utilised with few or no threats present, does not mean that this favourable relationship with the environment will continue. In fact, the underlying problem for the successful existence of contemporary Western organisations is the fact that the pace of environmental change is faster than the process of organisational adaptation.

Change is a difficult term to define. Expressed simply, it is any alteration in the *status quo*. This implies a change from a condition of stability to one of instability, a shift from the predictable to the unpredictable. It cannot be measured, and it causes insecurity. No single factor can be held responsible for change and in different places and communities it occurs in different ways and at different rates. Technological innovation, economic fluctuations, changing social values and demographic trends, political change, aggressive international competition and countless other variables are constantly changing the enterprise's environment, to such an extent that it not only affects the performance of organisations detrimentally but also threatens their existence. During the past decade the structure of South African society and its life styles, values and expectations have changed perceptibly. More and more of the Third-World characteristics which will dominate the South African environment of the year 2000 are beginning to appear. As a component of the environment the enterprise is therefore at the centre of environmental change and is constantly exposed to change. The result of this change is a new environment with new trends which can be classified into three groups:

- Trends which constitute **opportunities** for the enterprise. This refers to *a favourable situation in the environment in which the organisation has a distinct competitive advantage and possesses the necessary resources to utilise it.* The most important opportunities which result from change are probably the creation of new markets and the broadening of existing markets.
- Trends which pose particular **threats** to the organisation. This refers to *an unfavourable situation in the environment which may have a detrimental effect on the performance of the organisation if it is allowed to go on unchecked.*
- Trends which may appear but which hold no implications for the enterprise or the industry.

Successful enterprises that adapt to the environment are those who constantly scan the environment and adjust their strategies to keep abreast of change. Adjusting strategies is therefore those steps which management takes to gain a particular environmental fit for their organisations. Successful enterprises do this continuously. They are managed in a pro-active way, and their strategy adjustments are not delayed until such time as the environment has changed so drastically that nothing can be done about it.

In the early seventies Southern Sun identified the opportunities for hotels and entertainment in South Africa correctly, and developed a strategy to utilise the opportunities. During 1991 Sun International Bop reached the ninth position on the Business Times ranking of the 100 top South African businesses. In contrast to this, the property giant of the sixties and early seventies, Glen Anil, took no steps to ward off the threats in the property market. They disappeared from the property market in the early seventies.

A few remarks on the role of marketing management in environmental scanning are necessary before the composition of the marketing environment is examined.

2.2.3 Marketing management and the environment

Although the interaction between the enterprise and its environment is the concern of the entire strategic management team, marketing management probably plays the most important role in this interaction. Support for this statement can be found, first, in the existence of an enterprise's mission statement, an important component of which is the enterprise's position regarding its product–market relationship. This entails a broad but clear indication of the enterprise's product or service and the market in which it is operating. Both the enterprise's product development and its market are in the domain of marketing management, which necessitates marketing management's involvement in the development of the organisation's mission and strategy, as well as its involvement with the external environment.

The second reason for the importance of marketing management's involvement in the interaction between the organisation and its environment arises from the requirements of the marketing concept. It calls upon top management to determine the needs of the consumer and to satisfy those needs, instead of deciding unilaterally what the needs of the consumer are.

Marketing management thirdly plays an important role in the interface between the organisation and its environment since the latest research in strategic

FIGURE 2.1   A profile for management success: Success factors of successful enterprises

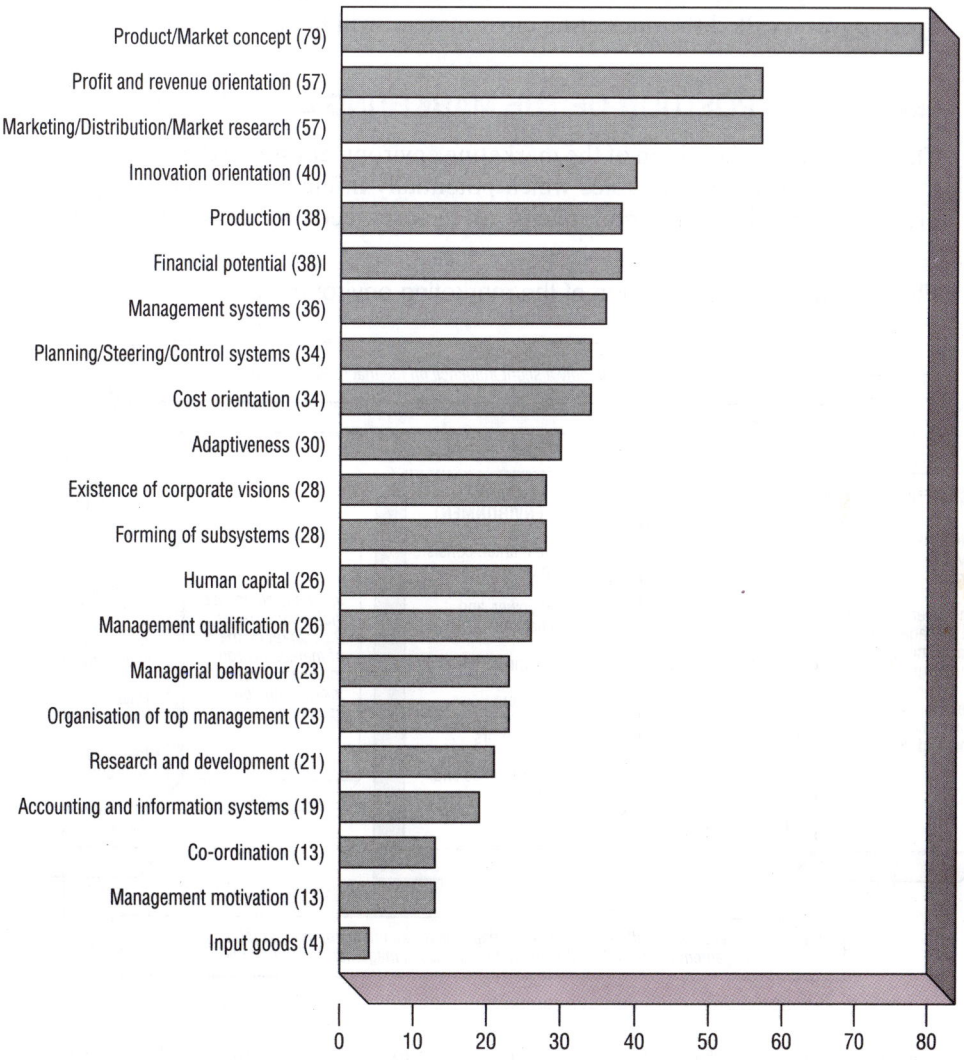

Source: Kruger, W. Patterns of Success in German Business, *Long range planning,* Vol. 22, No. 2, p. 105.

management indicates that successful enterprises are externally oriented — towards the consumer, the competitor, the market and the environment.[2] It must be borne in mind that corporate planners depend on marketing management for inputs regarding new products and market opportunities, and that the marketing strategy (product, price, distribution and marketing communication) plays a major role in the enterprise's total strategy. In fact, the most recent research on the success factors of an organisation took place in Germany. The research indicated that certain components of marketing management play a key role in the success of the enterprise. Figure 2.1 illustrates the so-called success profile of business organisations with the implementation of the marketing concept as the most important success factor, while marketing research and distribution are indicated as the third most important success factor for German enterprises.

The composition of the environment in which marketing management operates, also called the marketing environment, will be discussed next.

2.3 THE COMPOSITION OF THE MARKETING ENVIRONMENT[3]

The introductory definition of the marketing environment stated that it is the sum total of the factors or variables which potentially influence the marketing of a product or service. This multiplicity of factors needs to be scrutinised and

FIGURE 2.2   Composition of the marketing environment

The enterprise has only a slight influence on the macro-environment

MICRO-ENVIRONMENT
- Mission and objectives of the enterprise
- The enterprise and its management, eg marketing, financial, purchasing
- Resources, eg manpower, capital, know-how and information

Influence on market by its strategy

Direct influence by competitors, consumption expenditure etc

MARKET ENVIRONMENT
- The market, consisting of consumers, their needs, purchasing power, and behaviour
- Intermediaries
- Suppliers
- Competitors
- Opportunities and threats

Influence enterprise indirectly through the market by means of market environment, eg effects of taxation on consumer spending

MACRO-ENVIRONMENT
- Technological environment
- Economic environment
- Social environment
- Physical environment
- Institutional/political environment
- International environment

The macro-environment influences the enterprise directly, eg effects of interest rates on financial management or legislation that human resources management must comply with

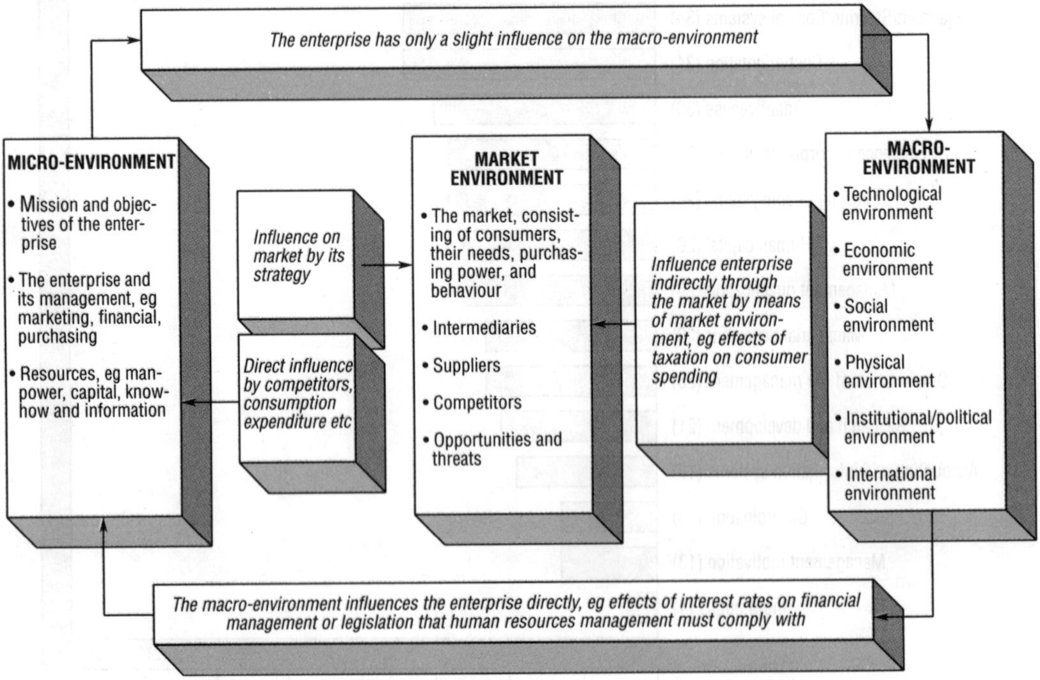

Source: Cronjé, GJ de J et al (eds). 1987. *Introduction to Business Management.* Johannesburg: Southern Book Publishers, p. 43.

rationally categorised to indicate those relevant to the organisation, and to identify distinct trends within each category or **subenvironment** for further analysis. Figure 2.2 shows the composition of the marketing environment.

2.3.1 The micro-environment

The first component of the total environment is the **micro-environment** or the internal environment which comprises the enterprise itself. Although this group refers to those variables which are largely under control of the enterprise's management, such as its mission and objectives, its management structure, its resources and its culture, it must be remembered that these variables are not solely under the control of marketing management. As already mentioned, marketing-management does have an important influence on these variables as it is responsible for the central input in developing the enterprise's overall strategies, but it must be clear that whilst top management controls certain micro-variables, marketing management can also control some variables in the micro-environment.

TABLE 2.1   Variables in the micro-environment controlled by top management.

VARIABLE	EXAMPLES OF ALTERNATIVES
1. Basic line of business (product or service)	
• Product/service category	Tourism, fast food, clothing, hotel industry
• Technology category	Manufacturer, distributor, wholesaler, agriculturist
• Geographic category	Neighbourhood, city, region, province, national, international
• Ownership category	Sole proprietor, partnership, close corporation, public corporation
• Specific business category	City Lodge (hotel industry, national)
	Premier Foods (food, manufacturer, national)
	Hatfield Bakery (bakery industry, city)
2. Overall goals	
• Sales	Certain percentage increase per year or percentage market share
• Profit (or return on investment)	Minimum percentage gross on nett profit (on sales), profit ratios per product (patents), geographic area or percentage return on investment.
• Customer acceptance	Environment-friendly products and socially responsible products (toys and medicine)
3. The role of marketing management	
• Importance in	Line of staff functions, extensive budget and resources
• Functions	Market research, planning, distribution, lease agreement
• Integration	Integration, decentralisation
4. The role of the other management functions	
• Manpower management	Determine responsibilities of each function, position of each
• Financial management	in the organisational structure, relationships between
• Operations management	functions, eg. should operations management be responsible
• Purchasing management	for purchasing or should purchasing do the procurement?

Although top management, that is the executive management, which includes the functional managers, focuses decision-making on the organisation's mission, goals and overall strategies, there are four basic top management decisions which closely involves marketing management, namely:

- the **basic line of business** (product or service) of the organisation;
- the **overall goals** of the organisation;
- the **role of marketing management**; and
- the **role of the other management functions** (such as purchasing and finance) in the attainment of the organisation's overall goals.

Table 2.1 gives a brief exposition of how these four top management decisions involve marketing management.

These decision areas, which fall under the control of top management, are expressed in the mission and overall goals of the enterprise.

From these decisions which top management takes, marketing management must determine the variables for which it is responsible and which fall under its control. Table 2.2 briefly illustrates the micro-variables which fall within the decision area of marketing management. In order to manage these variables effectively marketing management must be well-informed about the organisation's mission and top management's decisions regarding the overall goals and objectives of the enterprise. Marketing management must therefore constantly scan the micro-environment, as discussed in paragraph 2.4. Marketing management's activities must also support and complement top management's decisions for the organisation to function as a unit, internally as well as externally.

TABLE 2.2 Variables in the micro-environment controlled by marketing

VARIABLE	EXAMPLES OF ALTERNATIVES
1. Selection of target market	
• Size	Mass market, specific market segment, geographic area
• Characteristics	Male, female, young, old, conservative, liberal, east, west
2. Marketing objectives	
• Sales	Brand loyalty, new products, new markets
• Profit	Profit ratio per product, area, quantity
• Image	Quality, friendly, service
• Competitiveness	Competitive advantage through better quality, lower price, extensive promotion
3. Organisation structure	
• Type	Functional, product, area
4. Marketing plan	
• Product/service	One basic model, one colour, sizes, styles
• Distribution	Direct, wholesale, representatives
• Price	High, low, creaming
• Promotion	Advertising, personal selling, publicity
5. Control	Audit, research

Management decisions — including those made by marketing management — influence the **market environment** by extending or indeed curtailing the strategies employed to maintain the enterprise's market share.

2.3.2 The market environment

The second component of the marketing environment is the **market environment** immediately surrounding the micro-environment. In this environment all the variables depicted in Figure 2.2 become relevant for every enterprise since they determine the nature and strength of competition in any industry. The key variables in this environment are the following:

- **consumers** with a particular buying power and behaviour which in turn determine the number of entrants to the market;
- **competitors** in the market who want to maintain or improve their position, including existing, new and potential competitors;
- **intermediaries** who compete against each other to handle the enterprise's product;
- **suppliers** who supply, or do not want to supply, products, raw materials, services and financing to the enterprise.

All these variables give rise to particular **opportunities** and **threats**. Although marketing management can influence certain variables by adjusting its strategy, it normally has no control over the variables. The market environment has a strong influence on the success of the enterprise. A case in point is a strong competitor who possesses the necessary ability to enter into a price war or to launch a new substitute product. It is in the market environment that marketing management finds its most important task: to identify, assess, and take advantage of opportunities in the market; and to develop and adapt its strategies to meet competition. For these reasons the market environment is also called the **task environment.** The market environment is also influenced by developments and forces in the macro-marketing environment which works through the market to affect the micro-environment or the enterprise itself. This brings us to the third component of the marketing environment.

2.3.3 The macro-environment

External to both the organisation and the market environment is the **macro-environment,** which consists of six distinct subenvironments: the **technological environment**, which is responsible for innovation; the **economic environment,** in which such factors as inflation, recessions, exchange rates, and monetary and fiscal policy influence the prosperity of the enterprise and its community; the **social environment** in which consumer life styles, habits and values formed by culture, make certain demands on the organisation, particularly through consumerism; the **physical environment**, which consists of natural resources, such as mineral wealth, flora and fauna, and man-made improvements such as roads and bridges; the **institutional environment**, with the government and its political and legislative involvement as the main components; and lastly the **international environment,** in which local and foreign political trends and events affect the organisation as well as the market environment. The individual enterprise has no control over the macro-environment and its influence on these variables is negligible. The foregoing discussion on the composition of the marketing environment has brought certain general characteristics of the marketing environment to the fore.

2.3.4 Some characteristics of the marketing environment

Before we discuss the various subenvironments in more detail it is necessary to give a brief overview of the most important characteristics of the marketing environment. This will help to explain the nature of the marketing environment and it will also explain the importance of continuous scanning for the long-term success of the enterprise. The following are a few of the main characteristics of the marketing environment:

- **Environmental factors or variables are mutually related.** A change in one of the external factors may cause a change in the micro-environment or internal factors, and similarly a change in one external factor may cause change in the other external environmental variables. For example, **political events** caused the sharp decline in the value of the rand against foreign currencies in 1985, and that resulted in more economic change, including higher **inflation**, which reduced the **purchasing power** of consumers, which in turn led to **increased sales of second-hand cars**. At the same time the **price of fuel** doubled, which caused **holiday resorts** to suffer. Other businesses, such as Sasol, and exporters, benefited from this change in the macro-environment.
- **Increasing instability** is a second characteristic of the business environment. The consequences of interdependence in the environment are increasing instability and change. Although the general rate of change in the environment accelerates, environmental fluctuation is greater for some enterprises than for others. For example, researchers have found that the rate of change in the pharmaceutical and electronics industries is higher than in the automobile component and bakery industries.
- **Uncertainty** is a third characteristic of the business environment. This uncertainty about the environment is of course a function of the amount of information about the environmental variables and of the confidence placed by management in such information. If there is little information available, or if the value of the information is suspect, the uncertainty of management about the environment will increase, and vice versa.
- **Complexity** is a fourth characteristic of the environment. It comprises the number of external variables to which the enterprise has to react, as well as variations in the variables themselves.

These few outstanding characteristics of the environment show how important it is for effective management to know and understand the environment within which the enterprise is operating. With these facts in mind, let us consider the various business subenvironments, namely the micro-, market and macro-environments, in greater detail.

2.4 SCANNING THE MICRO-ENVIRONMENT

2.4.1 The importance of the micro-environment

The inclusion of a chapter such as this one is to emphasise the importance of environmental change. A company can be successful in an unstable environment only if it applies the principle of strategic management. This implies the allocation and deployment of the enterprise's resources towards threats and opportunities in such a way that the long-term profitability of the enterprise is maximised. More specifically it entails a survey of the enterprise's strengths and weaknesses so that a strategy can be developed to protect the weak points from environmental threats and to utilise the strengths for the exploitation of opportunities in the marketing environment. A successful strategy must comply with three critical conditions:[4]

- The strategy must first be formulated in terms of the market or the competitive environment.

- Secondly, the strategy must make realistic demands on the enterprise's resources and capabilities.

- Thirdly, the strategy must be implemented with great care.

It is especially the second condition which forms the basis for the scanning or evaluation of the internal or micro-environment, namely that a strategy must not be formulated in terms of management's perceptions and expectations of the market, but that the hard **facts about an enterprise's capabilities** be considered. Internal analysis or evaluation is part of the interactive strategic management process, as illustrated by Figure 2.3, and takes place while management keeps an eye on the external environment as well as the mission of the organisation. This all takes place with the aim of arriving at a particular strategy. It is not important whether the internal analysis or the external scanning is done first. It is, however, of the utmost importance that this exercise is done regularly. An internal analysis which results in a realistic organisational profile is a complex process which includes objective standard analysis as well as calculated guesses and subjective judgement. The latter often leads to a subjective personal opinion. It is therefore necessary to pursue a systematic internal analysis to construct an objective profile of the organisation so that a realistic strategy can be formulated. Before marketing management can pay attention to the choice of a particular marketing strategy, they must know what is going on in the organisation. This boils down to a systematic analysis of the enterprise's strengths and weaknesses. A few brief remarks will explain the concepts of strengths and weaknesses.

A factor can be regarded as a **strength** if it offers the enterprise a continuous **competitive advantage**. It is, in other words, something which the enterprise can do better than its competitors over the long run. (This aspect is also discussed in Chapter 19.) BIC, the French manufacturer of throw-away products, in this manner identified as its strengths in the throw-away market its abilities in the fields of mass production, mass distribution and mass advertising. A definite strength or

FIGURE 2.3   Internal analysis in the strategic management process

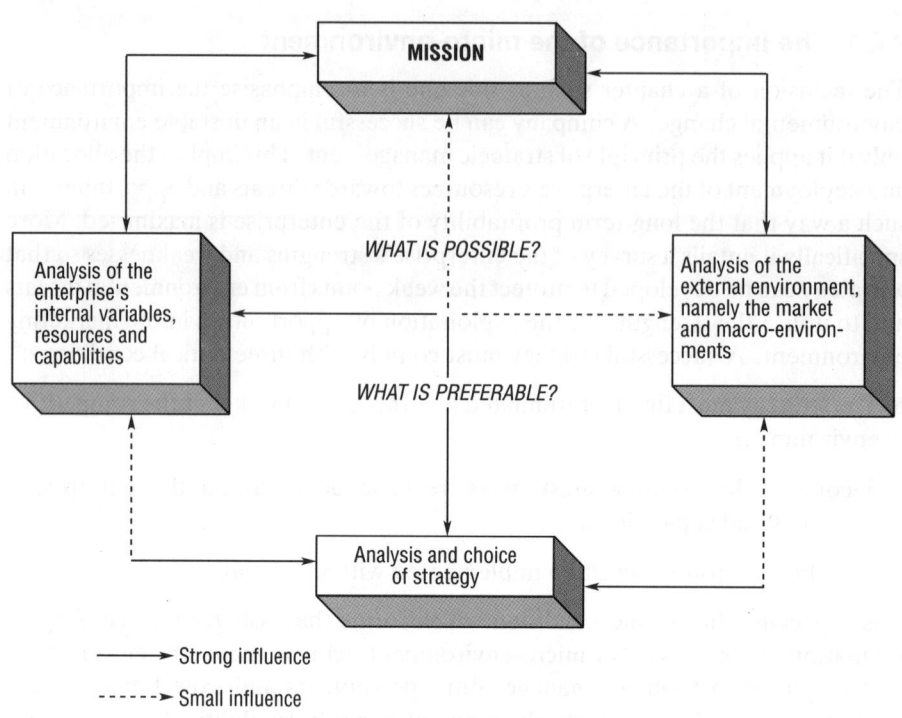

——————► Strong influence

------ ► Small influence

Source: Adapted from Pearce, JA & Robinson, RB. 1988. *Formulation and Implementation of Competitive Strategy.* Homewood, Illinois: Richard D Irwin, p 50.

strong point gives the organisation a competitive advantage in the market. A **weakness**, on the other hand, refers to the **inability successfully to do something**, while competitors possess the ability to do so successfully. Considering BIC's strengths, Scripto identified their obsolete production facilities and limited financial resources to back mass advertising as their main weaknesses in their race with BIC in the ballpoint pen market. The importance of internal analysis therefore lies in the identification of strategic and relevant strengths and weaknesses. An internal analysis which includes a long list of resources and capabilities does not necessarily contribute to the formulation of a realistic strategy. The internal analysis must therefore include only the *relevant* strengths and weaknesses. Figure 2.4 illustrates groups of strong and weak points which may be found in an enterprise.

The questions which now arise are the following:

• How does management **identify** strong and weak points in the enterprise?
• How must strengths and weaknesses be **evaluated**?

Answers to these questions will provide some guidelines for the process of internal evaluation.

FIGURE 2.4   Key internal factors: strengths and weaknesses

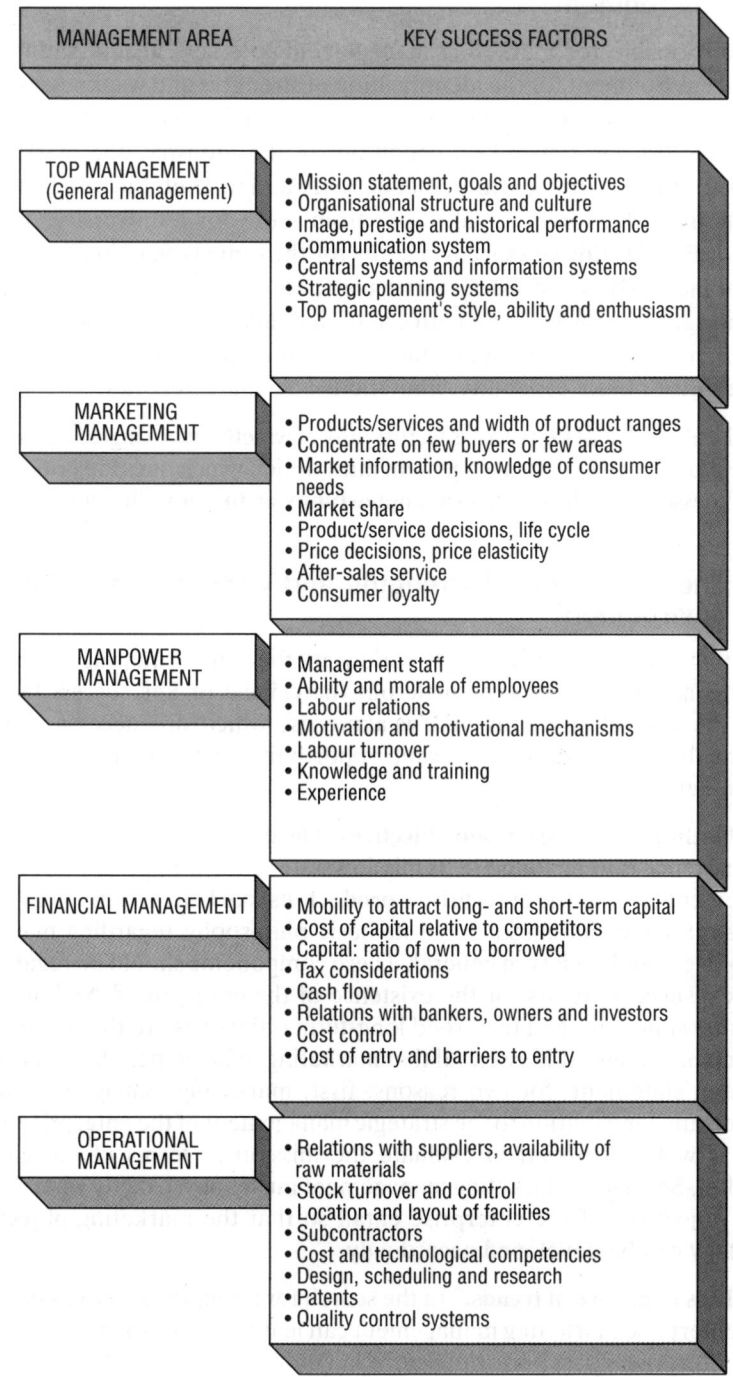

MANAGEMENT AREA	KEY SUCCESS FACTORS
TOP MANAGEMENT (General management)	• Mission statement, goals and objectives • Organisational structure and culture • Image, prestige and historical performance • Communication system • Central systems and information systems • Strategic planning systems • Top management's style, ability and enthusiasm
MARKETING MANAGEMENT	• Products/services and width of product ranges • Concentrate on few buyers or few areas • Market information, knowledge of consumer needs • Market share • Product/service decisions, life cycle • Price decisions, price elasticity • After-sales service • Consumer loyalty
MANPOWER MANAGEMENT	• Management staff • Ability and morale of employees • Labour relations • Motivation and motivational mechanisms • Labour turnover • Knowledge and training • Experience
FINANCIAL MANAGEMENT	• Mobility to attract long- and short-term capital • Cost of capital relative to competitors • Capital: ratio of own to borrowed • Tax considerations • Cash flow • Relations with bankers, owners and investors • Cost control • Cost of entry and barriers to entry
OPERATIONAL MANAGEMENT	• Relations with suppliers, availability of raw materials • Stock turnover and control • Location and layout of facilities • Subcontractors • Cost and technological competencies • Design, scheduling and research • Patents • Quality control systems

Source: Adapted from Pearce, JA & Robinson, RB. 1988. *Formulation and Implementation of Competitive Strategy*. Homewood, Illinois: Richard D Irwin, pp 208–9.

2.4.2 The identification of strengths and weaknesses in the micro-environment

It is not possible for marketing management to assess all the variables in the internal environment for the identification of strengths and weaknesses. They will rather isolate what are called the *key success factors* for a particular business. The success factors will depend on conditions in the industry, the market and the position of the enterprise within that industry and market. Success factors for the building industry, for example, differ from those for a university, a bank or a hospital. Besides this key success factors for the same type of business can differ. For instance, BIC's success factors have to do with mass production and mass advertising, while Parker's concern was design, image and distribution. Figure 2.4 gives an indication of the success factors found in most enterprises. It represents an enterprise's basic capability, limitations and characteristics.

From the above list of key success factors, any of which can be singled out as a strength or a weakness, marketing management must decide which ones are **critical** strengths or weaknesses to address a **relevant opportunity or threat** in the market.

2.4.3 The evaluation of strengths and weaknesses in the internal environment

Marketing management can apply various methods in evaluating the enterprise's strengths and weaknesses to single out the **critical** or **key success factors**, also called the critical strengths and weaknesses, which are necessary to meet a relevant threat or utilise a relevant opportunity in the market or the macro-environment.

- **Evaluation of the mission and objectives.** The enterprise's purpose or reason for its existence is to be found in its mission statement. Components of the mission statement refer to the enterprise's **product**, its **market**, its **technology** or ways in which it serves its market, and its basic philosophy regarding management, employees and society in general. These components should be regarded as the critical success factors for the existence of the enterprise.[5] And although the mission statement and the broad long-term objectives are the responsibility of top management, it is essential that marketing management keep an eye on the mission statement, for two reasons: first, marketing management makes an important contribution to the strategic management of the enterprise as a whole and is well positioned to evaluate the mission in terms of the enterprise's market. Secondly, marketing management must know exactly what the mission and objectives of the enterprise entail so that the marketing objectives and strategy can be developed accordingly.

- **Analysis of historical trends.**[6] In the search for strengths and weaknesses inside the enterprise marketing management can learn a lot by asking questions about the enterprise's past performance. What did the enterprise do particularly well in its marketing, financial or operations management? Did it have a great influence on performance? Was the sales department well organised? Were the right distribution channels used? Did the enterprise have the necessary financial resources to back its previous strategy? The analysis of historical data can be extended to analysis trends in sales, costs, profitability, product lines and sales territories. A detailed examination of the enterprise's performance history makes it possible to single out the internal factors which determine sales, costs and profitability. It can, for example, be found that 85 per cent of the enterprise's sales are produced by 25 per cent of its products, or that 30 per cent of its products are responsible for 78 per cent of its profits. In this way marketing management can identify the relevant key success factors and combine them in winning combinations.

- **The value chain.**[7] Another method of identifying key success factors in the internal environment is the so-called value chain method. The whole process through which a product goes until it reaches the consumer is divided into value-added stages. Each stage is then scrutinised and analysed to improve productivity, quality and so on. The identification and evaluation of the enterprise's strengths and weaknesses essentially amounts to an internal audit, as is discussed in Chapter 19. It must always be borne in mind that internal analysis is not an isolated process, and that marketing management must constantly keep an eye on the market and macro-environments, since a change in these areas may render the identified key success factors irrelevant.
- **The product–market evolution.** The requirements for success regarding the enterprise's product–market relationship change over time. Marketing management can thus apply the framework of the product life cycle (discussed in Chapter 18) to identify strengths and weaknesses in the internal environment as an ongoing exercise. Based on this concept, key success factors during the introductory phase of the product's life cycle will revolve around the marketing capabilities to create an awareness of the product, while key factors in the decline phase will encompass cost advantages, good supplier relations and financial control.
- **Compare the capabilities of competitors.** An important aspect in determining a business's strengths and weaknesses is comparison with those of existing and potential competitors. Businesses in the same industry often have different marketing capabilities, financial resources and production facilities. These varying capabilities can be relatively strong or weak points in a particular strategy. For this reason marketing management should compare the enterprise's internal capabilities with those of competitors when developing or chosing a strategy.
- **Success factors in the industry.** Each industry has specific success factors. The wine industry would single out capital resources and expertise in wine making as success factors, while the hotel industry would emphasise location and expertise in providing personal service. For this reason the key determinants for success in a particular industry must also be considered in the process of identifying the enterprise's strengths and weaknesses. The process of scanning the capabilities of competitors, consumer needs, vertical integration, distribution channels, cost barriers to entry, and the availability of substitutes and suppliers, will provide marketing management with a clear picture of the enterprise's internal capabilities.

- **Quantitative approaches.** The identification and evaluation of an enterprise's internal capabilities can also be accomplished by quantitative techniques, such as the use of comparative financial, marketing, manufacturing and other ratios which will point out strengths and weaknesses in the enterprise.

The environment immediately outside the enterprise is the **market environment** which, according to Figure 2.1, consists of the market, suppliers and competitors, and is a source of both opportunities and threats to the enterprise. To understand the interaction between the enterprise and its market environment clearly, it is necessary to examine the variables in the market environment more closely.

2.5 SCANNING THE MARKET ENVIRONMENT

2.5.1 Suppliers

An enterprise does not operate in isolation and requires inputs from the environment. The inputs required are mainly material, including raw materials, equipment, energy, capital and labour, which are provided by suppliers. When it is realised that sixty cents out of every rand paid out by the enterprise is spent on purchases from suppliers, the importance of suppliers as a variable in the market environment becomes clear. If an enterprise cannot obtain the necessary inputs of the required quality in the right quantity and at the right price for the achievement of its objectives, then it cannot hope to achieve any success in a competitive market environment.

In the case of **materials** practically every enterprise, whether it be in manufacturing, trading or contracting, depends upon regular supplies. As in the case of raw materials there are suppliers of **capital,** an input upon which the enterprise is dependent for its survival. Banks, building societies and shareholders are such suppliers. Small organisations often find it very difficult to attract the necessary capital.

2.5.2 Consumers

Consumers with their unique needs, purchasing power and behaviour patterns are the most important component of the marketing environment. Several meanings can be attached to the term 'market', and the subject is more fully discussed in Chapter 3. Briefly, however, it can be said that the *market consists of people who have needs to be satisfied and who also possess the financial means of satisfying them.*

2.5.3 Competitors

The present-day business, in the West at least, finds itself within the realm of the capitalist order, which functions on the basis of a free-market economy and is characterised by issues such as competition in the market environment. This means that every business trying to sell a product or a service in the market environment is constantly up against competition, and that it is often competitors rather than consumers who determine how much of a given product can be sold and at what price. Moreover, businesses compete for a share in the market for their product, and in addition they compete with other businesses for labour, capital and materials. As a variable in the market environment, competition may be defined as a *situation in the market environment in which several businesses offering more or less the same product or service compete for the patronage of the same consumer*. The result of competition is that the market mechanism keeps excessive profits in check, stimulates higher productivity, and encourages technological innovation. Although the consumer benefits from competition, it is nevertheless a variable that management has to take into account in its entry into and operations in the market.

In the assessment of competition marketing management must bear in mind that the nature and intensity of competition in a particular industry is determined by the following five factors:[8]

- The possibility of new entrants (or departures).

- The bargaining power of clients and consumers.

- The bargaining power of suppliers.

- The availability or non-availability of substitute products or services.

- The number of existing competitors.

FIGURE 2.5   Competitive forces in an industry

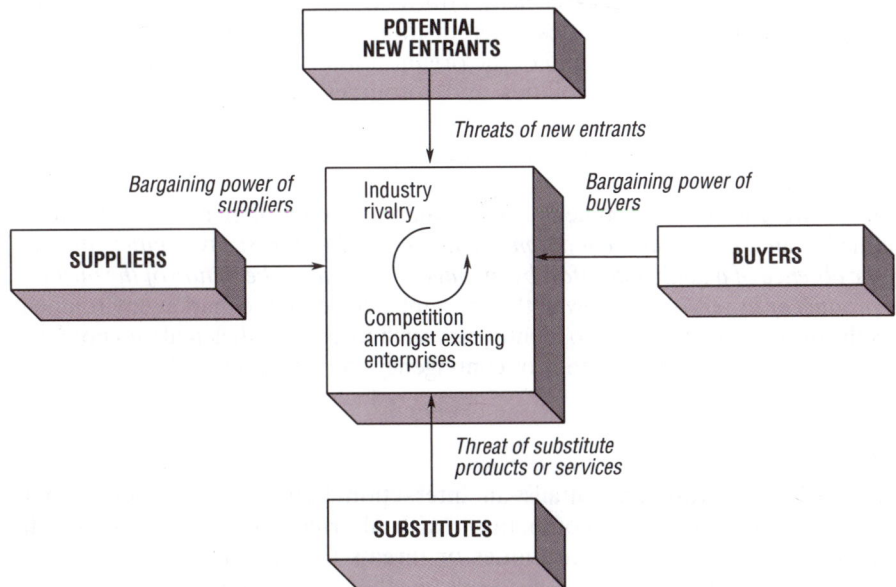

Source: Porter, ME. 'How Competitive Forces Shape Industry', adapted from Pearce, JA and Robinson RB. 1988. *Formulation and Implementation of Competitive Strategy*. Homewood, Illinois: Richard D Irwin, p 126.

Figure 2.5 illustrates the five forces responsible for competition in a particular industry. The collective strength of these five forces determines the competitiveness in the industry and therefore the profitability of the industry. Competition varies from intense, in industries such as tyres and retailing, to moderate in mining and cold drinks; the weaker the five forces, the better the chances of survival and good performance. It is therefore an important task of marketing management to find a position in the industry where the organisation can successfully defend itself against the forces of competition. The alternative would be to find a position where the enterprise can influence the forces of competition in its favour. Chapter 4 deals with market segmentation, target marketing and positioning, where these aspects are examined in greater detail. Continuous scanning of competition provides the basis for the development of a marketing strategy. It emphasises the critical strengths and weaknesses of the enterprise, gives an indication of the positioning strategy which must be followed, singles out areas where strategy adjustments can contribute to higher returns, and focuses on industry trends in terms of opportunities and threats.

2.5.4 Opportunities and threats in the market environment

The changes brought about in the market environment by the respective variables and their interactions, and the trends that constantly develop in the macro-environment, can ultimately be classified into two groups: those changes that offer an **opportunity** and those that pose a **threat**.

An **opportunity** may be defined as a *favourable condition or tendency in the market environment which can be utilised to the benefit of the organisation by means of a deliberate management effort.* It should, however, be clearly understood that the possibilities inherent in an opportunity always have to be assessed against the background of the organisation's resources and capabilities. Without the necessary capabilities and resources an opportunity cannot be properly utilised. The success of a business in making good use of an opportunity therefore depends upon its ability to satisfy the requirements for success in that particular market.

In contrast to an environmental opportunity, an environmental **threat** may be defined as an *unfavourable condition or tendency in the market environment that can, in the absence of a deliberate effort by management, lead to the failure of the business, its product or its service.* In view of the constant changes in the market environment, it is the duty of management to identify any such threats, both actual and potential, and to develop a counter-strategy or contingency strategy to meet them.

2.5.5 Conclusion

The market environment entails an interaction between a business and its suppliers, consumers, and competitors with alternate market offerings. This interaction can result in opportunities or threats to a business, and marketing management must be aware of trends in the market environment so that management can utilise opportunities profitably and avoid threats in good time. For this purpose environmental scanning, marketing research, and information management are the proper instruments.

2.6 SCANNING THE MACRO-ENVIRONMENT

2.6.1 The composition of the macro-environment

Apart from the market environment, which has a direct effect on the fortunes of a business, an organisation also operates within a wider macro-environment containing variables which directly or indirectly exert an influence on the business and its market environment. These variables constitute those uncontrollable forces in the environment that are sometimes referred to as 'megatrends'. As can be seen from Figure 2.2 the contemporary literature on management divides the macro-environment into six variables; these are technological, economic, social, physical, institutional or political, and international variables (or subenvironments) which the organisation has to observe and react to.

The macro-variables have an effect not only on the market environment and on decision making by management but also on one another, and this constantly causes changes in the business environment. The community (which is also the consumer), with its particular culture and values, decides what government it wants and gives it a mandate to form a certain political structure, which in turn determines the affairs of the community. Therefore politics is interwoven with the economy, which is influenced by the policies adopted and the economic measures taken to achieve political ends. The result is a particular standard of living for the community. Stimulated by the needs of the community, and with the support of the economy and the government, technology is mainly responsible for the rate of change in the business environment. Social trends also influence politics and the economy, and the international environment acts as a considerable force for change in the other variables, and therefore in the total business environment. The result of all this interaction is often a new business environment with new opportunities and new threats.

In the study of the macro-environment the emphasis falls on changes caused by the uncontrollable macro-variables, and their implications for marketing management.

2.6.2 The technological environment

Scientists estimate the age of the earth to be five billion years and the existence of man 250 000 years. History dates back 5 000 years. The products which exists today, excluding a few basic products, were developed during the past 60 years. And the latest products which have already become indispensable to modern society, such as laser surgery, robotics and robot factories, silicon protein molecules, fibre optics and 80 per cent of today's medicines, are the products of the past 10 years! This tremendous environmental change is largely a manifestation of technological innovation, a process which enlarges the capabilities of mankind.

Technological innovation originates in research and development by business and government, and results not only in new machinery or products but also in new processes, methods, and even new approaches to management that bring about change in the environment. Even the social and institutional progress in a company and the structures it possesses relate to technology. Technological innovation also affects other environmental variables. The economic growth rate is influenced by the number of new inventions. Social change, in which the appearance of a new product, such as television, brings about a revolution in people's way of life, is also partly the result of technology. These variables in turn influence technology, so that the process of innovation and change is repeated.

Every new facet of technology and every innovation creates opportunities and threats in the environment. Television was a threat to films and newspapers, but at the same time it presented opportunities for instant meals, satellite communication, and advertising. The opportunities created by computers in banking, manufacturing, transport, and practically every industry are innumerable.

Laser Technology saves South Africa Millions

- A German/South African firm has developed ultramodern laser technology to cut and drill diamonds in a split second compared to the traditional time it took. Diamonds are presently still being cut and polished in the same way as 400 years ago. It takes four hours to cut an average diamond and is therefore time-consuming and expensive. One expert diamond cutter with 40 cutting machines can cut approximately 80 diamonds per day with an average loss of 3,5 per cent per diamond. The new laser technology cuts an average diamond in something like $1\frac{1}{2}$ minutes with an average loss of only 1 per cent. The loss of diamond mass as a result of cutting will save De Beers $180 million per year.
- Laser technology is also responsible for opportunities and threats in the market environment. Laser technology can shorten the production cycle of products such as jewellery, motor-car components and medical components, such as artificial hip joints, by eighteen months. In the jewellery industry one of the biggest problems is the manufacturing of jewellery templates. An experienced designer can design only three to four templates or models per month. The laser machine can develop 400 ring models overnight when programmed to do so!
- For South Africa the implications of this technology is important. South Africa anually exports 600 tons of gold and only 4 tons are used by the local jewellery industry. Taiwan imports 134 tons of gold and is at present the world's eighth largest jewellery manufacturer. Italy has 14 000 jewellery manufacturers and has to import all its gold. Each 100 tons of gold which can be used locally will provide 100 000 jobs.

Source: *Finansies & Tegniek*, 20 December 1991, p. 20.

Moreover, technological innovation often has **unpredictable consequences**: the contraceptive pill meant smaller families, more women at work, and therefore more disposable income to spend on holidays and luxury articles, which would previously not have been possible. The most outstanding characteristic of technological innovation is probably the fact that it constantly accelerates the rate of change.

Business and government continually spend increasing amounts on research and development. In South Africa during the sixties and seventies expenditure on research and development increased by about 22 per cent a year. Furthermore, since the beginning of this century the **diffusion period** (see also Chapter 8), the time between the moment of invention and its commercial application, has decreased by 60 per cent. This time period is still being shortened so that the rate of innovation is constantly being speeded up too.[9]

Marketing management has a threefold involvement in the process of technological innovation and change. It first **promotes** technological innovation when it identifies new consumer needs and when it influences technology in such a way that it leads to the satisfaction of those consumer needs. Secondly, it **distributes** technological innovation throughout society by commercialising the innovation. Thirdly marketing management is involved in scanning the marketing environment for opportunities and threats posed by an increased **rate of technological innovation**. For example manufacturers of radiological scanners will profit by improved innovations which will increase the scanning rate of its products.

> The video revolution in South Africa has changed the behaviour and spending patterns of consumers. As a result of this revolution people are spending more time at home and less on bioscopes and 'Sunday driving'.
>
> Source: *Finansies & Tegniek,* 18 December 1987, p 13.

Marketing management therefore has a significant task to perform in managing the transition to a new technology, since technological innovation can have a fast and drastic influence on a product or even an industry. A case in point is the detrimental influence of quartz watches on the manufacturing of conventional watches. However, this does not mean that a certain technological innovation will render the older technology obsolete. Various observations have been made in this regard:[10]

- A new technology does not necessarily smother the old technology, but can even stimulate its growth because the threatened organisations improve their old technologies. Safety-razor sales have actually increased 800 per cent since the advent of the electric razor.
- In most cases firms involved in the old technology have a substantial amount of time to react to the new technology.
- It is relatively difficult to predict the outcome of a new technology, and it tends to create new markets instead of simply encroaching on the existing markets. For example, throw-away ballpoint pens created new markets without killing the market for refillable ballpoint pens.
- A further characteristic is the fact that technological innovations are unlimited and that they continuously affect the environment. Table 2.3 illustrates the possible technological innovations of the year 2000, and also the unlimited possibilities and threats which technology poses for business organisations.

In scanning the technological environment marketing management must keep the maturity of an existing technology in mind, and its possible replacement with a new technology. Technological innovation is especially possible when:[11]

- the physical boundaries of an existing technology are reached;
- research and development in a certain area becomes uneconomic;
- competitors start to experiment with expensive and risky technology.

Technological progress, therefore, affects the business as a whole, including its products, its life cycle, its supply of materials, its production process, even its approach to management, and ultimately its position in the market. These influences all require management to be increasingly on the alert for technological change.

TABLE 2.3   Possible technological innovations by the year 2000

STRONG POSSIBILITIES	LESS LIKELY POSSIBILITIES	HYPOTHESES
• Robots for domestic help • Genetic engineering to improve plant and animal strains through biotechnology • New sources of food and energy • 3D television • Practical electric cars	• Small flying cars • Automated motorways • Artificial cultivation of new limbs and organs • Large-scale use of rockets for transport	• Complete genetic control • Space tours and space colonies • Lifelong immunisation against disease • The use of nuclear power in mining and civil engineering

Source: Cronjé, GJ de J et al (eds). 1990. *Introduction to Business Management*. Johannesburg: Southern Book Publishers, p 54.

2.6.3 The economic environment

After technology, which is primarily responsible for change in the environment, follows the economy, which is influenced by technology, politics, and the social and international environments, while itself asserting some influence on these variables. All the time these cross-influences cause changes in the economic growth rate, levels of employment, consumer income, rate of inflation, and the general state of the economy, which is indicated by either prosperity or adversity. Ultimately these economic forces will have certain implications for marketing management. The most important interfaces between the economic environment and a business concern the economic growth rate, consumer incomes, inflation, monetary and fiscal policy, and fluctuations in these variables.

The economic well-being of a community is measured by the range and number of products and services produced. Expressed in monetary terms, this standard is equivalent to the gross domestic product, ie the *total value of finished articles and services produced within the borders of a country during a given period, normally a year.*[12] During the first thirty years after the Second World War the average real growth rate of the South African GDP was about 4,7 per cent per annum, after which, from 1970 to 1983, it declined to an average annual rate of 2,8 per cent and even to negative levels.[13] As a result of the shortage of foreign capital, it is also not expected that this growth rate will be improved in the near future. This excludes South Africa from the top economic achievers in the world. And the fact that South Africa's population growth rate of 2,9 per cent per year is higher than the GDP means a decline in real living standards. These trends have specific implications for marketing management.

The structural changes in the incomes of the different consumer groups are of great importance to marketing management, since they give rise to changed spending patterns with regard to products and services such as food, clothing, housing, and insurance. See Chapter 3 in this regard.

Although the economic growth rate has important consequences for a business and its market environment, it is the correct gauging of upswing and downswing phases of the economy that has the strongest influence on the strategy of a business. If a recession is expected a business can profit by reducing inventory in good time, since stocks could be difficult to sell, and by maintaining a state of liquidity, therefore avoiding the high costs of interest. Management can likewise defer any expansion. For an expected upswing the right strategy may be to build up sufficient inventory in good time and to carry out whatever expansion is necessary to meet increased demand.

Like economic growth, **inflation** is an economic variable that affects management decisions. Since the 1970s double-digit inflation has been a regular phenomenon, and has come to be regarded as a permanent condition in this country, a situation which is in contrast to those of its major trading partners. The average inflation level for the past 10 years is 14,6 per cent. It is therefore necessary to manage the effects of inflation on a permanent basis.

Marketing management must therefore constantly examine the effects of inflation on its marketing strategy. The example of how cars in South Africa are becoming too expensive for consumers serves to indicate the importance of this.

Consumers cannot afford cars

Most South Africans consumers can no longer afford a new car. By comparing the salaries of three profession categories from 1973 to 1990 with the increase in the price of motor cars over the same period, it becomes clear why a car is a luxury for the consumer. From the accompanying table it can be seen that a teacher needed only 3,77 months of gross salary in 1973 to buy a Ford Escort 1300. At the end of 1990 he needed 5,99 months' salary to buy a similar model.

In the case of a luxury car the same teacher would have had to work 10,16 months in 1973 for a Mercedes 230, and at the end of 1990 24,71 months.

The above calculations are based on gross salary. If it is taken into

Months necessary to pay for a car		
Graduated teacher	Ford Escort 1300	Mercedes 230
1973	3,77	10,16
1975	4,07	9,72
1977	5,01	13,89
1979	5,20	14,34
1981	6,65	14,20 *200
1984	5,46	13,10
1987	6,89*Laser	20,31
1990	5,99*Laser 1400	24,71

account that GST and VAT of 10 per cent has in the mean time been added, that interest rates on hire purchase agreements are about three times the rate in 1973, and that personal income tax has doubled, the number of months' salary needed to buy a car will probably be double the number indicated in the above table.

Source: *Sake-Rapport* 16 June 1991, p. 3.

The effects of inflation on a business are profound. It causes a situation of apparent profit, while the organisation's capital is being eroded all the time. It makes cost accounting and the financing of credit difficult. It forces the industrial buyer to build up supplies, while consumers adjust their behaviour to take account of keener price competition, increasing the importance of functionalism and buying early in anticipation of price rises — which often leads to another round of inflation. Inflationary pressures in South Africa are expected to remain high for the next ten years, the most pressure coming from Black wage demands. In the long term this will result in new consumer values, spending, and impoverishment. However, new values also mean new opportunities and new markets.

Another economic variable affecting a business and its market environment is the government's monetary policy, in accordance with which the money supply, interest rates, and the level of the rand relative to the currencies of other countries can be determined. Fiscal policy affects both the business and the consumer through taxation rates and tax reforms. Moreover, government spending in South Africa, as a percentage of gross domestic expenditure, rose from 18,6 per cent in 1980 to approximately 28,2 per cent in 1990. That in itself has brought about change in the economic environment. Drastic social intervention by means of privatisation will bring about still greater changes.

These economic trends, which are adduced simply as a few examples of economic change, without purporting to be exhaustive, demand a constant awareness by marketing management and regular reconsideration of the mission and strategy of the enterprise.

2.6.4 The social environment

The environmental variable probably most subject to the influence of other variables, especially technology and the economy, is social change. Precisely because it affects management indirectly through man as consumer and employee the ultimate effect of social change on the strategy of a business should not be underestimated.

Man is a product of his community. As a member of a particular society he accepts and assimilates its language, its values, its faith, expectations, laws and customs. The culture, the sum total of the way of life of a group of people, influences the individual's way of life, so that consumption cannot be explained solely in economic terms; the effects of culture and social change must also be considered. However, culture is not static. Over time a society's values, expectations, habits and way of life change.

It should also be clearly understood that the culture of any given country is by no means absolutely homogeneous. There are many subcultures based on such things as nationality, religion, population group or geographical area, each of which entails a distinctive change in the environment with consequent implications for the management of a business. A business stands in the centre of social change. On the one hand it contributes to social change, while on the other it should constantly be aware of the major influences of social currents on itself. Here are some observable social trends.

Demographic change, ie change in the growth and composition of populations, is probably the social variable that causes most change in the market by altering people's ways of life. Western societies are characterised by falling population growth rates and shrinking families, with the emphasis on smaller consumer units. There are growing numbers of one-person households, and consequently there is a growing demand for services. There is a growing population of ageing, and more affluent, persons and families over the age of 65, who create special marketing opportunities. And there are increasing numbers of one-parent families, with definite implications for the market and for the social responsibilities of a business.

In Shakespeare's time only 150 000 of the 450 000 words now part of the English language existed. Were he alive today, he would understand only five words out of nine.

Trends which hold certain implications for businesses are also observable among the population of South Africa. (See Chapter 3 in this regard.) Especially the changing population composition, the geographical distribution of people in urban and other areas, age structure, and educational levels play an important role.

Another social variable with clear implications for management is the changing role of women in Western society. As recently as 15 years ago 60 per cent of American women believed that a woman's place was in the home. Now only 22 per cent are of that opinion. In 1970, 72 per cent considered that children were the most important thing in their lives; now only 48 per cent think so. In South Africa the percentage of White women in the labour force rose from 23 per cent in 1960

Urbanisation in South Africa

The following are a few facts about the expected increase from 13,7 million to 30 million people in urban and semi-urban areas in South Africa.

- It means an increase of about 0,8 million people per year.
- About 40 % of the increase will be in the PWV area.
- About 14 % of the annual increase will be in the Durban-Pinetown-Pietermaritzburg area.
- There will be an increase of 5 % in the Port Elizabeth-Uitenhage area, 5 % in East London, and 13 % in the Western Cape.
- The remaining 23 % will probably flow into smaller centres such as Bloemfontein, Nelspruit and Pietersburg.

Source: Spies, P. 'South Africa in the year 2000: Society will decide' in *Energos: South Africa in the year 2000*. Vol 2. Johannesburg: Aviation Publications, p 155.

to 41 per cent in 1983, and the number of White women occupying managerial positions increased from 6,75 per cent in 1969 to about 14 per cent in the eighties.

These developments entail changes in the lives of women and consequently of their families, and also affect their buying patterns by shifting women's shopping hours mostly to weekends and causing women to favour shopping centres that cater for practically all their needs. This trend also puts new pressure on management to offer equal opportunities to women, and to provide day-care for the children of working mothers. The demand for 'convenience products' affects marketing management particularly.

A further social trend that has to be considered is consumerism, the social force that protects the consumer by exerting legal, moral, economic and even political pressure on management. This movement is a natural consequence of a better-educated public that resists such things as misleading advertisements, unsafe products, profiteering, and other objectionable practices, and presses for the rights of the consumer. These aspects are discussed in Chapter 3.

A final aspect of the social environment which warrants observation is the pressure which society exerts on the business organisation, forcing it to be **socially responsible**. This means that business organisations should constantly consider the consequences of their decisions and actions. In most instances criticism of such aspects as misleading advertising, dangerous products, pollution of the environment and exploitation of the consumer are levelled against marketing management. This is probably because marketing management is the final link between the organisation and the consumer.

'Just as a large company seeks to conserve its assets and ensure its future survival by re-investing part of its profits, so it should seek to conserve and improve the social environment in which it does business, in the hope that it will be able to continue to do business in the future, preferably in a better environment than it has at present.'

Source: Oppenheimer, HF. *Financial Mail Supplement.* 30 January 1987, p 9.

2.6.5 The physical environment

The physical environment embraces the limited resources from which a business obtains its raw materials. It is also the environment into which the business discharges its waste. This has a bearing on various forms of pollution. Since the 1960s there has been growing concern about our natural environment, particularly with regard to the exhaustion of resources; there has been protest against all kinds of pollution, and the destruction of the environment by opencast mining and the building of roads and dams; and there has been confirmation of the theories of Malthus and others about the overpopulation of the earth. Business itself has developed an awareness of the physical environment, because this can affect business in many ways. Some interfaces that present opportunities as well as threats to a business can be discerned.

- The *first* interface involves a broad range of resources which are becoming increasingly scarce, such as raw materials, energy and foodstuffs, and are of concern to management. Shortages affect the supply of goods, aggravate inflation, and cause severe price rises; they often necessitate different methods of production and a reorientation of marketing policy when management attempts to find substitutes for unobtainable materials.
- A *second* interface is the increasing cost of energy which also has a direct bearing on the environment, with consequent threats and opportunities for business. The rise in the price of oil, from $2 a barrel in 1970 to $34 in 1982, set in motion a frantic search for alternative sources of energy. Coal was once more in great demand, so that South Africa became second only to Poland as a coal exporter. Research on solar power, wind power and nuclear power was intensified, and the costs of nuclear power were studied. Tumbling oil prices in 1986–7 may once again turn the energy chart upside down. South Africa is fairly rich in energy sources, with 10 per cent of the world's coal reserves, 18 per cent of the Western world's uranium reserves, and some gas and oil off the Southern Cape coast.
- A *third* interface between business and its physical environment is not only the growing cost of pollution to the community in terms of destroyed living space but also the expense of preventing and remedying this while complying with the laws designed to minimise it. Here opportunities also present themselves in the form of new methods of producing and packing goods to reduce pollution to the minimum.

The destruction of plant and animal life by pollution, waste and noxious substances discharged into rivers, fouling the atmosphere and damaging forests, will mean a greatly impoverished environment for human beings in the long run. About 46 % of all urban waste consists of paper and paper products, 12 % of organic waste, 10 % of gas and plants, 10 % of glass, 8 % of metal, 7 % of wood, 4 % of plastic and 3 % of textiles. Since half of all the paper supplied is used for packaging, together with a proportion of glass, metal and plastic, **packaging** alone accounts for more than 50 % of urban waste.

Source: Mansen, RJ. 1983. *Business and the Changing Environment.* New York: McGraw-Hill, pp 28–32.

- The *fourth* interface between a business and its physical environment concerns environmentalism, which may be defined as *an organised movement of citizens and government institutions in defence of the natural environment.* Although the responsibility for a well-ordered ecology cannot be said to rest entirely with business organisations, they ought, nevertheless, to take care that their activities do not affect the environment adversely. Litter and harm to the ecology come from various sources, for example advertising boards and packaging materials in the form of beer cans, soft-drink bottles, and an infinite variety of paper containers, all of which cause pollution, as do substances harmful to man and his natural environment.

The weedkillers used by maize farmers, in the Western Transvaal particularly, to spray their crops constitute only one of many examples. They take years to break down chemically, and they adhere to the soil particles. The wind blows these polluted grains of sand on to blades of grass and the leaves of trees, and with the first showers the poisons are washed down and absorbed through the roots, killing off the flora. A further ecological objection is that excessive advertising and aggressive marketing give rise to greatly increased demand, leading to the plundering of sometimes scarce natural resources.

Business should respond timeously by taking steps to limit any deleterious effects on the community in so far as this is possible. If management does not show clear signs of a decent sense of social responsibility, it should not be surprised if hostile attitudes develop, which may threaten the survival of the enterprise. Therefore the packaging industry is developing containers to minimise pollution, the soap industry is carrying out research on less harmful chemicals, and the motor industry is being compelled by legislation to design exhaust systems which will minimise pollution.

2.6.6 The politico-governmental environment

Management decisions are continually affected by the course of politics, especially the political pressures exerted by the ruling administration and its institutions. As a component of the macro-environment government affects the business environment and business enterprise in a regulating capacity. By promulgating and enforcing legislation it creates order by means of political measures, steering agricultural and economic policy in a particular direction. The policy of the South African government is still (1992) based upon the maintenance of the benefits of the free-market system derived from free enterprise, private ownership, freedom of vocation, and a proper respect for the market mechanism, but with a readiness to intervene whenever monopolistic or any other conditions should obstruct the functioning of the market. Therefore the government intervenes in the total environment on a large scale and influences it by means of the annual budget, taxation, import control or lack of this, promotion of exports, import tariffs to protect certain industries against excessive foreign competition, price control for certain goods and services, the marketing of agricultural products, health regulations, incentives to encourage development in a specific direction, and so on.

Furthermore, the government influences the market both internally and externally: internally through government investment and externally through its political policy, which may determine the acceptability or otherwise of South African goods on international markets. Whenever the government acts as a producer, as in the case of numerous enterprises such as Iscor, Escom and Armscor, it competes with private enterprises for labour, materials and capital.

Privatisation, which takes place at a rather sluggish rate in South Africa, and which lacks credibility considering the fact that the public service workforce increased by 29 000 members in 1988, can also present opportunities and threats. Since 1979 the British government sold more than 40 per cent of its assets at a value of some R40 billion to nine million private investors.[14] China is also moving in the direction of a free-market system and through privatisation has maintained a growth rate of 10 per cent per year for the past eight years.[15] Russia is also moving in the direction of privatisation, which means that the large consumer markets of the future will be found in the East.

To an increasing extent it is the task of management to study the numerous and often complex activities of government as well as legislation and political developments, to determine their influence on the profitable survival of the business.

2.6.7 The international environment

While each of these factors to a greater or lesser extent exerts an influence on the business environment, the situation is rendered even more complex, with more opportunities and threats, if an international dimension is added to each of the environmental factors. Businesses that operate internationally find themselves in a much more complex business environment, because every country has its own peculiar environmental factors, with its own technology, economy, culture, laws, politics, markets and competitiveness, different from those of every other country. International and multinational organisations are susceptible to all kinds of international currents and trends.

The new economic order which is taking shape in Europe, namely the disappearance (removal) of trade barriers between Europe's twelve nations to form one consumer market consisting of 320 million consumers, presents new opportunities and threats to marketing management. With 320 million consumers Europe will overnight become the most affluent consumer market in the world. Some 300 regulations which limit intra-European trade are abolished. The expected results of a single market in Europe are an economic growth rate of seven per cent, a decrease of six per cent in consumer prices, and the creation of five million new jobs. At the same time it will improve Europe's global economic negotiating power, especially with the relatively 'closed' Eastern markets. South African marketers who have a traditional involvement with European markets should utilise opportunities of a single European market. Likewise the economic community which will replace the old Soviet Union, will offer marketing opportunities to Southern African marketers.

Nowadays, nations are also more dependent than ever on one another's technologies, economies, politics and raw materials, so that developments in these fields inevitably influence the decisions of management. Undeveloped countries depend upon technology imported from the developed countries for their self-development. Innovations are excellent export products; suffice it to mention only South African ability and experience in such fields as mining, exploration for minerals, oil-from-coal technology, and veterinary science. The influence of international economic and political developments on local enterprises, particularly in view of their closely interrelated nature, is multiple, and South African managers are acutely aware of the extent to which international influences are exacerbated by our domestic political problems.

2.6.8 Conclusion

In a free market system a business exists in a dynamic environment in which technological innovation, economic fluctuations, changing communities and ways of life, and political trends are continually altering the environment and ultimately affecting it. Awareness and understanding of trends and events in the environment and an ability to foresee how these will affect decision making are now assuming great importance, for in a rapidly changing environment experience of the past is often of little help in solving the new problems that confront management, and extrapolation from previous problems and solutions is therefore futile and counter-productive. Knowledge of currents in the environment, and the identification of issues that largely determine the course of development of a business are also necessary to make possible decisions that will maximise profitability. For that, scanning is a necessary management task. It enables management to identify threats or demands from the environment and, wherever possible, to turn these into opportunities.

2.7 METHODS OF ENVIRONMENTAL SCANNING

The degree to which the environment influences the management of a business depends largely on the **type** of business and the goals it proposes to attain. Moreover, environmental influences differ from functional area to functional area, and even at different levels of management. That means that the importance, scope, and method of scanning, ie the process dealing with the **measurement**, **projection** and **evaluation** of change in the different environmental variables, differ from one organisation to the next.

The importance of environmetal scanning may be summed up as follows:

- The environment is continually changing, so that purposeful scanning is necessary **to keep abreast of change**.
- Scanning is necessary to determine which factors in the environment pose **threats** to the present goals and strategy of a business.
- Scanning is also necessary to determine which factors in the environment present **opportunities** for the more effective attainment of the goals of a business by modification of its strategy.
  Businesses that scan the environment systematically are **more successful** than those that do not.

The scope and range of environmental scanning is determined by the following factors:

- The nature of the environment within which a business operates and the demands made by the environment on a business. The more unstable the environment and the more sensitive the business to change, the more comprehensive the scanning has to be. Increasing instability usually means greater risk.

- The basic relations between a business and its environment. Managers nowadays should constantly bear in mind the basic relationships of a business to its environment. The importance or otherwise of any one or more of these relationships to management will affect the scope of environmental scanning.

- The source and extent of change will also influence the extent of scanning significantly. The impact of change is rarely so 'compartmentalised' as to affect only one or two areas of an organisation. Change has an interactive and dynamic effect on several aspects of a business.

The *method* of environmental scanning is a much-debated subject. It will in any case be determined by the importance of the environment to the business and the measure of scanning required. The following are a few guidelines:

- The most elementary basis for scanning is to keep up to date with **relevant** secondary or published information obtainable from a vast wealth of sources, such as the media, the organisation's own data, trade publications, financial journals, statistics, associates in other organisations, banks, research institutions, and even employees. Such information may be added to the business information system of the organisation.

- A more advanced basis for scanning would be the addition of primary information, or special studies on particular aspects of the environment. Such studies can be carried out by members of the organisation's own staff or by consultants called in from outside.

- A much more advanced basis is the setting up of a scanning unit within the business with its own staff who scrutinise a broad range of environmental variables and make forecasts concerning certain variables. Economic predictions by economists using a number of models, assessments by market researchers of the market and of competition, and technological predictions by industrial analysts are only a few examples. Such a scanning unit is usually located in the planning department of management.

The question now arising is how all the collected information can be brought to the attention of the appropriate manager. There are many different opinions about this, the commonest being that information about the environment forms the basis of strategic planning, which is the responsibility of top management.

2.8 SUMMARY

A business and the community that it serves are not self-sufficient, closed entities: they depend on one another for survival. Together they form a complex dynamic business environment in which changes in the environmental variables continually determine the prosperity or otherwise of a business. Since these variables are often beyond the control of the business, it is the task of management to adapt the organisation to change. Sometimes the business operates pro-actively — management takes the lead and anticipates events — thereby accelerating and augmenting change. Knowledge of a changing environment through sustained scanning is a prerequisite for taking advantage of opportunities and averting threats.

REFERENCES

1. Aaker, DA. 1988. *Strategic Market Management*. New York: John Wiley & Sons, p 13.
2. Kruger, W. 'Patterns of Success in German Businesses' in *Long Range Planning,* vol 22, No 2, p 105.
3. This paragraph is based largely on Cronjé, GJ de J, Neuland, EW & Van Reenen, MJ (eds). 1987. *Introduction to Business Management*. Johannesburg: Southern Book Publishers, pp 45–55.
4. Pearce, JA and Robinson, RB. 1988. *Formulation and Implementation of Competitive Strategy*. Homewood, Illinois: Richard D Irwin, p 202.
5. Vasconcellos e Sá, J. 1988. 'The Impact of Key Success Factors on Company Performance' in *Long Range Planning,* vol 21, no 6, pp 56–64.
6. Pearce and Robinson op cit, p 207.
7. Ibid p 211.
8. Porter, ME. *How competitive forces shape strategy,* as quoted in Pearce & Robinson op cit, p 124.
9. Kotler, P. 1984. *Marketing Management*. Englewood Cliffs, New Jersey: Prentice-Hall Inc, p 100.
10. Aaker op cit, p 113.
11. Ibid p 114.
12. Lombard, JA, Stadler, JJ & Haasbroek, PJ. 1985. *Die Ekonomiese Stelsel van Suid-Afrika*. Pretoria: HAUM, p 286.
13. Ibid p 288.
14. Manning op cit, p 20.
15. Ibid.

CASE STUDY

TOYOTA'S ENVIRONMENT

Toyota South Africa, one of the biggest car manufacturers in the country, is constantly exposed to environmental influences. Some are internal management problems affecting decisions on its mission. These may take the form of internal pressure from shareholders and management to set a course in some particular direction, or of internal conflict and office politics, or of human resources having to be appointed or retrenched because of a recession. These are all influences of the micro-environment, but the management of Toyota is constantly influenced by the market and the macro-environment too. Management is affected directly by the market environment through the needs, preferences and purchasing power of consumers, and consequently it produces vehicles to suit these demands. Management also has to take into account the suppliers of components and materials, particularly with regard to their availability, quality and cost. Moreover, management must always keep a watchful eye on the activities of competing car manufacturers. Such factors may separately or collectively create opportunities (improved consumer purchasing power, more favourable rates of exchange making it possible to import components at a lower cost, competitors discontinuing a certain model) or a threat (declining purchasing power, suppliers raising their prices, marketing strategies of competitors becoming more effective) to management.

Toyota is indirectly affected by the macro-environment through technological innovation, for instance competitors may employ technological improvements in the mechanical and electronic fields in the production of their models, or new methods of production might be introduced, such as robot factories, that supplant other methods. Economic variables such as fluctuations in exchange rates in turn influence the cost of imported components, while monetary and fiscal policy will affect the purchasing power of consumers through interest rates, taxes and hire-purchase terms, causing them to spend more or less money on cars. Social trends, such as increasing urbanisation, also indirectly affect Toyota through their influence on the market. Indirect influences from the physical environment include the high price of imported fuel and the possible exploration of oil in Mossel Bay. Toyota is further affected all the time by the laws and regulations of the institutional environment, the demands of trade unions, and the influences of politics. Although these influences in the macro-environment do not affect the day-to-day activities of Toyota, the indirect influence of such factors, separately or collectively, needs to be constantly observed and considered by the management of Toyota to ensure survival and success in the long term.

Source: Cronjé, GJ de J et al (eds). 1990. *Introduction to Business Management*. Johannesburg: Southern, p 44.

QUESTIONS

1. List the potential threats in Toyota's external environment. How can Toyota counter these threats?

2. What is meant by internal strengths and weaknesses?

3. Toyota strives to ensure continued success in the long term. Does this mean that Toyota must sell as many automobiles as possible? Explain.

Enough dealers for after service care

CHAPTER 3

THE MARKET ENVIRONMENT

3.1 INTRODUCTION

The aim of this chapter is to describe the market environment, which is part of the total marketing environment. The internal and macro variables in the marketing environment received attention in the previous chapter.

The focus of this chapter is on the demand and supply side of the market environment with which marketing management is in close contact. In the market environment various opportunities and threats can be identified by marketing management whose task it then is to utilise these opportunities and to counter threats if at all possible.

A market has two sides, namely a **demand side** and a **supply side**. On the demand side are the potential consumers at whom the market offering is directed. On the supply side are all the enterprises competing for consumer patronage and the suppliers offering all kinds of products and services.

The South African market is complex. Nevertheless, marketing management must carefully scan this complex market and create market offerings to ensure that:

- consumer needs, demands and preferences are met;
- society is not harmed in any way;
- the struggle against competitors is won;
- profitability is attained.

After defining the concept of a 'market' this chapter continues with a description of the consumer market. Three questions can be asked:

- What is the nature of the market in terms of numbers and purchasing power?
- Why do consumers buy certain products and services?
- Where, how much, when and how do consumers buy?

All three questions are answered in this chapter.

ORGANISATION OF THE CHAPTER

Definition of the market concept: Different types of markets, the demand and supply sides of the market.

The nature of the consumer market: Demographic details of the consumer market, income and expenditure patterns.

Consumer behaviour: Individual, group and economic factors determining consumer behaviour.

Consumer decision making: Information processing, the decision making process, real, habitual and impulsive decision making.

Consumerism: The development of consumerism, problems, rights and responsibilities of consumers, the functions of the South African Co-ordinating Consumer Council.

3.2 DEFINING THE MARKET CONCEPT

3.2.1 Kinds of markets

The consumer market represents the demand side of the market environment and consists of final consumers (individuals and households), who purchase products for their own consumption. Marketing also takes place in other markets, namely the industrial market and the reseller's market. These institutions also purchase products and services, but not for their own use — rather to use in production processes or to resell at a profit.

The supply side of the market consists of competitors and suppliers who strive, each in their own area, to gain patronage of consumers.

This book, as indicated previously, focuses mainly on the marketing of consumer products to final consumers. In Chapter 20 the specialised application areas of marketing (such as marketing of industrial products and services) are discussed in more detail. Retail marketing is discussed in Chapter 21.

3.2.2 The supply side of the market

3.2.2.1 The competitors

On the supply side of the market many enterprises with roughly similar market offerings compete freely against one another for the attention and patronage of consumers. This free competition is one of the essentials for a free-market system.

In one sense all marketers therefore compete with all other marketers for the money in the consumer's pocket. The greater the demand for a specific market offering, the greater the chance of making a profit and therefore the fiercer the competition. This means that the threat posed by competition intensifies with increasing marketing success.

The greatest advantages of free competition from a marketing viewpoint are more satisfied consumers and a higher standard of living all round. Every competitor strives to offer new and better methods of satisfying consumer needs, thereby achieving its objectives of profitability and growth. These continued efforts lead to new and better products and services, innovation is encouraged, and lower selling prices may even result. It is true, therefore, to say that intense competition creates opportunities for enterprising marketers. Product positioning in a gap in the market is an example of the absence of competitors in a certain area creating a marketing opportunity for other competitors.

Competitors can be classified as **market leaders** who are always first with a specific market offering; **market followers** with 'me too' strategies; **challengers** who enter the market by starting price wars and employing aggressive advertising campaigns; and **avoiders** who avoid confrontation and strive to attain a state of peaceful co-existence.

Marketing warfare and competitive strategies are discussed in more detail in Chapters 18 and 19.

3.2.2.2 *The suppliers*

Suppliers offer raw materials, spare parts and services to the market and are therefore considered to be part of the supply side. Ordinarily marketing management is not involved in negotiations with suppliers, which is usually the task of the purchasing department. It cannot be denied, however, that the way in which this task is performed has a definite influence on marketing activities. If the supplier of packaging material delivers late, for example, the whole marketing effort suffers. Suppliers of services, such as advertising practitioners and market research agencies, can also directly influence the marketing of consumer products and services.

Enough said on the topic of supply. The remainder of this chapter focuses on the demand side of the market.

3.2.3 The demand side of the market

The demand side of the market consists of a relatively large number of individuals:[1]

- needing a specific product;
- having the ability to purchase;
- willing to purchase the product; and
- having the authority to purchase.

In a market all and not only some of these prerequisites must be met. Teenagers, for example, who are forbidden by law to purchase liquor, cannot be regarded as a 'market' for brandy even if they are willing to spend money on it.

The demand side of the market also involves other interested parties. There are government and other organisations guarding the interests of consumers and the general public. Many newspapers, for example, discuss consumer affairs, such as high prices, price increases, misleading advertising and other unethical business practices, on a regular basis. The South African Co-ordinating Consumer Council, which is discussed later in this chapter, is one such organisation which can and does influence consumer demand for products and services.

To summarise: the demand side of the consumer market consists of potential consumers who have the authority to purchase and who are willing to do so. Demand can, however, also be influenced by certain other organisations.

The demographic details of the consumer market, the behaviour patterns of consumers, consumer decision making and consumerism are discussed in the following sections.

3.3 THE NATURE OF THE CONSUMER MARKET   *STUDY OF STATS OF BIRTHS, DEATHS*

3.3.1 The significance of demographic characteristics   *DISEASE etc.*

The South African consumer market is difficult to describe because it consists of a large number of groups with diverse demographic characteristics. Demographics is a statistical study of the human population and includes aspects such as population composition, age, language and geographic structures. Demographic details indicate only how many individuals with certain characteristics are to be found in a specific group; if these numbers are monitored over time trends can be identified. Marketing management studies these trends to determine the nature of a future or potential market.

The question to be asked is why marketing management is so interested in these details. The answer is, first, because demographic characteristics indicate the size of a specific market and therefore the potential demand for a specific product, and, secondly, because changes in this market will give marketing management the opportunity to adapt plans accordingly. If, for example, statistics show an increase in the birth-rate over a period of a few years, this may create an opportunity for marketers of children's clothing and toys.

The baby boom

After the Second World War in 1946 the birth-rate in the United States of America increased sharply — it was referred to as the 'baby boom'. Through the years the baby boom created a market first for baby clothes and other necessities, then for children's clothing and toys, then for school books, then for fashion clothing and motor cars for teenagers, then for houses and furniture as the 'babies' grew up and their needs changed. Within the next 20 years there will probably be a demand for frail-care products and services for the aged.

3.3.2 The population

The total population in South Africa according to the 1989 census was 32 million — in 1990 it is expected to increase to 36 million, in 1995, 40 million, in 2000, 45 million and in 2035 between 94 and 119 million. The population which South Africa with its limited resources (land and water) can accommodate is 80 million. This means that the country will not be able to support its population growth from early on in the 21st century. Therefore people must now be persuaded to help stop the expected population growth by proper family planning.

Growing markets resulting from the increase in population offer good opportunities for marketers of a variety of products and services. The problem is to supply the right products at the right time, place and price to a growing population. If the resources to do this are inadequate the country will become poorer and poorer.

The South African population tends to concentrate in the large urban areas in search of housing, work and training opportunities. This leads to overpopulation in some areas and underpopulation in others and invariably to social problems. It serves no purpose to look at the various areas in general because they differ so drastically. In some areas population growth must be stemmed, in others it must rather be encouraged, in some areas illiteracy is a problem, in others a lack of employment opportunities is a problem.

Because the demographic characteristics of our population differ from area to area, it is necessary for marketers to study the nature of the area they wish to serve.

3.3.3 Characteristics of development areas in South Africa

Nine areas in which economic development must take place were delimitated in 1982. Since then the areas have been economically developed as units in the total South African economy. In determining the borders of the different areas no attempt was made to make all economically equal. The physical and economical characteristics were of overriding importance in the attempt to bring together that which naturally belong together. The development policy for all the areas is aimed at encouraging industrial development. Recently the Government announced that this policy will allow each area to select its own economic strengths on which to base its development efforts. In this way an area with exceptional scenic beauty can identify tourism as a potential strong point while one with the necessary raw materials available can concentrate on mining.

The PWV area (H) is economically the strongest — South Africa's economic engine — with area A in the second place. The three areas which are economically the strongest were responsible for 65,8 % of the total gross national product (GNP) in 1989. The other economically weaker areas are therefore economically dependent on these three. Area D for example cannot pay for its own social services and depends on the central government for funds. People in a specific area usually form a cultural and ethnic unity.

Population growth, standard of living, behaviour patterns of consumers and even age composition depend largely on the economic prospects of that area.

Figure 3.1 is a map of South Africa and the nine development areas marked from A to J. The contribution to the GNP is given in Table 3.1.

The Development Bank of Southern Africa has just introduced a publication which contains a variety of facts of importance to marketers. It must be kept in mind, however, that only averages are given and that deviations will definitely occur. The comparison for the areas is given in Table 3.2.

From Table 3.2 it can be seen that the Western Cape is now officially the land of the lazy. The population in this area has the highest life expectancy. At 65,5 years it is almost more than three years more than that in area B. Perhaps the longer life expectancy can be ascribed to the fact that more people retire in the Cape than elsewhere.

Area H has the biggest economy but its population is not better off than that of area F, for example, where the annual income per capita is the highest at R9 835. This area has also shown the biggest growth between 1970 and 1989. Area G's per capita income of R1 461 is only 14 % of that in area F.

As can be expected, area F has the lowest unemployment figure (8,7 % of the potential labour market), as well as the most productive workers. Each worker in area F contributed R25 650 per annum to the gross geographic product (GGP) in 1989.

It is very interesting to note that this successful area F has the lowest literacy level. Only 5,2 % of its population has had formal education at one stage or other. This compares to 81,3 % in area A.

Apparently people in the Cape do not work very hard. Despite the higher literacy level each worker could only manage to contribute R17 557 to the GGP of the area.

As if this is not enough the Development Bank says that life expectancy is a good measure of the quality of life!

FIGURE 3.1 Economic development areas in South Africa

TABLE 3.1   Area contribution to the total GNP (%)

AREA	1970	1980	1989
A	13.9	13.1	12.9
B	3.1	2.5	1.9
C	9.0	7.4	6.4
D	6.3	6.8	7.0
E	12.3	14.0	14.6
F	4.3	6.6	9.6
G	4.1	2.3	3.0
H	40.0	41.5	38.3
J	6.8	5.7	6.1

Source: Development Bank of Southern Africa.

TABLE 3.2   Comparison for the areas

THE AREA WITH THE:	AREA
■ biggest surface (259 915 m²)	A
■ highest population (4,3 million people)	G
■ highest life expectancy (on average 65,5 years)	A
■ lowest life expectancy (on average 62,5 years)	B
■ highest population growth (3,8 % p.a.)	G
■ lowest population growth (2,0 % p.a.)	B
■ highest population density (281 per m²)	G
■ highest urbanisation rate (3,7 % p.a.)	G
■ biggest part of population in urban areas (93 %)	H
■ highest literacy level* (81,3 % of population)	A
■ lowest literacy level (5,2 % of population)	F
■ highest dependency ratio** (4,8 per worker)	G
■ lowest dependency ratio (1,9 per worker)	H
■ biggest potential labour market (4,5 million people)	H
■ biggest gross geographical product (GGP) (R80 billion)	H
■ lowest GGP (R3,9 billion)	B
■ highest growth in GGP (average 1970-1989, 6,8 %)	F
■ lowest growth in GGP (1970-1989, 0,1 %)	B
■ highest GGP per capita of population (R9 855 p.a.)	F
■ lowest GGP per capita of population (R1 461 p.a.)	G
■ highest unemployment (25 % of potential labour market)	D
■ lowest unemployment (8,7 % of potential labour market)	F
■ most productive workers (GGP is R25 650 per worker)	F
■ most unproductive workers (GGP is R8 429 per worker)	G

 * Literacy level: Percentage of population with any form of formal education.
** Dependency ratio: Number of people supported by an economically active person (himself excluded).

Source: Development Bank of Southern Africa, as quoted in *Finansies & Tegniek*. 11 October 1991, pp 12-13.

3.3.4 Language

In South Africa 22 different languages are spoken, namely English, Afrikaans, Zulu, Xhosa, Venda, North Sotho, Tswana, Tsonga, Shaangaan, Swazi, Ndebele, Hindi, Tamil, Gugerati, Telegu, Urdu, Greek, German, Portuguese, Dutch, Italian and Chinese. In the rural areas 82 per cent of the Whites speak Afrikaans while the percentage in urban areas is 53 per cent.

The language spoken determines to a degree the consumer's cultural background, consumption patterns and buying habits. The language spoken is also important in the formulation of marketing messages. Obviously a message in an individual's mother tongue will have greater impact than in any other language. However, it is in practice impossible to translate marketing messages into 22 different languages. Usually marketing messages are presented only in English and Afrikaans, and the more well-known Black languages, namely Sotho and Zulu.

3.3.5 Age structure

It is a well-known fact that the needs of consumers differ from one age group to another. It is therefore important for the marketer of consumer products to know how many individuals there are in the different age groups.

Owing to its rapid population growth the average age of South Africans is relatively low in comparison with other countries where a substitution rate or even a no-growth rate is maintained.

> About 11 percent of the population of Japan of 124 million is now 65 years or older. With a declining birth rate and the longest life expectancy in the world this percentage will increase to 17 % by the year 2000 and to 21 % in 2010 (life expectancy is 75,5 years for men and 81,3 years for women).

> The "greying" of Japan will cause great social and economic changes in the years to come. Pension and health costs are expected to increase, tax pressure will be put on younger people and millions of people will have to be imported to alleviate the shortage of workers. In Japan companies insist that workers of 60 or 62 should retire.
>
> Source: *Finansies & Tegniek*, 25 October 1991, pp 53-54.

> In South Africa there are 51,5 % in the young group (16-19), 44,0 % in the adult group (20-64) and 4,5 % in the senior group (65+).
>
> Source: Central Statistical Services, as quoted in Nel PA *et al* 1988. *Researching the South African market*. Pretoria: Unisa, p 18.

3.3.6 Education

The higher the level of education, the higher the level of development. The dire need for education facilities in South Africa is generally recognised. Only a relatively small number of people is highly educated. This group's income and expenditure patterns differ from those of the far larger group with a lower level of education. Marketers must be aware of this distinction, especially in formulating complicated marketing messages which may not easily be understood by less-educated consumers. Table 3.2 shows that 81,3 % of the population in area A have had formal schooling compared to 5,2 % in area F.

3.3.7 Income and expenditure patterns

Income and expenditure patterns are important because they can give an indication of consumers' spending ability and the types of products and services required. Institutions like Market Research Africa (MRA) and the Bureau for Market Research (Unisa) often undertake nationwide surveys of these income and expenditure patterns. The well-known All Products and Media Survey (AMPS) of the MRA is an example. Research reports are also available at the Bureau for Market Research.

The South African population is getting poorer and poorer due to illiteracy, fast population growth, unemployment and inflation. Table 3.3 indicates how many people in urban and rural areas are living on earnings lower than the minimum subsistence level.

TABLE 3.3   Urban and rural population living on less than the minimum subsistence level

	URBAN	RURAL	TOTAL
Number	3 265 180	7 044 532	10 309 712
%	21,0	64,5	38,9

Source: Nel PA. 'n Evaluasie van voedingsintervensieprogramme. *Research report* No 88/19. Bureau for Market Research, Pretoria, p 88.

Spending patterns of persons in higher income groups differ from those in lower income groups. Persons in the last-mentioned group spend proportionally more on food but less on services than the more well to do. Generally speaking the main components of private consumer spending is as in Figure 3.2.

A living standard

A medium low-living standard for a family of five in a town in the PWV area was R870,72. The average expenditure was as follows:

Groceries	R349,70
Cleaning materials	24,62
Toiletries	23,36
Fuel	43,53
Medical expenditure	30,00
Clothing	139,42
Rent/School	110,00
Transport	63,10
Durable products	90,00

Source: *Finansies & Tegniek*, 23 June 1989, p 2 and 28 April 1989, p 14.

FIGURE 3.2   Main components of private consumption expenditure — 1985

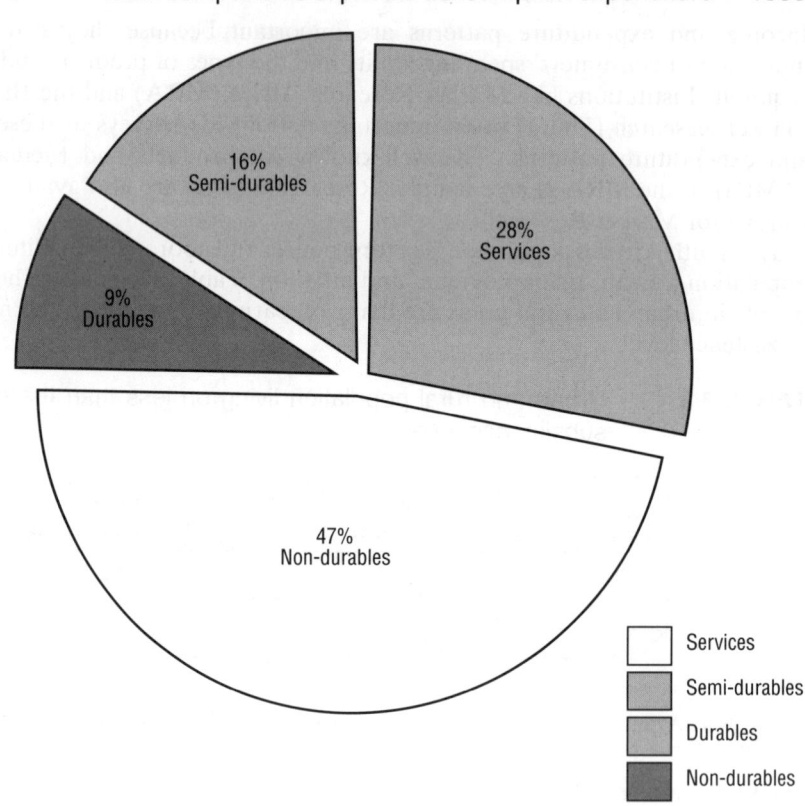

Source: South African Reserve Bank, as quoted by Nel, PA et al. 1988. *Researching the South African Market.* Pretoria: University of South Africa, p 8.

3.4 CONSUMER BEHAVIOUR

3.4.1 Defining consumer behaviour

Consumers are one of the most important components of the consumer market, and therefore knowledge of the general behaviour patterns of consumers and consumer decision making is of crucial importance to marketing management.

The study of consumer behaviour is directed at those factors that determine behaviour as well as the consumer decision making process underlying behaviour. The purpose of this study is to **explain** and to **forecast** human behaviour patterns in a purchasing situation. The marketer wants to know why a consumer decides to purchase one product rather than another. This knowledge is essential to the consumer-oriented marketer; it will facilitate marketing planning and help guide the development of a market offering which will provide better need-satisfaction to consumers than that of competitors.

Consumer behaviour consists of those acts of decision making units (families as well as individuals) directly involved in obtaining and using need-satisfying products and services, and includes the decision making process that precedes and determines these acts.[2]

From the above definition it is clear that consumer behaviour consists of both **overt** acts (buying and using products) and **covert** processes (decision making). Furthermore, consumer behaviour does not refer to a behaviour pattern of one individual only, as several family members may be involved in any single consumer decision.

The study of consumer behaviour resulted from the problems in matching mass consumption to mass production. It is therefore a relatively new field of study. The first textbook appeared only in 1966[3] but since then many writers have focused their efforts on this interesting and important subject.

3.4.2 Overview of the theory of consumer behaviour

An overview of all the variables involved in the theory of consumer behaviour is depicted in Figure 3.3 before the discussion proceeds in more detail.

Individual factors in the model refers to factors inherent in human behaviour. Motivation refers to a consumer's need to purchase a specific market offering. Perception entails the interpretation of a marketing message. The consumer also possesses an ability to learn need-satisfying behaviour patterns and to understand the marketing message. Attitudes refer to tendencies to act in a certain way. Personality and life style are variables that determine the combination of products and services which are likely to be purchased by a specific type of person, and thus his way of life.

How individual factors influence consumer behaviour

Motivation: The young girl needs (has a motive) to be pretty and to be loved by her boyfriend. She buys REVLON cosmetics.

Perception: The young man sees a cinema advertisement for CAMEL cigarettes. His interpretation is that smoking demonstrates masculinity. He buys a packet of CAMEL.

Learning ability: The housewife learns through experience that COBRA floor polish will put a shine on her floors. She remembers to purchase COBRA on her next shopping trip.

Attitudes: The teetotaller has a negative attitude to liquor. He does not even read the advertisement for brandy and never considers buying it.

Personality and life style: The man is ambitious. He buys books, travels overseas frequently, lives in a gracious home, plays golf and reads *Financial Mail* and other business publications.

FIGURE 3.3   A model of consumer behaviour

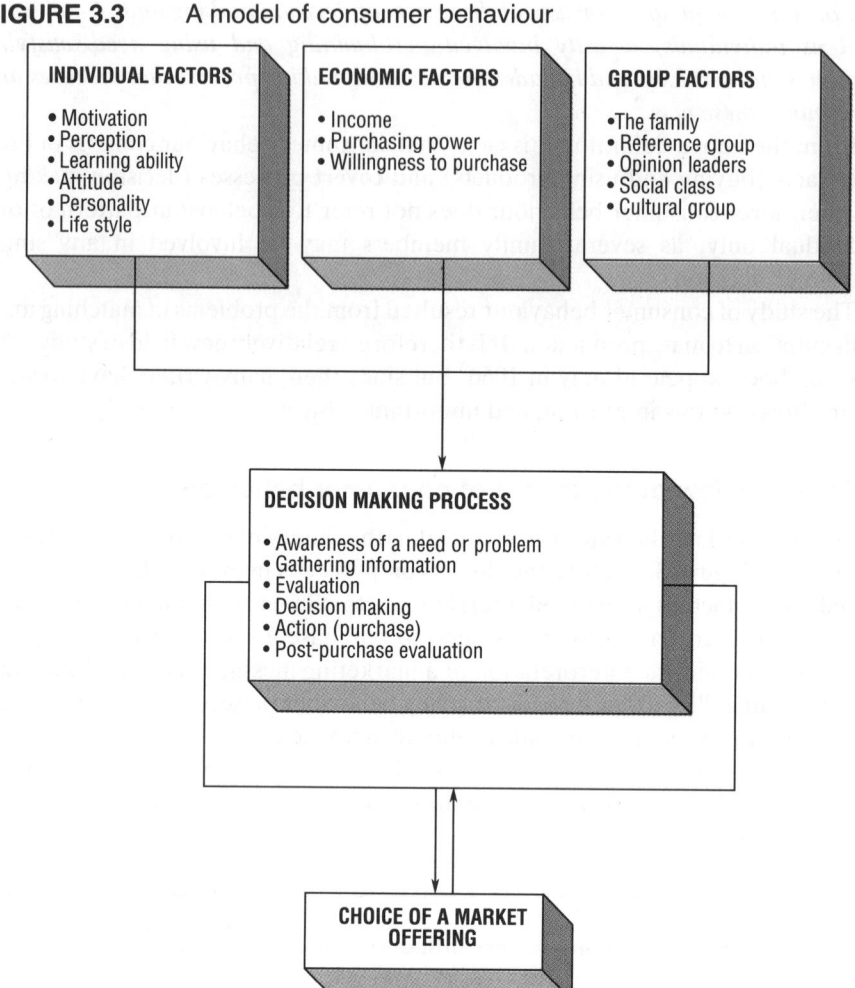

Group factors in Figure 3.3 refer to the cultural background, the social class and the immediate social environment in which the consumer must make purchasing decisions. The family, reference groups and opinion leaders are components of the consumer's immediate social environment.

How group factors influence consumer behaviour

Social class: People in the highest social class are usually wealthy. They tend to avoid products such as cheap jewellery.

The family: If the father in the family is the dominant personality, he will make most of the decisions regarding spending of money.

Cultural group: As a cultural group Jews tend to avoid eating pork and pork products.

Opinion leaders: The fashionable lady who has just returned from Paris is the opinion leader regarding the newest fashion trends. Her friends look to her for advice on fashion.

Reference group: The teenager is part of a reference group which prescribes what she should wear and what is unacceptable. She is unwilling to wear the dress her mother bought for her, convinced that she will appear ridiculous to her friends.

Economic factors refer to the income that enables the consumer to purchase a selection of products and services, and the willingness of the consumer indeed to spend this income.

The **decision making process** in Figure 3.3 consists of several successive steps and illustrates how a consumer goes about choosing how to spend his money. The first step is obviously that he must become aware of an unfulfilled need which can be satisfied by purchasing a specific product. He then gathers and processes information, evaluates alternatives, makes a decision and acts. Finally, the outcome of the decision is evaluated in the light of the consumer's experience with the purchased product.

Finally, Figure 3.3 shows that all these factors and decision making steps lead to the **choice of a specific market offering**. The nature of the market offering has been discussed in detail in Chapter 1. The product purchased by the consumer is not merely a physical object: the **place** where it is bought (distribution outlet), the **price**, and even the nature of the **marketing communication message** are all part and parcel of the total product. Purchasing a market offering provides new input to the next decision that must be taken.

The aforementioned components of the consumer behaviour model, as well as the underlying theory, can now be discussed in greater detail.

3.4.3 Individual factors determining consumer behaviour

3.4.3.1 *Motivation*

Motivation can be defined as the driving force within an individual which impels him to act in order to attain a certain objective. This driving force is the result of an unfulfilled need. Thus it can be said that unfulfilled needs motivate behaviour.

The best-known and also the most accepted theory of classifying the diversity of needs is that of Maslow. He classified human needs in a scheme in which the lower-level needs must first be satisfied, or partly satisfied, before the higher-level needs can fully emerge. Figure 3.4 shows Maslow's hierarchy of needs. The lowest-level needs are physiological, which help to ensure survival of the individual. The highest level is reflected in the desire for self-actualisation. According to this theory, the individual is motivated to fulfil whichever need is most strongly felt at any given time.

FIGURE 3.4   Maslow's hierarchy of needs

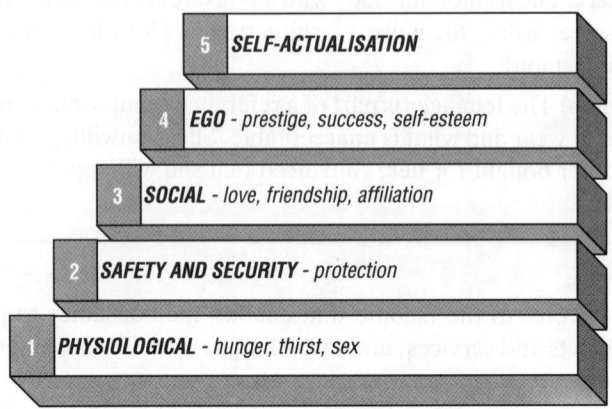

Source: Adapted from Maslow, AH. 1954. *Motivation and Personality*. New York: Harper & Row Publishers.

- The basic physiological need, hunger, impels the consumer to purchase bread and milk.
- Safety needs motivate the consumer to erect a security fence.
- Social needs underly a host of purchasing decisions, from cosmetics to deodorants.
- Ego needs impel consumers to purchase luxury products as symbols of status and success.
- Self-actualisation is the highest human need and has to do with personal development and individuality. It is unfortunately true that few people are in a position to satisfy this need. The buying of designer clothing is an example of an attempt to express individuality.

As is the case with the physiological and emotional motives, economic motives can also influence consumers to purchase. The economic motives are all rational by nature, dealing with technical functions and performance of the product, and are usually expressed in quantitative terms. These are in fact the functional motives underlying buying behaviour. Physiological, emotional and economic motives are depicted in Figure 3.5.

The fact that these motives are universal to all people does not imply that all human beings have the same needs, the same order of need-satisfaction, or even that the order of need-satisfaction will remain the same for any length of time.

Many advertising appeals are purely emotional in nature, promising a measure of need-satisfaction which cannot readily be obtained. Few consumers believe these promises literally and therefore they cannot be regarded as misleading. Economic advantages, especially those stated in quantitative terms, however, must live up to the consumer's expectation as it is relatively easy to compare the promise made in the appeal and the degree of need-satisfacation obtained in reality.

FIGURE 3.5   Motives of consumers

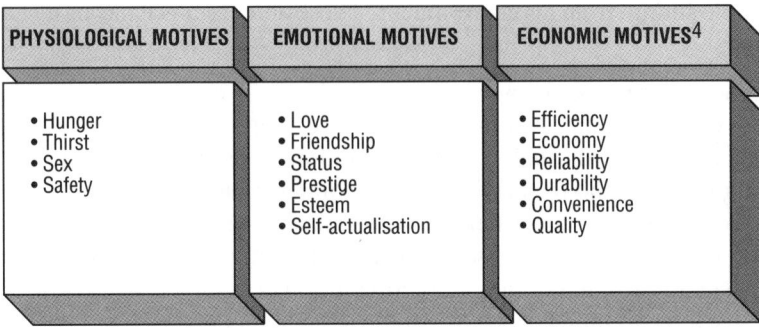

3.4.3.2 *Perception*

Perception involves seeing, hearing, feeling, tasting and smelling. These stimuli cause certain sensations which can influence a consumer to purchase or not to purchase.

Sensory stimuli

Seeing plays a role in purchasing jewellery.

Hearing plays a role in purchasing musical instruments.

Feeling plays a role in purchasing soft toys.

Tasting plays a role in purchasing sweets.

Smelling plays a role in purchasing perfume.

In purchasing a new motor car, virtually all the senses play a role in perception.

A consumer must pick up sensory stimuli from the environment before he will react. Perception also plays a crucial role in the interpretation of a marketing message. A consumer will perceive a certain market offering only after he has received sensory stimuli, especially after seeing or hearing the marketing message.

Perception can be defined as the process whereby an individual selects, organises and integrates stimuli into a meaningful and coherent overall picture.[5] The stimuli are picked up by the senses and relayed to the brain where they are interpreted. The consumer reacts according to his interpretation and not always according to objective reality. Subjective factors always play a role in perception. The experiences, values and prejudices of an individual colour his perceptions. This means that few people perceive things in exactly the same way.

Because so many, often conflicting, stimuli are received simultaneously the individual tends to defend himself. He may ignore some or distort the meaning of unwelcome stimuli. Such perceptual defence mechanisms protect a person against undesirable stimuli from his environment. These defence mechanisms include the following:

- **Selective exposure** occurs when a person selectively chooses to expose himself only to certain stimuli. A consumer can, for example, avoid unwelcome stimuli by quickly paging through a magazine and missing the advertisements or by turning off the radio or television when commercials come on.
- **Selective attention** occurs when the individual does not pay full attention to the stimuli picked up by the senses. Selective attention causes a consumer not to comprehend the content of a marketing message.
- **Selective interpretation** occurs when the stimuli are perceived but the message itself is not interpreted as it was intended to be. The consumer can interpret a marketing message incorrectly by distorting the meaning or by misunderstanding it.
- **Selective recall** refers to the individual's ability to remember only certain stimuli and to forget others which may be important. At the point of purchase consumers must therefore once again be reminded to purchase the product. The conclusion here is that the marketing message must be appropriately formulated to overcome the consumer's defence mechanisms.

3.4.3.3 *Learning ability*

The consumer's ability to learn also influences his behaviour.[6] He must for example know which product attributes relate to which brand and where it can be purchased. He must also be able to recognise the distinctive packaging. The consumer must remember the information supplied in the marketing message when he is in a position to act (purchase the product).

Learning can be defined as the result of a combination of motivation, attention, experience and repetition. Three elements are implied in this definition. In order to learn the learner/consumer must be **motivated**, he must give his full **attention** to the message (he must perceive and experience it) and there must be some measure of effective **repetition**. In proper combination these three elements result in a successful learning situation. Imbalance in any way invariably leads to failure.

The following learning principles are important when formulating marketing messages:

- Repetition is important to reinforce the message.
- A unique message is best remembered.
- A message which is easy to understand is easy to learn.
- The law of primacy states that the aspect mentioned at the beginning of the message is best remembered, but according to the law of recency the last-mentioned aspect is also remembered.
- Demonstrations facilitate the learning process.
- Promises of rewards (or threats of punishment) facilitate learning.

- Serious fear-producing appeals are avoided; consumers tend to distort such messages.

3.4.3.4 Attitude

A positive attitude to a product promotes brand loyalty but a negative attitude is virtually impossible to reverse.

Negative attitudes to products

- Conservationists abhor killing wild animals and maintain a very negative attitude to the wearing of fur coats.
- Members of some religious groups disapprove of the use of cosmetics.
- Health-conscious people exhibit a negative attitude towards the use of cane sugar.
- Teetotallers avoid liquor products.
- Conservative people have negative attitudes towards way-out fashions. They often forbid their children to purchase these fashions.
- Some men have negative attitudes towards using deodorants. They believe that such products are only for women.

Attitudes can be defined as relatively inflexible tendencies to perceive and act in some consistently favourable or unfavourable manner with regard to a given object or idea. Attitudes are learned as a result of experience. They determine behaviour patterns which are relatively inflexible. A consumer develops attitudes towards products, services, stores and advertising messages.[7]

3.4.3.5 Personality

Personality refers to those psychological characteristics of a person which both determine and reflect his reaction to environmental influences. Personality distinguishes one individual from another, and one group of individuals with similar characteristics from another group. There are several personality types, the classification of which by Karen Horney is best known.[8] She identified the following three types:

- **Compliant** individuals who move towards others. They desire to be loved and appreciated.
- **Aggressive** individuals who move against others. They desire only to excel.
- **Detached** individuals who move away from others. They are self-sufficient.

It is difficult to relate personality types to product choices. There are, however, indications that compliant individuals drink more wine than others, that aggressive individuals tend to shave with razor blades, while detached individuals prefer tea to coffee.

3.4.3.6 *Life style*

Life style refers to the way of living of individuals or families. The life style concept provides descriptions of behaviour and purchasing patterns, especially the ways in which people spend their time and money. Personality, motives and attitudes together influence life style.

The AIO classification[9] describes activities, interests and opinions of consumers. Figure 3.6 indicates some dimensions of life style often used to describe the attributes of a specific market segment (see Chapter 4, particularly Figure 4.2).

FIGURE 3.6   Life style dimensions

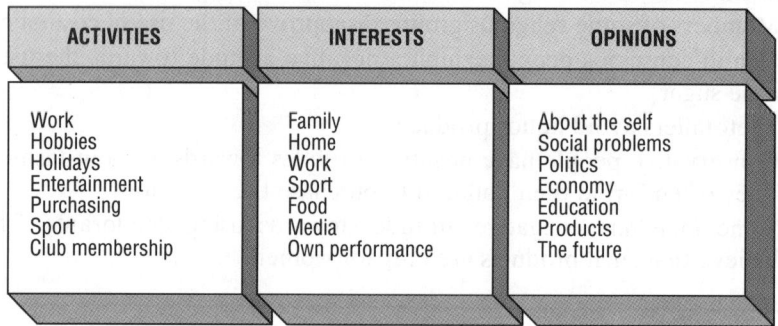

ACTIVITIES	INTERESTS	OPINIONS
Work	Family	About the self
Hobbies	Home	Social problems
Holidays	Work	Politics
Entertainment	Sport	Economy
Purchasing	Food	Education
Sport	Media	Products
Club membership	Own performance	The future

3.4.4 Group factors

3.4.4.1 *The nature of group influence*

The consumer is a human being who needs to be affiliated with other people in order to satisfy his social needs. Group membership will therefore influence the individual's behaviour patterns. Groups of individuals usually develop and maintain distinctive norms of behaviour. These norms include habits, mores, rules and regulations. Norms are in reality prescriptive with regard to what a person may or may not do. Sanctions (rewards or punishment) are used in formal and informal ways to ensure conformation.

Rewards such as social acceptance and approval encourage a person to conform to the prescribed norms of behaviour. Medals for bravery and degrees for academic performance are examples of formal rewards. Various forms of punishment can likewise be applied — ranging from, for example, a jail sentence for theft, to a frown of disapproval in response to a display of bad temper. Ridicule, contempt and ostracism are forms of punishment which are usually regarded in a serious light by most people. Subtle threats of this nature are often included in advertisements for toothpaste, deodorants, and skin lotions, the implication being that the person not using these products is in danger of being ridiculed, held in contempt or ostracised.

Taking into account the fact that every individual belongs to many groups, all of which maintain distinctive norms of behaviour, one can appreciate the degree of social pressure exerted on the economic activities of the individual by group membership. There are very few products which are without any social significance at all, and usually a consumer succumbs to the pressure of his social needs. The different groups that exhort a consumer to conform to group norms are the cultural group, social class, the family, and reference groups and opinion leaders.

3.4.4.2 *Cultural groups*

Culture comprises a complex system of values, norms and symbols which have developed in society over a period of time and in which all its members share.[10] The cultural values, norms and symbols are created by man and are transmitted from one generation to another to ensure survival and also to facilitate adaptation to the circumstances of life. Cultural values, norms and symbols are transmitted from parents to children. In this process the school, church and other social institutions also play an important role (this process is referred to as socialisation).

Each cultural group comprises several subcultures, each with its own norms, values and symbols. There are four main subcultures, categorised according to nationality, religion, race and geographical area of residence. Besides the four main groups smaller subcultures can develop, perhaps according to language, age, interests or occupation.

The South African society is fragmented into many cultural and subcultural groups. The White group dominates, not in terms of numbers but rather according to the influence of this group's norms, values and symbols on economic activities. Most advertisements therefore reflect the Western way of life.

The Black cultural group consist of many subcultures. Except for language differences these subcultures are regarded as homogeneous by marketing management. Because of the differences between the Black and White consumer groups with regard to norms, values and symbols, the advertising messages aimed at these groups also differ. Advertising messages aimed at Blacks are directed almost exclusively at the sophisticated urban Black consumer.

Black cultural subgroups have their own media such as magazines, newspapers, radio stations and TV channels. Specific product advertisements which appear simultaneously in the Black and the White media are usually variations on the same theme. Marketing management must, however, be careful not to use symbols which can be interpreted incorrectly (or differently), and not to portray unacceptable behaviour patterns. Effective communication can take place only if the theme of the advertising message reflects the cultural norms, values and symbols of the target market at which it is directed.

3.4.4.3 *Social classes*

In every society there is a tendency to classify its members in a certain order. High-ranking individuals enjoy more esteem than those of lesser rank. In this way social classes, which are relatively large homogeneous groups of persons, all with the same values and more or less similar life styles and consumption patterns, are established. Six social classes, as indicated in Figure 3.7, have been identified.

The same type of social class structure exists in South Africa, but there is very little information on the exact percentages in each class.

FIGURE 3.7   Social classes in the United States of America

- The **upper class** constituting approximately only one per cent of the population - mostly well-established, wealthy families.

- The **lower-upper class** constituting approximately 1,6 per cent of the population - mostly successful executives and professional people.

- The **upper-middle class** constituting approximately 10 per cent of the population - mostly less successful managers and professional persons all with a relatively high level of education.

- The **lower-middle class** constituting approximately 30 – 35 per cent of the population - mostly clerical and white-collar workers.

- The **upper-lower class** constituting approximately 40 per cent of the population mostly skilled or semi-skilled workers (blue-collar workers).

- The **lower class** constituting approximately 15 per cent of the population - mostly unskilled workers with a very low level of education.

Source: Adapted from Coleman, RP. 'The Continuing Significance of Social Class to Marketing'. *Journal of Consumer Research*. December 1983, p 267.

3.4.4.4 *The family*

Of all the groups influencing consumer behaviour the individual maintains the closest contact with his family. In family interaction the child learns behaviour patterns by means of the socialisation process.

The term 'family' refers to a social entity consisting of the father, mother and their children (included in this definition are the single-parent family and also the childless family). Each one of the family members has a greater or lesser influence on the consumer behaviour of the family. The family can be regarded as a nuclear group whose members live in close contact with one another and act as a decision making unit when they attempt to satisfy individual needs from one shared source (the family income). This fact implies that individual needs must necessarily be subordinated to those of other members to a greater or lesser extent. This leads to consultation and joint decision making among family members.

With regard to the influence of the family (as a decision making unit) on consumer behaviour, there are two aspects which are of importance to the enterprise in developing its marketing strategy: the family life cycle, and role differentiation between family members.

The family life cycle phases are the following:

- **Newly-wed phase**. Both members of this unit are usually economically active and pool their incomes, which means they can usually afford to buy durables and even luxuries.
- **Phase of family growth**. This phase starts with the arrival of the first child in the marriage, and markedly changes previous consumer behaviour patterns.
- **Maturity phase**. The children in the family have reached the adolescent stage where, in addition to their basic needs, they have also developed their own norms, preferences and life styles.
- **Post-parental phase**. All the children have left home and the parents spend proportionally less on basic household necessities. They have greater disposable income to spend on luxuries.
- **Sole survivor**. The consumption patterns and the life style of the surviving spouse change drastically.

Role differentiation and the influences exerted by family members on consumer decision making in the family are depicted in Figure 3.8.

FIGURE 3.8   Role differentiation in consumer decision making in the family

ROLES	FAMILY MEMBERS
The **initiator** is the person who makes the first suggestion regarding products to be purchased.	Teenagers often act as initiators.
The **influencer** is the person who implicitly or explicitly influences the final decision because this person's suggestions and wishes are reflected in the ultimate decision made by the family.	Children's preferences (for example for a certain kind of breakfast cereal) influence family decision making.
The **decision maker** is the person who actually chooses between alternatives and makes the decision.	This is usually the mother or the father.
The **purchaser** purchases the product.	It is usually the mother's responsibility to purchase the groceries.
The **user** is the person who actually uses the product.	The baby consumes the vegetable purée purchased by the mother.

Source: Adapted from McDaniel, C & Darden, WR. 1987. *Marketing*. Boston: Allyn & Bacon Inc, p 146.

3.4.4.5 *Reference groups and opinion leaders*

A reference group is any group against which a person can evaluate his behaviour patterns. In all groups there are distinctive norms of behaviour and members are expected to conform to these norms lest sanctions be applied against them.[11]

The following types of reference group influence the individual's consumer behaviour:[12]

- **Membership groups** are groups of which the person has obtained membership, for example friends or a social club.
- **Automatic groups** are groups of which a person is a member due to his age, sex, or occupation.
- **Negative groups** are groups with which a person does not wish to be associated. In such a situation a person intentionally avoids the norms of the negative group.
- **Associative groups** are those groups to which a person aspires.

An individual reveals his desire to belong to a certain group by distinctive consumption patterns.

Typical members of associative reference groups are often used as models in advertisements in order to show potential consumers the type of person who buys the product and also the way in which the product can be used. The advertising message attempts to persuade potential consumers to follow the example set by these models. Members of negative groups can also be used in advertising; for example, overweight models in a health food advertisement.

A reference group need not necessarily be a group of persons but can also be a reference person, an individual to whom others will look in forming opinions and taking consumer decisions. The reference person can therefore be regarded as an **opinion leader**. The opinion leader need not be well known or enjoy high status but can be an ordinary person, a stereotype, or even an imaginary person.

The influence of reference groups and opinion leaders

The pop music group is a **negative reference group** for a conservative farmer in Northern Transvaal.

A famous singer is a well-known personality. She acts as an **opinion leader** for the talented young singer.

The typical housewife in the OMO advertisement is the **opinion leader** for the inexperienced young housewife.

The motor-cycle gang is an **associative group** for the interested but poor teenager who cannot afford to buy a motor-cycle.

The executives of X-company form a **reference group** which expects of the new manager that he must conform to specific standards adhered to by the group. He must, for example, dress properly and acquire a genuine leather briefcase.

The members of a women's league apply **sanctions** by failing to invite the inexperienced housewife (who cannot even bake a cake) to their tea party.

The opinion leader has an important function in the marketing communication process. He acts as a go-between in what is known as the **two-step flow of communication**. Research results have indicated that information does not flow directly from the mass media to individual consumers in the target market but is channelled through a person, the opinion leader, who interprets and evaluates the information, relaying his acceptance or rejection of the message to other consumers in the target market.

The role of the opinion leader is especially important in purchasing high-risk new products. In the case of a new fashion, for example, the fashion opinion leader is willing to accept the risk of ridicule or financial loss which the ordinary consumer is usually anxious to avoid. The latter will only become interested after the new fashion has been vetted and approved by the opinion leader. This process of gradual acceptance is known as **diffusion and adoption**.

There is a great deal of overlapping of leader and follower roles. Every consumer is a member of several different reference groups and is influenced by these groups as well as by the opinion leaders in these groups. In the same way any one person can be an opinion leader in one group while being a follower in another. The marketer must identify the relevant reference groups and the opinion leader as this will ensure the effective communication of the advertising message and the acceptance of this message in the target market.

3.4.5 Economic factors

The income of the consumer, his willingness to spend money and his evaluation of the relative utility/benefit of alternative products available are all economic considerations in consumer decision making.[13]

Income determines what a consumer can buy and also what he can and cannot afford. This fact is reflected in the economic theory in which consumption is regarded as a function of income:

$$C = f(Y),$$

where,

C = Consumption

Y = Income

The gross income of a consumer is not fully at his disposal when he must decide between alternatives. There are certain necessities and contractual obligations which must be met, leaving the person with discretionary income (purchasing power) which is much less than the gross income. Marketing management can use information regarding the discretionary income of consumers in its target market to determine the potential of this market. Whether these potential consumers will actually purchase depends on other factors.

Marketing management can increase the discretionary income of the consumer in the immediate future by granting credit facilities and hire-purchase terms in order to put the consumer in a position to purchase. Invariably this will mean a decrease in the discretionary income in the following period because of the contractual obligation of the consumer to pay his debt.

The **willingness** of a consumer to purchase (or to save) is closely related to his economic expectations. If he expects his economic position to change for the better, he is optimistic and willing to spend money. The opposite also holds true: a pessimistic attitude may make him unwilling to buy. These expectations are presumed by economists to be one of the causes of cyclical changes in the economy, where a rising cycle is the result of general optimism and an increase in the willingness to spend, and vice versa.

Economists also attempt to explain consumer behaviour by means of the *utility theory*. According to the concept of utility the consumer is supposed to be able to rank those alternatives which are available to him according to their relative utility (benefit) and their relative prices. To maximise utility the consumer chooses products until the marginal utility (per rand) of all the products chosen is equal.

Utility is a subjective concept and a consumer cannot really quantify exactly the benefit of a specific product; therefore it is not easy for him to rank alternatives and to determine the marginal utility.

In conclusion to this section it can be said that individual, group and economic factors are determinants in consumer decision making.

3.5 CONSUMER DECISION MAKING

3.5.1 The nature of consumer decision making

Consumer decision making is regarded as a process consisting of several phases. Consumers display distinctive behaviour patterns in the various phases. Before discussing the details of the consumer decision making process it is necessary to obtain greater clarity on the way information is processed by the consumer because information is the basis of all decision making.

3.5.2 Information processing by the consumer

Information is a combination of symbols such as colours, forms, sounds and smells. It consists of facts, value judgements, forecasts and generalisations.[14] Facts are bits of information which cannot be doubted at all. Value judgements, forecasts and generalisations are all of dubious nature not accepted by all people. This means that information does not have the same meaning for everybody. No wonder, therefore, that consumers, exposed to the same information (on products or services), often perceive it quite differently.

Figure 3.9 shows the relationship between information, perception and the decision making process.

The flow of information (in Figure 3.9) can be explained by considering the effect of a television commercial. The advertising message contains facts, value judgements, forecasts and generalisations. It is created by means of colours, sounds and forms (words) which are picked up by the senses and relayed to the

FIGURE 3.9   The flow of information

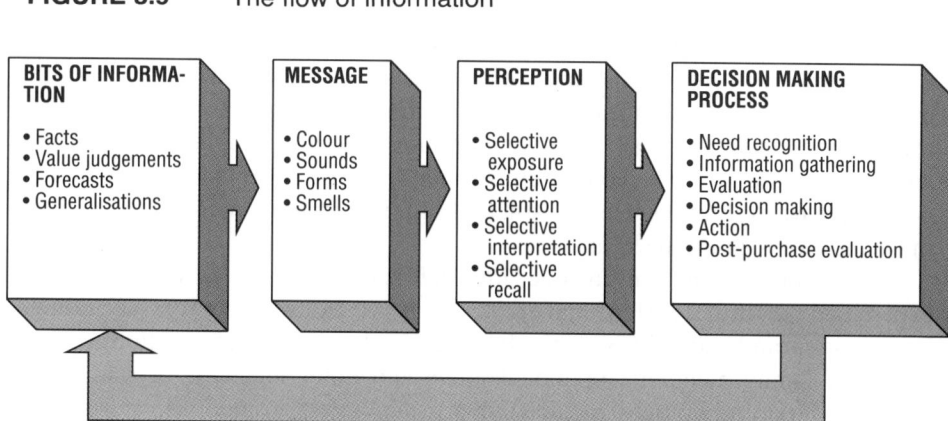

brain. Selective interpretation takes place if the individual chooses to pay attention to the message (this aspect is discussed in section 3.4.3.2). Thus the individual now becomes aware of a particular need — there is something that he lacks. He seeks more information on the advertised product, evaluates alternatives, decides on one, and purchases the product. Later at home, or while using the product, re-evaluation takes place. During this whole process new bits of information come to his attention. The consumer now knows from experience if the advertised product delivers what was promised in the message and whether it compares well or badly with other competing products. The flow of information is therefore a continuous process.

3.5.3 The decision making process

The important role of information processing during the decision making process is quite clear from the preceding discussion. It is now appropriate to look closer at the phases of consumer decision making.[15]

Need recognition

This phase is sometimes called the problem recognition or problem awareness phase. When an individual perceives a difference between the desired state of affairs and the actual state of affairs, an unsatisfied need is felt or recognised. A problem exists which must be dealt with as soon as possible.

Individual, group and economic factors influence need recognition. Advertising messages contribute to making a consumer aware of unsatisfied, perhaps dormant needs. It must, however, be emphasised that it is not possible for advertising alone to convince a consumer of the existence of an unfulfilled need if he does not experience it himself. Advertising messages cannot persuade any consumer against his inclinations.

Search for information

The search for information invariably follows need recognition, even if the search is conducted only briefly in the mind of the consumer. The search for information includes all the elements of learning and is not limited only to the second phase in the decision making process. In the other phases — evaluation, decision making and action — the consumer continues to search for more information. Even in the post-purchase evaluation phase he still looks for information in order to evaluate the decision which has been made.

Sources of information include internal sources, such as memory and experience of the decision maker, as well as external sources including interpersonal and marketing sources. Interpersonal sources of information are the advice of family members, opinion leaders and other members of reference groups. Marketing sources include advertising, sales promotions, store and window displays as well as advice from sales personnel. When the decision to be made is important, the search for information can be extensive.

Table 3.4 indicates the sources consulted in purchasing small electrical appliances. Udell found that previous experience is the most valuable source of information for the decision maker.

TABLE 3.4   Sources of information in order of importance in purchasing electrical appliances

SOURCE	% INDICATING THE SOURCE TO BE IMPORTANT
Previous experience with the brand	33,2
Advice of family and friends	18,7
Brochures and catalogues	10,2
Newspaper advertisements	9,6
Television advertisements	3,7
Magazine advertisements	2,4
Radio advertisements	0,4
Telephone enquiries at the store	1,0

Source: Williams, TG. 1982. *Consumer Behaviour Fundamentals and Strategies.* St Paul: West Publishing Co, p 33.

Evaluation

Evaluation entails the appraisal by the consumer of the attributes and benefits of various alternatives. A host of criteria may be used to evaluate products. The abundance of evaluative criteria involved in any major decision makes evaluation difficult indeed. The decision maker must also decide on the relative importance of often conflicting criteria. In Figure 3.10 some product and psychological criteria which can be applied in evaluation of alternatives are given.

FIGURE 3.10   Evaluation criteria

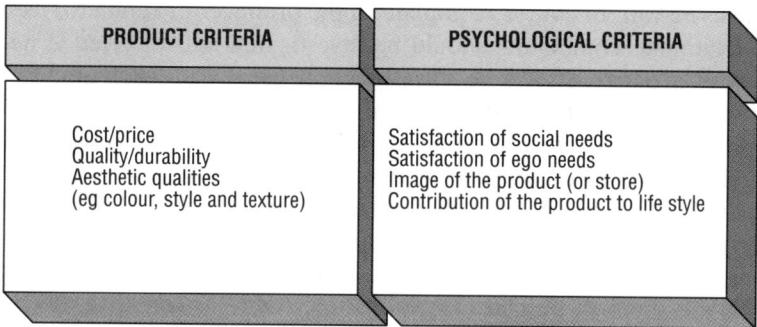

Some of the criteria in Figure 3.10 can be evaluated in an objective way. Price, quality and performance standards of alternatives can be compared objectively but personal and subjective factors play an important role in the evaluation of aesthetic qualities, the image of the product and the contribution of the chosen item toward need-satisfaction and life style. In the evaluation of alternative points of purchase (stores) the evaluative criteria may include the product assortment, hygiene considerations, the image projected by the store, and the conduct of the sales personnel.

Decision making

Decision making entails choosing that alternative which, according to the consumer, will satisfy all or most of the evaluation criteria. It is necessary to distinguish between decision making away from the point of purchase (at-home decision making) in which time elapses between the decision and the action, and final decision making, which occurs just prior to action. The elapse of a period of time between the decision and the action allows other influencing factors to interfere and to make the decision invalid. The time that elapses between decision making and action is important to the consumer because in this period the decision can be reversed in the light of new information which may have come to his attention.

Action

When the consumer is satisfied that he has made the correct and best possible decision, he acts accordingly. He can decide to purchase, not to purchase or to delay purchasing. Advertising at the point of purchase is often necessary to convert positive at-home decisions into appropriate purchasing action.

Post-purchase evaluation

After the consumer has acted a period follows in which the decision and the action are re-evaluated. If the product purchased lives up to expectations it may well lead to repeat purchasing at a later stage and the development of brand loyalty. If the purchaser has reason to be dissatisfied because of poor product performance or deficiencies he can, of course, complain to the producer or retailer. Needless to say, all legitimate complaints should be investigated and rectified if necessary because the negative effects of dissatisfaction usually are not limited to one consumer only. Negative interpersonal communication by one dissatisfied consumer can have a deterrent effect on many other potential consumers.

In making a choice the consumer had to forgo other attractive options. He also had to part with (perhaps a great deal of) money which could have been used for other purposes. It is no wonder therefore that the consumer often develops doubts regarding the wisdom of his decision. This negative feeling of doubt and uncertainty in the post-purchase period is referred to as **cognitive dissonance**.[16] Cognitive dissonance is a negative emotion stemming from a psychological inconsistency in the cognitions (the things that a person knows). The dissonant consumer will try to correct these psychological inconsistencies by attempting to convince himself that his original decision was correct and even very judicious. In order to do so he may rationalise by putting forward logical reasons for decisions taken. The dissonant consumer may also turn to others for approval and reassurance.

The post-purchase evaluation phase can be regarded as the beginning of a new decision making process. Will the consumer consider repurchasing the same product? Routine decision making develops when a brand-loyal consumer insists on purchasing the same brand every time. In such a situation it would be very difficult for a competitor to succeed in persuading the consumer to give attention to his marketing message and his product.

3.5.4 Real, routine and impulsive decision making

Real decision making can be regarded as a complex situation in which extensive problem solving takes place. The consumer must succeed in satisfying his unlimited needs with the relatively limited resources at his disposal. When an important or expensive product (a new house) is being considered the decision maker progresses relatively slowly through all the phases of the decision making process. Real decision making is characterised by conscious planning and occurs:

- when durable products, especially innovations, are purchased;
- when the purchase is important in terms of its cost and the purpose for which it is acquired;
- when previous experience in a similar situation resulted in disappointment;
- when the person becomes aware that his behaviour pattern differs drastically from that which is generally acceptable.

Routine decision making occurs when a consumer, without consciously thinking about it, consistently purchases the same branded products. This loyalty to specific branded products is the result of an extended decision making process of the preceding period. Routine purchasing reduces the necessity of repeating the decision making process each time an item is needed, thereby facilitating the purchasing task. Household necessities which must be re-stocked regularly, such as toiletries, detergents, margarine, coffee and tea, are often purchased on this basis.

Impulsive decision making[17] implies unplanned action on the spur of the moment, in contrast to the purposeful planning visible in real decision making. This is not completely correct. In impulsive decision making the consumer also progresses through all the phases of the decision making process. Usually action follows immediately after the decision has been reached, and to a bystander it seems as if the action was not preceded by planning (which includes purposefully searching for and evaluating information). Impulsive action viewed in this light indicates a decision made at the point of purchase and therefore cannot be regarded as an irresponsible approach to purchasing.

From the discussion in this section one can conclude that consumer decision making can be a long drawn-out process when the decision is important to the decision maker. It is also a process which can be concluded in the wink of an eye when an impulsive decision is made immediately after the consumer becomes aware of an unfulfilled need. In all decision making situations information processing plays a major role, but consumers often do not perceive marketing information as it was intended by the marketer. Even though some bits of information are lost, distorted or wrongly interpreted by consumers, it is still of cardinal importance for the marketer to give adequate information for consumer decision making. The lack of pertinent information and misleading marketing messages are some of the reasons for the development of a social movement known as consumerism (see section 3.6).

3.5.5 Where, how much, when and how consumers purchase

The consumer himself determines **where** he will purchase necessities. The reasons why consumers decide to purchase at specific stores are known as patronage motives. The most important of these are the following:

- the convenient location of the store;
- the grouping of stores (as in a shopping complex);
- adequate parking space;
- prices;

- services given by the store;
- politeness, knowledge and helpfulness of the sales personnel.

These aspects of the image a store projects are more fully discussed in Chapter 12.

Based on **how much** they purchase, consumers can be classified into four groups, namely non-users (who never purchase the product), light, medium and heavy users. The market may be segmented according to the usage rate (see Chapter 4). Information on usage rate is also important in market forecasting.

When consumers purchase is important in seasonal purchasing. Purchasing fashion clothing, for example, is sometimes planned a year previously by the store while consumers purchase during the season or even at the end of a season. When consumers purchase has recently become important for retailers to plan the so-called 'open hours'. There are also busy and less busy months and even days of the week. The retailer must know his consumers' time preferences and make the necessary arrangements to accommodate these preferences, such as having more sales staff on duty during peak periods.

How consumers purchase (method of payment) depends on the type of product and the preference of the consumer. In supermarkets the consumer usually pays cash (cheque or credit card). Durable products are often purchased on credit or hire purchase while financial institutions finance the purchasing of expensive products such as houses and motor cars. The consumer repays monthly over a long period of time (often 30 years in the case of a house) until the debt plus interest has been repayed. Each of these methods has advantages and disadvantages for the consumer and also for the dealer. The retailer must consider carefully how the method of payment will affect his cash flow. This is a financial matter and will not be discussed here any further.

The method of payment is an aspect often characterised by unethical marketing practices. Unsophisticated consumers can be tempted to purchase products that they cannot really afford if the retailer quotes very 'low' hire-purchase instalments. This is one of the reasons for legislation to protect consumers.

Where, how much, when and how consumers purchase are illustrated in Figure 3.11.

3.6 CONSUMERISM

3.6.1 Defining consumerism

In Chapter 1 reference was made to the fact that unethical sales methods, used in the times when management was sales- rather than marketing-oriented, eventually led to consumer resistance. In the United States of America this heralded the beginning of consumerism, a social force which now also presents problems to South African marketers.

Some enterprises still do not adhere to the stringent principles of the marketing concept, and they can be held responsible for the fact that dissatisfied consumers today are combining forces to seek redress. The unethical activities of these

FIGURE 3.11 Where, how much, when and how consumers purchase

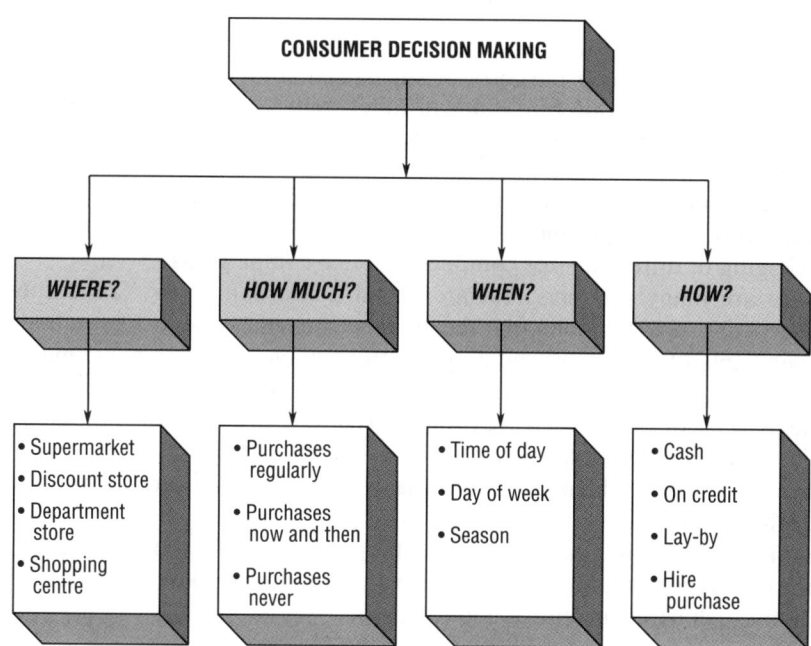

enterprises have caused the authorities to legislate in order to protect consumers from being exploited.

Consumerism is a **social movement** aimed at reconciling the **rights of buyers and sellers**. By applying legislative, moral and economic pressure on business enterprises, the movement strives to protect consumers against exploitation, and to compel organisations to heed consumer demands and provide adequate, accurate information which will enable judicious consumer decision making.

In the previous section it was pointed out that various individual, group and economic factors influence consumer decision making. These factors determine what a consumer will decide to purchase and what to forgo. The assortment of products and services bought by the consumer determines his standard of living and his life style. Thus it follows that unwise decisions to purchase inferior, harmful or extremely expensive products and services are wasteful of precious resources, leaving the consumer worse off than he would have been if he was better informed. Unwise decisions are often the direct consequence of a lack of information. The question is: whose responsibility is it to see to it that consumers are well informed? Before this question can be answered the consumer's dilemma must first be discussed.

3.6.2 Consumer's dilemma

The reasons for the consumer's dilemma are the following:

- There are many products and brands which are essentially identical serving more or less the same purpose. A superficial study of supermarket shelves indicates the many different kinds of toilet soap, toothpaste, deodorants and hand, body and sun tan lotions. How does the consumer determine which brand is best?
- The labels on most consumer products do not give adequate or even correct information on the product.
- Packaging of different sizes complicates price comparisons.
- There are many products that are harmful and dangerous. Sometimes the dangers are so well hidden that the average consumer does not even realise it, for example blankets and children's clothing made of inflammable material.
- Advertising messages are sometimes misleading, some appeals are questionable.
- The real cost of some expensive products is often but a fraction of the consumer price, such as some cosmetics.
- There are often hidden costs that the consumer is unaware of until he has bought the product.
- Conflicting information can confuse the consumer. A good example is the controversy surrounding the nutrition value and the supposedly harmful effect of food such as sugar, butter and red meat.

Not only marketers are responsible for the consumer's dilemma. The consumer himself has many conflicting needs and irrational prejudices. He is also subjected to social pressure to buy products which do not really contribute to his standard of living. Consumers being human, they sometimes are unreasonable, thoughtless and even downright greedy, and dishonest. In a classic article 'Consumers aren't all angels either'[18] the author gives some examples. Consumers steal the free gift inside breakfast cereal packs, they open bottles of baby purée to taste the contents, and they wear clothing taken out on appro.

3.6.3 The beginning of consumerism

A brief summary of the history of consumerism in the United States of America can help to promote a better understanding of this phenomenon.

In the period 1920–1940 consumerism, which started in the 1900s, developed further. A list of books in the topic appeared in this period. It is easy to deduce the nature of the contents from the descriptive titles.

Books on consumerism in the period 1920–1940

- *Your Money's Worth* (Chase & Schlink, 1927), which became a best seller.
- *100 000 000 Guinea Pigs* (Chase & Kallet, 1933), which pointed to the American consumer as a 'guinea pig' for many harmful or ineffective products.

- *Eat, Drink and Be Wary* (Schlink, 1934).
- *Our Masters Voice: Advertising* (Rorty, 1934).
- *Counterfeit* (Kallet, 1935).
- *Partners in Plunder* (Mathews & Schallcross, 1935).
- *American Chamber of Horrors* (Lam, 1936).

Source: Kelly, WT. 1973. *New Consumerism: Selected Readings.* Columbus, Ohio: Grid Inc, pp 20–3.

This period became known as the 'Consumer's Revolt' and was characterised by a general distrust of business enterprises. As a result the National Consumer-Retailer Council was established to promote better understanding between the trade and the consumer. The National Better Business Bureau started distributing information pamphlets such as 'Facts you should know', 'Buying used cars', 'Health cures', 'Advertising' and the like.[19]

This historic pattern of revolt and reaction repeats itself as regularly as economic cycles. There are periods characterised by consumer dissatisfaction followed by quiet periods of adaptation until once again new causes for dissatisfaction appear. In the 1960s Ralph Nader once again started a consumer movement that had serious consequences for many business enterprises in the United States. His book *Unsafe at Any Speed* (1965) caused General Motors to withdraw its Corvair from the market. After Nader proved just how unsafe this automobile was its sales declined by some 93 per cent.[20] Other campaigns lead by Nader were aimed at hidden costs, misleading advertising, poor service and harmful products. Many of his investigations lead to the promulgation of new legislation and fines for guilty parties. Nader used attorneys to help him with his investigations. They were called 'The Raiders'.

Ingredients of pork sausages

Nader found strange ingredients, such as 'insect fragments, insect larvae, rodent hairs and other kinds of filth' in pork sausages after they had been approved by inspectors.

Source: Kelly, WT. 1973. *New Consumerism: Selected Readings.* Columbus, Ohio: Grid Inc, p 57.

Contamination of rooibostee

Speculation about the source of *Salmonella* contamination found in rooibostee caused a public outcry in South Africa in 1985. A possible source was given as 'faecal matter, originating from rats, birds or cattle during the drying process'.

Source: 'Rooibostee. The story behind the scare.' *The Retailer.* January 1985, p 11.

Figure 3.12   Harmful effects of some consumer products

PRODUCT	EFFECTS
Patent medicines	
• Aspirin	Allergic reaction; can harm the kidneys.
• Cough syrup	The alcohol content can be as high as 25 %.
• Vitamins	Too much vitamin A and D can be fatal.
Cosmetics	
• Hair colourants • Deodorants • Soap	Contains chemicals that can cause allergies. Some ingredients can cause cancer and nervous disorders.
Aerosol cans	Can explode. The use of aerosol cans affects the ozone layer of the atmosphere causing unstable weather patterns.
Tobacco	Can cause cancer, heart complaints, chronic bronchitis and emphysema. Addictive.
Asbestos	Asbestos fibres can cause lung cancer.
Alcohol	Every drink reduces the flow of oxygen to the brain and destroys brain cells. Addictive.
Petrol and paint	Can cause lead poisoning, leading to brain damage and death.
Water	All water systems tested to date contains carsinogens ie substances which can cause cancer.

Source: A summary from Garmon, ET & Ecket, SW. 1979. *The Consumer World. Economic Issues and Money Management.* New York: McGraw-Hill, pp 161–86.

3.6.4 The rights of consumers

In 1962 President John F Kennedy laid down the following rights of consumers:[21]

- The right to safety — to be protected against the marketing of dangerous products or products detrimental to health.
- The right to free choice — access to competitive products and protection against monopolies.
- The right to a fair hearing — the assurance that consumer interests were being considered by the government and the parties concerned.
- The right to be informed — to be protected against misleading information, advertising or other malpractices, and to be provided with objective information so that the consumer can make a rational choice.

This last-mentioned 'right' is a controversial topic. Does the consumer really want to know everything about a product?

The ingredients of a hot dog

Rose Dewolf says:

'Frankly, I have to admit that I was a lot happier before packages of hot dogs had to admit right out in public that they contain ground-up cows' lips. Yechh. Do we have to know EVERYTHING?'

Source: Kelly, WT. 1973. *New Consumerism: Selected Readings.* Columbus, Ohio: Grid Inc, p 487.

In the United Kingdom a separate goverment department is responsible for enforcing these rights (Department of Prices and Consumer Protection). In the United States there are several institutions, such as the Consumer Advisory Council and the Federal Trade Council, keeping a close watch.

3.6.5 Consumerism in South Africa

The year 1970 was a historic year for the South African consumer. On 17 September 1970 the South African Co-ordinating Consumer Council came into being. The Council, with aid from the government, was established to further the interests of the consumer.[22]

The Council consists of 16 members appointed by the Minister of Economic Affairs. Representatives of the Department of Trade and Industry, Agriculture and the Bureau of Standards also sit on the Consumer Council.

The Council studies problems encountered by consumers and submits reports and recommendations to the authorities. Providing information is another important function of the Consumer Council. Information on a variety of subjects is supplied by means of lectures and publicity in the mass media. Brochures such as 'How to Complain' and 'How to deal with door-to-door Salesmen' are available from the Council. The *SA Consumer* is a free quarterly official publication of the Consumer Council. By these means the Consumer Council attempts to promote consumer awareness.

Purchasing a microwave oven

In the Third Quarter 1987 edition of *SA Consumer* there is a table of information on the different brands, availability, prices, sizes, capacities and other attributes of microwave ovens. The table also supplies information on cooking classes. Such detailed information facilitates consumer decision making.

Lectures are often given at schools and other educational organisations. The Consumer Council has offices in Pretoria, Bellville and Bloemfontein, and was involved in establishing the Small Claims Courts for consumer claims of less than R1 500.

Specially trained personnel are available to deal with consumer problems and complaints. Complaint statistics are kept in order to be able to identify and investigate problem areas. Organisations such as the South African National Consumer Union (SANCU) also submit complaints from their members. Virtually all women's organisations, the Automobile Association, the Federale Vroueraad, Catholic Women's League, Suid-Afrikaanse Konfederasie van Arbeid, South African Nursing Association and the Trade Union Council of South Africa are members of SANCU.

In virtually all magazines and newspapers articles in which consumer issues are discussed appear regularly. An example is Star Line of the *Star* newspaper. Educational radio and television programmes also help to inform the public and to teach members the necessary consumer skills.

The significance of consumerism to marketing can be summarised as follows:

- Consumer pressure is an unavoidable phase in the development of an economic system.
- Consumer pressure will continue in the form of permanent organisations.
- Consumer pressure will ultimately prove to be beneficial to the economic system.
- Consumer pressure is pro-marketing in the sense that it promotes adherence to the marketing concept.
- Consumer pressure creates new profit opportunities for responsible marketers.

3.7 SUMMARY

This chapter covers mainly the demand side of the market environment in which marketing management is to perform its marketing task. The supply side is discussed in less detail, but is again touched on in Chapters 18 and 19. Demographic details of the overall South African consumer market are given in the first part of the chapter. The size of the market, the population composition and distinguishing characteristics, such as language, sex, age, income and spending patterns, are discussed. The focus then moves to the individual consumer and the determinants of consumer behaviour. Individual, group and economic factors influence consumer decision making, described step by step.

The chapter concludes with a section on consumerism, a social force against consumer exploitation directed at those enterprises not adhering to the principles of the marketing concept. The South African Co-ordinating Consumer Council has been appointed to watch over the interests of South African consumers.

In Chapter 4 the different segments of the consumer market are studied further. Marketing management directs its market offering only to specific carefully selected market segments because it is virtually impossible to satisfy everybody with the same market offering.

REFERENCES

1. Marx, S and Dekker, HJ. 1982. *Marketing Management: Principles and Decisions*. Pretoria: HAUM, p 78.
2. Cronjé, GJ de J et al (eds). 1987. *Introduction to Business Management*. Pretoria: Southern Book Publishers, p 145.
3. This first book is Britt, SH. 1966. *Consumer Behaviour and the Behavioural Sciences*. New York: John Wiley.
4. Walters, CG. 1978. *Consumer Behaviour*. Homewood, Illinois: Richard D Irwin, p 53.
5. Van der Walt, A. 'Will the consumer be able to decode your advertising message correctly?' in Koekemoer, L. 1987. *Marketing Communications Management: A South African perspective*. Durban: Butterworths, p 298.
6. Based on Loudon, DL and Della Bitta, AJ. 1984. *Consumer Behaviour: Concepts and Applications*. New York: McGraw-Hill, p 459.
7. Ibid p 520.
8. Ibid p 501.
9. Based on Busch, PS and Houston, MJ. 1985. *Marketing: Strategic Foundations*. Homewood, Illinois: Richard D Irwin, p 190.
10. Walters op cit, p 451.
11. McDaniel, C and Darden, WR. *Marketing*. Boston: Allyn & Bacon Inc, p 146.
12. Ibid p 147.
13. Walters op cit, p 53.
14. Van der Walt op cit, p 29.
15. Based on Busch & Houston op cit, p 298.
16. Festinger, L. 1957. *A Theory of Cognitive Dissonance*. Stanford, California: Stanford University Press.
17. Marx and Dekker op cit, p 91.
18. Kelly, WT. 1973. *New Consumerism: Selected Readings*. Columbia, Ohio: Grid Inc, p 485.
19. Ibid p 33.
20. Ibid p 63.
21. Lucas, GHG. *The Task of Marketing Management*. Pretoria: Van Schaik, p 77.
22. The following section is based on information supplied by the South African Co-ordinating Consumer Council.

CASE STUDY

LEVI STRAUSS & CO.

When Levi Strauss immigrated to America in 1850 to join the Gold Rush, he did not discover gold but, instead, he came up with an idea that was to prove even more golden. From canvas that he had in surplus he fashioned pants for miners. Pleased, the miners quickly spread the word about the pants "of Levi's", and the orders came pouring in.

Levi continued to produce blue denim pants in the same basic style that has become a "classic" cut: low on the hips, tapering in the legs. As a major innovation pockets were reinforced with copper rivets in 1873.

The company continued in a dual role as a manufacturer of jeans (derived from "genes", the pants worn by Genoan sailors) and a regional wholesaler through to the end of World War II, at which time annual volume was little more than $8 million.

In 1961 it was $51 million, at which stage jeans became very popular with young people. In 1968 "Levi's for Gals" was introduced. The market quickly expanded to Europe. In 1970 net sales were $350, in 1975 $1 015 million.

One of the first major problems for the company occurred in 1973 with its European operations, when demand suddenly changed, resulting in large inventories of outdated styles, which had to be sold at drastically reduced prices.

During the period of rapid growth the company spent almost three per cent of its net income on social responsibility programmes such as day-care centres.

It is important to the Levi Strauss company to understand both the end user of the product and the behaviour of retailers in satisfying the needs and desires of consumers. Levi Strauss displays a philosophy of providing high-quality products at reasonable prices, backed by the company's guarantee of satisfaction. The success of the company can probably be ascribed to its ability to "read" the changing preferences of the youth market and to adapt to fashion changes. The original youth market gradually aged. Levi Strauss adapted by changing sizes and fittings.

Daniel Yankelovich, a researcher, undertook consumer research on a national scale in order to identify and describe the different life-style segments in his "Monitor". These were the following:

Traditionalists	14%
Retreaters	??%
New Conformists	33%
Forerunners	15%
Autonomists	??%

Levi Strauss decided after careful consideration to focus its market offering on three main segments. The description of these three groups can give an indication of marketing strategies to be followed:

PRODUCT LINES OF LEVI STRAUSS AND TARGET MARKET CHARACTERISTICS

Product	Target market characteristics
Classic	Age: 15-24 Outdoor, active men
Fashion Jeans	Age: 15-24 Higher income market
Levi's for Men	Age: 24-35
"Fresh Products" (newest styles)	Age: 15-24 High income market
Boys' Wear	Age: 2-14
Levi's for Gals	Age: 15-19 Small sizes 20-34 fittings
Signature Collection (designer collection)	Age: 18-24 High income, very fashion-conscious market

THREE TARGET MARKETS

The Traditionalists

- Traditional values
  (work before pleasure, savings-conscious)
- Materialistic
- Future-orientated
- Strong family ties
- Liberal sex attitudes
- Very social
- Friendly
- Teenagers involved in sporting activities and school organisations
- Fashion-conscious but conservative
- Read news magazines
- Interested in news programmes on television
- Like to buy at discount stores
- Like films
- Little support for unisex fashions

The New Conformists

- Modern
- Self-centered
- Adventurous, like excitement
- Family ties less strong
- Duty and the future not as important as to the traditionalists
- Very liberal sex attitudes
- Like to shop

- Very fashion-conscious
- Like to try new things
- Like a variety of television programmes
- Like to listen to the radio (especially music)
- Read fiction rather than magazines
- Prefer to shop at speciality stores
- Live in cities
- Like films
- Little support for unisex fashions

The Forerunners

- Not very materialistic
- Reject traditional values
- Intellectual
- Physical appearance less important
- Creative
- Live in cities
- Clothing must be comfortable and durable
- Realistic
- Television sport and news programmes very popular
- Listen to the radio
- Read art and craft magazines
- Love music
- Shop at discount stores
- Like films
- Little support for unisex fashions

Source: Summarised and adapted from Blackwell, R D, Engel, J F & Talarzyk, W W. *Contemporary cases in consumer behaviour.* Hinsdale Illinois: Dryden Press, pp 333.

QUESTIONS

1. Evaluate the results of research projects similar to that of Daniel Yankelovich.

   Note: Answer this question after you have studied chapters 4, 5 and 6.

2. Discuss the implications the characteristics and behaviour patterns (of consumers of jeans in the different groupings) have for marketing management in terms of the following:
   - Product decisions/product development
   - Pricing decisions
   - Distribution
   - Marketing communication decisions

CHAPTER 4

MARKET SEGMENTATION, TARGET MARKETING AND PRODUCT POSITIONING

4.1 INTRODUCTION

The discussion in this chapter centres on marketing management's approach to the market. The objectives of this discussion are, *first*, to weigh the relative advantages of market aggregation and market segmentation and, *secondly*, to indicate the bases for selecting a target market. Decisions on the four marketing instruments and the way they are co-ordinated in a specific marketing strategy are determined by the nature of the target market and the needs of consumers in this target market, as well as the competitive position prevailing.

The selection of a target market for the enterprise's market offering is preceded by an analysis of the market in order to determine whether it is homogeneous or heterogeneous in nature. In a homogeneous market more or less similar types of consumers make similar demands of the market offering. A heterogeneous market consists of different types of consumers with divergent needs, demands and preferences. In the light of the discussion in Chapter 3 South African consumers cannot be regarded as more or less similar in nature. This means that the mass market is not homogeneous but rather heterogeneous, consisting of many different market segments. The two major market segments in South Africa are the White consumer market and the Black consumer market. In this chapter it will become clear that there are methods of classification other than race according to which a market can be segmented. Only after the market has been divided into meaningful segments can marketing management select a target market. Selecting a target market to serve does not mean that the enterprise has an exclusive right to this segment. There will almost certainly be other competitors operating in the same segment, which will then compel marketing management to search for a special niche in the market. This simply means that the product is positioned where there are no, or only few, competitors. It is also possible deliberately to position a product in direct opposition to competitors, but in such a situation the product must have a differential advantage over those of competitors.

ORGANISATION OF THE CHAPTER

Market aggregation: The meaning of aggregation.

Market segmentation: Definition, concentrated market segmentation, differentiated market segmentation, merits of market segmentation, criteria for market segmentation, segment profiles, prerequisites for meaningful market segmentation.

Target marketing: Defining a target market, important factors, the market grid.

Product positioning: Aids to positioning.

Steps in the market segmentation process.

4.2 MARKET AGGREGATION

Market aggregation is also known as mass market strategy or a total market approach. Marketers following a strategy of aggregation presuppose that consumers needing the market offering have fairly similar demands and preferences. They are convinced that one specific market offering is suitable for all consumers. This is the case in the marketing of staple foods, because virtually all kinds of people need these products in more or less standard packaging.

Economies of scale result when an enterprise markets only one product in a standard package with only one basic marketing communication message. The lower cost of market aggregation arises from:[1]

- lower production costs per unit owing to larger production runs;
- relatively lower advertising costs as only one advertising campaign is usually launched; and
- lower marketing research costs.

When the market aggregation approach is taken by many marketers in the same market the result is intensive competition and lower profits. In such a situation the needs of the smaller segments within the aggregate market may remain unsatisfied.

A strategy of market aggregation was the norm until about 1950. The tendency was to offer the product in only one standard package to the mass market. Coca Cola also followed this approach up to 1950,[2] after which different sizes and kinds of packaging (bottles and tins) were used to differentiate the product. Banks and financial institutions used to offer undifferentiated services to the mass market until about 1970 in the United States of America and 1980 in South Africa. Today banks offer a variety of financial packages to investors, pensioners, students and even children. For every segment a separate marketing message is developed.

The tendency to segment the mass market and to develop differentiated products for each segment gave rise to a confusing array of models and variations of most durable products. The automobile market is a good example. Around 1970 there were 1 000 different automobile models in the American market!

The energy crisis, recession and inflation caused consumers to become increasingly price conscious. This resulted in a reaction against segmentation and a swing back to aggregation. Large numbers of people are now prepared to accept a basic product or model ('no frills') provided it is cheaper.[3]

4.3 MARKET SEGMENTATION

4.3.1 Definition of market segmentation

To ensure its continuity and growth the enterprise is dependent on inter alia the consumer and his needs. The consumer's needs are not satisfied for their own sake, but for the sake of achieving business objectives. It is thus evident that the higher the consumer's degree of need-satisfaction, the easier it will be to attain the business objectives. *Market segmentation can be defined as the process whereby the total heterogeneous market is divided into homogeneous market segments.*

The segmentation process can be <u>concentrated or differentiated</u>.

4.3.2 Concentrated market segmentation[4]

Concentrating the market offering on one specific segment can lead to greater expertise in production, distribution and marketing communication. A great disadvantage, however, is that all the eggs are now in one basket. The risk of product failure and non-acceptance of the product is thus concentrated in a single target market; should consumer preferences in this target market change or competitors take over the market segment with a new product, the results could be disastrous.

4.3.3 Differentiated market segmentation

Differentiated market segmentation[5] is also known as multisegment strategy, and means that marketing management have decided to serve two or more market segments and to develop a separate marketing strategy for each one (therefore separate product, distribution, marketing communication and price decisions). Previously it was said that the advantage of market aggregation lies in lower cost. Conversely, differentiated market segmentation brings about higher costs, for example:[6]

- **Product modification and product differentiation costs.** By modifying and differentiating a product for different market segments, relatively higher costs of research and development and the installation of machinery are incurred.

- **Production costs.** A high fixed-costs component makes it more expensive to manufacture m units of n different products than mn units of the same product.
- **Inventory costs.** It is generally more expensive to stock a variety of products than to stock only one type of product. The higher costs are attributable to, inter alia, more ledger accounts and higher stock control costs. A stockpile must also be held in reserve for each product.
- **Marketing communication costs.** Differentiated marketing necessitates that the various market segments have to be reached by different media. This requires inter alia the planning of special advertising campaigns for each market segment.

Differentiated marketing probably means that the consumer's needs are satisfied more fully than in the case of undifferentiated marketing. This increased need-satisfaction, however, occurs at a higher cost to the consumer.

To recap: differentiated market segmentation refers to a strategy where the market is divided into smaller homogeneous groups according to the divergent characteristics, needs and preferences of consumers in the different groups.

Figure 4.1 (1) shows that only one market offering is directed at the total market; 4.1 (2) shows concentrated market segmentation, with one market offering aimed at one segment of the total market. Figure 4.1 (3) indicates that three separate market offerings were developed for three separate market segments while segments 1 and 5 were not considered at all.

4.3.4 Merits of market segmentation

Market segmentation offers the following *benefits* to marketers:

- Segmentation leads to the identification of excellent marketing opportunities if research reveals an unexploited segment.
- Segmentation provides guidelines for the development of separate market offerings and marketing strategies for different market segments.
- A greater degree of consumer satisfaction can be achieved if the market offering is designed to satisfy consumers' needs, demands and preferences.

Market segmentation also has *disadvantages*:

- Development of separate models and market offerings is very expensive.
- Only limited market coverage is achieved.
- A very high degree of differentiation of the basic product leads to a proliferation of models and variations and finally cannibalisation. This happens when one product takes away market share from another product of the same enterprise.

The question that must now be answered is: on what grounds can markets be divided into different segments?

FIGURE 4.1   Approaches to the market

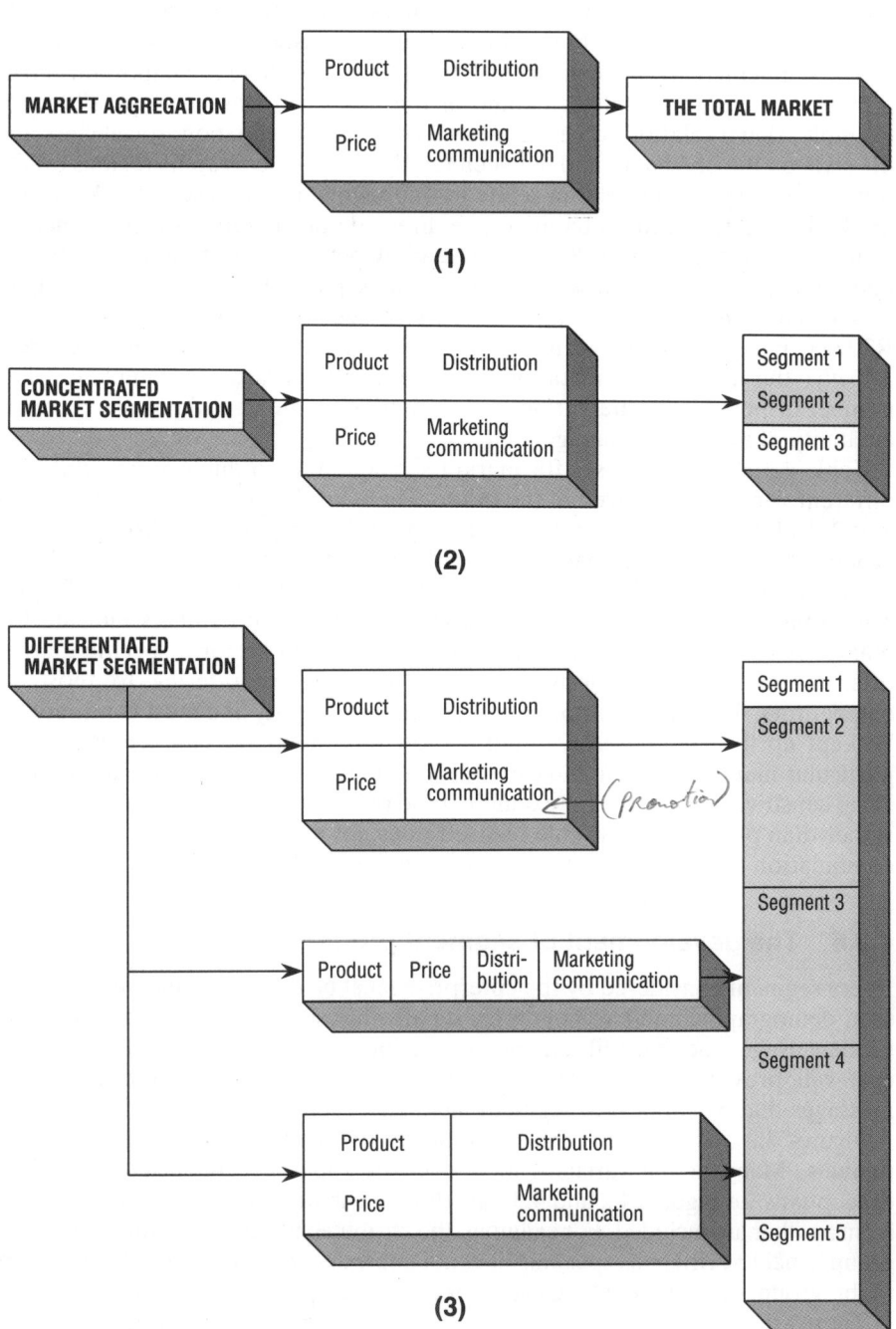

(1)

(2)

(3)

Source: Adapted from Cronjé, GJ de J et al (eds). 1987. *Introduction to Business Management.* Pretoria: Southern Book Publishers, p 151.

4.3.5 Bases for market segmentation

Marketing management can segment a market in different ways. Some geographic, demographic, psychographic and behaviouristic bases by which a market can be segmented are given in Table 4.1. Three aspects here are important. *First*, a mutual relationship between some of the bases can exist. It is possible, for example, that a relationship exists between income, occupation, social class and life style on the one hand, and between family size and geographic regions on the other. *Secondly*, needs seldom relate to one segmentation base only. A specific marketing strategy will probably not be directed only at persons with an income of between R15 000 and R20 000 per year. A better description of a particular market segment often utilises more than one segmentation base, for example: unmarried men between 20 and 34 years of age with an income in excess of R20 000 per year who live in the Pretoria-Witwatersrand-Vereeniging area. *Thirdly*, the market segmentation bases in Table 4.1 are not complete.[7] The number of possible segmentation bases are to a great extent determined by the creativity of marketing management.

Table 4.1 shows the bases for market segmentation in one column while the different variables are given in the other. There are five main groups. Groups 1 and 2 deal with the geographic and demographic variables that distinguish one group from another. Segmentation according to these variables indicates only the size of the market, in other words how many consumers in each group. (In Chapter 3 information is given about these variables.) The mere numbers indicate the market potential but not how many buyers there will be for a specific market offering or even why consumers prefer one market offering to those of competitors. This kind of information changes frequently and must continuously be kept up to date. Bases 3, 4 and 5 show the qualitative characteristics of a particular market segment and can indicate the reasons for specific preferences. Price-sensitive consumers, for example, tend to be motivated by economic factors rather than prestige. A variable by itself does not mean very much, but it is the combination of variables that serves to describe a particular market segment.

4.3.6   The development of segment profiles

Every segment considered by the enterprise must be described fully regarding its size, demographic and psychographic details, life style, behaviour patterns and product usage. Such a profile enables marketing management to develop products that will provide need satisfaction and to design marketing communication messages that will appeal to segment members.

Figures 4.2 and 4.3 are segment profiles in the white and the black consumer markets. Many of the variables mentioned in Table 4.1 are included in these descriptions. In Figures 4.2 and 4.3 only those attributes that distinguish one group from another are included. For example, the attribute indicating that the responsible group is mainly Afrikaans-speaking does not imply that there are no English speakers in this group; only that the language spoken by the majority is Afrikaans.

There are also other typical classifications besides those in Figures 4.2 and 4.3. The availability of this kind of information to segment the market can facilitate marketing decision making. Selecting a specific segment is, however, limited by important prerequisites and determined by specific evaluation criteria.

TABLE 4.1   Important bases for segmentation

BASES	POSSIBLE VARIABLES
1. Geographic	
Region	Pretoria-Witwatersrand-Vereeniging, Durban-Pinetown, Cape Peninsula, Natal, Remainder of Transvaal.
Size of city or town	Under 10 000, 10 000 to 20 000, 20 001 to 25 000, over 25 000 inhabitants.
Density	Urban, suburban, rural.
2. Demographic	
Age	Under 7, 7 to 13, 14 to 19, 20 to 34, 35 to 49, 50 to 65, older than 65years.
Sex	Male, female.
Family size	1 and 2, 3 and 4, more than 4 members.
Family life cycle	Young, married, without children; young married with children; older married couples with children; older married couples without children living in; singles.
Income	Under R5 000, R5 001 to R10 000, R10 001 to R15 000, R15 001 to R20 000, R20 001 to R25 000, more than R25 000 per annum.
Occupation	Professional and technical employees, clerical, employees in sales and related services, et cetera.
Religion	Protestant, Catholic, Muslim, other.
Social class	Upper class, middle class, lower class.
Ras	Blank, Swart, Kleurling, Asiër.
3. Psychographic	
Lifestyle	Conservative, liberal.
Personality	Gregarious, authoritarian, impulsive, ambitious.
4. Behaviouristic	
Purchase occasion	Regular occasion, special occasion.
Benefits sought	Economy, convenience, prestige.
User status	Non-user, ex-user, potential user, regular user.
Usage rate	Heavy user, medium user, light user.
Loyalty status	None, medium, strong, absolute.
Readiness stage	Unaware, aware, informed, interested, desirous, intending to buy.
5. Marketing decision sensitivity	Quality, price, service, advertising, personal selling.

Source: Adapted from Kotler, P. 1981. *Marketing Management: Analysis, Planning and Control.* 4th edition. New York: Prentice-Hall International, p 199, as quoted by Marx, S & Dekker, HJ. 1982. *Marketing Management: Principles and Decisions.* Pretoria: HAUM, p 104.

FIGURE 4.2 Segment profiles in the white consumer market

SEGMENT	KRITERIA	GROEPEIENSKAPPE
"The responsible me" (27 %)	*Geographic*	Spread over whole Republic.
	Socio-demographical	Afrikaans-speaking, over 50 years. Home owners. Lower education level.
	Psychographical • Personality • Lifestyle (avctivities, interests, opinions)	Hardworking. Avoidance of unknown innovations. Radio-listeners. TV-watchers. Very little reading. Interested in sport, angling. Church-goers. Camping and visiting.
	Product usage	Buyers of refined products (flour, sugar, rice, white bread). Low alcohol consumption (especially women), 42% smokers. Cash buyers. Little knowledge of financial services.
"The branded me" (23 %)	*Geographic*	Pretoria and Bloemfontein.
	Socio-demographical	Young. Single or newly-weds. Civil servants or artisans. Low education level. No university education.
	Psychographical • Personality	Materialistic. Status and recognition. Dislike being alone. Group memberhsip important.
	• Lifestyle (activities, interests, opinions)	Many interests and hobbies. TV and video watchers. Discos. Films. Popular fiction. Not interested in health foods or conservation. Rugby, boxing or wrestling. Women like cooking, men like angling and hunting. Servicing of own cars.
	Product usage	Expensive cameras. Beer drinkers, 50% smokers. Hire purchase. Support Edgars, Foschini, Checkers. Not brand loyal.
"The self-motivated me" (23 %)	*Geographic*	Johannesburg and Cape Town.
	Socio-demographical	English and Afrikaans-speaking. Between 20 and 44 years, 40% with tertiary education. High income. Flat dwellers.
	Psychographical • Personality	Smug. Demanding. Academic orientation. Creative. Non-materialistic. Patriotic. Self-confident. Avoidance of violence and aggression.
	• Lifestyle (activities interests, opinions)	Collect antiques, stamps or coins. Interested in art and cultural activities. Swim, tennis, sailing, hang-gliding (avoid contact sports). Informal. Conservationists. Health conscious.
	Product usage	Wine, whisky, sherry, liquers. Buy cheese, yoghurt, brown sugar, fruit juice. Buy time-saving equipment and computers. Support Pick 'n Pay and Woolworths. Cheque accounts. Credit cards. Do personal financial planning. Avoid hire purchase. Two motor cars; Mercedes or BMW.
"The innovative me" (27 %)	*Geographic*	City dwellers, mainly in Johannesburg.
	Socio-demographical	Males and career women. Between 16 and 34 years. High income. University education. Managerial posts in private sector.
	Psychographical • Personality	Aggressive. Leadership qualities. Non-church goers. Challenge and sensation. Impulsive. Ambitious.
	• Lifestyle (activities, interests, opinions)	Tennis, cricket, squash, bowling. Overseas travellers. Restaurants/discos/theatre.
	Product usage	Beer, wine, whisky. Support Pick 'n Pay. New products. Cheque accounts at Standard or Nedbank. Three motor cars, preferably German.

Source: Market Research Africa as discussed in Brits, RN & Reekie, WD. 1985. *Marketing in South Africa: Decision, Analysis, Theory and Practice.* Johannesburg: Macmillan, pp 149–60.

FIGURE 4.3   Segment profiles in the black consumer market

SEGMENT	CRITERIA	GROUP DESCRIPTION
Good neighbour (14 % of the population)	Geographic	One out of every two lives in urban areas.
	Social-demographic	Zulu or Xhosa. Understand English, Afrikaans. Young. Literate.
	Psychographic • Personality	Traditional. Peace-loving. Proud. Materialistic. Strives towards recognition. Law-abiding.
	• Lifestyle (activities, interests, opinions)	Personal appearance is important. Proud of their possessions. Maintains strong ties with family in rural areas. Like baking and cooking. Religious. Read newspapers and magazines. Listen to the radio. Sport loving.
	Product usage	Home owners. Brand loyal. Well known brands. Buy toiletries and cosmetics, paint, detergents and cleaners, rice and yeast. Own motor vehicle, radio, television and cassetteplayer.
Resigneds (16% of the population)	Geographic	One third lives in the cities.
	Social-demographic	Zulu and Sotho speaking. Semi-illiterate. Married. Low income.
	Psychographic • Personality	Life for this group is difficult. Resigned. Indecisive and apathetic. Practical.
	• Lifestyle activities, interests, opinions	Churchgoers. Believe in sangomas. Cooking, sewing, carpentry. Infrequent radio listeners. Do not believe in advertising messages.
	Product usage	Non-home owners. Poor housing. Cheaper brands. Irregular purchase of detergents. Secondhand clothing. Take-aways.
Emansipateds (16% of the population)	Geographic	Urban mostly Transvaal.
	Social-demographic	Educational level higher than average. Sotho speaking.
	Psychographic • Personality • Lifestyle (activities, interests, opinions)	Social, active, progressive. Like sport and entertainment. Read *Sowetan*, *Citizen*, *Star* and *Sunday Times*, as well as magazines. Positive about advertising,
	Product usage	Use financial services of banks and building societies. Buy prepacked and frozen products as well as a wide variety of consumer products including candy, chips, instant coffee, meat, colour TV, electrical appliances and cosmetics.

SEGMENT	CRITERIA	GROUP DESCRIPTION
Antis (16% of the population)	Geographic	Live outside main metropolitan areas, mostly in the OFS.
	Social-demographic	Sotho and Tswana speaking.
	Psychographic • Personality	Educational level and income above average. Literate. Negatively inclined. Social status conscious.
	• Lifestyle (activities, interests, opinions)	Read magazines. Listen to the radio. Buy on credit. Sport lovers.
	Product usage	Own motor vehicle. Buy furniture, preserved foodstuffs.
Moderns (14% of the population)	Geographic	Natal.
	Social-demographic	Nguni speaking. Virtually no knowledge of Afrikaans. Young. Educational level and income higher than average.
	Psychographic • Personality	Not socially inclined.
	• Lifestyle (activities, interests, opinions)	Interested in sport. Cooking, baking, sewing. Like to read. Education of children important.
	Product usage	Colour TV. Buy cosmetics, fridges, chewing gum, cigarettes. Savings account at bank. Insurance policy.
Traditionals (22% of the population)	Geographic	Small towns and cities specially in the OFS.
	Social-demographic	Illiterate. Sotho-speaking. Low income.
	Psychographic • Personality	Old fashioned. Traditional. Not interested in education and status.
	• Lifestyle (activities, interests, opinions)	Churchgoers. Gardening. Knitting and sewing. Not very social. Patronise sjebeens. Disinterested in the media and advertising.
	Product usage	Limited product usage. Save.

Source: Adapted from a research report of MRA (ten percent not classified)

4.3.7 Prerequisites for meaningful market segmentation

The *first* prerequisite for meaningful market segmentation[8] is that it must be possible to classify the total consumer market into groups with homogeneous attributes, needs, demands or preferences. It must be relatively easy to distinguish one group from the other.

The *second* important prerequisite is that the specific segment must be large enough for profitable exploitation. In South Africa, because of its fragmented population composition, many different segments can be distinguished. Some are, however, too small to be profitable.

The *third* prerequisite is that the market segment must be accessible. How can one, for example, reach Black women in the homelands with a marketing message if they do not read magazines or listen to the radio?

The *fourth* prerequisite is that it must be possible to measure and compare segments with regard to marketing costs, sales figures and potential profit.

When marketing management is satisfied that a specific segment answers to these conditions it can be evaluated before being chosen as a target market. *A target market is a specific segment chosen by marketing management and for which a separate marketing strategy can be developed and implemented.*

4.3.8   Evaluation of market segments

Before a specific market segment is selected as a target market it must first be evaluated according to three important evaluation criteria:

- *Segment size and growth possibilities*
  A segment need not necessarily be "big". A small segment can often be more profitable than one in which a large sales volume can be realised. Marketing management must be convinced that there are further growth possibilities and that investing in the segment under consideration does not have a mere short-term dimension.
- *Attractiveness and potential profitability*
  The attractiveness of a market segment lies not only in its size and growth possibilities but also in the promise of long-term profitability. Attractive segments attract competitors and intense competition can have a detrimental effect on future profits. Serious threats to attractive segments are aggressive competitors that can launch price wars or intensive advertising campaigns or even develop new substitute products. The growing power of buyers and suppliers also threatens attractive segments. If the threat is very serious, an enterprise that does have the necessary resources and skills can well decide not to avail itself of the opportunity to select the segment as a target market.

  A market segment is also attractive if it has some degree of interrelationship with other segments. Instead of serving a number of small segments it would be much better to combine interrelated segments. Interrelationship exists among segments that use the same raw materials, production methods or distribution channels.
- *The resources and skills of the enterprise*
  Promising segment opportunities that do not fit in with the long-term objectives set by management cannot be utilised. The same applies when resources and skills to exploit the opportunity are lacking. A segment can only be chosen as a target market if marketing management is fully committed to serving this target market better than any other competitor can. This implies that the market offering must have an undoubted differential advantage to target market members. If not, it would be better to rather commit the cost and energy to an alternative option.

4.4 TARGET MARKETING

4.4.1 Defining a target market

After the heterogeneous mass market has been divided into smaller homogeneous segments, marketing management chooses one or more of several promising segments as its target market(s). A market offering is then developed for each target market thus selected, taking into account the attributes of consumers in that segment. It is clear that target marketing can refer to the choice of several different market segments.

4.4.2 Important factors in target marketing

The following factors are of primary importance in the selection of one or several target markets:[9]

- When the resources of the enterprise with regard to labour, capital, natural resources or entrepreneurship are limited then one target market is the realistic choice.
- When the product is homogeneous, for example table salt in plastic bags, the market offering will be aimed at only one target market.
- If all consumers have the same preferences and similar reactions to the marketing strategy they are in fact all members of only one specific target market.
- Product items in a differentiated product range are directed at different target markets, for example Sta-Soft that is now available in different fragrances.
- In the beginning of the product life cycle the new market offering is aimed at only a few target markets, while many different target markets are served in the maturity phase. (The product life cycle is discussed in Chapter 18.)
- The marketing strategies of competitors also determine the enterprise's approach to the market. If competitors serve only one target market there are opportunities in the gaps thus created. But if competitors each develop separate market offerings aimed at many different target markets, the enterprise's competitive position will be harmed if it fails to do likewise.
- It is also possible to serve several target markets with one specific product. Baby talc is a good example. Besides babies, women and sportsmen use the same product albeit for different purposes. This means that three different target markets are involved. Except for the advertising message, the remainder of the market offering (packaging, price, distribution channels) remains the same.

4.4.3 The market grid

A market grid can be drawn up to facilitate target market selection. *A market grid is a description in qualitative and quantitative terms of the target market chosen by marketing management.*[10] Descriptive names are often given to the different target markets. Figures 4.2 and 4.3 are good examples of market grids. This method of classification is generally accepted and it is known that a research agency (Market Research Africa) has used this basic classification method to draw market grids for individual enterprises such as financial institutions. Such market grids contain details on geographic, demographic, psychographic (personality traits and life style) and product usage variables (see Table 4.1) and thus serve as full descriptions of consumers in a particular target market.

When the enterprise has succeeded in identifying a profitable target market, it does not necessarily follow that only this one enterprise has access to that market segment. In fact, market reseach would have indicated, at quite an early stage, the presence of competitors. In this competitive situation the enterprise must successfully position its product.

4.5 PRODUCT POSITIONING

Product positioning refers to the way consumers perceive a product in terms of its characteristics and advantages, and its competitive position. A *positioning map* can be drawn to illustrate the competitive position. Using the map will make it easier for marketing management to identify a gap or a niche where it can position its product. A product with differential advantages can be positioned in direct confrontation with competing products.

Figure 4.4 shows a positioning map in the automobile market in the United States of America. This positioning map indicates gaps in the area delimitated by variables 1 and 2. There are only two competitors in this market, namely BMW and Porsche. Also note the competition between Toyota and Volkswagen, which are in direct confrontation. This positioning map does not indicate the number of consumers in each target market, and neither, therefore, if it will be worthwhile positioning a product in a particular niche.

Figure 4.5 is a positioning map for beer marketing in the United States of America.[11] In this figure emphasis is placed on the relative size of the different market segments. There are eight market segments:

- A is the traditionalist group (25 % of the market).
- B is the beer drinker with a macho image (20 % of the market).
- C is the social drinker (13 % of the market).
- D is the status seeker (11 % of the market).
- E is the bargain hunter (10 % of the market).
- F is the true connoisseur (8 % of the market).
- G is the fitness-conscious consumer (8 % of the market).
- H is the occasional sipper (5 % of the market).

There are four variables in this positioning map, namely light/heavy taste and low/high price. In each segment there are two or more competitors. Most competitors centre around the traditionalist group A, which is the biggest group.

FIGURE 4.4   Positioning map — competitive position
Automobiles

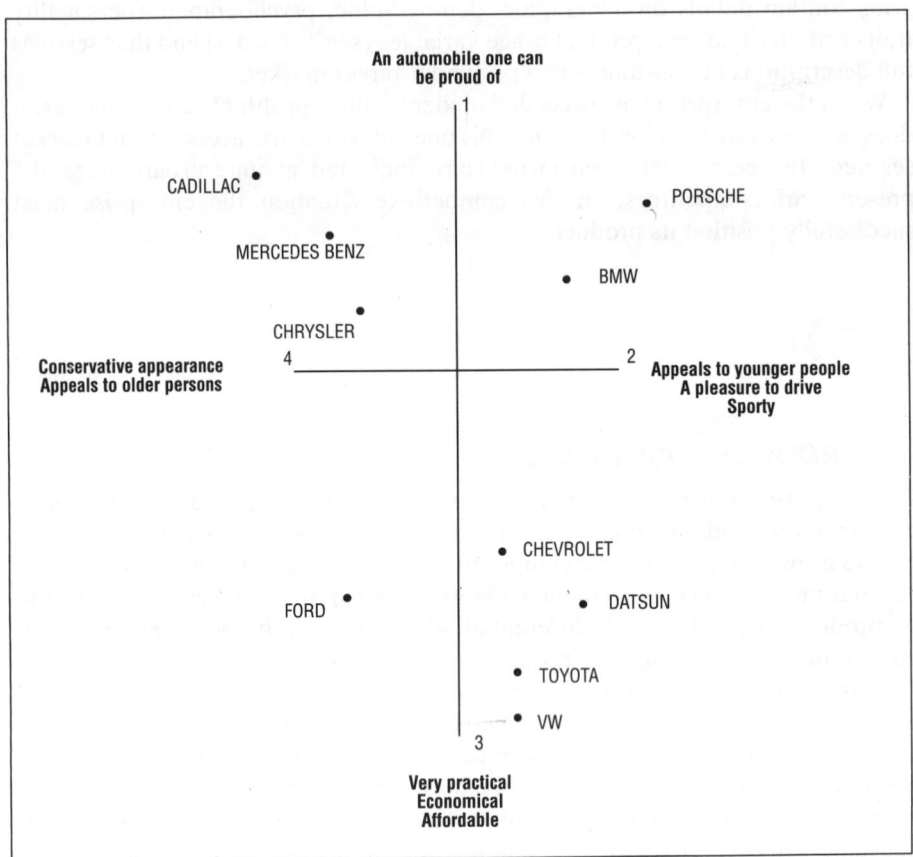

Source: Adapted from *Wall Street Journal*, March 1984, p 31.

According to the positioning map in Figure 4.5 the traditionalist group is situated right in the middle of the four variables. There are notably few competitors in the low price quadrants of the map. Although the occasional drinkers (H) are only a small segment, there are nevertheless three competitors competing in this market segment.

Many different variables can be used to draw similar positioning maps. Marketing management must determine what the critical variables are. The critical variables are those that serve to distinguish a product from those of its competitors. Marketing information and sophisticated statistical testing is necessary to draw positioning maps. They cannot be developed haphazardly or according to whim.

FIGURE 4.5   Positioning map — according to market segments
Beer

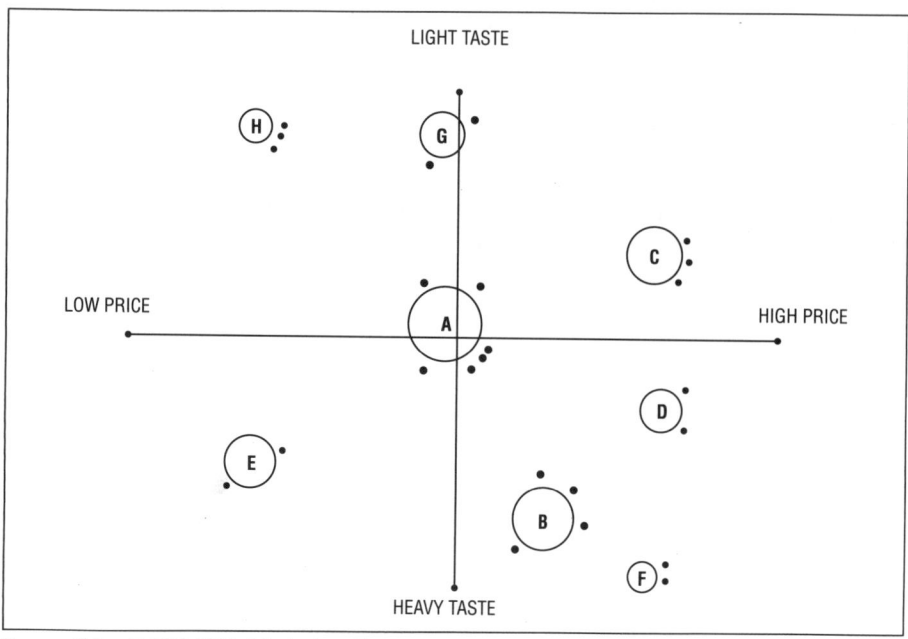

Source: Schoell, WF. 1985. *Marketing: Contemporary Concepts and Practices*. Boston: Allyn & Bacon
Inc, p 224.

4.6 STEPS IN THE MARKET SEGMENTATION PROCESS

As a summary of the preceding sections of this chapter the steps in market
segmentation are spelled out in logical sequence.[12]

Step 1: Define and describe the market

This is a broad definition in terms of the nature of the product and the market. For
a women's magazine the market consists of women in a specific language group.

Step 2: Analyse the characteristics and needs of potential consumers

Secondary and primary market information is used to describe the potential
consumers of a specific product in quantitative and qualitative terms.

Step 3: Investigate the enterprise's resources

Determine whether the enterprise has the necessary resources, abilities and
expertise to serve the chosen market.

Step 4: Identify the bases according to which the market can be segmented

Geographic, demographic, psychographic and product usage bases can be used to
segment the market.

Step 5: Evaluate potential segments

Determine the income potential and the cost involved in developing a market offering for a specific segment. Is the segment large enough to be profitable? (These aspects are discussed in Chapter 6 which deals with market measurement and forecasting.)

Step 6: Choose a target market

Choose a target market where the needs of potential consumers coincide with what the product has to offer. Draw up a market grid indicating both quantitative and qualitative attributes of the selected target market. Re-evaluate the enterprise's capabilities. Can marketing management deploy the necessary skills and resources?

Step 7: Analyse the competitive position

Investigate the nature of the competitive position and also consumers' perceptions of the competing products.

Step 8: Position the product

Position the product taking into account the number of potential consumers and the competitive position. Draw up a positioning map.

Step 9: Finalise the marketing strategies

Decide on the product, packaging, brand name, the distribution methods, the price and the nature of marketing communication for each individual segment.

Step 10: Monitor the marketing strategies

Reconsider carefully the marketing strategy and product positioning when necessary; for example, when competition increases or when a change in consumer demands or preferences are experienced. Identify new segments to approach. In the maturity phase of the product life cycle identification of new segments which can be served is of crucial importance.

    These steps are not necessarily the only ones or even in the correct sequence.[13] They nevertheless reflect the approach of this book in terms of the task of marketing management.

4.7 SUMMARY

The discussion in this chapter centres on the enterprise's approach to the market as well as its approach to the development of market offerings directed at specific market segments. The success of the marketing effort depends on the ability of marketing management to select profitable target markets in an ever-changing marketing environment. It is very important for marketing management correctly to judge the income potential of a specific market segment. The question of market measurement and market forecasting is discussed in full in Chapter 6.

REFERENCES

1. Marx, S and Dekker, HJ. 1982. *Marketing Management: Principles and Decisions*. Pretoria: HAUM, p 106.
2. Assael, H. 1985. *Marketing Management Strategy and Action*. Boston: Kent, p 231.
3. Ibid.
4. Ibid p 232. Other authors also refer to 'Concentrated marketing', Marx & Dekker, p 107, 'Concentrated strategy', Schoell, WF. 1985. *Marketing: Contemporary Concepts and Practices*. Boston: Allyn & Bacon Inc, p 190.
5. Schoell op cit, p 191.
6. Marx & Dekker op cit, p 106.
7. This section is based on Marx and Dekker op cit, pp 107–8.
8. This section is based on Cronjé, GJ de J et al (eds). 1987. *Introduction to Business Management*. Pretoria: Southern Book Publishers, pp 158–9.
9. This section is based on Marx & Dekker op cit, p 108.
10. Cronjé et al op cit, p 163.
11. Schoell op cit, p 223.
12. Based on Schoell op cit, pp 220–8.
13. See for example McDaniel, C and Darden WR. 1987. *Marketing*. Boston: Allyn & Bacon Inc, pp 212–13.

CASE STUDY

POSITIONING THE NEW BMW 3-SERIES

HISTORY OF THE 3-SERIES IN SOUTH AFRICA

Introducing the 3-series

Prior to 1983 the top segments in the South African car market were dominated by traditional executive and luxury cars such as Mercedes-Benz, Jaguar and BMW. The models offered by these manufacturers were generally medium and large-sized sedans. Compact cars were only available from mass manufacturers and in terms of specifications, features and engineering, these products were far removed from the traditional prestige cars.

When the 3-series was launched in the South African market in 1983, it created an entirely new market niche, as it had done in Europe in the previous decade. The 3-series comprised compact luxury sports sedans offering the design quality, engineering excellence and level of specification previously unavailable in a compact car. This concept met the needs and aspirations of executive car buyers, who had re-evaluated their motoring requirements following the energy crisis of the 1970s.

Positioning the 3-series

Owing to the new and unique product concept, it was essential to prevent the 3-series from being positioned in the consumer's mind in terms of some narrowly defined demographic market segment. For instance being perceived as 'the BMW for the woman' or 'the BMW for the young up-and-coming manager' would immediately have limited the wide appeal of the product and reduced the sales potential. The product was therefore aimed at consumers with a typical BMW psychographic profile and life-style irrespective of age, sex, or marital/family status. The well-known advertising slogan 'I want it because I want it' was designed to ensure wide appeal among higher-income earners, who for whatever rational or emotional reasons aspired to drive a compact luxury sports sedan.

Competitive developments

The 3-series was the 'original' and quickly developed a lucrative market niche. Its success was aided by systematic updating and expansion of the model range. Inevitably other manufacturers tried to share in the action. The mass manufacturers continually increased their efforts in this segment.

The success that other manufacturers have been able to achieve in the 3-series market segment is due to two considerations. The first is that the 3-series lost the outright performance edge, particularly with the four-cylinder models. Secondly, the limited interior space has excluded the 3-series as a practical alternative for some buyers and caused it to lose potential sales to certain price competitors. However, at the end of its life cycle the current 3-series is still achieving remarkable sales results despite the concerted efforts of competitors to exploit the product limitations.

MARKET PENETRATION

The 3-series share of the market rose from 0,75 per cent in 1983 to 6,10 per cent in 1987 and then declined to 4,80 per cent in 1991. It was decided to launch the new 3-series in 1992.

3-SERIES SHARE OF THE MARKET								
1983	1984	1985	1986	1987	1988	1989	1990	1991
0,75 %	4,05 %	4,85 %	5,82 %	6,10 %	5,83 %	5,80 %	5,67 %	4,80 %

PRODUCT CONCEPT: NEW 3-SERIES

The key elements of the product concept for the new 3-series are the following:

At the launch, three derivatives were to be introduced: the 318i, 320i and 325i, with manual and automatic transmission available in all models.

318i specifications and technical features

— M40, 4-cylinder 1796-cc engine, producing 85 kW and 165 Nm
— 5-speed manual transmission or 4-speed automatic transmission
— ABS braking system
— Power steering
— Central locking
— Tinted glass
— Air-conditioner
— Interior headlight adjustment
— Steering wheel height adjustment
— Anti-theft device
— Electrically operated windows
— Multiple function clock
— Rev. counter
— Rear window antenna
— Radio preparation kit (6 loudspeakers)

Options

Metallic paint
Electrically operated sun-roof
Leather trim
Sports seats
Radio/tape

320i specifications and technical features

— M50, 6-cylinder 1991-cc multivalve engine, producing 108 kW and 185 Nm
— 5-speed manual transmission or 5-speed automatic transmission

Features over and above the 318i

— Cassette holder
— Front centre armrest
— Active check control
— Grundig sound system
— Speed control (automatic only)

325i specifications and technical features

— M50, 6-cylinder 2494-cc multivalve engine, producing 138 kW and 240 Nm
— 5-speed manual transmission or 5-speed automatic transmission

Features over and above the 320i

— Leather steering wheel
— Front fog lights
— On-board computer
— Alloy wheels

The key elements of the product concept for the new 3-series are the following:

— Design
— Safety
— Engineers
— Transmission
— Suspension

CUSTOMER PROFILE

From BMW owner survey research, typical customer profiles for 3-series owners are the following:

- Over 25 years of age, but younger (predominantly up to 34 years of age) than 5 and 7-series owners
- Mainly upper-income group, having a monthly household income of at least R5 000
- English, married males, but compared to 5 and 7-series owners, relatively more Afrikaans, single and female
- Mainly management/executive and professional people, compared to 5 and 7-series owners, who are predominantly at director level and company owners
- Household consists of an average of 2,8 people
- Own an average of 2,4 cars per household, one being the BMW

Research conducted internationally indicates the possibilities of expanding the existing 3-series target market. The following profile groups for the new BMW 3-series show potential in attracting new business:

Young families

- May currently be driving another make for practical reasons, but aspire to BMW
- May have been limited with the 3-series due to the size

High-income singles (under 35)

- Fairly large disposable incomes and desire to acquire high-quality, prestigious products

Married couples (no children)

- Dual income, highly motivated and seeking quality, high-value contemporary products

Active retired persons

- New-found disposable incomes with a desire to maintain style, safety, quality and value

Successful self-employed individuals

- Motivated by rational and emotional stimuli which they associate with personal success and product selection

Females

- Emphasis on successful, independent income-earning women with a desire to express success in elegant and performance-orientated terms

PRICE POSITIONING THE NEW 3-SERIES

The new 3-series, with its improved interior space, advanced technology and safety, will be priced higher than the current range to compete in the upper luxury/performance segment on the basis of superior product substance rather than on price.

In image and value the new 3-series will allow the range to distance itself from the top end of the mass market, allowing for a pricing premium above some of the current competitors. The flagship 325i will compete among the executive sedans, priced in the bracket of the entry level of 5-series and M-Benz W124 ranges. The proposed launch pricing is as follows:

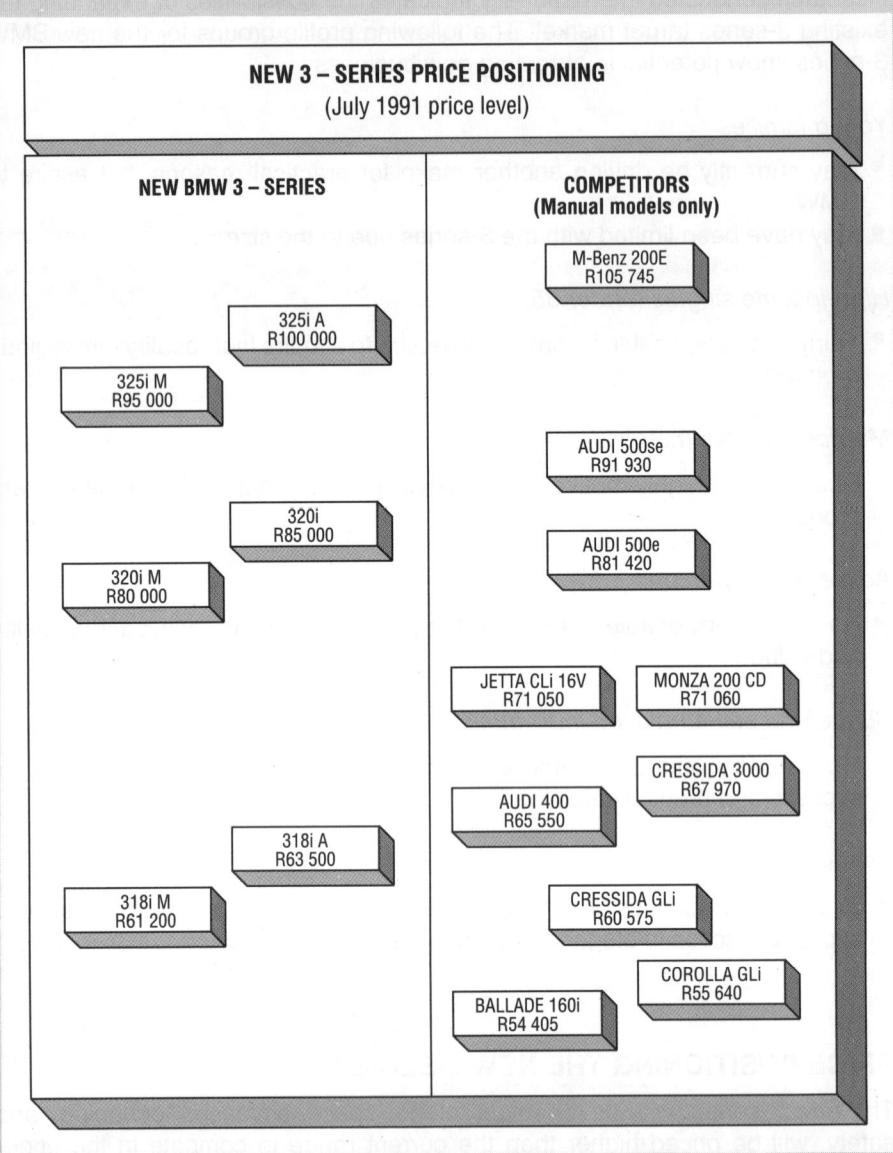

NEW 3 – SERIES PRICE POSITIONING
(July 1991 price level)

NEW BMW 3 – SERIES

COMPETITORS
(Manual models only)

M-Benz 200E
R105 745

325i A
R100 000

325i M
R95 000

AUDI 500se
R91 930

320i
R85 000

AUDI 500e
R81 420

320i M
R80 000

JETTA CLi 16V
R71 050

MONZA 200 CD
R71 060

CRESSIDA 3000
R67 970

AUDI 400
R65 550

318i A
R63 500

318i M
R61 200

CRESSIDA GLi
R60 575

COROLLA GLi
R55 640

BALLADE 160i
R54 405

COMMUNICATION OBJECTIVES

In creating advertisements for the new 3-series, product and brand image objectives should be taken into account.

The international *product* image objectives set for the new 3-series are the following:

- To establish a distinctive image for the new 3-series which clearly differentiates it from the 5-series

- To establish the new 3-series as the 'best-in-class' choice of compact luxury sports sedans in all aspects, maintaining the 'spirited original' image of the series

- To convey the increased size and presence of the new model

In addition certain brand image objectives have been identified:

- The new 3-series must serve to broaden the overall BMW brand image that is currently based largely on performance, which is most often associated with the 3-series.

- The new model must serve to evolve the current image of quality from a pure product perspective to an overall interpretation which permeates all aspects of the ownership experience.

- The new 3-series should reinforce BMW's leadership role through elements which communicate the heritage of success in innovation, of always being a leader in providing products to suit the requirements of the time.

SALES AND MARKET PENETRATION OBJECTIVES

Within the first three years, a market penetration of above five per cent is to be achieved.

Total 3-series	1992	1993	1994
% of market	6,47 %*	5,27 %	5,14 %

*Market penetration annualised, based on 8 months of May-Dec. 1992

The higher price of the new 3-series will have the effect of limiting the affordability of the entry level but the new character and better space offer of the car will also ensure a wider appeal. Therefore the volume lost at the lower end of the market segment will have to be substituted by a gain in the upper market share. This implies a challenging 'conquest' task for the new 3-series.

Source: BMW SA 1991. Information supplied by J P van der Walt.

QUESTIONS

1. How did BMW succeed in creating a niche for its 3-series back in 1983?

2. What were the problems that led to the development of the new 3-series?

3. On what key elements did BMW attempt to improve its new product concept? Explain.

4. "Income seems to be the main criterion for identifying potential target markets for the new 3-series". Discuss.

5. Discuss the emotional motives underlying a decision to purchase a 3-series.

6. List the rational reasons a customer can give for his decision to purchase a 3-series.

7. How did BMW position itself against competitors in terms of the 3-series range?

8. Which features and benefits should be mentioned in advertising appeals for the new 3-series and why?

9. List the criteria used to segment the potential market for the new 3-series.

10. Name a few competitors who tried to attack the 3-series niche segment.

11. You are an independent marketing consultant and have determined, by doing an ownership survey, that current BMW owners are potential buyers of the new 3-series. Write a report to BMW in which you explain your research results. Also point out the benefits of brand loyalty and recommend methods to appeal to this potentially lucrative target market.

   Note: Use your imagination. You will only be able to do this last question properly after you have studied all the chapters in the book.

CHAPTER 5

MARKETING INFORMATION AND MARKETING RESEARCH

5.1 INTRODUCTION

Marketing managers require timeous, accurate and relevant information to make effective decisions. The purpose of this chapter is to provide an overview of:

- the information needs for marketing decision making;
- the nature and extent of marketing information systems; and
- the application of marketing research as part of the marketing information system.

During the past two decades the availability of data and information has increased considerably, both in extent and speed of delivery. Our modern age is often described as the 'information era', and the consequent challenge of efficient information management is a reality. In the first part of the chapter the information needs of marketing management and the concept of information management are discussed. Thereafter the nature and composition of marketing information systems are discussed, and in the last part of the chapter the importance and process of marketing research, in particular, are highlighted.

The efficient management of marketing information and marketing research is today considered a strategic priority of an enterprise, since it can provide competitive advantages if accompanied by rational decision making.

ORGANISATION OF THE CHAPTER

Necessity of marketing information: Information requirements for marketing decision making, data increase and complexity, requirements for relevant information, management of information.

> **Marketing information systems:** Definition, relationship to the management information system, types of marketing information systems and their components, interaction between the components of a marketing information system, the advantages and costs of marketing information, status of marketing information systems.
>
> **Marketing research:** Nature of marketing research, types of marketing research and the marketing research process.

5.2 NECESSITY OF MARKETING INFORMATION

5.2.1 Information requirements for marketing decision making

In previous chapters it was made clear that marketing management should be future-oriented, in the sense that they should:

- anticipate environmental changes;
- forecast the direction and impact of these changes; and
- conduct their planning accordingly.

In order to implement these tasks, management requires information of the enterprise's various internal and external environmental variables. Figure 5.1 provides an overview of the major types of information requirements.

The nature of current fast-changing environmental conditions necessitates that every enterprise manages its marketing information as efficiently as possible. Examples of the pressure on information requirements are:

- Socio-cultural changes, such as the increasing urbanisation of the South African population, which impact on demand and consumption patterns.
- Technological trends, such as the increasing use of the computer.
- Heightening consumer pressures for product information, guarantees, service, etc.
- Competitive activities, which are in many instances intensifying because of trends toward privatisation of government enterprises and deregulation.
- Increasing complexity of marketing decision making, such as shorter product life cycles and consequently more product development, expansion to new markets, and the management of multiple distribution channels.

5.2.2 Data increase and complexity

Marketing managers often discover that the reason for their information problems lies in the great extent of available data, and not in a shortage of data. Data and information are not synonymous. *Data* refer to all available statistics, opinions, facts or forecasts, while *information* pertains only to data which are relevant for decision making. Because of technological progress in communication media and data processing the volume of available data has increased tremendously. In addition, the complexity of data has increased further owing to new data collection and presentation methods, which hinder the distinction between relevant data (in other words, information) and irrelevant data.

FIGURE 5.1   Major types of information requirements

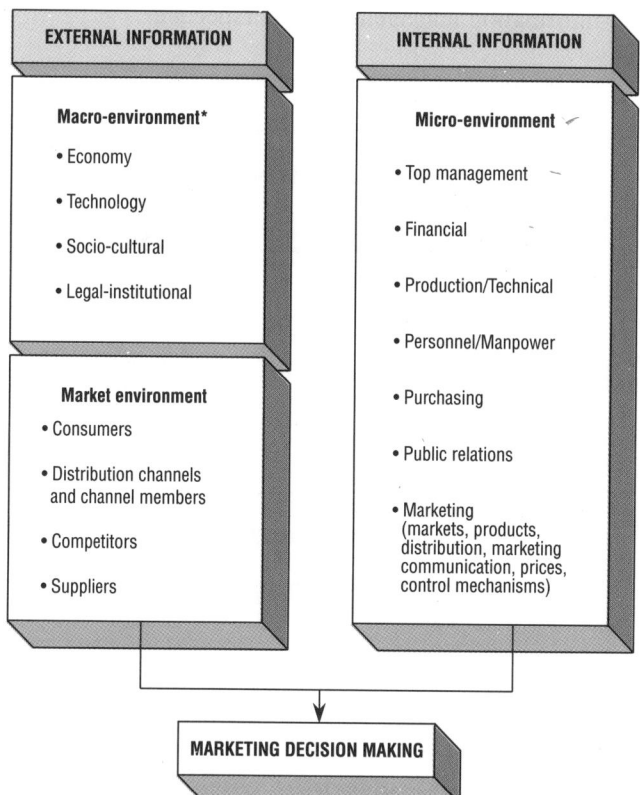

*See Chapter 2 for a discussion of the macro-environmental variables.

The degree of efficiency of a marketing information system is an important factor in the speed and accuracy of marketing decision making. A marketing information system should therefore have the objectives of filtering the massive inflow of data and providing information for decision making to the appropriate decision makers, when, where and in which form it may be desired.

5.2.3 The management of information

The efficient supply of information to decision makers has become so important that the term 'information management' is fast gaining popularity.[1] In a marketing context it means that the planning, organising, co-ordinating, leading and controlling of marketing information have to take place in such a way that the information requirements of marketing decision makers are optimally satisfied. Information requirements have to be continually monitored, data sources and availability have to be complete, data reduction has to take place efficiently, and the supply to decision makers has to be timely and in the right format. The marketing information system is the most important means to this end. Figure 5.2 puts the role of information management in perspective.

FIGURE 5.2   The role of information management

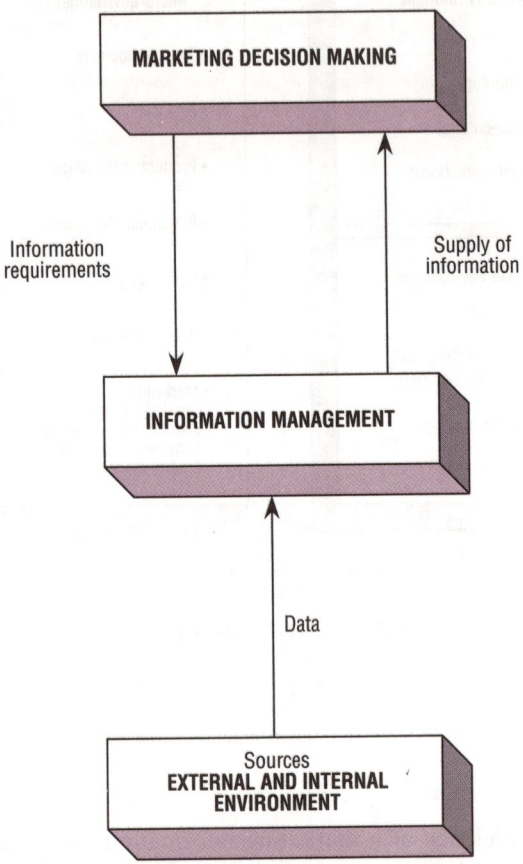

5.3 MARKETING INFORMATION SYSTEMS

5.3.1 Definition of a marketing information system

A prerequisite for efficient information management is a carefully planned marketing information system. A marketing information system can be defined as *a planned combination of ways and methods for continuous gathering, filtering, analysing, storing and flow of relevant information for the purpose of marketing decision making.*[2]

A marketing information system implies the interaction and interdependence of various elements which form a whole that is greater than the mere sum total of the individual elements. The ways in which the system functions refer to the human and non-human procedures and techniques that are applied. Together with the data inflow this forms the input of the system, and the process followed is the continuous filtering, analysing and flow of information. The eventual output of the system is timeous, relevant, accurate and comprehensible information for decision making. These components are illustrated in Figure 5.3.

FIGURE 5.3   Operation of a marketing information system

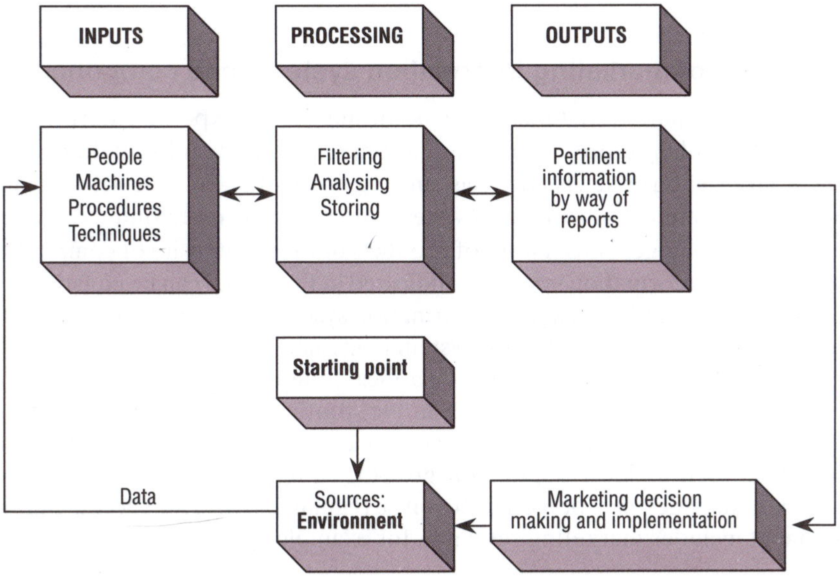

A marketing information system can be compared to military intelligence activity. Both gather data by various means, from different sources and by using different methods, process it and store it, and provide the information to decision makers. The information which a decision maker requires usually indicates a particular method of obtaining it. Modern information systems are especially characterised by the use of the computer and people who have quantitative-analytical and linguistic capabilities. The reason for this lies in the volume of data which is available, the high degree of sophistication that data collection and processing techniques have achieved, and the interrelationships which exist in such a system. The decisions by decision makers have a particular impact on the environment from which the data has originally been drawn (see the cycle illustrated in Figure 5.3).

5.3.2 The relationship between management and marketing information systems

The marketing information system forms part of the management information system of an enterprise. Each enterprise has a management information system, be it formalised or non-formalised. Usually only enterprises with separate marketing departments have a marketing information system. A management information system receives inputs from all the functional departments of the enterprise, such as finance, production, human resources, purchasing and marketing, with the purpose of generating information for strategic enterprise decision making. The marketing information system forms one of the most important parts of the management information system because of its strategic information outputs concerning markets, products and competitive conditions, which substantially affect the nature and direction of the enterprise's activities.

5.3.3 Types of marketing information systems and components

Marketing information systems differ according to the type of enterprise and industry. A small enterprise usually has a simple marketing information system, while a large enterprise usually has an extensive one. In industries such as agriculture and mining, information systems are generally more simplistic, due to the relatively homogeneous nature of products or lower intensity of competition.

A marketing information system as indicated in Figure 5.3 can be constituted in various ways. A simple marketing information system is illustrated in Figure 5.4.

A simple marketing information system consists of a routine data component and a special purpose component. For a local independent retailer the routine data component would include, for example, routine information from internal sources, such as sales, stocks, debtors and creditors. From external sources information such as local population growth, competitive activities and trade association statistics can be collected on a regular basis. The special purpose component includes marketing research, for example where the retailer engages

FIGURE 5.4   A simple marketing information system

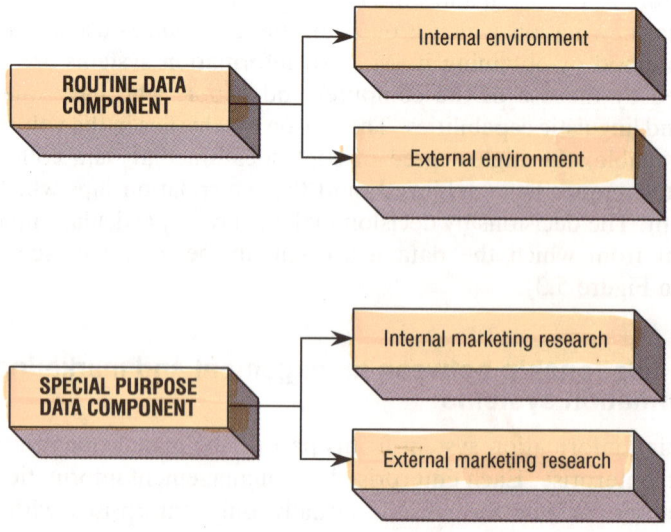

a marketing research organisation to determine the feasibility of a particular retail space in a new shopping centre (external marketing research). The retailer conducting certain research projects on his own, for example a survey among existing customers to determine their degree of satisfation with its services, constitutes internal marketing research (launched from internal sources).

Larger enterprises which have the necessary resources usually operate an extensive marketing information system. Figure 5.5 indicates the major components of an extensive marketing information system and the interaction among its components.[3]

FIGURE 5.5   An extensive marketing information system

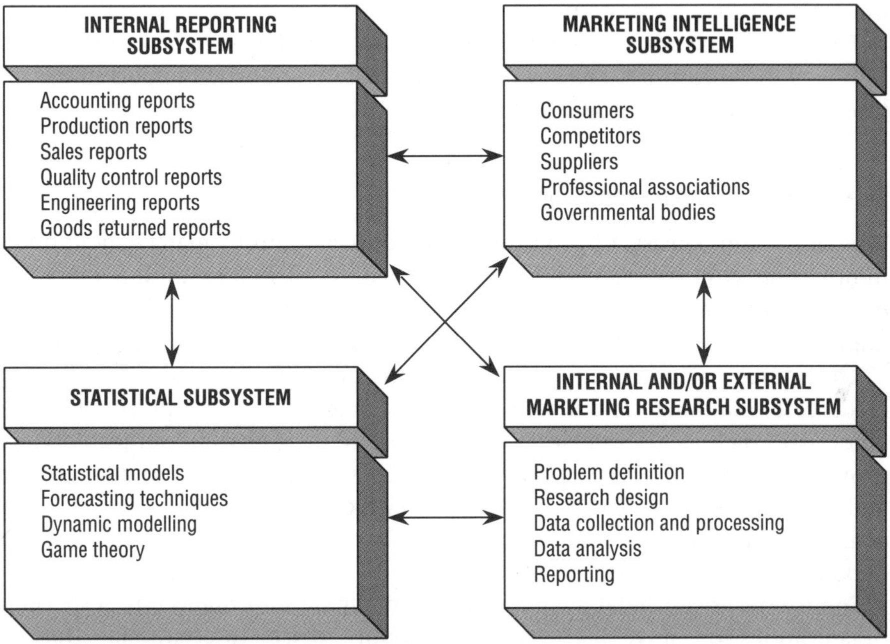

Source: Adapted from Kotler, P. 1988. *Marketing Management: Analysis, Planning, Implementation and Control*. Englewood Cliffs, NJ: Prentice-Hall, p 103.

The four major components of an extensive marketing information system, as indicated in Figure 5.5, are:

- an internal reporting subsystem;
- a marketing intelligence subsystem;
- a statistical subsystem;
- a marketing research subsystem.

The internal reporting subsystem

Various reports are prepared internally by enterprises. Important reports emanate from, among others, the accounting department, the production department, the sales department and the quality control department. Reports are prepared by, for example, sales representatives, brand managers, marketing researchers and stock controllers.

There are two important criteria for an internal reporting subsystem. The *first* is that the information has to be both necessary and useful for the decision maker. Marketing management has to distinguish between necessary and unnecessary information, and the information which is required has to be presented in a useful format. The *second* requirement is that it must be an interactive subsystem; in other words the necessary interaction between marketing, financing, production, purchasing and other functional divisions of the enterprise is incorporated in the system. In some large enterprises there is often a lack of appropriate interaction between departments and their personnel, which usually leads to a less efficient internal reporting subsystem.

The internal reports contain information about the historical performance results of the enterprise. By way of this information important opportunities and threats can timeously be identified.

The marketing intelligence subsystem

This subsystem consists of procedures and sources whereby management obtain information concerning current and relevant occurrences in the marketing environment. The information in this subsystem is often collected in a relatively unorganised way. Figure 5.6 indicates the sources of marketing intelligence.

The sources of marketing intelligence are extensive and can be utilised by resourceful planning. The most important source is often the personnel of the enterprise, such as sales personnel, who, despite their possible subjectivity, can provide important marketing information. Consequently, they should be trained and motivated to be sensitive to information which may be of relevance. A variety of information can also readily and with relatively little cost be collected from middlemen, suppliers and customers.

Some enterprises find it advantageous to purchase information from speciality organisations on a regular basis. In South Africa International Business Information Systems (IBIS), which has an association with the internationally reputable AC Nielsen company, is especially known for the retail audits which it regularly conducts. This information includes aspects such as market shares, retail prices, inventory levels and marketing communications.

The statistical subsystem

The statistical subsystem (see Figure 5.5) is a composition of a statistical data base and the application of advanced statistical procedures and techniques. The purpose of this subsystem is to create projections, scenarios and models which provide a better grasp of the alternatives for decision making. Decision making always takes place in conditions of risk and uncertainty. With this subsystem it is attempted to quantify the probable results of various possible actions of marketing management.

FIGURE 5.6 Sources of marketing intelligence

SOURCE	EXAMPLES
Customers/clients	Informal enquiries among customers, buyers of clients
Suppliers	Product suppliers, advertising agencies, banks, public relations enterprises
Middlemen	Retailers, wholesalers, agents, brokers
Enterprise personnel	Managers, sales representatives, engineers, buyers
Professional associations	Management, scientific and technical associations and meetings
Competitors	Annual reports, speeches, products, personnel advertisements, consultants
Other sources	Consultants, information speciality organisations, the media such as the press, radio and television

A variety of statistical data series is stored and regularly updated in the statistical subsystem. These serve as bases for the application of statistical techniques (with multiple variables), forecasting techniques (see Chapter 6), and the creation of models (for example, the creation of a model of consumer behaviour in a specific situation, which illustrates the probable effect of a change in a marketing instrument, such as price).

The marketing research subsystem

As already mentioned in the simplified marketing information system, the focus of marketing research is on specific situations or occurrences which require special investigation. Marketing research can broadly be defined as *the systematic process of investigating identified problems and phenomena in order to provide pertinent information for decision making.* It differs from the other subsystems of the marketing information system in that it is conducted on an ad hoc (discontinuous) basis, as the need arises. There could, of course, always be one or other marketing research investigation in process, but each project has a specific life span and ends with the completion of the investigation. Marketing research is discussed in greater detail in section 5.4.

5.3.4 Interaction among the components of a marketing information system

The dynamic interaction among the four subsystems of a marketing information system is best illustrated by way of a practical example. Figure 5.7 gives an example of a soft drinks manufacturer. Follow the figure by referring to both Figures 5.5 and 5.6.

FIGURE 5.7   Interaction of the components of a marketing information system of a soft drinks manufacturer

COMPONENT	INFORMATION	DECISION MAKING
Internal reporting subsystem	Sales reports for Natal indicate a 50 % decrease in sales for December	Ascertain the causes by way of the marketing intelligence subsystem
Marketing intelligence subsystem	Retailers mention a price reduction by the main competitor in Natal	Use the statistical subsystem to determine the probable effects of various alternative decisions
Statistical subsystem	Develop a model of the behaviour patterns of Natal consumers concerning soft drinks purchasing *Problem: Information about consumer preferences is not available*	Launch a marketing research project to determine the factors in Natal consumer demand for soft drinks, as well as their relative importance.
Marketing research subsystem	Give instruction to Market Research Africa to investigate and provide information	Marketing management makes appropriate decisions, for example: • change packaging because competitors' packaging is better • monitor sales on a weekly basis • launch a marketing communications campaign to strengthen brand loyalty among consumers • maintain price levels because consumers are not price sensitive

5.3.5 The advantages and costs of marketing information

All information has two important dimensions: the **quality dimension**, which refers to the quality of information, and the **cost dimension**, which refers to the price thereof.

The quality of information is a function of the accuracy, timeousness, adequacy, availability and relevance thereof. Accurate (valid) information refers to the realities of the situation. Timeous information simply means recent information which is available when desired. Adequate information means sufficient qualitative and quantitative information in order to make a better decision. The availability of information refers to its accessibility (in other words: can it be obtained?). Relevant information refers to the suitability of information for the decision which has to be taken.

No information can be obtained without cost. The cost of information consists of economic costs (direct financial, or indirect in terms of opportunity costs such as those which result from delaying a decision) and psychological costs (frustration of searching for information). For all types of marketing information in the marketing information system a value appraisal should be made in terms of decision making needs. Figure 5.8 indicates a simplified cost benefit formula.[4]

FIGURE 5.8   Value appraisal of marketing information for a decision

It is so that the determination of the value of information is not always possible. Nevertheless, marketing management should regularly consider the value of information in order to develop an efficient information system.

5.3.6 The status of marketing information systems

Marketing information systems have developed considerably since the days when they were known only as clerical activities. Today they are increasingly refined, especially with computer assistance, and enjoy high status in many enterprises. Because of the volume of data and information which is processed and presented, and the technical systems and procedures applied, problems often arise in managerial circles between information specialists and decision makers. Despite this the importance of marketing information systems should increase in the 1990s owing to:

- The increasing shift in emphasis from market status (the situation regarding prices, market share, etc) to market reaction (how factors react to change, such as price elasticity of demand and advertising reaction).
- The continuous advance in the power and capacity of the computer.
- The development of newer and more analytical procedures, methods and techniques in marketing information systems.
- The increasing need for information for strategic decision making by marketing management.

5.4 MARKETING RESEARCH

5.4.1 The nature of marketing research

Marketing research has previously been defined as a *systematic process of investigating identified problems and phenomena which require special attention.*

Although informal marketing research has been conducted since the earliest days of marketing activities, formal marketing research has developed only during the past seven decades. The key characteristic of the formal approach is that it is a **systematic** process. It is carried out in a methodical step-by-step fashion which results in reliable information for decision making. The focus is on the investigation of specific problems and phenomena which, as the first step in the process, are more precisely defined.

The American Marketing Association provides an extensive definition of marketing research:[5] *'Marketing research is the function that links consumer, client and public with the marketer by way of information — information that is used to identify and describe marketing opportunities and threats; to generate, specify and evaluate marketing activities; to monitor marketing performance; and to improve the grasp of marketing as a process.* Marketing research specifies the information which is required, designs the methods for data collection, implements and manages the data collection process, analyses the results, and communicates the findings and their implications.'

Marketing research assists marketing management to identify and solve problems. It can also help to identify marketing opportunities and to evaluate them. It is also important to distinguish clearly between the terms 'market research' and 'marketing research'. Marketing research is the wider activity that includes market research. Whereas the latter concerns only information about the size, nature, structure and other characteristics of *markets*, marketing research includes aspects such as product development, distribution channels, advertising effectiveness and pricing decisions.

FIGURE 5.9   Differences in characteristics between marketing research and the marketing information system

MARKETING RESEARCH	MARKETING INFORMATION SYSTEM
1. Application is on a project-to-project basis (discontinuous).	1. Continuous operation—a typical system.
2. Focus is on problem solving.	2. Focus is on prevention as well as solution of problems.
3. Handles especially external information.	3. Handles both external and internal information
4. Is only one source of information for a marketing information system.	4. Besides marketing research, includes other subsystems (see Figure 5.5).

Figure 5.9 indicates that there is also a clear distinction between marketing research and the marketing information system. The latter is a wider concept encompassing various information subsystems.

5.4.2 Types of marketing research

Marketing research is used by enterprises in all sectors of the economy, ie in the primary sector (for example, mining companies, agricultural producers), secondary sector (for example, television set manufacturers, textile companies) and the tertiary sector (for example, retailers, banks, travel agents). Because of the diverse nature of enterprises and their circumstances in the various sectors and industries, the spectrum of marketing research activities is wide. An indication of the types of marketing research used in the South African manufacturing sector is given in Table 5.1.

5.4.3 The marketing research process

Marketing research consists of a logical process, involving five major steps as indicated in Figure 5.10.

FIGURE 5.10   Steps in the marketing research process

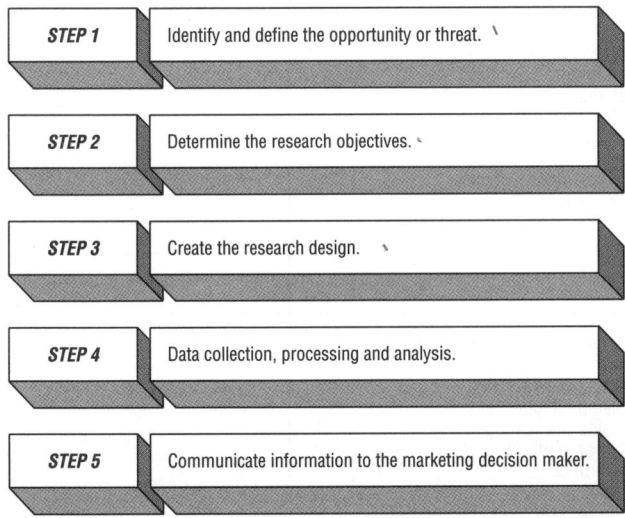

STEP 1	Identify and define the opportunity or threat.
STEP 2	Determine the research objectives.
STEP 3	Create the research design.
STEP 4	Data collection, processing and analysis.
STEP 5	Communicate information to the marketing decision maker.

These five steps are now discussed in greater detail.[6]

Step 1: Identify and define the opportunity or threat

No research project should be attempted before marketing management has clearly communicated the nature of the opportunity or threat to the researcher. A **threat** in the environment can, for example, be an increase in competition, a change in consumer preferences, or the withdrawal of retailers from the company's distribution system. These are symptoms of deeper-lying problems which have to be clearly defined. A weak diagnosis would lead to an inefficient solution.

TABLE 5.1   Types of marketing research used in the South African manufacturing sector, 1980

TYPES OF MARKETING RESEARCH	RELATIVE INCIDENCE	
	Major category %	Subcategory %
1. Research on products and services	28,0	
1.1 Brand and product preference		20,9
1.2 New product acceptance		20,0
1.3 Product design		12,2
1.4 Product display		6,2
1.5 Product usage		28,7
1.6 Formula testing (marketing aspects)		8,4
1.7 Use of by-products (marketing)		2,6
1.8 Other		1,0
SUBTOTAL		100,0
2. Research on markets	48,1	
2.1 General economic research		6,6
2.2 Current market potential		16,0
2.3 Market share		26,2
2.4 Market segmentation		15,1
2.5 Market forecasting		17,3
2.6 Dealer surveys		8,5
2.7 Buying and other patterns		6,2
2.8 Foreign markets		4,0
2.9 Other		0,1
SUBTOTAL		100,0
3. Research on methods and policies	23,9	
3.1 Advertising media		9,5
3.2 Advertising effectiveness		10,7
3.3 Advertising pre-testing		8,6
3.4 Distribution methods and channels		9,0
3.5 Distribution costs		9,8
3.6 Sales quotas		9,7
3.7 Location (of branches and depots)		9,2
3.8 Prices and pricing decisions		20,0
3.9 Settlement methods		6,2
3.10 Motivational research (attitudes, behaviour)		7,3
3.11 Other		0,0
SUBTOTAL		100,0
GRAND TOTAL	**100,0**	

Source: Adapted from Nel, PA, Rädel, FE and Loubser, M. 1988. *Researching the South African Market*. Pretoria: University of South Africa, p 55.

After the marketing manager has explained how he/she sees the threat, the researcher conducts an investigation into the real situation. The confirmation or rejection of the threat as stated by the decision maker is a critical phase of the research project. The researcher conducts this investigation by consulting with relevant experts, especially those who are directly involved. This aspect is especially important when the researcher is an external consultant. Solution of the problem situation enables the marketing manager to take steps to transform threats in the environment into promising opportunities.

Redefinition of a problem situation for the purpose of marketing research

The sales manager of a potato chip manufacturer notices that the sales of a specific brand have been declining two months in a row. He interprets the problem as 'inefficient advertising'. He instructs the marketing researcher to investigate the efficiency of the company's advertising campaign. The researcher conducts interviews with sales representatives, wholesalers and retailers, and discovers that retailer support declined because of a new competitive product which provides higher profit margins on sales. Retailers are therefore making more profit by selling the competitive product. This information makes it clear to the researcher that an investigation of advertising efficiency would not solve the problem. Redefinition of the problem is necessary, which subsequently is defined, in conjunction with the sales manager, as 'competitive pricing and profit margin tactics'.

Marketing research projects can also be aimed at the identification of **opportunities**. Positioning of a product in a particular gap (niche) in the market is an example of marketing research which is aimed at the identification and definition of an opportunity in the market (see Chapter 4).

Step 2: Determine the research objectives

A marketing research investigation could have one of four basic objectives, namely to explore, to describe, to determine causes, or to predict.

- **Exploratory research** is conducted when more information about a problem, opportunity or phenomenon is needed. The reason for this is often to collect data which can contribute to more meaningful research questions.

- **Descriptive research** is necessary when knowledge about a particular market or other marketing aspect is vague, for example the description of the conference market for a company who is considering entering the hotel industry, or where the nature of competition in a particular industry is vague. Descriptive research can describe opportunities or threats.

- **Causal research** is done to reveal a cause-and-effect relationship, for example increased advertising expenditure (cause) and increase in sales (effect). With descriptive research a possible relationship between certain variables is often revealed, while causal research confirms this relationship and its operation, or rejects it as false.
- **Predictive research** is conducted to forecast future values, for example sales income, market shares and retail orders. Both opportunities and threats which are expected in the future can be revealed by predictive research.

Step 3: Create the research design

The research design is the plan according to which the research investigation will be conducted. It specifies the data that will be required and the broad framework of procedures for the collection, processing and analysis of the data. This is an important step in the marketing research process, because from this an estimate of the costs of the investigation, which brings the desirability and feasibility thereof in relation to the potential value, can be made. The creation of a research design requires considerable ingenuity because it has to be planned specifically according to the particular requirements of the research project. Figure 5.11 indicates the six basic activities in the creation of a research design.

Determine the data requirements (Activity 1). The research objectives must be specified in areas of data requirements. Two broad groups of data requirements exist, namely primary data and secondary data. **Primary data** are data which have not previously been collected and thus have to be extracted by original research. Primary data collection is relatively expensive and slow, but the data are usually more relevant to the research objectives than secondary data. This type of data usually requires some or other form of survey.

Secondary data already exist, ie historical data which have been collected before, either by the enterprise itself or by outsiders. Researchers usually start by collecting and analysing secondary data, which may indicate that primary data are not necessary depending on the research objectives. Secondary data are usually cheaper and faster to obtain than primary data, but the researcher always has to consider its relevance, accuracy, reliability and timeousness.

Determine the data sources (Activity 2). Both primary and secondary data can be obtained from internal and/or external sources, as indicated in Figure 5.12. The marketing researcher should have a good knowledge of the available data sources in each data category, and determine the relevancy of each.

Determine the data collection approaches (Activity 3). This activity concerns the determination of how to collect the required data. The collection of secondary data is usualy simple, because the assistance of librarians and relevant government bodies, among others, could be used.

FIGURE 5.11   Activities in the creation of a research design

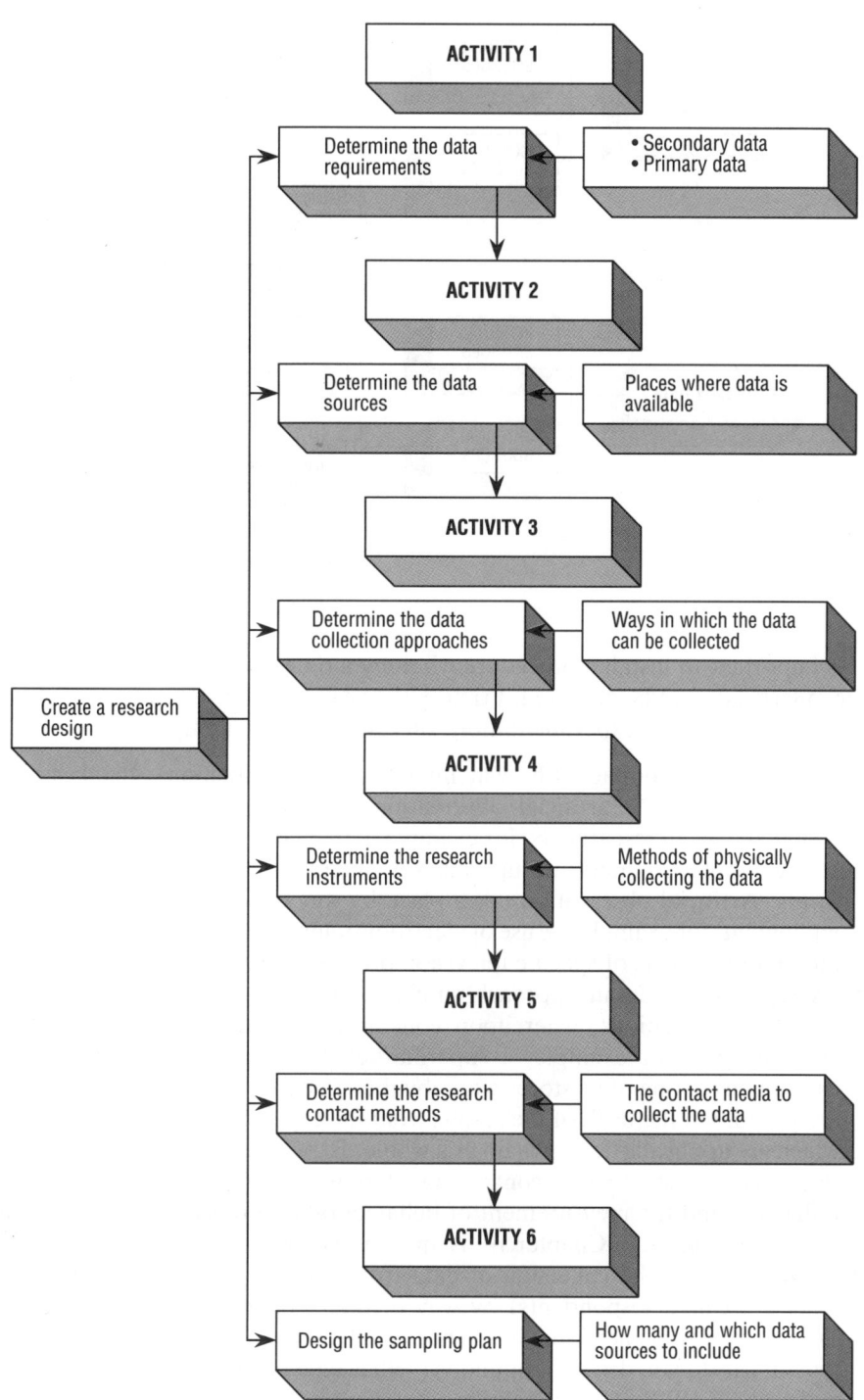

FIGURE 5.12   Examples of marketing data sources

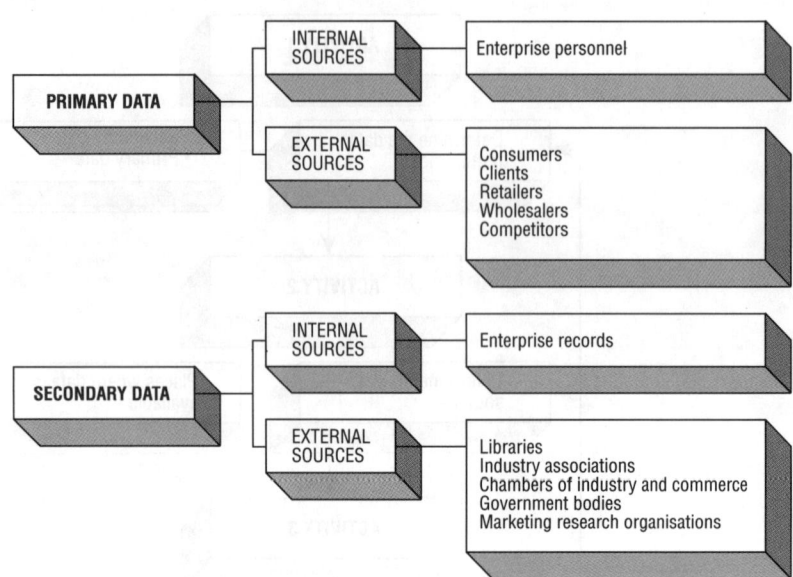

It is important to install a procedure whereby a timeous and continuous flow of secondary data can be obtained. Primary data can be collected by four methods, namely observation, experimentation, surveys and focus groups.

- **Observation** is conducted by watching people and situations. It takes place through human or artificial observation methods. Human observation is conducted when researchers, for example, personally monitor the number and behaviour of consumers in a supermarket, and register the data on predesigned forms. Artificial observation takes place by way of mechanical or electronic equipment, for example the use of electronic television meters to determine the number of viewers of specific television programmes.
- **Experimentation** is an approach similar to testing, and is implemented in controlled conditions, whereupon conclusions are drawn about the wider environment. For example, a supermarket chain store group conducts an experiment in one of its stores whereby the effects of a new display technique are tested. On the basis of the results from the experiment decisions are made which are applicable to the chain as a whole. Experimentation involves careful selection of test objects, controlling of other factors which may have an influence, and the measurement of behavioural differences. Test marketing, which is discussed in Chapter 10, is an example of experimentation.
- **Surveys** involve the collection of data from selected individuals (those who react are called respondents) by way of direct or indirect questioning (for example, a postal questionnaire). The type of data required can be facts ('What type of car do you drive?'), opinions ('What type of toothpaste tastes best?'), and motives ('Why do you holiday every year in Cape Town?').

- **Focus groups** are group discussions involving a number of persons, who spend a set time with an interviewer discussing a specific subject. For example, a housewife focus group's opinions are asked about their desires, preferences and buying behaviour concerning various types of cheese. The results of focus group research often present guidelines for more extensive research, for example a survey.

Determine the research instruments (Activity 4). Two types of research instruments for the collection of primary data exist, namely the questionnaire and mechanical/electronic equipment.

- The **questionnaire** is the most common instrument for the collection of primary data. With the design of the questionnaire careful consideration must be given to the type of questions, their format, wording and sequence. The nature of questions should be relevant and easily understandable by the respondent. The questions can be *open* (respondent replies in own words and extent) or *closed* (respondent selects one or more alternative replies listed on the questionnaire). The wording of the questions and instructions have to be simple, unambiguous and direct. The sequence of the questions has to be considered when structuring the questionnaire. For example, the introductory questions should arouse interest and ensure co-operation, while the difficult and/or more personal questions should be asked towards the end of the questionnaire. The pretesting of a questionnaire, in order to confirm that these considerations have been correctly implemented and to make adjustments if necessary, is always strongly recommended.
- **Mechanical/electronic equipment** involves the use of instruments such as galvanometers, tachistoscopes, cameras and electronic and mechanical meters. These instruments range from simple counting meters (for example, the number of people passing through a turnstile) to sophisticated reaction-measurement instruments (for example, emotional reaction to a specific advertisement).

Determine the research contact methods (Activity 5). The individuals involved in a research survey can be contacted by three methods, namely by telephone, by post or fax, and in person.

When the contact period is short, time limited, and funds scarce, the **telephone** is a logical choice. This method is quick, and problems or questions could be discussed directly. The disadvantages are that only individuals with telephones can be contacted, and that the contact period is necessarily short.

The **post or fax** is a better method when individuals do not like to give their opinions directly, and when the geographical contact area is relatively large. It also has the advantage that there is no pressure on the respondent to react quickly, and the contact person cannot influence the reaction. Post and fax contact methods, however, require clear instructions, and the rate of reaction (reponse) is usually low and/or slow.

The **personal** contact method involves a face-to-face situation. It has the advantage that more questions can be put and answered, and audio-visual aids (such as a tape recorder) can often be used with the approval of the respondent. However, it is an expensive method involving extensive planning and control.

Design the sampling plan (Activity 6). This last activity in research design is applicable in extensive surveys where the survey population (or universum) is too large for a complete survey, and a scientific sample is consequently necessary. Three basic aspects have to be considered, namely the sample unit, the sample composition, and the sample size.

- The **sample unit** involves a definition of the specific target market (for example, children who watch a particular television programme), as well as the specific characteristics of the sample unit (for example, only children in the age group 9 to 13 years).

- The **sample composition** has to be representative of the characteristics of the target market. Two methods of sampling exist, namely probability and non-probability sampling. In **probability (random) sampling** each unit of the population has a statistically accepted, equal chance of being included in the sample. Strict statistical rules are applied so that the eventual degree of confidence with which conclusions are drawn can be stated. In **non-probability sampling** the judgement of the researcher concerning the selection of sample units plays a direct role. This judgement of the researcher can be based upon factors such as convenience, relative importance of units, and recommendations of other experts. Although the degree of representativeness of the sample cannot be statistically evaluated in this instance, it is scientifically acceptable if the composition is knowledgeably and carefully made, and is relevant to the particular research situation.

- The **sample size** involves the number of units that are included in the investigation. No fixed rules exist concerning the number of units to be included. However, there are general norms and guidelines in this regard. Samples which are applied in consumer research can often be less than 1 per cent of the population, on condition that a probability sample and statistical formulae are used. In the case of industrial research larger samples are used because the number of industrial clients is considerably smaller than in the case of final consumers.

Step 4: Data collection, processing and analysis

The fourth step in the marketing research process (see Figure 5.10) involves the implementation of the research design whereby the data is collected. Data collection is often the most expensive aspect of the research process and the possibility of mistakes is high. The researcher consequently has an important control task to perform. Some of the problems which could arise are: respondents are not at home and substitutes have to be found; some respondents may refuse to co-operate; others may provide dishonest answers; the field worker may make mistakes or be dishonest. The control methods which the researcher applies have to envisage these aspects. Clear instructions and relevant motivational methods have to be used beforehand to ensure that respondents' and field workers' co-operation and honesty are as high as possible.

After the data had been collected, processing has to take place. The collected data has to be edited and codified to facilitate processing and analysis. With large surveys that require computer processing the questionnaires are coded beforehand for fast data input into the computer. At the designing of the questionnaire consideration should already be given to this.

Data processing is followed by analysis of the output. Various data analysis methods exist, which range from very simple (averages, measures of dispersion of data) to highly sophisticated (multivariable techniques, such as cluster analysis). The task of the researcher is to study the processed data and to transform it into relevant information for decision makers. The planning of data analysis methods starts already in the research design stage when the data requirements are considered.

A variety of computer programs to aid data processing and analysis exist, such as SPSS (Statistical Package for the Social Sciences), Statgraphics, SYSTAT and STATFORM. The assistance of speciality firms is often used for this purpose, even by large enterprises.

Step 5: Communicate information to the marketing decision maker

The final step in the marketing research process involves the interpretation of information for decision making purposes, and communication thereof to the relevant decision maker or instructor, usually in the form of a report. It is important that the decision making context is thoroughly grasped and that the communication takes place in an appropriate manner. This is because communication problems between researchers and line managers often arise because of their different backgrounds and work environments.

In the evaluation of the quality of a research report criteria such as understandability, relevancy, clarity, conciseness, organisation, timeousness, accuracy and comprehensiveness are applied.[7] Besides a written report an oral presentation is often made, which has to be planned and delivered according to the perception and requirement levels of the decision makers.

In the research report the problem situation is defined, and the information from secondary and primary sources analysed and interpreted. Conclusions and recommendations are made. It is not the researcher's task to make decisions or to implement them — that is the task of marketing management. The linguistic abilities of the researcher are of great importance in the writing of a good research report.

5.5 SUMMARY

In this chapter the strategic nature and importance of marketing information and marketing research has been outlined. The necessity of marketing information and information management, the types of marketing information systems and the components, and the steps in marketing research were stressed. In Chapter 6 the nature and methods of market measurement and market forecasting are discussed.

REFERENCES

1. Peter, JP and Donnelly, JH (eds). 1986. *Marketing Management: Knowledge and Skills*. Plano, Texas: Business Publications Inc, p 38.
2. Kurtz, DL and Boone, LE. 1984. *Marketing*. New York: The Dryden Press, p 154.
3. Kotler, P. 1988. *Marketing Management: Analysis, Planning, Implementation and Control*. Englewood Cliffs, NJ: Prentice-Hall, p 103.
4. Barry, TE. 1986. *Marketing: An Integrated Approach*. New York: The Dryden Press, p 198.
5. American Marketing Association. 1987. 'New Marketing Research Definition Approved'. *Marketing News*, vol 21, no 1, pp 1, 14.
6. Particulars concerning these six steps and the marketing research methodology are given in Nel, PA, Rädel, FE and Loubser, M. 1988. *Researching the South African Market*. Pretoria: University of South Africa, pp 88–101.
7. Ibid pp 410–57. Particulars concerning the writing and presentaton of the research report appear in this section.

ASSIGNMENTS

1. You are instructed to investigate the market situation (demand and supply) of your university/college restaurant, especially to determine the applicability of the market offering and the demand satisfaction among students. Discuss in detail the considerations you would give to each step in the marketing research process. Use practical indications as far as possible.

2. The Durban Town Council, after noticing a distinct change in the flow of tourists to Durban, instructed the Publicity Association to research the reasons for this change. Tourists visiting Durban increasingly came from the lower socio-economic groups, especially in developing societies. You must conduct this research project. Discuss how you would do it.

CHAPTER 6

MARKET MEASUREMENT AND MARKET FORECASTING

6.1 INTRODUCTION

In Chapter 5 it was emphasised that marketing information and marketing research are important to keep abreast of marketing opportunities, and to provide information for the solution of marketing problems. When an enterprise observes a new market trend, based on the information obtained, which holds potential marketing opportunities or threats, it is essential that the current size and future potential of the new market demand should be thoroughly determined.

The purpose of this chapter is to provide an overview of the principles and methods for the measurement and forecasting of market demand. Knowledge of market sizes and probable growth patterns provides the basis for the selection of attractive markets in which the enterprise would like to do business, gives an indication of possible new markets, and indicates pointers for relevant marketing strategies to achieve success in those markets.

Market measurement and market forecasting are management aids whereby the markets which are investigated are expressed in quantitatively measurable entities. These aids should be used in conjunction with instruments for qualitative market analysis (such as market behavioural characteristics). Market measurement focuses on the current market situation, while market forecasting pertains to the future market situation.

ORGANISATION OF THE CHAPTER

The nature of market measurement: Market levels, relevant markets, examples of application of market measurement information.

Methods of market measurement: Methods for the measurement of total market demand, measurement of market demand according to delineated

---

geographical areas, methods for the determination of actual industry sales and market shares of suppliers of products and services.

Market forecasting: Nature and role of market forecasting, methods based on historical information, methods based on current information.

Market measurement and forecasting in marketing strategy: The place and role of market measurement and forecasting in the marketing strategy.

6.2 THE NATURE OF MARKET MEASUREMENT

6.2.1 Market levels

The size of a market can be measured on different levels, and it is consequently important clearly to state beforehand what type of market is involved. The measurement of the market for Pepsi-Cola can take place on various consumer levels, product levels, spatial levels and time levels, as illustrated in Figure 6.1. Each of these levels represents a measurable market.

FIGURE 6.1   Possible levels of market measurement for Pepsi-Cola

CONSUMER LEVELS	PRODUCT LEVELS	SPATIAL LEVELS	TIME LEVELS
• Schools • Defence force • Fitness-orientated people • Sports meetings	• All sales of soft drinks in the RSA • Sales of Cola soft drinks in the RSA • Sales by the Pepsi-Cola Co • Sales of Pepsi-Cola in tins • Sales of Diet Pepsi-Cola	• Cape metropolitan area • Natal province • RSA • Southern Africa	• Monthly • Seasonally • Annually

From Figure 6.1 it is clear that many possible combinations of market measurement exist. The Pepsi-Cola Company would, for example, like to determine at a given point in time what the market demand for Diet Pepsi is in the Cape metropolitan area among fitness-orientated women in the summer. This information is required for, among others, the determination of competitive position and decisions concerning the marketing strategy.

From the foregoing it is evident that the *market* concept is seen here from a **demand** point of view. It is important to distinguish this concept from the concept of a market as a **physical place** where products are traded, and from the **supply** point of view which concerns the suppliers of products in the market. In this chapter the market concept refers in the first instance to **the total number of actual and potential buyers of a product**. Compare also the meaning of the market concept in this chapter with the definition given in Chapter 3.

6.2.2 Relevant markets

The types of markets which can be measured are not all relevant for a specific enterprise. It naturally depends upon whether an enterprise is actively involved or interested in particular markets or not. Consequently it is necessary to distinguish, besides the market level, the total market, available market, target market, and penetrated market.

- **Total market** (also termed *market potential*) pertains to all actual and potential buyers of a product type, if it is generally available and offered for purchase, and consumers have the ability to buy.
- **Available market** refers only to those actual and potential buyers of a product who have the interest, income and ability to buy the product at a particular point in time.
- **Target market** is that part of the available market at which the company has chosen to direct its marketing activities.
- **Penetrated market** refers to the number of consumers who have already bought the product.

For Pepsi-Cola the total market may, for example, be the Republic of South Africa, but the available market may include only the metropolitan areas where consumers are able to buy the product because of its availability and their income. The target market may include only those parts of the metropolitan population that fall into particular age groups and life style categories. The penetrated market is furthermore only that section of the target market who has already bought the product. Figure 6.2 illustrates the relationship and difference between these concepts.

6.2.3 The application of market measurement information

Market measurement is an essential aid to marketing planning, because it indicates the **sales performance** of the company in relation to various market norms. The total market demand can also be described as the **market potential** of a particular product type, if it is generally available and offered for purchase. The enterprise can now decide if it wants to increase the available market based upon the size of the market potential and profitability estimates. Another possibility is to maintain the available market, but to increase the target market.

If current sales are unsatisfactory, the enterprise could plan a variety of marketing actions without necessarily changing its target market or available market. Attempts could be made to gain greater market penetration by way of actions such as price reductions, improved distribution and/or more effective marketing communications.

FIGURE 6.2   Subsections of a relevant market for an enterprise

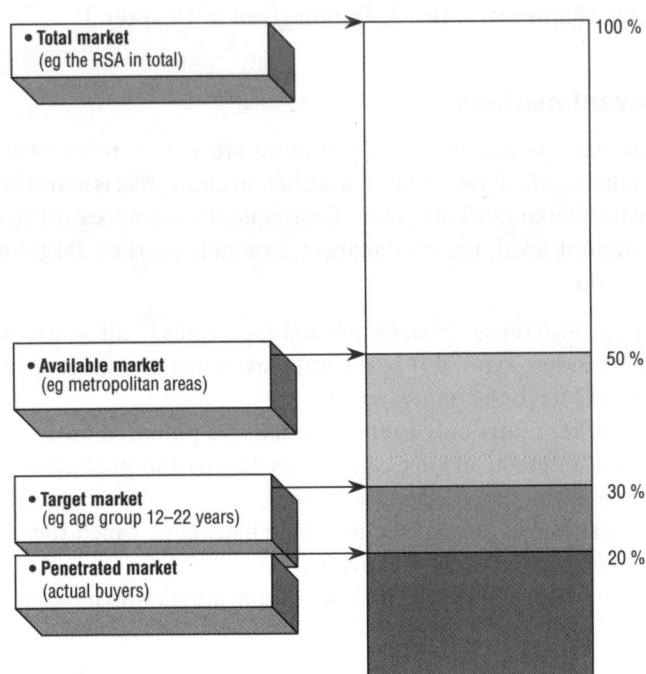

Market measurement information is also used in the determination of the enterprise's competitive position. This information is important for the regular evaluation of the efficiency of marketing efforts. In the evaluation process the calculation of **sales potential** and **market share** is relevant.

- *Sales potential refers to a quantitative indication of what the enterprise's probable sales in a total market, available market, and/or target market should be, taking into account various possible marketing efforts.* Where market potential indicates the size of the demand for a product type (offered by various enterprises), sales potential indicates the size of the demand for a particular enterprise's product or brand.
- *The measurement of market share indicates the relationship of an enterprise's sales to the sales of all comparable enterprises in the industry* (the particular enterprise included). A market share of 20 per cent of a market with sales of R5 million means that a company achieved R1 million sales, in relation to R4 million of the rest of the enterprises in the industry.

Various practical methods for the measurement of market sizes exist. They can be grouped according to purpose, namely:

- methods for the measurement of total market demand;

- methods for the measurement of market potential according to delineated geographical areas (area market potential); and
- methods for the determination of actual industry sales and market shares of suppliers of products and services.

These methods are discussed next.

6.3 METHODS FOR MARKET MEASUREMENT

6.3.1 Methods for the measurement of total market demand

The total market has already been broadly defined as all actual and potential buyers of a product type, if it is generally available and offered for purchase, and the particular consumers have the ability and willingness to buy. For the purposes of market measurement it is necessary to link this definition to a specific geographical area (for example, the Republic of South Africa), a specific time period (for example, 1990), and a specific marketing environment. The reason for this more extensive definition is to apply the market measurement methods correctly, ie without confusion about the dimensions of the market.

Two well-known methods are available, namely the basic method and the chain ratio method (which is a variation of the basic method).

The basic market measurement method

This method is the most simple one with which to measure total market demand (market potential). It is calculated by use of the following formula:

$$Q = n \times q \times p$$

where Q = total market demand

n = number of buyers in the market

q = average quantity purchased by a buyer per time period (for example, per year)

p = average price of the product per time period

Suppose 75 000 consumers annually buy music cassettes, that these consumers buy on average five cassettes per year, and that the average price is R20 per cassette. The total market potential for music cassettes is then estimated as follows:

$$Q_i = n \times q \times p$$
$$= 75\ 000 \times 5 \times R20$$
$$= R7,5 \text{ million per year}$$

Where the market potential is required only in units and not in rand value, the market potential would be 375 000 units per year.

The question which arises is how the various values in the formula are arrived at. The determination of average price is usually easy, but the determination of the number of buyers (n) and the frequency of purchasing (q) are more difficult. The number of buyers can be calculated by starting with the total population and systematically removing those who, according to reliable sources (such as the Bureau for Market Research):

- are not willing to buy;
- do not dispose of the purchasing power to buy;
- do not have the status (authority) to buy; and
- do not have the ability to buy.

Another method of determining the number of buyers and frequency of purchasing is by scientific surveys of the population, whereby sampling and statistical norms (see Chapter 5) are applied. Such surveys are undertaken by market research firms, such as Market & Opinion Surveys and Markinor.

The chain ratio method

A variation of the basic method is the chain ratio method, which entails the application of a series of successive calculations to a base quantity. The base quantity is often the total population, and to this figure a series of adjusting percentage calculations is applied.

For example: Suppose a wine producer wants to determine the market potential for a new low-alcohol wine. An estimate can be made according to the following formula:

Demand for the new wine = Population × personal disposable income per capita × average percentage of disposable income which is spent on food, beverages and tobacco × average percentage of the amount for food, beverages and tobacco which is spent only on beverages × average percentage of amount for beverages which is spent only on alcoholic beverages × average percentage of the amount for alcoholic beverages which is spent only on wine × expected percentage of the amount for wine which is spent only on low-alcohol wine.

These percentages can be obtained from reliable published sources (Reserve Bank reports, surveys of expenditure patterns by institutions such as the Bureau for Market Research, and industry publications) or by scientific surveys of the population. The final percentage applied concerns the expected percentage of consumers who will buy the new product, and is the most important but also the most difficult figure to calculate. It is essential that in the calculation of this figure the validity and reliability of the figure are carefully controlled. Figure 6.3 provides a practical example for a retail shoe store.

FIGURE 6.3   Determination of the market potential of a retail shoe store

---

STEP 1: Determine the **trading (catchment) area** of the store (logical area of servicing), for example, all residential areas located within a 15-minute drive from the store.

STEP 2: Determine the **total number of households** in the trading area: say 12 000.

STEP 3: Determine the **target market households** (for example, the percentage of households with average income of R40 000 per annum): say 4 000.

STEP 4: Determine the **average expenditure** on shoes by these households: say 1,0 % of income.

STEP 5: **Multiply** target market households (4 000) by average income (R40 000) by percentage expenditure on shoes (1,0 %) = market potential for the store = R1,6 million per annum.

STEP 6: **Control** with other knowledgeable parties for validity.

Important sources of information for the enterprise

STEP 1: Municipality/city council; city and town planning companies.

STEP 2: Municipality/city council; Retail Data Library (RDL).

STEP 3: Bureau for Market Research, Unisa; Central Statistical Services.

STEP 4: Bureau for Market Research, Unisa; Retail Data Library (RDL).

STEP 5: Own calculations.

STEP 6: Chambers of commerce; Afrikaanse Sakekamer; shoe retailers association; consulting firms (eg Doug Parker and Associates).

6.3.2 Methods for the measurement of market potential according to geographical area (area market potential)

Enterprises are often confronted with the problem of selecting the best areas and to allocate their marketing budget optimally according to these areas. Consequently it is necessary to determine the market potential of different geographical areas. Two methods are available in this regard, namely the **market build-up method** and the **market index method**.

6.3.2.1 *The market build-up method*

The market build-up method is mainly used by enterprises manufacturing industrial products. It involves the determination of all potential buyers in the target market and the quantities which each will buy. The multiplication of the two figures produces the market potential for the particular product in the target market. This method is relatively simple and easy to calculate if the potential buyers and the potential quantity that each will buy are known. In practice one or both of these entities are not generally available, and the following procedure for its determination should be applied:

Procedure for the determination of the number of potential buyers and buying quantities

- Use the Standard Industrial Classification of All Economic Activities (SIC)[1] of the Central Statistical Services to determine the possible relevant industries in which buyers may be present.
- Determine the relevant industries by:
  — ascertaining the industries from which buyers came in the past;
  — sending questionnaires to companies in those industries;
  — consulting with industry spokesmen and industrial associations.
- Determine the number of companies in each relevant industry by consulting the Industrial Index of the Bureau for Market Research and the Manufacturing Census of the Central Statistical Services. Industry associations and chambers of industry can also provide valuable information, although their membership lists do not include all enterprises in particular industries (membership is not compulsory).
- Calculate the potential (average) quantities that each company would buy per annum. This calculation can be based upon production volume, sales turnover or any measure which provides a reliable indication of usage rate. The figure can be controlled by sending questionnaires to all enterprises in each relevant industry.
- Multiply the number of enterprises identified as potential buyers by the average quantities which each potentially would buy per annum.

Figure 6.4 illustrates the use of the market build-up method for the marketer of a new gold ore grading instrument for the South African gold-mining industry.

6.3.2.2 *The market index method*

The market index method is especially applied by enterprises manufacturing consumer products in order to determine the market potential of a specific area or sub-area. The index which is calculated is a figure that indicates the proportion that a submarket forms of a total market. It is usually indicated as a percentage of the total market and is therefore an indication of relative (to other areas) market potential.

The market index of a particular area is calculated by combining (or adding) the various area indicators, such as the area's population, disposable income and retail sales. These indicators are expressed in terms of their particular shares of the total market. A typical formula for the calculation of the market potential for an area is:

$$Q_i = 0{,}2Y_i + 0{,}5r_i + 0{,}3p_i$$

where Q_i = market potential area *i* relative to the total market
               Y_i = percentage of national population in area *i*
               r_i = percentage of national disposable income in area *i*
               p_i = percentage of national retail sales in area *i*

The various coefficients (0,2, 0,5 and 0,3) represent the relative weights (and thus importance) allocated to the three indicators.

An example of the application of the market index method is given in Figure 6.5.

FIGURE 6.4   Determination of the market potential for a gold ore grading instrument

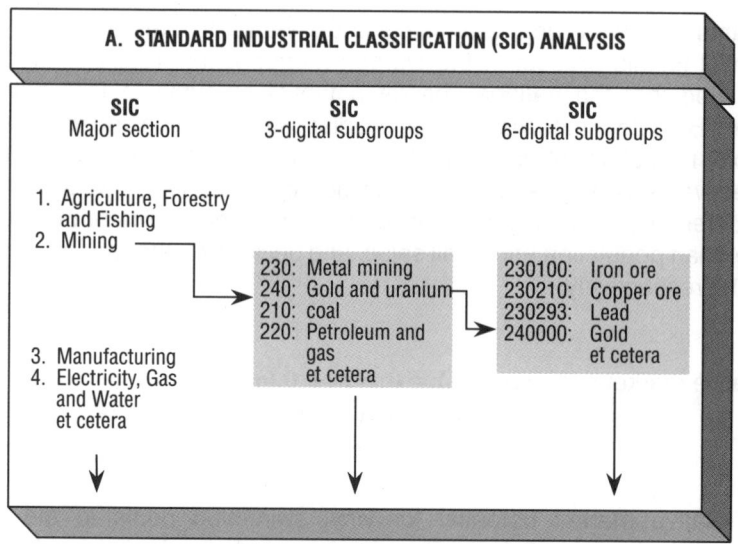

A. STANDARD INDUSTRIAL CLASSIFICATION (SIC) ANALYSIS

SIC Major section	SIC 3-digital subgroups	SIC 6-digital subgroups
1. Agriculture, Forestry and Fishing 2. Mining	230: Metal mining 240: Gold and uranium 210: coal 220: Petroleum and gas et cetera	230100: Iron ore 230210: Copper ore 230293: Lead 240000: Gold et cetera
3. Manufacturing 4. Electricity, Gas and Water et cetera		

B. MARKET POTENTIAL CALCULATION

Relevant SIC group	No of gold mines	Ave number of grading teams per gold mine	Potential number of instruments per team per year	Market potential in units per year
	(1)	(2)	(3)	(1 x 2 x 3)
240000 (lode gold)	45	10	12	5 400
240000 (alluvial gold)	5	1	10	50
			Total	5 450

FIGURE 6.5   Market index method for the calculation of the market potential for vinyl swimming pools in the Durban metropolitan area

A manufacturer of vinyl swimming pools wants to determine the market potential for his product in the Durban metropolitan area. He has already calculated that the national market potential amounts to R75 million per annum. He determines that population, disposable income and retail sales are reliable indicators of the area's purchasing power, and calculates the respective percentages of the national figures as 15 %, 21 % and 24 %. He also determines that disposable income is a stronger indicator of purchasing power than population and retail sales, and decides on the weights of 0,6, 0,2 and 0,2 respectively.

Relative market potential $(Q_i) = 0,2 \ Y_i + 0,6r_i + 0,2 \ p_i$
$$\therefore \quad Q_i = 0,2(15) + 0,6(21) + 0,2(24)$$
$$= 20,4$$

The relative market potential for vinyl swimming pools in the Durban metropolitan area is 20,4 %. The absolute market potential for the area is R75 million x 20,4 %, namely R15,3 million.

Important sources of information for the manufacturer:
1. Central Statistical Services.
2. Bureau for Market Research, Unisa.
3. Reserve Bank reports.
4. Durban Corporation (City Council).
5. Chamber of Commerce and Afrikaanse Handelsinstituut.

6.3.3 Methods for the determination of actual industry sales and market shares of suppliers of products and services

Besides the determination of total market demand and area market demand, an enterprise also wishes to determine what the total sales are of its product type (by all companies offering it) in the target market. Market share can then be determined by relating own actual sales to actual industry sales. The major sources of information concerning industry sales are:

- Industry associations, who often collect and publish industry sales figures.
- Bureau for Financial Analysis (BFA), University of Pretoria, who publishes industry-comparative figures of selected industries.
- Marketing research companies such as IBIS, who conduct extensive audits of total sales and brand sales of certain products (in retail stores).
- Ad hoc marketing research projects, either by own personnel or by private consulting companies.

6.4 MARKET FORECASTING   *Look at future.*

6.4.1 Nature and role of market forecasting

Whereas market measurement concerns itself with the determination of the size of the current market, market forecasting has to do with the determination of the size of the future market. Because the future is uncertain, forecasting concerns itself with the application of methods of predicting future market demand. In most markets the demand for and supply of products and services are unstable, which consequently makes good market forecasting a key success factor in the planning and implementation of marketing strategy.

Market forecasting forms the basis of a company's sales forecast, which in turn forms the basis of the company's production, financial and other forecasts (as reflected in the various budgets). Market forecasting does not usually form a separate activity, but is part of the company's overall forecasting activities, as indicated in Figure 6.6.

FIGURE 6.6   Position and role of market forecasting

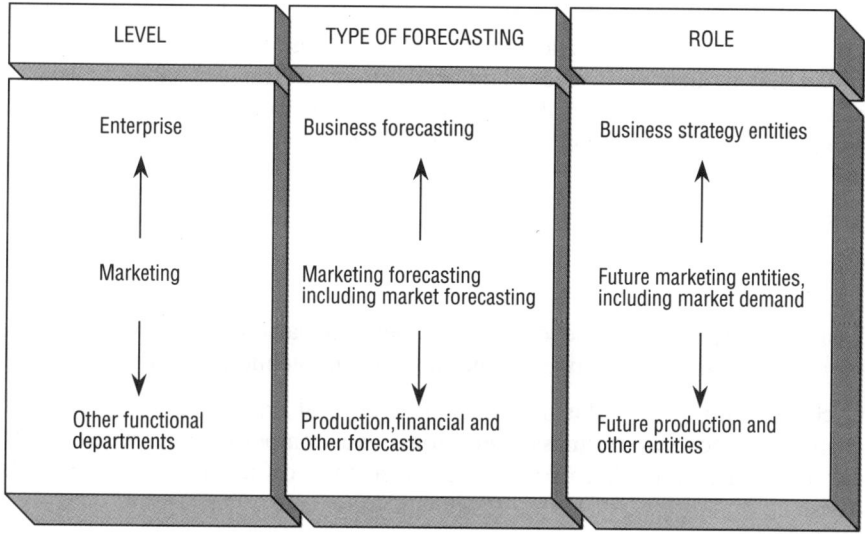

LEVEL	TYPE OF FORECASTING	ROLE
Enterprise	Business forecasting	Business strategy entities
↑	↑	↑
Marketing	Marketing forecasting including market forecasting	Future marketing entities, including market demand
↓	↓	↓
Other functional departments	Production, financial and other forecasts	Future production and other entities

Business forecasting includes environmental forecasting of factors such as the economy, technology, socio-cultural conditions, competition and legislation. On the marketing level market entities, such as especially market demand, are forecasted, while the other functional departments of the company rely to a large extent on the forecasted market demand as the basis for their own forecasts and budgets. Market forecasting should be clearly distinguished from the wider activity of marketing forecasting, in the same way as which market research should be distinguished from the wider activity of marketing research. **Market forecasting concerns itself only with demand**, while marketing forecasting involves entities such as products, prices, distribution and marketing communication. Various methods and techniques for the conduct of market forecasting exist, which can be grouped in two categories: methods and techniques based upon historical information, and methods and techniques based upon current information. The starting point of any market forecasting is usually historical information, ie sales of the past or derived sales figures of products with similar demand patterns, on which future projections are done. It is important to realise that history can indicate valuable trends, but that current information should additionally be used because history seldom repeats itself exactly.

6.4.2 Market forecasting methods based upon historical information

Two generally used methods are time series analysis and statistical demand analysis.

Time series analysis

Time series analysis is based upon the assumption that careful analysis of historical information could reveal certain causal relationships. It may, for example, be revealed that an increase in sales of umbrellas may be largely ascribed to weather conditions (heavy rain), but also to a lesser extent to an improvement in the general business climate. Such a relationship can then be used to forecast future sales.

A time series of a product's historical sales (Y) can be divided into four major components:

- Long-term trend (L) — the long-term underlying pattern of the change in sales based upon the basic changes in the population, technology and legislation.

- Cyclical trend (C) — the medium-term, cyclical pattern of sales owing to changes in general business conditions and competitive activities. Cyclical trends are difficult to forecast because they do not occur on a regular basis.

- Seasonal trend (S) — the regular, short-term (over a period of one year) sales pattern which can be ascribed to factors such as the weather, holidays or trade practices. A seasonal trend indicates a repetitive hourly, weekly, monthly, quarterly, or other time period (within a year) sales pattern.

- Coincidental trend (T) — the unpredictable coincidental happenings such as strikes, fires, wars, storms and droughts. The effect of this coincidental component of Y should be ignored in order to distinguish the normal (regular) sales trend.

The application of time series analysis involves the division (or decomposition) of historical sales (Y) into the components L, C, S and T. Thereafter the components are put together again in order to make the sales forecast.[2]

Example of the application of the time series analysis method

An insurance company sold 12 000 new ordinary life insurance policies in 1989. The company wants to forecast the sales in December 1990. The long-term trend (L) indicates an annual growth rate of 5 % in sales. This on its own points to sales for the year 1990 of 12 600 (12 000 × 1,05).

However, an economic recession (C) is expected in 1990, which would probably lead to a sales volume of only 90 % of the normally expected quantity. The sales of 1990 are therefore forecast as 11 340 (12 600 × 0,90). If the monthly sales should be the same for each month, a sales turnover of 945 (11 340 ÷ 12) per month could be achieved.

December is usually an above-average month for the sales of insurance policies, with a seasonal index of 1,30. The December 1990 sales could therefore be as high as 1 228,5 (945 × 1,30). No coincidental occurrences, such as strikes or terrorist attacks, are expected. The best forecast of policy sales for December 1990 is therefore 1 228,5.

Source: Adapted from Kotler, P. 1986. *Principles of Marketing*. Englewood Cliffs, NJ: Prentice-Hall, pp 256–7.

Statistical demand analysis method

Various factors influence the actual sales of a product, such as prices, income and marketing communication efforts. Whereas time series analysis considers the current and future demand as a function of time, the purpose of statistical demand analysis is to analyse the factors which influence actual sales, as well as their relative strengths.

Statistical demand analysis depicts sales (Q) as a dependent variable, and then attempts to explain sales as a function of a number of independent variables

$$X_1, X_2, \ldots, X_n;$$

$$Q = f(X_1, X_2, \ldots, X_n).$$

Various statistical methods, such as regression analysis, can be applied to measure the effect of an independent variable (such as advertising) on a dependent variable (sales).

Example of the application of the statistical demand analysis method

Pepsi-Cola uses the following formula for sales forecasting:

$$Q = +150 + 7X_1 - 3X_2$$

where X_1 = average annual temperature

X_2 = per capita income (R000).

The R-sales per capita in the Cape metropolitan area can be forecast as follows:

If the average annual temperature is 22 °C and the per capita income R2 000 in the Cape metropolitan area, then the forecast of sales is:

$$Q = +150 + 7(22) - 3(2)$$

$$= R298 \text{ per capita.}$$

Note: Per capita income refers to the income per head per 1 000 of the population. When per capita income increases, the factor of 150 would be more than proportionately adjusted.

Source: Adapted from Kotler, P. 1986. *Principles of Marketing*. Englewood Cliffs, NJ: Prentice-Hall, p 257.

6.4.3 Methods based on current information

Three methods based on current information are used, namely:

- Surveys of buyers' intentions.
- Opinions of sales personnel.
- Opinions of experts.

Surveys of buyers' intentions

Surveys of buyers' intentions are valuable when the buyers of specific product types, such as passenger cars, can formulate clear intentions, can realise their intentions and can describe them to interviewers. This method of market forecasting therefore concerns the determination of what buyers probably would do under a given set of conditions and circumstances.

Several research institutions, such as the Bureau for Economic Research at the University of Stellenbosch, conduct regular surveys of consumers' buying intentions. More specific surveys concerning particular product types and buyers are conducted by private marketing research companies, such as Market & Opinion Surveys (Pty) Ltd.

Several techniques for the surveying of buyers' intentions exist, such as buying probability scales, consumer confidence indices and measurements of buying sentiment. An example of a buying probability scale for passenger cars is as follows:[3]

Do you intend buying a car in the next six months?					
0,00	0,20	0,40	0,60	0,80	1,00
No possibility at all	Small possibility	Fair possibility	Good possibility	High probability	Absolutely certain

Surveys of buyers' intentions are made especially for durable consumer products and industrial products. It is also useful in the case of new products, where no historical data exist.

Opinions of sales personnel

Knowledgeable sales personnel, with the necessary experience, can be an important source of information concerning future sales, because they are the people who are in closest direct contact with consumers and buyers. Sales forecasts of sales personnel should, however, be carefully controlled, because they are possibly biased owing to their subjective involvement with the enterprise and its products. They could, for example, be over-optimistic or over-pessimistic, depending on the most recent sales performances. They also do not generally have a broader vision concerning the impact of expected economic and other conditions on market demand.

Sales personnel can be motivated to make more efficient estimates by offering them certain aids and incentives. Aids could, for example, include a list of historical forecasts in relation to sales, and a set of assumptions about environmental conditions for the forecast period. Incentives can, for example, be in the form of free holidays or specific monetary bonuses for the most accurate forecasts.

Opinions of experts

Experts include dealers, suppliers, marketing agents, industry spokesmen, industry associations, and research and consulting organisations. A manufacturer of television sets can, for example, conduct a regular survey among its dealers. It must, however, be borne in mind that these experts may be biased in certain instances, and forecasts should therefore always be controlled with other sources of information.

Some enterprises, especially large ones, make use of the services of speciality market research organisations to collect the opinions of experts. These market research organisations apply techniques such as focus group discussions and the Delphi technique to obtain information.[4] The Business and Marketing Intelligence (BMI) group is well known for its surveys of expert opinions, especially in industrial markets in South Africa.

6.5 THE PLACE AND ROLE OF MARKET MEASUREMENT AND MARKET FORECASTING IN THE MARKETING STRATEGY

In Chapter 1 it was clearly stated that marketing activities do not take place in isolation, but are part of a planned whole — the marketing strategy — which is aimed at the achievement of marketing objectives. Figure 1.10 illustrates the various interacting steps in marketing management, and a closer analysis thereof clarifies the place and role of market measurement and market forecasting in the determination of the current and future market.

The analysis of the extent of the current market demand, and the forecast of probable future market demand, are essential elements in the identification of marketing opportunities and threats. Furthermore, market measurement and market forecasting form the basis for decisions concerning the four marketing instruments, namely product, pricing, distribution and marketing communication. It is also important to realise that an enterprise's sales potential and sales forecast have meaning only when they are seen in the context of the company's strengths and weaknesses. The company's resources and its distinctive competences have to be borne in mind because promising opportunities in the market cannot be utilised if the company has not the ability to do it. Reliable market measurement information is an absolute prerequisite for the planning and implementation of the integrated marketing strategy and the various market strategies.

Market measurement and market forecasting also form the basis for decisions concerning competitive activities, with the eventual statement of market share goals. It is clear that a company's sales potential and its sales forecasting have meaning only when seen in the context of its particular abilities (strengths, weaknesses, distinctive competences) — especially in terms of its marketing abilities (product, price, communication and distribution abilities), technical abilities (production, technology, craftsmanship), and financial abilities (sources of capital, efficiency of capital employment, cost controls).

Example of market measurement and market forecasting in marketing strategy determination of the Volkswagen Citi-Golf

In 1981 Volkswagen introduced its new-generation Golf (Golf II) to the market. Marketing research indicated, however, that a substantial part of the young adult market, and to a lesser extent also the housewife market, continued to prefer the Golf I and would buy it if available. These markets consider the Golf I as a 'pleasure car' with a definite 'city roundabout' image.

Through market measurement it was determined that the market potential of the older model was large enough to make profitable utilisation of the abovementioned target markets. The market opportunities were determined, as well as the sizes of the target markets, and specific sales objectives were stated for each target market. The product now had to be correctly positioned. It meant that the image of the product had to be anchored in the minds of the target markets relative to competitive products by way of the right product, distribution, pricing and marketing communications decisions. Market forecasting had to indicate, among others, the number of products which had to be available at specific dealers at specific times.

6.6 SUMMARY

In this chapter the basic principles and methods of market measurement and market forecasting are discussed. The methods for the measurement of total market demand, the measurement of market demand according to delineated geographical areas, and methods for the determination of actual industry sales and market shares are analysed. Concerning market forecasting, various methods based on historical as well as current information are discussed. Finally, the place and role of market measurement and market forecasting in the planning and implementation of the marketing strategy are emphasised.

REFERENCES

1. Van Zyl, SJJ, Martins, JH and Steenkamp, HA. 1981. *A Guide to the Standard Industrial Classification of All Economic Activities*. Pretoria: Bureau for Market Research.
2. Kotler, P. 1986. *Principles of Marketing*. Englewood Cliffs, NJ: Prentice-Hall, pp 256–7.
3. Kotler, P. 1988. *Marketing Management: Analysis, Planning, Implementation and Control*. Englewood Cliffs, NJ: Prentice-Hall, p 271.
4. Berkowitz, EN, Kerin, A and Rudelius, W. 1986. *Marketing*. St Louis, Missouri: Times Mirror/Mosby College Publishing, p 213.

ASSIGNMENTS

1. You are considering opening a sports store in your city/town. You know that the population of the city/town is increasing and also that there are two other sports stores trading in the area. It is important for you to determine the current and future potential of the city/town as well as the sales potential of your proposed store.

   (a) Which methods would you use in market measurement?

   (b) Which sources of information would you consult?

   (c) Which other environmental variables would you take into account in your final decision?

2. An international manufacturer of shock absorbers for automobiles needs to investigate the South African market with a view to exports to this country.

   (a) Which technique for total measuring of market demand in the RSA would you apply and why?

   (b) Which procedure would you use in applying this technique?

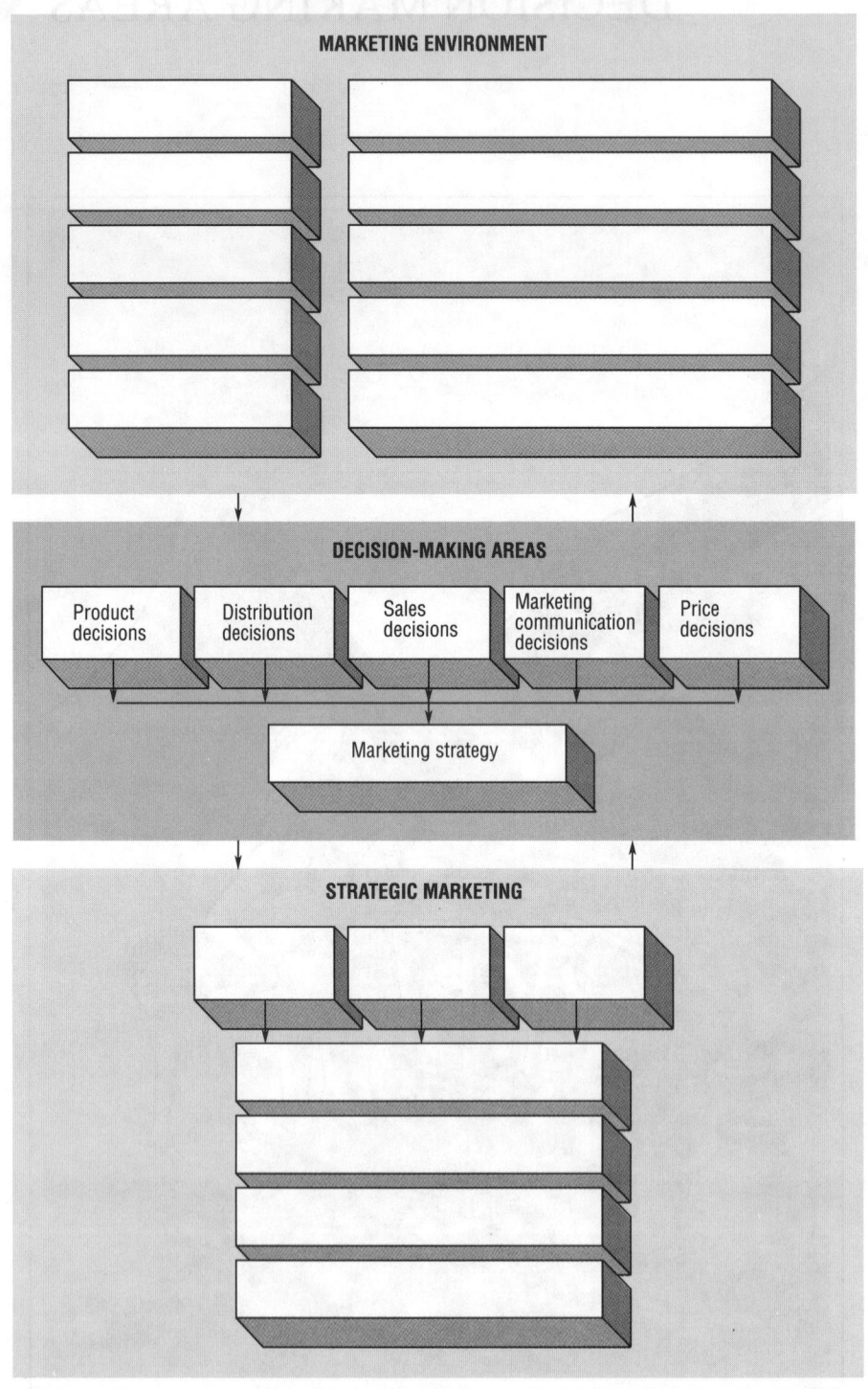

MARKETING MANAGEMENT

MARKETING ENVIRONMENT

DECISION-MAKING AREAS

Product decisions | Distribution decisions | Sales decisions | Marketing communication decisions | Price decisions

Marketing strategy

STRATEGIC MARKETING

CHAPTER 7

THE PRODUCT

7.1 INTRODUCTION

The aim of this chapter is to identify and describe the most important concepts generally used in connection with product decisions and the product mix. In this way the importance, nature, place and role of product decisions within the integrated marketing strategy are better understood.

The following concepts and their related components are discussed, as well as factors influencing decisions regarding the product mix.

ORGANISATION OF THE CHAPTER

The product and product concept: The formal product, the core product and the augmented product.

The product offering: The product mix, product lines and product items.

Some product decisions: Product diversification and product specialisation, simplification and product standardisation, product differentiation, product obsolescence, new products.

The width, depth and consistence of the product mix: The outcome of product decisions.

The ideal product mix: The contribution of product items and product lines to the realisation of business objectives, product portfolio analysis.

The classification of products and services: Industrial goods, commercial services, consumer goods consisting of convenience goods, shopping goods and speciality goods.

The factors influencing product-mix decisions: Business objectives, product leadership inclination, trading-up and trading-down, desire to change the image of the firm, changes in the target market, competitive actions, marketing considerations, production considerations, financial considerations.

7.2 THE PRODUCT AND PRODUCT CONCEPT

From a marketing point of view, a product in the broadest sense can be defined as a collection of need-satisfying utilities (perceptible and/or imperceptible) which is offered to a market (consumers) so that the market can pay attention to it, buy it or consume it. Physical objects, services, personalities, places, institutions and ideas are all products. Some observations on this definition are necessary.

For the marketer something becomes a product as soon as it leads to need-satisfaction in a target market. A product does not consist of a visible object only, but includes invisible qualities also. Thus anything which can be perceived by the human senses — hearing, sight, touch, taste, smell — and which provides need-satisfaction in the process of perception, is a product.

Different meanings, however, can be attached to products so that four basically different product notions or product concepts originate, namely the formal product, the core product, the augmented product, and the product image.

- The **formal product** is merely the physical object or service offered to the target market. Irons, motor cars, educational programmes and film stars, as such, are all formal products and are characterised inter alia by differing quality levels and features, styling, trade marks and packaging.

- The **core product** is the essential benefit or need-satisfaction that the consumer expects to obtain from the product. A housewife does not purchase a washing powder because of its specific chemical composition and other physical attributes — she buys hygiene, and praise from her friends; a handyman does not buy an 8 mm bit, but actually the holes that it can drill; women do not buy lipsticks, they buy beauty. Briefly, *people do not spend their money on goods and services, but on the need-satisfying attributes and value that, in their opinion, are inherent in what they purchase.*

- The **augmented product** consists of all the benefits that consumers receive or experience in perceiving, utilising, obtaining and applying the formal product. This embraces much more than merely the need-satisfying attributes which the product has as a result of the manufacturing process. Those which are added to the manufactured goods by means of packaging, service, advertising, customer advice, financing, delivery service, warehousing and other valued extras **convert the core product into an augmented product**. The augmented product concept presents considerable challenges and opportunities to the marketer. Only a few are mentioned. It requires a comprehensive consideration of the field in which the firm is now operating and will be operating in future (what business are we in?); new, inevitable and often expensive competitive strategies become necessary; consumer needs, going far beyond the core product, have to be analysed; and eventually it can offer unique opportunities to the firm which develops and markets the right augmented product concept.

- The **product image** encompasses all the above and refers to how the product is perceived by consumers. In the rest of this chapter the term 'product concept' is used to refer to the total product unless it is explicitly stated otherwise.

7.3 THE PRODUCT OFFERING

The product offering of a firm may consist of only one product item, a number of related product items (product lines) or a wide variety of widely divergent product items (product mix).

- *The **product mix** of a manufacturing firm is the total range of various kinds of products which it makes and markets.* In the distributive trade there is naturally no production as such, and the product mix here consists of the variety of products that are bought for resale.

- *A **product line** is a group of products within the product mix with one or more of the following relationships:* they satisfy similar needs (<u>toothpaste, deodorants, shampoos, toilet soap</u>); they can be used together (shirts, ties, socks, shoes, trousers, jackets); the products are bought by the same consumer group (toys for children); the products are marketed through similar channels (motor cars); the products fall within the same price class (all products with a selling price of, say, between R10 and R15).

[margin handwriting: Toiletries clothing etc]

- *A **product item** is a particular version of a product within the product mix of the firm, with a name peculiar to it.* For example, the Ford 6610 tractor is a <u>product item</u>, Ford tractors are a product line, and <u>all Ford products, such as tractors, motor cars, lorries and road construction equipment, are its product mix.</u>

It is important to note that the product decisions of a firm always relate to its product items, product lines and the product mix.

The product portfolio consists of a combination of product items, product lines or strategic business units (SBUs). This aspect is discussed more fully in Chapter 19.

7.4 SOME PRODUCT DECISIONS

Product decisions can be described as ==intentional== and ==purposeful== management decisions regarding the timely, economical and effective adaptation of the product mix to existing conditions and expected changes in the marketing environment. For the purposes of this book, product decisions, product strategies and product-mix decisions are regarded as synonymous.

[handwriting: Expansion of Product mix — Reduction (narrowing field)]

7.4.1 Product diversification and product specialisation

Product diversification and product specialisation are concepts normally used in connection with the product mix of an enterprise.

- For the going concern, **product diversification denotes the expansion of the product mix** *by adding new product items or product lines to the existing mix.*
- **Product specialisation** is the opposite of product diversification and for the going concern it **denotes the elimination of product items or product lines** *from the product mix in order to diminish or narrow the mix.*

Decisions regarding product diversification and product specialisation naturally are taken initially when the enterprise gets going. A firm entering the manufacturing and marketing of television sets has to decide whether it will deal only in colour sets (specialisation), or whether it will produce colour sets, monochrome sets, portable sets and video cassette recorders (diversification).

7.4.2 Simplification and product standardisation

Whereas the terms 'product diversification' and 'product specialisation' are used in connection with the **product mix** of the firm, the concepts of simplification and standardisation refer to **product items and product lines**.

- When a firm **simplifies**, *it purposefully limits* *the range of dimensions, shapes, qualities and other attributes which are possible in one product; in other words, only certain types of a product are manufactured.* For example, a manufacturer makes fridges in only four sizes instead of seven; a shoe factory makes men's shoes in six sizes, three colours and three styles only, instead of ten sizes, six colours and five styles; and motor cars are supplied in certain colours only.

- **Standardisation** *refers to the setting or acceptance by a group of firms or authorities, of* **specific dimensions, norms or standards** *whereby goods will be made or evaluated.*

Standardisation differs inter alia in the following ways from simplification: simplification refers to the product items and product lines of the individual firm, while standardisation involves the products of a specific industry and often occurs in co-operation with the authorities, experts and consumers. By simplification the individual manufacturer himself decides on the characteristics of the product. Standardisation actually is simplification across an industry, and requires co-operation between the various manufacturers regarding the product they are going to make; therefore the product characteristics for the individual producer are largely prescribed. This phenomenon can lead to limiting the competitive advantages of the individual firm, since product differentiation now becomes more difficult.

7.4.3 Product differentiation

Product differentiation is the endeavour of a firm to distinguish its product(s) physically and/or psychologically from other basically identical competitive products by way of shape, colour, dimensions, quality, packaging, brand name, image, status and other need-satisfying attributes, so that the consumer considers it to be a product(s) totally different from those of competitors.

Thus, product differentiation relates the product of a firm to that of similar competitive products in terms of the real and psychological differences. It enables a firm to move away from price competition, and uses non-price competitive strategies, such as advertising and product differences, to influence the marketing result. Product differentiation is normally implemented by firms which market reasonably homogeneous or similar products, such as toilet soap, toothpaste, cigarettes, liquor and petrol, to a broad undifferentiated (horizontal) market with fairly uniform needs for the specific product. Product differentiation is a distinctive version of product decisions in monopolistic competition.

7.4.4 Product obsolescence

In general *three* types of obsolescence can be identified.

- First, **physical obsolescence** occurs because the product wears out and becomes physically unfit for further use because of repeated use and exposure.

- Secondly, **psychological obsolescence** can arise from the development of a new competitive product which provides greater real or perceived need-satisfaction to the consumer, although the old product may physically still be effective. *(new painkiller (works faster))*

- Thirdly, **planned obsolescence** can result from a specific production and marketing strategy. New products are purposefully developed with a specific physical life span (planned technical obsolescence), while attempts are also made to replace the older product, which physically may still be effective, with a new product having minor technical modifications only (planned psychological obsolescence). This new product is usually supported by a powerful marketing communication strategy. Planned obsolescence occurs especially in the case of motor cars, durable household equipment and clothing, where new styles and fashions are often introduced annually. Considerable criticism can be levelled against planned obsolescence, especially because products which are physically still effective are thrown away, destroyed or fall into disuse.[1] Planned obsolescence, however, should not be confused with the development of new products which are necessary for the growth of the firm. *(New model car at in Japs)*

7.4.5 New products   *4 Types.*

For the purposes of marketing management **new products** *denote those products or product attributes which are new to the firm and in one or more respects are regarded by the target market as being significantly different from existing competitive products.* Four types of new products exist: products which are original and unique in every respect (the first motor car, radio, telephone and television); important alterations of existing products so that they differ significantly from the current product (instant coffee has replaced ground coffee and coffee-beans in many market segments); products which are new to the firm but not quite new to the market (a firm entering the toothpaste market with a product similar to those of competitors); and products which are new to the target market but not new to the firm. All four types of new product decisions are very important to the survival, profitability and growth of the firm. *(Siemens Cellphone phone.)*

7.5 THE WIDTH, DEPTH AND CONSISTENCY OF THE PRODUCT MIX

In section 7.3 the product mix was defined as the total range of product types which a manufacturer produces and markets. The product mix of a firm has width, depth and consistency, which are determined by numerous product decisions such as product diversification, product specialisation, simplification, standardisation, product differentiation and the procurement and/or development of new products.

- The **width** of the product mix refers to the number of product lines found within the mix. For example, the product mix of Stellenbosch Wine Trust Ltd consists of four product lines, namely natural wines, fortified wines, sparkling wines, and spirits and liqueurs.

    [handwritten: How many Product Lines]

- The **depth** of the product mix refers to the average number of product items which are available within each product line. For example, Stellenbosch Wine Trust Ltd's natural wines consist of, inter alia, Nederburg, Zonnenbloem, Taskelder, Oude Libertas, Autumn Harvest, Kellerprinz, Zonnheimer, Lieberstein and Virginia, and the sparkling wines include Grand Mousseux, Nederburg and 5th Avenue Cold Duck. The average depth of these and other product lines can be calculated to arrive at the average depth of the product mix of the firm concerned.

    [handwritten: Depth How many Products in one line]

- The **consistency** of the product mix refers to the relationship which exists between the different product lines in the mix regarding end use, production requirements, distribution channels or any other basis. Thus, with end use as a basis, a very close relationship and consistency exists between the different product lines in the product mix of Stellenbosch Wine Trust.

    [handwritten: Same price,]

Changes in the depth, width and consistency of the product mix normally influence the marketing result of a firm directly as follows:

- By increasing the **width** of the product mix (diversifying) the firm endeavours to benefit from its good reputation and skills in existing markets.
- By increasing the **depth** of the mix (specialising) the firm tries to attract the patronage of consumers with widely differing tastes and needs.
- By increasing the **consistency** of its product lines the firm tries to acquire an unparalleled reputation in a particular field of endeavour, for example wine production.

The relationship between the concepts of width, depth and consistency, and product items, product lines and the product mix, is illustrated in Figure 7.1. The product mix in the figure consists of *five* different product lines and an average depth of *three* product items per product line.

Figure 7.1 clearly brings to the fore *three* major facets of the product-mix decisions of a firm.

- *First*, decisions have to be taken on the number of items per product line, which entails questions concerning the addition, elimination and modification of product items.

FIGURE 7.1   Product mix of a hypothetical enterprise

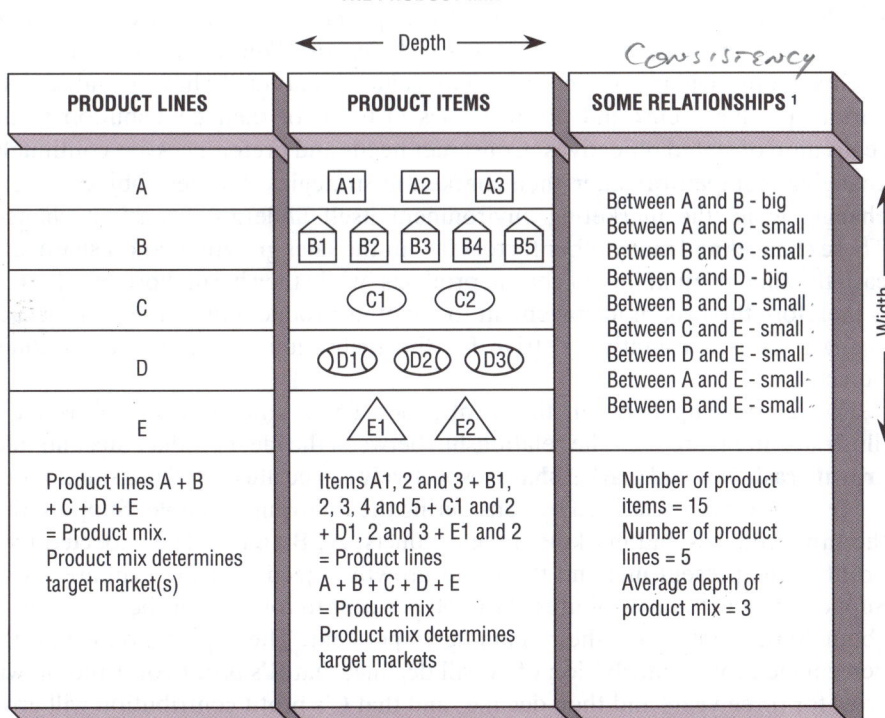

THE PRODUCT MIX

←——— Depth ———→

Consistency

PRODUCT LINES	PRODUCT ITEMS	SOME RELATIONSHIPS [1]
A	A1 A2 A3	Between A and B - big
B	B1 B2 B3 B4 B5	Between A and C - small
		Between B and C - small
C	C1 C2	Between C and D - big
		Between B and D - small
D	D1 D2 D3	Between C and E - small
		Between D and E - small
E	E1 E2	Between A and E - small
		Between B and E - small
Product lines A + B + C + D + E = Product mix. Product mix determines target market(s)	Items A1, 2 and 3 + B1, 2, 3, 4 and 5 + C1 and 2 + D1, 2 and 3 + E1 and 2 = Product lines A + B + C + D + E = Product mix Product mix determines target markets	Number of product items = 15 Number of product lines = 5 Average depth of product mix = 3

Width

1. The relationships are based on the shape of the symbols which represent the different product items. In this regard there is a big relationship between the shapes of product lines C and D.

- *Secondly*, decisions have to be taken on the number of product lines, involving the curtailment or expansion of the number of product lines.

- *Thirdly*, decisions have to be taken on the target market(s) in which the firm operates or intends to operate.

It is clear from the composition of the product mix that management can take only *four* basic product-mix decisions, namely the **maintenance**, **curtailment**, **expansion** or **modification** *of the existing product mix* (or a combination of these) by respectively maintaining, decreasing, increasing or modifying the existing number of product items and product lines. Evidently the *factors* which can lead to the maintenance, curtailment, expansion or modification of the product mix are numerous.

When management has to decide on alternative product mixes, emphasis should therefore not be placed on the mere maintenance, curtailment, expansion or modification of the mix per se, but rather on the objectives and the manipulation of the factors which may influence the composition of the product mix. This aspect is discussed in section 7.8.

7.6 THE IDEAL PRODUCT MIX

The ideal product mix is a dynamic entity and can be defined as the product mix which the firm *must continually have at its disposal in order to realise its objectives in terms of expected sales growth, market share, cash flow and profitability*.

Given a particular product mix, management continually has to evaluate the various product items and product lines in terms of their contribution to the realisation of stated objectives. Consumer needs and preferences are continually changing, competitors alter their marketing strategies, business objectives can change, while the marketing environment itself undergoes constant change. These changes and many other factors favour the sales growth, market share, and cash flow and profitability of certain products, while they harm those of others. It is therefore the task of management to adapt its product mix in the light of such changes so as constantly to strive for the realisation of the abovementioned objectives.

The relationship between the ideal product mix and the **profit objective** is illustrated in Figure 7.2. The relationship between the ideal product mix and **sales growth**, **cash flow** and **market share** respectively can be illustrated in a similar way.

Figure 7.2 can be clarified by considering the following example. Suppose that the firm produces and markets three products, A, B and C. The expected total profit of the present mix and the profit-growth objective of the firm are given. Suppose product A contributes about 60 per cent to total profit the first year, B about 30 per cent and C the remaining 10 per cent. The expectation is that the percentage profit contribution of A will decline, that B's profit contribution will grow for three years and then decline, and that C's profit contribution will grow annually. In year 6, C will be contributing most of the profit, followed by B and A. From the figure it is clear that the expected profits of the three products do not satisfy the profit-growth objective of the firm. Thus a profit gap (target gap) develops which can be *defined as the difference between the expected total profit of the present product mix and the profit-growth objective of the firm*. The profit gap has to be filled, inter alia, by developing new products, concentrating on the cash flow generated by established products, and eliminating older ones in order constantly to maintain an ideal product mix.

According to Drucker[2] the product mix of every firm can consist of *six* product categories in terms of their sales and profit contributions:

- tomorrow's breadwinners — new products or modifications of existing products;
- today's breadwinners — yesterday's new products and modifications;
- products which can make a profit contribution if drastic action is taken;
- yesterday's breadwinners — products with high sales volumes consisting of special offers, small orders and the like;
- the 'also rans' — products which did not come up to high expectations but did not fail outright; and
- the failures.

FIGURE 7.2   Relationship between ideal product mix and the profit-growth objective of the enterprise

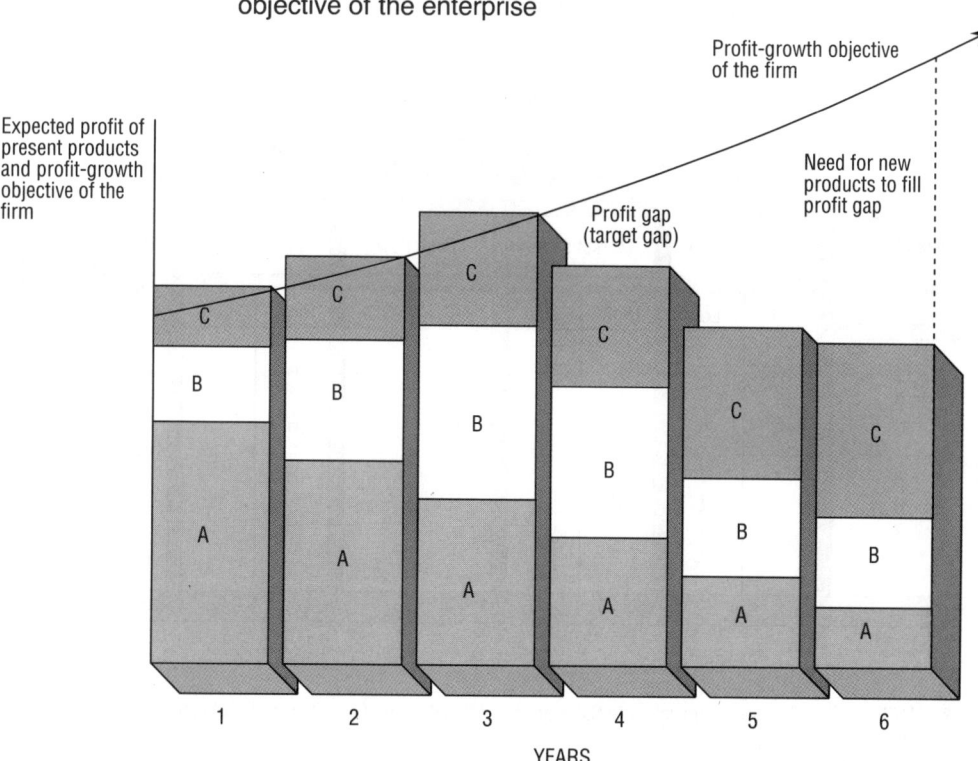

Profit-growth objective of the firm

Expected profit of present products and profit-growth objective of the firm

Need for new products to fill profit gap

Profit gap (target gap)

C
B
A

YEARS

Source: Adapted from Kotler, P. 1976. *Marketing Management: Analysis, Planning and Control.* 3rd edition. London: Prentice-Hall International, p 187.

If the firm does not develop new products and/or eliminate obsolete ones continually, it can eventually end up with an extremely unbalanced (non-ideal) product mix. The firm should therefore continually evaluate each product in terms of sales growth, market share and profitability. Table 7.1 illustrates a worksheet for product performance rating.

This product performance rating is especially useful to determine the present SMCP position (sales growth, market share, cash flow and profitability position) of each product, and what it can or should be in future. It can also serve as a basis for determining why SMCP is as it is, in terms of current marketing strategy, the competitive position, what the SMCP position should or will be, and what marketing strategy will be required to achieve this. For example, an existing HLLH product (high sales growth, low market share, low cash flow, high profitability) may be a successful new product which was launched in a highly competitive market and is at present in the growth phase of its life cycle. By means of an effective marketing communication strategy and by maintaining profitabil-

TABLE 7.1 Product performance rating in terms of sales growth, market share, cash flow and profitability

Possible alternative products	Sales growth		Market share		Cash flow		Profitability		Total SMCP[3] performance rating[4]
	PRODUCT PERFORMANCE RATING FORM								
	PERFORMANCE RATING IN TERMS OF:								
	High	Low	High	Low	High	Low	High	Low	
1	H[1]		H		H		H		HHHH product[5]
2	H		H			L[2]		L	HHLL product
3	H			L	H		H		HLHH product
4	H			L		L		L	HLLL product
5		L	H			L	H		LHLH product
6		L	H		H			L	LHHL product
7		L		L		L	H		LLLH product
8		L		L		L		L	LLLL product

1. H = High rating
2. L = Low rating
3. SMCP = Abbreviation fo Sales growth, Market share, Cash flow and Profitability
4. Total SMCP performance rating = Total Sales growth, Market share, Cash flow and Profitability performance rating
5. HHHH product = Product with high Sales growth, Market share, Cash flow and Profitabilty

ity, sales can grow so rapidly that a relatively high market share can be captured in due course. It is useful to define a possible alternative marketing situation for each SMCP position, and to indicate what marketing strategies will be necessary to move a product from one SMCP position to another.

Continual evaluation of the product mix, in order to bring it as close as possible to the ideal, is an important control task of marketing management. See also the composition of the product portfolio in Chapter 19.

7.7 THE CLASSIFICATION OF PRODUCTS AND SERVICES

We have already seen that the marketer considers products as being physical objects, services, personalities, places, institutions and ideas that satisfy one or more needs of a specific target market. However, products differ with regard to their particular characteristics, production and marketing methods, and the purpose for which they are used. Consequently, it is useful for marketing management to classify products into more or less homogeneous groups according to one criterion or another.

It is customary to divide products into *three* main groups, namely **industrial goods** (also called production goods), **commercial services** and **consumption or consumer goods**, with further subclassifications for each.

7.7.1 Industrial goods

Industrial goods are goods destined for use in a production process in order to generate other goods and services. Several subclassifications of production goods are possible, such as mining products, part-processed materials and components, installations, accessory equipment and operating supplies.

Mining products

Mining products, such as crude oil and iron ore, are found in the earth's crust and have their origin in its creation. Except for their having been mined, ie extracted from the earth, **they have not yet undergone further processing**. They are eventually used in the manufacture of other products, such as part-processed materials and/or components.

Part-processed materials and components

Products in this group eventually become part of the final product. In contrast with mining products, they have already been **partly processed**. Further processing is usually necessary, for example the use of pig-iron in the manufacture of steel, yarn woven into cloth, and flour used in baking bread. Components are assembled *without any further changes being made to their form*. Examples of components are, inter alia, spark plugs, fan belts and buttons.

Installations

Installations are **completed** industrial products (such as buildings, machinery and heavy equipment) and are usually long-lived and relatively expensive, and directly determine the capacity of the firm. The last-mentioned characteristic entails that the installations should be viewed in a broad context. A typewriter, if bought by a firm supplying secretarial services, can therefore be regarded as an installation because one typewriter directly increases such a firm's capacity. Products such as ships, agricultural machinery, office equipment, road graders and sewing machines differ from one another considerably, but are nevertheless part of the installations of the firms concerned.

Capital equipment forms part of installations and can be defined as the essential machinery and/or other important equipment used directly for, or contributing to, the manufacture of products and/or the rendering of services, and is directly related to the *major manufacturing activities* of the firms which use the equipment. Manufacturing activities have to be interpreted in the same way as production in a restricted sense, ie only the physical conversion process. Examples of capital equipment are inter alia road graders, coal-mining machinery, heavy earth-moving equipment, rock drills and water purification plants. All these products are characterised by a relatively *long life span* and *high prices*. Furthermore, they determine the production capacities of the firms where these products have a direct bearing on the major manufacturing activities.

Accessory equipment

Accessory equipment refers to industrial products which are used to **aid** the manufacturing process, but do not exert a significant influence on the production capacity. These products do not form part of the final product. The life span of accessory equipment is shorter than that of installations, but longer than that of operating supplies. Small power tools and fork-lifters are examples of accessory equipment. The preceding examples can, of course, also be regarded as installations and more specifically capital equipment, depending on the nature of the firm's major manufacturing activities.

Operating supplies

Operating supplies require no further processing, are relatively inexpensive, have a short life span and are purchased with the minimum of effort. Examples of operating supplies are cleaning materials, floor polish, stationery and toiletries for staff. In a sense operating supplies are the **convenience goods** of the industrial market.

7.7.2 Commercial services

Commercial services are independent, separate, identifiable, intangible, need-satisfying activities destined for ultimate consumers and industrial users, and are not necessarily related to the sale of a product or another service. Insurance, medical and dental services, entertainment, and communication services are examples. Commercial services differ from each other in the following ways:

- the degree of **durability**, which is indicative of the duration of the need-satisfaction (for example, the need-satisfaction provided by a cinema show is relatively short compared to that of life insurance);
- the degree of **tangibility**, which varies between purely intangible services, such as education, and the services of an architect, who provides a tangible product; and
- the period of **commitment**, which can vary from long-term commitment, such as insurance, to short-term commitment, such as urban public transport.

The following commercial services can be bought by institutional, industrial and intermediate buyers and final consumers.

- **Accommodation**, including the renting of hotel rooms, flats and houses.
- **Household services**, such as repair services for household appliances and cleaning of houses.
- **Recreation**, offered by institutions such as cinemas, holiday resorts, performing artists, theatres and sport clubs.
- **Personal services**, supplied by, inter alia, barbers, beauticians and dry-cleaners.
- **Medical services** provided by physiotherapists, physicians, dentists and private hospitals.
- **Educational services** other than those supplied by the authorities.
- **Professional services** performed by, inter alia, attorneys, accountants, management consultants, systems analysts and advertising practitioners.
- **Insurance and financial services** provided by institutions such as insurance firms and commercial banks.
- **Transport services** other than those supplied by the authorities.
- **Communication services** supplied by private firms, such as pocket paging systems for hotels, factories and building sites.

The marketing of services is discussed in Chapter 20.

7.7.3 Consumer goods

The emphasis in this book is mainly on the product decisions regarding consumer goods. The characteristics and marketing considerations of consumer goods are therefore discussed in somewhat more depth.

Consumer goods are goods destined for **direct use** *by households or ultimate consumers*. According to their **properties of durability** these goods can first be divided into durable and non-durable consumer goods. As the name indicates, durable goods are used repeatedly over a longer period of time (examples are stoves, clothing, motor cars and furniture). Non-durable consumer goods are goods with a short life span which are mainly destined for a single use or relatively few uses (examples are cigarettes, butter and toilet soap). This distinction has important challenges for the marketer. Products which are used rapidly and bought regularly (non-durable goods) have to be available at many outlets (intensive distribution), require a relatively low profit margin, and normally develop a strong trade mark (brand) loyalty. Durable products, on the other hand, require more personalised selling and service, carry relatively high profit margins, and often call for warranties from the seller.

Secondly, consumer goods can be divided into *convenience goods, shopping goods* and *speciality goods*, based on the **buying habits of consumers**. *Two* factors regarding buying habits that dominate in this classification are:

- the consumer's knowledge of the exact nature and characteristics of the product *before* he starts out on his shopping trip; and
- the satisfaction which he derives from searching for and comparing products, weighed against the time and effort required.

Convenience goods

Convenience goods are those consumer goods of which the consumer has **comprehensive knowledge** *before he goes out to buy them.* Normally the benefits which he derives from shopping around and comparing prices and quality do not justify the extra time and effort required. Trade mark preferences for convenience goods are normally not strong. Convenience goods are often subdivided into:

- *Staple goods.* These goods such as sugar, bread, vegetables, fruit, toothpaste and soft drinks are bought on a *regular* basis by consumers.
- *Impulse goods.* These are convenience goods which are normally bought without much preplanning and effort. These products are available at a variety of retail stores and the consumer often takes the decision to buy at the point of sale.
- *Emergency goods.* These goods are normally bought *immediately* when a need for it arises. Examples are towrope for motorcars, matches, torch batteries, sticking plaster and plastic raincoats.

The following marketing considerations apply to convenience goods

Since convenience goods have to be made available within easy reach of consumers, they require intensive distribution at retail level and normally also a long distribution channel (manufacturer → wholesaler → retailer) because it may be uneconomical for the manufacturer to sell directly to all retailers. Retailers usually stock several trade marks of specific convenience goods (toothpaste, for example) and they are not very keen to advertise individual trade marks.

Furthermore, the quality and prices of competitive convenience goods are reasonably uniform, the products do not call for much explanation to the consumer, and the retailer does not receive much incentive to promote one trade mark rather than another. Consequently, convenience goods are mostly marketed on a self-service basis and the entire marketing communication campaign is usually the responsibility of the manufacturer. Above all, the manufacturer has to advertise extensively to develop trade mark recognition and preference for his product. Self-service requires effective packaging, shelf space and point-of-purchase advertising, especially because many convenience items are bought impulsively.

Shopping goods

Shopping goods are those consumer goods which the consumer wants to **compare** *in terms of, inter alia, suitability, quality, workmanship, price and style in several shops before he buys.* Here the consumer does not have complete knowledge of the product attributes beforehand, and for that reason he is prepared to shop around to obtain this knowledge. He will, however, only continue *shopping* as long as the advantages of doing so are still greater than the effort and time required to visit several shops. Here trade marks play a relatively minor role. In fact, the very nature of shopping goods requires that the consumer compare a variety of products before he makes a decision. Examples of shopping goods are furniture, clothing and jewelry. Shopping goods normally have a higher unit value than convenience goods and are also bought less frequently.

The following marketing considerations normally predominate in respect of shopping goods

The consumer's buying habits with regard to these goods influence especially the distribution decisions and marketing communication decisions of both manufacturers and middlemen. Relatively few outlets (selective distribution) are required because the consumer is prepared to shop around for the goods. To make shopping easier for the consumer, manufacturers normally endeavour to distribute their products through retailers who deal in competitive shopping goods and who are situated close to each other. These retailers also prefer clustering together. Their individual attraction is thereby increased, while customers can be interchanged and intercepted. Normally close co-operation exists between manufacturers and retailers in the marketing of shopping goods, and wholesalers are not used to the same extent as with convenience goods. Because trade mark preference and insistence for shopping goods play a lesser role, the name of the retailer is often more important to the buyer of shopping goods than that of the manufacturer. Therefore, the retailer is willing to bear a large portion of the advertising, display and other selling costs, especially because the consumer does not care much who the manufacturer of a particular shopping item is.

Speciality goods

Speciality goods are those consumer goods with unique characteristics and/or trade mark insistence for which a significant group of consumers is habitually willing to make a **special purchasing effort.** As in the case of convenience goods the consumer has comprehensive knowledge of the particular product before he starts out on his shopping trip. The distinguishing and key characteristic of speciality goods is that the buyer *insists* on a particular trade mark and will accept only that one. Substitute products are therefore avoided even if the acquisition of the preferred trade mark requires considerable time and effort. Products such as motor cars, hi-fi and photographic equipment, and television sets are normally classified as speciality goods.

Some marketing considerations of speciality goods are worth mentioning

Normally only one outlet (exclusive distribution) in a specific territory or target market is used, and the manufacturer also markets directly to chosen retailers. The retailer and manufacturer of speciality goods are interdependent by nature of the marketing effort — the success of the one influences the success of the other. Trade marks are extremely important to speciality goods and, because relatively few outlets are used, both manufacturer and retailer have to advertise extensively.

Normally the manufacturer bears part of the retailer's advertising costs and the name of the retailer concerned also often appears in the manufacturer's advertisements.

It is important to note once again that the classification of convenience, shopping and speciality goods is based on the buying habits of the consumer. As buying habits regarding a specific product vary among consumers, the same product (for example radios) can be a convenience item for one, a shopping item for another, and a speciality item for a third person.

Table 7.2 contains a summary of the characteristics of convenience, shopping and speciality goods, as well as some marketing considerations which are generally applicable to each.

7.8 FACTORS INFLUENCING PRODUCT-MIX DECISIONS

Marketing management intending to use its product mix as an important marketing strategy should thoroughly acquaint itself with the factors which may influence the composition of the mix.

7.8.1 Business objectives as a basis for product-mix decisions

Business objectives are inextricably interwoven with product-mix decisions. It is a fact that the product mix, as the generator of income and profits, is the lifeblood of an enterprise.

Efforts apparently intended to stimulate the sales of obsolete products (which should have been eliminated earlier), such as relatively high advertising expenditure, unrealistically low prices and small profit margins, can seriously damage the profit position of the firm.

Product-mix decisions also form the basis for the stability and growth in sales and cash inflow of the firm. Existing products are maintained, new products are added, old ones are eliminated and existing products are modified with a view to enhancing stability and growth.

Product-mix decisions also have a direct bearing on the effective utilisation of the assets of the firm. New products usually require new investment in machinery and equipment; the immediate elimination of products creates spare capacity; obsolete and uneconomical products occupy capacity which can most probably be better utilised elsewhere.

In short, the entire profitability endeavour of the firm, and the extent to which it is achieved, is largely a result of product-mix decisions. The product-mix objectives, therefore, have to be derived from the business objectives. It can thus be said that the ultimate objective of product-mix decisions is the effective adaptation of the product mix to changing circumstances and the utilisation of opportunities so that the profitability endeavour of the firm, taking into consideration its socio-economic responsibilities, can best be served.

TABLE 7.2   Characteristics and some marketing considerations for convenience, shopping and speciality goods

CHARACTERISTICS AND MARKETING CONSIDERATIONS FOR CONSUMER GOODS	TYPE OF PRODUCT		
	CONVENIENCE GOODS	SHOPPING GOODS	SPECIALITY GOODS
Characteristics			
Time and effort devoted by consumer to shopping	Very little	Considerable	Cannot generalise. May visit nearby shop with the least effort and time or go to a distant shop which can require much time and effort
Time spent on planning the purchase	Very little	Considerable	Considerable
Course of time after need arises and when it is satisfied	Immediately	Relatively long time	Relatively long time
Comparison of price and quality	Less important	Very important	Less important
Unit price	Low	High	High
Frequency of recurring purchases	Usually frequent	Infrequent	Infrequent
Marketing considerations			
Length of distribution channel	Long	Short	Short to very short
Importance of retailer	The individual shop is unimportant	Important	Very important
Number of outlets	As many as possible - intensive distribution	Less than for convenience goods - selective distribution	Few - often exclusive distribution
Stock turnover	Relatively high	Relatively low	Relatively low
Gross profit margin	Relatively low	Relatively high	Relatively high
Responsibility for advertising	Mainly manufacturer's	Manufacturer's and retailer's on different levels	Joint responsibility
Importance of point-of-purchase advertising	Very important	Less important	Less important
Importance of trademark and shop name	Trademark reasonably important	Shop name very important	Both important
Importance of packaging	Very important	Less important	Less important

7.8.2 Product leadership inclination

The product leadership inclination of a firm entails striving always to be first on the market with a new product before competitors with similar or even better products enter the market. If the firm intends to remain the leader in a particular industry high demands will be placed on management to make the correct product-mix decisions. It calls, inter alia, for dynamic, progressive, creative and even adventurous management and willingness to accept risks, to vote considerable funds for product development, and continually to introduce new products into the market.

7.8.3 Trading-up and trading-down

Trading-up and trading-down pertain to the addition of new product items to existing product lines, but with specific objectives. Marketing management can see a special opportunity in **trading-up**, ie *to add a higher-priced prestige product item to the product line in the hope of increasing sales of an existing lower-priced product.*

> In the motor-car industry Nissan Motor Company introduced *inter alia* the Nissan Maxima 300 SE with the expectation that the sales of its lower-priced products would increase as a result of the prestige image of the Nissan Maxima 300 SE.

A firm employs **trading-down** *when it adds a lower-priced product item to its prestige product line in the hope that consumers who cannot afford the original prestige product will buy the new product item because it gains some of the prestige of the high-priced product.*

> Bayerische Motoren Werke (BMW) did this in 1975 when it added the less expensive 518 model to its product mix in the Republic of South Africa. This car was closely associated with the prestige image of its existing, more expensive BMW 528, 525 and 520 cars.

Obviously a strategy of trading-up and trading-down can have disastrous consequences for a firm, should it fail.

Trading-up and trading-down are visualised in Figure 7.3.

7.8.4 The desire to change the image of the firm

A change in the product mix in order to change the image of the firm is related to a strategy of trading-up and trading-down. The production and marketing of the same products year in and year out can easily lead to complacency, stagnation and indifference among the personnel of the firm, and marketing management should endeavour continually to rejuvenate the image of the firm by modifying its product mix.

FIGURE 7.3   Trading-up and trading-down

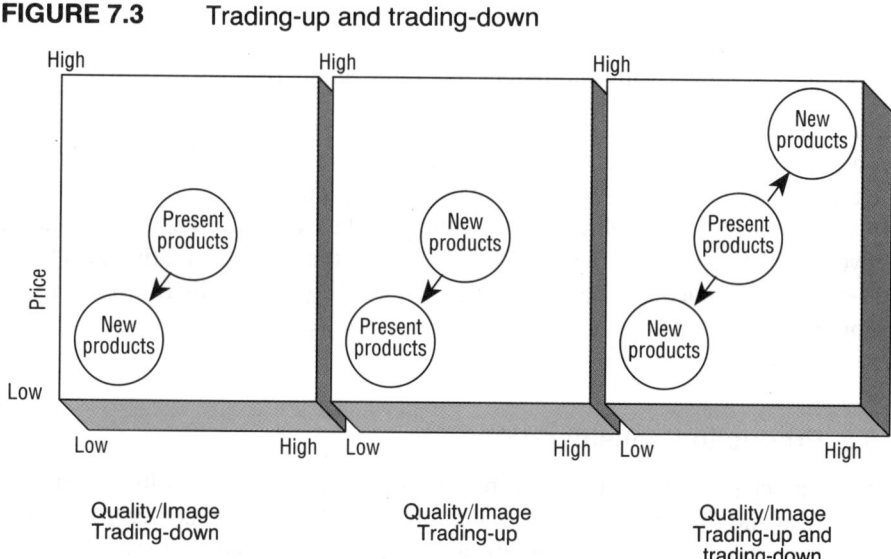

| Quality/Image | Quality/Image | Quality/Image |
| Trading-down | Trading-up | Trading-up and trading-down |

7.8.5 Changes in the target market

Markets can change in terms of **growth** (fewer children per family, more people in suburban residential areas, longer life expectancy due to better medical services), **buying power** (the principle of equal pay for equal work in the workplace has increased the buying power of women) and **consumer behaviour** (other forms of leisure spending and the aspiration to convenience). By adapting the product mix to accommodate these changes in the target market, marketing management is faced with unique opportunities and challenges which can lead to considerable benefits for the firm, provided they are spotted in time and can be utilised effectively.

7.8.6 Competitive actions and reactions

In order to compete more effectively, management can decide to differentiate (distinguish) its product mix from those of competitors so that price comparisons inter alia become more difficult. Furthermore, a firm can decide to diversify in order to move into markets where competition is less severe. However, if a firm enters a target market which offers relatively high profit possibilities with a new product, it can be expected that competitors will also enter the market in due course.

7.8.7 Marketing considerations

Two important marketing considerations exist in expanding the product mix.

- *First*, new products are **added** to the present mix in order to increase sales and profitability in existing and new target markets.

- *Secondly*, the present product mix can be **expanded** in order to make better use of the marketing skills and facilities of the firm, such as the sales force, warehouses, advertising campaigns and physical distribution networks.

A firm can also improve its marketing efficiency in certain cases by shrinking the product mix. With the existing mix the sales force may be spread too thinly over the target market; warehouse space may be occupied by products with turnover rates and market shares which are too low; and the existing physical distribution network may function inefficiently. By narrowing the product mix the sales force and warehouse space can be better utilised and the physical distribution can be rationalised.

7.8.8 Production considerations

A firm can change its product mix in order to make better use of its production capabilities and thus to lower its production costs per unit. In this way, prolonged spare capacity in machines, labour and management skills can lead to the development of new products to utilise these capacities.

Furthermore, the availability of by-products can also lead to the expansion of the product mix. Consider the variety of by-products of the South African Coal, Oil and Gas Corporation Limited (SASOL), such as butanol, acetone, benzole, creosote, pitch, tar and ammonium sulphate. These products originate in the extraction of fuel from coal.

7.8.9 Financial considerations

Various financial reasons exist for changing the product mix.

- *First*, the firm can **reduce its financial risks** by spreading them over a wide product mix — a matter of not putting all its eggs in one basket.
- *Secondly*, an **expansion** of the mix can contribute to a higher profitable sales volume and thereby even out seasonal fluctuations.
- *Thirdly*, the service division can be better utilised and generally **function more efficiently** with a relatively wide product mix.
- *Furthermore*, a widely divergent product mix, even one cutting across different industries, can **absorb recession shocks** in the firm because not all industries are equally sensitive to this economic phenomenon.
- *Lastly*, the narrowing of the product mix can also provide **financial advantages**. By eliminating products with a relatively low turnover rate and market share (such as exceptionally large and extraordinarily small shoe sizes), a slight drop in sales may occur but a substantial decrease in costs may be experienced. Smaller production runs with relatively high production costs per unit and relatively high stock-keeping costs (the so-called interest, space and risk costs) are inter alia eliminated.

From the preceding it should be clear that product-mix decisions are influenced by several factors which may change continually. To summarise: any change in the marketing environment which influences a firm's product mix can lead to specific product decisions. With these and possibly also other factors in mind, it is one of the tasks of management to aim at establishing an ideal product mix (see section 7.6).

7.9 SUMMARY

In this chapter some important concepts such as the product, product concept, formal product, core product, augmented product, product mix, product lines, product items, product diversification, product specialisation, simplification and standardisation, and product differentiation have been described. Furthermore, the width, depth and consistency of the product mix, the ideal product mix and the classification of products and services, and especially consumer goods, were reviewed. Attention was also focused on the factors which can influence product mix decisions.

REFERENCES

1. Packard, V. 1970. *The Wastemakers*. Harmondsworth, England: Penguin Books Ltd. The author especially points out the waste of resources and the sociological and psychological implications of a strategy of planned obsolescence. See also in this regard Galbraith, JK. 1968. *The Affluent Society*. Boston: Houghton-Mifflin Co.
2. Drucker, P. 'Managing for Business Effectiveness' *Harvard Business Review*, vol 41, May–June 1963, p 59.

ASSIGNMENTS

1. Clearly describe the **formal product, core product, augmented product** and **product image** of the following products/services:

   - A wrist-watch
   - Obtaining a B.Com. degree
   - Disco dancing
   - A savings account at a bank
   - An engagement ring
   - Toothpaste
   - A hotel holiday
   - Slimming food
   - A television set
   - Dental services

2. Take any five South African enterprises and **investigate** and **describe** the following aspects of their product mixes so that the meaning of each aspect is clear:

   - Product items
   - Product lines
   - Product diversification
   - Product specialisation
   - Simplification
   - Product standardisation
   - Product differentiation
   - Product obsolescence
   - New products
   - The width, depth and consistency of the product mix

3. Describe the **ideal product mix** for the following type of enterprises:

   - A manufacturer of toys
   - A programme series for a private television network
   - Fields of study of a Faculty of Economic and Management Sciences
   - A manufacturer of men's clothing
   - A motor-car manufacturer
   - A manufacturer of instant foods
   - A manufacturer of lighting equipment for private houses

4. Take any five different types of South African manufacturing firms and describe the following types of **industrial goods** which they use in their production processes:

   - Mining products
   - Part-processed materials and components
   - Installations
   - Accessory equipment
   - Operating supplies

5. Take five different types of South African service enterprises and describe the **service mix** (product mix) in view of the following:

- The degree of durability
- The degree of tangibility
- The period of commitment

6. 'It is important to note once again that the classification of convenience, shopping and speciality goods is based on the buying habits of the consumer.' Discuss this statement by investigating the buying habits of 20 final consumers regarding the following product types:

- Cigarettes
- Motor cars
- Television sets
- Washing powders
- Tomato sauce
- Fresh potatoes
- Insurance policies

Broadly describe the **marketing methods** used by South African businesses for each of the above-mentioned product types. Are these broad marketing methods 'correct' in view of your research findings on the buying habits of the 20 final consumers mentioned above? Motivate your point of view.

7. Give practical examples to indicate how the following factors influenced or probably can influence the product decisions of certain South African enterprises:

- Business objectives as a basis for product-mix decisions
- Product leadership inclination
- Trading-up
- Trading-down
- The desire to change the image of the firm
- Changes in the target markets
- Competitive actions and reactions
- Marketing considerations
- Production considerations
- Financial considerations

CHAPTER 8

PRODUCT DEVELOPMENT

8.1 INTRODUCTION

New products have been defined as those products or product attributes which are new to the firm and can in one or more respects be regarded by the target market as being significantly different from existing competitive products. Viewed in this way, *four* types of new products can be identified:

- products which are original and unique in every respect;
- important modifications of existing products so that they differ significantly from the original product;
- products which are new to the firm but not quite new to the target market; and
- products which are new to the target market but not new to the firm.

The following aspects of product development, which involve marketing management very closely, are dealt with in this chapter:

ORGANISATION OF THE CHAPTER

The importance of new products to the firm: Business planning starts with the product; maintenance of profit margins; prerequisite for business growth; increased standards of living, rapid technological development and more intensive competition; struggle for retail shelf-space; high costs and risks attached to product failures.

Some features of product development: Objective, luck, sequence, importance, risk, survival rate, development costs, all divisions contribute, timing.

The new-product matrix: Useful aid for the identification of possible alternative new products.

Steps in product development: The decision making process; organisation for the development of new products; the development of product ideas; the screening of product ideas; product concept development and testing consisting of the development of the product concept, product and trade mark positioning and product concept testing; the profitability analysis; the physical product development; test marketing of the new product; and commercialisation of the new product.

Role of research in product development: It covers the entire product development process.

The diffusion of innovation (new products): The macro- or diffusion process; the micro- or acceptance process; the innovators; the relationship between the diffusion of innovasion and the product life cycle.

Product development and the other functions of the firm: Relationship with production, financial, manpower, information, purchasing and external relations management.

8.2 THE IMPORTANCE OF NEW PRODUCTS TO THE ENTERPRISE

It has been said that never in the past has man thought so boldly and so far ahead as he does today. In a technological sense we stand at present like Adam on the threshold of a new world.[1]

"With the exception of a few basic products, most of the things bought and sold nowadays have come into existence during the past sixty years. Paul Kruger was completely unfamiliar with aeroplanes, radio, television or nuclear power. Jan Smuts was unfamiliar with antibiotics, personal computers, photostat machines or space flights. John Vorster did not know about robot factories, ordinary citizens as space travellers or silicon protein molecules that have already made the silicon chip obsolete. One reason for the constant rate of acceleration of technological innovation is the fact that 90 % of all the scientists who have ever existed are alive now."[2]

From this it is clear that the continual development and marketing of new products have become indispensable to the growth and survival of the modern firm. A variety of reasons (which are more important in some industries than in others) can be advanced for this. These reasons are discussed below.

8.2.1 Business planning starts with the product mix

The product decisions of a firm and especially its product development decisions determine to whom it will market in future, who its competitors will be and what technological and other skills it has to have at its disposal. The maintenance of an ideal product mix and the ability to obtain and/or develop new products constantly are important characteristics of a properly managed firm. The need for new products stresses the importance of continual analysis and proper evaluation of the changing market and technological environments in order to identify new consumer needs and acquire and/or develop new products to satisfy them.

Furthermore, business planning, marketing planning and financial planning are tied to product planning. The forecasting of sales, costs, capital investment, production facilities, personnel requirements and so on is virtually impossible without sound product planning.

8.2.2 The maintenance of profit margins

A continual flow of successful new products can form the basis of impressive profit opportunities for the firm. This statement is illustrated in Figure 8.1, which indicates the relationship between the sales and profit margin curves.

Generally, the sales and profit margin curves have more or less the same shape, but the gradients of the curves differ from each other at a specific point in the product life cycle. During the maturity phase sales still increase, but the profit margin shows a decreasing tendency, especially because intensive competition in this phase requires cost-increasing marketing efforts (particularly advertising and even price competition). Figure 8.1 clearly shows that new products are continually necessary to maintain and improve the profit and growth position of the firm (see also Figure 7.2). Therefore, it is more meaningful to base the firm's product-mix decisions on the profit margin curve rather than the sales curve.

FIGURE 8.1   The sales and profit margin curves in relation to the phases of the product life cycle

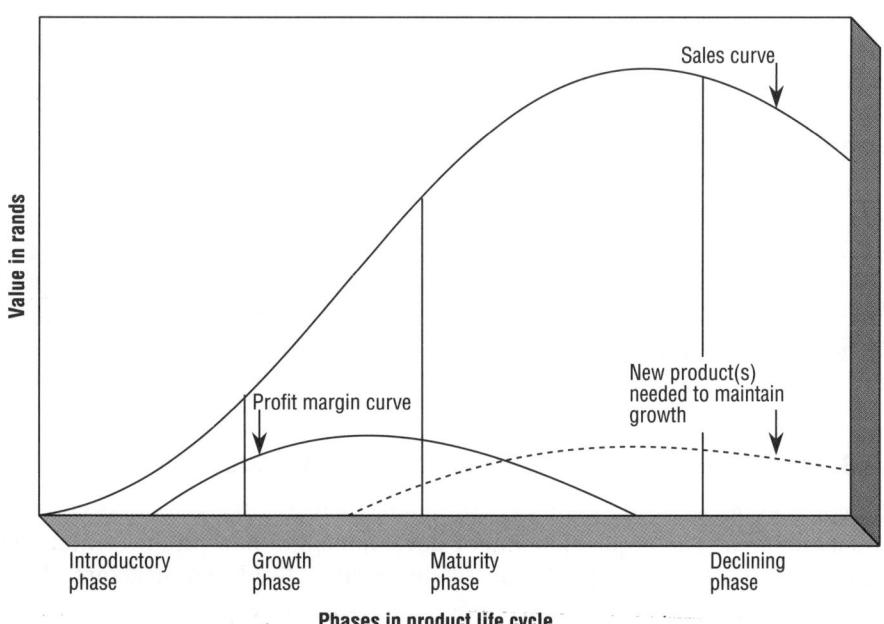

Source: Adapted from Booz, Allen & Hamilton. 'The Importance of New Products' in Berg, TL & Schuchman, A. 1965. *Product Strategy and Management*. New York: Holt, Rinehart & Winston, p 28. (Own caption.) For a discussion of the different phases in the product life cycle and the course of the sales and profit margin curves, see Chapter 18.

8.2.3 Prerequisite for business growth

It is general knowledge that fast-growing industries (such as the chemical and electrical equipment industries) spend relatively large amounts on research and development and thus are strongly committed to the development of new products. The relatively high growth rates in sales and profitability of these industries are accordingly mainly attributable to the regular launching of new products.

8.2.4 Certain environmental variables necessitate product development

It is generally known that the standard of living of the Western nations has improved substantially since the Second World War. Relatively large consumer groups in the middle, middle-high and high income categories, with significant amounts of disposable income and a variety of existing and slumbering needs which change continually, have developed. This phenomenon, together with rapid technological development, permits and also necessitates market segmentation, market targeting, and product differentiation in modern-day marketing. Technological development normally enables the manufacturer to satisfy the consumers' needs, but in the process competition naturally also intensifies. The acquisition and/or development of new products nevertheless remains one of the most effective methods by which to maintain and improve the competitive position, especially if supported by effective price, distribution and marketing communication decisions. The firm's product development therefore has to be **innovative** rather than **imitative**. Product development has to be directed towards *leading* competition rather than resisting it.

8.2.5 The struggle for retail shelf-space

The tendency towards one-stop buying by consumers and the continual flow of new products make it necessary for retailers, and especially departmental stores and supermarkets, to keep several thousand different product items on the available shelf-space, and here we can indeed talk of the struggle for shelf-space. Under these circumstances it is logical that products which are technically and/or psychologically obsolete will be the first victims, and the manufacturer continually has to develop new products in order to compete effectively for retail shelf-space.

8.2.6 The high costs and risks attached to product failures

The complex modern marketing environment increases the risks and costs of product failures. The acquisition and/or development of new products inter alia implies relatively large capital investment, a high fixed-cost structure, high break-even points and long capital pay-back periods. Moreover, compliance with government regulations regarding aspects such as pollution and product safety are also cost factors which have to be taken into consideration. The costs and risks attached to these and other factors stress the importance of effective product development and the dangers of product failures.

It is informative to note that product failures in the South African capital equipment industry are mainly attributable to:

- a defective market analysis;
- higher development costs than have been provided for;
- unforeseen actions of competitors;
- the product being too sophisticated for the South African market;
- technical shortcomings of the product; and
- an inadequate sales force.[3]

With a few exceptions these factors can be influenced directly by business management!

8.3 SOME FEATURES OF PRODUCT DEVELOPMENT

Product development inter alia has the following nine characteristics:

The objective

The *objective* of product development is systematically to adapt the technological dimensions of the product item to the opportunities and threats in the macro-, market and micro-environments. Each step in the product development process serves as a checkpoint to this end.

Luck

The principles of the scientific method are applied but the effectiveness and success of the product development process is sometimes reliant mainly on *luck*.

Sequence

The steps in the product development process occur in a definite *sequence*. The logical succession of the different steps cannot be changed without harming the effectiveness of the process. In most cases the output of one step serves as the input for the next.

Importance

The different steps may differ in *importance*. The relative importance of the various steps is determined by the type of product item being developed. In this way the physical product development step of an industrial product item (which is highly technical in nature) will, for example, be more decisive than for consumer goods.

Risk

Decision making takes place under conditions of *risk*. The product development procedure originates largely as a result of the high risks attached to possible product failures. In order to reduce these risks, management has developed a number of control points or steps where decisions must be taken either to drop the ideas or to take them to the next step. Thus, management is confronted time and again with a '*go/no go/don't know*' decision making situation.

Management's decision making objectives during product development are illustrated in Figure 8.2. As indicated, the decision making objectives are influenced by risk and profitability. During product development management looks for product items with low risks and high profitability. Thus, from a risk and profitability point of view, product items falling in the bottom right-hand corner of Figure 8.2 are ideal for development and marketing.

FIGURE 8.2   Management's decision making objectives during product development

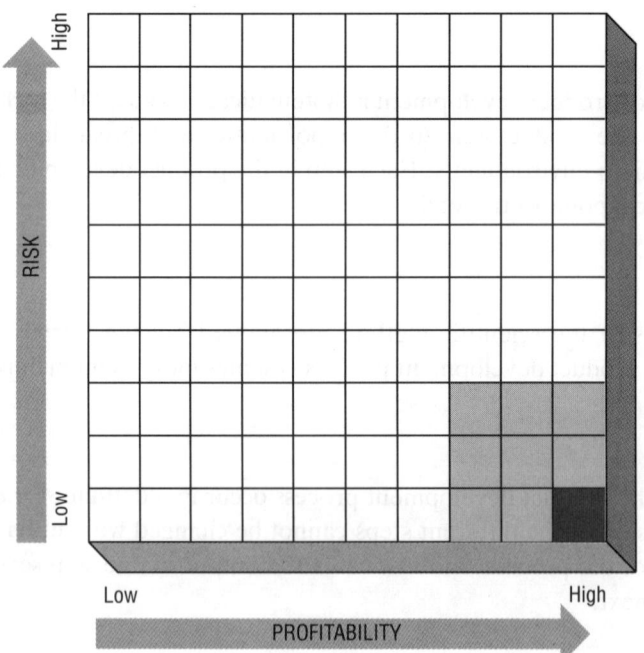

Source: Booz et al. 'A Program for New Product Evolution' in Berg TL & Shuchman, A. 1965. *Product Strategy and Management*. New York: Holt, Rinehart & Winston, p 345.

Survival rate

The relationship between the survival rate and development costs of new-product ideas is shown in Figure 8.3, illustrating that about 50 per cent of the ideas surviving a particular step are eliminated in the next step. It is therefore important to gather as many new-product ideas as possible.

FIGURE 8.3   The relationship between survival rate and development costs of new-product ideas

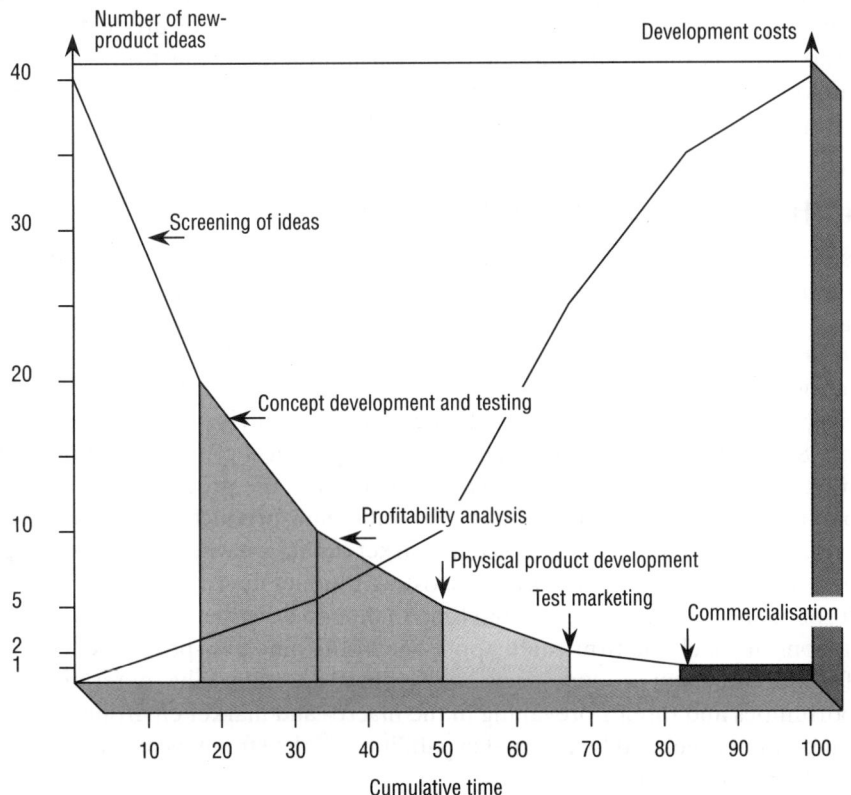

Source: Adapted from Pessemier, EA. 1977. *Product Management, Strategy and Organization.* Canada: John Wiley & Sons, p 16 and Booz et al op cit, p 343 (own caption).

Development costs

Figure 8.3 also indicates that the *development costs* of product ideas increase progressively with each step. To keep development costs as low as possible poor ideas must be eliminated rapidly. Effective screening procedures are therefore required at each step.

All divisions contribute

All divisions in the firm *contribute* towards product development. The importance of their contributions, however, varies between steps. The financial division, for instance, makes the most important contribution during the profitability analysis; the production division during physical product development; and the marketing division during test marketing.

Timing

The importance of *timing* in the product development process is often under-estimated. Poor timing is probably one of the main causes of product failures. Factors such as the availability of technical information, the firm's ability to accurately determine the needs of the market, and rapid decision making regarding risk influence the duration of development.

8.4 THE NEW-PRODUCT MATRIX

It is clear that the acquisition and/or development of new products are probably the most important methods by which the firm can achieve its objectives and satisfy the consumer's needs in a highly dynamic and competitive marketing environment. Management's motto must be: *Innovate or die*! A useful aid for the identification of possible alternative products with which the firm can fill its profit gap (see Figure 8.1) is the new-product matrix, which is depicted in Table 8.1. From Table 8.1 it is clear that new products can originate from the market dimension or the technological dimension of the product item, or both. From the new-product matrix basically nine new-product decisions can be identified. One strategy, for example, is market expansion where new markets are penetrated by modifying or changing existing product items.

It should be a useful exercise from time to time to describe practical marketing situations in which the firm could apply one of the nine new-product decisions.

The specific new-product decisions applied are inter alia determined by opportunities and threats prevailing in the macro- and market environments at a given point in time, and by internal capabilities, ie the strengths and weaknesses of the firm at that moment.

There are principally *four* ways to *utilise* specific new-product alternatives as identified in the new-product matrix. These are:

- manufacturing under licence;
- takeovers of other firms;
- internal product development; and
- establishing a new firm.

The first *two* go beyond the scope of this book and consequently only internal product development will be discussed. The establishment of a new firm for product development is an **organisational possibility** for the development of new products and is discussed briefly in section 8.5.2.1.

TABLE 8.1   The new-product matrix for internal product development

	Increase in newness of technology		
Product objectives / Market objectives	No technological change	Improved technology To make better use of the existing scientific knowledge and production facilities of the firm	New technology To obtain new scientific knowledge and production facilities for the firm
No change in the market	Maintain the existing position	Reformulation To maintain an optimum balance between costs, quality and availibility of raw materials in the specifications of the existing product mix of the firm	Replacement To replace the components or specifications of the existing product items of the firm with new technology
Deeper penetration into the market To develop the target markets of the existing product items of the firm more intensively	Improved marketing strategy To increase sales in the existing target markets of the firm	Improved product items To improve existing product items for greater need-satisfaction and better marketability	Expansion of product lines To expand the product lines which are sold to existing target markets with the aid of new technology
New markets To increase the number of target markets served by the firm	New uses To find new target markets which can use the existing product items of the firm	Market expansion To reach new target markets by modifying the existing product items	Product diversification To develop new target markets with the aid of new technology

(Left vertical axis label: Increase in newness of the market)

Source: Adapted from Johnson, SC & Jones, C. 'How to Organize for New Products' in Rothberg, RR. 1976. *Corporate Strategy and Product Innovation*. New York: The Free Press, p 180 (own caption).

8.5 STEPS IN THE PRODUCT DEVELOPMENT PROCESS

Product development is a process consisting of eight steps, namely establishing an organisation structure for product development, gathering product ideas, screening product ideas, product concept development and testing, profitability analysis, physical product development, test marketing and commercialisation.

Before these steps are discussed with a view to the development of successful products and the early elimination of poor product ideas, it is necessary to make some remarks on the decision making process in product development.

8.5.1 The decision making process in product development

For the individual enterprise, product development deals with the creation of new products. *It is the systematic process which has to be followed in order to create new products with the lowest possible sacrifices and risks and with the highest possible benefits to the enterprise, as well as the highest possible need-satisfaction for the target market.*

Innovation, product planning and even product diversification are often used as synonyms for product development. The term 'product development' is, however, to be preferred: innovation has a wide meaning and can include aspects such as technological and personnel development; product planning is only a part of product development because the latter process also has to be organised, co-ordinated and controlled, inter alia; and product diversification is possible without product development, such as can occur with the taking over of other firms.

The discussion in this section uses the development of a tangible product as a point of departure. A similar approach can, however, be followed for the development of intangible products, ie commercial services.

The sequence of and relationship between the various steps in an imaginary product development process are illustrated in Figure 8.4.

The task force, department, committee or person(s) responsible for product development has gathered ideas for twelve potential new products. During the screening phase five ideas are eliminated and thus seven enter the product concept development phase, where two more ideas are rejected. A profitability analysis is done for only five, and so on, until only one product from the 12 product ideas is ultimately manufactured and commercialised.

The nature of the decision making process in product development is obvious from Figure 8.4. At each step in the product development process the developers have to decide which ideas to drop and which to retain for the next step. Thus the developers are confronted time and again with a **go/no go/don't know** decision making situation. If the decision is *go* the idea advances to the next step; if the decision is *no go* the idea is dropped; and if the developers vacillate, ie if they cannot decide, additional information has to be gathered so that either a go or a no go decision can be taken.

It is also important to note that the product development phases and the product life cycle cannot be separated from each other. The author is of the opinion that the product life cycle actually starts with the gathering of ideas and not only at the introductory phase (see Chapter 18).

FIGURE 8.4   The sequence of and relationship between the different steps in the development process of an imaginary product

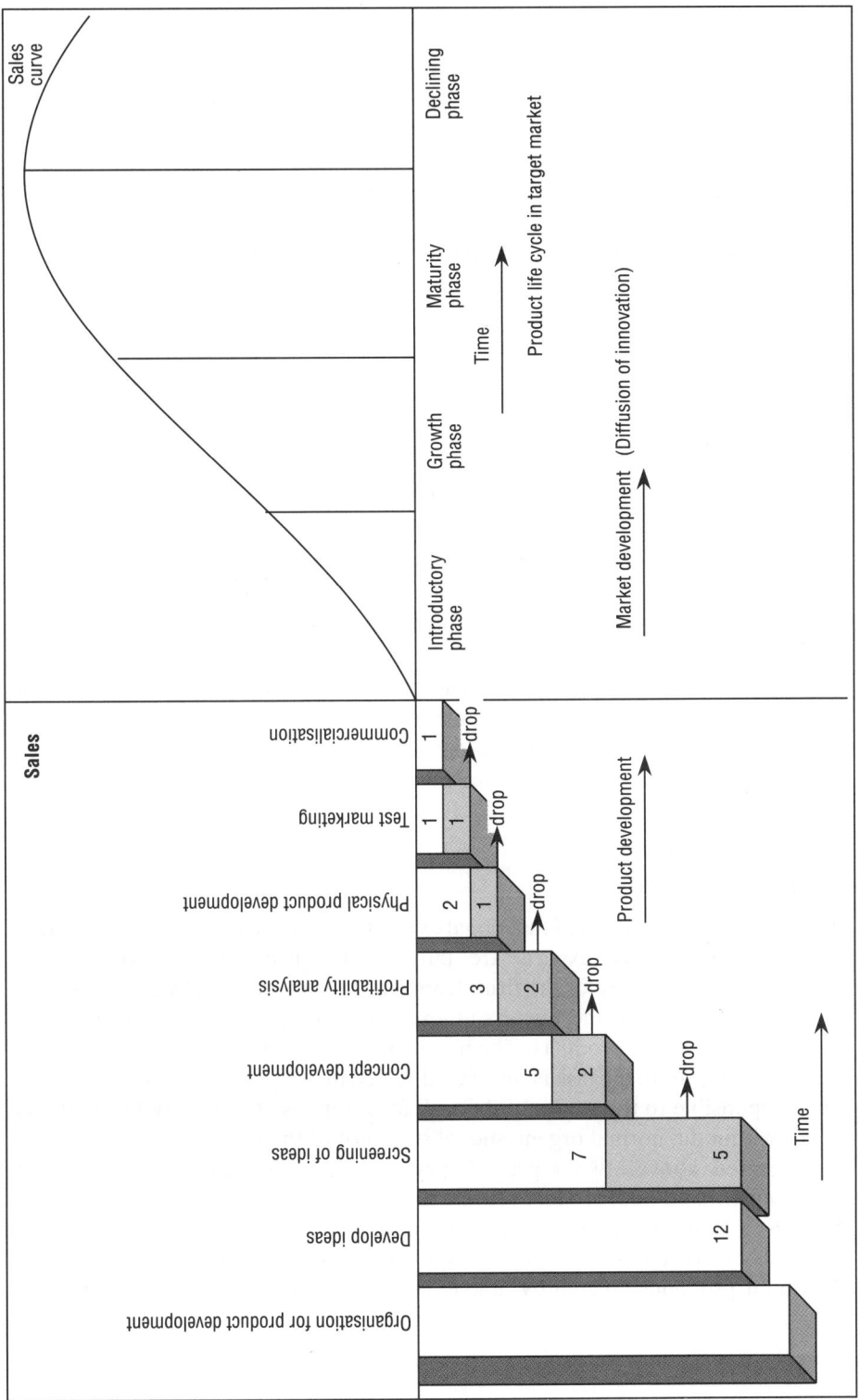

The various steps in the product development process are discussed below.

8.5.2 Organisation for the development of new products

The establishment of an effective organisation (with emphasis on the allocation of authority and responsibility), in which product development can be stimulated, planned, co-ordinated and controlled, is one of the most important prerequisites for successful product development. The *establishment* of an effective organisational structure in which product development can take place is the *first step* in successful product development.

Basically there are *six* different organisational possibilities for dealing with new products: the establishment of a new firm; special task forces consisting of project management and new-product venture teams; new-product divisions; new-product committees; new-product managers; and product managers.

The establishment of a new firm

If the *newness of the market* and the *newness of technology* for a specific new-product decision are relatively extensive and fall mainly outside the scope of present skills, know-how and capabilities of the firm (field of business), a new firm can be established for the development of the new product. New-product opportunities within the context of **product diversification** (see lowest right-hand square of the new-product matrix in Figure 8.1) can, for example, be utilised with the **establishment of a new firm**, particularly if manufacturing under licence and/or takeovers of existing firms are not possible.

The organisational possibilities discussed below, however, can be implemented in the **new** firm as well as the **existing** firm for the development of new products.

Special task forces

Task forces are composed of functional experts inter alia in marketing, production and financing. These experts are purposefully placed outside the normal organisational structure of the firm, from where they are directly responsible to top management for the successful execution of specific tasks such as the development of new products. The members of such a task force participate for different terms until the task is completed. Thus, in executing the task they are not only responsible to the leader of the task force but also to the various divisional heads within the normal organisational structure of the firm.

As stated above, two types of special task force exist, namely project management and new-product venture teams.

Project management is an effective method for the development of new products. Here the know-how and skills of various experts are mustered to surmount problems created by functional barriers. The project team is usually created for a well-defined, one-off task with a specific date of completion. This means that the composition of the team is unique and flexible. The success of the project (development of new products) depends on the abilities of the leader. Since he normally lacks sufficient authority for the effective execution of his task, he has to obtain the co-operation of the various divisional heads through persuasion.

New-product venture teams are normally used when the firm wants to develop new business opportunities falling outside its existing field. Product diversification is one such possibility (see Table 8.1). Like a project management team, a product venture team is composed of well-motivated functional experts: engineers for the product design and the development of prototypes; business economists for the business economic investigation; marketing experts for product concept development and testing, sales forecasting, test marketing, price determination and marketing communication; and financial experts for the cost, profitability and break-even analysis. Unlike project management teams, venture teams do not disband after the completion of each task. Specific product development projects are assigned to them, they possess the necessary authority for planning and full implementation, and the team has a more permanent composition. Organisationally the new-product venture team is usually separated from the rest of the firm and is directly responsible to top management.

New-product divisions

A new-product division is an organisational possibility in relatively large firms. This division is responsible for all the steps in product development — from the gathering of ideas to the ultimate commercialisation of the new product. Product development becomes a permanent and full-time activity in a formally organised new-product division. The head of such a division possesses substantial authority and is normally directly responsible to top management.

New-product committees

New-product committees can be appointed to deal with certain aspects of product development. Such a committee is normally constituted along functional lines with representatives from the marketing, production, financial, administrative and other divisions of the firm. The task of such a committee is usually not the actual development of new products, but rather a review and evaluation of the proposed product development plans. Members of these committees are often too engrossed in the affairs of their own divisions and too far removed from the actual challenges of product development to bear full responsibility for this task, and therefore the task cannot be delegated to them in its entirety. The committee system is time-consuming and expensive — individuals dominate the group, their sense of responsibility weakens and decisions are sometimes the result of a compromise, something which is not actually a solution to the product development challenge.

New-product managers

The use of new-product managers offers the opportunity for specialising in product development. These functionaries normally occupy positions in the lower management levels and thus do not always have the necessary authority or support from top management to deal with all product development challenges properly. Because their interest probably also does not extend beyond the modification and expansion of the present product mix for existing markets, product development opportunities which lie outside this area — but which are still within the capabilities of the firm — are not always noticed.

Product managers

The responsibility for product development is sometimes entrusted to the product managers of existing products. The limitations of this arrangement are obvious. Product managers are normally so engrossed in the management of existing products that they cannot give adequate attention to the development of new products. Besides, they do not always possess the essential knowledge and skills to develop new products successfully.

It is important to note that the ideal organisation for product development which applies to all firms and all circumstances, does not exist. The organisation which suits a particular firm best is inter alia determined by the marketing strategy of the firm, the nature of the new-product development, the size of the firm, the nature of the industry and products, the available technology, the management skills and know-how, the product development orientation, and the financial capability of the firm. Furthermore, it must be remembered that the ultimate responsibility for product development resides in the top management of the firm.

8.5.3 Development of product ideas

Product development starts with the product idea. Within the framework of the macro-, market and micro-environment of the firm, the responsible persons or divisions have to develop as many ideas as possible in a continual, purposeful, unswerving and effective way — ideas from which potentially successful products can eventually be developed. The search for product ideas embraces a combination of inspiration, perspiration and scientific method. It is a decisive step in product development since the ultimate new product cannot improve upon the original idea on which it was based.

The method of developing product ideas

A product idea comes into being as soon as a **perceived need in the market merges with a technological opportunity**. The method of developing product ideas usually starts with the identification of consumer needs which are presently not satisfied by available product items. The way in which the firm is going to satisfy consumer needs will depend on the nature of its internal strengths and weaknesses and its technological capabilities in particular.

Figure 8.5 reveals the relationship between the market and technological dimensions of a product item during the product idea development process.

According to Figure 8.5 the fusion (merger) of the market and technological dimensions is dependent on accurate information. This information is obtained through marketing research and technological research.

FIGURE 8.5   The relationship between the market and technological dimensions of a product item during the product idea development process

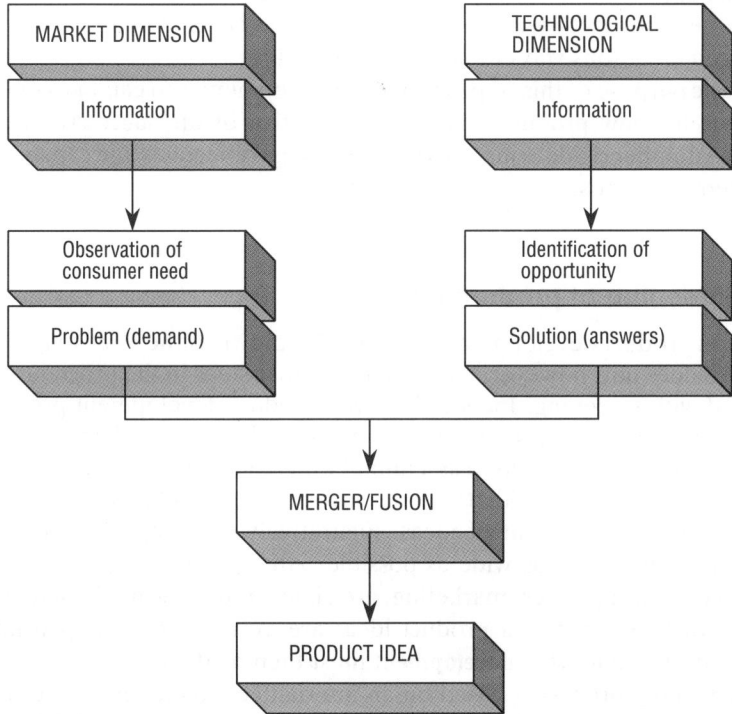

Sources of product ideas

The most important sources of product ideas are consumers, scientists, competitors, the sales force, retailers, top management and other persons employed by the firm.

In accordance with the marketing concept it is logical that the **consumer** and his needs should be the point of departure in the development of new product ideas. The present and latent needs of consumers which may possibly be satisfied by new products can inter alia be identified by means of direct consumer surveys, group discussions, suggestion systems and letters from consumers.

Scientists in a firm's research and development division often discover and develop ideas for new products and packaging, while attempts are also made to improve existing products and even to find new uses for them.

New products brought on to the market by **competitors** often spark off ideas for new products or the improvement of existing ones. Information on new competitive products can be obtained from middlemen, suppliers and the sales force, while the performance of these products in the market place can be determined by means of research services such as the Retail Index of AC Nielsen.

The **sales force and retailers** are particularly important sources of product ideas. Owing to their position in the distribution channel, they have first-hand knowledge of the consumers' unsatisfied needs and complaints and they are often also the first to become aware of new competitive products.

Top management can identify the most important product and market segments in which new product ideas can be searched for. *Other employees* can also be encouraged in various ways to devise product ideas.

The basic purpose of this step in product development is to gather as many ideas as possible for new products. The main objective of the successive steps is to reduce the number of ideas in terms of the business objectives and capabilities and the consumers' needs.

8.5.4 Screening of product ideas

This step in product development is specifically known as the *screening of product ideas*. This does not, however, mean that the other steps in the procedure are not concerned with screening. Indeed the *entire* product development procedure is, after the gathering of product ideas, composed of a number of successive screenings and can be visualised as a funnel with holes in its sides (see Figure 8.6).

From Figure 8.6 it is clear that as many new-product ideas as possible are looked for during the development of ideas. Figuratively speaking, it means that the funnel's *inlet* should be as wide as possible. All the other steps, from the first screening of ideas up to test marketing, are aimed at narrowing the screens in the funnel so that only the best product ideas are eventually developed into final products for which **market development** must then be done.

This screening process is based on an internal economic investigation during which each product idea is evaluated in terms of certain **qualitative business objectives** and the **functional skills and shortcomings** (such as in management, personnel, production, financing and marketing) of the firm.

A variety of methods and checklists have been developed for the first screening of product ideas. One such checklist appears in Table 8.2. The product idea is *first* evaluated in terms of its capacity to satisfy certain qualitative business objectives. *Secondly*, the competence of the firm to manufacture and market the product idea successfully is quantified.

The first column of Table 8.2 contains the factors (divided into qualitative objectives and business capabilities) which have to be considered in the evaluation of the product idea.

FiGURE 8.6   The screening stages in the product development procedure

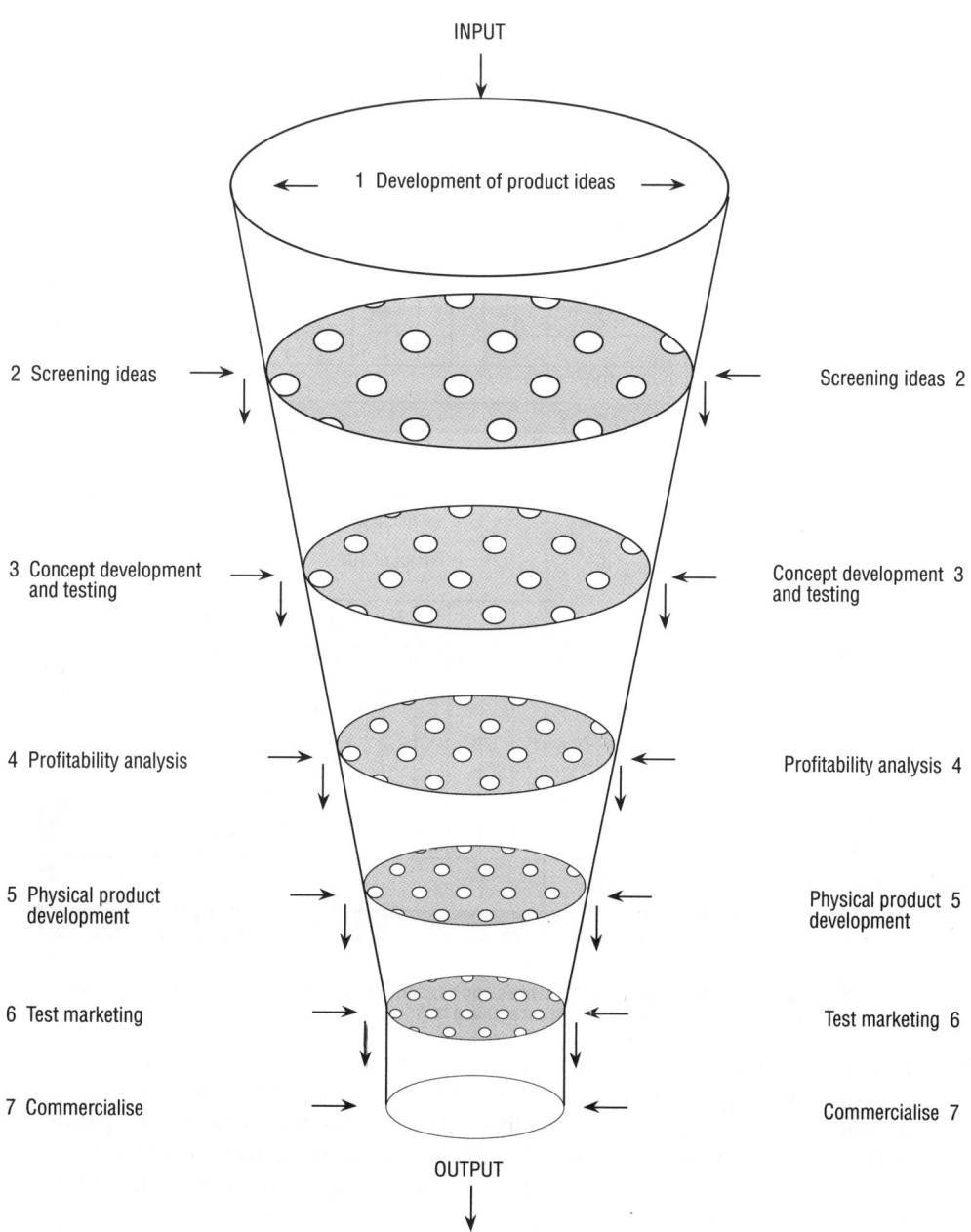

TABLE 8.2 Performance rating of product ideas in terms of qualitative business objectives and capabilities, based on internal economic investigation

Factors to consider in evaluation of product idea	Relative value (Out of 100) (A)	Contribution of product idea to objective (Out of 10) (B)											Performance rating (A) x (B)
		0	1	2	3	4	5	6	7	8	9	10	
Qualitative objectives													
Combat competition	30							X					180
Product differentiation	30											X	300
Sales stability	25								X				175
Business image	15							X					90
Total	100												745

Business capabilities	Relative value (Out of 100) (C)	Levels of business capabilities (Out of 10) (D)											Performance rating (C) x (D)
		0	1	2	3	4	5	6	7	8	9	10	
Management	20									X			160
Marketing	20								X				140
Production	20						X						100
Research and development	15							X					90
Finances	10									X			80
Personnel	5									X			40
Raw material resources	5											X	50
Administration	5											X	50
Total	100												710

Performance rating for business objectives and capabilities: 0 - 400, poor; 401 - 750, fair; and 751 - 1 000, good. **Present minimum acceptance rate:** 700

In the second column management has to allocate values to each factor according to its relative importance. In the third column the possible contribution of the product idea to the attainment of individual business objectives and the capability of the firm to convert the product idea into a successful product, are evaluated by means of a ten-point scale. The last column shows the total rating of the product in terms of the business objectives (745 out of 1 000) and capabilities (710 out of 1 000) of the firm. The present minimum acceptance rate for product ideas in the example is 700 and the idea concerned is thus transferred to the product concept development and testing phase.

8.5.5 Product concept development and testing[4]

Thus far the product idea has been viewed in a formal context only; in other words, the idea has been described and discussed only as something from which a potential physical object can possibly be developed. The marketer, however, is interested in the development of a need-satisfying product and the product idea has to be developed into a total product concept.

8.5.5.1 *The development of a product concept*

The development of a product concept hinges upon distinct **product attributes** and certain *quantitative* and *qualitative* **characteristics of consumers**. *Product concepts are formed by bringing together and integrating unique product attributes and certain consumer needs and actions.*

Product concept = market characteristics + product features.

This is explained by way of the following example. Suppose that a food manufacturer gets the idea of developing a powder that can be added to milk to improve its nutritional value and taste. This is a **formal product idea**. The consumer, however, is interested in a **need-satisfying product**. Therefore, this idea has to be developed into a product concept according to the following (and other) questions asked about the consumer and the product:

- **Who** can use the powder — infants, children, teenagers, adults under 60 years of age or adults over 60 years of age? (market characteristic)

- **What** unique attributes should the product possess — taste, nutritional value, refreshment value, energy-giving properties? (product feature)

- **When** is this drink mainly taken — breakfast, forenoon, lunch, afternoon, dinner, late evening? (market characteristic)

From the answers to these questions several product concepts for the powder can be developed. One is a nutritional instant breakfast drink (product feature) for adults under the age of 60 who do not want to prepare breakfast (market characteristic). Another is a bedtime health drink for adults over 60 years of age, and still another is a tasty drink for children as an afternoon refreshment. The food manufacturer now has to select one or more of these concepts in terms of information available on competition, market size, the far-fetchedness of the product concept, the influence on the current product mix, and so on. For each product concept chosen, product and trade mark positioning subsequently have to be done, especially to identify the **product versions** and **competition**.

8.5.5.2 *Product and trade mark positioning*

The choice of a specific product concept determines the position of the planned product in the market relative to that of competitive products. The competitors of an instant breakfast drink, for example, are bacon and eggs, instant cereals, coffee and sandwiches, cooked cereals and other breakfast foods. The *product concept*, and not the product idea, thus determines the nature of the competition.

- Suppose that the food manufacturer selects the instant breakfast drink as the product concept. A **product positioning map** can be drawn to indicate the position of the instant breakfast drink in relation to that of other breakfast foods, based on the **costs** and **speed** of preparation. This appears in Figure 8.7.

FIGURE 8.7   Product positioning of instant breakfast drink

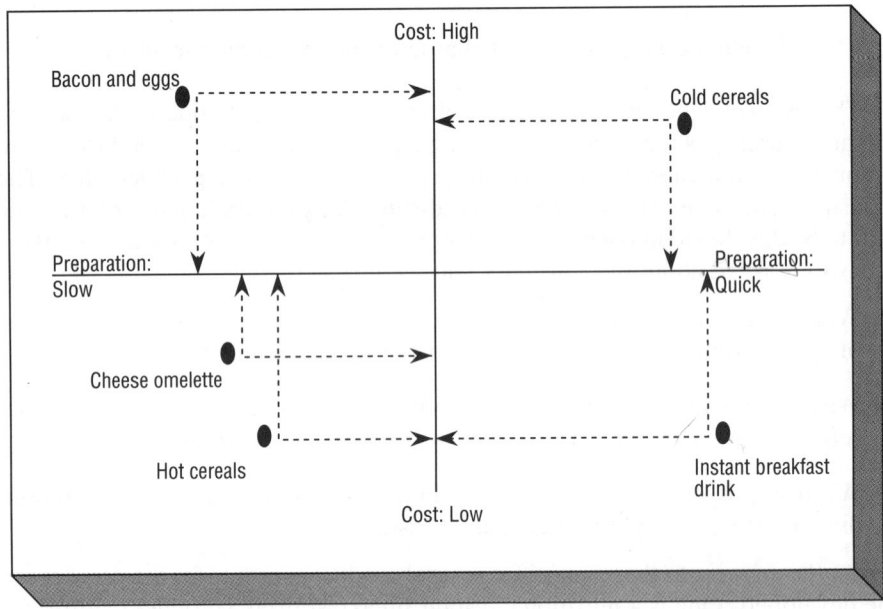

The instant breakfast drink, inexpensive and quick to prepare, thus has a distinctive position in the market — its nearest competitors are cold cereals and its most distant competitors are bacon and eggs.

- A product positioning map can also be useful in identifying the gap for potential new products in the market.
- Assume that there are already other manufacturers of instant breakfast foods. Now the food manufacturer also has to do a *trade mark positioning* for his product concept by means of a **trade mark positioning map**.

Figure 8.8 contains such a map for instant breakfast drinks, based on the assumption that there are three firms, A, B and C, who already have similar products on the market.

FIGURE 8.8   Trade mark positioning map for instant breakfast drinks

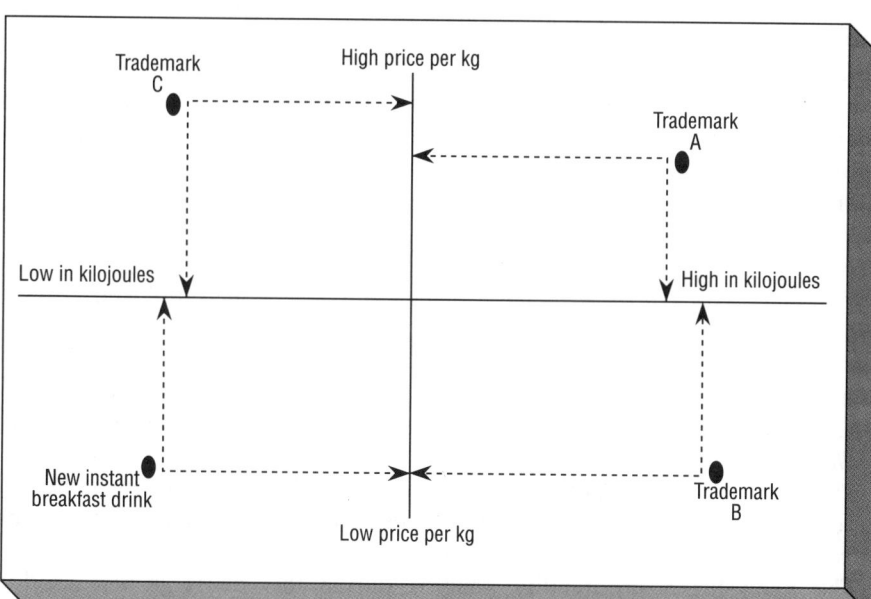

The manufacturer of the planned new instant drink now has to decide where to position his trade mark. One possibility is to develop a new product with a low kilojoule content in the low-price category, which will give the drink a distinctive position in the market.

The above procedure should provide the firm with viable product concepts which nevertheless have also to be *tested in the* **target market**.

8.5.5.3 *Product concept testing*

Product concept testing takes place when the planned product concepts are tested in a group of consumers from the target market in order to obtain their reaction to and opinion of the proposed product. Concept testing should give answers to questions such as: Is the concept clear and easy to understand? Does the planned product have definite advantages over similar products of competitors? Will consumers buy the product? Will the product satisfy a real consumer need? What suggestions have been made for further improvement of the product? This and other information enables the firm to improve the existing product concepts and to select the best ones for further development.

The product concept development has been discussed in terms of a specific example. This approach, however, can be followed for the concept development of any product, service or idea.

8.5.6 Profitability analysis

The most important attributes of, and the target market for the proposed product are known at this stage. However, before the product can be developed physically, a profitability analysis has to be performed; in other words, it is necessary to determine whether the **expected sales**, **costs**, **profit**, **asset employment**, **profitability** and **break-even point** of the product comply with the business objectives and fall within the capabilities of the firm. The following formula for profitability applies in this discussion:

$$\text{Profitability} = \frac{\text{Net profit}}{\text{Sales}} \times \frac{\text{Sales}}{\text{Assets employed}}$$

$$= \text{Net profit margin} \times \text{asset turnover}$$

The break-even point can be defined as that volume of turnover or production where the sales revenue of the new product is exactly equal to total costs and whereby neither a profit nor a loss is made.

The *ultimate objective* of the profitability analysis is to determine whether the expected profitability of the evisaged investment in the new product **at least satisfies the internal rate of return** of the firm.

The need for a profitability analysis during this phase in the product development strategy arises from the increased investment in production factors required by the next phases as well as the attendant increase in the risks attached to possible product failures.

The profitability analysis for new products is an extremely complicated challenge covering a wide field, and it can only be adequately carried out with expert assistance in the fields of market demand and business demand forecasting, and from the financial management of the firm. The magnitudes (such as sales, selling prices, costs, net profit and asset employment) involved in the profitability analysis are variable, mutually dependent and interwoven, and they cannot be considered in isolation. Moreover, the real sizes of these variables are also influenced by a series of manageable and non-controllable factors.

Only a few of these relationships are mentioned here. The expected sales are determined, inter alia, by the planned marketing strategy, timing of the product launch, its competitive position, and the economic climate. Then, in turn, the expected sales exert a direct influence on the total costs per unit (especially because of the existence of fixed costs), the net profit, the break-even point and the profitability. The profitability is further influenced by the extent of the asset employment (mainly via the turnover rate of these assets).

From the preceding it should already be clear that the profitability analysis in product development forms an integral part of the financial planning of the firm.

8.5.7 Physical product development and testing

If the proposed new product satisfies the profitability requirements of the firm, the product item, which thus far has been at most a product concept, has how to be developed into a concrete prototype. This phase in product development is extremely important especially because:

- *It represents the first effort to develop the product into a* **concrete physical object**.
- *This step requires relatively large investment — much* **time and money** *is needed for the eventual development of a technically effective product.*
- *At this stage it can be determined whether the product concept can indeed be developed into a technically effective and* **need-satisfying** *product.*

The success of the physical product development, which is mainly of a technical nature, is inter alia determined by the degree of co-operation between the technological research and development division and the marketing research division of the firm. It is the responsibility of the marketing researcher to see that the physical product development is directed towards the needs of the market, as well as continuously to monitor the external environment for changes. The influence of any change on the new product item must be determined, and the technological research and development division advised regarding the adaptations that must be made.

The **physical product development and testing** are *two activities which must be* **executed simultaneously**. In the following discussion these two activities are separated only for analytical purposes.

Physical product development

Physical product development covers at least *eight* broad aspects on which decisions have to be taken and implemented.

- **Technical research**, *engineer and technical testing related to establishing experimental models and the final product must take place.* The objective here is the development of a trouble-free prototype which can be manufactured economically and will meet with the approval of the proposed target market. A number of variations of the product are often developed before the most suitable alternative is found. This is a wide-ranging task covering divergent challenges regarding the product design, quality, sizes and colour which continuously crop up. This task is often also very complicated since in most cases special equipment for manufacturing the prototypes is not available. Different kinds of research are often used in this phase to improve the efficiency of decision making. Many prototypes are often *built by hand before the most suitable alternative is found*. It is essential that the prototypes should be accurate replicas of the final product in all respects otherwise problems will be experienced with the physical product testing and the production planning and control. This phase is sometimes very expensive and time-consuming, which does not, however, mean that only large and well-moneyed firms can do it effectively.
- *The implementation of dimensional and qualitative standardisation of certain technical attributes of the product have to be considered in order to utilise the advantages of standardisation.*

- *Consumer preference* **testing** *(market testing) has to take place.* This aspect is very closely related to prototype development, and the main objective is to determine which experimental model complies best with the need-satisfying requirements set by consumers for the product.
- *Patents have to be registered and care has to be taken that all legal requirements and regulations regarding the safety, ingredients, pollution, instructions for use and so forth applicable to the new product are fulfilled.*
- *Decisions have to be taken on the extent, duration and other clauses regarding the* **warranties and after-sales service** *(if applicable) of the new product.*
- It is advisable to submit the new product to the Design Institute of the South African Bureau of Standards for **evaluation** *and recording in the index of acceptable products.* Sound design is promoted by this Institute in order to raise the general standard of living aesthetically and functionally and to make South African products more competitive with imported equivalents on the local and export market.
- *A* **trade mark** *for the new product has to be selected.*
- *Decisions have to be made on the* **packaging** *of the new product.*

Because of the importance of trade marks and packaging from a marketing point of view, these two aspects are discussed in Chapter 9.

Physical product testing

Physical product testing is the control step of this phase. It takes place in a *continuous cycle after physical product development — the one cannot be executed effectively without the other. The objective is the early identification and rectification of any defects which can be detrimental to the success of the product item.*

The product item must be evaluated in terms of **technical as well as consumer standards**. This evaluation is done by means of *technical and consumer preference* tests. Great care must, however, be taken when interpreting the results of these tests because the data are gathered under artificial circumstances.

Technical tests

Technical tests deal with the physical features of the product item. It includes inter alia an evaluation of performance, stability and durability under circumstances of extraordinary stress; corrosion receptivity; energy consumption; and shock resistance.

The need for technical tests originates from the manufacturer as well as the consumer. The latter nowadays increasingly looks for **proof** that the **product item has been technically tested**.

The effectiveness of these tests depends on their comprehensiveness and completeness. In some cases laboratory testing is required with real-life usage conditions simulated as closely as possible. The establishment of test laboratories is often very expensive. Firms who cannot afford this, can establish a shared test laboratory, or they can use institutions such as the Council for Scientific and Industrial Research (CSIR) or the South African Bureau of Standards (SABS).

Consumer preference tests

The objective of consumer preference tests is to determine whether the features of the physical product item are capable of delivering consumer advantages in real-life circumstances to the same extent as was determined during the product concept development and testing phase.

A representative sample of the target market (compiled of potentially heavy, medium and light users) is consequently investigated by means of various marketing research techniques. In most cases unidentified samples of the product item are given to respondents to use. Hereafter the researcher asks them certain questions regarding the product item's need-satisfying capabilities.

8.5.8 Test marketing of the new product

Test marketing is the *seventh* step in product development. One should proceed to this phase only after all the previous steps have been finalised and management has had the opportunity to make a detailed study of the results. *Test marketing can be described as the marketing research method whereby the complete product item and its envisaged marketing strategy are, for the first time, subjected to relatively small but representative test areas or markets under normal competitive circumstances.* It is a method by which the risks of possibly wrong decisions (owing to the lack of reliable information) can be reduced.

Test marketing should never be a matter of routine in the firm. It is an extraordinarily expensive and time-consuming method of gathering information on the consumer's reaction to the new product item. Consequently, it should be used only as a last resort, when the risk of a potential financial loss attached to the failure of the new product item or its marketing strategy is bigger than the direct and indirect costs of executing test marketing.[5] Not all industries are in a position to use test marketing effectively. The size of the investment involved in the manufacturing of the new product item should determine whether it is necessary or not.

In test marketing there are at least five broad decisions requiring the serious attention of marketing management.

- It has to be decided whether test marketing is **necessary** or not. This decision is mainly determined by the nature and extent of the risks and the size of investment involved in the manufacturing and marketing of the new product. Test marketing will probably be unnecessary where the investment for manufacturing one unit is more or less the same as that for manufacturing many units, as with aeroplanes and motor cars. The mass marketing of new products also requires substantial expenditures (such as advertising expenditure and the remuneration of the sales force), while risks such as damaging the image of the firm and possible ineffective investment in production facilities are always present. If these important expenditures and risks can be postponed through test marketing until a more reliable estimate of the marketing result can be made, based on actual experience, test marketing is necessary.

- Management has to have clarity on the **objectives** of test marketing. Test marketing is normally conducted to gain more and better knowledge of expected sales, to test alternative marketing strategies, to locate possible product defects which may have slipped through during physical development, and to obtain a better idea of the reaction of the different market segments.

- It has also to be decided **by whom** the test marketing will be undertaken. This depends on the nature of the product, the size of the firm, and the characteristics of the consumer, and the scope and costs of test marketing. The firm itself can conduct it or the services of specialised institutions, such as marketing research and advertising practitioners, can be used.

- *Marketing management has to know* **what procedure** *and method to follow in test marketing, how many places/cities/towns/consumers will be involved, and what the duration of the test marketing will be.* Decisions on this are inter alia determined by the availability of skills to conduct test marketing, the number of marketing strategies to be tested, the geographical distribution and heterogeneity of the market, the average period between repetitive sales, the competitive position, and the costs attached to test marketing.

- *When the test marketing results are available, marketing management has to take decisions on the* **mass production and mass marketing** *of the new product.* Table 8.3 contains a summary of the alternative actions that can possibly be taken based on these results.

TABLE 8.3   Alternative actions based on test marketing results

TRIAL RATE	REPURCHASE RATE	ACTION
High	High	Commercialise
High	Low	Redesign product or drop it
Low	High	Improve advertising and/or distribution
Low	Low	Drop the product

Source: Kotler, P. 1976. *Marketing Management: Analysis, Planning and Control.* 3rd edition. London: Prentice-Hall International, p 222.

8.5.9 The commercialisation of the new product

This step embraces the **introduction** of the new product to the market. All weaknesses and deficiencies in the product and the planned marketing strategy which have been revealed during test marketing now have to be rectified. New equipment and manufacturing facilities for mass production have to be procured. Sales people must be appointed and/or trained if a sales force is to be used in marketing the product. The proper distribution channels have to be selected and the physical distribution organised, the price decisions have to be finalised and, if necessary, a comprehensive advertising campaign has to be launched in order to introduce the new product. This step, then, brings us to the first phase of the life cycle of the product (see Chapter 18).

8.5.10 The role of research in product development

Research as such has not been identified as a separate step in the product development process. This does not mean, however, that research has no role to play here. On the contrary, the entire process of product development (the gathering of product ideas, the screening of these ideas, product concept development and testing, profitability analysis, physical product development, test marketing and commercialisation) is structured on research covering a wide field and in which market and marketing research, financial research and technical research play a decisive role. Research thus covers the entire product development process. Whenever management has to take decisions but lacks adequate information, this management tool should be used.

8.6 PRODUCT DEVELOPMENT AND THE OTHER FUNCTIONS OF THE ENTERPRISE

The development and marketing of products are matters which affect the enterprise in its entirety and each function in particular.

- *First*, the development and manufacturing of new products present special **technical challenges** for the production management. Technical research and development; the construction, lay-out and organisation of the plant; the selection and use of machines, equipment and tools and the selection of production processes; production planning and control; quality control of the product; work study to discover the most effective methods, especially in the use of human labour; and stocking — all are important challenges which have to be dealt with in the development and manufacturing of new products.

- In the *second place* product decisions have a substantial influence on the **financial management** of the firm. For this reason financial analysis and control, the measurement and evaluation of the financial performance, the evaluation of the enterprise, the financial planning, and the need for capital by the firm are inseparable from the products which are developed, manufactured and marketed.

- *Thirdly*, product decisions directly affect the **personnel management** of the enterprise. The recruiting, selecting, training, remuneration, motivation, control and promotion of a large part of the work force are directly connected with the development, manufacturing and marketing of the product mix of the firm.

- *Fourthly*, product decisions also influence the **information management** of the enterprise. Aspects of bookkeeping (such as the recording and documentation of purchases and sales), statistics (such as the sales analysis), and cost accounting and control naturally hinge upon the product mix which the firm manufactures and markets.
- The **purchasing management** of the firm is affected in a special way by product development and other product decisions. The task of the purchasing manager is inter alia to provide and keep the firm supplied with the right machinery, raw materials and services, at the right time, in the right place and the right quantities. He must also see to it that this equipment and materials are available for the development and manufacturing of products.
- *Lastly*, information on the product mix which the firm manufactures and markets can be effectively used particularly by the **public relations officer** in his communication with the public (such as the labour market, financial institutions, shareholders, suppliers, markets and the government) whose judgement is important for the firm in reaching its objectives.

8.7 THE DIFFUSION OF INNOVATION

8.7.1 The nature of diffusion of innovation

The diffusion of innovation (market development process) starts where the enterprise's innovation process (product development process) ends. *It deals with the ways in which potential consumers become aware of, test and eventually accept or reject a new product item.*

In the following discussion of the diffusion of innovation, attention is given to four closely related aspects:

- The **diffusion process** on **macro level** — a social phenomenon which describes the distribution of a new product item from its source up to the broad consumer public.
- The **acceptance process** on **micro level** — a psychological phenomenon which describes the stages through which the consumer moves when she decides on buying the new product item.
- The **profile** of the innovators — those consumers who will be the first to buy the new-product item.
- The **relationship** between the diffusion and acceptance process and the product life cycle.

8.7.2 The diffusion process on macro level

Generally, firms endeavour to obtain the maximum diffusion of new product items, ie the distribution of the product item from its source to the broad consumer public in the shortest time. *This requires that the new product item, its price, distribution and marketing communication strategy must be adapted to the characteristics of the target market as well as those of the individual consumer.*

The economic conditions in the country, the interest of the target market in the product item, and the nature of the socio-economic group to which the target market belongs, influence the *rate of diffusion*.

The diffusion process consists of the following four elements:

- The innovation or **new product item**;
- which is communicated through certain **channels**;
- during a specific **course of time**;
- amongst members of a specific social system or **target market**.

The new product item

*The **nature** of the new product item influences the rate of diffusion.* The nature of the new product item in its turn revolves round the question of when a new product item is really new. This question can lead to a detailed classification of different degrees of newness. The newness of the new product item must be described in terms of the *consumer's* viewpoint of it. The consumer's vision of the newness of a product item and the rate at which she is going to adopt it are influenced by the features of the product item itself.

The rate of diffusion correlates *positively* inter alia with:

- The relative benefit offered by the product item.
- The degree to which it is reconcilable with the consumer's needs.
- The ability to communicate about it.
- The divisibility of the product item — in other words to use it in small quantities.

The rate of diffusion, however, correlates *negatively* with the complexity of the product item, ie the more complicated the product item is, the slower the target market will accept it.

Communication channels

*The way in which individual consumers **perceive** the product item determines whether it is a new product to them or not.* There is, however, a substantial difference between the consumer's view of the new product item and its eventual success in the market place.

The consumer normally first goes through a learning and decision making process before she buys. Consequently, rapid buying does not take place immediately after the launching of a new product, because the consumer needs time to gather information on the new product item.

The rate of diffusion depends to a large extent on the communication between the marketer and consumer as well as the communication between the consumers mutually (word-of-mouth communication). Thus it is necessary to give attention to the transfer of information regarding the new product item through the different communication channels. Furthermore, the *influence and impact* of the message and channel of communication on the acceptance or rejection of the new product item by the consumers should be considered.

There are basically two types of communication channels by which information can be transferred, namely **impersonal** communication channels which are controllable by the firm, and **personal** communication channels which are to a large extent not controllable. Regarding the transfer of information in general, it is probably true that most information diffused about the firm's products is uncontrollable by the firm.

Impersonal communication channels include mass communication media, such as newspapers, magazines, radio, television and the cinema. The most important feature of these channels is that they all endeavour to convince consumers to buy the product item by means of 'standardised' messages. Thus, these messages are not necessarily directed towards the needs of a specific individual. Repetition is consequently necessary to create sufficient interest at consumer level to move the consumer to buying the product.

Consumers do not rely only on impersonal communication messages and channels, but also on **personal (word-of-mouth) communication channels**. The latter's influence in most cases is stronger than that of impersonal communication channels because the credibility of the informers is often higher. As reference groups or persons, informers normally greatly influence the expectations and opinions of the consumer.

The importance of personal communication channels varies according to the risks experienced by the consumer during the buying process. Factors such as a high price, greater conspicuousness, complexity, and the lack of a yardstick for objective evaluation tend to increase these risks.

Each type of communication channel has a specific role to play during the transfer of information. They are therefore complementary and not substitutionary. Impersonal communication channels transfer information from the marketer to the target market and personal communication channels transfer information between consumers and the target market. The communication process is discussed in greater detail in Chapter 12.

The course of time

The course of time is probably the most important element in the diffusion process because it strongly emphasises the dynamic nature of this process. It affects the study of the diffusion process in three unique and interdependent ways, namely through the **buying time**, the identification of the different **groups of adopters**, and the **acceptance rate**.

Buying time

The buying time refers to the time that expires between the consumer's *first awareness of the new product item and the moment she decides to buy it or not to buy it.* The shorter the buying time, the more rapid the diffusion process and vice versa.

Groups of adopters

The rates of reaction of individuals to new ideas are known as their innovation propensity or new product propensity.

Innovation propensity thus *refers to the extent to which a specific individual adopts new ideas quicker or slower than the other members in his social group or class.*

A high innovation propensity means that the specific individual adopts new ideas relatively rapidly whilst a low innovation propensity indicates a relatively slow adoption of new ideas. Individuals in a particular target market can be classified in different groups of adopters according to their innovation propensities.

Figure 8.9 shows the groups of adopters of new product items, classified according to the duration of the diffusion process.

FIGURE 8.9   Groups of adopters of new products classified according to the duration of diffusion process

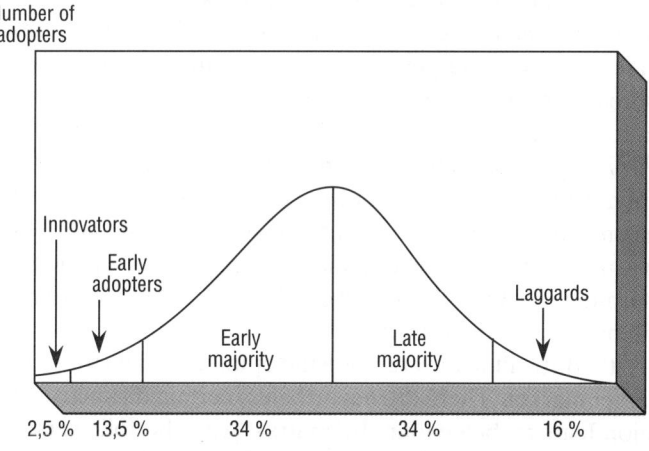

Source: Taken from Robertson, TS. 1971. *Innovative Behavior and Communication.* New York: Holt, Rinehart & Winston, p 31.

Figure 8.9 shows that the number of adopters of new products, when the graph is plotted over time, can be divided into a fairly normal distribution. Only a few people are innovators and the number of adopters increases rapidly as the benefits of the new product become known. Because of the normal distribution of the number of adopters, the innovators are defined as the first 2,5 per cent of consumers who adopt the product; early adopters as the following 13,5 per cent; the early majority as the next 34 per cent; the late majority as the 34 per cent following them; and the last 16 per cent as the laggards. Each of the abovementioned groups reveals unique characteristics in terms of certain independent variables such as age, social class, personality and communication behaviour.

The adoption rate

The adoption rate refers to the period taken for a new product item to be accepted by members of a specific target market. The adoption rate of a new product relates positively *inter alia* to the amount of money spent by the consumer on the item, the type of industry, the certainty or uncertainty regarding the future of the industry, and the new product item's ability to achieve savings for the consumer.

The target market

The diffusion of new product items usually takes place within a specific *target market*. The members of such a target market create the climate in which the marketer has to achieve consumer acceptance for his new product item.

The degree of integration and interaction between the members of a target market has a large influence on the adoption rate of the new product item. The marketer can influence this rate by adapting the features of the product item as effectively as possible to the needs and characteristics of the target market.

Certain individual consumers (opinion leaders) enjoy status positions and also play specific roles in each target market. Information on the new product item normally spreads from the source of new ideas through relevant, impersonal communication channels *to the opinion leaders, who in their turn inform their followers through* **personal communication** *channels about the product concerned*. These opinion leaders are persons in the target market to which others look for information and advice. The success of the new product item in the market place depends to a great extent on the acceptance thereof by the opinion leaders. They largely determine whether the followers (who are the majority in the target market) will buy the product or not.

However, it is difficult to differentiate the opinion leaders from the followers in a specific target market. There are nevertheless certain distinctive characteristics of the opinion leaders' behaviour. In contrast with the followers, they are to a greater extent exposed to and receptive to impersonal communication media. Furthermore, based on relatively limited knowledge, they are prepared to take risks when buying new product items. *The adoption of new product items is a function of the consumer's perceived risks, and the perceived risks in their turn are a function of the consumer's knowledge regarding the need-satisfying attributes of the product item.*

The amount of knowledge present in the product item's target market at a specific moment is a function of the nature and scope of communication that took place. Figure 8.10 shows the effect of personal and impersonal communication on the knowledge of the target market and the subsequent acceptance of the new product item, measured in terms of the cumulative percentage of consumers in the target market over a specific period. Figure 8.10 reveals that, as the amount of knowledge increases in the target market, the acceptance of the product item also increases.

FIGURE 8.10   The effect of personal and impersonal communication on the knowledge of the target market

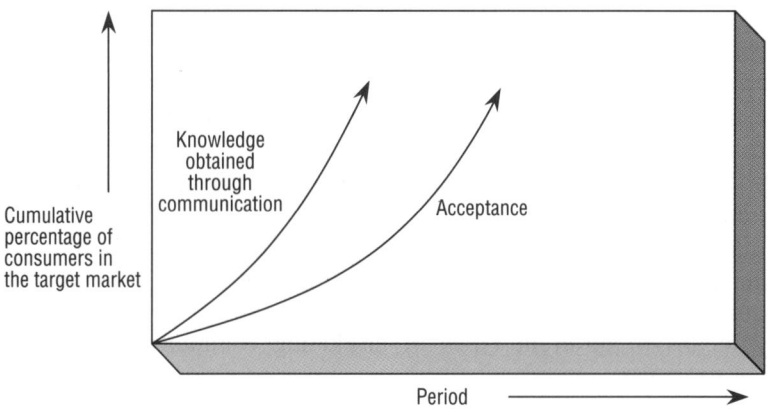

Source: Midgley, DF. 1977. *Innovation and New Product Marketing*. London: Croom Helm, p 37, Figure 2.7 (own caption).

8.7.3 The adoption process on micro level

The adoption process strongly relies on the individual consumer, because it is she who eventually has to decide whether the **adoption** of the new product item is the right decision or not. The diffusion process takes place in the target market, but the adoption process takes place in the mind of the individual. This process can be described as the psychological phases through which the consumer moves eventually to accept or reject the new product item. The phases in the adoption process are discussed next.

8.7.3.1 *Phases in the adoption process*

In the adoption of new products the potential consumer goes through *several* phases, beginning with the moment she first becomes aware of the product until she eventually decides to buy it regularly or to reject it.

These phases in the adoption process are classified as follows:

- **Awareness.** The person hears about the new product but has no information about it.
- **Interest.** The person starts seeking information about the product.
- **Evaluation.** The person evaluates the information and considers the utilities of the product.
- **Testing.** The person makes a trial purchase to determine the product item's utilities.
- **Adoption.** If the trial purchase proves to be successful the consumer decides to use the product regularly.

The value of the adoption process lies in the fact that it enables the marketer thoroughly to consider the potential consumers' adoption of the product item beforehand. It furnishes a framework whereby it can be determined what type of information sources are regarded as the most important by consumers during specific phases.

Advertising probably has the greatest impact during the early phases of awareness, interest and evaluation. Opposite to this, **personal influence** (word-of-mouth communication) is the most important during the trial purchase and adoption phases, where the consumer requires objective information for evaluation purposes.

The adoption process as a management tool is of special importance if marketing management knows which phase the potential consumers are in. Efforts can then be made to move them to the ultimate adoption of the product item by means of different types of marketing communication and other marketing strategies.

FIGURE 8.11 The phases in the adoption process

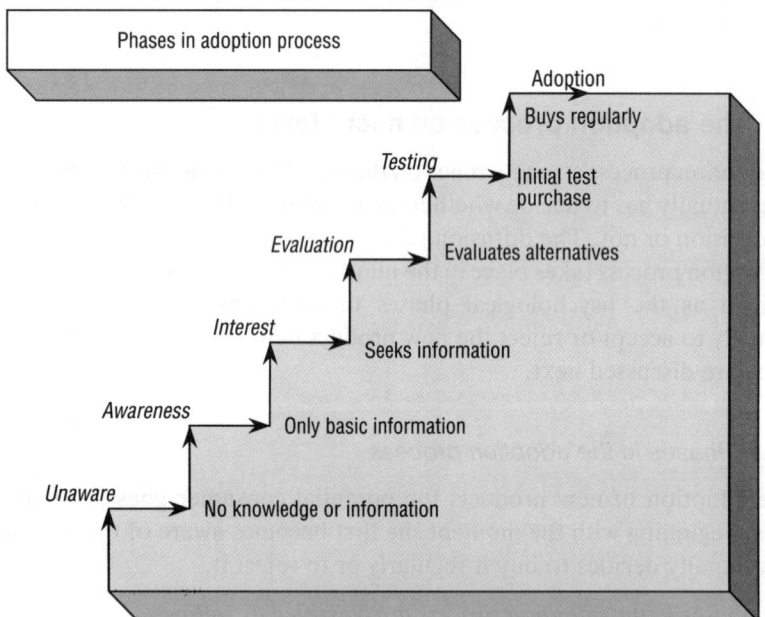

Source: Adapted from McDaniel, C and Darden, WR 1987. *Marketing*. Boston: Allyn & Bacon Inc.

8.7.4 The innovators as a third aspect of the diffusion of innovation

One of the most important tasks of the marketer during the introduction of the new product item is to *determine as accurately as possible the profile of the innovators*. Ideally, innovators should have the following four characteristics:

- They must be the first adopters of the new product item.
- They must be potential heavy users.

- They must be opinion leaders.
- They must be reached relatively inexpensively.

The identification of innovators is, however, difficult. To date a general personality profile for all innovators has not been determined because individuals are inclined to be innovators of certain product types and laggards for others.

In terms of specific product types it has been found that the profile of the innovators generally speaking drastically differs from that of the late majority.

A comparison between the profiles of innovators and early adopters and that of late adopters is made in Table 8.4.

TABLE 8.4 A comparison between the characteristics of the innovators and early adopters and those of the late adopters

CHARACTERISTICS	INNOVATORS AND EARLY ADOPTERS	LATE ADOPTERS
Interest in the product type	More	Less
Opinion leadership	More	Less
Personality:		
Dogmatism	Unprejudiced	Prejudiced
Social character	Introvert	Extrovert
Mobility in social groups	Wider	Narrower
Adventurous	More	Less
Perceived risk	Less	More
Buying and consumption		
characteristics		
Brand loyalty	Less	More
Transaction orientation	More	Less
Usage rate	More	Less
Media habits		
Exposure to periodicals	More	Less
Special interest periodicals	More	Less
Television	Less	More
Social characteristics		
Social integration	More	Less
Social ambitions	More	Less
Group membership	More	Less
Demographic characteristics		
Age	Younger	Older
Income	More	Less
Education	More	Less
Occupational status	Higher	Lower

Source: Taken from Schiffman, LG & Kanuk, LL. 1978. *Consumer Behavior*. Englewood Cliffs, New Jersey: Prentice-Hall Inc, p 425, Table 14-5 (partly own caption).

Table 8.4 shows that the innovators and early adopters are probably dynamic, independent, social, higher salaried and better educated persons. Furthermore, they are potentially heavy users and the opinion leaders which can be reached relatively inexpensively through the mass communication media.

Since the innovators are normally the opinion leaders from whom other potential consumers seek advice, their attitudes towards new products are often spread rapidly by means of word-of-mouth communication.

The timeous identification of the potential innovators (first and early adopters) of a new product item really holds great opportunities for the marketer. During the creation of the advertising message, attention should therefore be given to ways in which innovators can be supported to formulate their own oral messages in such a way that they can be transferred easily and clearly to their followers. As a prerequisite the product item must naturally be developed in such a way and even be unique so that people will readily talk about it.

FIGURE 8.12 The relationship between the cumulative and non-cumulative diffusion curves and the product life cycle curve

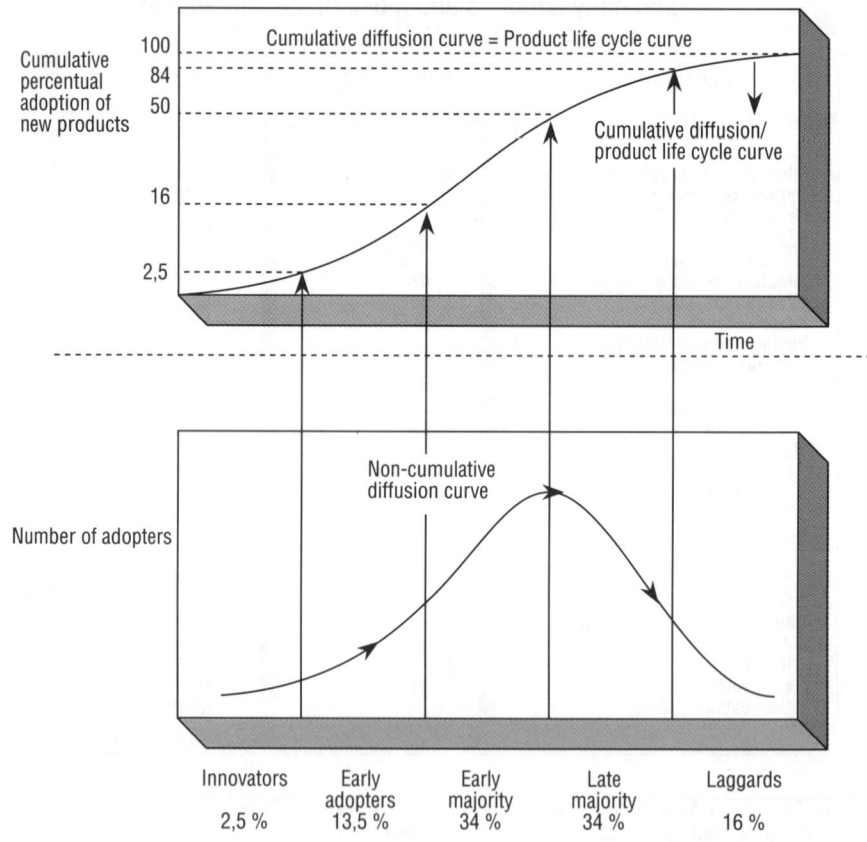

Source: Partly adapted from Howard, JA. 1977. *Consumer Behavior: Application of Theory.* New York: McGraw-Hill, p 198 (own caption).

8.7.5 The relationship between the diffusion of innovation and the product life cycle

The relationship between the diffusion of innovation and the product life cycle is obvious. *The diffusion process indicates the* **adoption of the new product item by the target market** *and can be represented by a cumulative diffusion curve and a non-cumulative diffusion curve.* The **non-cumulative diffusion curve** depicts the different adopters individually over time. The **cumulative diffusion curve** depicts the different adopters *added together* over time.

The product life cycle is the result of this cumulative adoption as it realises in the sales of the product item over time and can be represented by a *product life cycle curve.* The *relationship* between the diffusion curve and the product life cycle curve is illustrated in Figure 8.12.

Figure 8.12 shows that the cumulative diffusion curve (product adoption cycle) has the same shape as the traditional product life cycle and it is indeed the consumer with her buying behaviour who eventually is responsible for the product life cycle (see Chapter 18 for a further discussion of the product life cycle).

8.8 SUMMARY

Various aspects of product development are discussed in this chapter. The importance of new products to the firm, some characteristics of product development, the new-product matrix, and the steps in product development, consisting of organisation for product development, development of product ideas, screening of product ideas, concept development and testing, profitability analysis, physical product development, test marketing and commercialisation, are reviewed. Furthermore, product development and the other functions of the firm and the place of research in product development are also briefly explained. Owing to its importance, certain aspects of the diffusion of innovation are emphasised.

REFERENCES

1. Rupert, AE. 1967. *Leaders on Leadership.* Private publication, p 3.
2. Cronjé, GJ de J et al (eds). 1990. *Introduction to Management.* 2nd edition. Johannesburg: Southern Book Publishers, p 54.
3. Dekker, HJ. 1976. *Aspekte by die Bemarking van Kapitaaltoerusting deur Vervaardigers van Nywerheids-, Mynbou- en Konstruksiemasjinerie in die Republiek van Suid-Afrika, 1974.* Unpublished DCom thesis. Pretoria: University of Pretoria, p 133.
4. This section is partly based on Kotler, P. 1976. *Marketing Management: Analysis, Planning and Control.* 3rd edition. London: Prentice-Hall International, pp 207–9.
5. For a comprehensive discussion of the different marketing research techniques see, inter alia, Midgley, DF. 1977. *Innovation and New Product Marketing.* London: Croom Helm, pp 232–4; Pessemier, EA. 1977. *Product Management, Strategy and Organization.* Canada: John Wiley & Sons, pp 285–9.

ASSIGNMENTS

1. 'A useful aid for the identification of possible alternative products with which the firm can fill its profit gap is the new-product matrix.'

   Use a **new-product matrix** to identify alternative new-product decisions for the following types of South African businesses/institutions:

   - A farm
   - A steel processor
   - A manufacturer of aluminium products
   - A manufacturer of leather products
   - A pharmacy
   - A garage
   - A holiday resort
   - The Kruger National Park
   - A church
   - A political party

2. 'The development of a product concept hinges upon distinct **product attributes** and certain **quantitative** and **qualitative characteristics of consumers.** Product concepts are formed by bringing together and integrating unique product attributes and certain consumer needs and actions.'

   In view of this objective, design your own **practical** case where you develop and test a product concept for any new consumer product. (You are not, however, allowed to use breakfast cereals as a product.)

3. 'Physical product development covers at least eight broad aspects on which decisions have to be taken and implemented.'

   Explain step by step how you will deal with these eight broad aspects in the physical development of an electrically operated toothbrush.

4. 'The diffusion of innovation deals with the ways in which potential consumers become aware of, test and eventually accept or reject a new product item.'

   Take any **new product item** of your choice and describe how the process of the **diffusion of innovation** could possibly take place.

   Be very specific and organise your description under the following headings:

   - The diffusion process on macro level
   - The adoption process on micro level
   - The innovator's role in the diffusion of innovation

CHAPTER 9

TRADE MARK AND PACKAGING DECISIONS

9.1 INTRODUCTION

Trade mark and packaging decisions are particularly important product decisions. From time to time manufacturers and even middlemen want to establish a distinct identity for their products and contradistinguish them from those of competitors with a view to product differentiation. They can do this by using inter alia trade marks, symbols, distinctive shapes (as with motor cars) and packaging.

In this chapter emphasis is placed *first* on **trade mark decisions**. *Trade mark decisions are those product decisions which specifically deal with the identification and distinction of product items and product lines in the product mix.* Naturally, trade mark decisions are not isolated in this regard, but are interwoven with **packaging decisions** and **marketing communication decisions** of the firm. For this reason packaging decisions are discussed secondly. Packaging is especially important in the protection, storing and physical handling of products while it is also useful in certain marketing considerations such as product differentiation, consumer convenience and marketing communication. Marketing communication decisions per se are discussed in Chapters 12–15.

ORGANISATION OF THE CHAPTER

Trade marks: Terms used in connection with trade marks, the importance of trade marks, different phases of trade mark acquaintance and acceptance, trade mark decisions concerning manufacturer or dealer trade marks and family or individual trade marks (brands).

The selection of a trade name for the product.

> **Packaging:** A description of packaging, the tasks of packaging, the importance and objectives of packaging, some packaging decisions concerning the packaging of the product mix, re-usable packaging or not, multiple packaging or not, kaleidoscopic packaging or not, factors to consider in packaging decisions, labelling, bar coding and electronic scanning.

9.2 TRADE MARKS

9.2.1 Concepts used in connection with trade marks

The Trade Marks Act, Act 62 of 1963 (as amended by the Trade Marks Amendment Act, Act 46 of 1971) distinguishes between a **mark** and a **trade mark**.

This Act defines a **mark** as '. . . *a device, brand, heading, label, ticket, name, signature, word, letter, numeral or any combination thereof or a container for goods*'.

Example of a mark

A **trade mark** (brand) is '. . . *a mark used or proposed to be used in relation to goods or services for the purposes of:*

● *indicating a connection in the course of trade between the goods or services and some person having the right, either as proprietor or as a registered user, to use the mark, whether with or without any indication of the identity of that person; and*

● *distinguishing the goods or services in relation to which the mark is used or proposed to be used, from the same kind of goods or services connected in the course of trade with any other person*'.

Examples of trade marks

Thus a mark is the broad general concept while a trade mark is basically a mark which is allocated to the goods which are manufactured and marketed by a specific firm in order to distinguish them from similar competitive products.

A **device** is '. . . *any visual representation or illustration capable of being reproduced upon a surface, whether by printing, embossing, or by any other means*'.

A **trade name** has two meanings. *First*, it indicates the name under which a person or firm trades, and, *secondly*, it is the name under which a product is brought into trade. Vaseline is a *trade name*. Thus, in its second meaning the trade name refers to the *word(s)* in the *trade mark*.

Examples of trade names

First meaning

Second meaning

A **trade character** *is a mark that has been personified.*

Examples of trade characters

Trade marking (branding) is the process which a firm follows in the research, development and implementation of its trade marks.

Trade marks can be registered in terms of Act 62 of 1963 (as amended). Such registration protects the exclusive right to the use of a particular trade mark for a period of ten years. This protection can be extended from time to time but as soon as a trade mark has not been used for five years, a request can be made that it be struck from the register. Under certain circumstances South African law also recognises the existence of trade marks which originate through use and not through registration. When trade marks are accepted by the public as trade marks because of prolonged use and custom, they enjoy a certain measure of protection under common law.

9.2.2 The importance of trade marks

9.2.2.1 *Importance to consumers*

Trade marks can have the following advantages for consumers:

- They facilitate the identification of products at the point of purchase.
- They ensure consumers of a uniform quality standard which they can always rely on.
- They offer a measure of protection to consumers because they usually identify the manufacturer/supplier.
- Since the product is known, spare parts can be obtained with relatively greater ease.
- They give consumers greater freedom of choice in where to buy their products — strictly speaking, Dunlop tyres are Dunlop tyres regardless of where one buys them.
- They lead to improved products due to competition and continual product differentiation.
- They expedite the purchasing transaction because consumers are familiar with the trade marks.
- They can serve as a warning against repetitive purchases if the first purchase and use of a product did not comply with the requirements for need-satisfaction.

9.2.2.2 *Importance to marketers*

Trade marks can be used by manufacturers and middlemen in especially *four* ways to reach certain marketing objectives.

The trade mark often forms the **corner-stone** of the advertising and merchandising decisions. The product image is structured around the trade mark and to many consumers the trade mark can become more important than the name of the manufacturer. Especially products which are marketed on a self-service basis rely heavily on trade mark appeal. Products, and particularly the trade marks, have to be pre-sold through advertising so that the consumer will recognise and select them from among all the competitive products on the shelves of the retailers.

Trade marks can help the manufacturer or middleman to influence his **market share**. All successful sales promotional efforts regarding a specific trade mark benefit the owners of that trade mark while deliberate product substitution, against the will of the consumer or without his being aware of it, is basically impossible with trade marked products.

Trade marks **hamper price comparisons** between competitive products because products are no longer equal in all respects. Therefore trade marks facilitate the use of non-price competitve strategies, such as product differentiation, although, of course, price competition can never be eliminated completely.

Trade marks **facilitate product diversification** in certain respects. A new product item can, for example, be added with relatively greater ease to a known product line as compared with one which has no trade marks. Trading-up and trading-down especially come to mind in this regard.

9.2.3 The different phases in trade mark acquaintance and acceptance[1]

The acquaintance with and acceptance of a specific trade mark can differ considerably from consumer to consumer. In this way a person can be **unaware** of a specific trade mark, or can **recognise** it; find it **unacceptable**, or **acceptable** or **preferable**; or can even **insist** on it. From this knowledge and attitude of the consumer towards the specific trade mark, five phases in trade mark (brand) acquaintance and acceptance can be derived. These phases are indicated in Figure 9.1.

FIGURE 9.1   Phases in trade mark (brand) acquaintance and acceptance

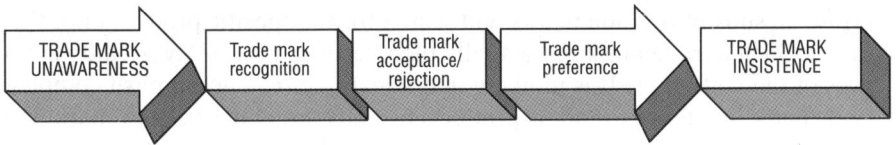

Source: Adapted from Schoell, WF. 1985. *Marketing: Contemporary Concepts and Practices*. Boston: Allyn & Bacon Inc, p 307. The explanation of Figure 9.1 is also based on this source.

Some explanatory remarks on Figure 9.1 are necessary:

- **Trade mark unawareness** and **insistence** represent the extreme limits or poles within which a person's acquaintance with and acceptance of a trade mark can vary.

- **Trade mark unawareness** means that the consumer views a specific product as being the same as other similar products because she does not even recognise the trade mark. Some examples are probably brooms, pins, eggs, tomatoes and hair brushes.

- **Trade mark recognition** exists as soon as the consumers have seen the trade mark and/or have heard about it, understand it and remember it. They can *identify* it amongst other similar products. *Trade mark recognition* is possibly the first phase in *trade mark acceptance or rejection*. Unknown new products are often introduced through free samples and discount coupons to move the product from the *unknown* to the *known* category. Trade mark recognition increases the probability of repetitive purchases should the consumer be satisfied with the first trial. If not, she rejects the product.

- **Trade mark rejection** literally means that the consumers reject the product and find it unacceptable. Even if they recognise the product they will still not buy it — probably because of the poor image of the trade mark. Yet the marketer can nevertheless attempt to alter this attitude of consumers by changing the product and/or the other elements of the marketing strategy, such as marketing communication and prices. The product can possibly be launched in another target market. Efforts to rectify a poor product image can, however, be difficult, expensive and time-consuming.

- **Trade mark acceptance** rules as soon as consumers consider a specific trade mark as one alternative and find it acceptable amongst similar products. The trade mark complies at least with the minimum expectations desired of the product.

- **Trade mark preference** follows trade mark acceptance. Based on previous experience with the product, consumers may prefer it to those of competitors if they are available. In this way a person may prefer Coca-Cola, but if it is unavailable, may be prepared to accept Pepsi-Cola or Fanta. An enterprise with products in the trade mark preference stage normally enjoys a favourable competitive position in the industry.

- **Trade mark insistence** is the final stage in trade mark acceptance. Consumers refuse all substitute trade marks and search for the specific product until they find it. Such a trade mark has actually then become a *speciality product* in the eyes of the consumer. It is unlikely that a marketer can accomplish complete trade mark insistence for all its products in all its target markets. A marketing strategy aimed at having available the *right products* in the *right places* at the *right times* in the *right quantities* and at the *right prices* for the *right consumers* will probably be more successful than a narrow trade mark insistence strategy.

Example of an enterprise that endeavours to accomplish trade mark insistence with advertising

Now you can be sure that the cushion vinyl floor covering you buy is real Novilon. Just look for the washable "Novilon" symbols on the surface of every Novilon floor covering and on the back of every sample. Novilon is the right floor choice for you — we guarantee it!

There may well be other cheaper vinyl floor coverings, and some that look rather like Novilon, but there is only one real, guaranteed Novilon.

Insist on it.

There's only one Novilon We guarantee it!

9.2.4 Trade mark decisions

We have already discussed some advantages that trade marks offer to both consumers and marketers. At present virtually no processed product is marketed without some form of identification or trade mark. Convenience goods, such as salt, sugar and bread, have trade marks nowadays, and even perishable agricultural products, such as milk, eggs, oranges, apples, tomatoes, potatoes and meat, are graded and are increasingly being marketed under some or other trade mark. Thus, for the modern marketer the use of trade marks is virtually a foregone conclusion and he has to take *two* decisions in particular regarding his trade marks:

- *First*, he has to decide in favour of either *manufacturer trade marks* or *dealer trade marks*.
- *Secondly*, regarding his own trade marks, he has to decide on either *family trade marks* or *individual trade marks*.

9.2.4.1 *Manufacturer trade marks or dealer trade marks*

The manufacturer may put his own trade marks or those of middlemen on his products. A mixture of these is also possible, where some of the products receive manufacturer trade marks and others receive dealer trade marks. Most of the trade marks in the Republic of South Africa are manufacturer trade marks, but the use of dealer trade marks, such as Pot O'Gold of the OK Bazaars and the no-name trade marks of Pick 'n Pay and the Rebel liquor store group, are becoming more significant.

Generally speaking, the manufacturer prefers manufacturer trade marks because they:

- often form the corner-stone of his advertising strategy;

- assist in controlling his market share;

- hamper price comparisons with competitive products; and

- facilitate product differentiation and diversification.

One of the implications of manufacturer trade marks is that the manufacturer has to bear the costs attached to **market development** largely by himself. Manufacturers do not always have the necessary funds for this at their disposal, and it may happen that producers completely or partly cede their own trade marks and manufacture all their products or some of them under dealer trade marks. With dealer trade marks, the manufacturer involved remains basically unknown. If conflict between the manufacturer and middleman develops the latter merely goes to another manufacturer, leaving the first manufacturer virtually without a market for his products.

Thus both manufacturer trade marks and dealer trade marks hold certain advantages and risks for the producer. The use of manufacturer trade marks or dealer trade marks, or a combination of both, is limited by the present and expected marketing and other circumstances of the firm, and one or other may be dominant from time to time.

Some remarks on **generic trade marks** are necessary. The use of generic trade marks means that products are literally stripped of trade names and the so-called 'no-name brands' come into being. The product is then identified only by its generic name or the name of the product type. 'No-name' trade marks or generic trade marks are noticeable among products such as tinned food, washing powders, and even toiletries, for example toilet soap. In the Republic of South Africa generic trade marks often appear as a special form of dealer trade marks. The retail chain stores such as Pick 'n Pay and Checkers are well known for their 'no-name brands' or generic trade marks.

Generally speaking, generic products are normally available in relatively few packaging sizes; they are often not of an exceptionally high quality or the highest quality; they mostly have simple blue-and-white or black-and-white packaging with labels indicating only the generic name of the products (such as washing powder, salted meat and peanut butter); they are not advertised aggressively; the greatest inducement to buy them is their relatively low price; they are often displayed as a separate group on the retailers' shelves; and they are mainly directed towards the price-conscious, cautious and judicious consumers who are sometimes inclined to accept a lower quality with the accompanying risks.

Example of Checkers' generic trade marks

9.2.4.2 *Family trade marks or individual trade marks*

Firms preferring manufacturer trade marks can follow at least four trade mark strategies:

- **Individual trade marks.** This strategy is followed by South African Breweries Ltd for its beer products (Lion Lager, Lion Ale, Castle Lager, Castle Milk Stout, Carling Black Label, Amstel, Shaft, Hansa Pilsener, Rogue and Guinness).

- **A family trade mark for all products.** This trade mark strategy is followed by the Barlows group for its Kelvinator household products, such as deep-freezers, refrigerators, stoves, washing machines and tumble driers.

- **A family trade mark for separate product lines.** Such a trade mark strategy is followed by OK Bazaars (1929) Ltd. Some examples are: Pot O'Gold food and related products; Caress toiletries; Dolores ladies', girls' and infants' wear; Curzon men's and boys' clothes; and Homecraft furniture, bedding and household linen.

- **The business name combined with individual product names.** The Kellogg Company of South Africa (Pty) Ltd follows this trade mark strategy for its products, for example: Kellogg's Raisin Bran; Kellogg's All-Bran Flakes; Kellogg's Hi-Bulk Bran; Kellogg's Corn Flakes; and Kellogg's Rice Crispies.

Individual trade marks have certain advantages for the enterprise:

- They do not involve the images of the other products or that of the firm, and the failure of a particular product does not easily damage the images of the other products or that of the firm.
- An individual trade mark strategy requires a new name for each new product, thus offering the opportunity for originality.
- Individual trade marks facilitate aggressive advertising efforts for individual products and the advertising message can also be attuned to the specific characteristics of the product and its target market.

Of course, individual trade marks are relatively expensive to market since a separate advertising effort, inter alia, is required for each product.

Family trade marks also have certain advantages for the marketer:

- The cost of introducing a new product under a family trade mark strategy should be lower than that of individual trade marks because high advertising expenditures are not actually necessary to obtain trade mark recognition and trade mark preference.
- The new product can also benefit from the popularity of existing products.

Family trade marks are preferable when:

- the products in the product mix have a high consistency;
- are more or less of the same quality;
- are marketed through the same channels; and
- lend themselves to the same marketing communication methods.

There are, however, exceptions to this rule. Consider, for instance, the trade mark strategy which South African Breweries follow for their beer products.

Like manufacturer and dealer trade marks, individual and family trade marks hold certain advantages and risks for the firm. Here also the particular choice is influenced by the present and expected marketing and other circumstances of the firm.

9.3 THE SELECTION OF A TRADE NAME FOR THE PRODUCT

As stated earlier, the trade name of a product is the name under which the product is brought into trade. The trade name is part of the trade mark and usually consists of a single word (Parker pens). Additional words (Peter Stuyvesant cigarettes) and even phrases (Good and Clean and Fresh washing powder) are also sometimes used as trade names. Consumers normally use the trade name to indicate their specific choice amongst competitive products (Nescafé coffee instead of Frisco, Ricoffy, Koffiehuis). The trade name forms part of the **product image** and should therefore be **distinguishable, meaningful** *and a* **symbol** *and* **strengthener of the product concept**. The impact of specific trade names can be so strong that some consumers identify the generic product with them (*Vaseline* for petroleum jelly, *Slasto* for slate and *Elastoplast* for adhesive plaster).

The following guidelines can be used in the selection of a 'good' trade name:

- It tells something about the product — its uses, ingredients, benefits and utilities (Naturelite, Appletiser, Wet Wipes, Budget Rent-a-Car).
- It is pronounced, spelled and remembered easily by the envisaged target market (Omo, Vim, Ford, Royco).
- It is 'versatile' and applicable to a product line or even the entire product mix (Defy, National, Kraft).
- It is original and distinguishable (Mustang, Satin Leaf).
- It creates a unique image of exclusiveness even if it is sometimes difficult to pronounce (Je T'aime, Elsève, L'Eggs, Camouflage, Musk Audace);
- It indicates high quality (Elite choice butter, Golden Crown margarine).

Some sources of trade names for the manufacturer are mentioned:

- When expanding the product mix, the **existing trade name** can be used for the new product item (Defy, National).
- Re-sellers can select their **own trade names** (Pot O'Gold, Caress, Dolores).
- If a completely **new trade name** is sought the following can be considered:

  — initials (Sanlam; BMW; Sasol; J & B Whisky; ABC washing powder);
  — numbers (Chanel No. 5; VAT 69; Five Roses; 2nd Debut);
  — mythological characters (Atlas tyres);
  — personal names (Peter Stuyvesant, Johnnie Walker, Rembrandt van Rijn);
  — geographical names (Blaauwkrantz cheese; Cedarberg);
  — animal names (Lion Lager; Tiger Oats; Penguin Pools; Black Cat peanut butter);
  — herb names (Five Roses);
  — celestial bodies (Sun Hotels);
  — common words (Sunbeam, Whirlpool);
  — foreign words (Nestlé, Lux);
  — combination of words (Good and Clean and Fresh).

Some aspects of packaging are discussed in the following section.

9.4 PACKAGING

Like trade mark decisions, packaging decisions form part of new product decisions of the firm. Packaging is especially important in the protection, storing and physical handling of products while it can also be useful in certain **marketing considerations**, such as product differentiation, consumer convenience and marketing communication.

The following sections deal with a definition of packaging, the importance and objectives of packaging, and some packaging decisions. Aspects of labelling are also considered briefly.

9.4.1 A definition of packaging

Packaging can be defined as that group of activities in product decisions which pertains to the design, manufacturing and filling of the container or wrapper with the product item, in such a way that the product item can be protected, stored, handled, transported and identified effectively, and marketed successfully. The word *'packaging'* sometimes refers only to the container of the product. The broader meaning, however, is preferred because certain packaging decisions, such as on the design, manufacturing and filling, have to be taken before the product physically exists. Thus, as defined, packaging mainly pertains to the individual product item in order to distinguish it from containerisation, where a large number of product items are normally put into one container with a view to effective protection, handling and transportation. Both technical and marketing aspects are involved in packaging. The manufacturing and filling (choice of packaging materials and packaging processes) are mainly technical challenges, while the design of the packaging is both a technical and marketing challenge. In what follows, attention is paid only to a few marketing aspects of packaging.

9.4.2 The tasks of packaging[2]

From a marketing point of view packaging has at least six roles to play, namely enclosement and protection, enabling re-usability, communication, market segmentation, co-operation with distribution channels, and product development.

TABLE 9.1   Tasks of packaging

TASK	DESCRIPTION
Enclosement and protection	Packaging facilitates the safe and easy dispatching, storing and handling of the product.
Re-usability	Packaging makes the product re-usable and easy to store. It can even be used after the contents have been consumed.
Communication	Packaging communicates a specific product image through its design, label, colour, trade mark and display. Packaging is an important instrument of communication.
Market segmentation	The selection of a package design, colour, shape, size and material enables the firm to direct its products to specific market segments.
Co-operation with the distribution channels	Packaging must satisfy the needs of the wholesaler, retailer and consumer.
Product development	A new package can be an important innovation for the firm.

9.4.3 The importance and objectives of packaging

These can be deduced from the tasks of packaging. It is especially important to the firm in *three* respects, and contributes to the achievement of certain objectives.

Products are packed so that certain **marketing activities**, such as the physical handling, storing and transportation involved in the flow of goods from the producer to the consumer, can be performed as economically as possible and with the highest possible degree of need-satisfaction for the consumer. In this regard the mode of transport, physical handling and storing of products by the consumer during purchase and consumption have to be carefully considered in packaging decisions. Aspects such as safety, convenient sizes, hygienic storing and convenience of re-use should receive particular attention in order to increase the need-satisfaction obtainable from the product.

Packaging is a useful instrument in the **market development** of the new product. Under certain conditions this, together with trade marks, can be the only significant way of implementing product differentiation (consider cigarettes, for instance). Changes in the packaging can often create the impression that the entire product has been changed; consequently it can be useful in the modification of existing products and the introduction of new ones. Furthermore, effective packaging has a sales promotional effect. Certain packaging characteristics, such as drip-free spouts, aerosol sprays, roll-ons or sticks (as with glue) and re-usable packaging (such as certain glass containers), can stimulate the sales of products packaged in this way. In a sense effective packaging can also serve as point-of-purchase advertising in self-service stores. Consider, for instance, preserved fruit in clear glass bottles and liquor in uniquely shaped bottles. Effective packaging can also be a useful tool in obtaining retail shelf-space, especially when it helps the retailer to realise maximum turnover or gross profit per running metre of shelf-space.

Packaging can also be used to increase the **profitability** of certain products. A particular type of packaging can be unique and so attractive that consumers are prepared to pay an extra premium for the product just to acquire the special packaging (for instance, wine in barrels and perfume in unique containers).

9.4.4 Some packaging decisions

With a view to reaching specific marketing objectives, management has to take inter alia different packaging decisions. Some of these decisions are discussed below.

9.4.4.1 *Packaging of the product mix*

Management has the choice of using either *family packaging* for all its products, or *individual* and *unique packaging* for each product line or product item.

Family packaging means that all products in the mix are more or less identically packed or have at least one or more important packaging characteristic in common (for instance, the packaging of Kellogg's products). Family packaging is connected with family trade marks, and the marketing considerations which apply to the choice of family trade marks normally also hold good for the selection of family packaging.

Example of family packaging

Individual packaging usually takes the form of speciality packaging where a manufacturer wants to create an image of distinctiveness and exclusiveness for the product. Certain types of liquor, for example, are packed in uniquely shaped bottles covered with raffia plaits, while jewellery and fountain pens are packed in gilded containers.

9.4.4.2 *Re-usable packaging or not?*

A firm can select and design containers for its products in such a way that they *can be used for some other purpose after the contents have been consumed*. In this way peanuts, biltong and spices are marketed in beer glasses, and washing powders and coffee sold in special plastic re-usable containers. This type of packaging serves as an additional incentive in the buying decision, especially if it does not increase the price of the product concerned excessively. Moreover, it can lead to re-buying since the consumer may feel inclined to collect a set of glasses or plastic containers.

Example of speciality packaging

Example of re-usable packaging

9.4.4.3 *Multiple packaging or not?*

With this type of packaging, *several products with a high consistency are packed in one container*. Deodorants, after shave lotions, shaving cream and hairspray for men; various types of confectionery; toothbrushes and toothpaste; razors and razor-blades; such products are often packed in one container. Multiple packaging is especially useful to introduce a new product and to obtain trade mark recognition. Furthermore, multiple packagings are often used as special offers (loss-leaders). Multiple packagings can also have certain cost benefits for the retailer since certain handling costs and the costs involved in the marking of goods should now be lower per product unit.

Example of multiple packaging

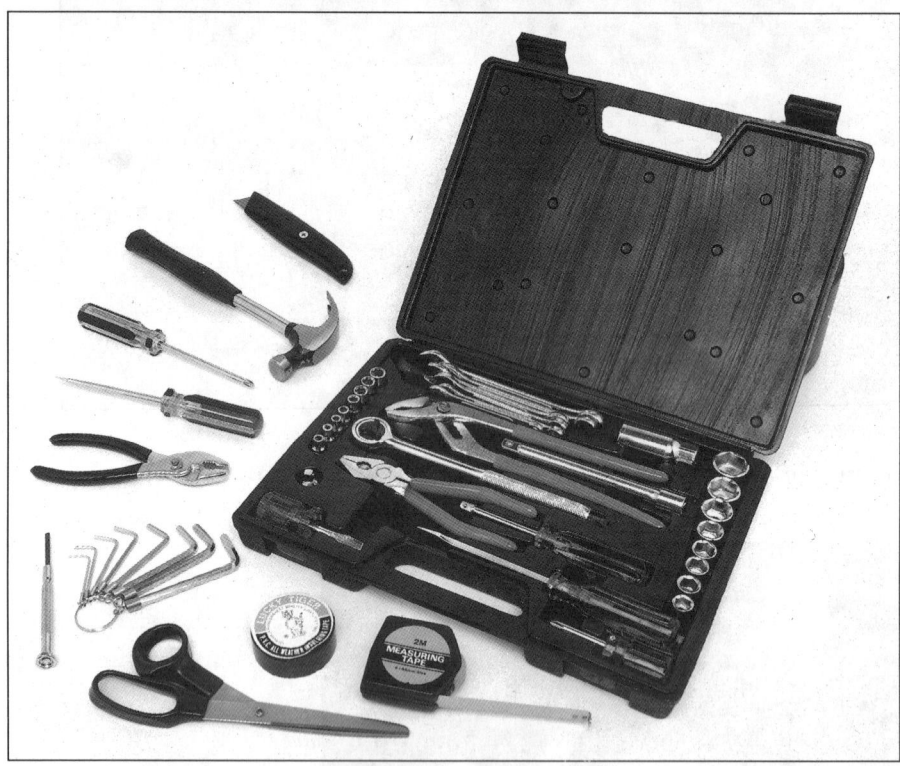

9.4.4.4 *Kaleidoscopic packaging or not?*

The term 'kaleidoscopic' is used to identify packaging decisions according to which certain aspects of the packaging are changed continually. Examples are a series of pictures of personalities which are printed on the inside of soft drink bottle caps, and a series of different animal species or other themes which are printed on the packaging of sweets (Sugus, for example). The basic idea behind this packaging decision is to create a demand for the product via the demand for the packaging.

9.4.5 Factors in the packaging decision

Package design has a direct impact on the image of the firm's products. It is, however, true that certain factors, such as packaging costs, durable materials, packaging sizes and packaging shapes, differ from product to product. Generalisations regarding the factors to be considered in packaging decisions are therefore not possible. A **check-list**[3] of factors which must to a greater or lesser extent be considered in all packaging decisions is nevertheless given below:

Check-list for packaging

- What product image is sought? ....
- Should family packaging be used? Yes No
- Should standardised packaging be used in all market segments?
   Yes No
- What should packaging costs be in total and per unit? Total packaging costs: R ....
   Packaging costs per unit: R ....
- What packaging materials should be used? ....
- How innovative/exclusive should the packaging be? ....
- What features/highlights should be incorporated in the packaging?   ....
- What sizes, colours and shapes should be used?
   Sizes: ....
   Colours: ....
   Shapes: ....
- How should the label and other inserts appear on the package? ....

- Should multiple packaging be used? ....
- Should items be individually wrapped within the package?
   Yes No
- Should the package be versatile/adaptable? Yes No
- Should the package contain a preprinted price and bar codes?
   Preprinted price Yes No
   Bar codes Yes No
- Should the package be re-usable? Yes No
- How should the package interrelate with the other marketing instruments? ....

This check list is particularly useful in packaging decisions for a new product.

9.4.6 Labelling

Labelling is an important aspect of packaging and trade marks. The label contains information about the product and/or manufacturer and is usually part of the packaging or is directly attached to the product by means of a ticket. Sometimes the label is directly attached to the product, as with fresh meat. Obviously a close connection exists between the packaging, the trade mark and the label of the product and they often form a unity. Labels mainly perform an informative function, and normally contain the trade mark, the grade, a description of the ingredients of the product, warnings, net contents, name and location of the manufacturer, and the directions for use. This information is especially useful when the product is purchased and used.

In general three types of labels can be distinguished:

- **Trade mark labels.** In this case only the trade mark appears on the product item or its package, for example the Outspan trade mark on oranges.
- **Grading labels.** The quality of the product is identified by means of a letter, number or word. Super AX, prime BX, prime BY, Grade A1Y, Grade B1Y and Grade C1X are, for instance, fixed on beef to indicate the quality thereof.
- **Informative labels.** These labels can inter alia give written and/or visual objective information on the product's ingredients, use, care, performance, life expectancy, precautions and nutritional value.

Certain information is nowadays increasingly incorporated on the package and/or label of consumer goods in particular by means of bar coding. Some remarks on this follow.

9.4.7 Bar coding and electronic scanning

9.4.7.1 *Background*

The South African Numbering Association (SAANA) is a non-profit association registered under Section 21 of the Companies Act. SAANA was formed in 1982 by leading retailers and the Grocery Manufacturers Association to promote the introduction of scanning in the Republic of South Africa by incorporating bar codes on all product items that pass through checkouts.

9.4.7.2 *What is bar coding and scanning?*[4]

Bar coding is the special numbering of a product item so that it can be read by an electronic machine. It consists of a series of bars and spaces of varying width according to a predetermined structure and standard. This combination (symbol) of bars and spaces can be read by laser scanners and other optical devices.

The standard number consists of 13 digits and is compatible with article numbering systems used inter alia in Europe, Japan, Australia and New Zealand.

- The **first three digits** (prefix) identify the number bank administered by the National Numbering Association. In respect of SAANA these three digits are 600.
- The **following four digits** are allocated by SAANA to the member or manufacturer.
- The **following five digits** are used by the manufacturer to identify the product item.
- The **final digit** is a check digit calculated over the previous 12 digits to ensure that the code is correctly composed.

The meaning of these digits can be summarised as follows:

Three digits	Four digits	Five digits	One digit
600	MMMM	11111	C
Prefix (SAANA)	Manufacturer's number	Product item code	Check digit

This is the structure of the standard 13-digit European Article Number, known as EAN-13, which is also used in the Republic of South Africa.

A shortened version, known as the EAN-8 code, is available on a directly assigned basis from SAANA for use on exceptionally small packages. The EAN-8 code is structured as follows:

Three digits	Four digits	One digit
600	1111	C
Prefix (SAANA)	Product item code	Check digit

Examples of the EAN-13 and EAN-8 symbols appear below:

9.4.7.3 *Implementation of bar coding*

The manufacturer incorporates the bar codes into the packaging of each product item. At the retailer the product item number is transmitted by a scanner to an in-store computer. This computer instantly relays the description of the product item and its current price back to the checkout cash register or terminal. This information will then be displayed electronically and simultaneously printed on the point of sale receipt for the consumer.

Example of a hand-held electronic scanner which transmits information on the bar codes without cords, cables, telephones or outside power sources to a central computer. This scanner is particularly useful for stocktaking.

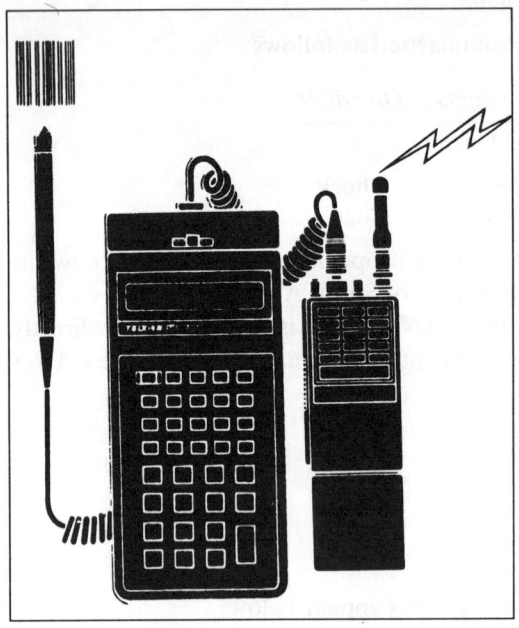

With computerised cash register systems the side of the product item on which the bar code appears is passed over the electronic scanner in any position. In less than one second the description and price of the product item are automatically retrieved from the central in-store computer and printed on the customer receipt or ticket. An example of such a receipt appears alongside:

```
         A B C
      SUPERMARKET
  KEEP THIS RECEIPT FOR
    FUTURE SHOPPING


IDEAL MILK   A      .44
MAYONNAISE   A     2.45
CAKE FLOUR   A     1.59
OXTAIL SOUP  A      .89
HEINZ BEANS A       .75
NESCAFE 125GAD     2.20
OIL OF OLAY A      1.25
TARTAR SAUCEA      2.99
   4   ONTY  a      .59
SARDINES     A     2.36
   6   ONTY  a      .69
BREAD ROLLS A      4.14
LAMB CHOPS   A    23.85
STEAK PRIME A     15.75
TAX1               3.52
TOTL              62.18

CASH              70.00
CHNG               7.82

  ITEM      20

A 005             10001
1665 10:55AM  4/19/88
```

9.4.7.4 *Benefits of bar coding and electronic scanning*

A summary of the most important benefits of bar coding and electronic scanning to the manufacturer, retailer and consumer is given below.

Benefits to the manufacturer

- **Standard product item numbers.** The use of a single, standard product item number in all distribution channels improves communication in the channels and reduces the incidence of errors caused by inaccurate product descriptions.
- **Retail acceptance.** For some retailers product items that are bar coded are more acceptable than those which are not bar coded. Indeed, certain retailers refuse to stock items that are not bar coded.
- **Feedback on product sales.** Feedback on the sale of the product item is improved. This feedback can come from a central clearing house as well as directly from the retailer, among others.
- **Feedback on new product performance.** Improved information on the product's sales performance helps the manufacturer to do better production planning.
- **Quicker identification of market trends.** Trends in the market can be observed much sooner due to the timeous and accurate information received from clearing houses and retailers.

Benefits to the retailer

- **Improved inventory control.** Bar coding and scanning can improve inventory control so that retailers can optimise stock holdings. This leads to a reduction in inventory costs and an improvement in stock turnover.
- **Improved utilisation of shelf-space.** Accurate sales information enables retailers to apportion shelf-space to products according to actual performance.
- **Improved productivity at cash registers.** Bar coding and scanning can lead to a reduction in the number of cash registers with a corresponding reduction in capital outlay, reduced staff costs and improved utilisation of floor-space.
- **Accurate pricing and indication.** The correct prices are charged to the buyer and the marking of product items with incorrect prices is eliminated.
- **Price-marking unnecessary — easy to make price changes.** The price-marking of each and every individual product item by the retailer becomes unnecessary. This saves on labour costs. Price changes merely require a simple entry into the in-store computer and a change in the shelf price label.
- **Elimination of malicious and deliberate underrings by cashiers.** Bar coding and scanning clearly indicate whether a transaction has been manually entered or whether an item has been scanned. In this way, inconsistencies in prices can immediately be noticed.
- **Improved shrinkage control.** Bar coding and scanning enable stock control for each product item. Store management is thus able to isolate those areas that are directly affected by shrinkage.

Benefits to the consumer

- **Quicker service possible at cash register control points.** Bar coding and electronic scanning should considerably increase the service speed of individual cash registers. Quicker service at cash registers will, however, be determined by the cash register policy of the retailer. If the same number of cash registers is maintained the service should be much quicker; if the number of cash registers is reduced to benefit from savings on capital investment and labour costs and better floor-space utilisation, the service can be quicker, the same or even slower. Whatever the case may be, at least a portion of the abovementioned savings should be passed on to the consumer by means of lower prices in general.

- **Descriptive sales receipt.** One of the tasks of a bar coding and scanning system is to print a unique description on the receipt of each product item purchased by the consumer. The description is sufficient clearly to identify each product item bought. This receipt is particularly useful to check goods after they have been bought.

- **Price comparisons.** The descriptive receipt is also useful for comparing prices between stores, and to monitor price changes over time at the same store. In this way stores with lower prices in general can be identified more easily.

- **Shopping list.** By retaining the descriptive receipt, the customer can use it as a shopping list during the next shopping trip.

- **Accurate pricing.** Scanning ensures that all product items with the same bar code symbol are sold at the same price. It prevents a price different from the one on which the customer's buying decision was based being read into the cash register.

- **Fewer out-of-stock situations.** Product items which are out of stock can be an embarrassment to the store and cause great inconvenience to consumers. A bar coding and scanning system enables effective stock control for each product item. Effective stock control means relatively few out-of-stock situations, which greatly eliminates the embarrassment and inconvenience mentioned above.

- **Elimination of product items not price-marked.** Customers waiting in a queue at a cash register are frequently inconvenienced because certain product items are not price-marked. These annoying events should be eliminated if bar codes which can be read by a scanner are incorporated on product items; prices of product items are kept in a file at the main computer. The computer is electronically linked with each cash register and automatically transmits the price as soon as the product is moved over the scanner.

- **Competitive prices.** Bar coding and scanning should make the prices in a scanning store compared to stores without this system more competitive due to various cost savings. Naturally, relatively low prices favourably influence the patronage motives of consumers.

9.5 SUMMARY

In this chapter different aspects of trade mark and packaging decisions were reviewed. The concepts used in trade marks; the importance of trade marks; the different phases in trade mark acquaintance and acceptance; trade mark decisions consisting of manufacturer or dealer trade marks and family or individual trade marks; and the selection of a trade name for the product, inter alia, were dealt with. With packaging, emphasis was mainly placed on a description of packaging; the tasks of packaging; the importance and objectives of packaging; packaging decisions, consisting of the packaging of the product mix, re-usable, multiple and kaleidoscopic packaging; and the factors to be considered in packaging decisions. Attention was also given to labelling, coding, and electronic scanning as important elements of trade marks and packaging.

REFERENCES

1. This section is based on Evans, JR and Berman, B. 1982. *Marketing*. New York: MacMillan Publishing Co, pp 287–8.
2. Adapted from Nickels, WG. 'Packaging — The Fifth "P" in the Marketing Mix'. *Advanced Marketing Journal*, Winter 1976 and Margulies, W. 1970. *Packaging Power*. New York: World Publishing.
3. For a discussion of these factors see Evans and Berman op cit, pp 291–4.
4. This section is mainly based on Pearcey, RM. *General Information on Bar Coding and Scanning in South Africa* and *Benefits to be Derived from Scanning*, both publications of the South African Numbering Association, Johannesburg. For further information see also *Retail Article Numbering and Symbol Marketing* and *Guidelines on the Location of Barcode Symbols*, publications of the South African Numbering Association.

CASE STUDY

PERSPECTIVES ON PACKAGING

Animal skins as packaging material

One can hardly imagine a world without packaging. From the earliest time man looked for methods to facilitate the transport of products. Primitive man was nomadic and probably used animal skins to transport belongings from place to place.

In early civilisations around 1500 BC in Egypt, Asia and Europe trading activities became more organised, necessitating the use of suitable containers to protect wares. Through the centuries traders tested clay pots, wooden boxes and barrels for this purpose.

Archaeological excavations reveal unusual examples of such containers. Egyptians, Greeks and Romans often used beautiful vases and urns. Stoppers were made to protect the contents of glass bottles. It is interesting to note that the glass-making techniques of the old Egyptians changed very little through the centuries. Glass is still an often-used material in modern-day packaging.

With the discovery of sea routes to Africa, America and the East effective packaging became a prerequisite for the protection of products during the long and hazardous journey.

By the end of the 18th century, hessian was used to transport grain, flour, sugar, coal and fertilizer. Paper also became an important packaging material. According to a brochure of the Packaging Council of South Africa, a Brit, John Dickinson, registered a patent in 1924 for a machine which could glue large pieces of paper to one another — and the first cardboard was made. Traders used this material to package large articles. They also used single sheets of paper to twist cones for products such as sweets and dried beans.

By 1830 tinned foods appeared in the stores in Britain. At first the packaging was simple but the Americans quickly used the opportunity to make the tins more attractive with interesting designs.

In 1870 corrugated paper was introduced in America as well as folded boxes for biscuits and the like. The emphasis was increasingly put on the protection of the contents of the package.

The packaging industry kept on growing and today it is large and sophisticated, providing jobs for millions of people. Packaging materials include plastics, metal, paper, aluminium foil and glass.

Packaging draws consumers to the stores

The packaging of a product is often taken for granted by consumers, but packaging is more than mere containers — packaging is also an advertising vehicle for manufacturers. When two products serving the same purpose are placed next to one another on the store shelf and there is no price difference, the consumer will most certainly opt for the package which is visually the most attractive.

Packaging must succeed in persuading the consumer to purchase the product on the store shelf. It must also contain information regarding the nature of the product. Much pressure is placed on the manufacturer by environmentalists and health-conscious consumers to provide adequate and correct information regarding the ingredients of food products. The package must also give the preparation method.

One of the main requirements is that a package must protect the product against contamination by bacteria, light, and dust, and the effects of handling, cold and heat. Care must be taken to ensure the freshness of the product in the hands of the consumer. Biscuits, for example, must not be stale and they must be intact. Nothing is more discouraging than opening a box of biscuits to find only crumbs. Packaging must be sealed to maintain flavour and aroma — like coffee. Sometimes the packaging must succeed in retaining moisture and sometimes it must keep moisture and air out.

In modern life consumers look for convenience like prepared meals that are ready for serving immediately. The manufacturer must provide suitable packaging that will help satisfy the demand for convenience products. Special containers that can be put into the oven have been developed. A housewife can purchase a pasta dish, put it in the oven and have a meal ready without even a dirty saucepan. Even here careful consideration must be given to suitable packaging for both conventional and micro-wave ovens.

Packaging must also be user-friendly for different groups of people. The needs of a single person who is responsible only for himself differ from those of a housewife who must care for a whole family. To a single person a giant-sized pack of cornflakes may prove to be an irritation while the housewife with four teenagers may well wish for double the size.

Tamper-proof packaging

It is sometimes extremely frustrating to open a tomato sauce bottle. The seal must first be broken or the plastic strip surrounding the cap must be removed, not to mention the difficulties with a product firmly sealed in a cardboard box, or a bubble pack or a tube of cream which needs a screwdriver to prick the metal-like seal.

Making containers difficult to open is required to protect the customer and the manufacturer against sabotage. In America, a deranged person opened bottles containing analgesic capsules (Tylenol) and added cyanide to some capsules. Many people died and the manufacturer had to withdraw 200 000 bottles of Tylenol from the stores. After this tragedy, ten years ago, tamper-proof packaging was developed.

A few years later bottles of baby food in British stores were contaminated with glass splinters, thereby making the use of tamper-proof packaging essential for these products.

In the case of Tylenol the carton container is now firmly sealed, the bottle cap is covered with plastic and the bottle opening is protected by foil. It is now difficult to tamper with the product while in the store. 'A packaged product without any protection can be easily opened. Even if sabotage is not intended a customer in a supermarket can open a bottle and taste the contents before putting it back. This is very unhygienic,' says Mr Jeremy Hele, executive director of the Association of Grocery Manufacturers.

'If a customer tampers with tamper-proof packaging, it is easy to see from the broken seal. If the seal is broken or the plastic covering torn the customer must avoid the product. It is a clear indication that somebody tried to open it,' says Mr Hele.

Many responsible manufacturers in South Africa use this safety measure but there are also those who do nothing about it.

Is it necessary to compel manufacturers by law to use tamper-proof packaging?

'It is a decision the manufacturer must take, depending on the nature of his product. If necessary he must take steps to ensure the safety of his product,' says Mr Hele.

Source: *Beeld*, Thursday, 18 June 1992 (free translation)

QUESTIONS

1. 'Packaging is a source of information in consumer decision making.' Discuss this statement.

2. How can a manufacturer of cough syrup demonstrate his responsibility to society by means of packaging decisions?

3. How can packaging be used in the marketing communication campaign?

4. How can packaging contribute to creating the 'total product' concept? Give examples.

ASSIGNMENTS

1. Take any **ten** South African manufactured products and answer the following questions on their *trade marks*. Motivate your viewpoint in each case:

   - In what phase of trade mark acquaintance and acceptance are these products in your opinion in their target market?
   - Are manufacturer trade marks or dealer trade marks used for these products? In your opinion are the correct/incorrect trade mark strategies used?
   - Are family trade marks or individual trade marks used? In your opinion, are the correct/incorrect trade mark strategies used?

2. Explain how you would select a **trade name** for a new product which successfully keeps dogs from lawns.

3. Take any five South African manufactured products and answer the following questions on their **packaging**. Motivate your viewpoint in each case:

- What packaging strategies are used for the product mix? In your opinion, are the right/wrong packaging strategies used?
- Is **reusable packaging** possible, is it being used, and why or why not?
- Is **multiple packaging** possible, is it being used, and why or why not?
- Is **kaleidoscopic packaging** possible, is it being used, and why or why not?

4. Obtain the following:

   - Five different trade mark labels
   - Five different grading labels
   - Five informative labels

   In your opinion, what purpose/value do these labels have for the consumer? Motivate your viewpoint.

5. Prepare yourself to debate the following statement:

   'In the marketing of consumer products bar coding and electronic scanning have many advantages for the manufacturer, the retailer and the consumer.'

6. 'Packaging and trade marks for new products are extremely important from a marketing point of view.'

   Explain how you would develop an effective trade mark and packaging strategy for the following types of products. Make all the suppositions you regard necessary on the firms involved as well as the macro and microenvironments. Indicate these in your answers:

   - Exclusive and expensive perfume for ladies
   - A new soft drink as a mixer in exclusive restaurants and hotels
   - A new unique washing-powder which must be measured precisely for the best results in automatic washing-machines
   - A unique ingredient which is added to the food of dogs and cats to effectively control external parasites (fleas, lice, mange, flies)

CHAPTER 10

DISTRIBUTION IN PERSPECTIVE

10.1 INTRODUCTION

Efficient marketing requires careful consideration and selection of the **most suitable outlets** to present the enterprise's products to its target market. At the same time consideration should be given to and a decision made on the **most economic way** in which products can be **distributed** to the various outlets. Therefore, in distribution two broad decisions are to be made, namely:

- decisions regarding the **transaction flow**, ie the **distribution channel** through which products have to move; and
- decisions regarding the **physical flow** of products from the producer to the final consumer.

Decisions on distribution channels, particularly those relating to **where, when** and **how** to present products to a specific target market, are an important and even critical facet of the total marketing strategy. Likewise, the physical movement of products requires careful decisions, especially in view of the comparatively high costs which are associated therewith.

ORGANISATION OF THE CHAPTER

The importance of distribution decisions for the marketing strategy: Influence of distribution on other marketing decisions, the long-term nature of distribution decisions.

The most important intermediaries in distribution channels: Typical distribution channels, sales intermediaries, resellers.

Intermediaries in perspective: Intermediaries' right of existence, justification of intermediaries' entering the distribution channel.

> **Combination of intermediaries in distribution:** The interdependence of intermediaries, vertical combination in distribution, horizontal combination in distribution.
>
> **Distribution trends in the Republic of South Africa.**

10.2 THE IMPORTANCE OF DISTRIBUTION DECISIONS

10.2.1 Explanation of important concepts

Figure 10.1 reflects the introductory remarks and shows the physical flow of products to the target market, and the transaction flow of money from the target market through the distribution channels. It is, however, necessary at the outset to explain a few basic concepts.[1]

- **Distribution decisions** entail the consideration of and choice between specific distribution channels and methods of physical distribution with the objective of optimally making available products or services to the target market in accordance with the marketing objectives.
- A **distribution channel** embraces all those **persons or enterprises**, from the producer to the ultimate consumer, who take title or ownership of products or who are directly involved with the transfer of title and who perform one or more marketing activities. The distribution channel is simply a 'pipeline' through which the products flow from the producer to the consumer — the producer places the product into the pipeline and with the help of intermediaries the product flows to the consumer at the other end of the pipeline.
- **Physical distribution** relates to the physical flow of products from the producer to the ultimate consumer and includes the performance of activities such as transport, storage and inventory holding to ensure this flow.
- The **distribution structure** is the sum total of all the enterprises concerned with the marketing of products and by whom certain marketing activities are performed. The distribution structure therefore comprises the **channel structure**, which includes **producers** and **intermediaries** such as agents, brokers, wholesalers and retailers, as well as the **physical distribution structure** with transport enterprises and warehouses as the most important components. Other auxiliary enterprises such as financial institutions, advertising practitioners and insurance enterprises are only indirectly concerned. For the purposes of this discussion these auxiliary enterprises will not be included.

It should be evident that a relationship does exist between these defined concepts. For example, it can be stated that marketing management has to select within the total distribution structure a particular distribution channel and methods of physical distribution.

FIGURE 10.1   Distribution in perspective

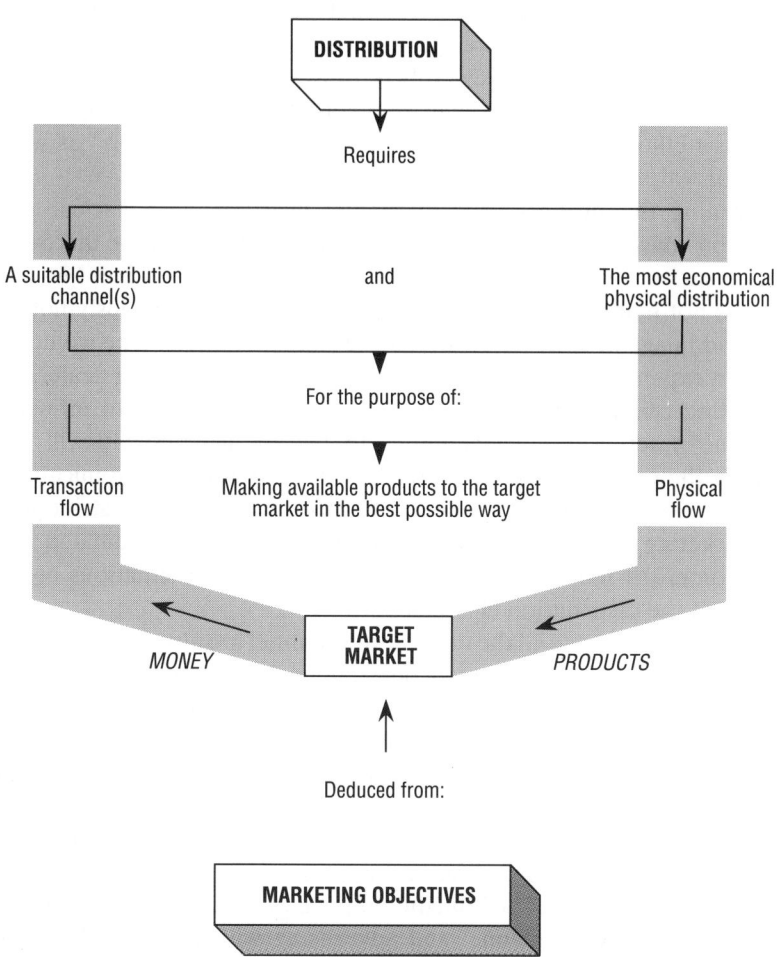

Therefore a thorough knowledge of the nature and operation of distribution channels and methods of physical distribution is of fundamental importance to marketing management.

It has been contended[2] that decisions regarding the distribution channels are of the most critical to be considered by marketing management. In the first instance, a certain distribution channel affects all the other marketing decisions, and, secondly, marketing management cannot easily change distribution channels in the short term.

10.2.2 Influence of distribution on the other marketing decisions

Before the effect of distribution on the other three marketing decisions, namely product, marketing communication and price, is discussed, it is necessary to refer only briefly to the particular market segment to which the marketing effort is directed.

The **target market** naturally gives direction for the development of the marketing strategy. Different target markets require different products, prices, promotion and distribution systems. Should the target market be industrial users, the distribution channel will inevitably be different (short) as opposed to low unit value convenience products (longer channels). Likewise, the target market will affect the method of physical distribution (rail or air transport) as well as the location of warehouses.

Concerning the **product** as a marketing instrument, it is clear that poor distribution may cause the failure of such a product, even if the quality and characteristics of the product are good and the price competitive. Moreover, if a product is not made available at the right places, it will obviously not sell. The quality and image of a product also require suitable outlets. One would certainly not sell an expensive and high-quality fur coat through general dealers.

Marketing communication and the distribution channel also influence each other. The practice of intermediaries to market aggressively will inter alia determine the extent of the enterprise's own marketing communication effort. Marketing communication should also be co-ordinated with distribution activities. Marketing communication which is not duly co-ordinated with the distribution effort may, for example, cause out-of-stock situations or excessive inventory in the distribution channel.

The **price** of products and the distribution channel are also interdependent. The general price level of a product will determine which distribution channels must be used. Distribution also entails cost and the more efficient the channel and physical distribution the higher the profit for the various members in the channel and the more favourable the competitive position for the enterprise as lower prices may then be quoted.

Furthermore, it should be noted that the retailer in particular is the enterprise's **point of contact with the ultimate consumer**. The retailer's location, the appearance and atmosphere within the shop, his product range, delivery facilities, credit facilities, sales personnel and advertising will influence the consumer's supporting behaviour. The consumer's image of the enterprise is largely determined by the quality of the outlets. This, in turn, can determine to what extent the consumer will react to the market offering of the producer. A further aspect which underlines the importance of distribution is that, together with the product, marketing communication and price, it **provides benefits to the consumer**, such as place, time and possession benefits, and therefore adds value to the product.

10.2.3 Long-term nature of distribution

Of all the marketing instruments, distribution is probably the one instrument which the enterprise changes the least in the short term. For this reason the view[3] is expressed that channel arrangements for the distribution of a product tend to be the most stable element in any producer's marketing mix. That is why marketing management must consider the correct constitution of the distribution channel very carefully. These considerations are discussed in Chapter 11. The various intermediaries in the channel will now be identified.

10.3 PRINCIPAL TYPES OF INTERMEDIARIES IN A DISTRIBUTION CHANNEL

A product can follow various possible paths from the producer to the final consumer. Figure 10.2 is a schematic representation of the main possibilities in the marketing of consumer products. Intermediaries can broadly be divided into sales intermediaries and resellers and each of these categories consists of various types, each with its own specific characteristics.

FIGURE 10.2   Typical distribution channels for consumer products

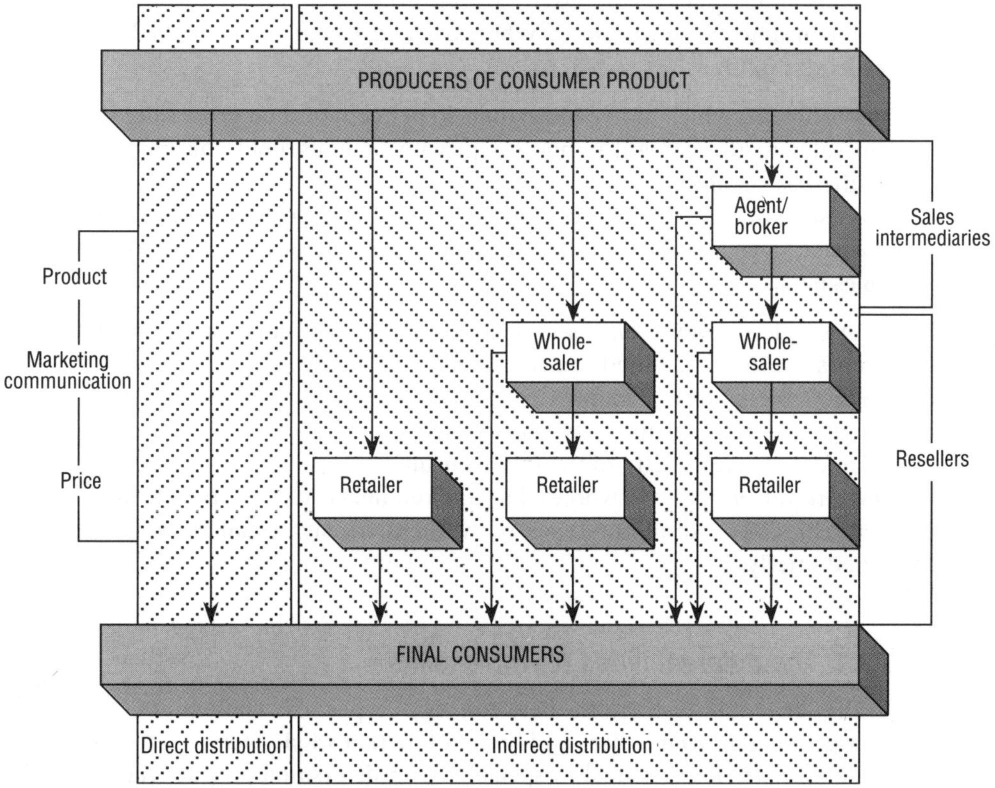

10.3.1 Sales intermediaries[4]

The most important role of sales intermediaries in the distribution channel is to act as a **link** between the other channel members, for example to bring producers and retailers into contact with each other **without effecting exchange of title** to products. Trade agents and brokers are the main types of sales intermediaries.

According to the Central Statistical Services, the main income of **trade agents**, including manufacturers' agents and sales agents, is in the form of **commission**. These agents can act on behalf of various principals and in some cases may even perform certain marketing activities such as storage and finance.

Brokers normally specialise in a specific product or service category such as wool, insurance or property, but normally perform only a very limited marketing task, the most important being to bring buyers and sellers together and to ensure that the **negotiations** between the parties flow smoothly. The party requesting their services is usually responsible for their remuneration.

10.3.2 Resellers

Wholesalers and retailers are the main types of resellers. These middlemen **take title** to the products which they handle. The basis for distinguishing between wholesalers and retailers is the extent to which their **sales income** is derived from the final consumer. The Census of Wholesale and Retail Trade of 1983[5] defines the traders as follows:

- Establishments which derive more than 50 per cent of their gross sales income from sales to the general public for private or household consumption are classified as **retailers.**
- Establishments deriving 50 per cent or more of their gross sales income from wholesale sales, ie sales to other businesses and institutions, are classified as **wholesalers.**

From these descriptions one can deduce that wholesalers may sell to final consumers but to be classified as a wholesaler, these sales may not exceed 50 per cent. Wholesalers market mainly to other resellers and as such they form a very important link in the chain between producers and retailers. Retailers, on the other hand, market directly to the final consumer.

There are various types of wholesalers and retailers each with its own particular characteristics. The different types of wholesalers and retailers will now be examined briefly.

10.3.2.1 *The different types of wholesalers*

Generally one can distinguish between two types of wholesalers, namely **full-service/function wholesalers** and **limited function wholesalers.**

Full-service wholesalers deal in specialised or diversified product ranges and offer a wide range of services to retailers such as repackaging, rearranging, delivery, financing and inventory holding. Limited function wholesalers, on the other hand, offer only a limited number of services to retailers. The following types of limited function wholesalers are encountered:

- **Cash-and-carry wholesalers** where retailers come to the premises of the wholesalers to fetch their requirements themselves and pay for them in cash. In other words no delivery or financing services are provided as in the case of Metro.

- **Rack-jobbers** administer shelf space in a retail shop. They stock these spaces or shelves with the products in which they specialise. The retailer then receives an agreed margin on all the items sold as in the case of Willards batteries.
- **Desk-jobbers** do not maintain any inventory themselves but actually only receive orders from retailers, mostly by telephone and then ensure that producers execute these orders. While they do take title to the products, they do not actually take physical possession of these products.
- **Truck-jobbers** specialise in speedy deliveries of perishable products in particular and normally travel from retailer to retailer.
- **Mail-order wholesalers** accept orders by post or by telephone according to catalogue and then despatch the products, often on a cash on delivery (cod) basis.

In conclusion then it can be said that the different types of wholesalers can be classified according to their degree of product specialisation, the variety of product ranges and the extent of services which they offer to retailers.

The Rusfurn Group Limited owns 100% of Rusfurn Management (Pty) Ltd.

Rusfurn Management (Pty) Ltd comprises 15 chains trading out of 432 stores throughout southern Africa.

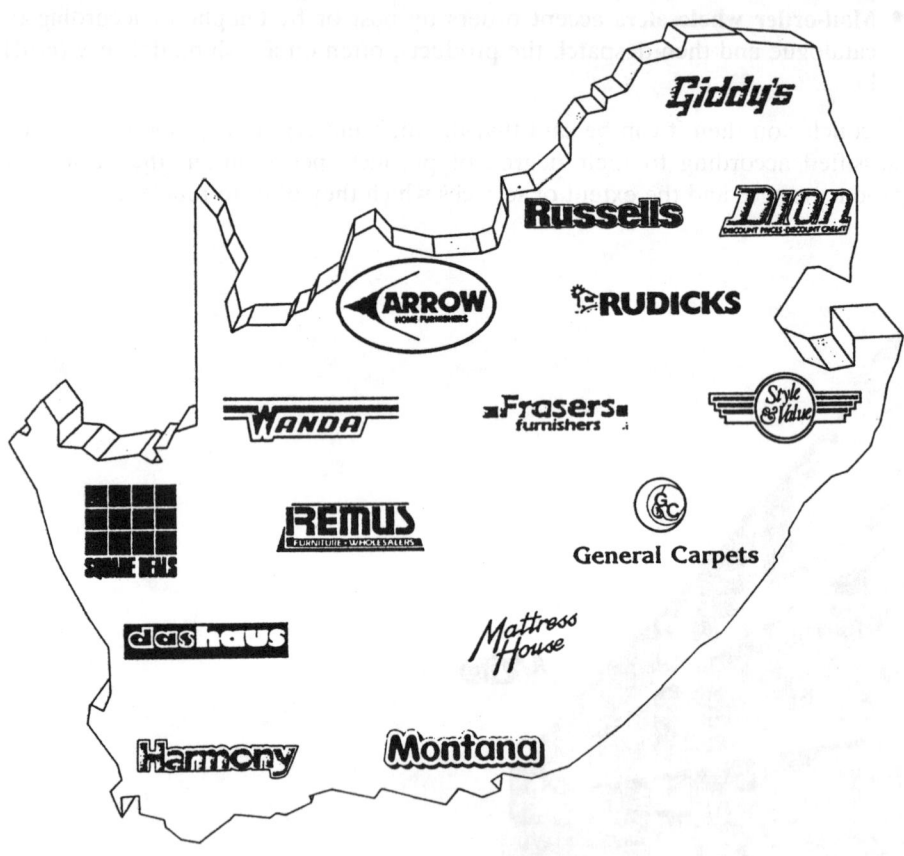

10.3.2.2 *Different types of retailers*

It has been mentioned earlier that retailers market almost exclusively to the ultimate consumer. The characteristics of and also the extent of service varies, however, from retailer to retailer. As such the following kinds of retailers can be distinguished:

- **General dealers** offer a wide and often diversified range of products in order to satisfy the various needs of consumers. They are found particularly in rural towns.
- **Departmental stores** are normally large stores and consist of various departments in which a variety of products with a relatively wide choice range are offered. A grocery department, a clothing department and a cosmetics department can thus be encountered within one store as in the case of OK Bazaars (1929) Limited.
- **Speciality stores** specialise in a limited product range but with a wide variety, that is, the product range is very narrow but very deep. Speciality stores are encountered chiefly in jewellery (Sterns), clothes and hardware.
- **Chain stores** consist of a number of more or less similar shops in various places all owned by one enterprise and all centrally controlled. Chain stores can include departmental stores, as in the case of Woolworths.
- **Supermarkets** operate on a **self-service basis** and because of this can compete on a price basis. Once again, in supermarkets there can be various departments such as hardware, groceries and clothing and they may also do business in various places, as in the case of Pick 'n Pay.
- **Discount houses** are characterised by relatively low fixed costs and relatively low prices. Their objective is to achieve a high rate of stock turnover in order to keep prices low. Discount stores can also consist of various departments and can often assume a departmental and/or chain store character, as in the case of Dions.
- **Hypermarkets** are a very recent retail concept in South Africa and are characterised by a large building, a wide product range, low prices, spacious parking facilities and a relatively **large geographical target market**. Other stores such as liquor stores, jewellers and stationers are often found in the same complex as the hypermarket as in the case of Pick 'n Pay's Stores Limited 13 hypermarkets.
- **Shopping centres** are usually found in large cities where a large number of different kinds of shops owned by various owners are found within one large building. In this way the consumer is able to effect shopping in one place as in the case of East Gate near Johannesburg or Menlyn in Pretoria.
- **Mail-order stores**, as their name indicates, use the mail to effect their marketing. Customers order products using catalogues, advertisements and order forms and usually pay with the order or on delivery of the products as in the case of Readers' Circle.

The South African Breweries Limited 69,0% of ordinary shares	The public 31,0% of ordinary shares

HOLDING COMPANY
OK BAZAARS (1929) LIMITED

187 departmental discount stores, supermarkets
and free-standing furniture stores
and 22 Hyperama, House and Home,
and service station outlets

SUBSIDIARY COMPANIES

OK Bazaars (Namibia) Limited Windhoek 100% owned	Property owning and name protection companies 100% owned	OK Bazaars (Swaziland) (Pty) Limited Mbabane and Nhlangano 100% owned

OK Bazaars (Ciskei) Limited Bisho 50% owned	OK Bazaars (Mitchells Plain) Limited Mitchells Plain 49% owned	OK KwaZulu Limited KwaMashu Ulundi 53% owned	Bophuthatswana OK Bazaars Limited Garankuwa, Mmabatho, Lehurutshe, Mabopane, Mogwase Mothibistad, Phokeng, Thaba N'chu 50% owned	OK Bazaars (Lesotho) (Pty) Limited Maseru 50% owned	OK Bazaars (Venda) Limited Thohoyandou 50% owned

It should be clear from the above review that the different types of retailers differ according to their divergent characteristics. It should also be clear that within a retail enterprise various combinations of retailers can exist. The **nature of service** can also assume different forms, such as:[6]

- **counter service** where the product is out of the customer's reach and is served by a counter salesperson, as would be the case with jewellery, motor spares or scheduled medical products;
- **self-service** where the customer selects a product and pays for it at a cash register, as would be the case with groceries, alcoholic drinks and hardware;
- **self-selection** where the customer can choose between the available products but still may consult a salesperson, whilst payment is made at a central cash register, eg in shoe shops (Edworks);
- **vending machines** which are coin-operated by the customers and they make their own choice of product, eg cigarette vending machines; and
- **door-to-door sales** where the marketing act takes place within the consumer's home by means of a demonstration of, for example, beauty products; it could also take the form of a tea party.

Apart from the nature of service, retailers can also be classified according to *other norms* such as, for example:[7]

- the **product range** — speciality stores carry a narrow but very deep product range, while departmental stores on the other hand carry a broad and shallow product range;
- the **price** — discount houses attempt to make low prices possible by relying on a high rate of turnover, while speciality stores normally charge higher prices but also offer specialised advice and personal service;
- the way in which the **consumer is reached** — some retailers reach the consumer indirectly as in the case of mail orders, while general dealers come into direct contact with the consumer;
- the **degree of control** over retailers — independent retailers decide for themselves what products they wish to offer, but in the case of chain stores decisions on the product range are normally made on a centralised basis at the head office;
- the **sales environment** — in the case of retailers in a shopping centre where there is a relatively high customer traffic, consumers tend to shop around in order to achieve comparison. Independent retailers, on the other hand, normally experience a more restful atmosphere and a more intimate customer/retailer relationship prevails.

It is obviously very important for the enterprise to understand the characteristics of the various intermediaries fully in order to be able to achieve the best possible combination between its product(s), the buying habits of its target market and the distribution channel.

10.3.2.3 *Profile of wholesale and retail trade in the Republic of South Africa*

A summary review of the South African distribution profile with regard to wholesalers and retailers appears in Table 10.1. The table is self-explanatory with regard to contents and a detailed explanation is thus not necessary.

TABLE 10.1 The South African distribution profile of wholesalers and retailers (Index: 1946/47 = 100)

Variable	1946/47		1960/61		1970/71		1983	
Number of enterprises: Wholesale Retail	3 883 (100) 29 752 (100)		5 486 (141) 36 330 (122)		7 021 (181) 52 149 (175)		11 518 (297) 53 644 (180)	
Number of retailers per wholesaler	7,7		6,6		7,4		4,7	
Employment: Wholesaler Retailer	71 386 (100) 168 904 (100)		123 838 (173) 215 876 (126)		191 377 (266) 368 272 (218)		302 740 (424) 440 964 (261)	
Employment per enterprise Wholesale Retail	18,4 5,7		22,6 (123) 5,9 (104)		27,3 (148) 7,1 (125)		26,3 (143) 8,2 (144)	

	Current prices	Index	Current prices	Index	Current prices	Index	Current prices	Index
Total sales: Wholesale (R'000) Retail (R'000)	850 930 747 222	100 100	2 095 107 1 500 860	246 201	5 569 130 3 769 873	651 505	43 485 369 24 564 520	5 110 3 287
Sales per person employed: Wholesale (R) Retail (R)	11 920 4 424	100 100	16 918 6 952	142 157	28 944 10 236	243 231	143 639 55 706	1 205 1 259
Sales per enterprise: Wholesale (R) Retail (R)	219 142 25 115	100 100	381 901 41 312	174 164	786 937 72 290	360 288	3 775 427 457 917	1 722 1 823
Private consumption expenditure (Rm)	1 264	100	3 381	267	7 698	609	50 703	321

Source: Compiled and calculated from Lucas, GHG. 'Ontwikkelinge in die Distribusiehandel in Suid-Afrika'. *Research for Marketing,* vol 4, June 1973, Table 2, p 34; Republic of South Africa, Central Statistical Services. 1977. *Census of Wholesale and Retail Trade 1977.* Report No 04-41-36. Pretoria: Government Printer; Republic of South Africa, *Census of wholesale and retail trade,* 1983, Reports Nos 61-01-01 and 62-01-01; Bureau for Economic Research. *Ekonomiese Tydreekse,* August 1975. Stellenbosch: University of Stellenbosch; Republic of South Africa, Central Statistical Services. 1980. *South African Statistics 1980.* Pretoria: Government Printer.
Note: Figures for 1977 — Transkei and Bophuthatswana excluded, Walvis Bay included.

10.4 INTERMEDIARIES IN PERSPECTIVE

10.4.1 Right of existence of intermediaries

Consumers often criticise intermediaries in that they accuse them of unnecessarily increasing prices and often also question their right of existence. In this section an attempt is made to place this criticism in perspective. The discussion revolves around the question: 'What is the use of intermediaries in the distribution of products?' An answer to this question lies in two arguments:

- the **function** or **marketing activities** performed by intermediaries; and

- the reduction in the **number of transactions** in the distribution of products.

Activities performed by intermediaries

In Chapter 1 the functional approach to the marketing problem was discussed, hence a detailed explanation of the various marketing activities is not intended here. For the purposes of this discussion, it need only be emphasised that the right of existence and purpose of intermediaries lie in the activities which they help perform in order to bridge the gap between producers and consumers.

The different gaps and the activities which intermediaries perform in order to bridge them, are illustrated as follows:[8]

Gap	*Activity*
Spacial gap	Transport (place utility)
Time gap	Storage (time utility)
Quantity and assortment gaps	Rearrangement, including both elements: accumulation and distribution (see Chapter 1)
Ownership gap	Buy, sell and financing (possession utility)
Information gap	Tracing of the producer or consumer by means of marketing communication and marketing research
Value gap	Standardisation, grading and risk bearing

In Figure 1.1 the major marketing activities are considered from the point of view of creating and servicing of the consumer demand.

It may be argued that producers are able to perform these various activities themselves and in this way eliminate intermediaries. However, the question is whether the individual producer can perform these activities at lower cost than the intermediary. Although this may well be the case regarding perishable consumer products, intermediaries are normally in a position to *perform these activities more economically than the individual producers*. For example, an intermediary such as a wholesaler can perform the joint storage for a large number of producers' products in one large warehouse at lower cost than the individual producers would be able to do. In this way distribution costs are minimised and in reality this is to the advantage of the consumer.

Reduction of the number of transactions

Intermediaries, because of their knowledge of the different manufacturers, are normally knowledgeable as to **who** supplies **what**. As a result they are able to effect purchases from the various producers and then supply the ultimate consumer. Should the consumers, however, wish to supply their needs by purchasing from the various producers themselves, there would be a marked increase in the number of transactions. Figure 10.3 indicates how the number of transactions (each of course bringing additional administrative costs) is affected before (16 transactions) and after (eight transactions) the introduction of an intermediary to the distribution channel.

The above hypothesis and the representation thereof in Figure 10.3 is of course postulated rather simplistically. Should we apply the same principle in reality the result would be much more remarkable.

10.4.2 Justification for intermediaries' entering the distribution channel

Not all distribution channels justify the entry of intermediaries. **The entry of an intermediary should be determined by business economic advantages.** These business economic advantages are based on three considerations which will determine whether an intermediary will enter the distribution channel. Each consideration is now discussed.

10.4.2.1 *Synchronising of needs*[9]

Consumers purchase products in accordance with their needs. Producers, on the other hand, produce according to their resources, know-how and ability a volume large enough to minimise unit cost. However, a specific offer from a producer is not necessarily reconcilable with the needs of the consumers. The synchronising of needs occurs by means of *reassortment*. The intermediary plays an important role here, namely to synchronise the assortments of producers and consumers.

The consumer usually needs a small quantity of a specific product at a time. The consumer will only benefit if the producer sells him a variety of products at a time. This does in fact take place when intermediaries rearrange the offers of different producers according to the consumers' needs, and the size of the transaction reduces the cost for the consumer. If the intermediary can achieve this, then his entry to the distribution channel is economically justified.

FIGURE 10.3   Reduction in the number of transactions by intermediaries

(a) Number of transactions without an intermediary

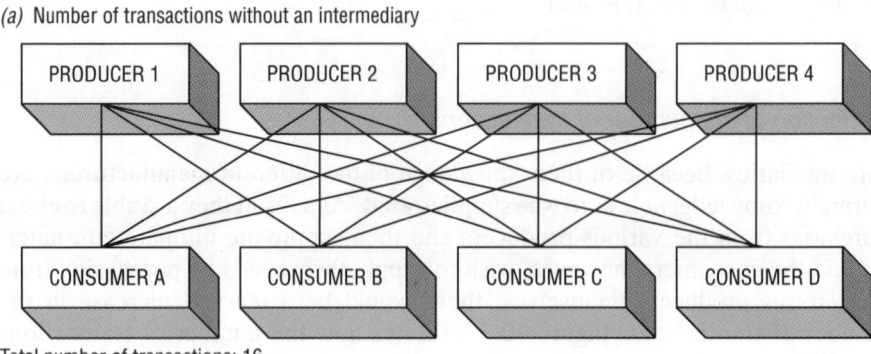

Total number of transactions: 16

(b) Number of transactions with an intermediary

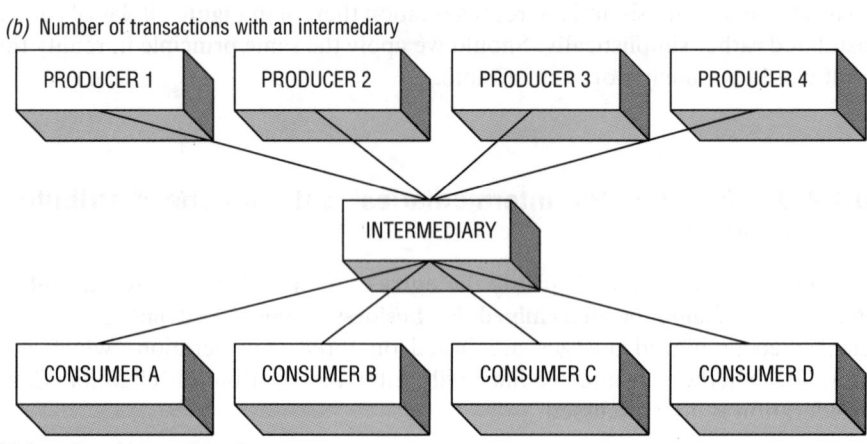

Total number of transactions: 8

10.4.2.2 *Opportunity for specialisation and division of labour*[10]

The execution of marketing activities such as storage and transport is subject to diminishing or increasing returns. **Increasing returns** imply that proportionally more outputs are realised in relation to applied factors of production and that the marginal costs at this larger level of activities subsequently decrease. In the case of **diminishing returns**, the position is reversed with a resultant increase in marginal costs.

Figure 10.4 shows a producer performing marketing activities at diminishing returns (curve BB_1) and an intermediary who, owing to the extent of the marketing activities which he is performing, achieving increasing returns and resultant decreasing marginal costs (curve AA_1). The intermediary is often in a favourable situation to **specialise** in certain marketing activities and in this way achieve increasing returns.

FIGURE 10.4   Entry of an intermediary to the distribution channel on the basis of increasing and diminishing returns

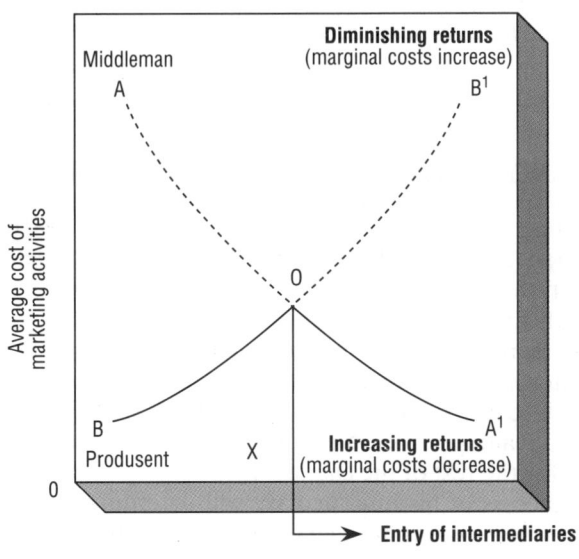

Extent of marketing activities

A situation is possible where diminishing returns of a producer are higher with regard to costs than the increasing returns of the intermediary (OB_1). From this point (X) the intermediary should theoretically enter the distribution channel because he can operate at lower cost (OA_1) than the producer, due to his specialisation in one or more marketing activities. The third consideration is concerned with the postponement and speculation theory.

10.4.2.3 *Postponement and speculation theory*[11]

This theory considers the question of **where** and **when** inventory holding, and thus entry to the distribution channel, will occur. Producers, intermediaries and consumers tend to postpone inventory holding until the product is required. This postponement of inventory holding means, however, that there is a risk of lost sales. Furthermore, a 'speculative' stock will be held by members of the distribution channel to satisfy the requirements of the next level in the channel if the cost of holding this inventory (space, interest and risk costs) will compensate for possible lost sales.

The degree of postponement or speculation will to a large extent be determined by the **delivery time**, ie the speed at which delivery must occur. The shorter the delivery time to the consumer, the greater the need for a speculative stock and the greater the merit for intermediaries to enter the distribution channel. However, when the delivery time for an enterprise is extended, the need for a speculative stock is diminished and so too the need for an intermediary.

In short, it can be stated that the entry of an intermediary to the distribution channel can be justified especially from a cost benefit point of view, on the one hand owing to the **specialisation** in the execution of marketing activities and on the other because of the holding of **speculative** stock in order to **satisfy consumer needs timeously**.

10.5 COMBINING OF INTERMEDIARIES IN DISTRIBUTION

Efficient marketing requires that the various levels in a distribution channel should not function as individual entities but rather as an interdependent system. This means that the members of the channel should link with each other meaningfully with the objective of achieving the most effective distribution of products to final consumers. The producer should also regard his distribution channel as an extension of his own marketing division within the framework of a system which will lead to a synergistic whole $(2 + 2 = 5)$ and which will be integrated to the advantage of all. A producer who maintains that what is good for him is also good for the rest of the channel is extremely short-sighted. He should realise that the success of his intermediary will determine his own success. An integrated distribution system has two dimensions, namely a vertical dimension and a horizontal dimension. These will be examined briefly.[12]

10.5.1 Vertical combination of distribution channels

The term 'vertical' refers to the **number of independent levels** occurring in a distribution channel and the mutual relationships between these levels. Successful distribution is largely dependent on the extent to which the various levels are synchronised. In practice, however, this is not always easily achieved. It often happens, therefore, that producers effect *forward vertical integration* by means of take-overs of retail distributors in order to ensure a more smooth flow in the distribution channel. In the case of Union Wine (a subsidiary of Pichold) the company has, besides its manufacturing interest, also an interest in the wholesale and retail of wine and spirits.

The opposite situation is obviously also possible in that intermediaries such as retailers effect *backward vertical integration* and in this way attain control over the supply (producers) of products. The Pep Stores group, for example, not only has its own retail outlets but its own factories supplying amongst other things shoes and clothing.

Apart from the absolute control of the various levels and distributing channels by means of vertical integration, **formal agreements** are also used in order to ensure better distribution. **Franchising** is one of the best-known formal agreements and gives the sole right to consecutive intermediaries to market products or services in a specific market environment according to certain prescriptions such as product presentation, marketing communication, target prices and shop layout. These arrangements can be between various levels in the distribution channel, for example with cooperation:

- between **producers and retailers** as in the case of the motor industry (Tiger Wheels);

- between **producers and wholesalers** as in the case of the soft drink industry where wholesalers receive the right to market and supply a concentrate (Coca-Cola) in a certain geographical area to retailers;

- between **original service suppliers and retailers** where the retailers receive the sole right to market the service in an area as in the case of Kentucky Fried Chicken in South Africa; and

- between a **wholesaler and retailers** as in the case of retail chemists (Link Chemists).

For this franchise right the franchisee pays a certain royalty, for example 5 per cent of his turnover (compare the abstract from *Finansies & Tegniek*).

The South African Franchise Association provides the following definition for franchising:

"A franchise is a grant by the franchisor to the franchisee entitling the latter to the use of a complete business package containing all the elements necessary to establish a previously untrained person in the franchised business and to enable him or her to run on an ongoing basis, according to guidelines supplied, efficiently and profitably."[13]

Even though the franchise business is relatively small in the Republic of South Africa compared to the United States of America, it's showing a steady growth. The fast-food industry especially is showing a notable growth. It has been said that 40 per cent of all fast-food retailers operate under a franchise system. More than 75 per cent of speed-printing is done by franchisees.[14] For example, it is estimated that for the year ended on 30 June 1990, total sales from franchising amounted to R25,4 billion whilst a figure of R60,6 billion is predicted for 1995.[15]

A franchise agreement offers certain advantages to the franchisee:[16]

- **Smaller risk.** Studies have shown that less than 5 per cent of franchises fail during their first year compared to 33 per cent in other business enterprises.

- **Management control** which includes supervision and general operating management.

PLEASURE FOODS LTD
SOUTH AFRICA'S LARGEST GROUP
OF FAST FOOD OUTLETS
ASSOCIATED TO SAFA SINCE IT'S INCEPTION

 *GO GRABBABURGER NOW!*

For full franchise details, please refer to page 83

For full franchise details, please refer to page 60

 **Fresh & healthy**

For full franchise details, please refer to page 72

Headin' for

For full franchise details, please refer to page 75

YOURS IN TOTAL GUEST SATISFACTION

For full franchise details, please refer to page 57

 **GET SET TO SIZZLE**

For full franchise details, please refer to page 58

 A COMPLETE MENU OF FAST FOOD FRANCHISES ALL UNDER ONE UMBRELLA

Source: The SA Franchise Association, 1990, The S.A. Franchise Association, P.O. Box 18398, Hillbrow, p. 67

- **Financial support and support in getting started**. The franchisor usually helps with the selection of the site, the store layout and the choice of premises, and is also helpful with its initial capital needs.

- **Training**. The franchisor often gives training to improve the management — anything from technical to administrative.

- Franchisors can get **discounts for bulk buying** and this is to the advantage of the franchisee.

- **Profitable incomes** are often attained sooner than would be the case with other new businesses.

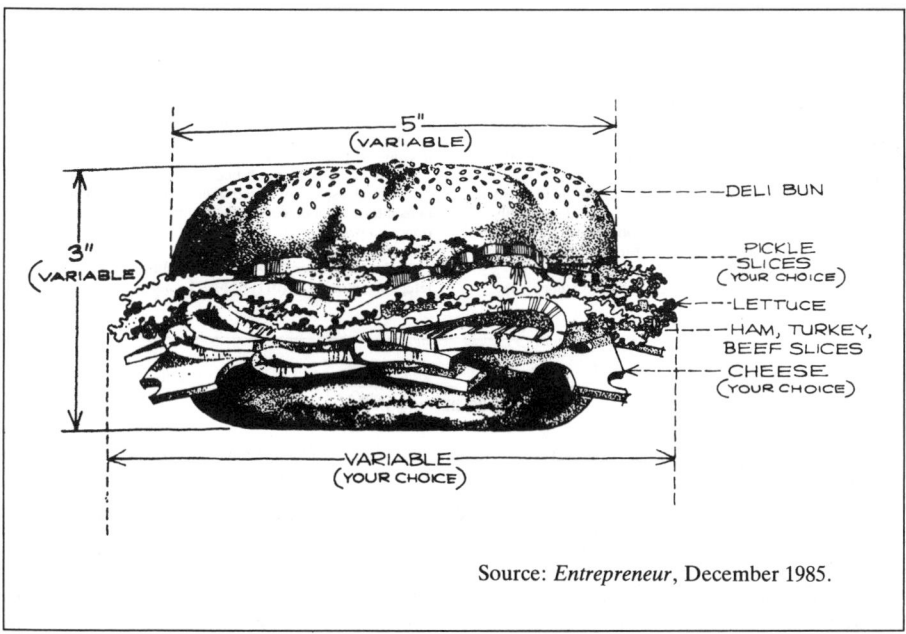

Source: *Entrepreneur*, December 1985.

Franchise agreements, however, also have certain disadvantages:

- **Ownership** of the franchise is usually limited to a time period — 20–30 years with an option to renew.

- **Prescribed work procedures** can be very time-consuming, especially if the business is run on a part-time basis.

- **Control** by the franchisor is often rigid and can leave no room for own initiative of the franchisee.

- The franchise right may require a **substantial capital investment**. Examples are: the franchise right outlay, royalties on sales, advertising contributions, and capital required to start off in accordance with stipulations.

How much does a concession cost?

A concession is a contract concluded between a concession holder and a concession company where the holder pays the company a specific amount of money in exchange for the company's management system and right to sell the company's service or product.

Concession costs are a once-off fixed amount generally paid when the concession contract is signed. This payment typically includes initial training of personnel and of the concession holder, assistance with choice of location and equipment, use of the name and trade mark and particularly the concession company's business expertise.

"Concession costs that are too high may mean that the concession company may not render the concession holder the necessary assistance, since it would already have pocketed a large amount of money and would not be too concerned about its percentage of monthly management fees," Mr Kurt Illetschko, executive director of the SA Franchising Association (SAFA), warns.

Capital costs are costs incurred by the concession holder to establish the concession. Costs vary according to the type of concession company, area, size of and necessary equipment for the building, estimated turnover and operating costs to be incurred, such as salaries of personnel during training.

Management fees is a fixed percentage of the monthly or weekly turnover to be paid to the concession company. It is the company's principal source of income from the concession holder.

Every concession holder makes a contribution to an advertising fund. This is also a fixed percentage of the monthly or weekly turnover paid to the concession company. It is paid into a central advertising fund used for publicity campaigns and other expenses related to marketing.

Most companies also assist the concession holder with publicity and campaigns in the local market.

In order to ensure corporate uniformity and quality, the concession holder has to buy certain products direct from the company. One advantage of this to the concession holder is that the products are purchased wholesale from the company and are therefore cheaper.

In some cases the concession company appoints outside companies from which products have to be purchased.

The contract period is generally fixed and the concession holder may choose whether or not to renew the contract after expiry of the period. Should the concession holder not have conformed to certain requirements and principles, the concession company generally has the right not to renew the contract.

All the companies approached by F&T provide training, which varies from a couple of days to a month and depends on the concession holder and his personnel's knowledge of the product and their general know-how. Should a new product or management system be introduced, the concession holder is duly informed and, if neces sary, provided with further training.

The majority of concession companies have brochures at their disposal that can be forwarded to interested parties on request. They contain information on the company's background and activities and, in some cases, an analysis of what it would cost to open a typical concession branch.

SAFA has recently published a manual of 128 pages that discusses all aspects of concessions in relative detail and contains information on concession companies, financial institutions and people in the legal profession who are members. The cost is R25,00 per copy.

SAFA's address is P O Box 18398, Hillbrow 2038, and its telephone number is (011) 642-2921 (mornings only).

Concession holding in SA

Concession company	Consession cost	Capital cost in R	Management service money	Contribution to advertising fund
Mike's Kitchen	R30 000	R500 000–R600 000	5% on turnover	2% on turnover
Steers	R12 000	R250 000+	5% on turnover	2% on turnover
Prontaprint	R31 500	R176 500	5% on turnover	5% on turnover
Rug Doctor PRO	R10 000	R16 500	6% on turnover	5% on turnover
Bread and Butter	R18 000	R162 000	5% on turnover	3% on turnover
Kardicor	—	R40 000–R60 000 plus R40 000– R60 000 for stock	4% on turnover	2% on turnover
Supa Quick	R20 000	R200 000	3% of purchases	4% of purchases

Concession company	Products which can be bought directly from the company	Contract period	Average turnover per month
Mike's Kitchen	None	Ten years	R100 000–R120 000
Steers	Most of the products	Unlimited	R55 000–R75 000
Prontaprint	Corporative packaging	Seven years	R25 000–R80 000
Rug Doctor PRO	All products	Ten years	R6 000 plus per machine
Bread and Butter	Corporative packaging	Five years	R50 000–R60 000
Kardicor	Must buy from approved suppliers	Same period as rental contract	R20 000
Supa Quick	Must buy from nominated suppliers	Five years	100 000 country 250 000 cities

Source: Translated from *Finansies & Tegniek*, 27 April 1990.

When obtaining the franchise the owner thereof must be totally committed because according to Collins off the SA Franchising Association:

Buying a franchising relationship

'In buying a franchise, you are not merely buying a business; you are buying a relationship with the franchisor. As with any relationship, this can be strained or healthy, lucrative or unprofitable and can end happily or in a painful, bitter lawsuit.'[17]

10.5.2 Horizontal combination in distribution

Horizontal aspects of distribution channels have to do with the **combining** of components or participants **at a specific level** with the object of more effective distribution. In this way economies of scale can be achieved by a group of retailers advertising jointly or transporting jointly. **Horizontal integration** thus occurs when a number of participants at one level in the distribution channel either **voluntarily** or **formally** co-operate by means of take-overs within the same enterprise, for example chain stores.

Voluntary co-operation occurs when a wholesaler effects mutual co-operation between independent retailers on the one hand to ensure himself of retail outlets and on the other in order to afford the participating retailers a united front against the larger groups. The well-known SPAR-Voluntary Trade Association in South Africa is an excellent example of voluntary co-operation. Independent retailers are voluntarily affiliated to the South African SPAR Groceries Association, which in turn is divided into independent wholesalers in different regions. Wholesalers supply affiliated retailers in the regional areas. A National Board of the Gild co-ordinates the needs of the different regional areas on a national basis. The National Board in conjunction with regional committees formulates a SPAR strategy to achieve the following objectives:

- **increased sales** of SPAR members through co-ordinated marketing communication;
- improving **group purchases**;
- improving **buying power** and improved price negotiations through a centralised buying department;
- negotiations with suppliers for **direct distribution** to various members on direct orders;
- supplying **training** facilities to achieve better trade operations;
- **improving members' business set-up**, e g display techniques, stockholding and administration systems.

Voluntary co-operation also occurs among **co-operative retailers** in an attempt to offer lower prices through centralised purchasing. In principle voluntary co-operation is aimed at achieving a better competitive position against the large chain stores.

10.6 DISTRIBUTION TRENDS IN THE REPUBLIC OF SOUTH AFRICA

Distribution during the nineteenth century was characterised by a structure consisting of independent retailers in the rural as well as urban areas. Although the self-service concept was experimented with early in this century, especially in the food trade, this distribution method only took off after the Second World War in the Republic of South Africa. The first of its sort was CTC Bazaars on the corner of Eloff and Market Streets in Johannesburg.[18]

Since then, however, the distribution structures and methods have changed drastically. Self-service was gradually accepted and supermarkets offering one-stop sales and wide product ranges at relatively low prices with limited service came into the picture. Where the traditional independent retailer supplied 200 different product items the present hypermarket offers more than 60 000 different items. The most important tendencies in distribution are discussed below.[19]

First, more **diversified product presentation** is present in distribution. Retailers are stocking more product types with a lower relationship. This phenomenon can be witnessed in the present-day grocery stores, where they also stock other products such as furniture, garden tools and clothes. There are several reasons for this trend, such as:

- consumer's need for **one-stop shopping**.
- the more intensive exploitation of **diverse distribution points** by manufacturers; and
- intermediaries are striving to **improve their income by stocking a bigger range**, especially products that utilise their floor space better.

Secondly, there is a trend among individual **chain stores** to gain a **bigger share** in the total retail business. Peter Dove, director of Pick 'n Pay, estimates that only 2 per cent of South African grocery stores are responsible for 68 per cent of total sales.[20] OK Bazaars already has more than 190 stores. Checkers has more than 170 and Pick 'n Pay, with the opening of their High Gate store on the West Rand, has 100 stores.[21] Obviously the chain stores have the power to demand bulk discounts and even 'confidential' discounts. Pick 'n Pay estimated that in 1989 three per cent or R2,6 million of its total income came from incentive and/or confidential discounts.[22]

A *third* trend is the so called '**pantry store**', which is specifically aimed at the housewife. Recently the price gap between supermarkets and pantry stores has declined to the extent that housewives are prepared to pay the premium for the added convenience: shorter queues at the tills mean a saving in time.

A *fourth* trend is the **cash and carry wholesalers**, known as Price Clubs. Those stores are finding favour in the **Black market** and are currently competing with well-established enterprises such as Metro and Score.

Photo: Courtesy of T. Rudman

There is *fifthly* a trend towards **speciality stores**. Enterprises are concentrating on certain product categories, for example the fashionable customer in a certain age and income bracket, and project an image of a sophisticated life style (eg Boardmans). It is claimed that these stores generate more sales per square metre and even higher profitability than other retailers.[23] *Finance Week* anticipates the following: 'If regional shopping centres promoted the retail revolution of the past 20 years, as profound will be the trend to specialisation in the decade ahead.'[24] With the growth in speciality stores there is the trend that departmental stores offering a multitude of products are fading. It has been estimated that departmental stores were responsible for 25 per cent of the retail sales 20 years ago. Today their share is a mere 1 per cent.[25]

A *sixth* development is the rise of the **informal sector** in the South African distribution structure. Even though figures as to the extent of this sector are difficult to establish and estimates differ substantially — from as high as 40% of the GNP to as low as 3% of the GNP, with 6,5 to 10% (1990) regarded as realistic — it must be accepted that the informal sector still holds a vast potential for further exploration.[26] As **privatisation and deregulation** gain momentum it can be expected that this sector will grow even more. The Central Business District (CBD) concept with a shopping centre may also provide some impetus to retailing.

A *seventh* trend that will grow over time is '**home buying**'. This is done with the help of Beltel and other computer-assisted methods. However, figures as to the extent hereof are not available.

As can be seen from the preceding, distribution is still undergoing important changes and will continue changing as long as opportunities in the marketing environment are exploited by the marketers.[27]

10.7 SUMMARY

The distribution decision of a producer has two important components — the choice of the most suitable distribution channel and the most economical physical distribution of products. Decisions concerning distribution are of particular importance for marketing management, especially in the light of the fact that they are not decisions which can normally be altered in the short term. Naturally there is a direct relationship between the distribution decision and the other marketing instruments.

Distribution of most consumer products occurs through various intermediaries. Intermediaries can be divided into resellers, wholesalers and retailers. Each of these intermediaries has specific characteristics which equip them ideally for specific marketing circumstances. A thorough comprehension of distribution channels is thus of particular importance for marketing management.

While intermediaries might often be criticised, their right to existence is to be found in the activities which they perform, often at a lower cost than the producer would be able to perform himself.

Intermediaries can co-operate or combine their efforts in various ways. Vertical combination involves the different levels in the distribution channel, while horizontal combination refers to co-operation between different enterprises at the same level. In both cases formal or informal co-operation can improve the efficient functioning of the distribution channel.

As circumstances change, the distribution channels also change. Several distribution tendencies have developed and they are aimed at satisfying servicing the consumer market.

REFERENCES

1. For a more detailed analysis of definitions of the distribution channel concept see Walters, CG, 1977. *Marketing Channels*. Santa Monica, California: Goodyear Publishing Company, pp 3–5; and Mallen, B. 'Understanding Marketing Channels'. *European Journal of Marketing*, 10, 2.
2. See for example Kotler, P & Armstrong, G. 1990 *Marketing — an Introduction*. Englewood Cliffs, New Jersey: Prentice-Hall Inc, p 324.
3. Guirdham, M. 1972. *Marketing: The Management of Distribution Channels*. Oxford: Pergamon Press, p 129.
4. For a broader explanation of trade agents and brokers consult Stern, LW & El-Ansary, AI. 1977. *Marketing Channels*. Englewood Cliffs, New Jersey: Prentice-Hall Inc, pp 135–6.

5. Republic of South Africa, Central Statistical Services. 1983. *Census of Wholesalers and Retailers, 1983*. Report Nos 62-01-01 and 61-01-01. Pretoria: Government Printer.
6. For a discussion hereof see Guirdham op cit, chapter 1.
7. See for example Mandell, MI & Rosenberg, LJ. 1981. *Marketing*. 2nd edition. Englewood Cliffs, New Jersey: Prentice-Hall Inc, pp 400–9.
8. For a discussion hereof see also Guirdham op cit, pp 103–6 for an informative exposition of the activities performed by intermediaries and the utilities for which they provide, see Hardy, KG & Magrath, AJ. 1988. London: *Marketing channel management* Scott Foresman and Company, pp 4–5.
9. See also Ibid p 107.
10. For a detailed explanation hereof see Stigler, GJ. 'The Division of Labor is Limited by the Extent of the Market' in Mallen, BE. 1967. *The Marketing Channel: A Conceptual Viewpoint*. New York: John Wiley & Sons, pp 56–62.
11. For a detailed explanation of this theory see Bucklin, LP. 'Postponement, Speculation, and the Structure of Distribution Channels' in Mallen op cit, pp 67–73.
12. See also Hardy, KG & Magrath, AJ. op cit, pp 22–26.
13. Consult South African Franchise Association, 1990, The South African Franchise Association Handbook, P.O. Box 18398, Hillbrow, 2038, p 5.
14. See *Finansies & Tegniek*, 11 December 1987, p 12.
15. See Illetschko, K. in *Entrepreneur*, June 1991, p 15.
16. See *Entrepreneur*, December 1985, p 6.
17. Loc cit.
18. Rainier, RL. 1975. *A Methodology for Strategic Planning for a South African Retail Organisation*. Unpublished MBL-thesis. Pretoria: University of South Africa, p 5.
19. See also Marx, S and Dekker. HJ. 1982. *Bemarkingsbestuur*. Pretoria: HAUM, pp 225ff.
20. See *Finance Week*, 7–13 April 1988, p 20.
21. Ibid. p 21.
22. Ibid. p 20.
23. Loc cit.
24. *Finance Week*, 20–27 October 1985, p 22.
25. Ibid. p 23.
26. See *Pretoria News*, 12 September 1988; Kirsten, M. 'A Qualitative Perspective on the Informal Sector in Southern Africa' *Development Southern Africa*, vol 5, no 2, 1988, pp 251–7 and Kruger, S. and De Bruyn, HEC, 1991, "'n Toekomsstrategie vir die Informele Sektor binne 'n Vryemarkstelsel", Paper read at the third yearly conference of the Southern Africa Institute for Management Scientists, 28 to 29 October 1991, University of Durban-Westville, pp 12–13.
27. For an informative preview of the distribution strategies for the nineties, consult Terblanch, NS. 1991. *Retailing Strategies in the Nineties — A Decade of Retailers Ahead?*, paper read at the third conference of the Southern Africa Institute for Management Scientists, 28 to 29 October 1991, University of Durban-Westville.

CASE STUDY

THE FRANCHISE ROUTE TO RESTAURANT OWNERSHIP

Mike's Kitchen was founded in 1973, with one outlet in Greenside, based on a totally untried route in the restaurant industry, with a family and fun orientation, and an unusual product mix including salad bars, spare ribs, kiddy meals and unique 'cottagey' menus and matching interior decor.

In ten years, Mike's Kitchen grew from one to fifteen outlets, the original Greenside operation being retained by the founder, and the others franchised to associates and investors.

By 1986, having been sold to David Lewis in 1983, the franchise had grown to a chain of 39 restaurants, with the only perceivable change in operational stance being a far greater emphasis on promotion, and the unique Mike's Kitchen Birthday Club, by then split into a kiddy and an adult section.

Looking at the present-day restaurant micro market, a dog-eat-dog situation has arisen, with a mass of competitive enterprises fighting for the available consumer spend.

Operating in this highly competitive environment, Mike's Kitchen has to be very specific in its offers, and its advertising must meet specific needs.

Market trends

The R1 billion South African restaurant industry operates predominantly in the White market, which for the owner/restaurateur was until recently an extremely profitable sector. High inflation, spiralling food prices (especially meat), and the recent advent of big business involvement have caused a rapid decline in profitability. This has created a mass of aggressive price oriented promotions within the sector. Even take-away operations represent a major threat, as price rather than value-consciousness accelerates. All this activity militates against the private operator, unless that operator is a franchisee.

But how does Mike's Kitchen operate in a market that appeals to an individual who is inclined towards personal ownership rather than being a corporate employee? Mike's Kitchen feels that it offers the best of both worlds ... a franchisee is not an employee, nor is he/she left on his/her own to face the slings and arrows of outrageous economic fortune!

The Mike's Kitchen market

Mike's Kitchen has defined its primary market as the '2 + 2', that is two adults and two children, but this tag does not cover all the factors that dictate the success of all Mike's Kitchens. In classical terms, the Mike's Kitchen market has to be broken down in a number of quantifiable ways.

Market stratification takes many forms. In Mike's case, it is largely demographic, with the psychographic aspects giving the individual franchisee rein for his personal attitudes and skills. This point may seem academic, for the Parktown outlet is born of the same operations manual as, for example, Mike's Kitchen,

Pietersburg . . . but the front-of-house approach varies to suit the catchment area and the needs of that area.

In demographic terms, a Mike's Kitchen franchise needs to match a number of fairly finite parameters:

Geographic — Any urban concentration which by population size, or commercial centre development, can support at least a 100 seat restaurant. Excluding the factor of office feed, a town or suburb of 20 000 homes is viable.

Demographic — Adults 24 to 40+, children 0 to 12, male and female equally, family unit income R1 000 to R3 999, and a host of other formal factors under occupation, race, language bias, etcetera.

The point we make is that the days of being all things to all people are long gone, and careful target market segmentation is essential to a longterm and secure future. At the same time, concentration on Mike's primary market would only keep us busy from 17h30 to 20h00 weekdays, and weekend lunchtimes. A secondary market must be addressed for weekday lunchtimes, weekday evenings after 20h00 and 'nights out', Saturday and Sunday, specifically business people, social singles and the youth market.

Over and above these formally defined target markets, Mike's Kitchen also boasts an exclusive and captive market of several hundred thousand birthday club members, but our usage of this captive audience is something of a trade secret!

What do you get with a Mike's Kitchen franchise?

The package that supports the franchisee is incredibly comprehensive. From exterior signage, through decor, to every aspect of point-of-sale; from three-month owner/manager training courses, through ongoing waitress training, to periodic franchisee workshops; from staff uniforms to uniform quality control; from TV advertising to the humblest of weekly special ads in local community newspapers, and involvement in family orientated sports like cycling, it is a package that few franchise operations in the world can surpass.

Mike's Kitchen is a fun family restaurant, typified by standardised signage, decor, service, food and even pricing. It's great strength in terms of trust, reliability and traditional values, puts it in a market niche of its own.

Consumer exposure

But, no matter the inherent or created strengths of a chain like Mike's Kitchen, the consumer is most exposed to the actual franchise holder, who either personally, or through a management/waitress team, meets, greets, seats and special-treats each guest. This front-of-house aspect is very much a priority when prospective franchisees are initially screened.

Put another way, the investment in each Mike's Kitchen is substantial, both by the franchisee and the franchisor, so the people relationship has to work from day one. Being a restaurateur is not an eight to five job. Only a particular breed of person can physically and mentally handle the strain of what can easily be an 8 am to 2 am life . . . with the rewards quite some way down the track.

Mike's Kitchen works as a team to support its selected franchisees. And it works, in about nineteen cases out of twenty. When it doesn't work, it's usually the customer that gives one the early warnings ... and it's usually the franchise company that springs into action with remedial training, task forces on food quality upgrading, local advertising and promotions, or any other activity that will address a specific problem.

Why be a franchisee?

The answer is almost a one-liner. In today's marketplace, to bear the costs of restaurant promotion on your own is almost impossible. And, to be able to source all the information and lessons of fifteen years of national experience is equally impossible. In fact, there is no way that an individual restaurateur can have access to the case histories of a franchise operation like Mike's Kitchen.

Go it on your own? No way!

Source: *Entrepreneur* August 1988.

QUESTIONS

1. What are the advantages of a Mike's Kitchen franchise?

2. Describe the target market for Mike's Kitchen.

3. Suggest a marketing communication campaign for a Mike's Kitchen in an up-market suburb.

4. How is the image for Mike's Kitchen created?

5. Describe the relationship between the franchisor and franchisee.

ASSIGNMENTS

1. 'It has been contended that decisions regarding the distribution channels are the most critical to be considered by marketing management.' Do you agree with this statement? Motivate your answer.

2. Suppose you have to categorise Woolworths Limited as a certain type of retailer. Explain the *type(s)* of retailer you would classify this enterprise as.

3. Suppose you are in the company of a few wine farmers hailing from the Western Cape. They have strong arguments concerning the low profit margin received on a bottle of wine. One of the farmers has the following opinion: 'It is all the middlemen's fault and it is they that receive all the profit with a low level of input from their side.' Another farmer expresses the viewpoint that these 'middlemen' need to be eliminated and farmers should undertake their own marketing.

You are invited to express an expert opinion on the matter. Supply a full explanation to the farmers regarding the implication of their 'own' marketing, as well as your evaluation regarding current use of other intermediaries.

4. Suppose, as an entrepreneur, you want to establish your own enterprise but circumstances dictate the closing of franchising agreements. *Discuss* the type of enterprise you will favour and how you will evaluate franchising agreements in terms of that form of enterprise.

5. Speculate on your expectations concerning tendencies in distribution which may manifest in the Republic of South Africa over the next decade.

CHAPTER 11

DISTRIBUTION MANAGEMENT

11.1 INTRODUCTION

In Chapter 10 a broad description of the nature and essence of distribution as a marketing instrument was given. It is, however, necessary that the planning, execution and control of distribution by marketing management should now be considered. To achieve this, purposeful distribution decisions are necessary.

In order to effect the successful integration of distribution into the marketing strategy the distribution channel and physical distribution must be managed efficiently. The producer should regard the distribution system as an extension of his own marketing division. The distribution system must function in such a way that mutual advantages for both producer and intermediaries are achieved. Consequently, the purpose of effective functioning in distribution is a smooth and continuous supply to distribution outlets, lower costs, including lower adminis-trative and physical distribution costs, as well as increased co-ordination in the distribution system.[1]

ORGANISATION OF THE CHAPTER

The nature of distribution management.

Distribution planning: Explanation of distribution planning, formulating channel objectives.

The selection of a distribution channel: The intensity of distribution, intensive, selective, exclusive distribution, factors determining the nature of distribution channels, the selection of specific intermediaries.

Executing distribution channel decisions: Division of tasks in the distribution channel, reasons why intermediaries are unwilling to co-operate, conflicts within the distribution channel, methods to improve co-operation in the distribution channel, leadership in the distribution channel.

Controlling the distribution channel: Control of channel members, evaluation of the total distribution channel.

Physical distribution management: The nature of physical distribution, the importance of physical distribution, the objectives, the selection of methods of physical distribution, co-ordination, control of physical distribution activities.

11.2 THE NATURE OF DISTRIBUTION MANAGEMENT

This chapter follows a dual approach. *First*, the management of the distribution channel is discussed, and, *secondly*, the management of physical distribution activities.

Figure 11.1 offers a broad framework for the **management of distribution**, and also serves as a basis for the discussion in this chapter. Figure 11.1 shows the decisions and activities which have to be performed in order to place the product in the hands of the final consumer.

Picture a consumer of wine in Pretoria who wants to buy a specific Nederburg wine which is produced in Stellenbosch. A 'path' is needed to bring the two parties together and to ensure an effective flow. Figure 11.1 offers an overview of this 'road', starting with planning and ending with control.

11.3 DISTRIBUTION PLANNING

11.3.1 Definition of distribution planning

Distribution planning incorporates the formulation of distribution objectives, and the selection of a suitable distribution channel and also methods of physical distribution to perform the necessary marketing activities efficiently.

In the preceding description the emphasis falls on two terms, **objectives** and **selection**. These two terms will be discussed in relation to distribution — first in terms of the distribution channel and secondly in terms of physical distribution.

11.3.2 Formulating distribution channel objectives

Distribution channel objectives should be focused on achieving the **marketing objectives** and ultimately on the **business objectives**. Marketing objectives will usually have a specific target market as basis and consequently the distribution channel decision must accommodate the target market in order to realise the marketing objective. The target market has to be served in such a way that the applied factors of production will ensure the highest profitability in accordance with the profitability principle (one of the managerial principles of the marketing concept).

FIGURE 11.1   Framework for the management of the distribution channel and physical distribution activities

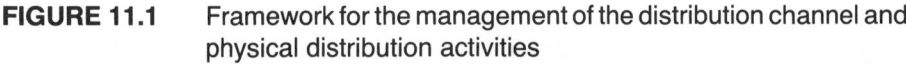

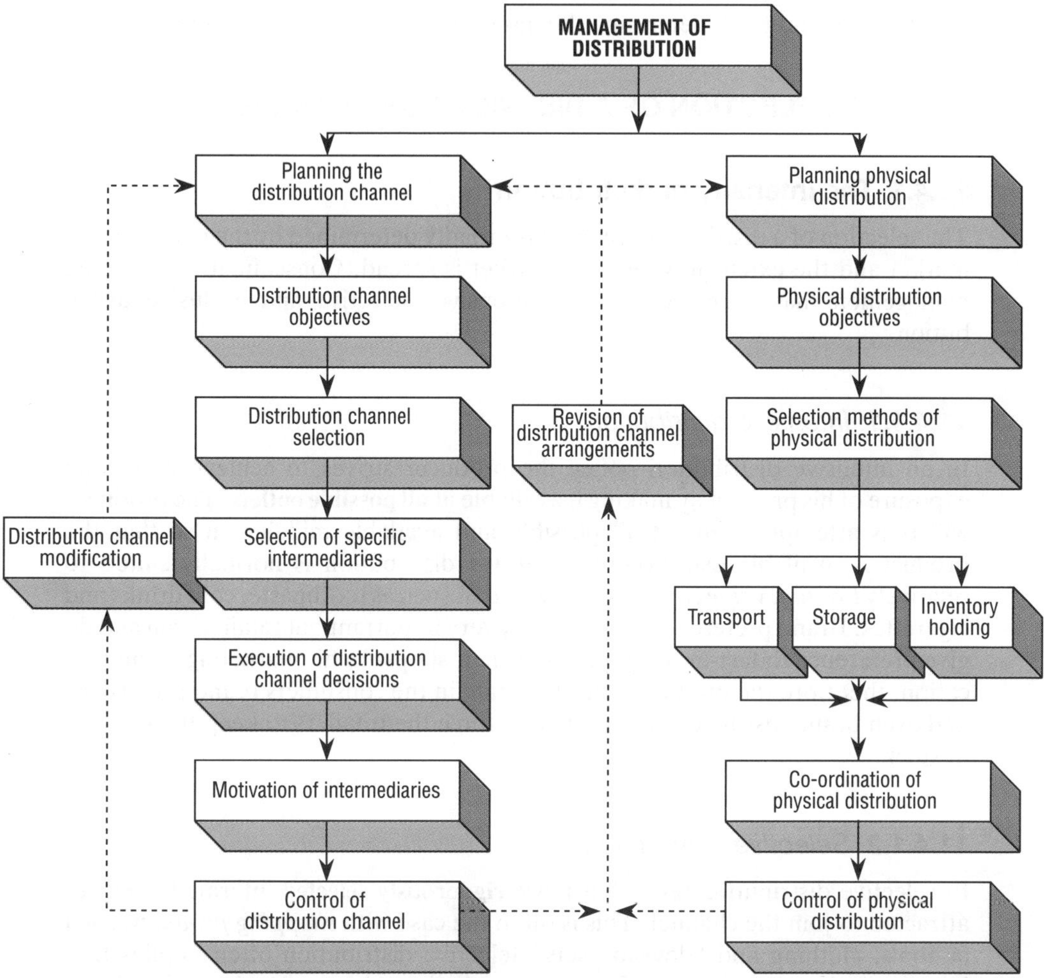

Source: Adapted from Sims, JT et al. 1977. *Marketing Channels: Systems and Strategies*. New York: Harper & Row, p 54.

An example of a specific distribution channel objective

Let us assume that a producer wishes to market a new convenience product to consumers in the Pretoria-Witwatersrand-Vereeniging area; a distribution objective could be as follows:

'To attain during 19X1 a distribution network in the PWV area whereby a minimum of 50 per cent of all housewives will be able through normal purchasing to obtain the grocery product A.'

A specific distribution objective which has been derived from the marketing objective offers a basis for the development of a specific distribution strategy. The distribution objective must thus, as in the example, be aimed at the target market. The target market will determine the **nature** and **intensity** of distribution.

11.4 THE SELECTION OF A DISTRIBUTION CHANNEL

11.4.1 The intensity of distribution

The selection of a distribution channel is broadly determined by the nature of the market and the extent to which the market is spread. Consequently marketing management has a choice between intensive, selective and exclusive distribution.[2]

11.4.1.1 *Intensive distribution*

In an intensive distribution policy the producer strives to achieve maximum exposure of his product by making it available at **all possible outlets**. The producer will thus attempt to attract all possible and available middlemen so that the product is available everywhere. Intensive distribution is normally suited to relatively *low unit value convenience products*, such as toothpaste, cold drinks and cigarettes. Brand preference is usually not very important but retailers can and do give preference to fast-moving brands in their shops. In his marketing communication, therefore the producer aims to create in the consumers brand preference and even brand insistence and this would force the retailers to keep the product in stock.

11.4.1.2 *Selective distribution*

In selective distribution **fewer** but **more rigourously selected** intermediaries are attracted to join the channel. This is often the case with *shopping products*, such as tools, clothing and television sets. Selective distribution often implies that intermediaries, especially wholesalers, are eliminated from the channel and that distribution is effected directly through selected retailers. A selective distribution approach will, as in the case of the other alternatives, offer guidelines to distribution decisions, for example in the choice of specific intermediaries.

11.4.1.3 *Exclusive distribution*

Exclusive distribution occurs when the producer **purposefully limits** the number of intermediaries for his product. Exclusive distribution is often found in formal co-operation, such as franchising, where it is stipulated where and how products must be marketed.

Exclusive distribution is often encountered in the marketing of *speciality products* such as jewellery and motor vehicles. In this approach the producer lays down certain conditions according to which the intermediary must operate, for example advertising, after-sales service, maintenance and financing. It should be clear that the producer plays a leading and often dominant role in the distribution of his products. Furthermore, it is important that the intermediary must be chosen carefully and co-operation should be evaluated continuously.

11.4.1.4 *Guidelines for the intensity of distribution*

Because marketing environments differ from producer to producer, the intensity of distribution and also the distribution channel will differ.

Sims and others[3] offer a number of guidelines which determine the intensity of distribution (intensive, selective or exclusive distribution), ie the number of distribution outlets, namely:

- **The unit value of products**. Low unit value products tend toward intensive distribution, while high unit value products require a more selective or even exclusive distribution.
- **Frequency of purchase**. Products with a high degree of repeat purchasing will normally be distributed intensively, while products bought once only, or very seldom, require a more selective distribution.
- **Price stability**. Products which are sensitive to price reductions tend to have intensive distribution, while products where the recommended price can be maintained tend to be distributed more exclusively.
- **Brand loyalty**. Products with a strong brand preference tend to be distributed more selectively, while those with relatively low brand preference can be distributed more intensively.
- **Product differentiation**. Products with relatively few distinguishing characteristics tend to be distributed intensively compared to those with strong differential characteristics where selective and even exclusive distribution are encountered.
- **Technical complexity**. Technically complex products which require specialised knowledge and training are normally distributed selectively or exclusively as compared to technologically simple products.
- **Selling requirements**. In a self-service outlet which is supported by attractive packaging and display, the consumer can be persuaded to purchase, hence intensive distribution is obviously the best method. However, where advice and sales assistance are required, the tendency will be toward selective and exclusive distribution.
- **Service requirements**. The greater the need for installation, maintenance and repair services, the greater the tendency will be toward selective and exclusive distribution.
- **Inventory holding**. A relatively low inventory holding is maintained with intensive distribution. On the other hand, selective or exclusive distribution entails a relatively higher inventory holding with the consequent risk of obsolescence.

It should be clear that the aim of intensive distribution is to achieve maximum market penetration so that products are available everywhere, while selective or exclusive distribution strives to eliminate direct competition with other brands at distribution outlets in order to increase sales. In the case of intensive distribution, the product must of necessity compete with other brands for, inter alia shelf-space and brand recognition. The intensity of distribution is usually associated with a specific *area*. For example, marketing management has to decide whether distribution will be intensive in the Transvaal and only selective in the Orange Free State.

Within the framework of a policy of intensive, selective or exclusive distribution, the choice of a distribution channel strategy requires a careful evaluation of the factors which determine the nature of a distribution channel. (The guidelines for the decision concerning either intensive, selective or exclusive distribution are also relevant here.) The following generally accepted factors merit further attention.

11.4.2 Factors influencing the nature of the distribution channel[4]

11.4.2.1 *Characteristics of the target market (consumers)*

A number of aspects pertaining to the target market affect the choice of a distribution channel. First, the **geographical characteristics** of the target market may influence the choice. A geographically dispersed market, for instance, will probably require more intermediaries and consequently a longer channel of distribution. However, when the target market is concentrated within a small geographical area, intermediaries can possibly be eliminated in favour of direct distribution.

In the second instance **consumer preferences and behaviour** may influence the choice of distribution channel. When final consumers purchase small quantities but with a high frequency longer distribution channels are preferable because administrative costs and execution of such orders make direct distribution uneconomical. In cases where large quantities are bought at a time, a shorter distribution channel may be more advantageous.

Thirdly, the **number of potential consumers** also influences the choice of the channel. When there is a large number of potential customers, the tendency will be to use a long channel and a large number of intermediaries will normally be required in the channel. If the product is to be marketed intensively, a longer distribution channel and consequently a large number of intermediaries will be used.

In the fourth instance the influence of the **kind of consumer** must be considered. If the product is intended for the final consumer market, retailers will be used almost without exception. Industrial consumers, on the other hand, often prefer to deal directly with producers, especially in the case of durable industrial products.

11.4.2.2 *Characteristics of the product*

Usually the following types of products will tend to have a shorter distribution channel or they will be distributed directly:

- products with a high unit value;
- cumbersome and bulky products;
- products subject to changes in fashion;
- products which require specialised service; and
- those produced according to specification.

Convenience and standardised products on the other hand, usually require a longer distribution channel.

The **extent** of the product range which a producer has to keep at the distribution outlet will also influence the channel choice. In this way a broad and deep product range with a high relationship would generally tend to be distributed through shorter and often direct distribution, for example where a variety of related product items are sold at a specific distribution outlet.

11.4.2.3 *Characteristics of the producer*

Enterprises with sufficient **internal resources**, such as capital, sales personnel and managerial know-how, are generally less dependent on the co-operation of intermediaries such as wholesalers. A financially strong company, for instance, would be able to perform its own distribution and also make credit available to retailers or consumers. The stronger the financial position of the producer, the greater the tendency to carry the intermediaries' financial burden, such as the financing of debtors and inventory.

Production-oriented producers often experience a **lack of marketing know-how** and are therefore virtually compelled to utilise the expertise of an intermediary. The producer may, however, feel strongly about the way in which the products are presented to the consumers. The greater the **degree of control** required by the producer, for example with regard to promotion, the shorter the distribution channel will tend to be.

11.4.2.4 *Characteristics of competitors*

The consideration and selection of an intermediary for the distribution of the product requires a careful study of the distribution channel(s) utilised by competitors. A producer may decide to use the same channel as that of competitors and thus compete directly for a market share or he may use an alternative distribution channel and so avoid direct competition.

Both strategies have their merits and for this reason the specific marketing circumstances will determine the choice. Some of the questions which could be asked at this point are:[5]

- How would our competitors react to the choice of channel?
- What advantages will competitors have by using the same or another channel?

- What will be the reaction of middlemen?
- Who will be the major competitors in each channel?
- Will the choice be successful in counteracting competition?

11.4.2.5 *Characteristics of the existing distribution structure*

The choice of a distribution channel will depend to a large extent on the **availability** and **quality** of existing intermediaries and their ability to perform specific marketing activities, such as storage, transport and financing, efficiently. Should a producer be in a position to establish his own distribution system, for example with the aid of his own retail distribution outlets, the existing structure is a given fact. Should his approach be to distribute **intensively**, he will have to try to utilise all possible outlets. On the other hand, if he wishes to distribute **selectively** or even **exclusively**, he can select from many alternatives.

11.4.2.6 *Environmental factors*

The environmental factors will exert a great influence on the choice of a distribution channel. In times of **economic recession** the producer may choose to utilise the shortest and most economical channel. **Technological innovations** will also exert a considerable influence on the distribution channel decision. Technological innovation in refrigeration, for example, has enabled perishable products such as fish to move through longer distribution channels with the result that more intermediaries can be used in the distribution channel.

The foregoing factors determine to a large extent the planning of a distribution channel. However, as the circumstances differ from producer to producer, a specific channel selection cannot be presented. These factors nevertheless do exert a considerable influence on the selection of specific intermediaries, which will now be discussed.

11.4.3 Selection of specific intermediaries

The selection of specific intermediaries in a distribution channel includes both **vertical** and **horizontal** dimensions.[6] The vertical dimension refers to the various levels (wholesalers and retailers) to be included in the distribution channel, while the horizontal dimension relates to the choice of acceptable intermediaries at a specific level, for example the specific retailers which will enable the accomplishment of the distribution objectives.

The vertical dimension of distribution channels (length) has already been discussed in the foregoing section. This discussion is, therefore, limited to the **horizontal dimension**, that is, the choice of specific intermediaries at a particular level of distribution.

When specific intermediaries are considered for inclusion in the distribution channel, the following factors should, inter alia, be kept in mind:[7]

- The ability of the intermediary **to reach the target market**. It is important to take into account how *frequently* the consumer purchases the product, the time and trouble he is willing to *sacrifice* in order to obtain this specific product and the *location* of the intermediary in terms of the target market.

- The ability of the intermediary **to satisfy the needs of the consumer**, for example with regard to the *variety* of products which he can offer; the *availability* of complementary products; the *ease* with which the consumer will be able to identify the product in the intermediary's shop; the *credit facilities* which he will be able to offer; his *delivery facilities*; his *after-sales service* and the general *appearance* of the shop.

- The ability to realise a sufficient **turnover** and turnover rate, in order to reduce the risk of stock obsolescence.

- The ability to provide the necessary **storage facilities** such as storerooms, containers and refrigeration.

- The ability and willingness **aggressively** to promote sales of the product, as indicated, for example, by the quality of his sales personnel.

- The ability to contend with **competition**.

- The intermediary's degree of **co-operation**, his acceptance of the marketing strategy of the producer and his willingness to execute this strategy. The intermediary often demands authority over the selling price of the product while the producer, in accordance with his marketing strategy, demands to recommend specific retail prices. The producer often expects the intermediary to perform the advertising for the product himself and the question is whether he will be willing to do this. The longer the distribution channel, the less the chance that the producer will be able to effect *realistic control* over it.

- The **creditworthiness** of the intermediary.

- The **managerial ability** of the intermediary.

Not all the aforementioned factors are of equal importance in specific marketing circumstances. Consequently the producer should identify those factors which he considers important for the specific channel of distribution decision. A quantitatively based selection can be performed by attributing relative values or 'weights' to the factors thus identified and evaluating individual intermediaries in terms of each factor; multiply the factor value by the intermediary's evaluation to arrive at a performance score for each factor. The scores can then be totalled and compared to identify the most promising candidate(s). Table 11.1 offers an example of this process.

According to Table 11.1 intermediary B achieves the highest performance while A performs least favourably. This example is extremely simple but should nevertheless serve to illustrate the broad approach.[8] Each evaluation should obviously be duly motivated.

After intermediaries have been evaluated and a final choice made, the execution of the distribution channel decision follows, with motivation of the intermediaries concerned to ensure co-operation in the distribution channel.

TABLE 11.1   Quantitative evaluation of middlemen

Evaluation factor	Weight out of 10	Rating of middlemen (out of 10)					
		A		B		C	
		Evalu-ation	Perfor-mance	Evalu-ation	Perfor-mance	Evalu-ation	Perfor-mance
• Target market penetration	10	7	70	8	80	5	50
• Store appearance	9	4	36	6	54	8	72
• Managerial ability	8	6	48	9	72	7	56
• Creditworthiness	7	5	35	8	56	6	42
			189		262		220

11.5 EXECUTION OF DISTRIBUTION CHANNEL DECISIONS

11.5.1 Division of tasks in the distribution channel

The execution of distribution channel decisions involves identifying and assigning the specific marketing tasks to be performed by the producer and the chosen middlemen, and promoting sound relationships between the various distribution channel members. It is thus concerned with the organisational arrangements in the distribution channel.

The first step in the execution of the distribution channel decision should be an **identification of all the tasks** which have to be performed for effective distribution and the requirements which are necessary for their execution.

In the *second* instance the various **tasks should be grouped** in a meaningful way so that related tasks are grouped together and are performed by a specific level in the distribution channel in the most economic way.

Thirdly, the identified and grouped tasks should be **allocated** to various intermediaries. At the same time intermediaries should be motivated to perform these tasks, naturally by means of a reasonable financial incentive. Should the producer, for example, allocate the storage task to the wholesaler, the wholesaler's recommended profit margin should allow for this.

Finally, **healthy relationships** between the various channel members should be promoted in order to ensure as little conflict as possible in the distribution channel and to ensure that a spirit of mutual dependence (an interdependent system) prevails.

The methods available to producers to ensure co-operation in the distribution channel, dealt with below, are relevant here. The execution of the distribution channel decision **should be settled formally**, ie the *arrangements should be in writing*, stipulating who is responsible for what. This can be done with the aid of a distribution channel scheme and guide, clearly showing who receives authority and responsibility for what.

Thus far the discussion has mainly centered on the planning of the distribution channel, and it has been accepted that all intermediaries can be considered and are willing to co-operate. Such an assumption is, however, not reconcilable with reality. It is often necessary to motivate and convince intermediaries to stock the producer's product and to strive towards a common objective.

11.5.2 Reasons why intermediaries are unwilling to co-operate

There are various reasons why a producer cannot simply accept that an intermediary will be willing to enter a distribution channel. First, many intermediaries regard themselves as **purchasing agents for their clients**,[9] and not necessarily as an extension of the producer's marketing department. Therefore intermediaries evaluate the product or products of producers carefully in the light of the needs of their clients. Intermediaries thus stock products which are in accordance with the needs and preferences of consumers and then choose the products of producers which they consider will satisfy their clients' needs.

A further reason why intermediaries are unwilling is that they already keep **other brands** in stock which provide need-satisfaction and therefore are not easily convinced of the merits of other products.

In the third instance it is possible that when a producer introduces a totally **new product** to the market, the intermediary may not be convinced that the product will be a success.

Fourthly, the marketing strategy of intermediaries may not be **reconcilable** with that of the producer, for example where intermediaries wish to use their own dealer brands or when they are not prepared to undertake any marketing communication themselves.

It should be clear that producers must endeavour to ensure co-operation in the channel on the one hand, and to eliminate conflict in the distribution channel on the other. Before various methods of ensuring co-operation are discussed, some sources of conflict in the distribution channel will be considered briefly.

11.5.3 Conflict in the distribution channel[10]

Intermediaries choose to enter a distribution channel mainly because of the advantages which it offers. By co-operating, the various participants expect that their profits will be greater than if they function separately. This joint attempt should thus lead to increased sales and income. The problem is to determine **what share** of the income each channel member should receive, but there is seldom agreement on this matter.

In general, vertical conflict in the distribution channel arises as a result of prices and various other factors.

Prices as a source of conflict

It stands to reason that sellers, for example producers, will attempt to obtain the highest possible price for their products. Buyers, such as retailers, naturally wish to pay the lowest possible price and sell at realistic prices in order to maximise their profits.

The intermediary also frequently offers a product at a cut price to serve as a 'bait' article, and in the process the image of the product may be harmed. Intermediaries may feel dissatisfied with the discounts which they receive while producers recommend specific selling prices. On the other hand, producers may feel dissatisfied when intermediaries deviate from the price and often even effect misleading price advertising. Intermediaries often complain about the complex price lists of producers and the delays in notification of price changes.

Other factors as sources of conflict

Producers may, in accordance with their marketing strategy, demand a specific selling method, such as display and shelf-space, while intermediaries are not prepared to do this. Producers often require information concerning the sales of their products while intermediaries do not wish to go to the trouble of supplying this.

Sometimes retailers are allowed to buy direct from the producer, and this may result in conflict between the wholesaler and the producer. In many instances the producer wishes to promote the sales of his product aggressively with the objective of attaining a larger market share, while the retailer is more passive and often only wishes to achieve a reasonable turnover.

Various other conflict situations may also arise, for example, when products are subject to late deliveries, inadequate packaging, inaccurate invoices or unsatisfactory handling of customers' complaints.

From the producer's point of view, it is imperative that conflict be eliminated as far as possible and that the distribution channel should function smoothly. Some methods which producers may use to ensure co-operation will now be discussed.

11.5.4 Methods of promoting co-operation in the distribution channel

Producers can apply various methods[11] in order to promote co-operation in the distribution channel. The following methods are considered the most important:[12]

- **Missionary salesmen** can identify bottlenecks in the distribution channel, analyse them and effect means by which they may be eliminated. They can, for example, offer training to the staff of intermediaries in order to ensure greater efficiency in the channel.
- Producers can assist with the intermediary's **planning tasks**, such as sales forecasting, marketing research, inventory planning and the development of marketing strategies for middlemen.
- Producers can provide intermediaries with **point-of-purchase advertising material** and if necessary even subsidise the advertising of intermediaries or engage in co-operative advertising with intermediaries.

- Producers can offer **managerial assistance** to intermediaries, such as accounting procedures, financial matters, information systems, personnel management, the choice of location and shop layout.
- Producers can establish a **distribution channel consultancy committee** on which all the involved parties are represented. In this way complaints and bottlenecks can be reported and steps taken to eliminate them.
- Producers can **eliminate uncooperative intermediaries** who may have a negative influence on others.
- Producers can organise **competitions** offering prizes to successful intermediaries.
- Producers can supply intermediaries with **free samples** to give to clients,

The foregoing methods aim to promote **voluntary** co-operation with producers. Producers can, however, also **compel** intermediaries to co-operate by:[13]

- effecting consumer **preference** or even consumer **insistence** for their products by means of advertising in order to persuade the intermediary to stock the product;
- entering into **formal agreements**, such as franchising with selected dealers, and in this way binding these dealers to operating in accordance with the agreement.
- means of **forward integration** whereby producers take over retailers and in this way effect full control over distribution outlets;
- **refusing to supply** intermediaries with products unless they agree to comply with the producer's prescriptions; and
- **spreading** the products over a number of intermediaries in order to be less dependent upon a specific intermediary.

The above discussion has been approached from the perspective of the producer, but it should be borne in mind that some intermediaries, especially the larger chain stores, often assume a dominant role in the distribution channel. In such cases the producer must convince intermediaries that their participation will benefit them and that they will find it profitable. The following arguments can be used:

- the fact that the producer's product offers more advantages than those of competitors;
- that marketing research and test marketing have identified consumer needs which can be satisfied by the product.
- that the sales potential of the specific product will justify keeping it in stock;
- that sufficient sales promotion will be done by the producer to persuade the consumer to purchase the product; and
- that the marketing strategy of the producer will ensure sufficient long-term profits for the intermediary.

11.5.5 Leadership within a distribution channel

The preceding discussion has considered the distribution channel from the producer's point of view, ie a situation where the producer is in a strong position and is able to modify the channel to suit his needs. In practice, however, it is *usually the intermediary who chooses the producer*. It depends on who is the **channel leader**. The channel leader will usually have the *power to control* the distribution channel.

Traditionally, in a distribution channel the **producer should be the channel leader**. This view is based on the postulation that the **producer knows his product better**, is more concerned with the characteristics of the product, provides **support services**, and in many cases is ultimately accountable for the **guarantee**.

The fact, however, is that a channel leader derives his status from his **financial strength** and his **marketing expertise**, including his present distribution network, market coverage and back-up service. An intermediary, for example, can command authority if he can dictate packaging, retail prices, stock levels and after-sales service. Similarly, the **reputation** of a retailer can influence his authority. Some of the big shopping chains, such as Pick 'n Pay, are in such a strong position that they can dictate in negotiations.

The extent to which a channel leader can control a distribution channel is, however, *limited*. A channel can be fully controlled only through formal co-operation arrangements, for example vertical integration.

The laws governing competition, such as the Act on Competition (Act 96 of 1979), are aimed at promoting healthy competition and to limit excessive integration.

Most distribution channels are characterised by mutual dependence. Even the strongest producers depend on intermediaries for the successful marketing of their products. The opposite is obviously also true.

The extent to which a channel member holds authority is usually limited over time, since dictatorship eventually leads to serious conflict. Once this has happened, there will be a total revision or modification of the roles in the distribution channel. The channel will eventually return to equilibrium.

11.6 CONTROLLING THE DISTRIBUTION CHANNEL

Marketing management must regularly evaluate and exercise control over the performance of the chosen distribution channels to maintain effective distribution. Control over the distribution channel should be exercised in accordance with the **objectives** which have been established for the various levels in the distribution channel and the contribution of the distribution channel to the achievement of the total **marketing strategy**.

The performance of individual members of the distribution channel should be evaluated as well as that of the distribution channel as a whole. Some remarks concerning both these aspects can now be made.

11.6.1 Control over members of the distribution channel

Control over the individual intermediaries should begin with the establishment of **performance standards** for measuring the achievement of distribution channel objectives by intermediaries. These standards can be quantitative as well as qualitative.

Examples of **quantitative** performance standards are, inter alia:

- sales figures per product;
- sales quotas achieved;
- income figures realised per product;
- extent of marketing communication;
- extent of distribution costs;
- promptness of payment;
- complaints received from customers; and
- inventory holding and out-of-stock situations.

Qualitative performance standards could, for example, include:

- co-operation afforded the producer;
- conflicts caused in the distribution channel;
- quality of market information and response by consumers provided;
- shelf-space and positions afforded to products;
- quality of marketing communication afforded the product;
- aggressiveness of the sales effort;
- attitudes of customers to the intermediary; and
- general progressiveness of the intermediary.

In order to evaluate the performance of an intermediary, a producer requires a system whereby information is supplied. In this way the **actual performance** can be observed, for example by means of **sales reports** and **retail audits**.

External information sources such as the so-called AC Nielsen surveys can naturally be applied fruitfully. Furthermore, **control lists** with specific reliable performance standards which usually characterise good intermediaries, and **rating scales** according to which intermediaries are rated, can be used (such as, for example, in Table 11.1). The rating scales can be used to identify certain qualitative characteristics of intermediaries and to evaluate them quantitatively.

Comparison of actual performance with the standard should be done at the shortest possible intervals, for example on a monthly basis. This is valid for especially the quantitative standards, and offers a timely indication of deviations and a basis for the necessary corrective action, such as a special attempt to ensure co-operation or the elimination of a specific intermediary.

11.6.2 Evaluation of the total distribution channel

In the evaluation of the total distribution channel, the original distribution objective should serve as the point of departure. Marketing management must determine to what extent this objective has been reached. Because the distribution objective has been derived from the **marketing objectives**, the distribution channel performance should be evaluated against a background of the degree to which the distribution decision has contributed towards the marketing objectives. Therefore **sales figures** per area and in total, as well as the **relative market share** achieved with this distribution channel, should be particularly important evaluation standards.

In those cases where alternative distribution channels have been used, it is possible to do **income** and **cost analyses** for each channel, and so the **contribution** of every channel to the realisation of the producer's profitability can be calculated. A comparison of the actual figures with the distribution budget can give further perspective to marketing management.

While the distribution channels of producers are normally relatively static in nature, the distribution channel performance or environmental changes can require an adjustment in distribution channels. Two kinds of action are possible, namely:

- a revision of distribution channel arrangements; and
- distribution channel modification.

Revision of distribution channel arrangements

A revision of distribution channel arrangements can, according to Matthews,[14] assume four forms. *First*, a **distribution channel shift** is possible, for example where the producer replaces his distribution channel with another separate channel. This may be the case when the producer decides to eliminate the wholesaler and to sell directly to retailers, or to develop and establish a totally new channel for a new market segment.

In the *second* instance, **distribution channel alteration** can occur, for example when a producer replaces a specific intermediary in the channel without influencing the other participants of the channel. This may be indicated where a particular intermediary performs unsatisfactorily.

Thirdly, **task modification** is possible, ie certain tasks which are performed by intermediaries are altered in such a way that additional marketing tasks are allocated to the existing intermediaries or removed from them, for example where the extent of the marketing task justifies this.

Lastly, distribution channel arrangements can be modified where the mutual **relationships** between channel members need to be **adapted**. This could, for example, occur where specific marketing tasks, such as storage, are transferred to a following level in the distribution channel in order to ensure more efficient distribution.

Distribution channel modification

Modification of existing distribution channels may become necessary because of changed circumstances or with the objective of achieving greater efficiency in distribution. The following circumstances could lead to channel modification:[15]

- When an enterprise or subsidiary is **taken over**.
- When a **new product or product range** is developed and the existing distribution channels are not suitable.
- **Changes** in the producer's **marketing strategy**, for example when he requires greater promotional and service support at retail level.
- When the producer wishes to reach a **new target market**, such as in the case of a product which has previously been marketed only to industrial users but for which a consumer market now exists.

- When the product enters a **new market phase in its life cycle**. During the introduction phase the producer may use particular incentives to convince intermediaries to stock the product while during the growth phase the producer may, as a result of increasing demand, be able to distribute on a more selective basis to more dynamic intermediaries who co-operate willingly.
- When the **actions of competitors** force the producer to change his distribution channel in order to counter competition.
- When the distribution structure **changes over time** and new, more profitable channels become available.
- When the possibilities of **more than simply the existing channels** (multiple-channel coverage) enable better exploitation of the market.
- When **new market segments** can be exploited.
- When further expansion of sales is limited by existing distribution channels and **alternative channels** offer possibilities.
- When **cost considerations** require a minimum order quantity and new arrangements have to be made with regard to smaller orders.
- When **legislation** forces the producer to modify his distribution channels.
- When **periodic reviews of the producer's business strategy** require a modification of distribution channels, as will be the case with the take-over of a retailer.

Any distribution channel modification should naturally be approached with great circumspection. Marketing management should still consider the long-term effects and should choose a distribution channel which will best exploit opportunities or resist threats. It should also be borne in mind that the distribution system must function smoothly in order to realise the enterprise's profitability and marketing objectives.

11.7 PHYSICAL DISTRIBUTION MANAGEMENT

11.7.1 The nature of physical distribution

Physical distribution is concerned with the physical flow of products from the producer to the consumer and the activities arising therefrom, such as transport, storage and sufficient provision of inventory. Even though those activities are seen by some marketers as 'the other half of distribution management', there is a tendency to see those activities as part of materials management or logistics management.

Advocates of the logistical management system[16] (under which physical distribution resorts) see the enterprise as a single business system aiming to minimise the cost of procurement (purchasing) and handling from the source of materials to the ultimate delivery to consumers. In this way all activities to do with materials are consolidated and placed under the authority of one logistics manager. **Total cost reduction** of material flow is the objective.

In this chapter the standpoint is taken that the performance of physical distribution activities is not necessarily the responsibility of the marketing manager, but that he has valuable inputs to make to ensure efficient functioning of the channel in order to achieve the marketing objectives. It is logical therefore that marketing management be a part of the planning, control and especially the co-ordination of physical distribution activities. Consequently the importance of marketing management in the physical distribution process is discussed.

11.7.2 Importance of physical distribution

The **general objective** of a physical distribution system is to ensure that *the right quantities of products are made available at the right time and in places where they are needed, but at the lowest possible cost*. Physical distribution thus represents an important link between the producer and his target market because the efficiency with which it is conducted determines inter alia:[17]

- the **service rendered** to consumers and the **satisfaction** of customers by making products available at the right time;
- the extent of **marketing costs** (distribution costs) and eventually the profitability of the various members in the distribution channel;
- the extent of **co-operation** that will exist in the distribution channel;
- the **condition** of the product when it arrives at its destination; and
- the **marketing success** of the producer compared to that of competitors.

Although physical distribution has always been regarded as an important cost centre, the importance thereof from a marketing cost point of view has not always been properly assessed. Particularly since the 1960s, authors[18] have drawn attention to the **cost saving possibilities** of physical distribution. Physical distribution has, for example, been referred to as a last frontier for cost saving.[19] Findings[20] in the United States of America show that physical distribution costs as a percentage of sales amount to 21 per cent. In the RSA it has been estimated that the cost of logistic activities (of which physical distribution is the largest element) represents 21 per cent of wholesale food prices compared to 16–18 per cent in Western Europe.[21]

Physical distribution is naturally also **closely related to the other elements of the marketing strategy**. For example, the physical form and packaging of a product may influence the mode of transport. Price determination should also take physical distribution costs into account. The speed with which delivery to the consumer is conducted may also fruitfully be used in marketing communication. Even if marketing management has an excellent product of good quality and with an attractive package at its disposal, and even if a competitive price is quoted and promotion is effective, sales will be hampered if products are not made available in the right quantities, to the right places and at the right time in order to meet the demand. From the viewpoint of marketing, physical distribution should therefore be seen against the background of the marketing opportunities it offers and not purely as a cost centre.

11.7.3 Activities of physical distribution

The physical flow of products in a distribution channel entails a variety of activities. The following list contains the main activities in order of their relative importance from a cost point of view:[22]

- transportation
- storage
- inventory holding
- receipt and dispatch
- packaging
- administration
- ordering.

The **sequence** of the abovementioned activities starts with the receipt of an order, after which the products are packed and dispatched, and by way of the most suitable mode transported to warehouse(s) where they are received and stored. In each activity documentation (administration) is involved. Figure 11.2 broadly illustrates the various activities and course of physical distribution.

FIGURE 11.2   Activities of physical distribution

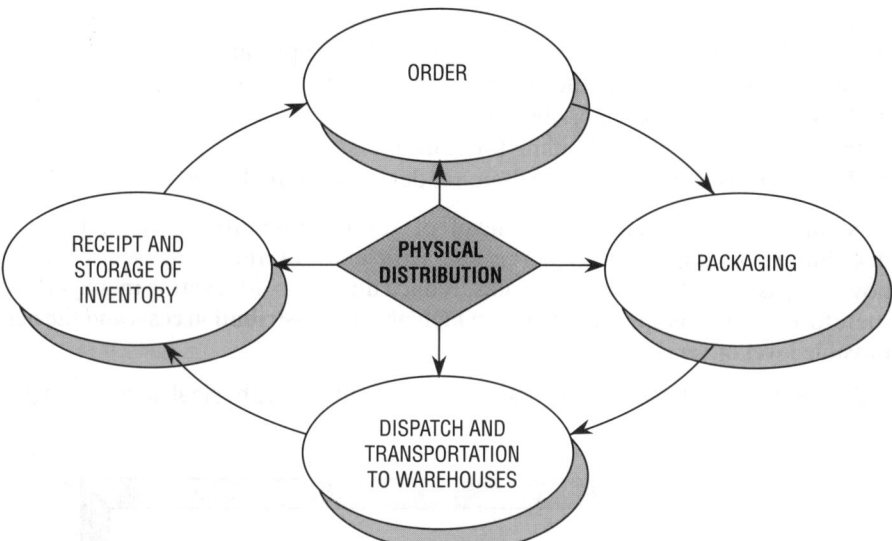

It should be clear that activities of physical distribution may have different relationships within the distribution channel. In some cases the producer may, for example, be responsible for packaging, dispatching, storage, inventory holding and transportation of products to intermediaries. In other cases, some of these activities may be allocated to intermediaries, especially where specialisation makes their execution more economical (see Chapter 10, section 10.4). The allocation of activities will be aimed at minimising costs, and simultaneously at the best possible utilisation of marketing opportunities.

In section 11.3.1 a description of distribution management was given and a reference was made to the nature of physical distribution. The management of physical distribution will now be discussed in greater detail. (Refer to Figure 11.1 for the sequence of the steps, starting with physical distribution objectives.)

11.7.4 Objectives of physical distribution

The objectives of physical distribution are naturally derived from the marketing objectives. From an operational point of view, two divergent issues are of particular importance:

- rendering the best possible **service through physical distribution** to attain marketing objectives; and
- the reduction of **physical distribution costs**.

Rendering of service through physical distribution

The rendering of service through physical distribution implies satisfying consumers' needs in the best possible way. This may include several means, such as:

- the speed with which orders are executed;
- the willingness to accommodate urgent orders;
- the care with which products are handled to ensure that they reach consumers in good condition;
- the willingness to take back and replace defective products;
- the availability of after-sales service and spares;
- the variety of delivery possibilities;
- the extent of inventory holding for consumers;
- the extent to which services will be rendered without charge.

It should be clear that a high level of service rendered through physical distribution would incur higher costs. Efficiency in rendering service may, however, as a result of increased sales, reduce unit costs. Marketing management therefore seeks a **compromise between high physical distribution costs and the best possible level of service.**[23]

FIGURE 11.3   Relationship between service through physical distribution and sales

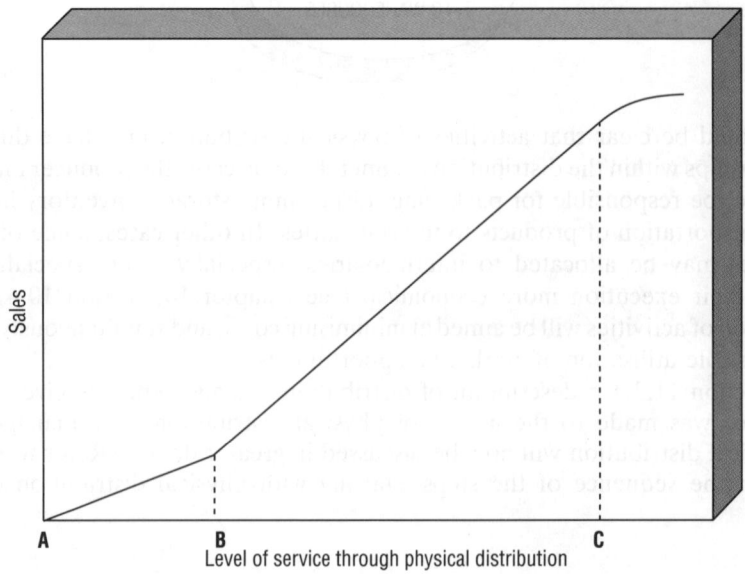

The level of service rendered and its effect on sales is shown in Figure 11.3, which indicates that sales will increase as service improves, but not in a linear relationship. A point (C) is reached where improved service will produce a relatively smaller increase in sales.

The optimal level of service through physical distribution cannot be deduced from Figure 11.3. In order to do that, the cost of rendering service should also be taken into account.

Cost of physical distribution

The intensity of the service rendered through physical distribution requires costs such as larger inventory holding, better (and more expensive) modes of transport, and larger warehouses. This implies that physical distribution costs will probably increase as the level of service increases. This is illustrated in Figure 11.4.

Figure 11.4 shows that the cost of physical distribution will increase relatively faster as the level of service increases. The reason why the curve rises progressively is that effective control of physical distribution becomes increasingly difficult and costs inevitably increase as the level of service increases. The question arising again from a cost point of view is what the level of service should be in terms of cost. The answer, at least in theory, is to be found in a combination of the costs and the sales resulting from the level of service rendered through physical distribution.

FIGURE 11.4   Relationship between service through physical distribution and physical distribution cost

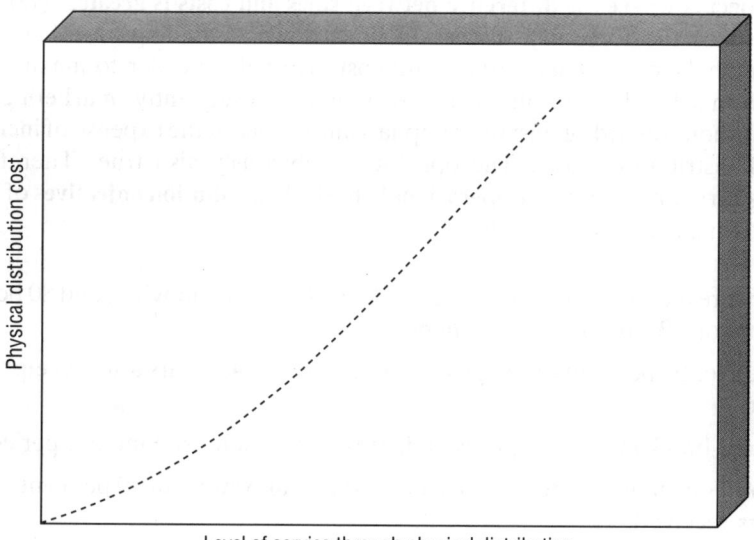

FIGURE 11.5   Optimal level of service rendered through physical distribution

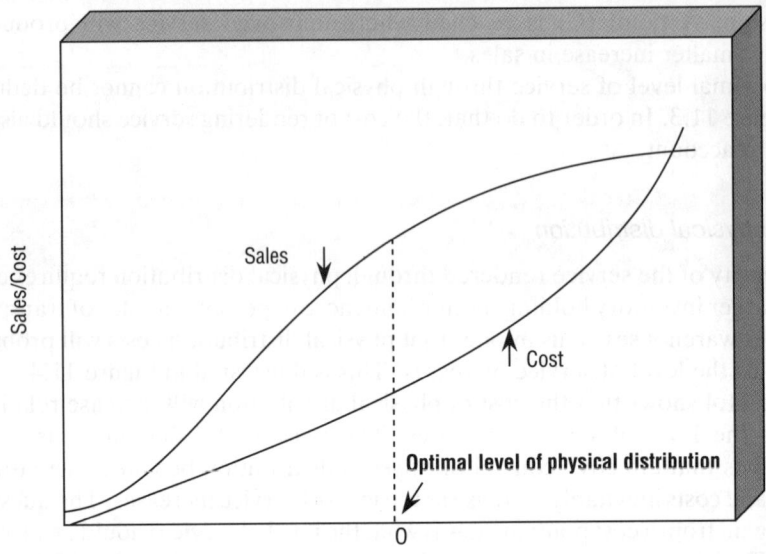

Level of service through physical distribution

Optimal level of service rendered

Figures 11.3 and 11.4 reflect the response of sales and costs in relation to the level of service rendered through physical distribution. When the two curves are related, the theoretical optimal level of physical distribution can be deduced. Figure 11.5 illustrates this. From this figure it appears that the optimal level of service occurs **where the difference between sales and costs is greatest** (O).

In essence the foregoing discussion boils down to finding an efficient and economic balance between service and cost elements in order to maximise the profit from sales through physical distribution. Consequently, marketing management should guard against overemphasising service at the expense of increased physical distribution costs. The opposite is obviously also true. Therefore it requires formulating **realistic operational physical distribution objectives** of which the following are some examples:

- To ensure that 95 per cent of category A products (fast-moving) and 80 per cent of category B products are available.
- To deliver 95 per cent of the product range within 48 hours after receipt of the order.
- To limit breakage during physical distribution to a maximum of 2 per cent.
- To limit outstanding orders (back orders) to a maximum of 10 per cent of total orders received.
- To limit out-of-stock situations to a maximum of 3 per cent of the stock demanded.

Such specific physical distribution objectives should naturally be accounted for from a cost point of view to optimise the balance between service and cost.

In the above discussion costs have been considered in total. It is, however, necessary to analyse the planning of the main components of physical distribution strategy separately in order to place the physical distribution problem in perspective.

11.7.5 The selection of physical distribution methods

11.7.5.1 *The activities of physical distribution*

The activities of physical distribution, such as the handling of orders, packaging, receipt and dispatch, as well as their administration are all important. However, for the purposes of this presentation, the discussion will be limited to the three main components of the physical distribution strategy, namely:

- Selection of warehouses. ⌐
- Selecting the most suitable mode of transport. ⌐
- Selecting optimal inventory holding levels. ⌐

It should be stressed that a compromise between the aforementioned components must be aimed for in terms of **cost and service**. This implies that the **total physical distribution system** should operate efficiently and cost-effectively, and not that the efficiency of only one component should be optimised. For example, rail transport, owing to its relatively lower cost, may be preferred, but this may bring about delays in delivery which hamper service and may even require higher inventory holding with increased capital costs. The inventory department possibly wishes to use cheap containers for packaging to save cost but this may lead to a higher breakage rate and dissatisfied consumers. Likewise, the inventory department would like to keep inventory to a minimum and even to eliminate warehouses to reduce inventory holding costs. This may, however, lead to out-of-stock situations or expensive speed deliveries, and may even provide competitors with an advantage. The point of departure is therefore the optimal co-ordination of all the components in an integrated physical distribution strategy with the aim of minimising costs but also to ensure an efficient level of service.

The main components of the physical distribution strategy are now discussed.

11.7.5.2 *The selection of warehouses*

The basic purpose of warehouses is to ensure **better service** to consumers on the one hand, and on the other hand to **save costs**, especially transport costs. Selection of warehouses or distribution outlets requires a compromise between the distribution of the market and the producer's location(s), the characteristics of the product(s) (for example perishable or bulky), available warehouses, the transport alternatives and costs to and from the various warehouse alternatives.

As far as the producer's location(s) and **distribution of the market** are concerned, warehouse planning is particularly important, especially where production is geographically concentrated but the target market is geographically dispersed. The problem here is whether warehouses should be provided on a centralised or decentralised basis.

Centralised warehouses naturally offer the advantage of better planning and control of inventories, more rapid reaction by the producer to special requests and generally the improvement of efficiency. However, the disadvantages are that transport costs may increase and order cycles may extend, something which can hamper service.

In the case of **decentralised warehouses**, the question is whether such warehouses are to be erected and financed by the producer **himself** or whether **public** warehouses will be used; whether a **comprehensive range of services** will be provided at warehouses or whether they will be used only as **depots**; and the **location** of the warehouse.

The choice of warehouse locations requires the consideration of a variety of factors, such as:[24]

- construction costs including the cost of acquiring the premises;
- property taxes and other levies of local authorities;
- labour situations and availability of labour as well as the general wage structure in the area under consideration;
- availability of services such as water, electricity and refuse disposal;
- the attitude of the local community towards the project;
- zoning restrictions which may be applicable to the proposed warehouse;
- availability of transport facilities such as railways and roads; and
- possibility for later expansion of warehouse facilities.

In the case of public warehouses and warehouse specialists, such as Frasers International, Rennies and Freight Services, the choice is naturally based on the storage tariffs and physical characteristics such as the state, amenities and layout of the building. Where an enterprise provides its own warehouse facilities, provision can be made in the planning thereof for its particular needs from a physical distribution point of view.

Apart from the location problem regarding warehouses, a further issue concerns the **number of warehouses** which will be needed. In general terms, the optimal number of warehouses required is to be deduced from the other cost elements of physical distribution, ie inventory holding costs and transport costs as well as the costs of warehouses, particulary operating and capital costs. Figure 11.6 illustrates how the optimal number of warehouses can be determined.[25]

Figure 11.6 shows that as more warehouses are used, delivery costs to consumers (curve A) decrease, but that the cost of transport from the producer to warehouses, warehouse costs and the inventory holding costs (curve B) increase gradually. The point at which total physical distribution costs (curve C) are at their lowest indicates the optimal number of warehouses.

In summary, with regard to the planning of warehouses the number and location depend to a large extent on the nature and distribution of the target market, the nature of the product, the financial ability of the producer and the relative costs. Warehouse planning therefore requires counterbalancing the **advantages** of several warehouses close to the target market (speedy service) and the **cost-increasing implications** thereof as expressed by larger inventory holding, increased operating costs and smaller transport quantities.

FIGURE 11.6   Optimal number of warehouses in physical distribution

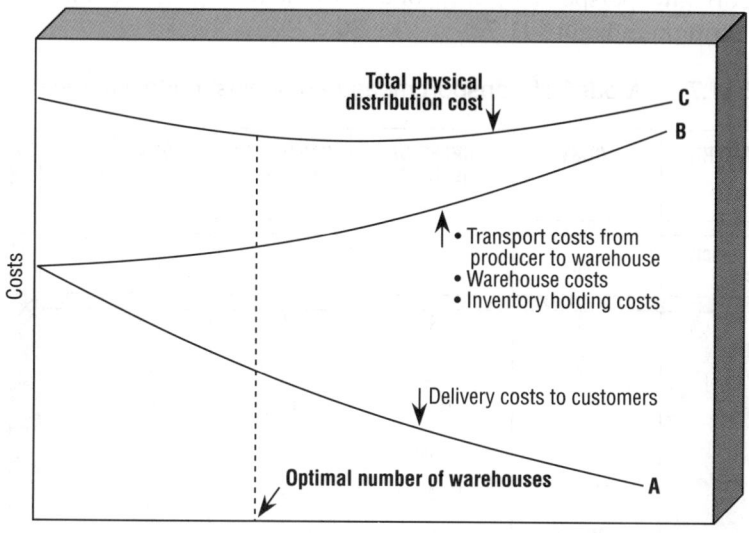

Number of warehouses

11.7.5.3 *Selection of the most suitable mode of transport*

The main problem which marketing management has to deal with in planning transport, is **what mode of transport** or combination of modes would be the most suitable for physical distribution purposes to bring about the movement of products from one place to another. The choice of a particular mode of transport depends on, inter alia:

- The **nature of the product**, such as the weight, unit value, perishability and whether the consumer needs it urgently. A product with a low unit value and weight which is not perishable and not subject to quick consumption, such as cereals, will probably be transported by a slower mode of transport.
- The relative **cost** of the various modes of transport. The cost applicable to air transport is, for example, much higher than transport by train.
- The level of **service** the enterprise wishes to render. The quicker delivery has to take place, the more the enterprise is committed to a fast mode of transport such as air transport.
- **Legal regulations**. In South Africa certain regulations govern, for example, the extent to which private road transport is allowed.
- The **nature of the enterprise**. Enterprises with limited funds can obviously not afford their own warehouses and large inventories, and consequently they are to a larger extent dependent on more effective and reliable transport.

- The **nature of the need** for transport. Where transport between warehouses is needed to supplement stocks, road transport may be suitable, while emergency needs of consumers should obviously be satisfied by way of air transport.

It should be clear that certain marketing circumstances require a particular mode of transport. In order to place the characteristics and merits of the various modes of transport into perspective, each one is evaluated against a few important transport criteria in Figure 11.7.

FIGURE 11.7   Modes of transport measured against certain criteria

CRITERION	COST	SPEED OF DELIVERY	CAPABILITY IN MASS	LOSS AND DAMAGE
Character-istic	High	Fast	Most	Least
Mode of transport ↑	Air	Air	Water	Pipeline
	Road	Road	Rail	Water
	Rail	Rail	Road	Air
	Pipeline	Pipeline	Air	Road
	Water	Water	Pipeline	Rail
	↓	↓	↓	↓
Character-istic	Low	Slow	Least	Most

Source: Adapted from Mandell, MI & Rosenberg, LJ. 1981. *Marketing.* 2nd edition. Englewood Cliffs, New Jersey: Prentice-Hall Inc, p 430.

Figure 11.7 shows clearly that each mode of transport has certain strong points. The choice of a particular mode of transport will nevertheless depend upon the relative cost on the one hand, and the need for physical distribution from the point of view of marketing on the other. Furthermore, the speed with which delivery should take place also applies, as do the regularity of delivery, the reliability of the mode of transport, the capability to handle a particular product and the extent to which a specific destination (including warehouses) can be reached effectively.

The effectiveness with which products are transported has a definite effect on the quality of service to consumers. For example, a transport problem will increase inventory holding costs and may even cause out-of-stock situations resulting in lost sales.

11.7.5.4 *Selecting the optimal level of inventory holding*

A further dimension of physical distribution decisions is the planning of the right **quantities** of inventory which should be kept at the various warehouses. In principle marketing management would prefer to hold just enough inventory. The lower the investment in inventory, the less capital is required, and the greater the possibility of a high inventory turnover. This may ultimately increase profitability. Theoretically the ideal situation would be if supply and demand are synchronised to such an extent that no inventory need be kept. This, of course, is not possible in practice.

The main reasons for inventory holding within the distribution system are:

- Inventory ensures **better customer service**, prevents out-of-stock situations and consequent loss of sales, thereby improving an enterprise's competitive position.
- Inventory holding may enable **transport** of large quantities.
- Inventory protects the enterprise against **uncertainties** in the demand for products, for example, when an exceptional increase in demand is experienced.
- Inventory serves as a precaution against any **contingencies**, such as strikes or acts of God.

It should be clear that the existence of inventory holds definite advantages for an enterprise. Holding inventory, however, also implies costs and therefore an **optimal solution** should be striven for between:

- the ever-increasing demand for **better consumer service**;
- the maintenance of an **uninterrupted flow of products**; but
- the elimination of an **unnecessarily large investment** in inventory.

The first two factors obviously require more inventory, the last less inventory. The question now arises: 'How can the optimal level of inventory be determined?'

Optimal inventory level

In determing optimal inventory size, the **basic costs** associated with inventory holding should firstly be analysed. Broadly, three basic cost categories are important, namely the cost of **carrying inventory**, the cost of **too low an inventory** and the cost of **ordering and inspection of inventory**.

The main elements of inventory carrying costs are:

- the cost of capital for inventory financing (opportunity costs);
- storage cost;
- insurance cost;
- property tax; and
- depreciation and obsolescence.

These costs are often referred to as **interest, space and risk costs**.

The cost of too low an inventory or out-of-stock costs entail the following:

- cost as a result of lost sales;
- cost as a result of forfeited sales;
- cost as a result of a decrease in consumer support.

The costs relating to ordering and inspection of inventory are represented by:

- the cost of placing an order to supplement inventory, such as the salaries of personnel and administration concerned;
- dispatch, handling and inspection costs;
- the cost relating to the checking of invoices and dispatch documents, as well as comparing them with the actual products received; and
- the follow-up of queries where differences may occur.

The behaviour of the abovementioned cost categories is divergent. While out-of-stock costs which are not always quantifiable decrease as more inventory is kept, the inventory carrying costs increase as inventory increases. Therefore, **inventory carrying costs are variable**: the more inventory kept, the higher the cost.

The **ordering and inspection costs** on the other hand are more **fixed**: the cost per order remains constant irrespective of the size of the order, but will increase gradually (more inspection) with larger inventory holding. It can thus be deduced that the total cost curve will reveal first a declining and then an increasing tendency as is shown in Figure 11.8. From the figure the optimal inventory size can also be determined from a cost point of view.

FIGURE 11.8   Basic costs relating to inventory holding and the optimal inventory size

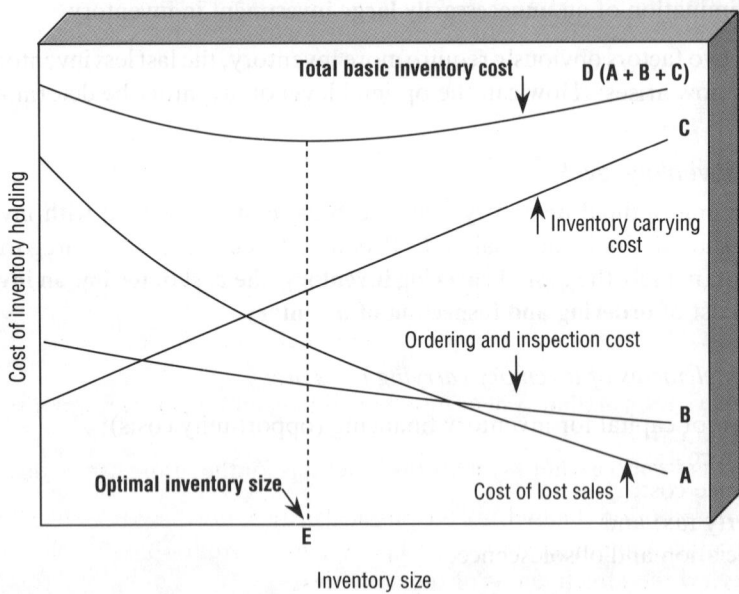

Inventory size

Figure 11.8 shows that the optimal inventory size occurs at E. At this point the total cost of inventory holding, ie inventory carrying cost, order and inspection cost and the cost of lost sales, is at its **lowest**. Although the latter cost (lost sales) is difficult to quantify, it should nevertheless be taken into account in determining the optimal inventory size.

11.7.6 Co-ordination and physical distribution

Good co-ordination requires a rational synchronisation of activities. Poor co-ordination between marketing management and logistics management can have serious implications as far as the effective marketing of a product goes. Poor co-ordination could lead to **out-of-stock situations** which could in turn put intermediaries in a bad light and/or may result in dissatisfied customers. All the above could lead to **serious conflict** in the distribution channel, even to the point where intermediaries refuse to stock a producer's products.

Usually the marketing department is responsible for the transaction flow, but if there is a lack of co-ordination between the transaction and physical flows the marketing effort could be wasted. It has been alleged[26] that **good customer service** represents the mutual importance of the marketing and logistical tasks. Many enterprises have a competitive advantage as a result of their good customer service. It is here also necessary to emphasise the mutual objective: the maximising of the enterprise's long-term profitability.

Co-ordination between marketing management and physical distribution is needed at the following levels:

- **price decisions**, for example, lower transport costs as a result of bulk transport can be important when determining prices and discounts;
- **product decisions**, for example, the nature of packaging needed to protect products or to make economic packaging possible;
- **marketing communication decisions**, for example, the speed of delivery could convince intermediaries and customers to buy the product;
- the **promotion of co-operation** in the distribution channel, for example, mutual responsibility for stock levels so that supplies are provided on time.

To ensure effective co-ordination a formal structure should be created consisting of:

- a **central management committee** where deliberation and planning occur regularly;
- an **effective information system** supplying timely and regular information to all interested parties;
- a **budget committee** where synchronised actions for the future can be discussed.

Once the distribution channel and the physical distribution have been planned and executed, marketing management and people in control of physical distribution should review the effectiveness of the activities.

11.7.7 Controlling the physical distribution activities

Control over physical distribution is considered here against the background of an efficient physical distribution system. In broad terms, marketing management should on the one hand determine the efficiency of the **service** which physical distribution produces and on the other hand what the **costs of physical distribution** are. In order to do this, physical distribution must be measured against certain standards.

An obvious standard for the evaluation of physical distribution is the initial objectives (see earlier) set for physical distribution. However, **specific performance standards** can also be used to evaluate the operational efficiency of the physical distribution system, such as:

- **warehouse cost** as a percentage of the total marketing cost;
- **transport cost** as a percentage of the total marketing cost;
- **inventory holding cost** as a percentage of the total marketing cost;
- **losses** resulting from damaged products as a percentage of the total value of products handled;
- the number of **speed deliveries** performed as a percentage of total orders;
- the number of **late deliveries** of products at their destinations;
- the number of times when the **safety stock** had to be used;
- the number of **out-of-stock situations** at warehouses or points of distribution;
- the real inventory compared with the **planned or stipulated inventory** levels in the distribution system;
- the average **inventory turnover** at each warehouse;
- the average **time elapsed** since inventory has been ordered to the time it was delivered at the destination; and
- the nature and extent of **complaints** concerning physical distribution received from consumers.

The above are only a few examples of performance standards which may be developed for evaluating the physical distribution system and should provide an indication of fields in which control of physical distribution can be exercised. Corrective action should naturally be taken if there are problems or if there is a deviation from performance standards. Consult Chapter 19 where the evaluation and control of marketing activities are discussed in more detail.

11.8 SUMMARY

The producer's distribution channel should be seen as an extension of his own marketing department. Careful planning, execution and control of the distribution channel are required. The target market will to a large extent determine the distribution channel decision. Such a target market is an expression of the marketing objectives and these objectives in turn determine the distribution channel objectives.

In principle marketing management must choose between intensive, selective and exclusive distribution. Each has its place depending on the marketing conditions, and provides broad guidelines for distribution channel decisions.

Several factors must be taken into account with regard to distribution channel decisions, such as the specific target market, the product, the capabilities of the product, competition, the present distribution structure and environmental changes. Once those factors have been carefully considered, intermediaries must be selected and motivated to co-operate. Distribution channel management must also make provision for continuous control of the channel. Both quantitative and qualitative measures can be used to evaluate middlemen.

Purposeful marketing requires meaningful co-operation with physical distribution. On the one hand, marketing opportunities can be exploited by good physical distribution; on the other, physical distribution has become an important cost centre. Through physical distribution a compromise must be reached between good service and low physical distribution costs. The physical distribution decisions mainly entail planning of warehouses, modes of transport and optimal inventory sizes. With each of these the service/cost aspect is an important consideration. The nature and extent of each component requires careful planning and must also be co-ordinated with the marketing strategy.

In conclusion it can be said that effective physical distribution requires continuous control over the physical distribution activities. Suitable evaluation measures should be developed to measure the performance of physical distribution on a continual basis. The ongoing adaptation and revision of performance standards will naturally lead to improved physical distribution.[27]

REFERENCES

1. See also Ferrel, OC and Pride, WM. 1982. *Fundamentals of Marketing.* Boston: Houghton Mifflin Co, p 244.
2. Some authors regard the intensity of distribution as distribution objectives (see Walters, CG. 1977. *Marketing Channels.* Santa Monica, California: Goodyear Publishing Co, p 184) or as part of the selection of distribution alternatives (see Kotler, P. 1988. *Marketing Management: Analysis, Planning, Implementation and Control.* 6th edition. Englewood Cliffs, New Jersey: Prentice-Hall Inc, pp 537–8. For a more comprehensive exposition consult Hardy, KG and Magrath, AJ. 1988. *Marketing Channel Management: Strategic Planning and Tactics*, London: Scott Foresman & Co, pp 22–26.
3. Sims, JT et al. 1977. *Marketing Channels: Systems and Strategies.* New York: Harper & Row, pp 138–40, referring to Cannon, JT. 1968. *Business Strategy and Policy.* New York: Harcourt Brace Jovanovich, p 244. For a concise but illuminating table on the relationship between intensity of distribution and the type of product and shop see Stern, LW and El-Ansary, AI. 1977. *Marketing Channels.* Englewood Cliffs, New Jersey: Prentice-Hall Inc, p 369.
4. For a more comprehensive view see Walters op cit, pp 173–89.
5. Ibid p 187.
6. See also Guirdham, M. 1972. *Marketing: The Management of Distribution Channels.* Oxford: Pergamon Press, pp 137–40.

7. Loc cit. See also Hardy KG and Magrath, AJ. op cit, chapter 9.

8. For an exposition of more complex methods see Stern and El-Ansary op cit, pp 355–9.

9. For a comprehensive discussion consult McVey, P. 'Are Channels of Distribution what the Textbook say?' *Journal of Marketing*, vol 24, January 1960, pp 61–5.

10. For a concise but elucidatory discussion see Mallen, BE. 'Conflict and Co-operation in Marketing Channels' in Mallen, BE. 1967. *The Marketing Channel: A Conceptual Viewpoint*. New York: John Wiley & Sons, pp 125ff, Sims et al op cit, pp 208–23 and Hardy, KG and Magrath, AJ op cit, chapter 2.

11. For example see Weiss, EB. 'How much of a Retailer is the Manufacturer?' *Advertising Age*, vol 29, 21 July 1958, p 68 as referred to by Walters op cit, p 496.

12. See also Guirdham op cit, p 132.

13. For a comprehensive discussion consult Revzan, DA. 1967. 'Evaluation of Channel Effectiveness', in Mallen op cit, pp 219–21 and Guirdham op cit, chapter 12. See also Christopher, M. 1986. *The Strategy of Distribution Management*. London: Heinemann, chapter 5.

14. Matthews, WE. 'Challenge for Industrial Marketers: Changing Channels of Distribution' in Kelly, EJ and Lazer, W (eds). 1973. *Managerial Marketing: Policies, Strategies and Decisions*. Homewood, Illinois: Richard D Irwin, pp 401–13 as referred to by Sims et al op cit, pp 200–1.

15. See Guirdham op cit, pp 129–30.

16. See Dobler, DW, Burt, DN and Lee, L. 1990. *Purchasing and Materials Management*. 4th edition. New York: McGraw-Hill, pp 20–21.

17. See also Husty, RW and Will, RT. 1975. *Marketing*. San Francisco: Canfield Press, p 224.

18. See Perreault, WD and Russ, FA. 'Physical Distribution Service: A Neglected Aspect of Marketing Management' in Walker, BJ and Haynes, JB (eds). 1978. *Marketing Channels and Institutions: Selected Readings*. Columbus: Grid, pp 119–20.

19. Parker, DD. 'Improved Efficiency and Reduced Cost in Marketing'. *Journal of Marketing,* April 1962, pp 15–21, as referred to loc cit.

20. See Stock, JR and Lambert, DM. 1987. *Strategic Logistics Management*. 2nd edition. Homewood, Illinois: Richard D Irwin, p 12. Compare also Hardy KG and Magrath, AJ. op cit, pp 195–196.

21. See Prinsloo, GC. 1978. *Fisiese Distribusie: Begripsbepaling en Kosteontleding binne die Voedselvervaardigings/voedselverspreidingsbedryfstakke*. Unpublished DComm dissertation. Johannesburg: Rand Afrikaans University, p 152.

22. See Kotler op cit, p 577 and Hardy KG and Magrath, AJ. op cit, p 196.

23. The subsequent discussion is largely based on Guirdham op cit, pp 181–3.

24. Consult also Ballou, RH. 1992. *Business Logistics Management*. Englewood Cliffs, New Jersey: Prentice-Hall Inc, p 566.

25. See Buskirk, RH. 1970. *Principles of Marketing*. 3rd edition. New York: Holt, Rhinehart & Winston, p 344, and Coyle, JJ & Bardi, EJ. 1980. *The Management of Business Logistics*. 2nd edition. New York: West Publishing, p 161.
26. See Stock and Lambert op cit, p 44.
27. In compiling this chapter liberal use was made of Van Rooyen, DC in Lucas, GHG (ed). 1984. *The Task of Marketing Management*. Pretoria: Van Schaik.

ASSIGNMENTS

1. Suppose you decide to import an exceptionally powerful calculator from Japan and market it in South Africa. The suggested retail price is R1 350. Your landed cost of the product is R835. A three year guarantee is to be supplied by you and you also have to undertake the repair or replacement of parts.

   Explain the following with the necessary rationale:

   (a) The measure of **intensity** you will adopt when choosing a distribution channel

   (b) How the **factors** influencing the nature of the distribution channel may exert an effect on your choice of intermediaries

   (c) Which factors will hold a large measure of importance in the choice of **specific** intermediaries

2. Suppose you, the producer of beauty products, is considering the marketing of a new two-in-one shampoo. It requires small retailers to supply prominent shelf-space for the product and to advertise the product in local newspapers. You have already launched an intensive marketing campaign on national level to establish brand preference. You are not receiving the expected co-operation from retailers. Closer investigation reveals the existence of competing brands with larger profit margins enjoying favourable shelf-space positions.

   Explain the steps you will take to improve on the apparent advantages enjoyed by competitors.

3. Critically evaluate the following statement: "As a result of the fact that the producer manufactures the product and enjoys superior knowledge of the product, the producer should be the channel leader.'

4. Suppose your company markets the same product via two small retailers in a countryside town. Given the need for rationalisation you want to conduct business with one of the retailers. **Explain** which criteria (performance standards) you will utilise to choose the particular retailer to distribute your company's product.

5. Why, in your opinion, is efficient physical distribution of particular importance in the successful marketing of convenience goods?

CHAPTER 12

THE MARKETING
COMMUNICATIONS PROCESS

12.1 INTRODUCTION

The aim of this chapter is to outline the nature of marketing communications, the various communications models and the elements of marketing communications, to discuss the role of other marketing instruments and their influence on marketing communications, and to indicate the types of marketing communications objectives.

In the broadest sense marketing communications include activities such as advertising, personal selling, sales promotion and publicity. **Advertising** is mass communication which is non-personal and paid for by an identified sponsor. **Personal selling** is person-to-person communications where the seller attempts to persuade prospective buyers to purchase his product or service. **Sales promotion** includes all those activities to stimulate quick buyer action, such as coupons, premiums and free samples. The abovementioned three marketing communications activities are those over which the marketer has control. In the case of publicity the firm has little or no control over what appears in the media. Publicity is also non-personal communications aimed at mass consumers. In contrast with advertising the marketer does not pay for publicity. Publicity usually comes in the form of news or editorial comment about a company's product or service. On occasion companies can instigate publicity through the release of controlled news items (ie a press release) to the media.

Other communications elements which must be co-ordinated with the overall marketing communications strategy are the product itself, its price, where it is available, and all other company actions which consumers may perceive as communications about the product or service.

ORGANISATION OF THE CHAPTER

Communications models: Components of the communications model, interpersonal communication, verbal communication, mass communication.

Elements of marketing communications: Advertising, personal selling, publicity, contact with the public relations department.

The role of the other marketing decisions: Marketing communication through product decisions, marketing communication through distribution decisions and through price decisions.

Marketing communication objectives.

12.2 THE NATURE OF MARKETING COMMUNICATION[1]

The consumer normally acts to satisfy his needs. In this action he often has to be informed, reminded and persuaded through communication. In this sense **marketing communications** can be defined as:

- *The personal and impersonal transmission of a message;*
- *regarding any need-satisfying product, service, personality, place, institution or idea;*
- *with the manufacturer, producer, owner, intermediary and consumer as possible senders and/or receivers of the message;*
- *with a view to informing and/or reminding and/or persuading the receivers of the message to take a specific action.*

Five aspects of this definition need further explanation.

- *First*, the message can be transmitted by **human beings** (personal) or the **mass media**, such as radio, television and the press (impersonal).
- In the *second place*, the message can be sent by more than one type of **sender**. For example, the producer can advertise his products; the supplier of a service can tell his clients about the service; the owner of a holiday resort can send out a brochure; intermediaries can advertise their firms and products; and consumers can tell other consumers about the product or service (word of mouth).
- *Thirdly*, the message can be received by more than one type of **receiver**. Sometimes the manufacturer, for example, aims his advertising at the intermediaries involved in the marketing of his products and often at the consumers and potential consumers of his products. The manufacturer himself, however, can be the receiver of messages when industrial goods are marketed. Compare, for instance, the buying of machines for the manufacturer's plant.
- In the *fourth place*, marketing communication has a **definite objective**. The message has to be inter alia of such a nature that it broadens the receiver's knowledge about the product or service; it reminds the receiver about the

existence of the product or service and its need-satisfying attributes; and it exerts a calculated influence on the receiver's buying behaviour in the sense that it persuades the receiver to do something. The strongest form of persuasion probably takes place when the consumer, on the grounds of the message, decides to buy the product. Persuasive communication is an aspect inherent in competition and, although it is possible to shift demand from one product to another, it can intensify the competitive process — with resulting advantages to the consumer.

- *Fifthly*, the marketing communications process can also be **reversed**. This means that a message, say about the defects of a specific product, can at times flow back from the consumer (now the sender of the message) to the manufacturer (now the receiver of the message). Intermediaries, who are in close touch with consumers and their needs, often play an important role in this inward marketing communication (feedback). This communication can be regarded as a marketing data-flow and marketing information flow.

12.3 COMMUNICATION MODELS

12.3.1 Components of the communication model

The components and functioning of the marketing communications process are discussed with reference to figure 12.1.

FIGURE 12.1   The communication model

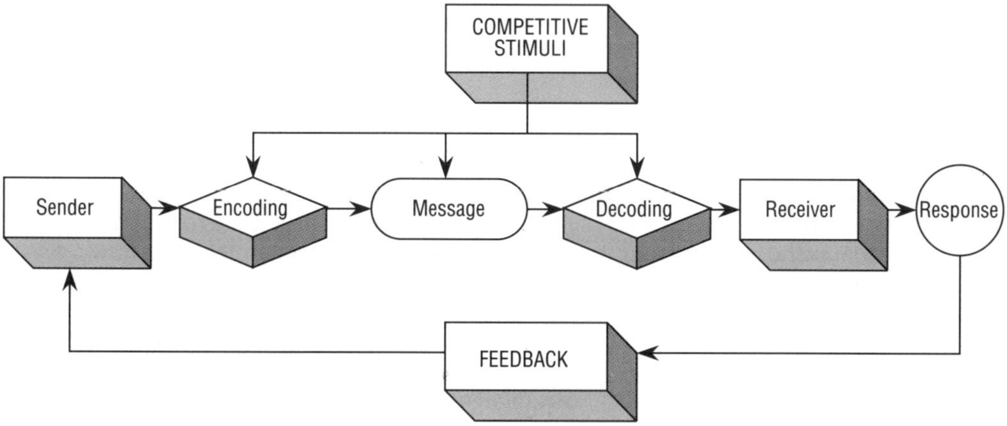

Source: Adapted from Engel, JF, Warshaw, MR & Kinnear, TC. 1983. *Promotional Strategy — Managing the Marketing Communications Process*. Homewood, Illinois: Richard D Irwin, p 16.

- The **sender** is the person (producer, supplier, owner, intermediary or consumer) who sends the message to the receiver. He is sometimes also called the **communications source** or **communicator**.

- The **encoding** of the message (formulation) refers to the process of compiling the message in words, pictures and sounds, or a combination of these.
- The bearer of the **message** (medium) is the method which will be used to send out the message. Here *two* broad possibilities exist, namely the **mass media** (such as television, radio and the press) and **personal conveyance** (such as the sales force and other consumers).
- The **receiver** of the message (target audience) is the person(s) (producer, intermediary, consumer) who receives the message from the sender.
- The **decoding** of the message (interpretation) refers to the meaning that the receiver attaches to words, pictures, and sounds, or their combination.
- The **response** of the receiver (reaction) determines whether the communication process was successful or not, ie is the receiver now better informed, reminded and persuaded as planned?
- The **feedback** of reaction indicates the degree to which the sender is aware of the reaction he evokes from the receiver through the marketing communications process. This communication can be regarded as marketing data and marketing information flow.
- **Competitive stimuli** indicate noise and other interference which negatively affect the successful transfer of the message.

12.3.2 Interpersonal communication[2]

12.3.2.1 *Between seller and buyer*

The communication between seller and buyer is often crucial in the selling process. The seller evaluates the personal interaction situation, establishes what will motivate the buyer and then uses those communication techniques that will motivate him to buy the product or service.

Example of a personal interaction situation

Gert is talking to Susan. He is a salesman marketing a range of pots and pans and Susan is a recently married housewife who cooks dinner for her husband every evening after work. Gert establishes that she has little time to prepare the meal but does not want to risk cooking an unappetising meal. He now demonstrates to her the unique features of his range of pots and pans and tells her how easy it is to use them. 'But what about the price?' asks Susan. 'Don't worry,' says Gert, 'this is the best investment you will ever make, and because we want to help newlyweds like you, we have a special offer just for this month — 20 per cent off.' Susan signs the contract and Gert is highly satisfied.

What happened in the interaction between Gert and Susan? Gert as **sender** of the message encoded his message in such a way that he proved he could place himself in her shoes and that he knew what would motivate her. *That* is the success of interpersonal communication. There are two requirements for Susan to receive and accept the message: it should attract her attention, and it should contain symbols which are understandable and meaningful.

A common field of reference as illustrated in Figure 12.2 is a feature of successful interpersonal communication.

FIGURE 12.2   Overlapping of fields of experience

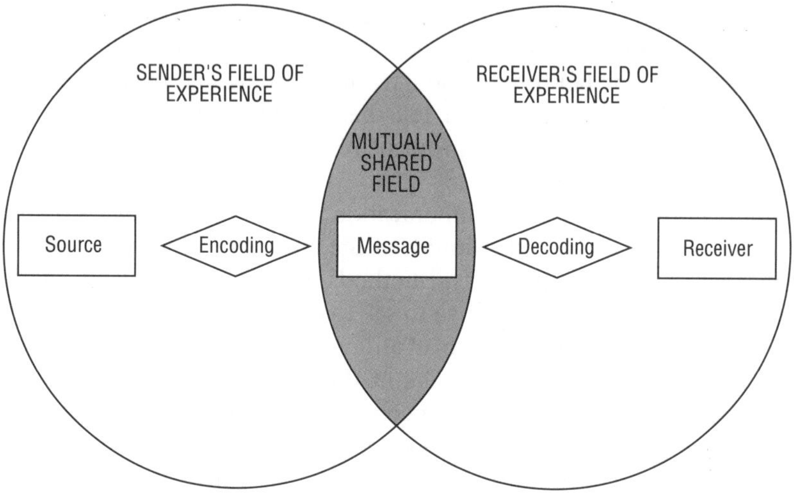

Source: Koekemoer, CL. 1978. *Print Media Advertising: Some Basic Principles*. Johannesburg: Insight Publications, p 9.

It is noteworthy that the message communicated between sender and receiver contains not only the spoken word but includes non-verbal signs such as body language, voice qualities, and clothing.

12.3.2.2 *Verbal communication*

Verbal communication, in the context of marketing communication, can be defined as being *informal conversations between persons* about:

- *the need-satisfying attributes of the product, service, place, institution or idea;*
- *the places where it is offered for sale;*
- *the price thereof;*
- *the ways in which the marketer communicates with the target market.*

The **objectives** of verbal communication are inter alia:

- to exchange more information on the abovementioned aspects;
- to remind persons of the abovementioned aspects; and
- to encourage or discourage persons to take a specific action in view of the abovementioned aspects.

Internal verbal communication and word-of-mouth communication between consumers always happen informally and can only partly be controlled by marketing management. **Internal verbal communication** refers to informal conversations taking place between employees of the firm and also between employees and outsiders about the abovementioned aspects. The possible circumstances under which internal verbal communication can take place are many. For example, an engineer of a motor-car manufacturer tells his friends how well the motor cars of his firm are made; a sales lady uses the perfume produced by her firm and talks to her friends about it, and by doing so proves her confidence in the products involved; a lecturer tells his friends about the good education offered by his university and, as proof of his views, sends his children to this university.

The value of internal verbal communication is probably not always realised by manufacturers. The views and attitudes of the employees about the firm and its products, prices of the products, methods of distribution and marketing communications, and what they have to say to one another and to outsiders, can have a very favourable but often also an unfavourable influence on the marketing communications and marketing results of the firm. This communication is an informal component of the marketing communications mix of the firm which is difficult to control, quantify and measure. The positive or negative nature of internal verbal communication within a firm is probably strongly influenced by the level of the *morale* of its employees.

Verbal communication between consumers ('word of mouth') refers to informal conversations between the consumers of a product or service, and between consumers and potential consumers of the product or service. The possible circumstances under which this communication can take place are numerous. For example, a consumer who wants to buy a new motor car makes inquiries among friends and other persons about the strengths and weaknesses of a particular model, the service of the retailer, the warranties, and many other aspects of the model; a person who wants to attend a particular performance at a theatre tries to gather all possible important information about the programme from those who have already attended the show; consumers who have visited a particular country, holiday resort or hotel, inform their friends in detail about their pleasant and unpleasant experiences during their visit.

12.3.3 Mass communication

Mass communication is much more complex than interpersonal communication between seller and buyer or word-of-mouth communication between consumers. Mass communication implies that a single message is sent via a medium to a large number of receivers. These receivers could be readers of a magazine or newspaper, radio-listeners, television-viewers, or cinema-goers.

Each firm should communicate with its target market about its products and the needs they can satisfy, the prices of the products and the places where the products can be bought. This marketing communications task is not the responsibility of

FIGURE 12.3   Mass communication

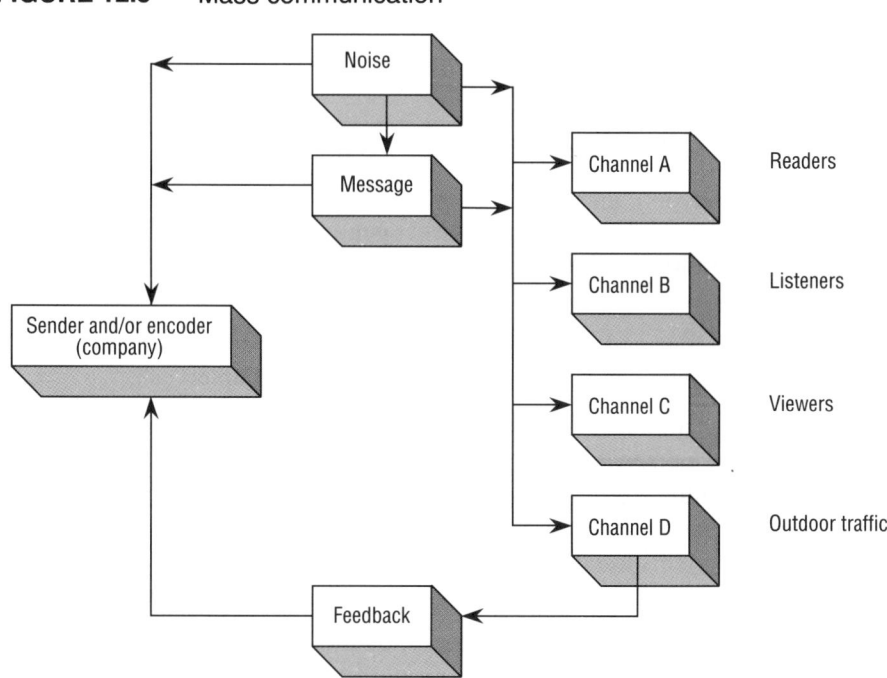

Source: Adapted from Engel, JF, Warshaw, MR & Kinnear, TC. 1983. *Promotional Strategy —
Managing the Marketing Communications Process*. Homewood, Illinois: Richard D Irwin, p 23.

only certain persons in the firm. In the marketing-oriented firm everything and
everyone in the firm should in a certain sense communicate with persons and
institutions in the market and macro-environment. In this way the products,
prices, employees, appearance, delivery vehicles, advertisements and the
behaviour of sales representatives of the firm — in short, the entire **image** of the
firm — convey a specific message to the target audience.

Marketing communication has become so important to the modern firm that the
firm:

- gives special training to its **sales force** in communication and salesmanship;

- appoints **advertising practitioners** to launch its advertising campaigns;

- uses **public relations specialists** to help promote the overall image of the firm;
  and

- spends relatively **large sums of money** on its total marketing communications
  strategy.

Thus each firm needs a unique marketing communications system for performing its marketing communication, and this system is inter alia determined by:

- the type of product (consumer products, agricultural products, capital equipment or mining products);
- the size of the firm;
- the target markets of the firm (final consumers, industrial, institutional or intermediary buyers); and
- the marketing strategy of the firm (market penetration, market development, external integration or diversification).

Each firm should have at least one or more of the components of the marketing communications system contained in its own mix, for example:

- The **enterprise** (producer) uses its marketing communications mix, consisting of advertising, personal selling, sales promotion methods, publicity, other forms of communication and verbal communication to inform, remind or persuade intermediaries, consumers and other institutions in the market and macro-environments to take a specific action.

- **Intermediaries** use their marketing communications mixes, consisting of advertising, personal selling, sales promotion methods, publicity, other forms of communication and verbal communication to inform, remind or persuade consumers and other institutions in the market and macro-environments to take a specific action.

- **Consumers** and **other institutions** in the market and macro-environments are also part of the marketing communication system and use verbal communication to inform, remind and persuade each other about the products and prices of the firm/intermediary, and places where the products can be bought. Verbal communication between consumers and potential consumers is particularly important.

Viewed comprehensively, this mix consists *first* of **internal** components, which can be influenced to a great extent, as follows:

- the **advertising, personal selling, sales promotion methods** and **verbal communication** of the manufacturer in which marketing management, through marketing communications decisions, is directly involved;
- **publicity** by the producer in which public relations is directly and marketing management is indirectly involved;
- aspects such as **packaging, brands** and **product image** in which the manufacturer's marketing management, through product decisions, is directly involved;
- aspects such as **retail outlets** where the product is available and the display of the product, in which the manufacturer's marketing management, through distribution decisions, is directly involved;

FIGURE 12.4 The internal and external sources and components of the marketing communications mix of a producer

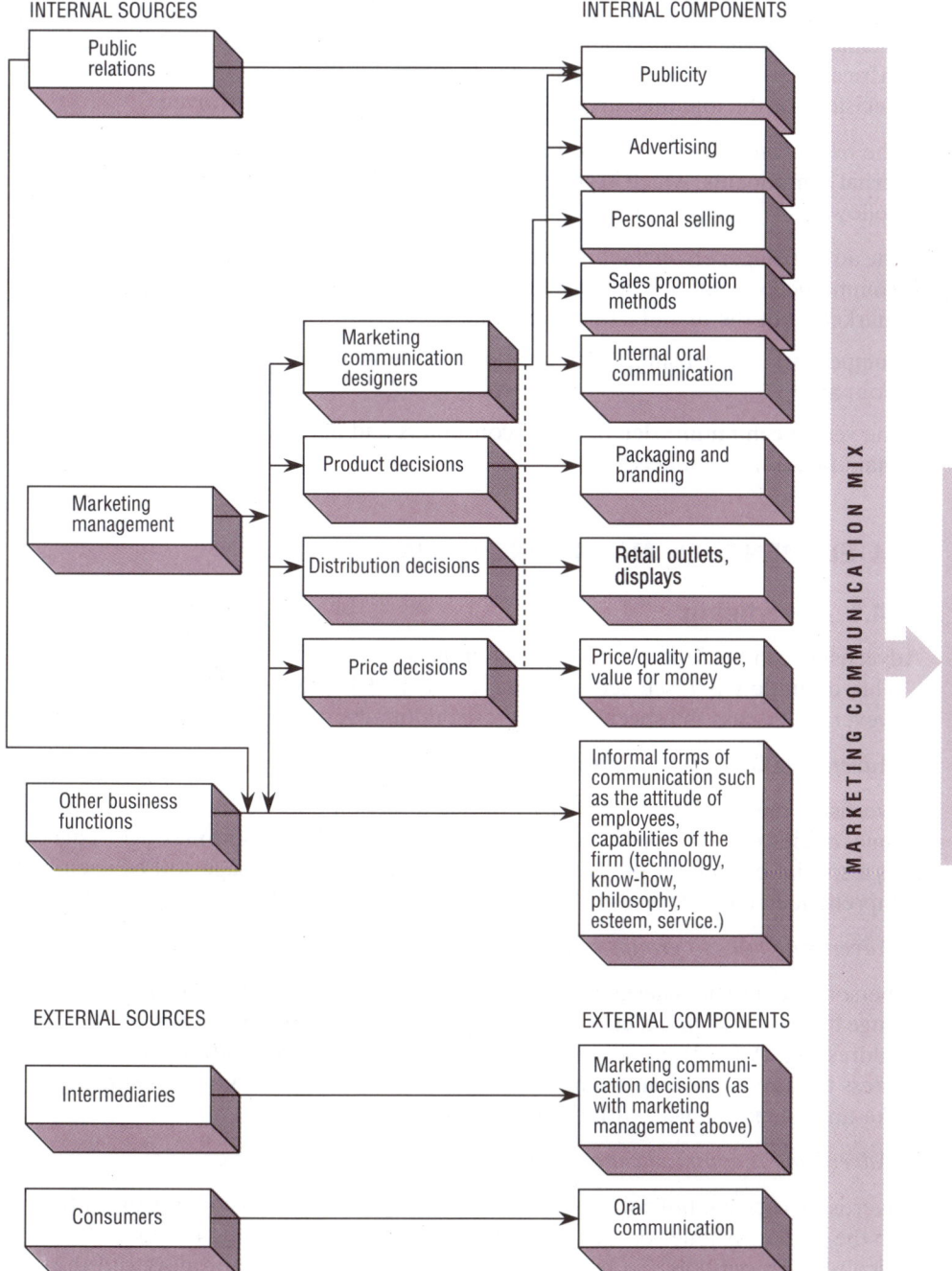

Source: Marx, S & Dekker, HJ. 1982. *Marketing Management: Principles and Decisions*. Pretoria: HAUM, pp 264–5.

- aspects such as **price/quality image** of the product in which the manufacturer's marketing management, through price decisions, is directly involved; and

- aspects such as the **attitude of employees**, the **capabilities** of the firm, the **technology** at the disposal of the firm, its **know-how**, its **philosophy** ('buy South African') and its **strategic importance** in which all the business functions and decisions of the manufacturer are directly and/or indirectly involved.

In the *second place* the manufacturer's marketing communications mix consists of **external** components, which in general cannot be influenced by the manufacturer, as follows:

- the advertising, personal selling, sales promotion methods, publicity and verbal communication of the **intermediaries** (usually middlemen) involved in the marketing of the manufacturer's products;

- **competitors'** advertising, sales promotion, publicity and verbal communication; and

- the **verbal communication** between consumers and potential consumers of the manufacturer's products.

12.4 ELEMENTS OF MARKETING COMMUNICATION

12.4.1 Advertising

Advertising can be defined as: *Any paid impersonal conveyance of a message.*

This definition is discussed in more detail in Chapter 13. It is important, however, to discuss the specific characteristics of advertising:[3]

- *Advertising is one-way communication*

Advertising messages move primarily in one direction only because the reader, listener or viewer has no opportunity to comment on the advertising message. This puts a special burden on the advertiser to ensure that his message will be seen, comprehended and adopted.

- *Advertising talks to groups of consumers*

In personal selling the salesman talks to one person, or perhaps to two, and he can change his approach and tactics to fit the specific situation or type of person(s) he is addressing. Advertising, however, is non-personal communication and has to address thousands of men, women and children, each with a unique personality make-up and experience, with the same message.

- *Advertising is communication that depends on symbols*

Advertising uses symbolic words, pictures and sounds to convey ideas in order to help the reader, listener or viewer to identify with the advertising message. It is difficult to use symbols. To be effective symbols should fit the product and the target audience. Symbols should be understood and must make sense to the target audience.

● *Advertising is low-cost mass communication*

Advertising is that means of communication which enables advertisers to deliver a message to a large number of potential customers at the lowest possible cost. By delivering frequent and economical messages, the advertiser is able to speak to thousands of consumers in a matter of a few days or even a few hours. This reduces the cost per consumer substantially.

● *Advertising is selective communication*

Readers, listeners and viewers act selectively when reading magazines or newspapers, when listening to the radio, when viewing television, or in a cinema. A reader of a magazine can test himself by paging through it and trying to remember which advertisements were seen and what their messages were. (In this regard see section 3.4.3.2, Chapter 3.) The reader will find that he selectively reads only those advertisements which are relevant to him at that stage and those which create interest. Circumstances can, however, change quickly, and when the reader goes through the magazine again he may be looking specifically for a different type of advertisement. Let us assume that this person is promoted and now qualifies for a company car. He will suddenly search for advertisements about cars, while he may have ignored such advertisements previously.

● *Advertising communication is the transfer of important information*

In most cases products or services are advertised. Information about the product or service is important to enable the consumer to decide which product to buy. Advertising is usually used to communicate the product's quality features, advantages and a specific brand image.

● *Advertising is persuasive communication*

To persuade the consumer is the ultimate aim of the advertising message. An advertisement will only persuade the consumer that this product is the best choice if it attracts attention, creates interest, communicates relevant important information about the product, if the information is perceived to be credible, and if the product is seen to be strategically better than competitive products.

● *Advertising is commercial communication*

Advertising is an expense to the advertiser that must be justified. Effective advertising at the lowest possible cost-per-message may stimulate demand and help assure the advertiser to maintain profitable sales in the long term. If the advertising does not achieve its objectives, a lot of time and money can be wasted.

12.4.2 Personal selling

Personal selling can be defined as the verbal and personal presentation of a need-satisfying product, service, personality, place, institution or idea to one or more potential buyers with a view to concluding a sales transaction.

Personal selling mainly concerns the relationship and interaction between the seller and buyer. In this relationship there are two important aspects, namely **personal salesmanship**, and the steps in the **personal selling process** which need further explanation. These aspects are also discussed in Chapter 14 in which sales management receives attention.

12.4.2.1 *Personal salesmanship*

Personal salesmanship is the ingenuity and skill which the seller uses during the personal selling process. Viewed in this way, personal selling can be defined as:

- the ability of the seller to interpret the characteristics of the product, service, personality, place, institution or idea in terms of the utilities and advantages it contains for the potential buyer; and
- persuading and motivating the potential buyer to buy, visit, utilise, use or accept the specific product, service, personality, place, institution or idea.

Each seller thus has a unique **salesmanship** or **selling style**. Salesmanship is, however, not limited to personal selling only. Advertising and publicity, inter alia, also use certain principles of salesmanship to inform, remind and persuade the target audience, and in this regard is referred to as impersonal salesmanship.

Salesmanship thus literally means the *art of selling*. In a sense this art is inborn, but can also be learnt to a great extent. The art of selling is, however, not the same for all sales transactions. It can vary from simple selling situations which require no personal salesmanship to complex selling situations where highly sophisticated personal salesmanship is required.

The types of selling situations, the role of the seller, and the nature of personal and impersonal salesmanship necessary for each situation, are summarised in Table 12.1.

A very important but somewhat hidden aspect in Table 12.1 is the type of selling situation where personal salesmanship dominates and where the impersonal message in the form of advertising is decisive. This aspect is very important in the composition of the marketing communications strategy of the individual firm.

The **principles** of personal salesmanship are interwoven with the steps of the personal selling process. This aspect will subsequently receive attention. Unless explicitly stated otherwise, the terms 'salesmanship' and 'selling process' further on in this chapter refer to personal salesmanship and the personal selling process.

12.4.2.2 *Steps in the personal selling process*

Seven steps in the process can be identified: the prospecting of the potential buyer; preparation for contact with the potential buyer; the contact itself; presentation and demonstration; dealing with objections; closing of the transaction; and following up. The relationship and sequence of these steps appear in Figure 12.5.

TABLE 12.1   Types of selling situations, the role of the seller, and the nature of personal and impersonal salesmanship

Type of selling situation	Role of seller	Nature of personal salesmanship	Nature of impersonal salesmanship
1. Self-service.	Virtually no role.	None.	Aspects such as packaging, display and point-of-purchase advertising very important.
2. Delivery.	Delivery of products such as milk, bread and fuel.	Virtually no personal salesmanship.	Impersonal salesmanship in the form of advertising beforehand, can be very important.
3. Order-taking *inside* the outlet.	Takes orders only - usually stands behind the counter.	Relatively little personal salesman-ship.	Impersonal salesmanship in the form of advertising beforehand, can be very important.
4. Order-taking *outside* the outlet.	Takes orders only - usually visits potential buyers such as soft drink distributors and dry-cleaners.	Relatively little personal salesman-ship.	Impersonal salesmanship in the form of advertising beforehand, can be very important.
5. Orders are not taken. Seller must, for example, develop goodwill or train the potential customer.	Does not take orders, develop goodwill or train buyers and potential buyers. Example is medical representatives who visit doctors.	Personal salesman-ship very important.	Impersonal salesmanship relatively unimportant.
6. Durable industrial goods. Emphasis falls mainly on technical know-how.	Must advise the potential buyer and thus plays mainly the role of consultant to the buyer.	Sophisticated personal salesmanship very important.	Relatively little or no impersonal salesmanship.
7. Durable tangible consumer goods such as fridges, motor cars and caravans.	Creative problem-solver of the potential buyer.	Sophisticated personal salesmanship very important.	Impersonal salesmanship in the form of advertising beforehand, can be very important.
8. Intangible goods and services such as insurance and educational programmes.	Creative problem-solver of the potential buyer.	Sophisticated personal salesmanship very important.	Impersonal salesmanship in the form of advertising beforehand, can be very important.

Source: Marx, S & Dekker, HJ. 1982. *Marketing Management: Principles and Decisions*. Pretoria: HAUM, p 269.

FIGURE 12.5   Steps in the personal selling process

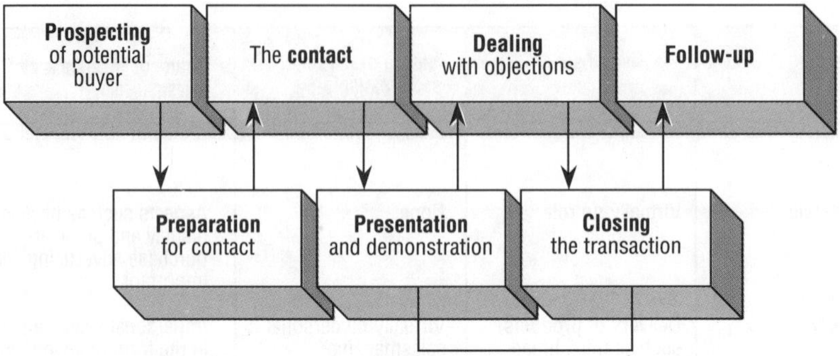

Source: Marx, S & Dekker, HJ. 1982. *Marketing Management: Principles and Decisions*. Pretoria: HAUM, p 270.

12.4.3 Sales promotion

Sales promotion methods can be defined as personal and non-personal sales promotion in order to:

- encourage consumers to purchase the product or service;
- encourage the middlemen to purchase and resell a product or service;
- encourage sales representatives to sell a product or service.

Thus *three* sales promotion methods can be distinguished, namely those aimed at consumers; those directed at middlemen; and those that focus on sales representatives. Marketing management must take decisions about the nature of these sales promotion methods. Consult Chapter 15 for more details on these methods.

12.4.4 Publicity

Publicity can be defined as the personal and impersonal stimulation of demand for a product, service, personality, place, institution or idea by making available their commercial news value to the mass media such as the press, radio and television, and where the sponsor normally does not pay for the placement/broadcasting of the message.

Publicity is a part of the public relations (liaison) effort of the firm which can be used effectively by making available news of events in the firm with a commercial and sales-stimulating value to the mass media for placement/broadcasting. Publicity is relatively inexpensive since the sponsor (sender) normally does not pay for the space/time taken up by the news item. Except for the man-hours involved in compiling the news item and persuading the media to place it, there is not much other cost involved. However, it does sometimes happen that certain media are more willing to use a news item as editorial material if the sponsor also places advertisements in those media.

If something happens in the firm and this event really has **commercial news value** which can be used by the mass media, it can mean publicity for the firm equal to advertisements worth many thousands of rands. News reports normally are also more credible than advertisements. Publicity is discussed in more detail in Chapter 15.

Examples of publicity

- The development of **new unique products**, such as an internal combustion engine using sunflower oil as fuel, or a cure for cancer, can mean front-page news in newspapers and main reports on radio and television news. Such news space and time are not available for advertisements, hence the value of this publicity is incalculable.

- Such publicity can help to stimulate the **morale and enthusiasm** of employees and middlemen. In this way, news reports on a new product (a tasty, nutritious slimming food) before it is introduced commercially can help sales representatives to persuade middlemen to stock the product.

- For some products the **credibility** of the unique claims made for the product is an important factor in the buying decision. If the claims are used in a news report their credibility can be increased (consider the claims that are made for certain hair-growth stimulants, slimming foods and toiletries).

- In cases where the firm has a relatively **small marketing communication budget** it can, by means of imaginative publicity, compete effectively with competitors with relatively large communications budgets, at least in the short term.

12.4.5 Contact with the public relations department

Every company and its products have a particular image as perceived by its customers and institutions with which it has direct or indirect contact. This overall image is created, inter alia, by the company's advertising, sales promotion, publicity, and personal selling, its products, services and prices. It is important for the marketer to create favourable relations between his company and its target publics, and to ensure that the right image is projected for the company. The image could be projected by marketing communication methods or by public relations. The public relations department aims to soften up the target, as it were, for the attack of marketing communication. Marketing communication efforts should be planned in co-operation with the public relations department to ensure harmony when, for example, a price increase is announced. Advertising could state how big the increase will be while public relations could explain the reasons why it will be such. When planning an advertising campaign it is essential to involve the public relations department so that editorial support could be planned by this department. Editorials are usually more credible than advertising because the consumer perceives advertising as an effort by the marketer to influence him directly while editorial commentary is perceived to be objective information supplied by the medium. Consult Chapter 15 in this regard.

12.5 THE ROLE OF OTHER MARKETING DECISIONS[4]

12.5.1 Marketing communication through product decisions

Certain product characteristics which are the result of product decisions, such as packaging, quality, brand name, colour and styling, communicate a particular message to consumers and potential consumers. This message could inform, remind or persuade the consumer towards the desired action. A product, then, is the sum of everything it communicates, often unconsciously, to others when they look at it or use it. Consumers do not purchase a physical product, they purchase psychological satisfaction. Women, for example, do not only purchase cosmetics, but also the promise of beauty.

The *packaging* of the product often conveys important marketing messages. With the advent of supermarkets and other self-service outlets, packaging has taken on functions beyond the traditional ones of containing and protecting the product. Seen as the 'silent salesman', packaging can often make or break a producer in the self-service market of today. It must communicate the advantages of the product, and provide information on usage methods, price, ingredients, quality, storing, mass and colour to the consumer, to mention but a few. The packaging must be so attractive as to say 'buy me'. Packaging is discussed in more detail in Chapter 9.

Symbolism in packaging

Packaging relies upon the use of symbolism. People react more to images and symbols than to ideas. A symbol is any form, shape, or colour that within the social context of the shopper is meaningful. Whichever symbol is used by the marketer, it should communicate a meaningful message and must be acceptable to the consumer.

Components of packaging containing verbal and symbolic communication elements include colour, design (shape, lines), brand names, labels and lettering. All these components must interact harmoniously to evoke within buyers the image intended by the firm. The notion underlying good packaging is gestalt; ie people react to the whole, not to the individual parts of a situation.

Colour in packaging

A very important component of packaging is *colour*. Down through the ages people have associated colours with certain things. Yellow is associated with the rays of the sun, red with fire, blue with the sky and water, and white with purity. The effect of colour is more emotional than rational. For example, red is the most appealing to the appetite. Orange is more juicy than the other colours, while green and blue are associated with coldness, for example frozen foods. Yellow is a warm colour and has a friendly connotation. Green's connotation is abundance, health and coolness while blue is the coldest colour and also has the widest appeal.[5] The use of contrasting colours or colour combinations is often very popular, for example, black and red, black and gold, green and yellow, and orange and yellow.

Packaging design

The *design* and *shape* of the packaging often communicate important aspects. A good packaging design is one which permits easy eye flow and provides the consumer with a point of focus. Lines are often used in packaging, and the following types of lines could be identified: a horizontal line suggests restfulness; vertical lines evoke feelings of strength, confidence, and even pride; slanted lines suggest upward movement because one reads from left to right; thin lines symbolises femininity and thick lines masculinity. In the same way the shape of the packaging can evoke emotional responses. A round package symbolises femininity whereas sharp, angular objects suggest masculinity. Washing powders, although mainly bought by women, have been found to sell better in a pack that symbolises masculinity.[6]

FIGURE 12.6   Packaging lines and shapes

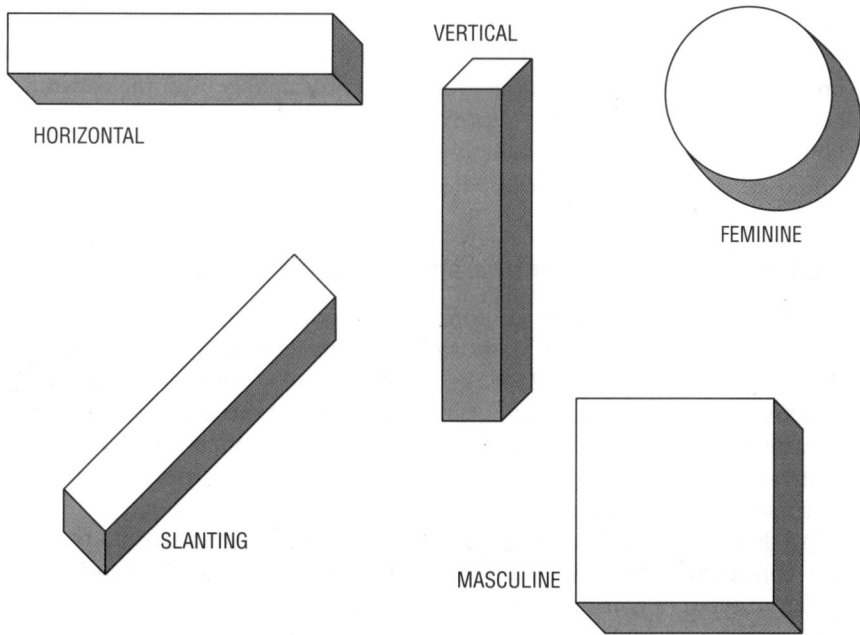

HORIZONTAL

VERTICAL

FEMININE

SLANTING

MASCULINE

Source: De Lozier, MW. 1976. *The Marketing Communications Process*. New York: McGraw-Hill Book Company, p 179.

Brand names on packaging

The brand name is, perhaps, the most important single element in packaging. It identifies the product and differentiates it from others on the market. There are *six* fundamental requirements in selecting a brand name. A brand name should:

- distinguish the product from its competitors;
- describe the product or its benefits whenever possible;
- help motivate the consumer to purchase the product;
- be compatible with the product;
- be compatible with the design, shape, and colour of the product; and
- help create and support a brand image.

Think, for example, about Texan for a man's cigarette, Mum for a woman's deodorant, Bernina for a sewing machine and Toyota Conquest for a car. A good brand name projects a feeling of confidence, or security, or strength, or durability, or speed, or status.

Labels

Product information is given on the label. In a sense, all the previous components — colour, design and brand name — inform consumers about what is inside the package. Product information refers here to verbal key words and other visual symbols on the label. All of us are aware of the words 'new', 'improved', and 'free' which are used on labels. These words are often put on brands to stimulate immediate trial purchases of the brands and presumably offer the consumer what he wants — something new, improved, or free. Even the letter type used on the label can convey a symbolic meaning to the marketing message. Block-lettering is supposed to be masculine, while flowing handwriting is more feminine.

12.5.2 Marketing communication through distribution decisions

Distribution decisions play an important role in deciding on the *place* where a product or service will be made available and *how* it will be made available. Aspects such as convenient location, pleasant buying atmosphere in the shop, the effective merchandising of products, and the type of service offered communicate a particular message to current and potential consumers. This message could motivate the consumer to act in a particular way. Distribution decisions are discussed in detail in Chapter 10.

All distribution outlets (stores as final outlets) project a personality or image to the consumers. The same store could, however, have different images for different types of consumers. For the high-income group a particular store could look stylish and elegant while the lower income group could perceive it to be snobbish and expensive. A store's image is created by a multitude of variables which can usually be controlled. These image creating variables are now briefly discussed.

Architecture and exterior design

A store's physical size can communicate strength, power and security if it is large. The shape and architecture can have subtle meanings to consumers; for example a new building could be perceived as modern if a lot of glass has been used and if it has a modern, futuristic shape. The store's front is important as it immediately communicates a feeling of coldness and emptiness or a feeling of warmth and a pleasant buying atmosphere. Outside lighting creates a particular buying atmosphere, and it could tell the prospective consumer that this is an elegant shop, offering a pleasant buying experience, a homely atmosphere and security. The entrance to the shop could enhance or limit consumer traffic. Entrances should preferably be wide and welcoming to invite the consumer into the shop.

Interior design

Once the prospective consumer is in the door, the store must communicate the right image. Aspects relevant here are the colour scheme, fixtures, lighting, the aisles, even the music being played. The colour scheme can be controlled and a store with sophisticated clientele would use more subtle colours while a store aiming at the middle to lower income groups would probably use brighter colours. The fixtures such as shelves and counters where products are displayed also project the desired image. Neat displays are more suitable for the higher-income groups, while a slightly more untidy display could create a more comfortable buying atmosphere for the middle to lower-income consumers. Lighting plays an important role because lighting enables consumers to see the product, shoplifting is reduced and certain displays are highlighted. Lighting should be co-ordinated with the overall theme used, and the aisles should be wide enough to create a pleasant buying experience.

Store personnel

One of the dominating aspects of a store's image is its personnel. Friendly, courteous, trained and informed sales personnel will develop a favourable image towards the store. Particular care should be given to the recruitment of the right staff because this will be determined by the type of customers a store would like to attract. A mature person may not want to be waited on by a young salesperson. In some cases people feel uncomfortable if they are attended to by members of the opposite sex. In general it can be stated that when salespeople are similar to their customers with regard to age and socio-economic group, the customers will usually feel comfortable.

Merchandise offered

The type of products offered in terms of quality, price, variety and quantity usually tell the consumer what type of store he is dealing with. A store that carries high-quality, high-priced merchandise usually communicates to the consumer that he is dealing with a store that would like to attract high-income consumers. A store that carries a wide range of products tells the consumer: 'We have everything, plenty of it, and if we don't have it, nobody does.'

Logo

The logo of a store tells the consumer something about the store's personality. The logo design and colours used could, for example, suggest 'bargain' or 'prestige'.

Advertising

Over and above the content of a store's advertising messages, the general style and tone of its advertising is very important. Consumers forget quickly what the advertiser said in his message but they retain a feeling about what was communicated. A store which constantly advertises low prices will develop the specific image of a low-price store. On the other hand, if more emphasis is placed on friendly service and reliability rather than price, its image would be completely different.

Store location

The physical location of a store can affect its image in two ways. The *geographical* location can help to segment its market. If a store is located in a high-income suburb, its clientele are likely to be in the higher-income bracket. A store's location *within* a shopping complex is also an important factor influencing its image. If the shopping complex contains stores projecting images consistent with each other, the effect is likely to be sympathetic, resulting in greater success than when stores aim at different target markets.

Post-purchase communications

Communications are not only important before purchases are made but often also after the sale is made. The purpose of post-purchase communication is to help consumers reduce cognitive dissonance during the post-purchase period. There are *three* aspects which can help to curtail post-purchase cognitive dissonance: good advertising, letters and a follow-up telephone call (see also Chapter 3, section 3.5.3).

Other factors affecting store image

The following *four* factors can influence a store's image: service (credit, deliveries, returns and the policy regarding exchange of damaged goods); store displays; word-of-mouth communication between consumers; and the store's name.

The name of the store

The name 'Fair Lady Boutique' projects an image of a store with tasteful clothing while 'The Penny Savers' projects the image of a store selling products at bargain prices.

12.5.3 Communication through pricing decisions

Price plays an important role in most buying decisions made by consumers. Price can at times be an important indicator of the quality of the product (for example, expensive motor cars), and certain psychological aspects of price, such as the use of odd numbers (R4,99 instead of R5,00), can probably persuade the consumer to take a specific action. In this regard certain pricing decisions become part of marketing communications. Consult Chapters 16 and 17 for a discussion of price determination and price decisions.

How can a marketer use price as a marketing communication tool?

Price gives an indication of the attributes of a product

When there is a real difference in the quality of two products, marketers can use price as a cue for higher quality or lower quality. Sometimes the product is a component, for example a spare part or something that is added, for example, spices: in this case the contribution made by the spices to the meal is relatively more important than the difference in price between high-quality and low-quality spices. The higher price then is an indication that the quality of the product is higher.

In the case of a gift a higher price is an indication to the buyer that the quality is better, for example in the case of perfume. The brand name also serves as an indication of quality because certain products have become synonymous with quality: Mercedes-Benz cars, Bernina sewing machines and AEG stoves.

Price gives an indication of the characteristics of the consumer

Consumers have different experiences with products. Consumers with little knowledge of products use price as an indication of the quality of the product especially where there is no personal selling involved. Some consumers use the price of a product to project their status or prestige. The price then has snob value.

In many cases a consumer really cannot decide between two products and the price will then act as an indication of which product is of the higher quality.

12.6 MARKETING COMMUNICATION OBJECTIVES

Advertising objectives are discussed in great detail in Chapter 13 and it will suffice here to briefly discuss the relationship between marketing communication objectives and business objectives. This is outlined in figure 12.7.

The overall business objective is, for example, to increase the earnings per share by R1, the marketing objective is to achieve 25 per cent market share in the next year. This marketing objective can be achieved if the marketing communication can be achieved, that is:

- an advertising objective to increase awareness of the product to 80 per cent of the target market;
- the sales promotion objective is to persuade 40 per cent of the tarket market to try the product;
- the personal selling objective is to recruit 100 new accounts.

The reseller support objective is to get 80 per cent of the retailers to display the product at gondola ends (end-aisle displays) and the public relations objective is to get 85 per cent of the shareholders to believe that the company is dynamic and profitable.

FIGURE 12.7   Relationship of marketing communication objectives to other company objectives

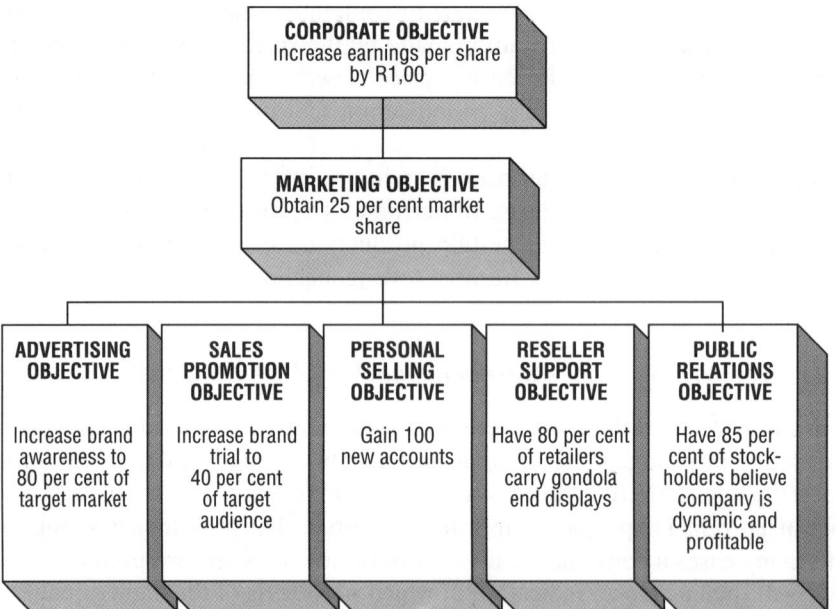

Source: Engel, JF, Warshaw, MR & Kinnear, TC. 1983. *Promotional Strategy: Managing the Marketing Communications Process*. Homewood, Illinois: Richard D Irwin, p 180.

12.7 SUMMARY

In this chapter the nature of marketing communication was outlined, the different communication models, the elements of marketing communications, and the role of the other marketing tools were pointed out, and the types of marketing communication objectives that could be set were briefly discussed.

REFERENCES

1. The following sections are largely based on Marx, S & Dekker, HJ. 1982. *Marketing Management: Principles and Decisions*. Pretoria: HAUM.
   The nature of marketing communications: Marx & Dekker, pp 255–7.
   Communications models: Marx and Dekker, pp 266, 267 and 276.
   Elements of marketing communications: Marx & Dekker, pp 263, 266–76.
   Marketing communications through distribution decisions: Marx & Dekker, p 277.
2. The following sections are based on Engel, JF, Warshaw, MR & Kinnear, TC. 1983. *Promotional Strategy: Managing the Marketing Communications Process*. Homewood, Illinois: Richard D Irwin.
   Interpersonal communication: Engel et al pp 20–3.
   Mass communication: Engel et al pp 23–6.
3. Koekemoer, CL. 1978. *Print Media Advertising: Some Basic Principles*. Johannesburg: Insight Publications.
4. The following sections are based on De Lozier, MW. 1976. *The Marketing Communications Process*. New York: McGraw-Hill Inc.
   Marketing communications through product decisions: De Lozier, pp 174–88.
   Marketing communications through distribution decisions: De Lozier, pp 201–7, 210–13.
   Communications through pricing decisions: De Lozier, pp 190–9.
5. Ibid p 174.
6. Ibid p 179.

CASE STUDIES

1. ADVERTISING CEMENT

Advertising cement is not easy. It's a commodity-type product which consumers don't ask for by brand.

Even builders probably don't buy on anything but price. But awareness of the name of SA's largest cement producer, PPC, must have been massively increased through a commercial created by Bernstein Loxton Golding & Klein. It's a commercial which B L G & K is pinning its hopes on for this year's International Advertising Film Festival in Cannes.

The PPC 'bridge' commercial was made in 1989. It features the 'old' Van Staden's River bridge near Port Elizabeth. B L G & K's deputy creative director Paul Curtis gave the bridge a place in SA's ad history, plus a hefty boost for PPC, which supplied the cement used in the construction.

The commercial features a host of historical scenes involving the old bridge. Crossing the bridge in the course of the commercial are soldiers marching off to war, the last governor-general of the Union in his Rolls-Royce, the first car assembled in SA and a host of other characters who each represent a bit of history. And that's besides what crosses under the old cement bridge — including 'the floods of '68'.

Having established the longevity of the bridge and its place in history, the story line notes that when a new Van Staden's bridge was planned, who better to approach for cement than PPC, which supplied the material for the old structure — which not only is still standing but is still used? The cameras move back, and the massive new concrete arch bridge is seen, high up the ravine behind the old one.

The commercial is not telling any tall tales. 'What's amazing about the ad,' says Curtis, 'is that the old bridge is still there and that PPC supplied the cement for both.'

Indeed, the research went further. Curtis notes that even down to the buttons on the soldiers' tunics, authenticity was total. 'The whole commercial was carefully researched . . . even the pennant on the governor-general's car was real.' And to ensure there was no question of the era, even the telephone lines near the bridge were removed for the five-day shoot!

But you can't please everyone. B L G & K account executive, Jill Merrifield, recalls a Durban man who challenged the scene of soldiers marching across a bridge. A company of soldiers, he advised, always breaks step when crossing a bridge.

That's quite true because the marching could cause the bridge to resonate and become damaged. But the 'inaccuracy' was not critical because on a short concrete bridge, the army told B L G & K, perhaps the soldiers would not have been instructed to break step. But what the letter from the viewer told the agency is that the ad was certainly watched, and watched carefully.

For PPC, the commercial must have been satisfying. While it may not change the way in which people buy cement, it has given the group a secure and benevolent profile with staff and with potential employees.

As for the agency, the commercial's been a creative success. It's picked up Loeries, Clios and other awards.

Source: Media and Marketing Focus. *Finance Week*, 27 June-3 July 1991.

QUESTIONS

1. Why did the advertisers take so much trouble to make the advertisement seem authentic?

2. What was the main objective of the PPC advertising campaign? Give reasons for your answer.

3. Explain the difference between brand advertising and company image advertising.

2. THE MISSING SALES FIGURES

The scene is the foyer of a marketing enterprise. The marketing director, Mr Rumble, comes out of his office and goes towards the receptionist, Miss Maud Awesome, who is trying to answer calls and attend to customers.

Mr Rumble calls across the foyer, 'Maud, have the sales figures arrived yet?'

Maud is already flustered and is on the telephone, so she does not answer immediately.

Mr Rumble waits, tapping his fingers on the counter.

Maud finishes her call and goes on serving a customer. Mr Rumble has given specific instructions that customers always come first. He asks, 'Maud, have the sales figures arrived?'

'Which sales figures?' asks Maud.

'I told the sales manager to instruct the sales representatives to let me have the sales figures by 10 this morning.'

'So why should I have them then?'

'Well, I haven't received them yet and I was wondering whether they had left them with you,' says Mr Rumble.

'Oh,' says Maud, shrugging and continuing to serve the customer.

'Well, get a memo to each sales representative instructing that I need them immediately,' he says, frowning while walking off.

Source: Adapted from Adey, A D & Andrew, M G. 1990. *Getting it right: The manager's guide to business communication*. Cape Town: Juta, p 10.

QUESTIONS

1. Identify the different communication processes in the case study.

2. Evaluate the effectiveness of the communication process between Mr Rumble and Maud in terms of the components of the communication model.

3. Evaluate the other communication processes in the case study in a similar way.

4. Give examples and explain the meaning of the non-verbal communication symbols included in the case study.

5. 'Mr Rumble is not consumer-orientated at all.' Discuss the statement critically.

6. What are the main shortcomings in the communication examples given in the case study?

CHAPTER 13

ADVERTISING

13.1 INTRODUCTION

The aim of this chapter is to provide an overview of advertising and to give attention to defining advertising, the role of advertising in marketing, advertising objectives, management of the advertising campaign, the role of the advertising practitioner and advertising control in South Africa.

In Chapter 12 it was seen that a simple communications process consists of a sender of a message on the one hand and a receiver on the other. Advertising is, however, more complex because verbal and non-verbal symbols are sent via media to the receiver. Advertising essentially has to do with **who** says **what** to **whom** through **which medium** with **what effect**.[1]

The *who* is the sender. The *what* is the advertisement. The *whom* is the target audience. The *which medium* could be television, radio, newspapers or magazines, and the *what effect* could be the number of viewers/listeners, readers reached, how the message changed the target audience's attitude, or the extent to which they were motivated to buy the advertised product or service.

ORGANISATION OF THE CHAPTER

Defining advertising.

The role of advertising in marketing.

Advertising objectives: The importance of advertising objectives, the requirements which advertising objectives have to fulfil, themes for advertising objectives.

Management of an advertising campaign: Steps in the management of an advertising campaign.

The role of the advertising practitioner.

Advertising control in South Africa.

13.2 DEFINITION OF ADVERTISING[2]

Advertising can be defined as:

- *Any paid impersonal conveyance of a message;*
- *regarding a need-satisfying product, service or idea;*
- *by an identifiable sponsor;*
- *to a specific target audience;*
- *with the objective of informing and/or reminding and/or persuading the target audience to take a specific action.*

Certain concepts in this definition require further explanation:

- **Paid:** This concept distinguishes advertising from publicity; the advertiser has control over the contents, time and course of the marketing communication process, while this is not the case in publicity.
- **Impersonal conveyance of a message:** This phrase signifies that advertising takes place in the form of outward communication from the advertiser to the target audience by means of impersonal mass media (the press, radio, television, mail, posters, cinemas, et cetera). This concept distinguishes advertising from personal selling.
- **Need-satisfying product, service or idea:** This phrase points to the fact that the message can contain information on the product and its need-satisfying attributes, the place where it can be bought or its price. It is, however, not necessary that all this information always has to be present in an advertisement. Sometimes advertising can deal with a personality or an institution.
- **Identifiable sponsor:** This concept means that the target audience (receiver of the message) can identify the sender (sponsor) of the message on the basis of the brand or name of the product, service, personality, place, institution or idea.
- **Specific target audience:** This concept means that the message has to be directed to a specific target audience. This specific target audience is the result of market segmentation and market targeting.
- **To inform:** One of the most important tasks of advertising is to inform the target audience of the need-satisfying attributes, availability, and price of the product, service, personality, place, et cetera.
- **Remind:** Advertising also has to remind the target audience continually about the need-satisfying attributes, availability, and price of the product, service, personality, place, et cetera.
- **Persuade to take a specific action:** Advertising has to try to persuade the target audience to prefer the product, service, personality, place, et cetera — based on its unique need-satisfying attributes, the place where it is available and its price — above that of competitors. Advertising can naturally also encourage the target audience to take other action such as: asking for more information; visiting a specific retailer; driving safely; saving fuel; preventing veld fires; and conserving nature.

13.3 THE ROLE OF ADVERTISING IN MARKETING

Successful marketers know their customers and know what products/services to offer to satisfy the needs of the consumers. The mere availability of a product is not enough. The consumers should be informed, reminded and persuaded. This is what advertising does. There should be regular analyses of the market and its needs as well as how consumers react to products, prices, distribution outlets and advertising. There is therefore a two-way information flow in successful marketing as depicted in Figure 13.1.

FIGURE 13.1   The relation between marketing and marketing communication

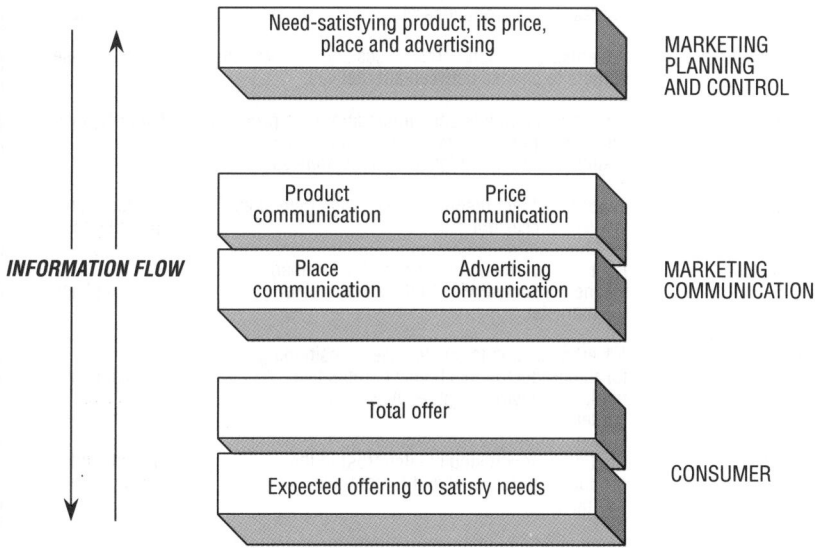

Source: Adapted from De Lozier, MW. 1976. *The Marketing Communications Process*. New York: McGraw-Hill Inc, p 167.

Ultimately the consumer perceives a 'total offering' based on the product, price, place and advertising communication which he then compares with what he expects from the product to satisfy his needs.

Advertising plays an important role in the different phases of the product's life cycle (see Chapter 18) and to help sales representatives in their task. These two aspects will now be discussed.

Specific roles which advertising plays during the different phases of a product's life cycle can be summarised as in Figure 13.3.[3]

FIGURE 13.2   Advertising during the product life cycle

Role	Description	Life cycle application
Create awareness	Advertising creates awareness of the product/service, the solution to the consumer's problems or possible need-satisfaction.	Introductory phase
Inform consumers	Advertising informs consumers about what the product/service can do for them, ie. what it is, what it does, how it can be used, its price and where obtainable.	Introductory phase
Create interest	Advertising calls on the consumer's need and creates interest in the product/service.	Introduction and growth phase
Develop preferences	Advertising develops preferences and enables consumers to choose between alternatives.	Growth phase
Remind	Advertising reminds consumers about the product, the years of using it, its price, where available. It aims to achieve a high level of awareness.	Maturity phase
Generate leads	Especially direct response advertising generates leads to successful sales.	Introduction and growth phases
Image building	Regular advertising builds a particular image for the product/service to the advantage of the marketer.	Growth phase
Positioning	Advertising aims to create a clear positioning for the product in this highly competitive marketing environment, eg Avis's "We try harder".	Growth phase
Create trust	Continued advertising creates trust in the product to purchase it and to continue buying it.	Growth and maturity phases

Advertising also plays an important role in helping sales representatives and retailers. Sales representatives have more confidence when selling a well-advertised product because the awareness has already been created. The customer is informed that the product has a particular image and positioning, the customer's interest is aroused, preferences have already been developed and the customer hopefully trusts the product.

Advertising creates consumer demand which helps the retailer. Good advertising actually pulls the product through the distribution channel because the consumer wants the product and may even insist on it.

13.4 ADVERTISING OBJECTIVES

13.4.1 The importance of advertising objectives

Considering and planning advertising objectives start with the target audience. The target audience could be the current or potential consumers of the marketer's products, opinion makers or innovators in the target market.

The target audience could consist of individuals, certain groups or the general public. The quantitative and qualitative features of the target audience have a strong influence on **what** will be said in the advertising, **why** it must be said, **how** it will be said, **when** it will be said, **where** it will be said, and **who** will say it. Answers to these questions centre in the overall objectives of marketing communications, ie **to inform**, **remind and persuade** the target audience.

Advertising objectives are especially important because they:

- help to fit the advertising decisions into the product, distribution and price decisions;
- help to make more effective decisions on the advertising budget and the selection of advertising media;
- are necessary for measuring advertising effectiveness. The results of an advertising campaign cannot be measured if they are not evaluated in terms of specific advertising objectives.

13.4.2 The requirements which advertising objectives have to fulfil

Advertising objectives must:

- Be **specific** about the product/service/personality/institution/idea to be advertised: The entire advertising campaign basically hinges upon the item to be advertised. In this way the product/service, greatly determines the target audience, advertising media, the contents of the advertising message and the duration of the campaign.

- Have a **specific theme**: The theme of an advertising objective is basically that aspect which has to be changed in the target audience, such as brand awareness, brand preference, image of the enterprise, buying season and patronage behaviour.
- Be **measurable**: Advertising objectives have to be formulated in specific and clear terms. It has to be precise about the communication result envisaged for the theme. For example, if 10 per cent of the target audience is presently aware of product X, an awareness of 25 per cent among the target audience can be set as part of an advertising objective.
- Have a **bench-mark**: This requirement has already been presumed above. It means that a specific advertising objective can be formulated only if the present position is known. In the abovementioned example the present 10 per cent awareness of the product among the target audience is such a bench-mark.

- Have a **target audience**: The target audience at which the advertising objectives are aimed has to be defined very clearly. The target audience is the result of market segmentation and market targeting. In this way one can communicate with all students at South African universities; married males between 24 and 35 years of age; all chemists in the Republic of South Africa; all white teachers in Transvaal and Natal; and all owners of private residences in the Pretoria/ Witwatersrand/Vereeniging area. Clarity on the target audience is particularly necessary for the selection of advertising media and the creation of the advertising message.

The **theme** of advertising objectives, is particularly important in the management of an advertising campaign. This forms inter alia the core of the measurement of advertising effectiveness. As a matter of fact, the theme is probably the only variable in the advertising objective which one *wants* to change purposely by way of the advertising campaign. Advertising objectives can, however, have different themes for the *informing, reminding* and *persuading* of the target audience.

13.4.3 Themes for advertising objectives

The following are some examples of themes for advertising objectives (the cores of the themes are printed in bold type):

- **reminding** the target audience **to buy**;

- **stimulating impulsive buying** among consumers visiting grocery shops;

- **effecting direct sales and encouraging enquiries** by mail advertising to farmers;

- **introducing** a new washing powder to housewives;

- **creating larger brand awareness** for rugby boot X among rugby players;

- **developing a favourable image** for restaurant A among movie patrons;

- **putting right wrong impressions and wrong information** about fuel X among owners of private motor cars in the Transvaal;

- **improving co-operation** with men's outfitters in the Republic of South Africa;

- **attracting new students** to University B;

- **asking for more information** regarding road safety;

- **increasing confidence** in insurance company H.

13.5 MANAGEMENT OF THE ADVERTISING CAMPAIGN

An advertising campaign is the intentional, purposeful, effective and impersonal dissemination of messages regarding a need-satisfying product, service, personality, place, institution or idea, and/or the place where it is available, and/or its price, by an identifiable sponsor to a specific target audience with the objective of informing and/or reminding and/or persuading the target audience to take a specific action. Thus, an advertising campaign is advertising in full swing.

The management of the advertising campaign consists of nine interdependent steps:

Steps in the management of the advertising campaign

- Analyse the present situation.
- Determine the advertising objectives.
- Draw up an advertising budget.
- Select the advertising media.
- Develop the advertising messages.
- Pre-test the advertising campaign.
- Conduct the actual launch of the advertising campaign.
- Co-ordinate the advertising campaign with other marketing and business activities as well as outside institutions.
- Review and measure the effectiveness of the advertising campaign.

From the point of view of the advertising practitioner, there is a very important step preceding these nine, namely the advertising briefing.

The advertising briefing usually outlines the following for the advertising practitioner:

- the product/service's strengths and weaknesses, its image and positioning;
- the target audience, their needs and usage patterns;
- what should be said in the advertising, ie the objectives of the advertising; and
- the advertising budget.

The nine steps are now discussed in more detail.

Step 1: Analyse the current situation[4]

An analysis of the current situation includes an analysis of the market, the product/service and the selected target audience.

Market analysis: An analysis of the market includes an analysis of the target audience, their usage patterns, preferences and especially their needs. The marketer does not, however, operate in isolation and therefore attention is paid to the companies who market similar products (ie the competitors): market shares, image perceptions, sales trends, advertising expenditure, and new products being planned.

Analysis of the product/service: Usually two analyses are conducted: a SWOT analysis and an analysis of the product/service's image and positioning. The SWOT analysis includes an analysis of the product's strengths, weaknesses and the opportunities and threats found in the marketing environment.

S : Strengths
W : Weaknesses
O : Opportunities
T : Threats

The analysis of the product's image and positioning supplies information about how the consumer experiences the product and how the product differs from competitive products. It is important for the advertiser that his product/service has a favourable image and a positioning that is unique. In this regard see Chapter 4 for the product positioning guide.

Analysis of the target audience: The target audience consists of people or decision making units to be reached with the advertising to inform, remind and persuade them. It is important to establish the following about the target audience:

- who they are (demographics and psychographics);
- where they are (geographics);
- market size;
- purchasing and usage habits;
- knowledge and image perceptions of competitive products;
- attitudes to competitive products/services, their prices, selling outlets and advertising;
- specific needs and/or problems facing the target audience.

Step 2: Determine the advertising objectives

Advertising objectives should be outlined in detail and should preferably be:

- written;
- valid for a particular period, for example one year;
- measurable and quantifiable;
- planned considering the attributes and needs of the target audience and the amount of money available in the advertising budget.

Step 3: Plan the advertising budget

The advertising budget can be defined as the *determination of the total amount of money required to execute each activity in the advertising campaign.* Viewed in this way, the advertising budget has two sides, namely the determination of the *total amount* to be spent on advertising, and *how* this money will be appropriated.

FIGURE 13.3   Steps in the management of the advertising campaign

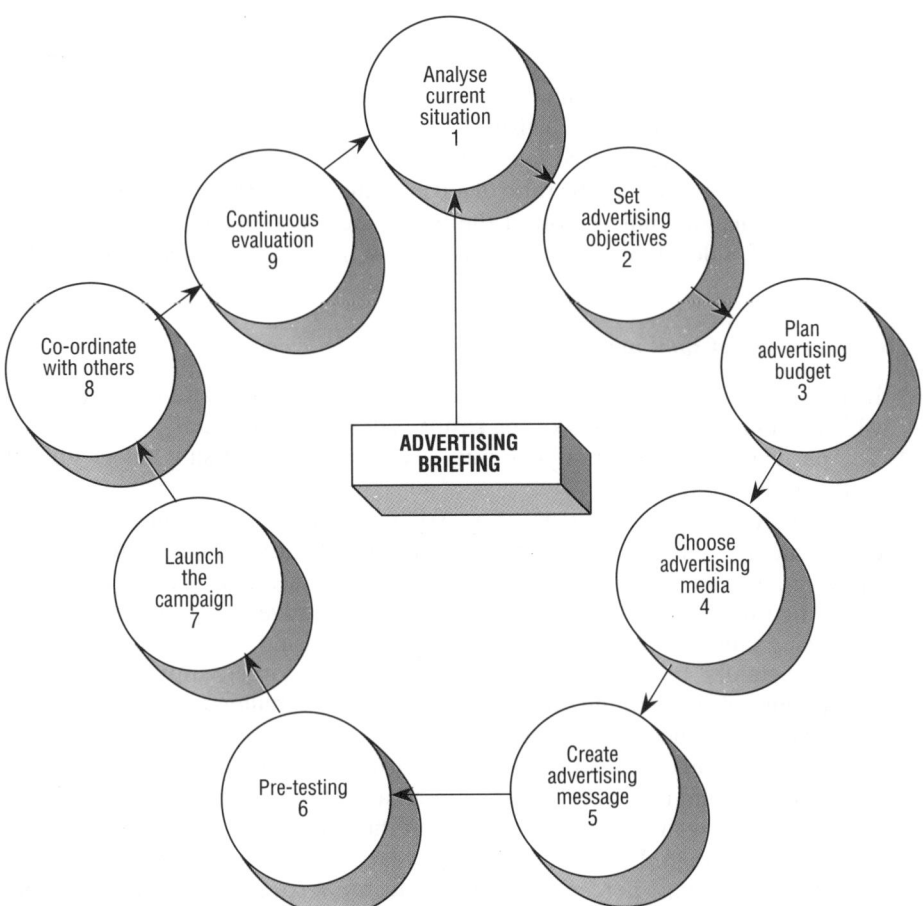

The advertising budget thus has a source side and an application side. These two sides of the advertising budget are discussed in detail.

The source side of the advertising budget

The source side of the advertising budget can be determined according to a **breakdown** or **build-up** method. In the **breakdown method** the total advertising amount is determined according to a certain method(s) and thereafter amounts of money are allocated as costs to the different advertising activities (broken down). In the **build-up method** the total advertising amount is built up from the costs of the various advertising activities which have to be performed to achieve certain advertising objectives.

Four breakdown methods are identified, namely the percentage-of-sales method, the units-sold method, the expenditures-of-competitors method and the what-can-be-afforded method.

Percentage-of-sales method

From the point of view of calculation, this is the easiest method to determine the total amount of money for advertising. The difficulty, however, is the determination of the real **percentage** of sales which has to be calculated. The size or the percentage is often based on the ratio of advertising to sales in the past, advertising to expected sales, a combination of the foregoing, or, if available, the average percentage of sales that similar firms in the particular industry spend on advertising.

The percentage-of-sales method has the following deficiencies:

- It does not consider changes in the macro-, market and micro-environments which can influence the marketing result (sales) of the firm.
- The particular marketing opportunity/threat which advertising has to utilise/deal with is ignored.
- This method makes an error of reasoning because it assumes that sales **determine** advertising, instead of advertising **influencing** sales. This method therefore provides a smaller amount of money for advertising during times of declining sales and a larger amount of money for advertising during times of increasing sales. In view of the influence of advertising on sales, the situation should actually be the opposite, ie a relatively larger appropriation for advertising with declining sales and a relatively smaller appropriation for advertising with increasing sales.
- Taking the average percentage of similar firms means that the individual firm can hardly extend its market share with an advertising campaign. It depends, however, on how the actual percentages of the firms in the industry are spread around the average. If there is a relatively large number of firms which spend *less* than the average percentage of the industry, a specific firm which accepts the average percentage of the industry can probably extend its market share at the expense of these firms.

Units-sold method

By the units-sold method a specific amount for advertising is added to the cost of the product. The total advertising amount is thus determined by the number of units sold. Therefore this method has the same deficiencies as the percentage-of-sales method.

Expenditure-of-competitors method

This method is a refinement of the percentage-of-sales method, where the percentage is based on the average percentage of similar firms in the industry involved. If the information is known, a firm can **follow the example** of its main competitor by spending the same, or a higher, percentage of sales on advertising.

Spending the same percentage of sales for advertising as that of the most important competitor points to a **market share maintenance strategy** while a higher percentage can possibly be an effort towards **extending market share**.

The expenditure-of-competitors method has the following deficiencies:

- Two firms are seldom, if ever, identical in size and internal capabilities and their appropriation for advertising amounts should therefore not purposefully correspond.
- The competitor's appropriation for advertising is probably also not optimally determined and the firm can actually follow a poor example.
- The competitor may, for good reasons, apply his appropriation for advertising differently on advertising media and types of advertising than the imitator. If the imitator, with similar good reasons, were not to use the same advertising media and types of advertising as the competitor, this imitation will be meaningless. Such similar conditions probably seldom exist in practice in any event.

What-can-be-afforded method

The what-can-be-afforded method for determining the total appropriation for advertising uses the amount of money that the firm can afford to spend on advertising as point of departure. This approach is relatively conservative since management inter alia wishes to ensure strict control over advertising costs by way of this method. The advertising amount budgeted for under these circumstances is usually expressed as a certain percentage of the net profit or current assets of the firm. If this amount is calculated too conservatively, the firm runs the risk of not achieving its advertising objectives effectively.

Similarly, the what-can-be-afforded method can also lead to a relatively optimistic approach in determining the amount of money for advertising if management were to follow a **go-for-broke strategy.** Here the what-can-be-afforded method is taken to the utmost limits of optimism and management inter alia has a firm belief in the ability of advertising to influence the marketing results favourably.

The task method

The build-up method for determining the amount to be spent on advertising is the **task method.** The point of departure of this method is the desired **advertising objectives.** For this reason the task method is also known as the **objectives method.** Thus the question is: What advertising activities have to be performed in order to achieve the advertising objectives and what is the cost of each task?

The task method consists of four steps:

- Describe the **advertising tasks** necessary to achieve the specific and clearly formulated advertising objective as derived from the marketing and sales objectives.
- Determine the **type** of advertising required to achieve the objective.
- Determine the **scope and intensity** of each type of advertising.
- Determine the **cost** of each advertising activity and add up the costs of the various activities to arrive at the **total costs** of the advertising campaign.

Example of the task method

Suppose a marketer of caravans sets his marketing objective for 1993 at 20 per cent of the market demand of 1 000 caravans in Pretoria. Thus the sales objective is 200 caravans (20 per cent of 1 000). Experience has proved that one out of every five enquiries, based on a full-page advertisement, leads to the purchase of one caravan. A total of 1 000 enquiries (100 caravans × 5 enquiries) is therefore required to achieve the sales objective. It was further found that a full-page advertisement on a Friday leads to an average of 20 enquiries. One full-page advertisement therefore leads to the sale of 4 caravans. Thus, 50 full-page advertisements (200 caravans divided by 4 caravans per advertisement) have to be placed on 50 Fridays during 1993 to achieve the sales objective of 200 caravans. Suppose, further, that the cost of placing one full-page advertisement in the local newspaper is R8 000. The total cost of the advertising campaign is thus R400 000 (50 advertisements × R8 000).

In theory the task method for determining the advertising amount has no deficiencies. The practical application reveals, however, the following **problem**:

It is often difficult to determine the **relationship** between an advertisement, the number of enquiries based on it and the ultimate purchases which are in turn based on the number of enquiries. Experience in the past, however, can be useful in this regard.

Other factors, such as the nature of the product (its newness, durability, complexity), the prevailing and expected economic conditions (growth, recession, inflation), the internal capabilities of the firm (availability of funds), the actions of competitors (aggressive counter-advertising), and the net profit margin per product unit, naturally also influence the total advertising amount.

The application side of the advertising budget

Advertising costs are running expenses incurred by a firm. It is, however, not always clear what cost items have to be included in the advertising budget. These cost items can be divided into *three* groups: cost items where there is no doubt; cost items where there is sometimes doubt; and cost items sometimes wrongfully included in the advertising budget.

The most important cost items which undoubtedly have to be included in the advertising budget are the following:

• The costs of **advertising space** in advertising media such as magazines, newspapers, business periodicals, consumer periodicals, consumer catalogues, farming publications, outdoor advertising, material for point-of-purchase

advertising, direct mail advertising, posters, placards, brochures, vehicle panels, and posters at bus stops, stations, alongside roads and at other places.
- The costs of **advertising time** on media such as radio, television and cinema.
- **Administrative costs** directly related to advertising, such as the salaries of personnel in the advertising department, costs attached to office and other equipment in the advertising department, and subsistence and travelling expenses of advertising personnel.
- The **production costs** attached to the creation of advertisements, such as artwork, artists, photographic work and the advertising aspects involved in the design of packaging.

Cost items where there is sometimes doubt as to whether they are part of the advertising budget or not are the following:

Samples, point-of-purchase demonstrations, shows, premium products, depreciation on advertising vehicles, market research on advertising, advertising allowances for co-operative advertising and catalogues for the sales force.

Cost items which are not part of the advertising budget include:

Gifts (not samples) given away, donations to welfare organisations, labels, cartons, price-lists, bonuses for middlemen, special discounts, membership fees paid to industrial associations, entertainment costs of customers, and the subsistence and travelling expenses of sales representatives.

Step 4: Select advertising media

Requirements of media selection

The selection of advertising media is part of the advertising budget because the major part of the appropriation for advertising is used for payment of the advertising media to be utilised in the advertising campaign. The selection of specific advertising media thus has an important influence on the application of the appropriation for advertising.

An important requirement for successful advertising is to convey the right message at the right time in the right media to the right target audience. The following procedure in selecting advertising media has to be followed to comply with this requirement:

- Consider what **type** of advertising medium should be used, such as newspapers or periodicals.
- Decide on the specific **group** within the type of medium, for example, agricultural periodicals.
- Select **specific** advertising media from this group, such as *Farmer's Weekly* and *Landbouweekblad*.

However, carrying out this procedure in practice requires a sound knowledge of the most important characteristics of the advertising media and the factors which have to be considered in selecting media. These two aspects will be discussed next.

Most important characteristics of advertising media

Each type of advertising medium has features peculiar to itself. No single advertising medium can be regarded as the best under all circumstances.

Advertising media can be classified into **printed media** and **audiovisual media:**

- **Printed media** consist of inter alia newspapers, periodicals, consumer periodicals, pamphlets, brochures, direct mail advertising, outdoor advertising, such as panels and posters, and point-of-purchase advertising.
- **Audiovisual media** consist mainly of the various commercial radio networks, television networks and cinemas.

The characteristics of the different types of media, especially in terms of their strengths and weaknesses, are summarised in Table 13.1.

Factors to be considered in selecting advertising media

These factors can be divided into **internal business factors**, **external factors** and **media factors**.

The following mutually dependent internal factors have to be considered:

- The financial and in particular the **liquidity position** of the enterprise. An enterprise which does not possess sufficient cash, or can obtain it only with great difficulty, is rather restricted in respect of advertising and the selection of specific media.
- The **nature of the product**. Certain products, for example, require demonstration, and only television and cinema advertising can be used for this purpose.
- The **nature of distribution channels and market coverage** of the enterprise. In this way a product which is marketed intensively and country-wide through the agency of retailers may require different types of advertising media compared to a product that is marketed exclusively by retailers and in certain regions/cities only.
- The nature of the **marketing communication mix** of the enterprise. If the enterprise uses mainly personal selling to market the product, relatively expensive advertising media, such as television and the press, will probably not be considered.
- The nature of the **advertising objectives** and the matching **advertising message**. An advertising message which, for example, entails motion and profuse detail naturally cannot be conveyed effectively by radio.

The following external factors have to be considered:

- The **reading, listening, viewing** and **buying habits of the target audience** and the ways in which the target audience has been segmented definitely have a very important influence on the selection of specific advertising media. Here it is important to know **who** is the target audience, **where** they are, **what** their reading, listening and viewing habits are, **what** they buy, **why** they buy, **how** they buy, **when** they buy, and **where** they buy.

TABLE 13.1 The characteristics of the different advertising media in terms of their relative strengths and weaknesses

TYPE OF ADVERTISING MEDIUM	STRENGTHS	WEAKNESSES
1. Print media Direct advertising including direct mail advertising	• Reaches a selective group • Especially flexible • Can be made personal • Can be used within a small budget	• Relatively expensive per reader per message • Is often ignored and waste takes place • No editorial support • Lists of addresses difficult to obtain and seldom up-to-date
Newspapers	• Enable illustration and explanation • Suitable for high frequency • Flexible in the event of change • Relatively cheap per reader • Geographically selective • Buyers use it as a guide	• Bad reproduction • Short life span • Is read cursorily • Reaches a general audience • Many advertisers, little chance to dominate
Magazine	• Good reproduction • Longer life span • Reaches specific segments • Usually loyal readers • National coverage	• Limited flexibility because of long lead times • Many advertisers and little chance to dominate
Outdoor advertising	• Cost per passer-by low • Suitable for high frequency • Geographically selective • Gives support and serves as a reminder of other advertisements • Large product presentation	• Short time in which to convey message • Necessarily a short message • Reaches the general passer-by • Space relatively more limited • Detrimental to aesthetics of environment
Point-of-purchase advertising	• Stimulates impulsive purchases • Gives support and reminds • Can ensure better co-operation with middlemen	• Dealer can refuse preference for a specific manufacturer's point-of-purchase advertising • Is sometimes placed in poor locations
2. Audio-visual media (a) Radio	• Is a personal medium • Geographically selective in regional services • National coverage with certain transmissions • Can reach specific audiences at certain times • No literacy necessary • Listening habits sometimes habitual	• Limited availability • No back reference to message • No illustration possible • Only a short message • Is a background medium
(b) Television	• Involves the most senses • Viewer transfixed and cannot ignore message • Good in case of demonstrations • Wide coverage • Prestige value • Can involve the whole family	• Limited availability • No back reference to message • Relatively expensive medium • Reaches a general audience • Relatively lengthy preparation • Repetition can irritate viewer • Only national
(c) Cinema	• Involves the most senses • Viewer transfixed and cannot ignore message • Good in case of demonstrations • Geographically selective • Receive message in a relaxed atmosphere • High quality reproduction	• Reaches a general audience • Relatively expensive medium • Limited message • Relatively lengthy preparation necessary

Source: Adapted from Van Rooyen, DC. 'The Management of the Advertising Campaign' in Lucas, GHG, et al (eds). 1980. *The Task of Marketing Management*. 1st edition. Pretoria: Van Schaik, p 486.

- The advertising media which **competitors** use also influence the choice of advertising media. A particular firm can use more or less the same media as its competitors or it can select other advertising media. Here it is difficult to make generalisations. Whether to imitate competitors or not is inter alia determined by the nature of the product, the nature of the target audience, the capabilities of the firm, and the availability of advertising space and/or time in the various media.

The following media factors have to be considered:

- The **availability and accessibility** of the medium to the marketer. In radio and television the time available for advertising is limited, and it is furthermore **inadmissible** to advertise certain products on television (liquor and cigarettes) or in certain periodicals.
- Advertisements used in retail advertising, for example, **change** continually. To counter this problem, a medium which can **adapt** at short notice is very important, such as local newspapers.
- Certain advertisers probably have the **sole right** to the inside front page, the middle pages, inside back page or back page of a specific periodical. If such space is important in advertising decisions and it has already been taken up by other advertisers, a sole right eliminates the medium involved for consideration.
- The **cost per thousand target audience receivers** of the message in a specific medium also influences the media choice. The cost per thousand:

$$= \frac{\text{Total costs of the advertisement}}{\text{Target audience receivers of message in thousands}}$$

The application of the cost-per-thousand yardstick, however, is relatively complex in selecting media. Advertising media not only differ from one another regarding the cost per thousand, but inter alia also in respect of impact, circumstances under which they communicate with the target audience, and the quality of the artwork and reproduction (compare a colour advertisement in a newspaper with the same colour advertisement in a glossy periodical). These factors detract from the significance of a comparison of the cost per thousand target audience receivers of the message between different media.

- The **price decisions** of the different media can also influence the choice of media. Certain media, for instance, grant a quantity discount on advertisements which are placed for a relatively long period and which remain unchanged.
- The **costs of using the media**, in view of the funds at the disposal of the enterprise for advertising, also influence the choice of media. If the available appropriation for advertising is relatively small, relatively expensive media such as television will probably not be considered.
- The **coverage**, frequency and continuity of the advertising media also play an important role in media selection. **Coverage** *denotes the total number of persons in the target audience exposed at one time to the advertisement.* **Frequency** *refers to the number of times that a person can receive the advertising message during a specific period, such as a day, week or month.* **Continuity** *refers to the period*

for which a specific advertisement is placed in a specific medium. The longer the period, the bigger the **cumulative audience** should be. For products with a relatively short and high repurchasing rate, continuity is an important factor in the choice of media, especially with a view to reminding the target audience.

In conclusion it can be said that the *reading, listening, viewing and buying habits of the target audience* and the *characteristics* of the firm probably are the most important factors which have to be considered in selecting the available advertising media. This means that those advertising media should be selected which are attuned best to the reading, listening, viewing and buying habits of the target audience and which fit the characteristics of the firm best. This attuning can be accomplished by relating the *characteristics and possibilities* of each advertising medium to the reading, listening, viewing and buying habits of the target audience and the characteristics of the firm.

Step 5: Create the advertising message

Dimensions of the creative process

This step makes great demands on the creative abilities of the advertising artist and it is the field of the specialist *par excellence.* The remarks on the creation of advertisements are therefore aimed at the **evaluation** of advertisements rather than furnishing *guidelines for creation.* Furthermore, the printed advertisement appearing in newspapers and periodicals is taken as the main basis for discussion.

With the reading, listening, viewing and buying habits and lifestyles of the target audience, the characteristics of the specific product, and the particular medium in mind, the copywriter must answer the following questions: *What must be said/written/visualised? How must it be said/written/visualised in order to utilise the advertising space effectively and to achieve the advertising objectives?*

The creation of an advertisement has *three* mutually dependent dimensions, namely **copywriting, visualisation** and **copy layout**. The reasoning behind, and mutual relationship between the three dimensions appear in Figure 13.3.

It is noteworthy that the advertising objectives of informing, reminding and persuading are also based on the attention, interest, desire, credibility, action and satisfaction of the AIDCAS concept.

Based on Figure 13.4 the three dimensions involved in the creation of an advertisement are discussed below.

Copywriting

Copywriting pertains to the use of words to arouse attention, interest and desire, to achieve credibility, to stimulate action and to ensure satisfaction in the target audience, and consists of copy research, copy structure and copy style.

- **Copy research** *must inter alia be done in order to find a motivational factor which will be used in the advertisement.* The motivational factor is a unique and original persuasive proposition (often a selling proposition) made to the target audience. The motivational factor can be found in the **characteristics** of the **product or service** (stain-free guaranteed; the plaster that breathes;

FIGURE 13.3   The reasoning behind and the mutually dependent dimensions of copywriting, visualisation and copy layout in creating an advertisement

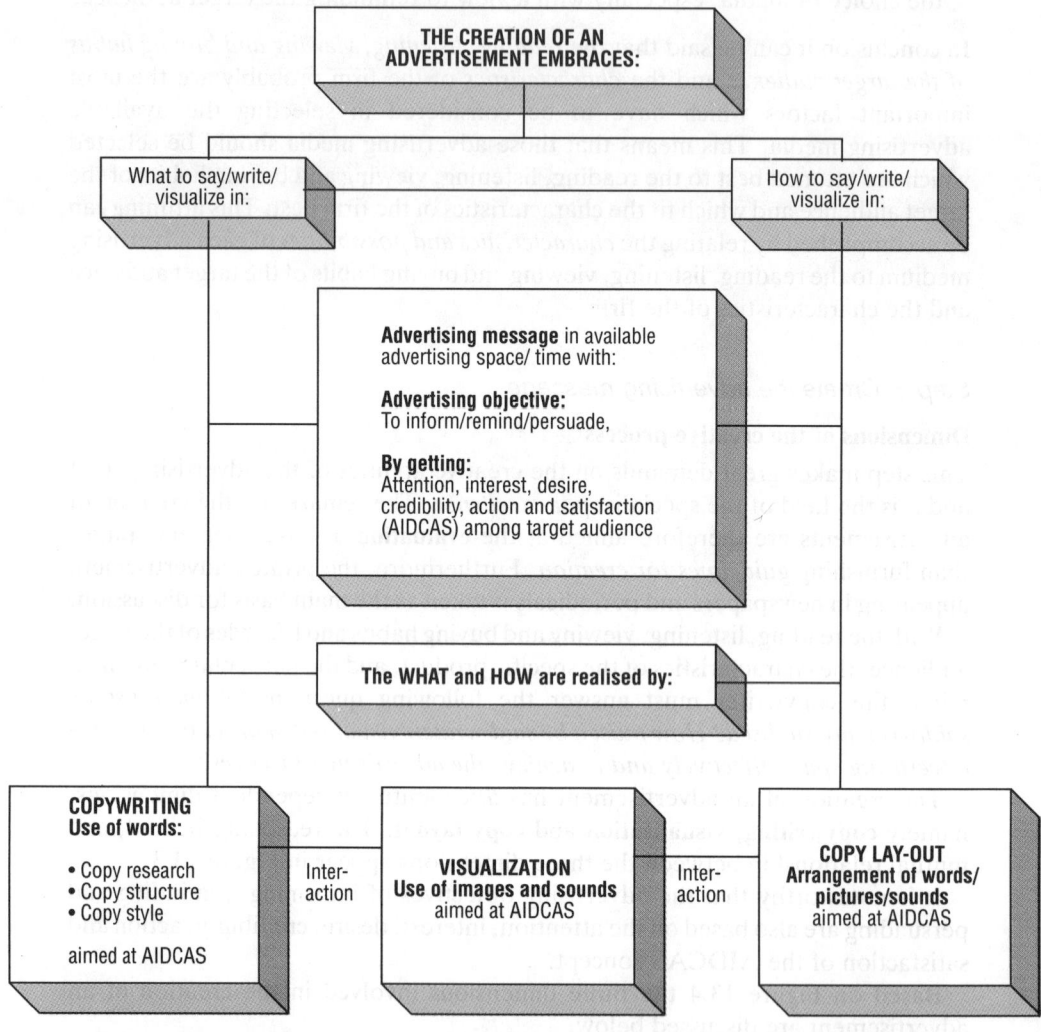

Source: Marx, S & Dekker, HJ. 1982. *Marketing Management: Principles and Decisions*. Pretoria: HAUM, p 310.

will not peel or perish; clean-burning economy; each product a masterpiece; golden-oak mellowed; one-stop service; the biggest helping hand in the land) and/or in the **need** which the **product satisfies** (after-action satisfaction; lion pleasure; finger-licking good; serious about money; noise-free reception; pure driving pleasure). Thus, the copywriter is looking for an **original motivational factor** which he can use to differentiate the product or service concerned from those of competitors.

Copy structure *is the content and scope of the text to be used in the advertising message*. It usually consists of a main headline, the text itself, and the conclusion which frequently suggests a specific action. The main headline is very important because it is often *all* which many people read in an advertisement. The extension of the headline normally explains or qualifies the main headline. The text contains details on the product or service and its need-satisfying attributes as well as the need of the consumer that can be satisfied. The conclusion suggests an action which should lead to a particular form of satisfaction — after-action satisfaction and pure driving pleasure.

Copy style *refers to the style in which words are presented*. The style can be **rational**, ie objective and factual information on the product, how it is made, what it is, what purpose it serves, and what utility it contains. An **irrational** or subjective style can also be employed in the use of words; that is to say, the style is emotional and subjective in nature and endeavours to fire the imagination of the target audience so that the reader/listener/viewer identifies with the events depicted in the advertisement.

Visualisation

Visualisation involves arousing attention, interest, and desire, achieving credibility, stimulating action and ensuring satisfaction in the target audience through sounds and pictures. Visualisation and copywriting supplement each other, and have to form a unity in order to strengthen the AIDCAS concept and to increase the impact of the advertisement as much as possible. Here the creative abilities and originality of the advertising artist play a particularly important role.

Copy layout

Copy layout embraces the effective arrangement of the different elements of the copy (words, sounds and pictures) within the available advertising space in order to increase the measure of attention, interest, desire, credibility, action and satisfaction in the target audience as much as possible.

The following aspects have to be borne in mind with regard to copy layout:

- **balance** in design of the advertisement, ie the harmonious distribution and placement of the words and pictures in the available advertising space;
- **continuity** in the advertisement, in other words the pictures and words have to be arranged in such a way that they form a logical sequence which enables the reader/listener/viewer to receive and understand the entire advertising message;
- the layout has to form a **unity**, ie the words and pictures have to supplement each other and should not conflict or create an impression of confusion;
- the layout has to be **simple and easy to understand** for the target audience; and
- good layout **emphasises** the most important words and pictures in the advertising message.

There are many adjectives which can be used in an attempt to **evaluate** the advertising message. Vague generalisations, such as that the advertisement has to be dramatic, distinguishing, simple, meaningful, authentic, realistic and surprising, do not help much if the advertising message cannot achieve the **advertising objectives**.

After having been created, the advertising message, together with the other aspects of the advertising campaign, have to be tested before the actual launch of the campaign.

Step 6: Pre-test the advertising campaign

From a management point of view, the pre-testing of the advertising campaign is an important **preventative control task**, ie control is exercised to prevent deviations from the plans.

In a sense an advertising campaign is a relatively expensive and irreclaimable activity for the firm. This means that relatively high costs, such as the production of advertisements, have to be incurred *before* the advertisements appear in the mass media. In order to reduce the risk of these costs being mere waste, the advertising message and other strategic aspects of the campaign have to be tested beforehand. *The advertising message is tested in order to gauge its communication ability under normal marketing conditions.*

A brief discussion follows of some methods which can be used in pre-testing an advertising message.

Methods of pre-testing advertisements

- *Copy testing*

  The advertisement is shown to a number of respondents in the target audience to assess *what* it communicates and how credible the message is perceived to be.

- *Control lists*

  A variety of control lists exist which contain different control questions. The ultimate aim of all the control questions is to determine whether the advertisement arouses attention, interest, and desire, achieves credibility, stimulates action and ensures satisfaction in the target audience as planned.

- *Consumer panels*

  A consumer panel is a group of consumers selected from the target audience who are exposed to the advertising message in order to gauge their reaction to the advertisement. Consumer panels are especially used when the best choice among a number of advertising messages has to be made. Members of the panel are usually requested to rank the advertisements in order of importance according to their impact.

- *Test marketing*

  The use of the advertisement in test marketing can furnish the marketer with reasonably reliable indications of the manner in which the advertisement should perform in a mass marketing situation. Test marketing is also particularly useful when testing other aspects of the advertising campaign, such as the choice of media, timing, and advertising objectives. (See Chapter 8 regarding the test marketing of new products.)

- *Enquiry tests*

  Persons in the test market can be requested, by means of a coupon system, to make enquiries about a special offer made in the advertisement. If the intention behind such a special offer is not too obvious, the enquiries can give a reasonable indication of the success of the advertising message.

- *Split-run exposure tests*

  If the marketer has to make a choice between two advertisements, for example, he can place one advertisement in one part of a newspaper supplement and the other advertisement in the remaining part of the edition. After members of the target audience have been exposed to the advertisements, they are questioned on aspects of the advertisements such as *what* they have seen and *what* they can remember of the contents.

If necessary, the advertising message should be revised. Subsequently the actual launch of the campaign can take place.

Step 7: Launch the advertising campaign

It should be clear by now that the advertising campaign consists of a variety of divergent but nevertheless mutually dependent activities.

Time, however, is of decisive importance in any advertising campaign and wrong timing can jeopardise the entire advertising campaign. Completion dates must therefore be laid down for each activity in the advertising campaign. In this way the analysis of the present situation, the setting of advertising objectives, the drawing up of the advertising budget, the selection of advertising media, the creation of the advertisement and the pre-testing of advertisements have to *start* at specific times and have to be *completed* at specific times so that the advertisements can appear at the appointed times in the mass media.

It so happens that certain activities can be executed simultaneously (the analysis of the present situation and setting of objectives); certain activities can only follow after others have been completed (creation of the advertisement can only take place after media selection); and certain activities precede others (the creation of an advertisement before pre-testing). Most advertising departments of large firms and advertising practitioners have so-called **traffic departments** which have to see to it that the course of the campaign runs according to schedule. With the actual launch of the advertising campaign the **media plan** has to serve inter alia as a point of departure and the agency works back from the date when the first advertisement is scheduled.

Step 8: Co-ordinate the advertising campaign with other relevant parties

Co-ordination entails obtaining co-operation between individuals and groups in order to act in harmony as a team in the pursuit of a common goal. In managing an advertising campaign co-ordination on at least *four* levels is necessary: with top management; between other departments in the firm *outside* the marketing department; between sections *inside* the marketing department; and with outside institutions.

Co-ordination with top management

- **Approval** of the nature and scope of the advertising campaign is probably the most important aspect to be co-ordinated with top management.
- Top management will probably expect to be **informed** from time to time on the course of the campaign.
- After completion of the advertising campaign top management should be informed about its **effectiveness**.

Co-ordination with other departments in the enterprise

- Co-ordination with the **financial department** is of special importance in order to ensure that the right amount of money is made available at the right times for the financing of the campaign.
- Co-operation with the **production department** is also very important. The unique persuasive proposition which will be used in the advertising message is often derived from the technical attributes of the product. Then it must be ensured that the production department can timeously handle the increased demand which will probably flow from the advertising campaign. It can inter alia happen that the capacity of the plant has to be enlarged.
- Co-ordination with the **purchasing department** can at times be important. If the increased demand flowing from the advertising campaign results in increased production, it will most probably also lead to increased purchases of raw materials.
- Co-operation with the **public relations department** is very important because the advertising campaign can often be combined with a publicity campaign.

Co-ordination inside the marketing department

- Co-operation between the advertising department and the **marketing information department** is important throughout the advertising campaign. As a matter of fact, the entire advertising campaign is based on data and information on the present situation of the firm, the characteristics of the target audience, the availability of media, the search for a motivational factor, and the actions of the competitors. Here the marketing information system of the firm plays a decisive role.
- Co-ordination with the **sales force** is an obvious requirement. One of the *themes* of an advertising campaign can be to provide sales representatives with a point of departure, and they have to be aware of this. Furthermore, they have to possess sufficient information on the advertising campaign so that they can inform middlemen about the campaign.
- Co-ordination with the **physical distribution department** is essential in an advertising campaign. Just imagine the dilemma and embarrassment if the advertised products are not available at retail outlets because of transport and other bottle-necks in physical distribution.

Co-ordination with outside institutions

At the launch of an advertising campaign co-ordination with many outside institutions is necessary. Only a few are mentioned.

- Co-operation is necessary with **middlemen** and with retailers in particular. The retailers have to be informed about the advertising campaign so that they can place their orders in good time, arrange for point-of-purchase advertising and co-operative advertising if necessary, inform their sales personnel about the new campaign, and deal effectively with consumers' enquiries about the advertised product.
- Co-ordination with the envisaged **advertising media** cannot be over-emphasised. In certain media, such as radio, television and cinema, the time available for advertising is limited and early negotiations in this regard are necessary. Then also, certain media wish to evaluate the advertisement before placement and early contact is therefore required to accomplish this.
- Co-ordination with other outside institutions such as **advertising practitioners**, **marketing research institutions** and **financial institutions** can at times be very important if the firm itself is not going to launch its advertising campaign or when outside financing is to be used for the campaign.

Co-ordination of the advertising campaign with the abovementioned individuals, groups and divisions is not a one-off process, but has to be repeated continually.

While the advertising campaign is in swing and also after its termination, control has to be exercised over the activities. This brings us to the next step in managing the advertising campaign.

Step 9: Revision of the advertising campaign

The pre-testing and revision of the advertising campaign and the measurement of the advertising effectiveness is part of the **control task** in managing the campaign. Thus, control has to take place on *three* occasions: before the campaign is launched (**control before the fact**); while the campaign is in swing (**control with the fact**); and after the activities have been completed (**control after the fact**). The purpose of control before the fact is to *prevent* deviations; the aim of control with the fact is to *rectify* deviations in *good time*; and the goal of control after the fact is to serve as basis for *future planning* and the prevention of similar deviations in future. For each type of control the steps in control naturally have to be followed:

- setting standards at strategic points;
- measuring and recording the actual performance at strategic times and places and comparing the actual advertising activities and performances with the planned activities and performances;
- evaluating the differences between the actual and planned activities; and
- deciding on future action.

Pre-testing has already been discussed and attention will here be given to selected post-tests developed for measuring the advertising effectiveness. **Recall tests** and **recognition tests** are probably the two methods used most frequently.

- In **recall tests** persons who are regularly exposed to the medium involved are questioned from time to time in order to determine what they remember of the advertised product in terms of the advertising theme. The recall performance is then gauged in view of the answers of the respondents and this can be used to quantify the communication impact of the advertisement in terms of the advertising theme.

- **Recognition tests** are based on a sample from the target audience. This sample consists of readers of a specific edition of, for example, a periodical in which the advertisement has appeared. The readers are questioned on what they can remember of the specific advertisement. The answers are divided into *three* groups, namely those readers who said that they had seen the advertisement; those who had read a part of the advertisement and who could give the name of the product; and those who said they had read more than half the contents of the advertisement. From this information an indication can be obtained of the communication impact of the advertisement in terms of the advertising theme.

13.6 THE ROLE OF THE ADVERTISING PRACTITIONER

Advertising practitioners are specialised and skilled firms responsible for managing relatively large advertising campaigns on behalf of their clients. Their task consists mainly of the *commencement, preparation, launching* and *evaluation* of advertising campaigns for the product or service of a client.

Advertising practitioners are especially suitable for managing advertising campaigns because they have specialised skills for executing complicated and sophisticated advertising activities; they usually pursue a more objective approach than that of the internal advertising division; and they receive a media commission from media owners which enables them to render many services to clients.

Services such as a study of the product or service, analysis of the present and potential market, a study of the available media, copy instructions to media, control over the correct publication of advertising material, and the handling of invoices for advertising space or time and invoices from suppliers of production material, are paid for from the media commission and are thus rendered free of charge to clients.

Advertising practitioners can be organised in various ways and normally they have a division for client services which mainly consist of account supervisors; a division for marketing services which usually has subdivisions for media, research and sundry liaison services; a creative division which consists of subdivisions for copywriters, artists, copy production and a traffic division; and a management and finance division which oversees office management, personnel, administration, bookkeeping and finances.

Advertising practitioners make an important contribution to the marketer's marketing activities as they do not specialise in advertising, but they give advice whilst being objective. No marketer can be totally objective about his product or service. The advertising practitioner has an objective view of the marketer, his products/services and the needs of the market.

13.7 ADVERTISING CONTROL IN SOUTH AFRICA[5]

The advertising industry in South Africa is an industry which aspires to professionalism in the conduct of its members and to enhance the credibility of advertising by imposing self-regulation rather than legal restrictions or government intervention.

The ASA (Advertising Standards Authority) was established in 1969 as an independent body, set up and paid for by the advertising industry. All the main organisations within the advertising industry, including the media, are members of the ASA and have subscribed to its Code of Advertising Practice.

This Code is based on the British Code of Advertising Practice and the code of the International Chambers of Commerce, which are accepted internationally. The objective of the Code is threefold. For those in advertising it lays down criteria for professional conduct, it prevents the advertising industry being discredited, and to the public it gives the assurance that advertising is honest, legal, in good taste and is prepared with a sense of responsibility towards the consumer.

The main provisions of the Code are:

Decency: Advertisements may not contain verbal or visual presentations offensive to the standards of decency prevailing among those who are likely to be exposed to them.

Honesty: Advertisements may not abuse the trust of the consumer or exploit his lack of knowledge or experience.

Fear, superstition, violence and illegality: Advertisements may not exploit fear or superstitions. Advertisements should not contain anything which might lead to acts of violence or lend support to criminal or illegal activities.

Truthful presentation: All descriptions, claims and comparisons should be capable of substantiation. Advertisements may not contain anything which directly or by implication misleads the consumer.

Denigration and disparagement: Advertisements may not attack or discredit other products. Brands may not be compared in an advertisement.

Exploitation of name: Advertisements may not without permission make use of the name of an enterprise, person or product. An advertisement may not look or sound like another advertisement and thereby create confusion or mislead the consumer.

Other: Specific provisions exist with regard to guarantees, children, medicines and other products and services such as hair products, liquor, cigarettes and many more.

Members of the advertising industry as well as members of the public, in fact anybody, may appeal against an advertisement which is perceived to be illegal, misleading, dishonest, an untruthful presentation or in bad taste. Such an appeal should be handed in at the ASA in writing and should be accompanied by the relevant advertisement. The following procedure is followed when the ASA receives a complaint:

- The executive director receives the complaint, considers it, refers it to the advertiser or advertising practitioner and if he believes the complaint is justified, he refers it to the Copy Committee. If not, he responds in writing to the complainant stating why it is not justified.
- The Copy Committee consists of members selected from the advertising industry and the Consumer Council. They meet at least once a month to consider complaints. After considering a complaint the complainant can be informed that the complaint is not justified; or if it is justified, the advertiser or advertising practitioner is informed that the advertisement should be stopped with immediate effect or it should be modified. Any person/institution/practitioner who is unhappy about the verdict of the Copy Committee could appeal to the Appeal Committee.
- The Appeal Committee consists of a chairman and a number of members selected from the advertising industry and the Consumer Council. The Appeal Committee considers the appeal, both parties (complainant and defender) have the right personally to state their case, and the Appeal Committee gives its verdict. This verdict is final.

In many cases one advertising practitioner lodges a complaint against the advertisement(s) of another practitioner. In such a case it is expected of the two practitioners to discuss the matter and to sort it out among themselves in a responsible way before a complaint may be sent to the ASA. Consumers could, however, go straight to the ASA and the ASA will always refer the complaint to the relevant advertiser and/or advertising practitioner who created the advertisement for his commentary before it will be referred to the Copy Committee.

Fines are not imposed by the ASA but guilty parties could be instructed to withdraw the advertisement(s) from the media, never to place such an advertisement in the media again, to publish the facts which will put the guilty party in a poor light, and in extreme cases advertising practitioners could forfeit their privileges or they could be asked to stop producing advertising.

13.8 SUMMARY

In this chapter advertising was discussed and emphasis was placed on the role of advertising in marketing, how advertising objectives should be set, the management of the advertising campaign, the role of the advertising practioner and how advertising control is applied in South Africa.

REFERENCES

1. Koekemoer, CL. 1978. *Print Media Advertising: Some Basic Principles*. Insight Publications, p 8.

2. The following paragraphs are largely based on Marx, S and Dekker, WJ. 1982. *Marketing Management: Principles and Decisions*. Pretoria: HAUM.
  Defining advertising: Marx and Dekker, pp 266 & 267.
  Advertising objectives: Marx and Dekker, pp 283, 295–7.
  Management of the advertising campaign: Marx and Dekker, pp 289 & 290.
  Plan the advertising budget: Marx and Dekker, pp 297–302.
  Selection of advertising media: Marx and Dekker, pp 303–7.
  Creating the advertising message: Marx and Dekker, pp 309–12.
  Pre-testing of the advertising campaign: Marx and Dekker, pp 312–13.
  The actual launching of the advertising campaign: Marx and Dekker, pp 313 & 314.
  Co-ordination of the advertising campaign with other relevant parties: Marx and Dekker, pp 314–16.
  The revision of the advertising campaign: Marx and Dekker, pp 316–19.
  The role of the advertising practitioner: Marx and Dekker, pp 320 & 321.
3. Koekemoer, CL (ed). 1987. *Marketing Communications Management*: *A South African Perspective*. Butterworths, pp 23–30.
4. Ibid pp 126–9.
5. See also ibid pp 48–76.

CASE STUDIES

1. MEDIA SELECTION IN SOUTH AFRICA

It's an understatement to say that media is a megabuck business. In 1991, R2,3 billion was spent advertising in the media (Adindex). TV and print took the major share. Radio still remains the medium of choice.

What makes some mediums more powerful than others? Impact! Reach! Frequency! It is really a case of sheer numbers and, if not, how can quality be seen to prevail over quantity? What are some of the innovations on offer by the mighty media which are certain to bring advertising rands their way?

Radio has come into its own as a stable medium which continues to have extensive reach and which gets results for advertisers. To its 13 million daily listeners, SABC Radio is an inherently intimate, one-to-one form of communication, says Radio Active's Carole Darkins.

'To the advertiser, it's a cost-effective medium offering immediate and flexible advertising. Through careful selection of specific target markets for each station, SABC Radio has established a solid audience penetration. The power of radio in the black market is well known, attracting a daily audience of nine million listeners and 12,4 million throughout the week. However, few advertisers realise that radio is also rated superior to other media types. About 96% of the white population listens to radio each day for over four hours.

The picture is even more dramatically in radio's favour between 6 am and 6 pm ⸱ during which times radio achieves 73,4% reach, as opposed to 35,7% for TV. It's during these productive buying/selling/shopping hours that radio's tremendous reach and length of listening time pay important dividends by delivering the advertising message closest to the actual point of purchase. Darkins adds that radio commercials can be produced in a fraction of the time it takes to produce ads for other mediums.

'Radio can no longer be seen merely as a support medium which conveniently provides that 'high-frequency-low-cost-per-thousand' formula. Whoever the advertiser, chances are he will get a better return on investment with radio than any other media type.'

A regional radio, 702 serves the PWV and upper income adults in the 25-49 age group. 702's format is an intimate one-on-one form of communication — this means one-on-one selling for advertisers. Listeners depend on 702 for information, so advertisers messages reach listeners as part of that information and not as an interruption.

Selling an audience over the television

The bottom line of electronic marketing is selling the presence an audience to an advertiser. TV1 is currently the only station which consistently delivers the biggest audiences at extremely cost-effective prices.

The power of TV1 lies not only in its programming and programme schedule, but also in expectations surrounding the programming. For instance, the 1991

Bankfin Currie Cup final was broadcast live on both TV1 and M-Net. Because of the expectations surrounding the broadcast, 75% of M-Net decoder owners watched the match on TV1!

A Telmar analysis of January and February 1992 points out that TV1 consistently delivered the biggest audiences — including demographics like children (89 out of 100), housewives (97 out of 100) and AB-income males (95 out of 100). These audiences are also delivered cost-effectively. It is audiences the advertiser wants, not programmes. For advertising purposes, programmes serve as vehicles carrying audiences of varying sizes, tastes and profiles. Whilst it is true that the environment in which a commercial is placed is important, it should be noted that TV1 offers the advertiser a variety of such environments.

TV1 dominates television audiences and will continue to do so by offering its audiences the very best in entertainment, sports and news coverage.

TV opportunities

M-Net's very clear positioning for 1992, in terms of its pricing policy, has resulted in audiences being delivered at very competitive prices and, in these tough economic times, that's exactly what advertisers and marketers are looking for. Media planners openly punt M-Net as being a delight to work with — prompt, efficient, approachable.

'Open Time' locks target markets into the best of locally produced and overseas programming. There's the launch on April 6 of what promises to be another Frans Marx blockbuster — a locally produced bilingual tele-serial called Egoli, starring big names. M-Net projects a minimum 25% growth in audiences for this programme. Loving continues to dominate the battle of the soaps between 17h30 and 18h00.

The Monday to Friday 18h00-19h00 time channel features a host of top American sitcoms and great sporting action in the World of Panasonic on Fridays. There's also great sport on Saturdays in Open Time, while Sunday's line-up of the Wonderful World of Disney in M-Net Family Time is proving to be a hit. The Open Time formula is successful, delivering consistently high ratings across a selected range of target markets very cost-effectively.

Despite dramatic growth into some 690 000 homes, the positioning for encoded time remains very clear. M-Net delivers 'full colour' viewers (defined as households earning R5 000+ pm) more cost-effectively than any other station. A Markinor Image Tracking Study reveals that M-Net subscribers spend 65% of all their viewing time tuned to M-Net.

Increasingly, marketers and advertisers are looking for exciting and innovative ways of communicating their message and growing brand awareness. The sponsorship experience fills the gap and gives the advertiser the opportunity to 'own' an event.

Magazine mix

The success of Nasionale Tydskrifte in the magazine market can be directly attributed to its long-term marketing strategy. Its motto: 'Dedicated to editorial excellence and advertising effectiveness' clearly spells this strategy out.

Nasionale's titles all enjoy number one positions in their respective markets. Collectively, they comprise 60% market share of the total consumer magazine advertising cake. Annually, the company sells 55 million magazines and over five million adults read one or more of its eight consumer titles. Strategically developed with minimal overlap, the magazine mix allows for the broadest consumer appeal in South Africa's three major consumer markets — Afrikaans, English and black.

Nasionale's titles were developed to provide major advertisers with the broadest coverage of their most sought-after consumer markets — female aspirational, female service and family entertainment, for example *Sarie, Fair Lady, True Love, You, Huisgenoot, Women's Value* and *Drum*.

With over two million readers and reaching 40% of people over 16 in its primary target market, the Sunday Times Magazine is South Africa's biggest English language magazine. In the PWV, the magazine reaches one in five of all races and its reach at the top end of the market is higher than average for a consumer magazine.

Business Day is ranked by South Africa's top business executives as the premier daily news medium. Research conducted for TML by Markinor shows that 94% of chairmen, MDs and chief executives, financial directors, company accountants and stock-brokers in the Johannesburg/Reef/Pretoria area read Business Day every weekday. Among accountants and stockbrokers in particular, the reach is 100% — an almost unprecedented result for a research survey.

South Africa's most widely-read financial weekly, the Financial Mail, has an 85% subscriber base. This makes it the country's most highly subscribed consumer publication, percentage-wise, says Marketing and Sales Manager, Fulvio Cassuto. 'We have always had a high subscriber ratio and our most recent research analysis, prepared by TML from Markinor research to determine page traffic and attitudes, simply confirms this.'

Whichever way you look at it, South Africa wields some major media clout. The media continues to grow by leaps and bounds. As the mass public becomes a massive consumer public, the need for viable media increases accordingly.

The advertiser's media shopping basket is full.

Source: Adapted and summarised from an investigative article by Terk, J. Media Power. *Professional Marketing Review*, April 1992, pp 21-24.

The above excerpt from the *Professional Marketing Review* gives a particularly good overview of the major media in South Africa. Advertisers require this type of analysis of the characteristics and impact of the media in media selection.

Questions

1. Why is it more effective to advertise simultaneously on the radio, on TV and in magazines? Discuss critically.

2. Explain in detail why television is an effective communication method by referring to the communication model.

3. What are the advantages of advertising on local radio stations? Mention five products which cannot effectively be advertised on the radio. Give reasons why not.

4. Select the most suitable medium (only one) in which to advertise the following:

   - The Hypermarket's 'specials for the week'.
   - Toys for five to six-year-olds.
   - Baby-care products.
   - The newest fashions from France.
   - The local hardware store in Pietersburg.
   - Expensive jewellery.
   - A well-known brand of toothpaste.

   Give reasons for your answers.

5. Describe the typical life styles of the target markets for the products mentioned in question 4.

2. THE SUCCESS STORY OF *FINANSIES & TEGNIEK*

Finansies & Tegniek originated in the Rembrandt group where the need was felt that an Afrikaans-speaking executive must be able to read about topics that interest him in his mother tongue. *Tegniek*, as the magazine was originally known, was later sold to Sanlam and then taken over by Nasionale Pers.

In 1986 it was decided that *Finansies & Tegniek* must be a weekly magazine rather than a monthly because the format of a monthly is not suitable for the intended contents, namely business news.

In this time Nasionale Pers also purchased the Afrikaanse Handelsinstituut news magazine, *Volkshandel*, and incorporated it in *Finansies & Tegniek*. The direct advantage of this deal was a doubling of the circulation within a year. It now became worthwhile for advertisers who wished to reach the Afrikaans executive market with advertising campaigns to include *Finansies & Tegniek* in the media mix.

Traditionally magazines are sold through cafés, supermarkets and the CNA. The target market for *Finansies & Tegniek*, however, does not patronise these venues. It was therefore decided to mail the magazine to subscribers. This strategy is still followed, with the result that *Finansies & Tegniek* is unique with regard to its readers' profile. Nearly 90 per cent of readers receive the magazine through the mail. A courier system is used because of time limitations. The magazine is printed in Johannesburg and mailed on the same day in all the main centres in the country.

The slogan of *Finansies & Tegniek*, 'VERSTAAN HOE SAKE STAAN', is justified by the many awards received by its journalists, who do not write their stories in a vacuum; research is a continuous process enabling the magazine to give priority to preferences of readers. The reaction to a story in *Finansies & Tegniek* is never 'so what?'. The content is always meaningful to its target audience.

Research indicates that *Finansies & Tegniek* is accepted and regarded as an authoritative source of business news. This perception is valued and great care is taken to verify all facts before they appear in print. The magazine succeeded in scooping the Information scandal and the Vermaas fiasco. It has been threatened by interdicts on several occasions but prides itself on the fact that it has never been found guilty of misrepresenting facts. Because of the readers' profile, wide circulation and high reliability index, *Finansies & Tegniek* is a much sought-after advertising vehicle. It's high realiability index helps to sell the magazine to readers who are eager to buy a reliable source of news and information, rather than just another business magazine.

The management style at *Finansies & Tegniek* cannot be regarded as the usual traditional magazine style. At *Finansies & Tegniek* there is close interaction among the editorial, advertising and marketing departments. Each department is autonomous but management is in daily close contact. The result is a homogenous approach directed at the further growth of the magazine. The last few years before the change of the century present new opportunities for an Afrikaans business magazine. An increase in the Afrikaner executive target market is expected and *Finansies & Tegniek* is positioned to continue to satisfy the needs of its readers.

Source: Information supplied by H Kruger, Marketing Manager, *Finansies & Tegniek*.

Questions

1. Describe the product concept of *Finansies & Tegniek*.

2. Which advantages are there for advertisers using *Finansies & Tegniek* as an advertising vehicle?

3. Describe the target market of *Finansies & Tegniek*.

4. It is said that research is a continuous process. What type of research is referred to?

5. Which marketing communication elements are used to promote the magazine?

CHAPTER 14

PERSONAL SELLING

14.1 INTRODUCTION

The success of the marketing effort is determined by the interaction between the seller and the buyer. The objective of this chapter is to summarise the role of interpersonal communication between the sales representative who acts as the seller, and the customer, who wants to buy the product. Personal selling is only one of the elements of the marketing communication decisions. Together with advertising, sales promotion techniques and publicity, it has to communicate the enterprise's marketing message to the target market. The communication process is discussed in Chapter 12, which indicated that the marketing message can be transmitted more effectively through interpersonal communication than through communication in the mass media. In the first section of this chapter the most important characteristics of interpersonal communication are once again emphasised. Thereafter, the nature of personal selling, the selling process and the task of sales management will be discussed.

ORGANISATION OF THE CHAPTER

Interpersonal communication: The meaning of interpersonal communication, application of the communications model to personal selling.

The nature of personal selling: Personal selling in the enterprise, the task of sales representatives and sales management, types of selling situations, different sales theories, the steps in the selling process, formulating the sales message, methods to improve the performance of sales representatives.

Sales management: Environmental scanning, the planning task, organisation in the sales division, control of the execution of the sales task.

14.2 INTERPERSONAL COMMUNICATION

14.2.1 The meaning of interpersonal communication

Interpersonal marketing communication plays an important role in planning and executing the task of the sales representative. This is so because, first, personal selling forms part of the marketing communication decisions that are made in the enterprise, and secondly, because personal selling is to a very large extent based on interpersonal communication, which involves a two-way action (dyad) between the sales representative and the potential buyer.

In this section, the nature of the interpersonal communication between the sales representative and his customer will be discussed. In the personal selling situation, it is through interpersonal (face-to-face) communication that a potential buyer is persuaded to buy a product. The sales representative should therefore be familiar with the principles involved in interpersonal communication as well as with the way in which interpersonal communication should be adapted to be effective in the different selling situations. Interpersonal communication between a customer and a sales representative who has to sell a highly technical industrial product will, for example, differ greatly from the situation where a sales representative has to sell a consumer product to a reseller.

The importance of personal selling

'Nothing happens until somebody sells something.'

Source: Frain, J. *The Principles and Practices of Marketing.* London: Pitman Publishing Ltd, p 311.

14.2.2 Application of the communication model to personal selling

The communication process and model have already been discussed in Chapter 12 and therefore this section will deal mainly with the application of the communications model to the personal selling situation. Basically, the communication model entails that a communicator (marketing management) wants to send a specific message to the receiver(s) (a specific target audience) through a communication channel. In this case the two-way action of the communication involved in personal selling makes the application of the communications model unique. An additional distinguishing characteristic of personal selling is the exclusive and selective form of communication which enables the marketer to adapt the persuasive message to the specific needs of the receiver and the demands of the situation.

In reality, the **communicator** is the marketing management of the enterprise, who is the source or origin of marketing communication. Marketing management tries to convince the receiver by means of a message transmitted through the sales representative. Consequently, marketing management is responsible for formulating the message as well as the selection and training of the sales representatives who have to transmit the message. Marketing management also interprets the reactions of the receiver of the message, as transmitted by the sales representative, and this feedback is used when formulating the new message. In the case of personal selling the sales representative is the spokesman for the enterprise through which the enterprise makes direct personal contact with the consumer.

The **message** is transmitted verbally by the sales representative to the receiver who can respond directly to the message, while the sales representative has the opportunity to answer questions and solve discrepancies. This two-way communication is unique to personal selling, which gives it a special persuasive potential not found in the other instruments of marketing communication.

The **communication channel**. In personal selling the message is mainly transmitted verbally. The spoken word is therefore the channel through which the marketing message flows. The sales representatives also use brochures and other printed material to make the message more persuasive. In contrast to the other elements of marketing communication, the communication channel works in two directions and the sales representative can receive feedback from the receiver almost immediately. An additional aspect which is unique here is the fact that the sales representative can adapt the message to the demands of the situation. This gives the message greater power of persuasion, but the communications process is much slower as only one receiver (or at the most a few receivers) is exposed to the message at one time. Through advertising in the mass media many receivers are reached by the same message.

The **receiver** is the eventual destination of the message. In the case of personal selling, the potential customer is usually an individual (which is often the case in the consumer and reseller markets) or a small group of people (as in the case of industrial purchases). The sales representative has to take thorough note of each receiver's situation to ensure that he can adapt the message effectively in order to give it the necessary power of persuasion.

The **feedback** in the communications model is directly obtained by the sales representatives from the target audience and enables marketing management to determine whether the message has been interpreted correctly or not. Disturbances in the communications process can also contribute to the fact that the message may not be interpreted correctly by the target audience. As the message is transmitted directly to the receiver, and the sales representative has the opportunity to test the reaction, interpersonal communication is usually more effective than mass communication. In mass communication there are more disturbances, a greater danger of misinterpretation and a longer time lapse between the receipt of the message and the feedback process.

In the following section personal selling will be put in perspective by looking at the sales task more closely.

14.3 THE NATURE OF PERSONAL SELLING

14.3.1 Personal selling in the enterprise

Personal selling plays an important role in almost every type of enterprise because all enterprises must, to a greater or lesser extent, make use of the services of sales representatives. Manufacturers use sales representatives to sell products to retailers and wholesalers, while financial institutions use agents or brokers to sell financial services to potential consumers. Various enterprises also use sales personnel to sell products on a door-to-door basis. In shops it is the task of the sales personnel to sell products to consumers over the counter. This chapter deals mainly with the sales task of sales representatives. The principles which will be discussed can to a greater or lesser extent also be applied to door-to-door sales and counter sales, although personal selling on this level is often regarded as a mere distribution task.

The American Marketing Association defines sales management as the *planning, execution and control of personal selling, including recruitment, selection, training, supervision, remuneration and motivation of the selling corps.*[1] The sales manager therefore has a marketing task as well as a personnel task.

As part of his marketing task, the sales manager must help with the planning process, execute the sales task and exercise control over it. This does not only entail the formulation of the persuasive sales message, it also includes the organisation of all the activities connected to the selling of the enterprise's products. As part of the personnel task, the sales manager and his personnel fulfil a liaison function between the enterprise and its customers. Personal contact is extremely important for establishing an extended distribution network for the marketing of the enterprise's products. The sales representatives execute these tasks under the leadership of the sales manager (or managers). It is important to realise that the personnel in the sales department form part of the marketing team and are partly responsible for the planning and implementation of the marketing strategy. Basically, sales representatives can be divided into three categories according to the tasks which they should execute:

- **Recruiters** are sales representatives who only recruit customers.
- **Order takers** are sales representatives who engage in routine visits to get orders.
- **Supporters** are sales personnel who provide their support to the sales representatives in the other two categories.

All these tasks can, however, be performed by a single sales representative (especially in small enterprises).

14.3.2 The task of the sales representative in perspective

14.3.2.1 *The sales representative as mouthpiece of the enterprise*

The sales representative is the mouthpiece whereby the enterprise communicates with potential buyers. In many cases this represents the only contact of the potential buyer with the enterprise. This contact can sometimes be very brief but still cost a lot of money for the enterprise. It is consequently necessary that the sales representative exploit this contact opportunity to the full.

A popular conception exists of a "born" salesman as a dynamic, extrovert, highly assertive person. Although these qualities can be helpful in many selling situations, experience has taught that many other factors determine sales success.[2] Key among these factors is the ability to relate to others in effective and productive ways.

14.3.2.2 *The sales representative as link in good relationships*

The sales representative forms a connection between different persons in the enterprise and the buyers. One of the most important tasks of the sales representative is consequently to maintain healthy relationships with buyers as well as people inside the enterprise. The sales representative must build up healthy relationships with the management of the enterprise as well as persons inside the enterprise offering supporting services for sales and the consumers.

14.3.2.3 *The sales representative as image bearer of the enterprise*

The sales representative must constantly remember that he projects the enterprise's image. The image portrayed by the sales representative consists of different aspects, all of which in some or other way form part of verbal or non-verbal communication.

Relatively recent studies in the field of communication revealed that words play a surprisingly small part in the communication process.[3] Only 10% of our understanding comes from spoken words, about 40% from what we hear (how it is said: tone of voice, volume and speed of delivery) and about 50% from what we see or feel (facial expression, clothing, posture, eye contact, touch and gestures). A positive message can be communicated to the potential buyer with a smile, a firm handshake and good eye contact. A pat on the shoulder can communicate the message that the representative agrees with what the buyer said. The representative can also indicate that he is listening to the buyer and understands his problems by just nodding his head now and then. The ways in which and the extent to which the representative uses these non-verbal elements depend on the specific selling situation, which will be discussed in the next section. Credibility is gained when actions and words correspond.

A few general guide-lines, which are applicable in most selling situations, are given below:

- The **dress and grooming** of the sales representative usually convey the first impression, which the buyer can use to make certain assumptions about the representative. The potential buyer will probably base his conclusions on aspects such as type of clothing, length and style of hair, nail care, jewellery and perfume. The representative must develop a feeling for the preferences of his target market. There are, however, some basic guide-lines:[4] Clothing must not be extravagant, but must convey simplicity; flashy colours and clothing must be avoided because these are not associated with the seriousness of the business world; clothing must be appropriate for the type of business, environment and climate; and the representative must wear good-quality clothing which fits him and gives a tidy appearance. Research by the Research Institute of America indicates that 82,5% of respondents judged the enterprise by its salesperson's appearance.

- The **facial expression** of the sales representative reflects his inner feeling and conveys a message to the potential buyer even before words are spoken. The consumer continuously looks for congruency between words and facial expression. The consumer can easily detect whether the enthusiasm about the product or interest in this needs is genuine by looking to see whether the words and facial expression of the representative support each other.

- The **voice** of the sales representative is one of the most important aspects in communication with the consumer because it is the medium used by the representative to convey his words. Voice is especially important over the telephone, where other aspects are hidden to the consumer. You cannot trade the voice with which you are born, but you can use it better by taking the following guide-lines into consideration:[5]
  - **Do not talk too fast or too slowly**. Rapid speech is associated with high-pressure sales techniques and slow talking can make the consumer impatient.
  - **Avoid a speech pattern that is dull and colourless** because it may not convey enthusiasm.
  - **Do not talk too loudly or too softly**. The consumer must be able to hear clearly what you say but must not be overwhelmed by a noise.

- The **handshake** of the sales representative is probably the first as well as the only physical and the most intimate contact between the sales representative and the potential buyer. Without the use of words a handshake can convey a strong message. A firm handshake conveys a caring but steadfast attitude, while a weak grip communicates indifference and a dubious attitude. Eye contact during the handshake can enhance the positive impact of the handshake. The representative must, however, try to ensure that his hands are not sweaty when shaking hands. A clammy hand may repel some people and may also convey an impression of nervousness.

- Good **manners** are indispensable in any sales situation. There is no substitute for good manners. Although every person has a reasonably good idea of the meaning of good manners, we sometimes unintentionally do things which can irritate others and be regarded by them as bad manners. The sales representative must consequently be sensitive to aspects that can be regarded by others as bad manners, for example:[6]
  - Do not smoke in the presence of a customer, without obtaining permission.
  - Do not visit a customer without an appointment, especially at difficult times of day.
  - Do not address the customer too soon by his first name. Wait until a good business relationship has been established. It may be taken as an indication of respect and may avoid irritation.
  - Do not offend others by remarks, stories and jokes. Remember that your value systems and those of the customer may differ.

— Do not make political or religious remarks. These topics usually contain sensitive and emotional aspects that may put the customer in a bad mood.
— Always show your sincere appreciation for the time and /or purchase of the consumer.

In certain situations, all the abovementioned tasks can be executed by just one sales representative (for example, in very small enterprises). These three basic tasks are executed in a variety of selling situations. Selling situations are distinguished according to the nature of the potential buyers, the type of product, the amount of money involved and the time required to conclude the sales transaction. There are four types of selling situations.[7]

14.3.3 Types of selling situations

14.3.3.1 *Consultative sales*

Consultative sales are characterised by the fact that the sales representative, in order to sell the product or service, has to negotiate with the higher levels of the hierarchy in the enterprise. This is done primarily because the sales decision has to be approved at a high management level as large amounts of money are involved, and not necessarily because specific technical knowledge is required. The selling process usually takes very long, sometimes even months. Consultative sales also include professional sales to people such as doctors and architects.

Product examples of consultative sales

Complicated and sophisticated computer systems, management consultations, civil engineering projects and other products or services which are expensive and must be applied specifically to the specifications or circumstances of the buyer.

14.3.3.2 *Technical sales*

Technical sales involve sales situations where the technical aspects of the product are of primary importance and where the sales representative should have a higher level of technical knowledge. This selling process is normally of a shorter duration than that of consultative sales. This situation usually involves specific persons in the purchasing enterprise who, as a result of their specific technical knowledge regarding the products that must be purchased, act as buyers. Technical sales are also referred to as industrial sales.

Product examples of technical sales

Printing machines, weaponry, personal computers and technical apparatus used in production.

14.3.3.3 *Commercial sales*

Approximately 50 per cent of all sales representatives are involved in commercial sales, which include non-technical sales to various types of enterprises. Commercial sales are sometimes referred to as trade sales. Sales representatives are trained to conclude the purchase transaction during the first visit, if this is at all possible. The level of training required is lower than in the case of consultative or technical sales.

Product examples of commercial sales

Many different branded items sold to wholesalers and retailers (for resale).

14.3.3.4 *Direct sales*

Direct sales deal directly with the final consumer. This includes door-to-door sales and the so-called party plan schemes.

Product examples of direct sales

Insurance, motor cars, encyclopaedias, house improvements, time-share schemes, household items such as waterless cooking equipment, linen, lingerie and beauty products.

The selling process is usually very short and the sales representatives are trained to try and conclude the sale during the first visit, although this is not always possible. The sales representative used here normally has strong powers of persuasion and enthusiasm. The high pressure persuasive techniques which are sometimes applied in direct sales often scare consumers and make them hesitant or even unwilling to give the sales representative the opportunity to state his case. Direct mail advertising is often used to stimulate interest and to reassure the prospective buyer, thereby making the sales representative's task easier.

Direct sales of a time-share scheme

In order to overcome the resistance or unwillingness of the target audience, the marketers of Port Owen Cabanas included the following paragraph in their direct mail advertising to prospective buyers:

'We can assure you that you will enjoy the experience without any gimmicks or high pressure activities. Therefore please feel free to contact me.'

The purpose of direct mail advertising is to convince the target audience to make an appointment with the sales representative in order to make it possible for him to sell this time-share scheme.

Personal selling in all the abovementioned examples has developed into a fine art. In an attempt to determine what the underlying principles of a successful sales transaction are, a number of theories have been developed. Some of these theories will now be discussed.

14.3.4 The different sales theories

14.3.4.1 *The AIDAS theory*

The letters in AIDAS represent the various steps through which a potential buyer proceeds during the decision making process, namely: Attention, Interest, Desire, Action, Satisfaction. The sales representative must guide the potential buyer through all these phases, and therefore he must structure the sales message in such a way that it will help the buyer to make a decision, convince him to take action and promote satisfaction after the purchase. Advertisements are often used to attract the attention of prospective buyers and to arouse interest. The sales representative can then concentrate on the other phases.

14.3.4.2 *Right-set-of-circumstances theory*

This theory is also known as the situation response theory and presupposes that the situation in which the sales transaction takes place can influence the persuasion of the buyer. This implies that if the sales representative correctly chooses or manipulates the situation (external factors) in which the persuasion must take place, this will have a positive influence on the complaisance of the potential customer. The sales representative could, for example, invite the customer for a meal and try to conclude the transaction during the meal. The danger, however, exists that the sales representative will rely too much on the manipulation of the external factors and that the internal factors, such as the transmission of an effective sales message, will be neglected.

14.3.4.3 *Buying-formula theory*

According to this theory attention is focused on the needs and problems of the buyer. It is the task of the sales representative to help the buyer to satisfy his needs and solve his problems. In contrast to the preceding theory, this theory attaches a lot of importance to the internal factors which direct the purchasing decision, but the external facts are not discounted completely. The buying formula consists of the following variables:

$$\text{Need (or problem)} \rightarrow \text{solution} \rightarrow \text{action} \rightarrow \text{satisfaction}$$

The solution entails the decision about the specific product (or service) which can be bought to satisfy the need or solve the problem. The sales representative will obviously try to convince the buyer that his specific product will satisfy the need and solve the problem. If the product does fulfil these promises the purchase will lead to the satisfaction of the buyer, and it will serve as motivation for repeat purchases and the development of an established buying habit. If this happens the task of the sales representative will be considerably eased as his follow-up task will be reduced.

A change in any of the variables in the buying formula necessitates a corresponding adjustment of the sales message. The sales representative in this case therefore cannot transmit a previously constructed sales message; he should first determine the circumstances, needs and problems of the potential buyer and then adapt the sales message accordingly.

14.3.4.4 *Learning theory*

This theory is also called the behavioural-equation theory. Personal selling is viewed as a learning process where the sales representative is the teacher who should motivate the buyer to react to stimuli.

The behavioural model is compiled as follows:

$$B = P \times D \times K \times V$$

where B = buyer's reaction (purchase action)

P = buyer's receptiveness

D = buyer's need

K = degree of satisfaction that the product can provide

V = intensity of the stimuli

The nature of the formula (multiplication instead of addition) implies that all four variables must be positive before the buying action (B) will take place. In other words, if one variable has a zero value there will be no purchasing action. Hence, in formulating his sales message the sales representative should attend to all four variables in the learning theory. The learning theory will be successful when the buyer automatically reacts every time he receives a stimulus (as soon as he experiences the need, he buys the specific brand or contacts the sales representative).

Conflict and dissonance experienced by the prospective buyer are reflected in the values of the variable V (intensity of the stimuli) and K (degree of satisfaction that the product can provide). The conflict and dissonance experienced by the buyer can for example have a negative influence on the intensity of the stimuli received by the buyer during the learning process and the degree of need satisfaction which the product can provide. Before deciding to purchase the product the buyer will be in conflict about the many alternatives (other brands) from which he must choose. After the buying decision has been taken dissonance will be experienced which means that the buyer will be uncertain as to whether he has made the correct decision or not. Both these phenomena will weaken the values of V and K and will impede the learning process. It is the sales representative's task to lessen the conflict before, and the dissonance after, the buying decision. If he succeeds, the buyer will be able to justify (rationalise) his decision to himself and others and there will be a greater probability that the behavioural formula will be positive in the future. Conflict must be resolved otherwise a prospective buyer will never make a positive decision. Likewise cognitive dissonance must be counteracted otherwise the buyer will never buy the product again.

The learning theory forms the nucleus of the present-day art of salesmanship and is reflected in the selling process. The selling process, which will be discussed next, consists of a series of successive steps. These steps can be applied to all selling situations and all categories of consumers.

14.3.5 The steps in the selling process

14.3.5.1 *Prospecting*

Prospecting basically entails the search by the sales representative for potential buyers. This task, to a large extent, entails the follow-up of leads. Leads can originate from various sources such as telephone directories, customer references, friends and many more. All these services can be divided into three categories, namely new recruits (cold canvassing), recruiting with the help of mass communication, and references.

New recruits

Finding new recruits entails that the sales representative should try to contact every possible potential buyer in a specific area. The sales representative can go from house to house, but this is very expensive and time-consuming, and not always effective. Using a telephone, for example, is much more cost-effective. The sales representative's approach will depend on the type of product he sells. In some cases (where the product is used by almost all households, such as insurance and house improvements), telephone directories or personnel lists of large enterprises will be used to 'take some shots in the dark'. In cases where the product does not have such a wide market, as with sales to a wholesaler, the sales representative will have to be more selective. He can find leads in the Yellow Pages, circulation lists of specialised magazines, and membership lists of organisations and societies.

Recruiting with the help of mass communication

Such recruitment entails the placing of advertisements in the press, obtaining publicity in the mass media, and direct press advertising to which potential buyers can react in order to identify themselves. When using this recruitment method the qualification of potential buyers will to a large extent already have been done.

No cold-canvassing for Reeva Forman cosmetics

'We only see a potential customer when it is by appointment. In our advertisement we ask the customer to phone or write to us and she will receive, in her home, a free facial make-up lesson from a professionally trained consultant. This has given us tremendous credibility and a unique position in the market place.'

Source: Reeva Forman in *Marketing Mix,* May 1986, p 10.

References

References can originate from various sources, but a satisfied buyer is the most effective and most important. The advantage here is that because they have a mutual 'friend', the sales representative will not be regarded as a stranger by the potential buyer. References are particularly valuable with purchases where reasonably large expenses and/or risk are involved. References help to increase the credibility of the sales representative and his enterprise (in reality it is a type of publicity).

Data bases on computer

It is possible to combine the product characteristics and the needs of different buyers with each other by means of electronic data processing. Many enterprises develop their own data bases. In other cases it may be more economical to purchase a data base. These data bases can be purchased from, for example, enterprises specialising in gathering such information or manufacturing or distributing similar products.

14.3.5.2 *Qualification of potential buyers*

Before the sales representative can continue with the selling process he must first determine whether the potential buyer qualifies. In this way valuable time is not wasted on buyers who do not really want to buy or cannot buy. Four questions can be asked in the qualification process:

- Does the prospective buyer really have a **need** for the product or service which is being offered?
- Does the prospective customer have the **ability** to buy? In the case of individuals, expenditure ability is determined by purchasing power and in the case of industrial buyers it is determined by a budget.
- Is the potential buyer **eligible** to make a decision and to conclude the purchase transaction?
- Can the product be sold **profitably** to the buyer?

14.3.5.3 *Presentation of the sales message*

The presentation of the sales message can be seen as the nucleus of the selling process. The sales message can consist of a previously constructed, structured presentation ('canned' presentation) or a flexible presentation which can be adapted to the buyers' needs during the purchasing process. Structured presentations are often found with direct sales of simple consumer products.

The sales message can be formulated according to the learning theory which was discussed in section 14.3.3.4 and consists of the following components:[8]

- **An introduction.** The objective of the introductory section of a sales message is, first, to create a relaxed atmosphere in which a feeling of trust is created between the two parties. In this way the buyer will regard the sales representative as a friend and adviser who can help him solve his problems and satisfy his needs. Secondly, the sales representative will start to develop empathy for the buyer's situation. Thirdly, the buyer's interest in the presentation is stimulated.
- **Identification of the problem and need.** This can be done by asking the prospective buyer questions or by giving him an opportunity to describe the problem from his viewpoint. In both cases the prospective buyer gets the opportunity to participate in the presentation and this confirms the position of the purchaser as adviser and problem solver.
- **The demonstration.** The objective of demonstrations is to indicate to the buyer how a particular product can solve his identified problems and satisfy his identified needs. Demonstrations stimulate interest and reduce the observed risk which faces the prospective buyer. The buyer can sometimes participate in the demonstration himself and experience for himself what the characteristics and use of the product are. Demonstrations are a valuable aid to persuasion.
- **Handling of objection.** During this phase the buyer is given the opportunity to raise objections as to why he should purchase the product. These objections can be handled by, for example, referring to similar experiences of third parties or to easy credit facilities.

The objections raised revolve mainly around the need, the product, the supplier, the price or the time, as illustrated in the following example:[9]

Type of objection	*Example*
Need	"My old car still provides good service."
Product	"The car does not have the latest advanced electronic accessories."
Supplier	"Will you be able to assist us with any problems in using the computer as well as repairs or will we get someone else?
Price	"R15 000 is actually a very big one-payment expense for a swimming pool."
Time	"Perhaps we should rather buy the new car next year when I have saved more money."

Objections can be dealt with in four different ways:

- **Objections** can be converted into a question. If the prospective buyer raises an issue about, for example, price, the objection can be converted into a question of value for money for benefits offered by the product.
- **Third party stories** are used to, for example, illustrate that other buyers have experienced the same problems or offered the same objections and then describe how they were resolved.
- The **boomerang technique** is used to convert an objection into an advantage for the consumer. The objection that the car does not have the latest electronics can be converted by emphasis on the greater reliability and lower price.
- **Comparisons** can best be used when the prospective buyer refers to competitive products. The representative must use discretion not to demean the products of competitors. He must rather emphasise the unique features of the product that he is selling. A good method is a side-by-side listing on a piece of paper of the features and benefits of the representative's product against the competitive product to enable the prospective buyer to draw a conclusion.

Various approaches can be followed in order to overcome the buyer's resistance:

- The **direct close** can be used in instances where the buyer has received the sales message in a positive way and is ready to make a decision. The sales representative can, directly ask the buyer, for example: "Must I write an order for you? or "Have you decided on a model yet?". This approach must not be used on buyers who are uncertain, indecisive or hesitant.
- The **assumptive close** is based on the assumption that the prospective buyer has decided to buy and can be used where the prospective buyer is indecisive or uncertain. The representative can ask, for example: "Must we deliver the product?", "How many cases do you want?" or "When did you want the product?".
- With the **summative close** approach the sales representative sums up the advantages and recaps the points of the agreement, touching all key elements of the decision and leaving nothing for the prospective buyer except to commit to the purchase.
- With the **negative close** the sales representative attempts to put pressure on the prospective buyer to decide now, based on some imminent negative event, such as an impending price increase, possible accidents or a shortage in stock. The sales representative must be careful with this approach because it may increase the buyer's tension.

14.3.5.4. *Closing the purchase transaction*

The sales representative must encourage the buyer to conclude the purchase transaction because buyers are often hesitant to take action as a result of the risk connected to the purchase. The buyer can be reassured by, for example, again giving counter-arguments to his objections and by referring him to other comforting aspects, such as guarantees.

14.3.5.5 *Follow-up*

After the purchase the sales representative should ask the buyer whether he is fully satisfied and he should also attempt to rectify to the best of his ability any other aspects which might present problems. Through this process cognitive dissonance is reduced and repeat purchases and brand loyalty are promoted.

The selling task which has been discussed here is executed by sales representatives under the leadership of the sales manager who manages the selling task, ie he plans, organises and controls the activities. These aspects will be discussed in the following section.

14.3.6 **Methods for improving the sales performance of sales representatives**

14.3.6.1 *General*

Sales representatives, more than most other business professionals, are measured and rewarded by results. It is therefore important for them as well as the individual sales representative to seek ways of developing and improving sales performance. Govoni[10] is of the opinion that the following four may have the biggest influence on productivity:

- Building good customer relations.
- Improving selling skills.
- Improving personal attributes.
- Effective self-management.

14.3.6.2 *Building good customer relations*

It has already been emphasised that the development of good human relations is a key factor in the successful execution of the selling task. Good customer relations may result in, for example, repeat purchases and referrals.

The most important aspect in good relations between the sales representative and the customer is *trust*. The sales representative must earn this trust by dealing with customers in an honest, straight forward and trustworthy way. This can be accomplished by, for example, being on time for appointments, fulfilling promises and showing a sincere interest in the satisfaction of the consumer's needs. The sales representative must always remember that he is rendering a service. A service is inseparable from its quality, which goes hand in hand with the characteristics of the person rendering it.

14.3.6.3 *Improving selling skills*

The quality of the selling skills of the sales representative depends on his knowledge and insight concerning key aspects such as knowledge of the consumer and his behaviour patterns, the enterprise, the product and selling techniques.

Knowledge of the consumer

The sales representative's selling skills can be enhanced immensely by a thorough knowledge of the basic aspects of consumer behaviour, especially consumers' decision-making processes and the motives prompting them to take decisions. Selling skills increase as the sales representative's knowledge grows concerning the following aspects of the consumer in the target market: needs and desires; and characteristics such as fears, self-image, intelligence, purchasing habits, motives, purchasing influences and organisational structure (in the case of organisational buyers).

Knowledge of the enterprise and the product

The sales representative must have a thorough knowledge of the policy, objectives, procedure and strong and weak points of the enterprise. He must also have a thorough knowledge of the total market offering of the enterprise and how it compares to the market offering of competitors.

Knowledge of selling techniques

A thorough knowledge about selling techniques is a key for the effective application of all the other methods for improving sales performance. Achieving selling knowledge is not a one-time task, but a continuous process which adapts to the evolution of the enterprise and competition. The sales representative must evolve in this process.

14.3.6.4 Improving personal attributes

Listening

The successful sales representative in an attentive listener in contrast with the image of a glib talker. By listening attentively the sales representative gathers information which can assist him in his selling task and the sales presentation.

Drive and empathy

Drive and empathy should be balanced in the sales representative. He must, for example, have enough drive to close a sale, not to be discouraged by opposition, to trump competition and to convince the consumer. On the other hand, the sales representative must have the necessary empathy to place himself in the position of the buyer and develop understanding for the buyer's situation and his decision-making process.

14.3.6.5 *Effective self-management*

As result of the nature of personal selling the sales representative must frequently work independently and with self-discipline. Self-management determines the productivity with which the sales representative performs his task. The sales representative can manage himself by applying the following four steps:

- An **analysis** of aspects in his sales territory, such as the sales potential, products, competition and needs and attitudes of consumers.
- The **planning** of his route, visiting patterns and time schedule, which depend on the preceding analysis.
- The **execution** of the planning, which involves *inter alia* the sales representative adhering strictly to the programme and appointments and keeping record of his selling activities.
- Lastly, regular **evaluation** of the execution of his activities and planning of corrective steps, if necessary.

The principles of self-management are especially applicable to the management of the following four areas: time, territory, reports and stress.[11]

14.4 SALES MANAGEMENT

14.4.1 Environmental scanning

The management task of sales management is indicated in Figure 14.1. The sales decisions are discussed systematically and step by step as they appear in Figure 14.1.

Environmental scanning is the starting point of managing the sales division and it is the background against which all further decisions should be taken. The environmental variables discussed in Chapters 2, 3 and 4 with regard to internal strengths and weaknesses and external opportunities and threats can also be applied to sales management. Information about consumers, target markets and competitors is of utmost importance for the planning and execution of the sales task. The internal financial ability and expertise of the enterprise also determine the way in which the sales task will be executed. Figure 14.1 further indicates that the three main elements of sales management are planning, organising and controlling.

14.4.2 The planning task

14.4.2.1 *Steps in the planning process*

The planning task involves the following steps:

- Formulating the sales objectives.
- Compiling the sales budget.
- Formulating the sales message.
- Determining the type of sales personnel required.

FIGURE 14.1 The task of sales management

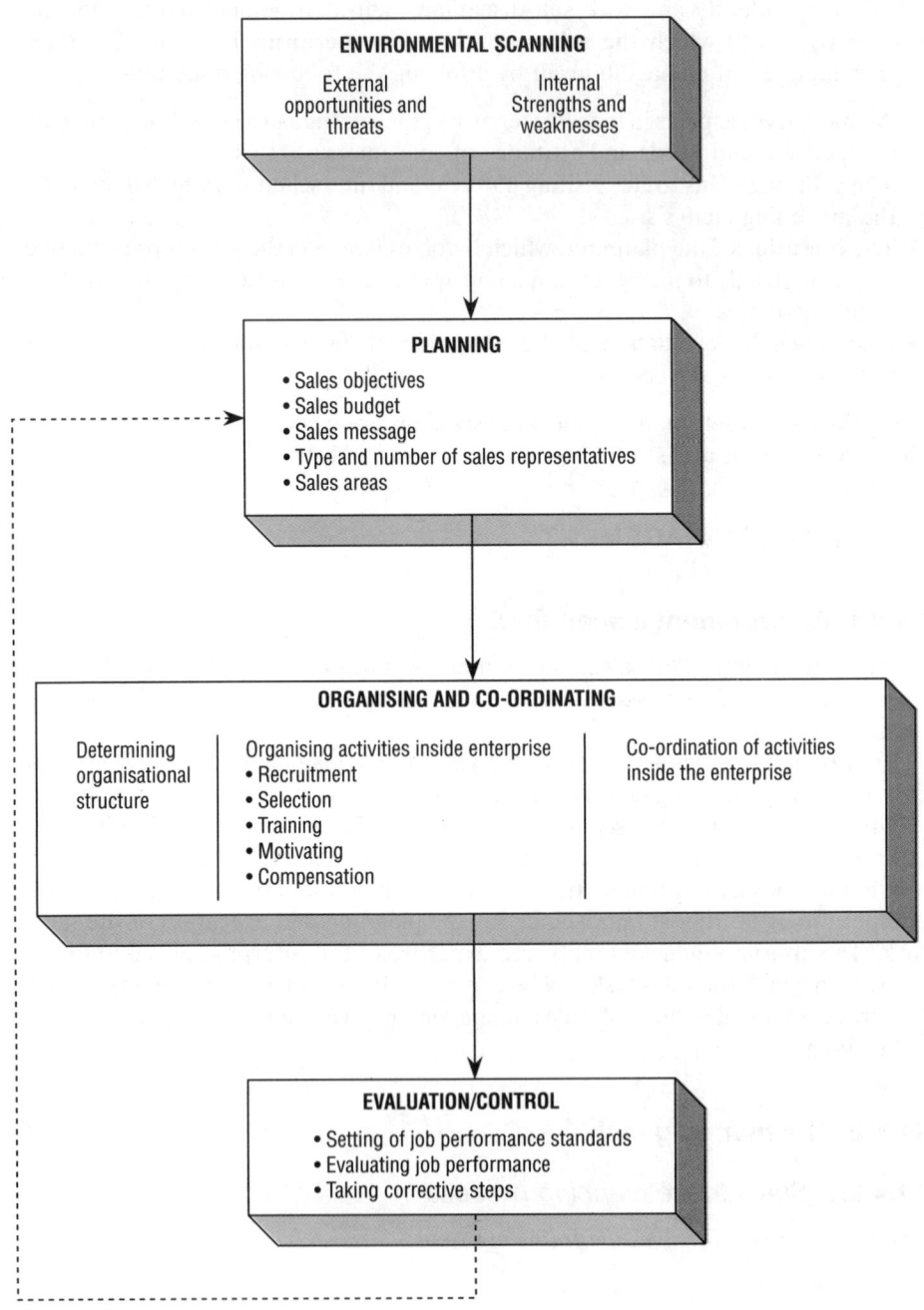

- Determining the size of the sales force.
- Allocating sales areas.

These steps do not necessarily follow each other in this sequence, but it is important to note that no decision can be made before environmental scanning has taken place and sales objectives have been formulated. Sales areas cannot be constructed or allocated before decisions concerning the sales personnel have been made. (The management tasks are discussed in greater detail in Chapters 1 and 19.)

14.4.2.2 *Formulating the sales objectives*

Sales objectives cannot be determined at random, but are derived from the enterprise's hierarchy of objectives. The marketing objectives (and objectives of the other functions in the enterprise) are derived from the overall business objectives, while the objectives of the marketing communication instruments (such as personal selling) are derived from the marketing objectives. These objectives increase co-ordination between the various functions and divisions in the enterprise and are indispensible guidelines when making decisions. In order to make them more specific and operational, all these objectives are also based on the information obtained from environmental scanning. Uncertainty about the objectives is further limited by putting them in writing.

Sales objectives can be formulated only after the task and role of personal selling as part of marketing communication has been put in perspective, because personal selling must contribute towards promoting the sale of the enterprise's product through communication with potential buyers. The basic elements which should be included in the sales objectives include, with regard to each product, aspects such as the following: the potential buyers, sales areas, time limits, intended sales message and intended sales volume.

14.4.2.3 *Compiling the sales budget*

As discussed in Chapter 12, various budgeting techniques exist according to which the total marketing communication budget can be compiled and allotted to the communication instruments. Here it is important to concentrate more specifically on the role of sales management with regard to the communications and sales budgets.

There are two methods according to which the sales budget as part of the communications budget can be approached. The first is the **breakdown method** where the communication budget is derived from the sales budget. The main advantage here is that senior marketing personnel are involved in the allotment, but the weakness of the method lies in the way in which the budgeted amounts can be allotted. The ideal is to obtain the inputs from sales management before the allotment is done. This is in fact done in the second method.

The second method is the **build-up method** where the total communication budget is built up out of the various communication elements. According to this method sales management first decides which tasks must be done in the specific budget period and also determines the costs involved. This method is very popular because it enables sales management to link the costs directly to the tasks necessary to reach the intended sales objectives. The question which arises here is: What will happen if the total amount determined in this way by all the communication instruments is more than the amount which the enterprise can make available for communication? To solve this problem a combination of the two methods is sometimes used. Various budgeting techniques, as discussed in Chapter 12, can be used for both methods.

14.4.2.4 *Formulating the sales message*

The formulation of the sales message takes place against the background of the specific sales situations and sales theories (which have been discussed in a previous section of this chapter). It must also be borne in mind that in personal selling unstructured flexible sales messages are mostly used, which enables the sales representative to tune the sales message very finely to the receiver's circumstances. This approach makes use of the two-way character of personal selling.

The sales representatives are not only responsible for the transmission of the sales message per se. The name of the enterprise and the logo appears on all the sales material and often even on the vehicle with which sales visits are made. Sales representatives are also often involved with point-of-purchase promotions and they are sometimes responsible for the installation of special display shelves, refrigeration facilities and overhead display boards. The message transmitted by the sales representative is therefore much more than a mere sales offer.

14.4.2.5 *Determining the type of sales representatives*[12]

Sales management must decide about the type of sales representatives who will be able to transmit the message effectively, ie the requirements which the sales representative must meet with regard to the different selling situations and products. These decisions serve as guidelines during the recruitment, selection and training of the sales representatives. The decision about the required type of sales representatives is preceded by the following activities, which are carried out step by step.

Conduct a job analysis

A job analysis basically involves collecting and analysing data to determine which activities and responsibilities will constitute each sales position. The collected data will answer the following questions:

- What are the objectives of the sales position?
- What are the general responsibilities and duties of the position?
- Which specific selling activities form part of the position?
- What is the relationship of the specific position to the other positions in the enterprise?

Develop a detailed job description

The job description is based on the results of the job analysis and entails the accurate description of all the activities which must be carried out by the person filling the position, as well as the responsibilities which have been assigned to him. The objective here is for all parties to understand the exact extent and nature of the duties and responsibilities of each sales position. Job descriptions are very handy during the recruitment, selection and training of sales personnel. Job descriptions consist of the following elements:

- Job title.
- Statement of job objectives.
- The relationship of the position to others in the enterprise.
- Detailed description of the tasks, responsibilities and activities of the position.
- Nature of the authority and supervision.
- The remuneration plan.
- Criteria for evaluating posts.

Determine the job specifications

The job specification identifies all the personal characteristics and qualifications which an individual should possess in order to function in the specific position and it is derived from the data collected during the previous two steps. The following job specifications can be stipulated:

- Type and level of educational background.
- Basic intelligence level.
- Necessary personality characteristics, such as interest, ambition and motivation, emotional stability, initiative, self-confidence and ability to get on with others.
- Previous sales experience in terms of product, area and customer.
- Physical attributes such as health, general stamina and appearance.

Figure 14.2 indicates some of the characteristics required for successful sales representatives with regard to each of the four selling situations.

14.4.2.6 *Determining the number of sales representatives*

The number of sales representatives[13] required is derived from four fundamental considerations, namely the number of prospective customers, the buying potential of the customers, the geographic distribution of the customers, and the financial resources of the enterprise. Various methods exist according to which the required number of sales representatives for the enterprise can be determined. The following methods are the three common approaches:

FIGURE 14.2   Characteristics of sales representatives in each of the four sales situations

TYPE OF SALES SITUATION	CHARACTERISTICS REQUIRED OF SALES REPRESENTATIVES
Consultative	• Smooth approach • Personality compatible with achieving a few large successes periodically • Ability to gain strong confidence of the client
Technical	• Very strong product knowledge • Strong interest in detail • Rational approach in utilising sales techniques
Commercial	• Strong self-organisation • Ability to reach decision-maker in organisation • Ability to make smooth presentation and close sale
Direct	• Strong ability to close sale on first call • Strong persuasive ability • Ability to quickly identify a prospect's buying motives

Source: Based on Storholm, GR. 1982. *Sales Management.* Englewood Cliffs, New Jersey: Prentice-Hall, p 47.

The sales potential method

The following formula is used in the sales potential method to determine the required number of sales representatives:

$$N = S/P + T(S/P)$$

where: N = number of sales representatives

S = estimated sales volume (R-value)

P = estimated productivity of one sales representative (what he can handle per year)

T = provision for the turnover rate of the sales representatives

It is clear that the formula will give only an estimated indication of the number of sales representatives who should be employed.

The work load method

This method, which is also known as the build-up method, enables sales management to make use of the following aspects to determine the number of sales representatives to be employed:

- The visit frequency to each customer category.

- The number of customers in each category.

- The average number of sales visits which a sales representative can make in one year. This figure is influenced by the length of the sales visit.

The required number of sales representatives can then be determined in the following way: **multiply** the visit frequency by the number of customers in each category; then add the different categories together and divide this by the average number of sales visits which a sales representative can make in one year.

This calculation must be performed step-by-step.[14]

Step 1:*Determine the amount of time available to the sales representative on an annual basis.*

Example: 52 weeks × 5 days per week × 8 hours per day = 2 080 gross hours per year. Make provision for leave, illness and other time off, for example for attending courses. Suppose that this provision amounts to 5 weeks (5 × 20 hours = 200 hours), then 1 800 hours remain for selling activities.

Step 2: *Determine the time that the sales representative really devotes to selling.* Make provision for non-selling actitivities, such as travelling and administrative tasks. Suppose that the representative spends 60 % of this time on selling (60 % × 1 880 = 1 128 hours).

Step 3: *Categorise the customers according to the level of sales effort needed.*
The sales effort with regard to some customers requires more time than in other cases. The classification can be done as follows:

Category/Sales effort	No.
Extremely heavy	10
Heavy	30
Medium	150
Little	250

Step 4: *Determine the call length and frequency for each category of customer.*
Example:

Category/Sales effort	Call length/visit	No. of visits/yr
Extremely heavy	80 mins	40
Heavy	60 mins	30
Medium	40 mins	30
Little	30 mins	50

Step 5: *Determine the amount of time necessary on an annual basis to serve the customers.*
The following is an example based on the data above and summarising the calculations:

Category/Sales effort	Time/visit (mins)		Frequency/visit (per year)		Time/customer (hrs/yr)		No. of customers		Time/category (hrs)
Extremely heavy	80	×	40	=	53	×	10	=	530
Heavy	60	×	30	=	30	×	30	=	900
Medium	40	×	30	=	20	×	150	=	3 000
Little	30	×	50	=	25	×	250	=	6 250
									10 680

Step 6: *Determine the number of sales representatives required.*
The 10 680 selling hours from step 6 are now divided by the annual number of selling hours that the sales representative has at his disposal (1 128), as calculated in step 2. The enterprise therefore needs 10 sales representatives.

A direct relationship exists between determining the number of sales representatives, identifying and determining the number of sales areas, and the allocation thereof to sales representatives.

14.4.2.7 *Allocating sales areas*[15]

Sales areas are identified during the planning phase. Specific sales areas are then allocated to the sales representatives. A sales area can be defined as the grouping of existing and potential customers who have been assigned to an individual sales representative. A sales representative must be able to reach this group of customers easily and economically. Because of this, it is possible and sometimes also preferable for such groups to be limited to certain geographical areas. Geographic factors are, however, not necessarily the only basis for this division. Different types of products and customers can also be used as a basis. A combination of these factors is also often used.

There are various reasons for allocating certain sales areas to sales representatives. The following are the most important:

- It ensures better market coverage.
- It facilitates and promotes control of sales activities.
- It eliminates uncertainty, duplication and overlapping of areas.
- It makes specialisation possible.

The allocation of sales areas occurs step by step:

Step 1: Decide on the basis for the distribution of units. Every unit is known as a control unit and must preferably be kept as small as possible.

Step 2: Determine the sales potential of each control unit.

Step 3: Combine the control units in preliminary areas. To determine the size of the preliminary areas, the total sales potential of all the areas can be divided by what a sales representative can handle per year (productivity per average sales representative per year). In this way the sales areas are divided amongst the sales representatives.

Step 4: Adjust the preliminary areas to ensure that full market coverage is achieved. The sales potential is very seldom distributed evenly over a preliminary area. A rural and an urban area can, for example, have the same sales potential, but the cost and difficulty of covering each will definitely differ. An optimal area combination can be achieved when areas have been combined in such a way that the increase in sales per rand spent is equal between areas.

Step 5: Allocate areas to sales representatives. Every sales representative is allocated a certain area where he can use his ability, background and qualifications to make the best contribution to the profit of the enterprise.

14.4.2.8 *Planning travel patterns*

After the sales areas have been allocated planning must take place as to how each sales representative will be able to serve his area most effectively timewise. Travel costs time and money and can make contact with buyers very costly. By planning travel patterns sales management tries to ensure the optimum use of time and other resources by means of which the required level of contact with the buyers can be reached. The sales management must try to minimise travel time and maximise selling time. The following basic travel patterns, illustrated in figure 14.3, were developed for this purpose:[16]

- The **circular route** is best when the customers are evenly distributed and when there is a need for a uniform degree of contact with those customers.

- The **straight line** is a route on which the sales representative visits customers on a straight line, for example between Johannesburg and Pretoria or Johannesburg and Durban.

- The **clover leaf route** consists of a number of routes arranged like the petals of a flower around the enterprise. Each route begins and starts at the the enterprise. The situations for which this is applicable are more or less the same as in the case of the circular route. The difference is, however, that the sales representative serves the different petals in turn. He will, for example, cover one petal each week in order to cover all the petals in one month.

- The **wedge-shaped route** is used especially where each sales representative is responsible for a segment in an urban area. The point of the wedge starts in the city and becomes wider as it extends into the surburban areas.

The decisions made during the planning phase must now be implemented in the planned way. First of all it is necessary to indicate, by means of an organisational structure, who is responsible for what.

14.4.3 Organisation in the sales division

14.4.3.1 *The organisational structure*

Two aspects are involved in organising, namely organising activities and the organisational structure. Organising is the process by which the functions in the division are arranged as the personnel will function better jointly, in defined relationships with each other, than individually. The organisational structure is the result of organising and is normally indicated in the form of an organisational chart. During the planning phase a considerable amount of decisions are made and many aspects are analysed which can serve as guidelines for organising the sales division.[17] The formal organisational structure facilitates the allocation of

FIGURE 14.3   Travel patterns of sales representatives

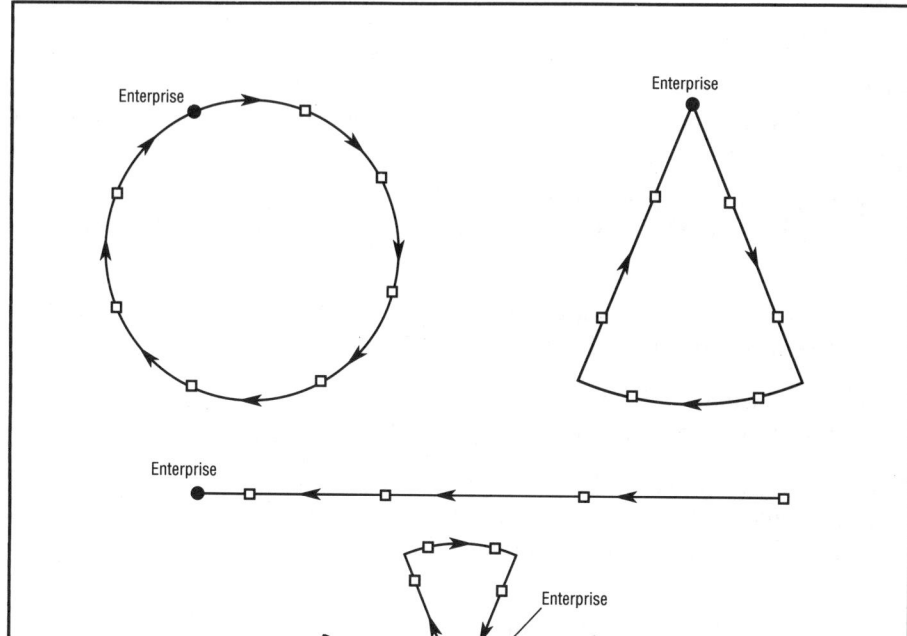

responsibilities and the exercising of authority. A general sales manager who reports to the marketing manager is normally at the top of the organisational structure. Three types of organisational structure and lines of authority normally exist in an enterprise:

- Line organisation.
- Line and staff organisation.
- Functional organisation.

It is easiest to demonstrate each type of structure visually with the help of an example in the form of a simple organisational chart, as indicated in Figure 14.3.

It is important to note that the management function of leading (see Chapter 1, section 1.5) is the responsibility of the sales manager. He plans, organises and controls the sales activities as well as seeing to the internal and external co-ordination thereof. There are usually a number of sales managers in a large organisation reporting to the general sales manager. These managers are responsible for organising all activities in the sales department. Most medium-sized and larger enterprises find it advantageous to construct their organisational structures on a specialisation basis in order to enable the sales representatives to do their work more effectively. Sales managers who fall under the line authority of a general sales manager can be divided according to the following specialisation bases:

- **Geographical area.** Sales managers (falling under the general sales manager) are appointed for each geographic area (for example Sales Manager: Northern Natal).

- **Product.** Sales managers are appointed for different types of products (for example Sales Manager: Trade Vehicles).

- **Type of customer.** Sales managers are appointed for different types of enterprise (for example Sales Manager: Industrial Market).

- **Sales task.** In this case, different deputy managers can report to the general sales manager (for example Customer Development and Maintenance, Tele-marketing and After-sales Evaluation).

A combination of the abovementioned structures is often found.

The organisation of the sales force, in such a way that everyone knows what to do and how to do it, entails the following activities: recruitment, selection, training, remuneration, and motivation of the sales representatives.

14.4.3.2 *Organising the activities in the sales division*

Recruitment and selection of the sales representatives

Recruitment and selection procedures differ from one enterprise to another. They are, however, all based on the guidelines included in the job analysis, job description and job specification and the required number of sales representatives (see sections 14.4.2.5 and 14.4.2.6). The type of organisational structure determines, inter alia, which people will be responsible for recruitment and selection, which can be managed by the sales division or the personnel division. Each enterprise should in any case make use of the exchange of information as well as consultation between the sales and the personnel divisions (irrespective of the formal organisational structure in use).

Recruitment involves the search for suitable people to employ. As a result of uncertainty as to when sales representatives will be needed, a reservoir of suitable, available people is created for employment. The names of people to be included on this list can be obtained from various sources, such as responses to advertisements, internal personnel, personnel agencies and educational institutions. The differences in the recruitment attempts of different enterprises normally lie in the recruitment sources and methods, which are based on sales

FIGURE 14.4   Simple organisational structure in the sales division

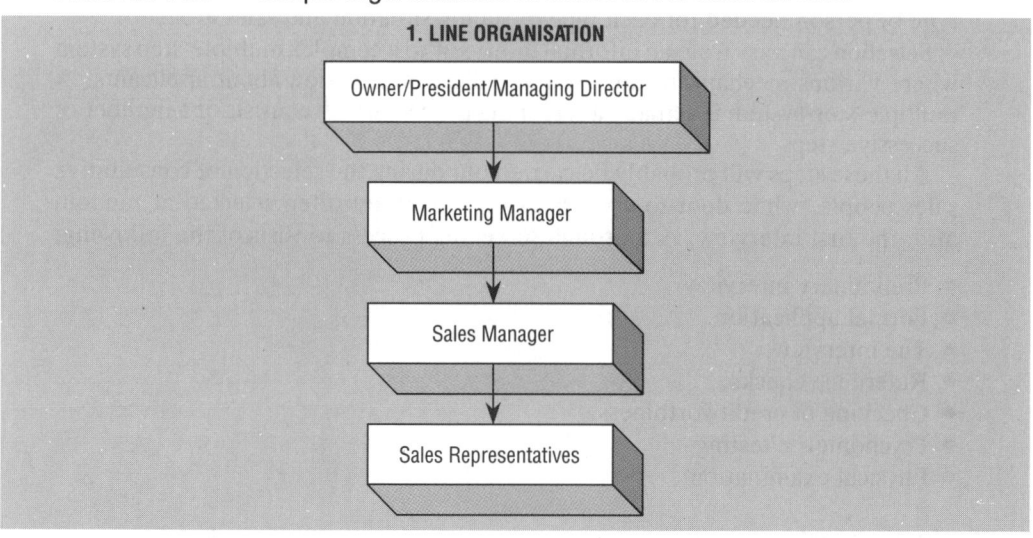

1. LINE ORGANISATION

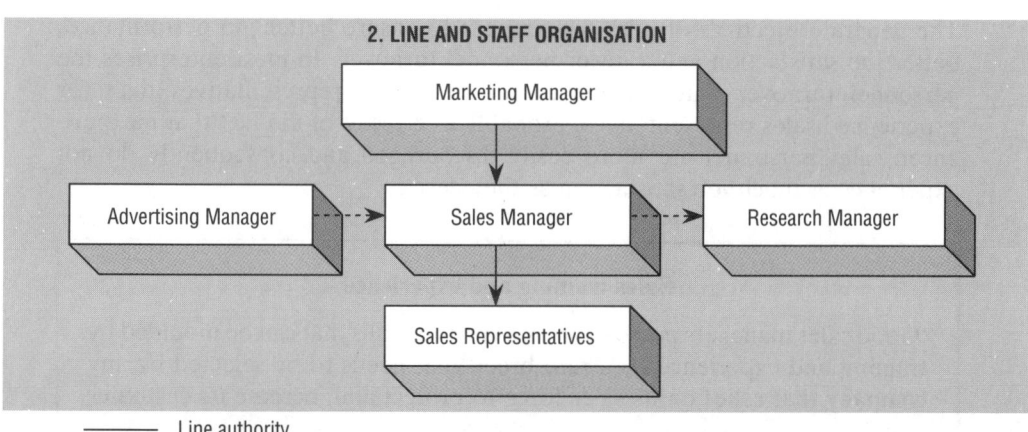

2. LINE AND STAFF ORGANISATION

——— Line authority
- - - - - Staff relationship

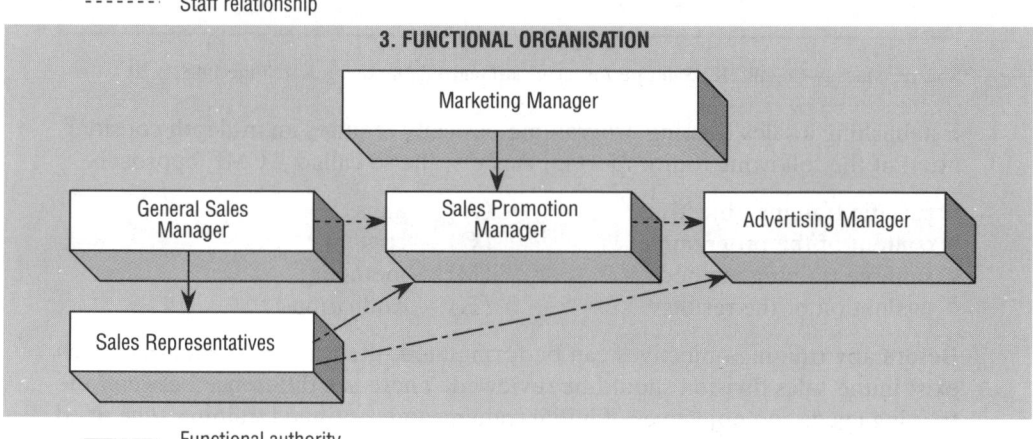

3. FUNCTIONAL ORGANISATION

— - — Functional authority
——— Line authority
- - - - - Staff relationship

management's sales plan where a decision has already been made regarding the type of person needed for each type of selling situation and sales area.

Selection can vary from an informal interview to a complex multiple-step system where various mechanisms are used to collect information about applicants. A multiple-step system is actually a screening process which consists of a number of successive steps.

All these steps will probably be carried out during the selection of consultative sales people, while door-to-door sales personnel are often selected at random after the first interview. A thorough screening process consists of the following:

- Preliminary interview.
- Formal application.
- The interview.
- Reference checks.
- Checking of creditworthiness.
- Psychometric testing.
- Physical examination.

Training of sales representatives

The general objectives of sales training are to ensure better job performance, better job satisfaction and a lower personnel turnover. In most enterprises the personnel turnover figure is higher for new sales representatives than for experienced sales representatives, probably as a result of the fact that inexperienced sales personnel are more easily discouraged and consequently do not experience as much job satisfaction as they desire.

Sales training and experience

'Good sales managers possess inherent people skills that can be moulded by training and experience — a rare breed that needs to be selected by any company that relies on its sales force to protect and increase its customer base.'

Source: Mackay-Coghill, K. 'Sales performance strategies.' *Marketing Mix*. June 1988, p 20.

Establishing a sales training programme basically requires an in-depth consideration of the following four important aspects, the so called ACME approach:

- specific training objectives   (A) — aims
- content of the programme   (C) — content
- suitable training methods   (M) — methods
- evaluation of the results   (E) — evaluation

Before any training objectives can be formulated, the training objectives which exist in the sales division should be reviewed. There is a difference between the training needs and objectives of initial training and continued training. The need for and the objective of initial training can be derived, inter alia, from the identified job specification, the background and experience of the individual applicants, and the marketing strategy of the enterprise. The objective of continued training is normally to improve existing knowledge or to introduce new products, methods and techniques.

The **content** of the sales training programme will be derived, inter alia, from the training needs and objectives and the nature of the training which candidates already have. Initial sales training programmes are normally considerably broader in extent than continued training. The initial training programme usually covers the following aspects: product data; sales techniques; markets; and information about the enterprise.

A wide variety of training **methods** is available and the method chosen depends on the contents of the training programme. In the case of the marketing of computers, demonstrations and practical workshops will be much more valuable than a formal lecture. Role playing can be used to show sales representative/customer relationships, while case studies are particularly useful for improving decision making and problem solving abilities. A combination of the different methods can also be used to complement each other. Further on-the-job training is necessary to round off the training programme. The following training methods are often used in sales training programmes:

- Lectures.
- Demonstrations.
- Practical workshops.
- Role playing.
- Case studies.
- Impromptu discussions.
- On-the-job training.
- Programmed learning.
- Correspondence courses.

The use of **learning material** and **training aids** depends on the contents of the training programme as well as on the training methods being used. Learning material includes printed lectures, diagrams, questionnaires and textbooks. Training aids include the following: blackboards, overhead projectors, video machines and projectors, and computers. It is important for the sales representative who will use certain aids during the sales presentation to be trained with these aids. This can improve his skill in using these aids.

Training in the use of sales aids

It has been proved that the use of sales aids can increase recall by the receiver by as much as 80%.

Source: *Marketing Mix*. August 1987, p 43.

It is also important for sales representatives to be informed about the enterprise's marketing strategy during training. The sales representatives should not only be knowledgeable about products and prices — they should also be involved in developing the advertising message and designing the sales promotion material. An internal marketing programme should therefore form part of the training programme.

Evaluation entails the comparing of results to the objectives of the training programme. Methods which are used differ from case to case, for example tests, observation by instructors, and evaluation by the students themselves.

Motivating the sales representatives[18]

The objective of motivation is to encourage sales representatives and to persuade them to perform their task to the best of their ability. Underlying motivation are aspects such as need-satisfaction, reward, independence and communication.

Research by the behavioural sciences has indicated that every human activity is directed at **need-satisfaction**. The individual's behaviour will therefore depend on the nature of his fulfilled and unfulfilled needs. Maslow's hierarchy of needs can for example also be applied here (see Chapter 3). It is sales management's task to determine at which level of the hierarchy a sales representative is, so that suitable motivational measures can be arranged, if this is in any way possible. The social and ego needs especially can be satisfied in a sales situation.

McClelland's view of money as a motivating factor

'Money is a tool among many for managing motivation. It is a treacherous tool because it is deceptively concrete, tempting many managers to neglect variables in the work situation and climate that really affect productivity. In the near future there will be less and less excuse for neglecting these variables, as the behavioral sciences begin to define them and explain to management how they can be manipulated just as one might change a financial compensation plan.'

Source: Storholm, GR. 1982. *Sales Management*. Englewood Cliffs, New Jersey: Prentice-Hall, p 140.

The relationship between reward and motivation is very complex. Behavioural scientists are of the opinion that reward has a low priority as a motivating factor. The place which reward fulfils as a motivating factor depends entirely on the individual and the level of need-satisfaction which has already been achieved. According to Herzberg's theory, the so-called hygiene factors (for example money, supervision and working conditions) can result in dissatisfaction, but they cannot motivate employees to do their jobs to the best of their abilities. Real motivation lies in aspects such as the job itself, recognition and decision making freedom. Reward is viewed as a hygiene factor which cannot effect job satisfaction, but merely prevents dissatisfaction. According to McClelland's theory every individual has a need to achieve, a need for affiliation and a need for power.[19] The need for achievement is characterised by the setting of objectives, willingness to take moderate risks, and the need for concrete feedback about performance, all behavioural characteristics which are reconcilable with activities in the enterprise. Most sales representatives' need for achievement is higher than normal.

Within the traditional organisational situation the head (in this case the sales manager) possesses the authority to allocate specific tasks to his subordinates. (See Chapter 1, section 1.5.) Whether his policy and instructions will be carried out is a function of the relationship between himself and his subordinates. The latest trend is to develop self-reliance and a degree of **independence** in this relationship, as decision making freedom is a motivational factor without an equal.

Effective **communication** between the sales manager and sales representatives is indispensable for high morale and productivity. Communication can be written or interpersonal. Good communication involves good communication channels and implies a free exchange of opinion, which is rated very highly by sales representatives. Communication is also a very good motivating factor. There should also be communication between the marketing manager and sales representatives. Internal marketing has already been referred to. An internal marketing programme aimed at sales representatives who deal directly with customers will ensure their interest and involvement with the marketing task in general.

Effective managers are leaders rather than slave drivers. They succeed in obtaining and maintaining the voluntary co-operation of the sales representatives. They also succeed in ensuring that the sales division's objectives are realised through motivation.

Reeva supports motivation

Reeva Forman emphasises the importance of the motivation aspect:

'Unless you are giving the people who work for your company a fair deal, either in a more conventional sort of business where they are sharing in the profits, or as in direct selling where their earnings are appropriate to the effort they put in, your growth is going to be limited.

Employees need recognition, they need praise. There is no such thing as lazy staff or people who don't want to work. It's the self-image those people have been given. If I thought that there was no future for me in my company . . . I too would be lazy.'

Source: *Marketing Mix.* May 1986, p 11.

> ### The importance of internal marketing
>
> It often happens that sales representatives see the advertising campaign of their enterprise at home for the first time. They might also hear about plans for expansion or special new products in news reviews for the first time. This is extremely demotivating for sales representatives who, in this case, cannot make any contribution to transmit the marketing message further.

The remuneration plan

A good remuneration plan[20] meets the following seven requirements:

- It covers the cost of living.

- It is synchronised with the rest of the motivation plan.

- It is justifiable.

- It is straightforward and easy to understand.

- It provides for adjustments, if necessary.

- It is economical to administer.

- It helps to realise the objectives of the sales division.

The remuneration plan of sales representatives basically consists of four elements: a fixed element, usually in the form of a **salary**; a variable element, normally in the form of **commission**; an element which makes provision for repaying the **sales expenses** incurred by the representative; and an element which involves **fringe benefits**. These four remuneration elements can be combined in various ways. It is sales management's task to decide on the combination of elements which will best serve both the enterprise and the sales representative. It is traditional for commission on sales to make up a large part of the sales representative's remuneration package. Commission is supposed to motivate sales representatives to sell as much as possible. The salary part is meant as security for sales representatives. It must therefore be adequate to fulfil the basic living needs in those times when no sales are realised. If the commission part is too large the sales representative may be tempted to go after sales at all costs, perhaps to the disadvantage of the customer.

The remuneration plan is drawn up after sales management has studied the job descriptions and analysed the general remuneration package in the enterprise, as well as the remuneration patterns in similar enterprises. The final decision about the remuneration level and the combination of elements is taken by considering the needs and problems inherent in the enterprise and by asking the advice of present sales representatives. The remuneration plan must be revised continually so that shortcomings can be identified in time.

14.4.4 Controlling the execution of the sales task

14.4.4.1 *The evaluation process*

The job performance standards of sales representatives must be defined and measured quantitatively as well as qualitatively. Effective supervision forms part of this measuring or evaluation process. The fact that sales representatives are not office bound or time bound obviously makes supervision and control of their activities difficult. However, supervision is necessary, but it should not be over-emphasised or neglected. For evaluation, the actual performance should first be recorded before it is compared to the set standards. If deviations occur which should be rectified, corrective steps should be taken. Job performance standards should therefore be set after the sales task of each sales position has been carefully analysed within the context in which it was executed. The evaluation process is therefore not something which should be forced on sales representatives from the top. Their co-operation in the initial setting of standards should rather be obtained.

Quantitative job performance standards

Quantitative job performance standards involve the nature and desired level of job performance expressed in quantitative terms. The setting of sales targets[21] not only facilitates the evaluation task, it can also continually encourage sales representatives to reach the sales target or to exceed it.

Various types of targets exist, for instance the sales volume target (focuses on number of units), budget target (money value), activity target (number of visits), and a combination of these. Use of these targets differs from one enterprise to another.

Since a target is a control measure, it is often unpopular. If it is not instigated and administered very discretely, the attitude of the sales representatives might negatively affect its effectiveness. To be effective, the following two requirements should be met:

- Targets must be accurate, just and achievable.
- Managers must ensure that sales representatives understand and accept targets and the procedures for determining targets.

Qualitative job performance standards

There are certain aspects of job performance that are not easily quantifiable, but which nevertheless have an influence on the realisation of objectives in the sales division. There are various qualitative criteria which should be taken into account in the evaluation process, for example:

- Willingness to perform tasks (other than the sales task).
- Ability to maintain good relationships in the sales division and the marketing division.
- An ability to solve customers' problems.
- Insight and interest in the objectives and activities of the enterprise.
- Enthusiasm.

As subjective judgement applies in all the abovementioned cases, it is preferable to combine quantitative and qualitative standards in the evaluation process.

14.4.4.2 *Corrective action*

The control task of sales management is a continuous process which culminates in decision making about future behaviour.

If it is found in the evaluation process that job performance is not satisfactory, corrective steps should be taken. At management level corrective steps entail reconsideration of job specifications, sales areas or sales quotas — if these are the reasons for the substandard performance. However, if the fault lies with the sales representative, a tactful and constructive reprimand would be the best measure.

When the evaluation process shows positive results, the necessary recognition should be given to those responsible. Recognition of performance is a strong motivating factor which will possibly lead to a favourable evaluation in the following evaluation period.

14.5 SUMMARY

The unique two-way nature of communication in personal selling is successful if the selling task is planned thoroughly, organised well and controlled effectively. Particular attention is given to sales representatives because they communicate directly with the consumers of the products. If this link is weak, it will negatively influence sales and therefore also the profit motive of the enterprise.

The sales manager, who is at the head of the sales division, is responsible for the job performance of the sales representatives. He, in turn, falls under the line authority of the marketing manager. This ensures that decision making in the sales division will make a contribution to the marketing communication decisions with regard to advertising, sales promotion and publicity. The sales and advertising messages thus form a unit with a specific objective, directed at a specific target market. These messages are further strengthened by sales promotion and publicity.

In the following chapter the last-mentioned two marketing communication elements will be discussed in greater depth.

REFERENCES

1. Still, RR, Cundiff, WE and Govoni, NAP. 1981. *Sales Management*. Englewood Cliffs: Prentice-Hall, p 5.
2. Manning, GL and Reece, BL. 1987. *Selling Today: A Personal Approach*. Dubuque, Iowa: Brown Publishers.
3. Adler, RB, Rosenfeld, LB and Towne, N. 1983. *Interplay — The Process of Interpersonal Communication*. New York: Holt, Rinehart & Winston, p 111.
4. Manning and Reece op cit, pp 114–117.
5. Manning and Reece ibid, p 119.
6. Based on Manning and Reece *ibid*, pp 121–122.

7. Based on Storholm, GR. 1982. *Sales Management*. Englewood Cliffs: Prentice-Hall, pp 40–49.
8. Based on Govoni et al. 1986. *Promotional Management*. Englewood Cliffs: Prentice-Hall, pp 306–310.
9. Based on comprehensive discussions in Govoni et al op cit, pp 308–310, Manning and Reece op cit, pp 334–341 and Patty, RC and Hite, R. 1988. *Managing Salespeople*. New Jersey: Prentice Hall, pp 414–422.
10. Govoni et al op cit pp 313–317.
11. A good and comprehensive discussion of the four areas of self-management appears in Manning and Reece op cit, pp 421–437.
12. Based on Govoni op cit, pp 320–328.
13. For a comprehensive discussion, see Churchill, GA, Ford, M and Walker OC. 1981. *Sales Force Management: Planning, Implementation and Control*. Homewood, Illinois: Richard D Irwin, pp 160–167.
14. This process is explained well by Govoni et al op cit, pp 337–340.
15. The whole issue concerning the identification, choice and allocation of sales areas is placed into perspective by Churchill et al op cit, pp 174–204.
16. This whole process is discussed by Govoni et al op cit, pp 337–340.
17. A good discussion on organizing the sales department appears in Stanton, WJ and Buskirk, RH. 1987. *Management of the Sales Force*. Homewood, Illinois: Richard D Irwin, pp 61–79.
18. See Storholm op cit, pp 134–145 and Stanton and Buskirk op cit, pp 271–291.
19. Storholm op cit, p 140.
20. Stanton and Buskirk op cit, pp 301–346 provide a good discussion about this.
21. Still op cit pp 614–616.

CASE STUDY

PROBLEMS AT COSMIC COMPUTERS

Cosmic Computers is an enterprise selling computers and accessories, such as printers and computer programs. The enterprise started six years ago with only two persons, grew and now has four sales representatives and six other personnel. Mr Dickens, has recently been appointed as the first sales manager of Cosmic Computers. The enterprise presently mainly serves the Pretoria/ Witwatersrand area as well as customers in a few other areas.

Up till now Cosmic Computers handled the sales representatives in a haphazard way because not one has had training in this area, but rather have a technical computer background.

During the last few years Cosmic experienced various sales management related problems. Cosmic Computers appointed you as marketing consultant to make suggestions about solutions for the problems experienced in this area. Mr Dickens prepared a report concerning the problems as well as the activities and performance of Cosmic Computers.

REPORT OF COSMIC COMPUTERS

Summary of problems

We experience the following problems:

1. We allocated quotas to our representatives, but we don't know whether we did it right. Must we allocate a larger quota to the person who can do more or not?

2. One of our biggest problems is to know whether our sales areas has been compiled correctly and sales representatives been allocated correctly to the areas. Our representatives are so different. Are there any guidelines for compiling of sales area and the allocation of sales representatives to specific areas. Please make suggestions about the allocation of our sales representatives to specific sales areas.

3. Our sales representatives are generally slightly demotivated and feel that they should be able to do better. What can we suggest to the sales representatives in order to improve their sales performance? What can we further do to increase their motivation? Will financial compensation be adequate?

4. Do you regard it as necessary to train the sales representatives in the different aspects of sales management or must they learn from experience? If we train them, what should we teach them? They are so different and then the customers are different too.

5. The sales representatives complain that they spend too much time in travelling to and fro and that valuable selling time is lost in this way. How can we improve this problem?

BACKGROUND INFORMATION

Sales representatives

Ivan Sellers

He looks like the typical born salesman. He is 33 years of age and is still unmarried and lives for travelling around and selling. He has previous sales experience. He appears like the typical 'YUPPIE'. He previously worked for a wholesaler as computer programmer.

Peter Marinkowitz

He is 24 and has just completed his technikon training. He is of the know-all type who do not like to be prescribed or taught. He is perhaps still a bit of a windbag and slightly immature. This is expressed in his extrovert and extravagant clothing as well as an ear ring. One sometimes wonders whether you can be relaxed to let him work on his own away from the office for long periods of time. His sales are not very good.

John McCarthy

He is 30 years of age, married, and has one child. He is very talkative, enjoy cracking jokes, dress only in the best and is very flamboyant. He is very seldom serious, but also very seldom depressed. He is an active sportsman, very fit and has an excellent working capacity. He had previously sold life insurance for a short period before he stated his own computer business.

Jan Venter

He is 36 years of age, has four children and appears like the typical family man. He enjoys his work, but does not want to be away from home for long. He joined Cosmic after the closure of the computer section of a Government Corporation where he was employed. His sales are not satisfactory and he therefore earns little commission. He consequently has many financial worries and must do many things at home by himself. He is nevertheless a committed, conservative person who strives to do everything perfect. He is at ease with people and his appearance is always good.

Sales areas

A   Urban, visiting point close to each other, customers mainly large enterprises. Estimated sales potential is plus minus R100 000 per month.

B   Urban as well as certain suburbs, visiting points close to each other, customers mainly smaller enterprises. Estimated sales potential is R120 000 per month.

C   Peri-urban areas, smaller towns and suburbs as well as places in rural areas, cover nearly the whole of Transvaal and the Orange Free State. Estimated sales potential is R160 000 per month.

D   Intercity, different towns on or near the N3 highway between Johannesburg and Durban. Different smaller enterprises as well as some large enterprises in Durban. Estimated sales potential is R140 000 per month.

QUESTION

Compile a report for Cosmic Computers in which you attempt to answer their problems and in which you recommend solutions.

CHAPTER 15

SALES PROMOTION METHODS AND PUBLICITY

15.1 INTRODUCTION

The aim of this chapter is to discuss the role of sales promotion and publicity as elements of marketing communication. First a general outline is given as regards the meaning of each of the elements and how they integrate with the other elements of marketing communication. The task of marketing management in respect of the planning, implementing and evaluation of sales promotion methods and publicity will also be explained.

The first part of the chapter is devoted to sales promotion methods, while the second part describes and discusses publicity. The topics and subdivisions that will be discussed include the following:

ORGANISATION OF THE CHAPTER

The nature of sales promotion: Definition of sales promotion, strengths and weaknesses of sales promotion, the status of sales promotion in South Africa.

Management of a sales promotion campaign: Formulation of objectives, choice of sales promotion methods directed at the consumer and intermediaries, implementation and co-ordination of the programme, evaluation of the methods.

Publicity: Nature of publicity, different types of publicity, development of a publicity plan.

15.2 THE NATURE OF SALES PROMOTION

15.2.1 Definition of sales promotion

Sales promotion is often described generally and rather vaguely as all activities and material other than advertising, personal selling and publicity, used to stimulate sales and co-operation amongst distributors. This definition places the emphasis on what sales promotion methods are not rather than on what they actually involve.

A number of attempts to define sales promotion from a more operational viewpoint are considered in Figure 15.1.

FIGURE 15.1   Definition of sales promotion

Wright[1] indicates that the meaning of sales promotion methods can be derived from the two elements comprising the term, namely sales and promotion (advertising). Sales promotion methods embody something of each element and co-ordinate and support both.

Luick & Ziegler[2] are of the opinion that sales promotion methods are a direct inducement which offer an extra value or incentive to the sales force, distributors or consumers.

Stanley[3] considers sales promotion methods to be attempts made to ensure that products move through distribution channels, by means of additional incentives offered to sales personnel, intermediaries and consumers.

Ailloni-Charas[4] defines sales promotion methods as inducements designed to accelerate selling and buying functions in the marketing process and to supplement the basic product/service-in-use satisfaction anticipated by both ultimate and intermediate consumers.

Kotler[5] distinguishes between the following aspects of sales promotion methods:

- communication which is specifically directed at the consumer, to inform him and attract his attention;
- incentives to do business;
- an invitation to buy.

From these definitions of sales promotion the following is apparent:

- Sales promotion supplements advertising and personal selling as elements of marketing communication.
- Sales promotion serves as an incentive for three parties, namely sales personnel, intermediaries in the distribution channel, and the final consumer.
- Sales promotion comprises a variety of activities such as competitions, free samples, discount coupons, exhibitions and point-of-sale advertising.
- Sales promotion is result-orientated and stimulates immediate reaction.

15.2.2 Strengths and weaknesses of sales promotion

As a method of marketing communication, sales promotion possesses both strengths and weaknesses. These strengths and weaknesses are displayed in Figure 15.2.

FIGURE 15.2   Strengths and weaknesses of sales promotion

STRENGTHS

A positive attitude towards the product is stimulated within distributors as well as consumers.

Distributors and consumers feel that they are getting something extra.

Immediate action can be stimulated via sales promotion.

This medium is most adaptable.

It is a multi-purpose medium. For example, it can be used to introduce a new product, to support a sales message or to attract attention, to convince or result in action.

Sales promotion is exceptionally effective when a new product is being introduced, when product improvements are being announced, when intensive distribution is required, and when it supports an advertising campaign.

WEAKNESSES

Results of sales promotion are short term in nature

They cannot be used without the support of other marketing communications methods.

A specific sales promotion method cannot be used continuously.

Too many sales promotion efforts can be disadvantageous for the image of the brand.

The effect of a sales promotion method can be eliminated easily by competitors.

Sales promotion methods are often viewed as a form of bribery.

15.2.3 The importance of sales promotion as a means of marketing communication

The use of sales promotion as a means of marketing communication has increased dramatically in the last few years. In the USA in 1988 an estimated $124 billion was spent on sales promotion in comparison with $118 billion spent on advertising.[6] In the United Kingdom, spending on sales promotion (the so-called 'below-the-line' spending) has increased by 250 per cent, in comparison with a 63 per cent increase in other marketing communication spending (the so-called 'above-the-line' spending). In the United States of America, spending on sales promotion methods overtook that of other 'above-the-line' expenditure at the beginning of 1970. This same phenomenon occurred in the United Kingdom in 1976. Koekemoer[7] is of the opinion that, if they were available, South African statistics would probably reflect a similar development pattern. An investigation undertaken by Market Research Africa, involving 170 of the top advertisers in South Africa, revealed that firms had budgeted to spend 38,8 per cent of their entire budget on sales promotion methods in 1988. Of this amount, 72 per cent will be aimed at the consumer and the balance at intermediaries in the distribution channel.[8] Table 15.1 indicates the most popular sales promotion methods from the point of view of the respondents.

TABLE 15.1   Top advertisers' preferences for various sales promotion methods

METHOD	% OF RESPONDENTS
Sales conference	63,6
Product introduction promotions	63,1
Contests and sweepstakes	60,3
Sales incentives	57,5
Point-of-purchase displays	56,9
Direct advertising	48,6
Trade deals and promotional allowances	46,9
Gifts	45,2
Free samples	35,1

Source: *Marketing Mix*, January 1988, p 21.

There are, however, two laws which restrict the use of sales promotion methods, namely the Gambling Act (Act 51 of 1965) and the Trade Practices Act (Act 76 of 1976 as amended). The Gambling Act prohibits any game of chance, for example bingo, lotteries, and the forecasting of the outcome of an event. The Trade Practices Act prohibits any form of business practice which may deceive or exploit the consumer. Until 1984 the use of trade coupons was prohibited by the latter Act. However, with the amendment of the Trade Practices Act the use of trade coupons became legal practice in certain circumstances. The amendment was worded in such a way that it could be interpreted in many different ways. Koekemoer suggests that when an institution is assessing the legality of a promotion, advice should be sought from professionals in this field.[9]

15.3 THE MANAGEMENT OF A SALES PROMOTION PROGRAMME

15.3.1 Steps in the management of a sales promotion programme

As is the case in any other marketing activity, it is the task of marketing management to manage the sales promotion programme. This implies that decisions need to be made concerning aspects such as:

- the aim of the programme (objectives);
- who will accept responsibility for the programme;
- what methods will be used;
- the execution of the programme;
- the co-ordination of the programme with other marketing communication methods; and
- how control will be exercised over the programme.

The steps to be taken in the management of a sales promotion programme are illustrated in Figure 15.3.

Ten sales promotion commandments

- Thou shalt not plan sales promotion without first specifying objectives and budget.
- Thou shalt select only the right sales promotion techniques to attain specific objectives.
- Thou shalt direct thy sales promotions to thy target audience.
- Thou shalt not use confusing, complicated consumer copy.
- Thou shalt not be greedy in consumer purchase requirements.
- Thou shalt support sales promotion with advertising when merited.
- Thou shalt test any major programme in which there is no brand experience.
- Thou shalt not wait 'till the last minute to plan'.
- Thou shalt always honour the 'kiss philosophy', that is 'Keep it Simple Stupid'.
- Thou shalt always consult with promotion specialists when planning sales promotions.

Source: Adapted from Ailloni-Charas, D. 1984. *Promotion: A Guide to Effective Promotional Planning, Strategies and Executions*. New York: John Wiley & Sons, p 42.

15.3.2 Formulation of sales promotion objectives

Sales promotion can be used and applied by business for a variety of objectives. A single sales promotion method can be used to achieve one or several objectives, or a variety of sales promotion methods can be used to achieve one specific

FIGURE 15.3 Steps in the management of a sales promotion programme

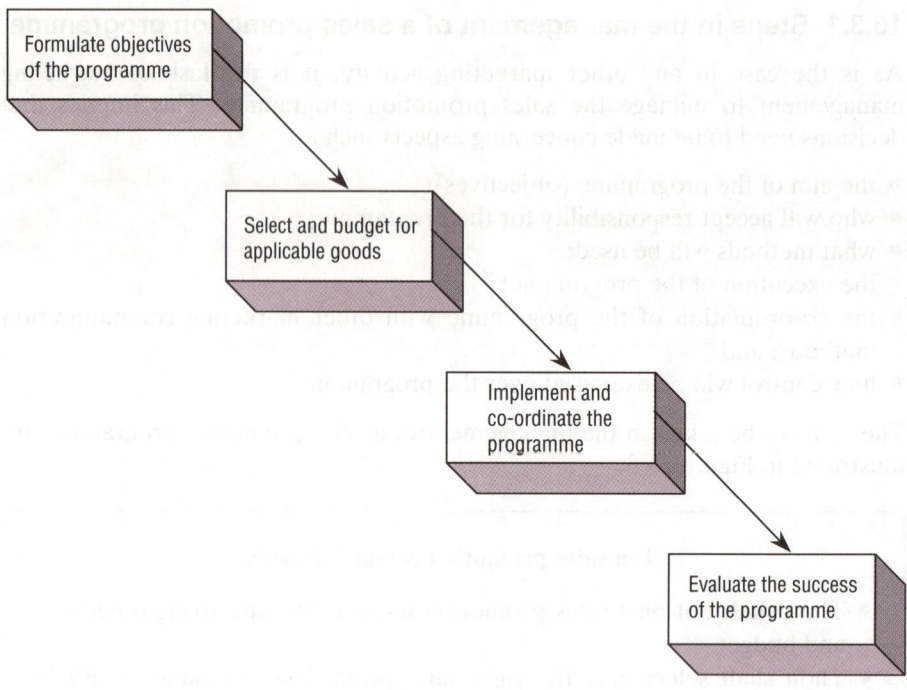

objective. The objectives of a sales promotion programme must continually be aligned with the marketing communication objectives which, in turn, originate from the marketing objectives for a specific product or product range.

A list of objectives that can be striven for is illustrated in Figure 15.4. These objectives usually have one or more of the following in mind:

- to increase the consumption rate of existing consumers;

- to attract new consumers;

- to convince intermediaries to distribute the product and/or pay special attention to the distribution thereof;

- to motivate and involve sales personnel in the marketing action.

From the above it is obvious that sales promotion activities can be directed towards three main groups:

- potential or existing consumers of the product;

- dealers who must support the marketing activities of the company;

- the sales force, whose actions need to be supported.

FIGURE 15.4   Specific objectives of sales promotion

To track down and attract new consumers.

To introduce a new product.

To increase the number of users of a particular brand name.

To increase the consumption rate of existing consumers.

To inform consumers of product improvements.

To attract more consumers to a business/retailer.

To increase inventory turnover.

To counteract competitors' marketing actions.

To obtain improved shelf and display space.

To obtain co-operation from intermediaries.

To support sales personnel.

Sales promotion methods aimed at final consumers

Sales promotion methods that focus on consumers can be directed towards two segments, namely **existing consumers**, ie persons already using the product, and **new/potential consumers** who do not know about the product yet, or who use another brand.

Sales promotion methods which focus on existing consumers have the following objectives:

- to increase the loyalty of consumers;

- to strengthen or change the image of the product;

- to stimulate repeat purchases;

- to encourage regular use of the product; and

- to stimulate the demand for larger containers or more luxurious variations of the product.

The sales promotion methods for existing consumers can be divided into two groups, namely those aimed at the **building of consumer loyalty** in the long term, and those aimed at **increased sales**, largely in the short term. The first-mentioned method combines a product with an attractive deal, for example a free sample of the product with an associated sales message. The short-term methods simply offer a deal, for example a discount coupon. It is these short-term objectives that have resulted in the perception that sales promotion methods are often considered to be defensive strategies and marketing actions taken by the marketing management if problems are experienced with the sale of a product. (The offensive and defensive strategies will be discussed in Chapter 18.)

Sales promotion methods used for an offensive marketing strategy are more effective when they are used in conjunction with an advertising campaign. Advertising informs the consumers of the sales promotion actions via the advertising message, which also includes the aim of the sales promotion methods. Both long- and short-term advantages result from such a combined campaign.

Sales promotion warfare

A large Checkers Warehouse was erected diagonally opposite a Pick 'n Pay Hypermarket that was 11 years old. This was the first time that two giant shopping centres were erected opposite one another and had to compete for market share.

Each of the two giants in Brackenfell looked forward to the defeat of the other by using millions of rands' worth of advertising.

The obstinate struggle between Pick 'n Pay and Checkers is raging to gain the purchasing power of almost half a million people living in the Cape Town region, who are inundated with offers of bargains and entertainment.

Advertising campaigns are guarded like state secrets and intricately planned strategies are formulated in order to invite the most popular artists before the competitor can.

It was at the opening of Warehouse City that singer Bles Bridges was used to attract the guests to the Pick 'n Pay Hypermarket — and this only days after his performance at Warehouse City.

Source: 'Winkelreuse kruis swaarde in Brackenfell'. *Finansies & Tegniek*, 2 December 1988, p 16.

Sales promotion methods focusing on dealers

The success or failure of many a product is dependent on the amount of support received from dealers. It is, for example, the retailer who decides whether or not he is going to stock the product and how much support he is going to give to the product. Consequently, promotions to the trade are essential to the success of a product, as producers gain the co-operation and active support of dealers with regard to aspects such as:

• special price offer promotions; and
• general support.

Sales promotion methods focusing on the sales force

Sales promotion activities directed at the company's sales force, for example competitions, sales seminars, and brochures, aim at motivating the sales force to spend extra effort in the pursuit of increased sales goals. Increasing the overall level of sales is the broad goal of these efforts, but they may also accomplish the following short-term goals:

- securing new dealers;
- promoting and increasing sales of a specific item or brand;
- introducing special promotion methods to dealers;
- increasing order size; and
- increasing profitability and lowering sales costs.

15.3.3 Selection of sales promotion methods

15.3.3.1 *The sales promotion budget*

Figure 15.3 indicates that the budgeting for and selection of suitable sales promotion methods is the second step in the planning of a sales promotion programme. The sales promotion methods that are selected must be of such a nature that they will best achieve the objectives set for the sales promotion programme. The various sales promotion methods which can be selected are divided into two groups, namely those methods aimed at the **final consumer** and those aimed at **dealers**. As discussed earlier, methods directed at the consumer are essentially instituted to attract consumers to a particular retailer, to introduce a new product, and to stimulate sales directly. On the other hand, the sales promotion methods directed at dealers strive to convince wholesalers and retailers to stock the manufacturer's product(s) and to market the product(s) aggressively. The marketing communications budget will determine the amount of funds available for expenditure on sales promotion as well as the combination of methods that can be selected for a specific promotional programme.

The **budget** for sales promotion can be drawn up in one of two ways. First, a build-up procedure can be used. In using this method, individual sales promotion methods are selected and the costs involved to implement each of these is estimated. When this estimation is made, the following also need to be taken into consideration: administrative costs (printing, distribution and advertising costs); and the costs of the particular activity (eg discounts, samples, or free items). Secondly, more general guidelines can be used, for example a percentage of budgeted/expected sales; a percentage of the total marketing communication or advertising budget; or that which remains after the advertising budget has been finalised.

The various sales promotion methods focusing on the consumer and interme-diaries respectively will now be discussed.

15.3.3.2 *Sales promotion methods directed at the consumer*

Coupons, competitions, samples, special offers, exhibitions, demonstrations and point-of-sale displays are examples of methods aimed at consumers to encourage them to buy or to buy more of the product(s).

Coupons

Coupons have, for many years, been the most widely used of all sales promotion methods. Coupons are certificates distributed by manufacturers to consumers, redeemable at retail outlets, giving the consumer a specified price reduction on a particular product. Examples include a 15c discount on a tube of toothpaste, a 25c discount on washing powder and two cinema tickets for the price of one.

Coupons can be distributed in various ways, namely:

- as part of an advertisement in newspapers or magazines;
- as supplements in newspapers or magazines;
- by door-to-door distribution;
- by direct mail;
- in or on the packaging of a product; and
- together with another product manufactured by the same manufacturer or even another manufacturer.

Research regarding the use of coupons in the United States of America revealed the following:

- Approximately 120 billion coupons are distributed annually.
- An average household receives approximately 1 400 coupons annually.
- As much as 50 per cent of these coupons are not redeemed.
- In 20 per cent of all coupons redeemed, fraud is involved.

Source: Kincaid, WM. 1985. *Promotion: Products, Services and Ideas.* Columbus, Ohio: Charles E Merrill Publishing Co, pp 343–6.

Competitions

The variety of competitions which can be used is virtually endless. Basically, competitions as a sales promotion method require the participant (usually the consumer) to do something, for example completing or creating a slogan, answering a question, collecting caps, or submitting a recipe. Participants must then usually also submit proof of purchase of the manufacturer's brand or product either to a retailer or to the manufacturer itself. A variety of prizes can then be won by the lucky winners of the competition.

Free samples

Sampling is a method which is especially popular with the introduction of new products. Sampling places a free product in the hands of the consumer for trial, with the idea of letting the product sell itself, and to encourage consumers to purchase the product on a regular basis. Samples are smaller versions of the actual product, and must contain a sufficient amount to enable consumers to make informed judgements of the product's attributes. On the other hand, the sample must not be so large that it delays the purchasing of the product by consumers. A number of alternatives exist for the distribution of samples to potential users, for example direct mail, door-to-door delivery, and point-of-purchase give-away, perhaps in conjunction with another product or an in-store demonstration in shops.

The distribution of free samples can be particularly effective in the following situations:

- if the product possesses an easily demonstrated superiority over its competitors;
- if the product returns a reasonably high profit margin;
- if the product's primary advantage and key attributes are difficult to communicate by means of advertising;
- if the product's promotional budget allows for sufficient advertising support for the sampling effort.[10]

Consumer deals

Consumer deals are short-term promotions offering consumers a saving or a bonus (premium) on the purchase of a product. Examples of consumer deals include the following:

- Direct price reductions usually take the form of a 'cents-off' reduction appearing on the product label or package. They are also particularly effective in stimulating sales of products during off-seasons.
- Bonus packs — a bonus pack deal offers the consumer an opportunity to purchase more of a product (in volume or quantity) with no increase in the product's regular price (for example, buy four cakes of soap for the price of three). A variation of the standard bonus pack deal is the combination bonus pack offer, which allows the consumer to purchase two different, but related, products at a combined price that is lower than the total of the two items if sold separately (eg a paint brush and a tin of paint).
- Discount offers and free offers to a consumer who can produce evidence of having purchased a certain amount of a product, for example a free weekend for a family after twenty nights have been spent in a specific hotel group's hotels, or a free aeroplane ticket after a specified number of paid flights.

Premiums

Premiums are articles of merchandise provided free or at reduced prices to consumers as incentives to encourage the purchase of a specified product.

The objectives of premiums include the following:

- to entice consumers into switching from a competitor's product;
- to introduce new packaging of existing products;
- to build brand loyalty;
- to offset seasonal slumps;
- to stimulate impulsive buying;
- to serve as a form of product differentiation.

The following types of premiums (bonus articles) can be distinguished:

- On-pack premiums: These are also known as banded premiums. They are usually attached to a product's package or are included in a special package. For example, a container containing fire lighters attached to a packet of charcoal.
- In-pack premiums: These premiums are found inside the actual package of the product. For example, a free teaspoon in a tin of instant coffee, or toys in breakfast cereals.
- Container premiums: A container premium is a re-usable container which serves as the product's package. For example margarine packed in a plastic container, or cookies in a plastic bucket.
- Continuity coupon premiums: These are articles of merchandise for which the consumer receives a premium by collecting coupons, proof-of-purchase stamps, special labels and stickers.
- Free give-aways: Here the dealer gives certain articles to the consumer directly at the time the product is purchased. For example, a free bottle of cooldrink when purchasing petrol at a filling station.

Point-of-purchase displays

Producers make use of existing displays to attract the attention of the consumers in the store and stimulate them to purchase the product. These displays encourage impulsive purchasing to a large extent and they are normally closely related to the advertising campaign. Specifically, it involves the use of display materials such as posters, banners, shelves, signs, mobile displays, price cards and special display facilities. This material is usually provided by the manufacturers and displays are constructed in co-operation with retailers.

Demonstrations in stores

Manufacturers often use demonstrators in retail stores. During demonstrations the consumer is shown how to use the product, how effectively it works, and its important points or merits. In some demonstrations the consumer is invited to try out the product or to taste the sample prepared. These demonstrations are usually restricted to large stores and products such as foodstuffs, cosmetics and electrical appliances.

Specialities

Specialities are valuable articles on which the firm's name or the advertising slogan or logo appears. These articles are handed out free of charge to selected individuals and include articles such as calendars, pens, ashtrays, keyrings, T-shirts, pocket diaries, files, stationery, hats, peaks and handbags. This method contributes to the creation of the goodwill of the firm and exposure of the firm's name, logo, or slogan.

A summary of the strengths and weaknesses of each of the abovementioned sales promotion methods is depicted in Figure 15.5.

FIGURE 15.5 Strengths and weaknesses of the various sales promotion methods

METHOD	STRENGTHS	WEAKNESSES
Coupons	• More effective than a direct price decrease • The price is only temporarily decreased • A greater psychological effect than normal price decrease • More regular and larger volume of purchases are encouraged • Introduces new products • New consumers can be convinced to try the product	• Competitors can easily eliminate the effect of coupons • Consumers of coupons are already loyal supporters of the product • Fraud can result • Retailers are not always willing to co-operate • Many coupons are not redeemed - this leads to waste
Competitions	• Attract consumers to stores • Causes consumers to be involved and interested in the product • Attention is focused on the firm/product	• Consumers are lax in executing the task that the competition requires of them • Poorly planned competitions can cause the consumer to react negatively towards the product • Requires an aggressive advertising campaign to introduce the competition • Effect is short term in nature
Free samples	• Consumers are given the opportunity to test the product • Can be used as an offensive or defensive mechanism • Suitable for the introduction of new products or to attract new consumers for the product	• Very expensive promotion method • Not suitable for expensive and slow-moving items • Wasting of the product occurs (as much as 20 % of the samples are wasted) • Potential consumers are not always reached; samples often end up in the wrong hands
Consumer deals	• Effective in the testing of new products/brands • Stimulates the demand for products in off-season times or in the maturity of the product life cycle • Encourages and stimulates impulsive buying • Stimulates repeat purchases or support	• Retailers can buy the product at normal prices • Results in increased packaging costs • Brand loyalty is not necessarily created • Can be harmful to the image of the product
Premiums	• Effective in stimulating the support of a store or a product • Support is not directly linked to a price discount; the consumer receives something of value in return for his support • Repeat purchases are encouraged • Stimulates impulsive buying	• Not all products are suited for this type of sales promotion • Difficult to select a suitable premium article that is exceptional • Causes additional administrative burden and costs • Repeat purchases decrease as soon as consumers have collected enough premium articles
Point-of purchase displays	• Stimulates impulsive buying • Serve as a supplement to the advertising campaign • Ensure that the product is uniformly and attractively displayed	• Retailers are often inundated with these materials and are not always willing to co-operate • Retailers also want to gain advantage from this attempt; they therefore only allow displays where they too can gain • Sufficient space for an effective display is often not available
Demonstrations in stores	• Effective in attracting the attention of consumers and convincing them to purchase the product • Advantages of the product can be observed easily	• Relatively expensive • Mainly limited to large stores • Limited to products that can be easily demonstrated

15.3.3.2 *Sales promotion methods directed at dealers*

Manufacturers who primarily make use of dealers to distribute their product(s) to the final consumer usually employ sales promotion methods aimed at the middleman. The objectives of these methods are the following: first, sales promotion methods are used to convince middlemen to stock a particular product, to stock sufficient supplies, and possibly to carry a portion of the holding costs. Secondly, these methods are used to convince retailers to devote special attention to the supplier's products and to allocate sufficient shelf-space for the product(s). Thirdly, sales promotion methods assist the dealers in communicating with the consumer.

A number of sales promotion methods directed towards dealers will now be discussed.

Co-operative advertising

Co-operative advertising is the result of an agreement between the retailer and the manufacturer in which the manufacturer undertakes to settle a specified portion of the retailer's advertising expenses if he advertises the manufacturer's products in the local market.

Co-operative advertising holds the following advantages for the manufacturer:

- A greater amount of advertising results.
- Advertisements can be 'localised' or custom-tailored to adapt to specific target markets.
- Consumers are informed as to exactly where the product is obtainable.
- Contributes to improved dealer relations and better co-operation between producers and dealers.

For the dealer, co-operative advertising offers the following advantages:

- The retailer can advertise on a regular basis.
- Retailers can benefit from a well-designed co-operative programme because the manufacturer provides it.
- The quality of advertising is usually much better than what the retailer could afford.

Trade deals and promotional allowances

Trade deals are sales promotion devices which a manufacturer uses to encourage and secure retail distribution for a product or to generate extra promotional support and attention for products by middlemen. Trade deals usually take the following forms:

- Discounts and buying allowances, based on the quantity purchased, the time of the purchase and additional orders placed.
- Free goods are usually supplied for purchasing a specified amount of a particular product, eg one free case of beer for every twelve cases ordered.

- Advertising allowances are incentives which usually take the form of a monthly payment to middlemen for advertising a maufacturer's product, equivalent to a percentage of gross product purchases per specified time period.
- Display allowances are allocated to retailers who build special displays for a manufacturer's products according to specifications laid down in a formal contract between the parties.

Competitions

Competitions as a sales promotion method attempt to increase the motivation and productivity of sales personnel and dealers through an appeal to their competitive spirit. The goals of competitions can vary from increasing the level of total sales and profitability to the promotion of slow-moving or seasonal items, stimulation of a specific model or product line, securing new consumers, stimulating special displays or pushing new products. Competitions are popular in the life insurance, cosmetics, motor, and petroleum industries.

Two important considerations in making a sales competition successful are the duration and nature of the competition. While there are no established guidelines, the competition duration should provide sufficient time to build enthusiasm and provide all participants with a reasonable chance of success. The largest single disadvantage of competitions is that the benefits of competitions are short term in nature, and sales decrease the moment the competition ends.

Sales conferences

Sales conferences involving sales personnel or intermediaries are an effective means of disseminating information and stimulating greater effort. They provide an opportunity for the company to accomplish the following specific goals:

- to introduce new products, models or product lines;
- to explain an advertising campaign;
- to announce specific sales promotions and announce changes and explain the reasons for changes;
- to discuss problem areas;
- to provide training;
- to develop team spirit.

Sales brochures

Sales brochures provide manufacturers with the opportunity of presenting detailed information regarding the variety of models, styles, colours, optional features and technical specifications of its products. These brochures provide a wealth of information to dealers, as well as providing information to consumers when they make enquiries about certain products.

Trade shows and exhibitions

Several manufacturers of consumer and industrial goods make use of trade shows and exhibitions to exhibit their products. They provide the opportunity for introducing new products and new models, and the conducting of demonstrations.

The third step in the management of a sales promotion programme (see Figure 15.3) is the implementation and co-ordination of the programme. This important step will be discussed in the following section.

15.3.4 Implementation and co-ordination of the programme

15.3.4.1 *Implementation*

After the objectives of the sales promotion programme have been formulated and methods for achieving these objectives have been decided upon, the programme must be implemented. In this phase, attention must be devoted to the delegation of authority and responsibility, the execution of the sales promotion programme and the co-ordination of activities in the organisation to ensure that individuals accomplish their tasks in a thorough, professional and timely manner.

The **delegation of authority and responsibility** for the execution of the sales promotion programme is especially important when the firm's organisational structure does not cater for a separate department with the responsibility for sales promotion methods. In this case, the responsibility for sales promotions is usually distributed among the marketing communication and sales managers. Thus marketing communication management can be responsible for coupons, premiums (special offers), competitions, brochures and co-operative advertising, while sales managers are responsible for trade shows and exhibitions, sales conferences, trade deals and allowances, displays and demonstrations in stores. In some cases, the services of institutions such as advertising agencies, consultants and pamphlet distributors can be utilised.

An important facet requiring attention during the implementation phase is the **formulation of conditions** which intermediaries and consumers must satisfy in order to be eligible for the advantages of sales promotion methods.

The following examples are prerequisites or requirements which require attention:

- minimum purchasing quantities;
- displaying conditions;
- trade-in conditions for intermediaries;
- specifications as to who may participate;
- producing evidence of purchases;
- expiry dates.

The **time span** of sales promotion programmes can vary. Some programmes are of a shorter duration than others, for example those used to get rid of slow-moving inventory, or the introduction of a new packaging method for a product. Some programmes can be more long term in nature, while others can even continue for an indefinite period of time. The time span of a sales promotion programme must be linked to the objective of the programme. Research has revealed, however, that if the duration of a specific sales promotion programme becomes too drawn out the stimulation ability of the attempt will be damaged, with the result that consumers will consider it a normal purchasing condition and not a sales promotion method. The optimum duration of the sales promotion programme should be the same as the average purchasing cycle of the product.[11]

15.3.4.2 *Co-ordination*

Each of the sales promotion programmes must be co-ordinated in such a way that they are linked to the other marketing communication programmes of the enterprise. For example, sales promotion material must be available in good time for sales conferences, coupons must be ready for use when the packaging of a product is printed or when the product is packaged, special displays in stores must coincide with advertising campaigns in the media. This interdependence with other marketing communication efforts makes co-ordination imperative and contributes to the attainment of synergistic advantages for the various pro-grammes. An advertising campaign providing information can be supplemented by a persuasion element from sales promotion methods. Sales personnel can then also act as co-ordinators of sales promotion programmes.

Specific weak points can be identified in the co-operation between advertising and sales promotion methods. Integration of sales promotion programmes and advertising campaigns is often lacking because of the fact that several different persons or departments are responsible for advertising and sales promotion. Moreover, short-sighted budget considerations can also be disadvantageous to the integration of campaigns.

Another weakness is that often no attempt is made to research the influence of corporate campaigns, with the result that synergistic advantages are not always identified and utilised.

The equilibrium between advertising and sales promotion methods is determined by the following factors:

- **Phase of the product in its life cycle.** Both advertising and sales promotion methods are important in the introduction and maturity phases, while advertising plays a more important role in the growth phase. (The product life cycle will be discussed in Chapter 18.)
- **Consumer loyalty.** Advertising will be dominant in situations where consumer loyalty is apparent, while sales promotion methods will be prominent if consumer loyalty is low or absent.
- **Business strategy.** The business strategy will determine the ratio between these two marketing communication elements.
- **Behaviour of competitors.** When competitors launch sales promotion pro-grammes the enterprise is forced to seek methods that will negate the attempts of competitors to gain entrance into its target markets.
- **Target markets at which marketing efforts are aimed.** Some target markets can be reached more effectively by using sales promotion methods than advertising.

It is the task of marketing management to co-ordinate the various marketing communication actions and allocate the marketing communication budget effectively. The last step in the management of a sales promotion campaign is the evaluation thereof.

15.3.5 Evaluation of the sales promotion programme

The evaluation of the results of a sales promotion programme is extremely difficult. *On the one hand* sales promotion methods normally form part of a total marketing communication campaign and, *on the other hand,* a sales promotion programme often consists of a variety of methods. Thus the effect of a specific sales promotion method cannot be easily isolated. In spite of the abovementioned complicating factors, genuine attempts need to be made in order to determine the effectiveness of such a promotional programme.

Prior evaluation of a sales promotion method must be initiated in order to identify any deficiencies or potential problems so that these may be rectified before a full-scale campaign is introduced. The objective of prior evaluation may also be to select various methods that will be used. This is usually accomplished with the aid of panels, focus groups or experiments.

Results evaluation takes place either after the completion of the programme, or during the period in which it is in full swing. This evaluation can be performed by considering the following:

- reactions of the sales personnel (sales force);
- reactions of dealers;
- sales patterns;
- changes in market share;
- opinions of consumers;
- number of coupons or other sales promotion material redeemed or received.

Programme evaluation occurs when the total sales promotion programme is reviewed in order to determine whether:

- objectives have been achieved;
- the campaign was cost-effective;
- the co-ordination was effective;
- deficiencies have emerged which need to be rectified for future campaigns; and
- success factors were apparent which can be repeated in future campaigns.

In conclusion, it is clear that sales promotion methods are important marketing communication elements and they therefore need to be thoroughly planned, implemented and evaluated. The management of a sales promotion programme thus demands intensive reflection in order to benefit from the synergistic advantages that exist in a well-co-ordinated marketing communication programme. Publicity is the fourth marketing communication element that will be discussed. It is apparent that creativity in the selection of sales promotion methods can earn publicity for the enterprise, especially because of the fact that exceptional methods are often most newsworthy.

15.4 PUBLICITY

15.4.1 Nature of publicity

Publicity embraces the non-personal stimulation of demand for a product of the enterprise by making available to the mass media actual newsworthy information and, in so doing, obtaining a favourable and free coverage of the enterprise and/or its products in the relevant media.[12] The primary objective of publicity as a communication method is to inform the public and to develop an awareness of the enterprise, its products, and its services. Other specific objectives are also set for specific publicity programmes.

Sometimes the aim of publicity is to establish and improve a firm's image. For example, a business can establish an image of social involvement if it receives wide publicity for its work in upgrading the less privileged groups of society. Development of a specific image for a product can also be the objective of publicity. For example, the vehicles that participate in the Total Rally gain publicity by means of creating a quality image for the vehicle (especially for the winner). In the case of negative publicity experienced by a business (eg impurities are discovered in the product, or the product is declared unsafe, or the advertising campaign is declared unrealistic), the aim of the publicity campaign will be to negate the unfavourable reactions and perceptions that have developed. Corrective press declarations in these circumstances are welcomed by news media.

Publicity offers the following advantages:

- The business does not usually pay directly for publicity. This does not imply that there are no costs involved in publicity; there are in fact indirect costs such as salaries of personnel, the arranging of news conferences and receptions. Some newspapers insist on the placing of an advertisement together with the news report.
- The credibility of the publicity message is high because it is supplied by an independent medium (eg newspapers, the radio, television or magazines).
- The news component in the media is more acceptable and believable to the public than advertisements.
- A mass audience is reached within a short period.

But publicity also has the following disadvantages:

- The enterprise has almost no control over the message which is finally broadcast or published. Although a carefully edited press release can overcome this difficulty, it remains the particular medium's privilege to decide what news it is going to publish concerning the product or service. Mistakes as a result of misinterpretation often occur. The enterprise also has no control over the specific placing of the report, nor over the other reports and advertisements that are placed alongside its report.
- Unfortunately, negative events often have more publicity value for news media than do positive events. A disaster or an unfortunate occurrence will receive coverage far easier than, for example, the opening of a new store.
- It is also difficult to ensure that publicity will be given at the correct time. News of the opening of a new shop published only some days after the event is far less effective than coverage on the day of the opening.

15.4.2 Types of publicity

An enterprise can obtain publicity via news or press releases, sponsorships, articles, conferences and letters.

News or press releases usually consist of a description (one to two pages) of a newsworthy occurrence that is made available to the media. If necessary, the press release can be supplemented with relevant photographs.

Sponsorships are a popular means of gaining publicity, for example sports sponsorships for tennis (Standard Bank), rugby (Bankfin) and cricket (Panasonic).

Publicity can also be obtained through an **article** in which a particular aspect is discussed in detail. This type of article is usually written for a specific newspaper or magazine, for example an article regarding the launch of a new motor model.

News or press conferences are usually arranged for a specific or exceptional announcement. They are held at a central venue where the press is present, and an opportunity for questions is given after a senior personnel member has made the announcement. A package of information is usually also made available at a media conference, for example the procedure followed by Eskom with the announcement of tariff increases.

Letters can be written to the editor of a newspaper or magazine in which a business states its point of view concerning a particular issue, imparts information, or rectifies a misunderstanding.[13] Such letters often evoke reaction.

15.4.3 Development of a publicity plan[14]

The total publicity effort needs to be carefully planned to ensure maximum advantage from the communication method used. The various steps to be taken when formulating a publicity plan are shown in Figure 15.6. Each of these steps is discussed below.

Formulation of publicity objectives

The objectives of publicity can be twofold. On the one hand, the objective can be to **stimulate the demand** for a product by providing information or by means of a persuasive message. On the other hand, publicity can have as its objective the **furtherance and/or protection of the image** of the enterprise.

Allocation of responsibility

Enterprises have various alternatives to select from as to who will accept responsibility for publicity. The enterprise can arrange its own publicity or it can make use of other external sources for assistance (eg advertising practitioners or a public relations consultant).

In a marketing-orientated business, the **marketing department** is closely linked to the market. Marketing management is aware of the plans of competitors and continually monitors the reaction of consumers. This department is responsible for the planning of the entire marketing communication campaign and thus it is also responsible for publicity, which forms part of this campaign. The realisation that publicity has a communication role to fulfil and must effect marketing advantages is very clear to the marketing department. It is for these reasons that one can assume that the marketing department is largely responsible and should be responsible for the publicity plan. The public relations department in the enterprise must assist in making arrangements, drawing up the news release, negotiating and corresponding with the media, and in the execution of action plans. The disadvantage of this alternative is that it is expensive to employ communications professionals in the various departments (areas) on a permanent basis. Usually only large enterprises can afford this luxury.

The use of **external institutions** has many advantages. They usually have an independent and objective approach to publicity and usually have good relations with the news media. An advertising practitioner (agent) or a public relations consultant can draw on a wide range of skills found in this type of business. They usually have access to a variety of specialist services, such as graphic artists, photographers, copywriters and marketing researchers. Publicity services are often required on an ad hoc basis and therefore it is cheaper for a business to make use of an external institution than to employ personnel on a permanent basis.

FIGURE 15.6   Steps in the formulation of a publicity plan

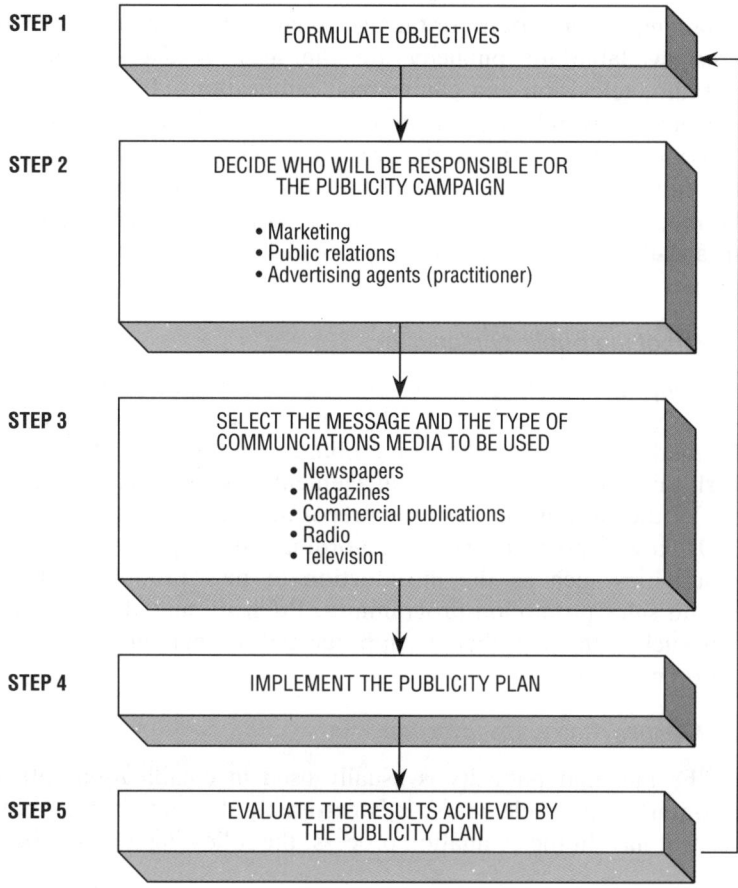

It is also possible for the marketing department to execute the publicity plan **in co-operation** with an external institution. This is the obvious manner in which to execute the publicity plan since it is the responsibility of marketing management to manage the publicity plan, especially in cases where the product or the sales thereof can be affected.

Selection of the message and media type

The selection of the message and the media type to be used is the third step in the drawing up of a publicity plan. In order to achieve the objective that has been set for the publicity plan, the publicity event must be carefully selected and the message must be well formulated. The event that will receive publicity must be identified, and if necessary publicity must be created. In the first case, an attempt is made to identify newsworthy events and then provide the press with this information. Examples of newsworthy events are for example, the promotion of personnel, or the announcement of financial results (annual reports). Publicity can also be created by, for example, sponsoring a newsworthy event such as a sports event, entertaining senior citizens, or taking orphaned children on excursions.

The media available for publicity are the mass media — newspapers, magazines, radio, television and commercial publications. In some cases, for example in general press releases, an attempt is made at obtaining news coverage in all possible media. In contrast to this, certain publicity messages can be more target-orientated and then the choice of the specific media type is important, because the medium selected (motor vehicle news in motor vehicle magazines rather than a daily paper) must reach a particular target audience in the best possible manner.

Implementation of the publicity plan

This fourth step in the formulation of a publicity plan requires careful management which must be particularly aimed at ensuring that publicity is actually obtained in the media and that it is obtained at the correct time. In order to accomplish this, it is necessary for management to know what the needs and practices are of the various media in the preparation and provision of publicity messages. Of key importance is the co-ordination of publicity with other marketing activities such as the introduction of new products, advertising campaigns, and sales promotion programmes. Publicity must be arranged and organised in such a manner that it supports and strengthens the marketing communication message.

Evaluation of results

Because of the fact that publicity is usually used in combination with other marketing communication elements, it is extremely difficult to determine the specific effects it has. In the evaluation process, the following needs to be taken note of:

- The **number of exposures** obtained in the media. This method does not provide any indication of how many people were exposed to the report.

- The **change in awareness or attitude** that has been effected by the publicity plan. This type of evaluation demands market research, in which the level of awareness or attitude is determined both before and after the implementation of the publicity plan.
- The **influence on sales**. Sales can be monitored when the objective of the publicity plan was a direct sales reaction.

15.5 SUMMARY

In this chapter sales promotion methods and publicity, as elements of the marketing communication process, were discussed. The nature of each of the two methods was discussed and a broad explanation was given on how marketing management should plan, implement and evaluate these elements. The eventual success attained with each of the methods will depend on the manner in which they are integrated with the advertising and personal selling elements of marketing communication. In this way synergistic advantages can be achieved which will have a larger effect than the individual activities.

REFERENCES

1. Wright, JS et al. 1977. *Advertising*. New York: McGraw-Hill, p 629.
2. Luick, JF and Ziegler, WL. 1968. *Sales Promotion and Modern Merchandising*. New York: McGraw-Hill, p 4.
3. Stanley, RE. 1977. *Promotion*. Englewood Cliffs, New Jersey: Prentice-Hall, p 308.
4. Ailloni-Charas, D. 1984. *Promotion: A Guide to Effective Promotional Planning, Strategies and Executions*. New York: John Wiley & Sons, p 11.
5. Kotler, P. 1986. *Principles of Marketing*. Englewood Cliffs, New Jersey: Prentice-Hall, p 499.
6. Assael, H. 1990. *Marketing: Principles and Strategy*. Chicago: The Dryden Press, p 449.
7. Koekemoer, L. 1987. *Marketing Communications Management: A South African Perspective*. Durban: Butterworths, p 453.
8. *Marketing Mix*. January 1988, p 21.
9. Koekemoer op cit, p 454–5.
10. Govoni, N, Eng, R & Galper, M. 1986. *Promotional Management*. Englewood Cliffs, New Jersey: Prentice-Hall, p 417.
11. Kotler, P. 1984. *Marketing Management: Analysis, Planning and Control*. Englewood Cliffs, New Jersey: Prentice-Hall, p 666.
12. Lucas, GHG (ed). 1983. *Die Taak van die Bemarkingsbestuur*. Pretoria: Van Schaik, p 400.
13. Govoni op cit, pp 464–5.
14. Evans, JR and Berman, B. 1985. *Marketing*. New York: MacMillan Publishing Co, p 513–516.

CASE STUDY

HIGH STREET MOTORS

Background

Piet van Zyl, after completing high school, decided on a business career but his father wished him to study further. Piet, however, bagan working as a salesman in Edgars and was quickly promoted to sales manager of the Western Transvaal area. He worked as a sales manager for four years.

During March 1990 Piet's father, who was a prosperous farmer in the Nothern Free State, told Piet that a well-known automobile service station in town was to be sold. The previous owner of High Street Motors was liquidated only two years after he took ownership.

Piet had good business acumen and after evaluating the opportunity carefully he left Edgars and bought the service station with the financial assistance of his father. He was of the opinion that the service station, despite its neglected appearance and weak image, could be a success with the right product line, good service and good management. Piet took over the Toyota agency from the previous owner. The town in which High Street Motors was located had been in existence for over fifteen years (under a different name), was known for its large number of automobile dealers and road cafés because it was on the main road from the PWV to the south. High Street Motors was the first service station on the south entrance to the town and also had adequate facilities for heavy trucks. It was next to a very popular take-away fast-foods restaurant.

Competition

Piet immediately realised that there were many competitors in the market. Besides the Nissan, Volkswagen and Delta dealers there were also eight other garages and service stations in the town. When scanning the market before deciding to purchase High Street Motors it became clear to Piet that the Volkwagen and Nissan dealers were busy with aggressive marketing campaigns and were also improving on service quality. The service offered by the other competitors was poor, their attitude being that they were doing automobile owners a favour by helping them.

The market

A superficial market investigation showed that Toyota had 35 per cent of the light commercial vehicle market and 25 per cent of the passenger automobile market in town and surrounding areas, the biggest competitors being Volkswagen, Nissan and Delta.

The population of the town and district was, according to the last census, 8 880 whites and 18 500 other population groups. The town was popular with pensioners, who made up about half of the white residents.

The automobile market mainly consisted of a farming community, which was suffering badly under a severe drought. The drought had a direct influence on the purchasing of new automobiles. Other economic indicators, however, were positive. Gold and coal mines were to be opened in 1993 while Eskom was planning a large electrical supply station.

Marketing

After having bought High Street Motors, Piet tried his utmost to increase his turnover. He found the first year very satisfying as it was a new beginning and a new career for him. He soon became anxious about the fact that sales of new motor vehicles started to stagnate. Many whites, especially farmers, had withdrawn their patronage from High Street Motors because of the bad service given by the previous owner. High Street Motors still had a negative image. Whites also tended to favour other automobile models.

Previously the service station had been well known, for more than ten years, under the name South End Motors. During this time marketing was never considered important as the previous owner was quite satisfied with the support he received and regarded marketing as an unnecessary expenditure. The man from whom Piet bought High Street Motors cancelled the weekly advertisement in the local newspaper and refused to sponsor any activities and ventures of the local community. He regarded them as unnecessary as he could in any case rely on support because he was the only Toyota dealer in town as well as being the first service station on the southern entrance to town.

Piet's experience at Edgars, however, made him aware of the importance of marketing and the role of special promotions to encourage sales and patronage. Customer satisfaction had his first priority and he actively tried to improve customer service.

Future

Piet wanted to do everything in his power to market his enterprise actively by utilising sales promotion methods and improved service quality. He was aware of the following threats and problems:

— The continuing rise in prices of new vehicles which influenced sales negatively. The negative influence, however, presented a challenge to the service workshop as vehicles and implements were brought in for repair services. Owners rather had them repaired than buy new ones.
— The new highway currently under construction, to be completed by 1993. This project would cause the traffic flow to bypass the town. About 60 per cent of High Street Motors' petrol sales were to customers currently travelling through the town.

QUESTIONS

1. Identify and evaluate the market segments on which High Street Motors should in the future concentrate its efforts.

2. Which sales promotion methods could Piet van Zyl utilise to stimulate the turnover of new vehicle and petrol sales as well as that of the service workshop?

3. Which long-term marketing strategies could be considered by Piet van Zyl to counter the threats confronting his venture?

CHAPTER 16

PRICE AND PRICE DETERMINATION

16.1 INTRODUCTION

The purpose of this chapter is to explain the concept 'price' as well as to describe the process of price determination from the firm's viewpoint. This chapter enables the reader to understand:

- the meaning of price for the consumer and the firm;
- why prices are important for the firm and the community;
- the pricing objectives of a firm;
- why not all firms determine the selling prices of their products; and
- how firms determine prices.

From the consumer's viewpoint the approach by firms towards prices is often confusing. Some of the reasons are:

- The same products are often available at varying prices from different retailers.
- Many retailers consult a price list and thus do not themselves determine the selling prices of their products.
- In many large firms the selling prices of products are not even known to top management, and these prices are often determined by the application of particular formulae by lower managerial levels.
- With bar coding the prices do not even appear on the products but are read by electronic scanners at the till and printed on the cash register slip (see Chapter 9, section 9.4.7).

From the marketer's viewpoint the behaviour of the consumer in respect of prices is similarly bewildering because:

- Some consumers purposely select expensive products.

- Other consumers patronise only those retailers known for their exclusivity and high prices.
- Another group of consumers is brand loyal and buys the more expensive products even if cheaper trade marks of the same type of product are available.
- Other consumers are born bargain hunters. Should the retail price of a product represent a bargain to them, they will buy the product, even if it is not really required for the satisfaction of an immediate need. In this case it is the low price itself which actually offers the consumer need-satisfaction.
- Yet another consumer group will refuse to buy a particular product if its selling price is in their opinion too low — the product is then considered to be of dubious quality.

Prices of some products and services are designated by a variety of terms.

Price terms

Product/service	Term indicating price
Land	Rent
Labour	Wage/Salary
Capital	Interest/Dividend
Entrepreneurship (successful)	Profit
Entrepreneurship (unsuccessful)	Loss
Transport	Fare
Electricity	Tariff
Insurance	Premium

ORGANISATION OF THE CHAPTER

The meaning of price: To the consumer and to the firm.

The importance of prices: To the firm and to the community.

Price-takers: Why enterprise are price-takers, price control, price maintenance, price leadership.

Objectives of the enterprise and the role of price: Objectives of the firm, role of prices in the earning and sharing of profits.

Pricing objectives: Profit objectives, sales volume objectives.

Market forms: Characteristics of the different market types, price determination under perfect competition, oligopoly, monopoly and monopolistic competition.

Elasticity of demand: Price elasticity, income elasticity.

Determination of basic price.

> **Cost as a basis for pricing:** Cost terms, total cost as a basis for pricing, variable cost per unit as a basis for pricing, desired contribution ratio as a basis for pricing, desired profitability as a basis for pricing, cost of the scarce production factor as a basis for pricing.
>
> **Demand as a basis for pricing:** Influence of the micro-, macro- and market environments on demand, the demand band.
>
> **Competition as a basis for pricing:** Identifying the competitors, price changes by the marketer, decisions following a price change, reaction by competitors to price changes.

16.2 THE MEANING OF PRICE

The meaning of price to the final consumer and to the firm is discussed next.

16.2.1 The meaning of price to the consumer

The consumer unconsciously attaches two meanings to a price and these depend on his interpretation of value. The **return value** is the need-satisfaction which the product provides to the consumer, and the **replacement value** is the amount of money which he has to pay in exchange for the product — the price the consumer has to pay for the product, or the retail price.

The price which a consumer pays for a product is theoretically lower than the price he would be prepared to pay rather than going without the product. The consumer's need-satisfaction from the product is thus greater than the need-satisfaction he sacrifices by paying the price for the product. This surplus need-satisfaction is known as the **consumer surplus** and is illustrated in Figure 16.1.

In Figure 16.1 a consumer's demand curve for a product is DD₁ and he buys OQ units at a price of OP each. The return value of the last unit which the consumer buys is equal to its replacement value; in other words the price of the product is apparently just as much as the value of the product to the consumer. According to the law of diminishing returns all the previous products offer more utility to the consumer than the last unit. The consumer nevertheless pays the same price for all the product units and the previous units thus provide a surplus need-satisfaction. The consumer surplus in Figure 16.1 is thus PDE. The consumer surplus is the difference between the amount the consumer would be willing to pay for OQ units, namely ODEQ, and the amount he actually pays, namely OQ units at OP, that is OPEQ. (This analysis calls for various assumptions, such as a steady marginal utility of money and the measurability of need-satisfaction or utility.)

FIGURE 16.1   Consumer surplus

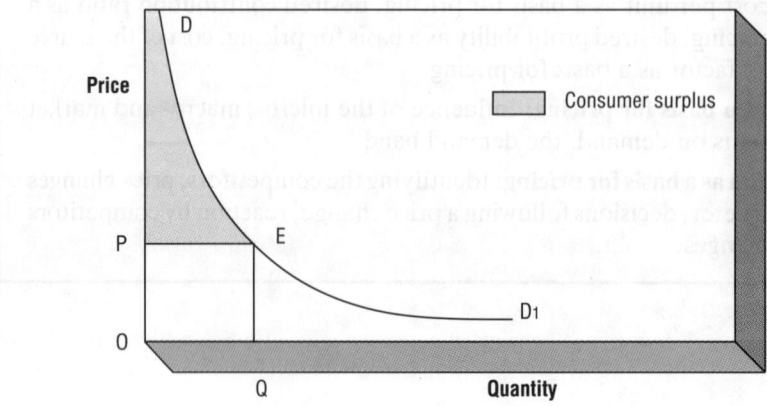

16.2.2 The meaning of price to the enterprise

The same simple explanation does not suffice when price is considered from the viewpoint of the firm. Many firms are multi-product firms, and charge different prices for different products. It is therefore possible, for example, to calculate an average selling price for the product mix. Even firms marketing only one type of product often quote different prices for different clients because of different qualities, the quantities bought, the conditions of sale, and the geographical location of the buyers. For such firms the price of their products is an average price realised from the prices at which products are sold to different buyers.

The importance of prices is subsequently discussed from the viewpoints of the individual firm and the community respectively.

16.3 THE IMPORTANCE OF PRICES

16.3.1 The importance of prices to the individual enterprise

The profitability formula can be expressed as:

$$\frac{\text{total income} - \text{total cost}}{\text{total assets employed}} \times \frac{100}{1.}$$

Selling prices have an influence on the extent of profitability because they have a direct influence on the three components of the profitability formula, namely the total income, the total cost and the total assets employed.

Total income is obtained by multiplying the number of products marketed by their selling prices. The number of products marketed is influenced by all the product, distribution and marketing communication decisions of the firm *as well as* the selling prices of the products. A general guideline applicable here is the theory of demand. According to this theory the consumer normally buys less of a product when the price is high and more when the price is low.

Total cost is the sum of total fixed costs and total variable costs. Total variable costs are obtained by multiplying the number of products manufactured by their variable costs per product unit. As mentioned above, the number of products produced and marketed, and thus the total variable costs, are influenced by the selling prices of the products. The extent of the total variable costs influences the total cost directly. Total fixed costs are determined by the production volume, and the latter directly influences fixed costs such as depreciation, salaries and rent. Setting up a specific production volume necessitates the application of particular assets.

Total assets employed are influenced by selling prices (and vice versa) because the selling price of a product has a considerable effect on the method of production, and consequently also the type and cost of production facilities (assets). The following example is oversimplified but illustrates the preceding statement.

Let us suppose that either one of two production methods, A and B, enables a manufacturer to produce and market 10 000 units of product Z. The following data apply to the two production methods:

Item	Production method	
	A	B
Total assets required	R16 000	R40 000
Annual total costs	R28 000	R25 000
Number of Z products produced	10 000	10 000
Profitability at a selling price of:		

	A	B
R2,50	−18,75 %	0 %
R2,80	0 %	7,50 %
R3,00	12,50 %	12,50 %
R3,20	25,00 %	17,50 %

Production method A requires manually operated machines and skilled labour (compare the annual total costs), while production method B calls for automatic machinery but unskilled labour. If product Z sells at R3,20 per unit, production method A will result in a profitability of 25 per cent and production method B in a profitability of 17,5 per cent. The profitability of production methods A and B at different selling prices of product Z are shown in Figure 16.2.

FIGURE 16.2   The profitability of production methods A and B at various selling prices of product Z

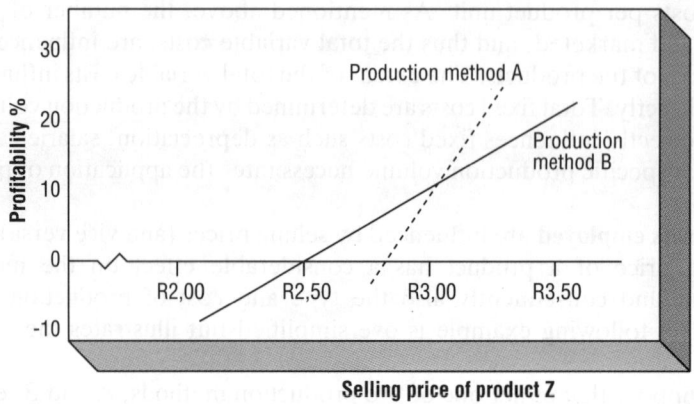

Figure 16.2 shows that production method B will offer a greater profitability than production method A if the selling price of product Z is lower than R3,00. Production method A on the other hand offers a greater profitability than production method B when the price of product Z exceeds R3,00.

16.3.2 The importance of price to the community

Viewed in a macro-sense and in a perfect free-market system, prices are inter alia responsible for the optimal allocation of the available factors of production among the members of the society. Prices determine inter alia how much and what is produced, how it is produced, and for whom it is produced. These aspects form part of the study of economics.

In a centrally planned economy the authorities plan the what, how much of, for whom and how something is to be produced. The price, however, is used to allocate the resources.

Perfect free-market and perfect centrally planned systems are, however, not to be found in practice; one finds systems containing features of both perfect free-market and centrally planned systems. In the Republic of South Africa, for example, the price of bread is set by the authorities while the price of fresh carrots is determined exclusively by demand and supply.

It is a fact that not all marketers make real price decisions. In order to decide, a choice among various options must at least be possible. The focus in this chapter is on firms which themselves determine the selling prices of their products. Attention is, however, focused first on price-takers, those firms for which the selling prices of their products can be regarded as given.

In the next section the reasons for the existence of price-takers as well as price control, resale price maintenance and price leadership in the Republic of South Africa are discussed.

16.4 PRICE-TAKERS

16.4.1 Reasons for the existence of price-takers

Some firms are largely price-takers. These enterprises, for various reasons, have very little influence on the selling prices of their products. A few examples are mentioned:

- The output of a particular product of an enterprise is relatively so small that it cannot have a meaningful influence on the supply of the product. Such situations are typical of the markets for primary products, such as fresh vegetables and fruit.
- The product is subject to price control. The present situation regarding price control in South Africa is set out in section 16.4.2.
- Resale price maintenance. Resale price maintenance is discussed in section 16.4.3.
- The price can be regarded as given because of a price leader in a particular industry. Price leadership is discussed in section 16.4.4.

16.4.2 Price control in the Republic of South Africa

Price control was introduced in the Republic of South Africa soon after the outbreak of World War II. The authorities at that time were of the opinion that the abnormal conditions of supply and shortages could create the opportunity for unfair high prices for some scarce goods and services. These special war measures were replaced by the Price Control Act, Act 25 of 1964. This Act makes provision for inter alia a price controller. The price controller can inter alia:

- fix maximum prices for certain products or services at which one person may sell to another;
- fix maximum prices for certain products or services at which one person may buy from another;
- prescribe the maximum amount of any deposit required for the return of a container in which the goods are sold;
- prescribe maximum gross profit margins for middlemen; and
- freeze prices at certain levels and on specific dates.

Price control can be formally or informally applicable to an industry or a single firm. In the case of informal price control an arrangement is made with an individual firm or with an industry that it will not unilaterally effect increased prices without the consent of the price controller. In the case of formal price control concerning an industry, a notice in this regard appears in the *Government Gazette*. Where only an individual firm is involved the price controller advises it thereof by letter.

The consequences of a price increase above the maximum price or cost plus the maximum profit margin of the approved price, namely legal prosecution, are the same whether the product is subject to formal or informal price control. With formal price control immediate steps can be taken against infringer(s), and with informal price control steps can be taken after the control has been formalised by a notice in the *Government Gazette* or by letter.

The number of products subject to formal and informal price control has declined considerably over the last few years. The introduction of price control in the past most probably centred around socio-political rather than economic considerations, and it is the declared policy of the present authorities to abolish price control in those cases where it is no longer necessary. For all practical purposes price control in terms of the Price Control Act does not exist. Soft drink bottles are the only products subject to formal price control (November 1991) and only the producer prices of black tea and the industrial prices of sugar are subject to informal price control.

Formal and informal price control in terms of the Price Control Act is administered by the Department of Trade and Industries. The prices of inter alia paraffin, petrol and power-paraffin are administered by the Department of Mineral and Energy Affairs, whilst the prices of some agricultural products, such as bread and maize, are fixed in accordance with the Marketing Act (Act 59 of 1968).

Marketers of products subject in one way or another to price control are price-takers with regard to their maximum prices. The Departments of Trade and Industries and of Mineral and Energy Affairs and the various agricultural control boards in terms of the Marketing Act of 1968 specify only maximum prices and gross profit margins. Firms which market at prices lower than these maximum prices can be regarded as price-makers.

16.4.3 Price maintenance in the Republic of South Africa

Vertical and horizontal price maintenance can be distinguished and can be applied individually or collectively. **Vertical price maintenance** occurs when an individual producer or group of producers prescribes to middlemen at what prices the product manufactured by the producer must be sold to the final consumer. If the middleman does not comply with this directive, the producer can inter alia withhold stocks from the middleman. **Horizontal price maintenance** usually occurs when all the enterprises on the same distribution level agree to charge a specific selling price for a particular product or service.

Price maintenance was at one stage common in the Republic of South Africa. From 1 July 1969, however, price maintenance was prohibited by Government Notice No 1038. This notice, however, excluded magazines, books and newspapers, inner tubes, tyres and fuel from the prohibition. Since then price maintenance on magazines, books, inner tubes and tyres has also been abolished, and fuel and newspapers were the only products in the Republic of South Africa legally subject to price maintenance.

On 2 May 1986 (Notice No 801, *Government Gazette* No 10211 of 2 May 1986) the then Minister of Trade and Industries (now the Minister of Trade, Industry and Tourism), in terms of section 10(1)*(d)* of the Maintenance and Promotion of Competition Act, 1979 (Act 96 of 1979), prohibited:

- resale price maintenance;
- horizontal price collusion;
- horizontal collusion on conditions of supply;
- horizontal collusion on market sharing; and
- collusive tendering.

The prohibition of 2 May 1986 is of the utmost importance to all marketers in the Republic of South Africa. Contravention of the prohibitions and subsequent conviction in a criminal court is punishable with a fine of R100 000 or five years' imprisonment.

The prohibitions apply to all goods and services, as well as professional and financial services, including goods and services supplied by the State. The aforesaid five practices were chosen because they occurred with regularity in the economy and have a serious restrictive effect on competition. Only the first two restrictive practices, namely resale price maintenance and horizontal price collusion, are discussed briefly.

Resale price maintenance

'. . . *(a)* means any agreement, arrangement, understanding, business practice or method of trading which has, or is likely to have, the effect of directly or indirectly compelling or inducing a reseller of any commodity to charge a particular, or a particular minimum resale price, whether or not such price is determined or is to be determined by calculation or by reference to any discount; and

(b) excludes the recommendation, by an individual supplier, of a resale price as a guide for the convenience of the reseller who may reduce such price at his discretion and which is not directly or indirectly enforced by means of the withholding of supplies, the denial of distribution rights or by means of any discriminatory sales condition or a penalty or by any other method likely to have such effect: Provided that where a recommended resale price appears on or in relation to a commodity, the words "recommended price" shall appear with such price.'[1]

Recommended or suggested prices, ie retail prices suggested by the producer to the middlemen, are not illegal. One of the results of this arrangement is that the retail prices of some products, such as cigarettes, at various types of retailers and in various places are more or less the same.

Horizontal price collusion

. . . *(a)* means any agreement, arrangement or understanding between or among two or more suppliers of any commodity, or of substantially similar commodities, to —

(i) charge a particular, or a particular minimum price; or
(ii) use in any way, any price as a recommended price or as a guide, whether or not such price is determined or is to be determined by calculation or by reference to any discount;

(b) includes the use of an association or of a company, close corporation or other juristic person in which such suppliers have an interest, to effect the horizontal price collusion in any way; and

(c) excludes, in respect of a professional service by members of an organised profession, the issue of a tariff of recommended fees as a guide for the convenience of the members of such profession and which is not directly or indirectly enforced or any structure of tariffs or fees authorised by law.'

The provisions of the prohibitions contained in Government Notice 801 do not apply in respect of any agreement, arrangement, understanding, business practice or method of trading between or among

'*(a)* a holding company and its wholly-owned subsidiary, or between companies which are the wholly-owned subsidiaries of the same holding company;

(b) close corporations which have only the same person or persons as members;

(c) companies of which all the shares are held by the same person or close corporation, or between such close corporation and such companies; or

(d) to exports (except to the BLS-countries).'[2]

On the recommendation of the Competition Board the Minister may, in a particular case, in terms of section 15(5)*(b)* of the Maintenance and Promotion of Competition Act, in writing grant exemption from any prohibition contemplated in this notice to such extent and subject to such conditions as may be specified in the exemption. A number of exemptions have already been granted by the Minister. The exemption that is probably a matter of common knowledge is that granted to the cement cartel in regard to horizontal price collusion, horizontal collusion on conditions of supply, and horizontal collusion on market sharing.

16.4.4 Price leadership in a particular industry

Price leadership is encountered when the selling prices of a particular firm(s) are followed by other firms in the industry. The price leader is usually the largest firm in the industry. The price leader attains his position informally, because a formal agreement on selling prices among the members of an industry may be regarded as price collusion by the authorities.

Price followers (price-takers) do not necessarily market their products at the same prices as those of the price leader, but maintain a consistent difference between their own selling prices and the selling prices of the price leader.

Most firms in the Republic of South Africa are relatively small and can be price followers for the reasons set out below:

- The smaller firms accept that the price leader is better equipped to determine selling prices.
- The smaller firms assume that the price leader is the most effective firm in the industry and that they have to follow his selling prices to be competitive.
- Price following can be the most convenient pricing method for smaller firms. By leaving the fixing of the price to the price leader, the price followers probably save time and money.
- Smaller firms often manufacture the same types of products by using the same production methods as the price leader does. A natural consequence of this decision is also to follow the selling prices of the price leader.
- The smaller firm can operate at full capacity. Under such circumstances a selling price of the price follower's products lower than that of the price leader's will serve no purpose, as the price follower cannot in any case execute additional orders.
- It is often expedient for a small firm to follow a price leader rather than to involve itself in a price war.

The explanation above does not imply that all small firms are price-takers. Many of the biggest firms in South Africa are also price-takers, especially when an industry is dominated by a single firm. Usually the world price of the product is followed, for example the LME prices (London Metal Exchange). The following of prices is not limited to metal prices only but also applies to a large number of other products.

In the following section a short discussion of the objectives of the firm is followed by the role of prices in the enterprise's objectives. Pricing objectives are directly related to the firm's objectives.

16.5 THE OBJECTIVES OF THE FIRM AND THE ROLE OF PRICE

16.5.1 Objectives of the enterprise

It can be stated that it is at times possible for a firm to have more than one objective, and even to aim at a collection of objectives. Because of particular circumstances emphasis can therefore be placed on one objective at one time and at other times on the other objective(s). The firm's objectives can be grouped in three phases:[3]

- *First,* the firm has capital at its disposal (partly obtained from the shareholders) which must be maintained to ensure the firm's **continuity**. Without continuity the next two phases are not possible.

- In the *second* place the firm must enlarge the available capital. A particular profit must be **earned** to make the next phase possible. This profit is usually expressed as a percentage of the capital required to earn the profit — the profitability.
- In the *third* phase the firm must **distribute** the profit among the persons to whom the enterprise has a responsibility to justify its right of existence over the long term. In the main this distribution takes place between the shareholders (dividends) and the community (inter alia sponsorships, bursaries and grants to universities, technikons and welfare institutions).

Only when the enterprise has secured its continuity can it earn and distribute.

16.5.2 The role of prices in relation to the objectives of the enterprise

Price, just as any other activity of the enterprise, influences the firm directly. Price, for example, influences inter alia the cash flow, the competitive situation, the stock turnover, debtors, the quality strategy, and eventually the objectives of the firm. Three aspects are distinguished: the role of prices in the earning and distribution of profit; the pricing objectives; and the relative unimportance of prices in the marketing strategy.

16.5.3 The role of prices in the earning and distribution of profit

Prices are important in profit earning and the collective objectives of the firm are important in the distribution of profit. The following are reasons why prices are important only in the profit earning process and why it is unscientific to apply low selling prices for the benefit of the community (the profit distribution process):

- In the *first* place the firm carries **risk** and it is extremely chancy to distribute profit before it is earned. Such action can prejudice the firm's continuity.
- In the *second* place it is possible that the consumer, who is supposed to benefit from low prices, could **reject** the low prices and a potential transaction is thus not realised.
- *Thirdly*, the **replacement value** (cost) of the product at the moment of exchange is unknown; consequently a price that satisfies the consumer and enables the firm to make a profit on the product is unknown.

The role of prices during the profit earning process should thus be aimed at a particular profitability objective. Only after this objective has been reached is it possible to realise the community objectives (profit distribution objectives).

16.6 PRICING OBJECTIVES

The ultimate objective of prices is to actualise the objectives of the firm (a particular profitability and responsibility towards the community). These objectives are usually pursued over the long term, and in the short term the pricing objectives serve as a frame of reference within which decisions on the selling price are taken. The choice of pricing objectives is influenced by inter alia the objectives of the firm and prevailing market conditions.

The following pricing objectives are discussed: profit, volume, and other pricing objectives.

16.6.1 Profit objectives

The following profit objectives are distinguished, namely maximum profit, target profit, satisfactory profit and profit on each product, and are dealt with in this section.

Maximum profit as a pricing objective

This particular profit objective does not mean much for control purposes, because the maximum is usually not quantifiable and thus no standard exists for judging the real profit performance. Maximum profit as a pricing objective can attract additional competitors and can also possibly damage the image of the firm.

Target profit as a pricing objective

A target profit usually starts with a planned profitability which the firm wants to attain.

Example of a target profit as a pricing objective

Number of units	100 000
Desired profitability	30%
Total assets	R2 000 000
Thus planned profit	R600 000
Planned profit per unit	R6
Total cost	R1 000 000
Thus total cost per unit	R10
Selling price per unit	R16
Margin on cost price	$\dfrac{16-10}{10} \times \dfrac{100}{1}$
	$= 60\%$

The greatest drawback of this pricing objective is that it is not always possible to apply a uniform margin on all the products of a multi-product firm. The various products in the product mix do not always have the same cost structure, demand, and competitors.

Satisfactory profit as a pricing objective

Satisfactory profit as the objective basically means that firms set a minimum objective, such as 10 per cent profit on the total assets employed. The 'satisfactory profit' can change in the course of time. An enterprise, for example, which wants to increase its production capacity but does not want to attract foreign capital for this purpose (to maintain inter alia the liquidity of the firm), will have a higher satisfactory profit than in a case where the conditions of a larger production capacity and the maintenance of liquidity do not apply.

Therefore, it seems that in practice there is no meaningful difference between a target profit and a satisfactory profit as pricing objectives. Just as the satisfactory amount of profit depends on the circumstances in which the firm finds itself, and also on its future expectations, so the target profit aimed at will also be influenced by the same circumstances. It can be assumed that a firm which attains its target profit in a particular year, but expects a decrease in the profits in the following year because of a recession, will set a lower target profit for the expected poor year. In the same way a firm aiming at a satisfactory profit will, under the same circumstances, set its satisfactory profit at a lower level compared with that of the previous year.

Profit on each product

A profit on each of the products of the firm is logical only if the firm manufactures one type of product. It is possible for firms with a wide product mix to show a greater total profit on all the products put together, even though showing a loss on one particular type of product. An example here is the well-known loss-leader which is used to increase the total turnover and profit of a retailer.

16.6.2 Sales volume objectives

The sales volume objectives discussed are the maintenance or increase of the market share, and the maximising of sales.

Maintenance or increase of the market share

Enterprises which want to increase their market shares by specific price decisions have to bear in mind inter alia the price elasticity of demand for their products and the reaction of competitors. A relatively inelastic demand for their products and competitors following a price cut can wreck any effort to increase the market share through the decrease of prices.

Maximising sales

The firm can aim at maximising its sales, taking into consideration a certain minimum profit level. Such action, however, is possible only if the firm has excess capacity and can make price decisions without being influenced by competitive action.

16.6.3 Other pricing objectives

Other pricing objectives which the firm can strive for are inter alia the prevention of competitive action, reasonable prices, low prices, continuity of the firm, growth, and social responsibility. These pricing objectives could, of course, also be included in the collection of objectives which the enterprise pursues at times.

Before discussing the determination of the basic price, it is necessary to pay attention to two aspects of economic theory, namely price determination in the different types of market, and the price elasticity of demand. These two aspects have an influence on the basic price.

16.7 ASPECTS OF THEORETICAL PRICE DETERMINATION AND PRICE ELASTICITY OF DEMAND

16.7.1 Market types

This section highlights a few aspects of economic theory on prices. It is synoptic and should not be regarded as an attempt to trespass on the field of micro-economics. Price determination and the interrelationship between the demand for and the price of a product (price elasticity of demand) are discussed in subsequent sections.

According to economic price theory the price of a product is determined by the supply of the product, represented by that part of the marginal cost curve above the average cost curve, the demand for the product, and the degree and extent of competition, expressed as the type of market in which the firm operates. The following discussion emphasises the last factor, namely the type of market. Ten different types of market, set out in Table 16.1, are distinguished.

Table 16.1 shows that the number of buyers and sellers in a particular marketing situation determine the type of market in which a firm conducts business. For example, a relatively small number of sellers and a relatively large number of buyers operate in an oligopolistic market. A particular situation develops where many buyers and sellers operate in a market. Perfect competition exists if the products are homogeneous, and monopolistic competition occurs where many buyers, many sellers, and product differentiation are found.

TABLE 16.1   The different types of markets as determined by the number of buyers and sellers in each market type

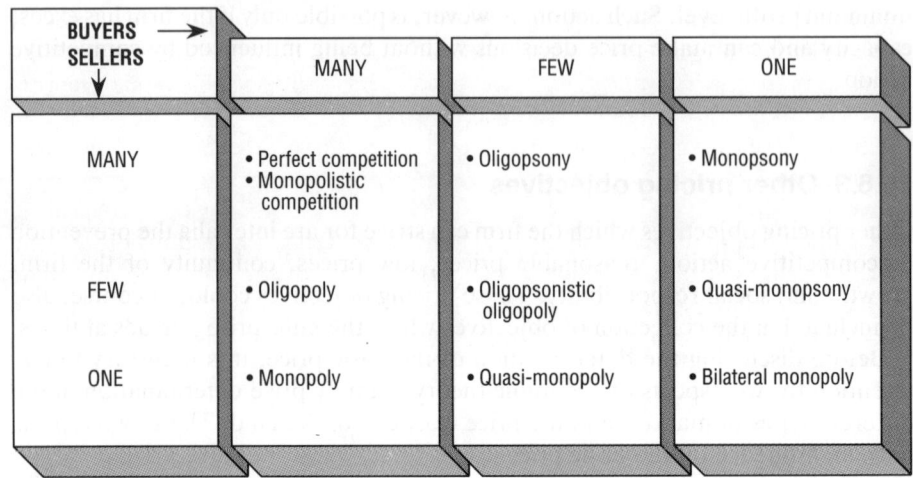

BUYERS → SELLERS ↓	MANY	FEW	ONE
MANY	• Perfect competition • Monopolistic competition	• Oligopsony	• Monopsony
FEW	• Oligopoly	• Oligopsonistic oligopoly	• Quasi-monopsony
ONE	• Monopoly	• Quasi-monopoly	• Bilateral monopoly

Source: Adapted from Schumann, CGW, Franzsen, DG & De Kock, G. 1957. *Ekonomie — 'n Inleidende Studie*. Stellenbosch/Grahamstown: Universiteitsuitgewers en -boekhandelaars (Pty) Ltd, p 201. (Own caption.)

The influence of each of the ten market types on the determination of the price will not be discussed here. Because the final consumers are usually a large number of buyers, it will suffice to remark briefly on pricing under conditions of perfect competition, oligopoly, monopoly and monopolistic competition.

16.7.2 Price determination

The theoretical analysis and description of pricing differs for each of the four market types to be discussed. What all the market types have in common is the fact that interaction between the demand for and the supply of a product determines its price.

The following assumptions regarding the supply of a product apply. The enterprise:

- has as its only objective the maximising of profit;
- produces and markets only one type of product, and in multi-product firms the products are continuously produced and marketed in the same ratios;
- knows what the total cost at each level of production is; and
- knows how many products it can market at each possible selling price.

The following assumptions apply regarding the demand. The consumer:

- is aware of the price and quality of all available goods and services;
- takes only the present situation into consideration when making a decision to buy and is not influenced by his learning experience or his expectations of the future; and
- plans his purchases in such a way that he derives maximum need-satisfaction.

Pricing under perfect competition

Under circumstances of perfect competition the individual marketer has no influence on the quantities supplied and hence the price. The products offered by the marketers are largely homogeneous, thus it makes no difference to the consumers from which marketers they buy. The suppliers in this type of market are price-takers rather than price-makers.

The price of the product under perfect competition is determined as indicated in Figure 16.3.

In Figure 16.3 MC is the marginal cost curve, AC the total average cost curve, and MI the marginal income curve. The MI curve is horizontal because the marketer can sell any number of the product at a fixed price per unit. The marketer maximises his profit should he produce and market OQ products at a price of OP each because the MC of the last product unit at this point is equal to the MI thereof.

Pricing under oligopoly

The price formation model of the oligopolist uses the familiar kinked demand curve shown in Figure 16.4. In Figure 16.4 the marginal cost curve, MC, crosses the marginal income curve, MI, at any point on the vertical part thereof, namely between Q and R. The oligopolist maximises his profit should he produce and market OQ products at a price of OP each. The vertical part in the MI curve is attributed to the kink in the demand curve (the average income curve, AI).

It does not pay the oligopolist to change the price of his product. Should the price be adjusted below OP, all the oligopolist's competitors follow suit and everybody is worse off than before. Should the oligopolist unilaterally increase his price above OP, his competitors do not follow suit and consequently the oligopolist loses customers to his competitors. At a price above OP the demand curve AI is relatively elastic and at prices lower than OP the demand curve is relatively inelastic.

Pricing under monopoly

Pricing under monopoly is illustrated in Figure 16.5. The monopolist maximises his profit at that number of products and price per product where the marginal cost is equal to the marginal income. In Figure 16.5 the marginal cost curve, MC, crosses the marginal income curve, MI, at quantity OQ and price OP.

The monopolist is in the fortunate position of being able to determine the price and the quantities offered of a particular product. Because there is only one supplier there is no question of product differentiation. In the Republic of South Africa monopolies exist in those cases where the authorities regard them to be in the public interest. From a marketing point of view a perfect monopoly cannot exist, because all marketers in a sense have to compete for the rand in the consumer's pocket.

FIGURE 16.3 Price determination under perfect competition

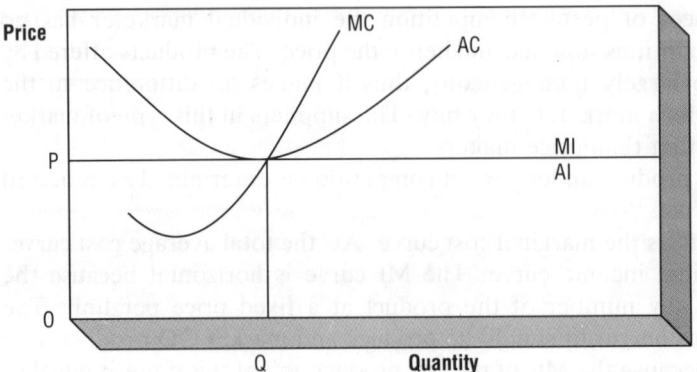

FIGURE 16.4 Price determination under oligopoly

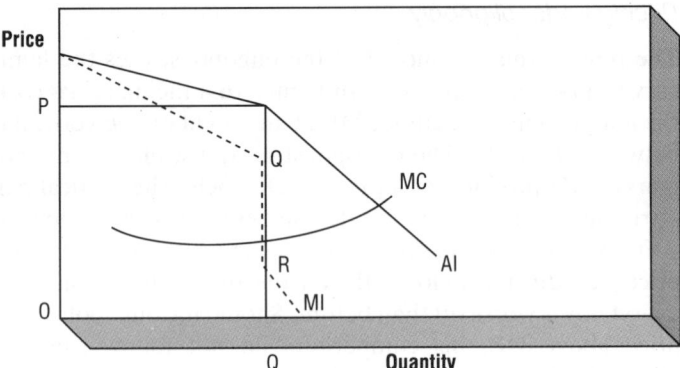

FIGURE 16.5
Price determination under monopoly

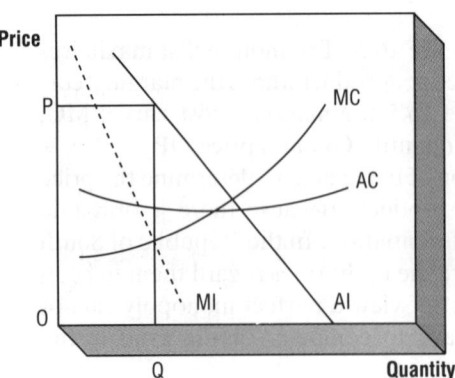

FIGURE 16.6 Price determination
under monopolistic competition

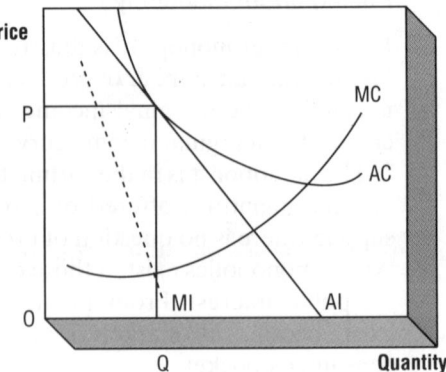

Key: MC = Marginal cost; AC = Average cost; MI = Marginal income; AI = Average income

Pricing under monopolistic competition

The degree of product differentiation in the Republic of South Africa causes the extensive incidence of monopolistic competition as a type of market. In this type of market individual competitors exert greater influence on the prices they can negotiate, as compared to perfect competition. Through marketing communication, brands, packaging, design and a host of other marketing decisions, competitors under monopolistic competition try to differentiate their virtually homogeneous products physically and/or psychologically from those of their rivals (product differentiation). As a generalisation it can be stated that the greater the consumer's brand insistence, the greater the degree of pricing freedom afforded a particular marketer under conditions of monopolistic competition. Pricing under monopolistic competition is illustrated in Figure 16.6.

In Figure 16.6 the marketer under conditions of monopolistic competition maximises his profit at a price of OP per product and at a production volume of OQ products. At this number of units the marginal cost curve (MC) crosses the marginal income curve (MI).

Pricing under monopolistic competition is similar to pricing under pure monopoly. Because of the competition under conditions of monopolistic competition the average cost of the products is equal to the average income thereof. Under pure monopoly (see Figure 16.5) the average income of the product is much higher than the average cost thereof.

16.7.3 The elasticity of demand

16.7.3.1 *Introduction*

According to traditional economic price theory more units of a product will be purchased by the buyer if the price is low and fewer will be bought if the price is high. This generalisation is described by the various price elasticities of demand. The quantity bought will also depend on the consumer's income and the price of, inter alia, substitute or complementary products. These generalisations are described by the price elasticity of demand, the income elasticity of demand and the cross elasticity of demand respectively. These aspects are discussed briefly.

16.7.3.2 *Price elasticity of demand*

The price elasticity of demand measures the sensitivity of the demand for a product in reaction to changes in the price of the product, and is obtained by dividing the change in the quantity demanded by the change in the price of the product.

Example:

If Q_1 = original quantity demanded;
Q_2 = new quantity demanded;

P_1 = original price; and
P_2 = new price,
the price elasticity of the demand (Ed) is:

$$\frac{Q_2-Q_1}{Q_1} \div \frac{P_2-P_1}{P_1}.$$

Five price elasticities of demand are identifiable:

- **Perfect price elasticity.** In this case the value of Ed is $-\alpha$. A very small price change will result in an infinitely large change in the quantity demanded.
- **Relative price elasticity.** The value of Ed lies between $>-\alpha$ and <-1. A price change will result in a more than proportional change in the quantity demanded.
- **Price elasticity of one.** The value of Ed is -1. The change in the quantity demanded will be proportionate to the change in price.
- **Relative price inelasticity.** The value of Ed is >-1 and <0. A price change will result in a smaller than proportional change in the quantity demanded.
- **Perfect price inelasticity.** The value of Ed is 0. The quantity demanded does not react to changes in the price.

It is possible that the price elasticity of demand for a product type, such as cigarettes, can be inelastic, while the price elasticity of demand for cigarettes of a particular brand (product item) can be elastic. The frequency of purchase, the necessity of and need for the product, and the comparability between brands count among the factors exerting an important influence on the price sensitivity of individual brands (product items) within a product type. This can be explained as follows:

- Individual brands in product types, such as baby foods where the **frequency** of purchase is high, tend to be price sensitive.
- The **necessity** of the product type for the consumer often has the result that changes in the selling prices of all brands will not affect the demand for the product type. If the product type in general is relatively unimportant to the consumer (such as potato chips and ice-cream as snacks), the demand, especially in the short term, will be adversely affected by price increases.
- The **comparability** of brands also influences the price sensitivity of brands. Consumers are usually less price-conscious about heterogeneous products (such as breakfast cereals) than other products which are more or less homogeneous (such as other grocery products). Breakfast cereals differ from each other with regard to inter alia packaging, size and type, thus complicating price comparison for the consumer.

Although the price elasticity of demand has limited practical application, it nevertheless offers some guidelines in the pricing of a product. Thus, price reductions in cases where the price elasticity of demand is perfectly or relatively price inelastic will probably result in a lower total income.

16.7.3.3 *The income elasticity of demand*

The income elasticity of demand measures the sensitivity of the demand for a product according to changes in the consumer's income, and is calculated by dividing the quantity demanded by the change in the consumer's income.

Example:
If Q_1 = original quantity demanded;
$\quad Q_2$ = new quantity demanded;
$\quad I_1$ = original income; and
$\quad I_2$ = new income,
the income elasticity of the demand (EI) is:

$$\frac{Q_2 - Q_1}{Q_1} \div \frac{I_2 - I_1}{I_1}$$

Three income elasticities of demand are distinguished, namely:

- An income elasticity >0 **and** <1. In this case the product becomes less important in the consumer's spending pattern as his income increases. The expenditure on the product therefore increases proportionally less than the income.
- An income elasticity >1. The product becomes more important in the consumer's spending pattern as his income increases, and demand therefor increases proportionally more than the income.
- A **negative** income elasticity means that the expenditure on the product decreases as the consumer's income increases. This happens in the case of so-called inferior products.

16.7.3.4 *Cross elasticity of demand*

The cross elasticity of demand measures the sensitivity of the demand for a product in reaction to changes in the price of a substitute or complementary product, and is obtained by dividing the change in the quantity demanded by the change in the price of the substitute or complementary product.

Example:
If AQ_1 = original quantity demanded of product A;
$\quad AQ_2$ = new quantity demanded of product A;
$\quad BP_1$ = new price of product B, and
$\quad BP_2$ = new price of product B,
the cross elasticity of demand for product A is:

$$\frac{AQ_2 - AQ_1}{AQ_1} \div \frac{BP_2 - BP_1}{BP_1}$$

If the cross elasticity is large and positive, products A and B are good substitutes for each other. Products A and B are complementary to each other if the cross elasticity is negative.

With substitute products a price decrease of product B results in a decrease in the demand for product A; a price increase of product B results in an increase in the demand for product A.

If products are complementary to each other a price reduction of product B will result in an increase in the demand for product A, and a price increase of product B will result in a decrease in the demand for product A.

16.7.4 Conclusion

The theory of price determination has, because of the impractical assumptions in the analysis, limited practical application for the marketer. Nevertheless, it offers some guidelines in the pricing of a product, such as:

- A low price of a product results in higher sales.
- A low price of a product which has substitutes results in lower sales of the substitute product.
- The sales of 'inferior' products decrease if the consumer's income increases.

16.8 DETERMINATION OF THE BASIC PRICE

The basic price of a product is simply that price obtainable from a specific price determination method. Stated differently: The basic price is the result of the method of price determination and the decision on the basic price is guided by the pricing objective. Deviations from this basic price occur because of, inter alia, quantity discounts and the geographical location of the buyers. These aspects are discussed in Chapter 17. To avoid repetition, price in this section refers to the basic price unless stated otherwise.

It is possible to draw up an impressive list of factors influencing the price of a product. However, it may be stated that within the framework of the marketing environment (especially the economic environment), the objectives of the firm and the pricing objectives, a price-maker has to consider mainly three factors in the determination of his price: the cost of the product; the demand for the product; and the degree and extent of competition. These three factors combined thus determine the price of a product to a great extent.

No practical formula exists to determine an ideal price for a product or service which will simultaneously satisfy the business objectives and also embrace all aspects of the cost of the product, the demand and competition. Different approaches can be followed to determine different prices for a particular product. Price calculation methods can be regarded as a scientific approach to pricing. The choice of the right price for a product is the art of pricing. In sections 16.9, 16.10 and 16.11 the cost of a product, the demand and competition as factors to consider in pricing are discussed. Guidelines on the manner in which these three factors individually influence the pricing decision are especially emphasised.

16.9 COST AS A BASIS FOR PRICE DETERMINATION

16.9.1 The role of cost

In a previous section supply (offer or cost) was identified as one of the factors which determine the price of a product. This offer is represented in theoretical price determination by a particular section of the marginal cost curve. Put differently: The manufacturer incurs cost in the marketing of a particular product (supply) to a specific market segment.

It is necessary to consider what is offered to the market before cost as a basis for the determination of prices is discussed. The enterprise's offer (supply curve) finds expression in the price, distribution, marketing communications and pricing decisions which are taken (decisions by marketing management). These decisions by marketing management are made possible by the decisions of production, personnel, public relations, purchasing, administrative, financial and general management. The implementation of all these decisions results in need-satisfaction and cost.

Cost plays a dual role in pricing decisions.

- *First*, the firm has to use its cost data to judge the **acceptability** of the price of a particular product. This course of action especially applies to price-takers for whom the selling prices of products are given. The only way the gross profit per unit can be increased is by reducing the cost per unit. This can be accomplished by increasing turnover with the existing total fixed cost, or increasing efficiency in the application of the production factors, or a combination of these two methods. The price-taker cannot therefore use cost as a basis for price determination. He can at best use it as a basis for evaluating the price in the light of an acceptable profitability.
- *Secondly*, cost can be used by price-makers as a basis for **price determination**.

The way this is done is discussed in Chapter 17 (17.6).

Prices are evaluated and determined for the future marketing of products. The relevant cost data which the marketer uses for the evaluation and/or determination of prices should therefore, in view of relatively high inflation rates and other cost increases, be based on the replacement value of the production inputs.

Cost is a collective noun for many types of cost. In illustrating cost as a basis for price determination it is necessary to discuss two cost concepts briefly. These are fixed costs and variable costs. In the following discussion these two types of cost are used by way of illustration. A more correct approach would be to distinguish between inter alia direct variable costs, direct overheads, general factory overheads, and variable and fixed sales and administrative costs, other general costs and standard and real costs. The proposed approach, however, illustrates the relevant principles without necessitating a detailed discussion of costs.

- Total fixed costs of an enterprise are those costs which remain unchanged in total, over a certain time period and with a given capacity, irrespective of the level of production and marketing. The fixed cost per product unit, however, decreases as the production volume increases, because the numerator (the total fixed costs) remains constant while the denominator (the number of units manufactured) increases. Total fixed costs are allocated to all products to obtain the fixed cost per product unit. An increase in the volume of products manufactured within a certain capacity brings about a smaller share of the total fixed costs allocated to each product.
- Total variable costs are those costs which increase more or less proportionally with the scope of production. The variable costs per unit therefore remain constant irrespective of the number of units manufactured. Material and direct labour costs are well-known examples of variable costs.

The preceding explanation of fixed and variable costs is quantified in Table 16.2.

TABLE 16.2 The influence of the number of products on the total cost and the cost per product unit

PRODUCT (Units)	TOTAL COST			COST PER PRODUCT UNIT		
	Fixed	Variable	Total	Fixed	Variable	Total
	R	R	R	R	R	
0	1 000	0	1 000	∞	0	∞
1	1 000	5	1 005	1 000	5	1 005
10	1 000	50	1 050	100	5	105
100	1 000	500	1 500	10	5	15
1 000	1 000	5 000	6 000	1	5	6
2 000	1 000	10 000	11 000	0,5	5	5,5

It is important to note that all decisions of the firm exert an influence on the total cost of a product. For example, product decisions about the uniqueness, durability, packaging, standardisation, form, dimensions, and quality of the product mix directly influence the total cost of the product. In the same way decisions about distribution and marketing communications of a product influence its total cost. Furthermore, the implementation of decisions by production, personnel, public relations, purchasing, administrative, financial and general management influence the total costs of the enterprise and eventually the product mix of the enterprise.

16.9.2 Total cost as a basis for price determination

A pricing method commonly used in the Republic of South Africa is to calculate the total cost of a product (absorption cost) and add to this a certain percentage mark-up to determine the selling price.

Price determination based on total cost

Assume a 10 % mark-up is required by the seller of the product in Table 16.2. If the sales forecast for the product is 2 000 units, the price will be R6,05 ((R5,50 × 110) + 100) and the total gross profit R1 100. This gross profit will materialise only if 2 000 units are actually sold. The gross profit, for example, will be R50 if only 1 000 units are sold.

Total or absorption cost as a basis for price determination results in the total cost of a product being dependent on the budgeted (forecast) production and marketing volumes. During periods of declining demand for the product the cost and thus the price increases. In prosperous times, characterised by a greater demand for the product, the cost and thus the price decreases! The marketer intuitively suspects (probably because of the traditional price theory) that his prices should increase in prosperous times and decrease when the demand for his products decreases. The price calculations are correct, but the pricing decision looks suspicious!

Allocation of fixed costs to more than one type of product

The use of total cost as a basis for pricing is exceptionally complicated when fixed costs have to be allocated to more than one type of product. In order to recover the total cost in the price, each type of product has to carry its share of the fixed costs. A generally accepted method of allocating total fixed costs to individual types of product does not exist, and there are probably many methods which can be used. Different allocation bases can result in different cost prices per product unit (and thus selling prices). The allocation basis of total fixed costs therefore determines the price of a particular product to a great extent! Table 16.3 depicts the influence of different allocation bases on the selling price.

It is evident from Table 16.3 that the different allocation bases of total fixed costs can result in considerable differences in the calculated cost prices (and eventually selling prices) for the same products. The selling prices of product A vary between R23,37 and R28,94, and that of product C between R13,76 and R17,46.

The following **objections** inter alia can be raised to the three allocation bases for fixed cost as indicated in Table 16.3:

TABLE 16.3   The influence of various allocation bases on the selling price of a product

Item	Basis	PRODUCT A	PRODUCT B	PRODUCT C	Total for product mix
1. Products	Number	2 250	7 500	1 500	11 250
2. Total labour costs	R	18 000	22 500	7 500	48 000
3. Total material costs	R	20 250	67 500	7 500	95 250
4. Total variable costs (V)	R	38 250	90 000	15 000	143 250
5. Total fixed costs (F)	R				71 625
Allocation bases for the total fixed costs					
6. Allocate (F) by taking 149,2 % of item 2	R	26 859	33 574	11 192	71 625
7. Allocate (F) by taking 75,19 % of item 2	R	15 227	50 758	5 640	71 625
8. Allocate (F) by taking R6,36 for each product	R	14 325	47 750	9 550	71 625
Variable cost per product unit					
9. Labour cost	R	8	3	5	
10. Material cost	R	9	9	5	
11. Total variable cost	R	17	12	10	
Fixed cost per product unit per allocation basis					
12. Item 6 ÷ Item 1	R	11,94	4,48	7,46	
13. Item 7 ÷ Item 1	R	6,77	6,77	3,76	
14. Item 8 ÷ Item 1	R	6,37	6,37	6,37	
Total costs per product unit					
15. Items 11 + 12	R	28,94	16,48	17,46	
16. Items 11 + 13	R	23,77	18,77	13,76	
17. Items 11 + 14	R	23,37	18,37	16,37	

- The first allocation basis in Table 16.3 (item 6) assumes in the first place a direct ratio between fixed costs and the direct labour cost for all products. It is possible in practice that products which incur very little labour cost require huge amounts of fixed costs and vice versa. Compare the production of plastic bottles with hand-made glass containers. Secondly, the calculated cost price of products manufactured by expensive machinery using few and inexpensive labour inputs is probably too low. The material cost per product of products A and B is R9 each, while the labour cost per product (item 9) is respectively R8 and R3. The cost of the machines is in no way taken into consideration in the cost price calculations! Thirdly, the allocated overheads should increase if the labour costs increase, but the biggest portion of the overheads are fixed over the short term. This procedure can result in an over-recovery of fixed costs, increased selling prices, and a shorter order book. A decrease in the number of orders can in turn result in higher prices — and a still shorter order book!
- In the second allocation basis (item 7) the cost of the product is determined by its material content. Although it is possible that products A and B are manufactured by different machinery (inter alia fixed costs because of depreciation), this allocation basis implies that the fixed costs per product unit are the same for both products. Products with a high material content and cost and which utilise little fixed costs will nevertheless (according to this allocation basis) have to carry a high amount of fixed costs per product unit. Expensive materials can also result in the final products having unnecessarily high prices, while products manufactured from inexpensive materials are marketed at too low prices.
- The third allocation basis in Table 16.3 (item 8) can probably be applied without too much risk (except a poor sales forecast) by a firm which manufactures only one type of product. The illogical consequences of this allocation basis for a multi-product firm are obvious from the table. Products A, B and C each carry the same fixed costs per product unit (item 14) despite the probable different utilisation of fixed costs.

Objections to absorption cost as a basis for pricing

The following objections can be raised against using absorption cost (total cost) as a basis for pricing:

- Demand and the competition are not taken into account.
- Total cost per unit and thus price per unit are largely influenced by the utilisation of capacity (lower total cost per unit is possible by manufacturing more products — see Table 16.2).
- Total cost per unit and price per product are influenced by a somewhat arbitrary allocation of total fixed costs.
- During unfavourable economic conditions the prices of products are increased.
- During favourable economic conditions the prices of products are decreased.
- No provision is made for the extent to which production facilities are utilised.

Notwithstanding these objections absorption cost as a basis for pricing is commonly used by firms. The reasons for its popularity are discussed next.

Reasons for the popularity of absorption cost as a basis for pricing

The following reasons can be put forward for the popularity of absorption cost as a basis for pricing:

- The administration of the cost-plus method is *relatively simple* and ensures an apparently predetermined profit margin. This method also makes it unnecessary to judge each product on its own merits. Once the mark-up is determined (perhaps on a seasonal or annual basis) no further decisions are necessary. The whole issue of prices can be delegated to middle and even lower management.
- Managers on all levels (top, middle and lower management) are often attracted (lulled) by formulae and guidelines which hold the promise of correct and *fast solutions* to their problems.

16.9.3 Variable cost per product unit as a basis for pricing

Using variable cost per product unit as a basis for pricing is also known as the contribution approach, and here the total fixed costs are not taken into consideration in price calculations. Obviously no firm can sell its products over the long term at a price which covers only variable costs. In the long run all products have to be marketed at prices which cover total fixed and total variable costs in such a way that the difference between total sales and total costs is positive and represents an acceptable rate of return on total assets. The desired profitability aimed at does not imply that each product type which the firm markets has to cover its particular total cost.

The contribution approach to pricing can be applied under the following conditions:

- In the case of new products total fixed costs can be covered by the existing products. The price of the new product can then be determined by using the contribution approach.
- The firm employs highly skilled labour and the demand for the firm's products decreases. Rather than dismissing some employees, the firm could in the short term base its prices on the variable cost of the products.
- The firm is prepared to recoup only total variable cost in order to penetrate a certain market segment. In this way the firm tries to capture a certain market share by means of a low selling price.

Pricing aimed at attaining a particular contribution ratio can now be discussed.

16.9.4 Desired contribution ratio as a basis for pricing

Some firms calculate the basic price of their products in such a manner that a particular contribution is achieved. Consider the following example:

Data: Variable cost per product unit   R5,00
                Desired contribution ratio   0,30
Required: Calculate the basic selling price
Solution: Contribution ratio $=$ $\dfrac{\text{Selling price} - \text{Variable cost per unit}}{\text{Selling price}}$

thus: Selling price $=$ $\dfrac{\text{Variable cost per unit}}{1 - \text{Contribution ratio}}$

$$= \frac{\text{R5,00}}{1-0,3}$$

$$= \text{R7,14}$$

Derivation of the formula

Contribution ratio $=$ $\dfrac{\text{Selling price (P)} - \text{Variable cost per unit (Vc)}}{\text{Selling price (P)}}$
(CR)

$$CR(P) = P-Vc$$
$$-CR(P) = -P+Vc$$
$$P-CR(P) = Vc$$
$$P(1-CR) = Vc$$
$$\text{thus } P = \frac{Vc}{1-CR}$$

An enterprise (often a workshop) that receives more orders than it can manufacture can possibly turn down those orders which do not obtain a particular minimum contribution ratio.

16.9.5 Desired profitability as a basis for pricing

A price can also be calculated which covers total fixed and total variable costs, while also providing a particular profitability on total assets employed. This calculation is possible for firms manufacturing and marketing only one type of product or for multi-product enterprises.

Desired profitability as a basis for pricing for a firm marketing one type of product

The following is an example of pricing for a desired profitability by a firm marketing one type of product:

Data:		
	Number of products	1 500
	Variable cost per product unit	R10,00
	Total fixed costs	R25 000
	Fixed assets	R125 000
	Current assets	40% of sales
	Selling price	x

Required: Calculate a selling price that will yield a
profitability of 20% on total assets.

Solution:

$$\text{Profitability} = \frac{\text{Total income} - (\text{Total fixed costs} + \text{Total variable cost})}{\text{Total fixed assets} + \text{Total current assets}}$$

$$0{,}20 = \frac{1500x - \{\text{R25 000} + 1500\,(\text{R10})\}}{\text{R125 000} + 0{,}4\,(1500x)}$$

$$0{,}20 = \frac{1500x - \text{R40 000}}{\text{R125 000} + 600x}$$

$$0{,}20\,(\text{R125 000} + 600x) = 1500x - \text{R40 000}$$

$$\text{R25 000} + 120x = 1500x - \text{R40 000}$$

$$-1380x = -\text{R65 000}$$

$$x = \text{R47,10}$$

The advantage of this pricing method is that the extent of the capital required by the particular product is taken into account. The method partly uses absorption cost as a basis for pricing. The objections to this method were discussed above.

Desired profitability as a basis for pricing of a multi-product firm

Manufacturers utilise materials, men and machines in the production process. In the short term labour and other production costs (conversion costs) are probably a fixed cost and material costs a variable cost. Nevertheless, capital is tied up in material and conversion costs. The turnover of capital tied up in materials is inevitably higher than the turnover of capital tied up in conversion facilities. Any pricing formula should make provision for this difference; if not, the price calculation does not hold water. The following example shows why:

	Product A	Product B
Material cost	R5	R15
Conversion cost	R15	R5
Total cost	R20	R20

If product A and product B are marketed at the same prices (their total costs are the same) their respective contributions to fixed costs will be the same. Product A requires a conversion cost of R15 to convert R5 worth of materials into a product, while product A requires a conversion cost of R5 to process materials worth R15 into a product. Product A is labour intensive and product B materials intensive. It should be clear that product A makes more use of production facilities (eventually capital) than product B. The price of product A should thus be higher than that of product B. Intuitively it seems if product B is overpriced while product A is priced too low. Yet the success of a manufacturer is not determined by the value of the materials he uses, but by the efficiency with which he converts materials into final products.

Product A and product B should thus not command the same price in the market. In the following a pricing method is developed in which two mark-ups are calculated, namely a mark-up on materials and a mark-up on conversion cost.

Assume the desired profitability of a firm manufacturing and marketing products A and B is 30 per cent. The material turnover rate is five times per year. If a mark-up of 6 per cent (desired profitability divided by the turnover rate: $30 \div 5$) is set on the material content of the product a profitability of 30 per cent per year on the investment in materials will be attained (on condition that the budgeted number of products are marketed). The mark-up on the material component of the product has now been calculated and next a mark-up on the conversion cost and eventually the price must be calculated.

Data for products A and B

	Product A	*Product B*
Budgeted sales (units)	40 000	60 000
Budgeted raw material cost (R)	200 000	900 000
Budgeted conversion cost (R)	600 000	300 000
Other data:		
Desired profitability (%)	30	
Total assets (R)	5 000 000	
Total fixed costs (R)	1 800 000	

Required:
Calculate selling prices for products A and B which will yield a profitability of 30 per cent on the total assets.

Solution:

- The mark-up on the material components of products A and B was calculated at six per cent. The total required material cost for the year is R1 100 000. The material component of products A and B will thus be 'sold' at R1 166 000 (R1 100 000 × 1,06).
- To obtain a profitability of 30 per cent the total sales value of products A and B must be R5 300 000 (total sales = total costs + profit). The total costs and profit are:

Fixed costs	R1 800 000
Total material cost	R1 100 000
Total conversion cost	R 900 000
Desired profit	R1 500 000
Total sales	R5 300 000

- The mark-up on the conversion cost is:
  - the difference between the total desired sales minus the 'sales value' of the material component contained in products A and B;
  - divided by the total conversion cost.

Thus, $\dfrac{5\ 300\ 000 - 1\ 166\ 000}{900\ 000}$ = 4,593 . . . or 4,59.

The price per unit of product A then is:

Material cost R5 × 1,06	=	R 5,30
Conversion cost R15 × 4,59	=	R68,85
		R74,15

and that per unit of product B:

Material cost R15 × 1,06	=	R15,90
Conversion cost R5 × 4,59	=	R22,95
		R38,85

Proof:

Sales: 40 000 units of product A		R2 966 000
60 000 units of product B		R2 331 000
	Total	R5 297 000

Minus:

Total material cost	R1 100 000	
Total conversion cost	R 900 000	
Total fixed costs	R1 800 000	R3 800 000
Total profit		R1 497 000
Profitability	=	$\dfrac{1\ 497\ 000}{5\ 000\ 000} \times \dfrac{100}{1}$
	=	29,94 per cent

The realised profitability differs by 0,06 per cent from the desired profitability because the mark-up on the conversion cost of 4,593 . . . was approximate to 4,59.

This pricing method is more practical than the method whereby only one mark-up on total variable cost is used to calculate the price. Products A and B have the same total variable cost, but product A needs more production facilities compared to product B. The calculated price of product A is thus much higher compared to the calculated price of product B.

16.9.6 Cost of the scarce production facility as a basis for pricing

All the pricing methods so far discussed implicitly assume that the supply of the marketer's products is greater than the demand for the products. However, a shortage of particular production facilities can at times result in the demand for a product exceeding its supply. Production facilities must be viewed in a very wide context and include inter alia: limited machinery, production hours and man-hours; insufficient financial resources and material. The latter shortages will probably increase in future because of its limited availability.

The pricing method now discussed applies in a situation where limited available production hours is a problem. Assume a firm manufactures product A in standard lots of 1 000 units and markets these products at R15 each. The following data apply:

Total sales: 1 000 units at R15 each		R15 000
Less:		
Variable costs:		
Setting-up cost (5 hours at R50 per hour)	R250	
Machining cost (20 hours at R15 per hour)	R300	
Material cost (R5 per unit)	R5 000	R5 550
Total contribution income		R9 450
Total hours required (5 + 20)		25
Contribution income per hour		R378

Assume further that the firm receives a special order from a client for 2 000 units of product A. The client will probably demand a quantity discount and the quotation will of necessity be for a price lower than R15 per product unit. On the other hand, the limited production hours entails that the firm would like to maintain the contribution income of R378 per hour on all orders.

The price per product unit for an order of 2 000 units is calculated as follows:

Total variable costs:		
Setting-up cost (5 hours at R50 per hour)	R250	
Machining cost (40 hours at R15 per hour)	R600	
Material cost (R5 per unit)	R10 000	R10 850
Desired contribution income:		
Number of hours × marginal income per hour thus		
(5 + 40) × 378		R17 010
Total sales of 2 000 units		R27 860
Price per unit product		R 13,93

16.9.7 Concluding remarks

In this section several methods of determining the price of a product were discussed. All these pricing methods are based on the cost of the product. The most important disadvantages of these pricing methods are:

- The cost is based on budgeted production volumes and budgeted cost. If the realised production volumes deviate from the budgets the calculated cost per product changes.
- The demand for the product is not considered.
- The reaction and action of competitors are ignored.

There are various factors which can possibly influence the demand for a particular product, such as the characteristics of the product and its price, substitute products, the income and preferences of consumers, the number of consumers, the temperature, and many more. To summarise: the combined influence of the micro-, the macro- and the market environments determine demand. It is not easy to describe the combined effect of all these factors on the demand for a product. In the following sections attention is focused on only some aspects of these environments and demand.

16.10 DEMAND AS A BASIS FOR PRICING

16.10.1 The influence of the micro-environment on demand

The most important variables in the micro-environment which influence the demand for a product are the decisions on the product and its price, distribution and marketing communications. The exact influence of all these decisions on demand is equally difficult to determine, and thus **only pricing decisions** are discussed briefly.

Traditionally it was assumed that the price of a product represented the acquisition cost and nothing more. This view presupposes that the consumer prefers a low price rather than a high price for a particular product. Any deviation from this viewpoint was ascribed to ignorance of the consumer and speculation on future price developments.

At present the view is that the consumer's reaction to price also influences the demand for a product, in other words price influences the consumer's judgement of the product's return value. Sometimes consumers use the price of a particular product to judge its quality, for example. This use of price differs depending on the type of product, retailers and socio-economic groups. A number of research reports confirm this phenomenon.[4]

Some aspects of the price/quality relationship are discussed next.[5]

Price/quality relationship

The following are reasons for the use of price as an indicator of quality: It is a convenient judgement criterion, has snob value and influences the perceived risk.

- The price of a product is a convenient judgement criterion. A product inter alia serves as a combination of guidelines for the consumer. These guidelines are inter alia the style of the product, the trade mark, the colour, the packaging, the quality, **and the price** of the product. The price of a product is a concrete and measurable guideline. The consumer trusts price as guideline more than other guidelines which are directly linked to quality, such as the quality of spare parts and the tensile strength of the metal or thread of cotton. The following aspects make it difficult for the consumer to use other quality guidelines rather than price. In the *first* place the modern consumer is not an expert buyer (compare the product assortment women buy on behalf of the household). The consumer uses guidelines to judge the quality of some products, such as the size of the firm, the image of the firm, the combination of guidelines of the product, and the price. Price is probably the most convenient judgement criterion. *Secondly*, self-service and self-selection make it difficult for the consumer to obtain information regarding the product other than its price.

● Prices have snob value. To the extent that high prices are an indication of scarcity (for example gold and diamonds), it can also create an impression of individuality and prestige. In a society characterised by a high standard of living and status often associated with material prosperity, it is possible that scarcity and prestige (high prices) are factors which some consumers consider when making a purchasing decision.

● Prices influence the perceived risk. A prospective buyer consciously or subconsciously considers the price of the more expensive product against the risk of the expected low quality of a less expensive product. Consumers often buy the more expensive product to avoid the risk of a poor-quality product. The cost and quality of a spare part or component also influence consumer attitude towards risk. The cost of a spare part or component could be relatively small compared to the total cost of the final product, but the spare part, component or ingredient can play a decisive role in the quality of the final product. (Compare gaskets in engines and yeast in bread.) The consumer may tend to buy the more expensive spare part or component in such cases to ensure that the quality of the final product is acceptable.

16.10.2 The influence of the macro-environment on demand

The macro-environment is the sum of all the variables outside the firm and its markets which have an actual or potential effect on the marketing of a product, and which are not at all or to a very small extent influenced by management. The macro-environment consists of a number of interacting subenvironments, namely the economic, technological, institutional, social, political, physical and international environments. The influences of all these subenvironments on demand are not discussed. The subenvironment which most probably has the greatest influence on demand is the economic environment.

The influence of the economic environment on demand

The economic environment includes various economic factors and phenomena, such as economic growth, the trend of the business cycle, inflation, fluctuating interest rates, and levels of investment and unemployment. These and other economic factors can all have an actual or potential effect on the demand for a particular product. In what follows attention is focused on·aspects of pricing and demand during the business cycle and inflation.

The following aspects of demand and pricing during the growth phase of the business cycle are important:

● Generally speaking demand increases because of an increase in economic activity. Pricing in this phase is relatively easy compared to pricing in the declining phase.

- Although it is possible that the demand for the products of a particular firm could increase, the firm could also be subject to keen competition because of new entrants to the industry or because existing competitors have increased their production capacities.
- The input costs could increase in this phase because of greater demand. As a generalisation it can be stated that during the growth phase of the business cycle firms place more emphasis on cost as a basis for pricing compared to the declining phase.
- Cost increases are often used by firms to motivate price increases. It is, however, possible, because of greater demand, that total cost per unit could decrease.

Some aspects of declining demand and pricing during the declining phase of the business cycle are the following:[6]

- A long-term strategy could include drastic price reductions to rid the industry of marginal producers and thus to maintain demand for the products of the own firm.
- A short-term strategy could be directed at stealing a march on price cutters.

Aspects of demand and pricing during inflation:

A salient feature of inflation is a decrease in the buying power of money. This decreased buying power:

- decreases the demand for some products, such as motor cars, holidays and entertainment;
- increases the demand for other products — this occurs especially when consumers try to protect the buying power of their money by buying products such as Persian carpets, paintings and stamps.

Depending whether demand for the products of a firm increases or decreases during inflationary periods, the prices of these products could increase or decrease.

Winkler[7] suggests the following rules of thumb for either a price increase or a price reduction by the firm.

Rules of thumb for price increases by the enterprise:

- Where possible, increase prices when general price increases occur in the industry.
- Avoid frequent price increases.
- Allow a short respite of payment on the price increase to the most important buyers, especially the important middlemen.

- Give ample notice of the proposed price increase to enable middlemen to supplement their stock.
- Offer a price reduction on products with a low stock turnover.
- Motivate the price increase by explaining how cost increases necessitated the price increase and how the firm tried to absorb the cost increases through increased productivity.
- Introduce a lower-quality and lower-priced model of the product.
- Offer alternative conditions of payment.

Rules of thumb for price reductions by the firm:

- Cut prices when the competitors expect it least, and preferably if the competitors increase their prices.
- Do not give notice of a price reduction, and communicate the reduction intensively to the target market.
- Important middlemen should not be overstocked before the price reduction.
- Reduce prices only if the reduction can be maintained over a relatively long period of time.
- Price reductions should be considered only if the demand is relatively price elastic.
- Do not reduce prices as an emergency measure. This applies particularly when profits are low and demand is declining. In oligopolistic circumstances competitors will follow a price reduction and start a price war.
- The price reduction should be large enough to be regarded as significant by the market — in most cases a 15 per cent price reduction is necessary.

16.10.3 The influence of the market environment on demand

16.10.3.1 *The nature of the market environment*

The market environment comprises the market (the demand), competition and consumerism. The influence of competition on demand is discussed in section 16.11. The market and consumerism influence the demand for a product, but their individual and combined effects on demand are not exactly determinable. (See Chapter 3 for the various aspects regarding the market and consumerism.) The demand band is discussed next.

16.10.3.2 *The demand band*

According to traditional economic price theory the price of a product is established where the supply and demand curves meet. This position is illustrated in Figure 16.7.

FIGURE 16.7 Theoretical determination of price

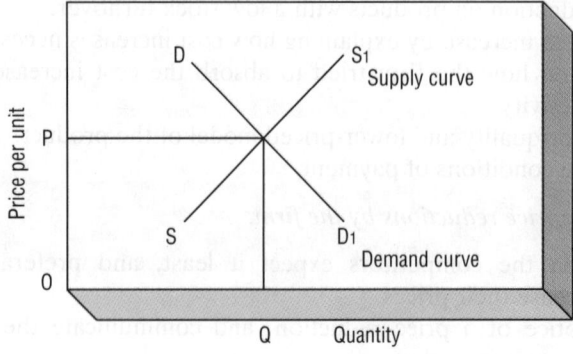

The supply curve SS_1 in Figure 16.7 runs from the left-hand side below to the right-hand side above. The reasoning is that the higher the price, the more products the producer is prepared to manufacture and offer on the market. The demand curve DD_1 runs from the left-hand side above to the right-hand side below and reflects the situation that the consumer is likely to buy more products at a lower price. The equilibrium price is established at price OP and at this price a quantity of OQ products will be offered and taken up by the market. Should the price of the product be just higher than OP, the consumer would not be prepared to buy the quantity OQ. This deduction is not quite logical and a more acceptable alternative is presented by the demand band in Figure 16.8.

FIGURE 16.8 The demand band

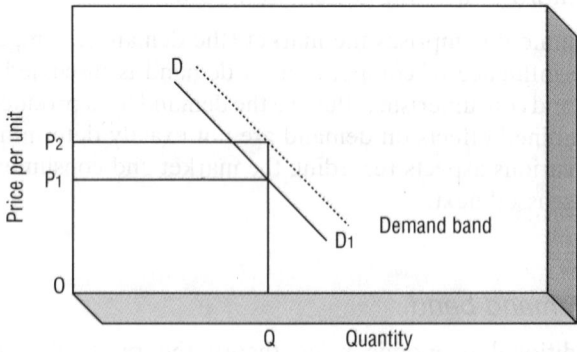

The demand band DD_1 in Figure 16.8 depicts the same trend as the demand curve in Figure 16.7. The demand band, however, shows that the consumer will buy quantity OQ even if the price should vary between OP_1 and OP_2. This view possibly reflects the consumer's buying habits more accurately.

The demand band shows that the consumer approaches a market for a particular product consciously or even subconsciously with two prices in mind. *First*, an **upper price limit** exists and prices higher than this limit are regarded as too expensive by the consumer. *Secondly*, a **lower price limit** exists. Prices lower than this limit are too cheap for the consumer; in other words, the consumer distrusts the quality of a product which, in his opinion, is too cheap. This aspect is of utmost importance to the marketer, as products cannot only be too expensive, but also too inexpensive.

The upper and lower price limits of the demand band for a particular product can be determined by inter alia marketing research. Research on price limits is discussed next.

16.10.3.3 *Research on price limits*[8]

The existence of price limits is confirmed by introspection, ie an examination of one's own purchasing behaviour, and by the results of a number of studies. The price limits can be determined by asking a representative number of respondents in a target market what the highest price is they are prepared to pay for a particular product and what the lowest price is at which they will still buy the product. The price limits set by the various respondents should be similar, but not identical. Differences are inter alia due to social status, income, age, education, taste and habits of the respondents. From the price limits obtained from the respondents, the percentage potential at various prices of a product can be determined. Table 16.4 reflects the results of a fictitious investigation regarding the suggested prices of product Z.

According to Table 16.4, 80 per cent of the consumers are prepared to pay 13 cents for product Z, and nobody will buy product Z at a price of 9 cents and lower or at 17 cents or higher.

The pricing research methodology briefly set out relates mainly to functionally identical and functionally similar products. A functionally identical product is, for example, a new brand of toilet soap, and a functionally similar product is, for example, a new type of textile fibre. The selling prices of existing brands and types of products could be used as benchmarks by the consumers, and the consumers are aware which needs can be satisfied by the products.

Functionally unique products are products for which there are no direct substitutes. These products are new and unique in the true sense of the word. It seems that research on price limits for this type of product is of limited practical value and may even be misleading.

- *First*, because of limited funds, a firm can only test-market a limited number of product concepts. Should the wrong product concept be tested, the product may be unacceptable for reasons other than price.

TABLE 16.4 The percentage of potential consumers at different suggested prices of product Z

Price of product Z (cents)	% consumers who will buy the product	% consumers who will not buy the product	Cumulative % who will buy the product
9	0 % at ≤ 9 cents		0
10	5 % at 10 cents		5
11	18 % at 11 cents		23
12	43 % at 12 cents		66
13	21 % at13 cents	7 % not at ≥ 13 cents	80 (a)
14	12 % at 14 cents	31 % not at ≥ 14 cents	61 (b)
15	1 % at 15 cents	44 % not at ≥ 15 cents	18 (c)
16		16 % not at ≥ 16 cents	2 (d)
17		2 % not at ≥ 17 cents	0 (e)

(a) 66 % + 21 % - 7 % = 80 % (d) 18 % - 16 % = 2 %
(b) 80 % + 12 % - 31 % = 61 % (e) 2 % - 2 % = 0 %
(c) 61 % + 1% - 44 % = 18 %

- In the *second* place the available areas for test-marketing limit the number of product concepts which can be tested.
- *Lastly*, pricing research on functionally unique products determines the consumer's reaction to prices of products which are unique to him. It is difficult for price researchers to simulate conditions whereby the consumer can judge the value of such a functionally unique product with confidence.

16.11 COMPETITION AS A BASIS FOR PRICING

16.11.1 The nature of competition

Two factors which can influence the price of products, namely cost and demand, have been discussed. The costs of the firm are available internally and are relatively easily quantifiable. The lower and upper price limits for a particular product can be quantified by inter alia research.

The third factor which influences pricing, namely competition, is highly subjective and qualitative, however. It will therefore remain relatively difficult to develop a practical formula for the pricing of products which will also make provision for the competitor's reaction. The reason for this is that the type and extent of competitors' reactions to a particular price or a change in the existing price is not known before the actual reaction itself becomes known.

In any competitive situation the marketer and the buyer can enter into negotiations to determine the selling price. It goes without saying that in a particular marketing situation the competitive advantage rests with either the marketer or the buyer. Where the competitive advantage rests depends inter alia on the following:

- number and size of the marketers and buyers;
- availability of substitute products;
- extent of and trend in demand;
- perishability of the product;
- financial ability of the negotiating parties; and
- negotiation abilities and skills of the participants.

The competitive advantage inclines to the marketer:

- in situations of relatively few marketers;
- where substitute products do not exist;
- if the demand shows an increasing trend;
- if the product is not perishable; and
- where the marketer is in a better financial position than the buyer.

The following aspects are discussed in this section: the identification of competitors; price changes by the marketer; consequences of a price change; and the reaction to price changes by competitors.

16.11.2 The identification of competitors

All firms who compete for the rand in the consumer's pocket can be seen as competitors. Thus, for example, a consumer could spend part of his money on an overseas visit (and the competitors are all the airlines which fly passengers from South Africa), a swimming pool (the competitors are all the local builders of pools) or a motor car (the competitors are all the local and possibly foreign firms who market motor cars). It is, however, doubtful whether a manufacturer of canned fruit regards a manufacturer of lipstick as a competitor. It stands to reason that a firm is not a price competitor if a change in his prices has no influence on the prices and sales of other firms.

Competitors are identified only from the viewpoint of prices for purposes of this chapter. A price-maker determines the prices of his products himself and also bears the consequences of his pricing decisions. The competitors determine to a large extent what these consequences will be.

The firm can be prevented from dropping its prices by the competitor simply by following any price reduction. The intention to charge the same or lower prices than the firm is often communicated to the consumers (and also to the firm, if its marketing information systems function efficiently), for example 'nobody undersells us'.

If the firm intends charging more than the competitor for a product, the competitor can put a spoke in the wheel by increasing his price to the same level. The situation set out above clearly indicates who the price competitor is.

16.11.3 Price changes by the marketer

The marketer can at times increase or decrease the price of all or some of his products. The following factors can necessitate a *price reduction*:

- The firm has excess capacity and increased sales cannot be attained through more or better outlets or marketing communications. The effects of a price reduction on the gross profit of the firm have to be kept in mind. For example, a firm with a gross profit of 20 per cent on its sales and which reduces its prices by 5 per cent, has to increase its physical sales volume by 33,33 per cent to maintain the same gross profit in rand.

Before price reduction:

Gross profit = Total sales − Total costs

(Assumption R20) = 100 units (R1 each) − 100 units (80 cents) each.

Price reduction of 5 per cent:

Set new sales volume equal to x

Gross profit	= Total sales − Total costs
R20	= x(0,95) − x(0,80)
0,15x	= R20
x	= 133,33 units.

Thus the increase in physical units is 33,33 per cent.

In Table 16.5 the percentual increases in the physical sales volume to maintain the gross profit for some percentage price reductions are given.

Any increase in the physical sales volume will of course entail higher transport, storage, financing and risk costs, and will consequently lower the net profit.

- Another reason for price reductions is that the market share of the firm is decreasing and demand is relatively price elastic.
- The marketer wants to dominate the market through lower total cost per unit. Through lower selling prices the firm attempts to increase its sales volume and this causes a lower total cost per unit, mainly because of a decrease in the fixed costs per unit. Under these circumstances the firm must of course have excess capacity.

TABLE 16.5 Percentual increase in the physical sales volume to maintain the same gross profit, arranged according to the price reduction and gross profit in percentages

Gross profit (%) Price reduction (%)	5	10	15	20	25	30
1	25,0	11,1	7,1	5,3	4,2	3,4
2	66,7	25,0	15,4	11,1	8,7	7,1
3	150,0	42,9	25,0	17,6	13,6	11,1
4	400,0	66,7	36,4	25,0	19,0	15,4
5		100,0	50,0	33,3	25,0	20,0
6	—	150,0	66,7	42,9	31,6	25,0
7	—	233,3	87,5	53,8	38,9	30,4
8	—	400,0	114,3	66,7	47,1	36,4
9	—	900,0	150,0	81,8	56,3	42,9
10	—		200,0	100,0	66,7	50,0
11	—	—	275,0	122,2	78,6	57,9
12	—	—	400,0	150,0	92,3	66,7
13	—	—	650,0	185,7	108,3	76,5
14	—	—	1 400,0	233,3	127,3	87,5
15	—	—		300,0	150,0	100,0
16	—	—	—	400,0	177,8	114,3
17	—	—	—	566,7	212,5	130,8
18	—	—	—	900,0	257,1	150,0
19	—	—	—	1 900,0	316,7	172,7
20	—	—	—	—	400,0	200,0

The marketer often *increases* his selling prices in order to quell the demand for the product and to keep pace with inflation. Some of the methods which can be applied to adjust to inflationary circumstances are the following:

- the inclusion of escalation clauses in contracts;
- pricing the accompanying services in the marketing of products separately;
- the reduction and/or elimination of discounts;
- increasing minimum order quantities; and
- lowering the quality of the product.

In the preceding section price changes by the marketer were discussed briefly, and in the following section decisions which follow a price change come under review.

16.11.4 Decisions which follow a price change[9]

A decision to change the price of a product has particular consequences for the firm. The following are some examples:

- *Firstly*, special arrangements must be made to support the price change. Salesmen must be informed from which date the price change is effective; price lists must be revised; and advertising is probably necessary to inform consumers about the price change. The first consequence of a price change is thus changes in the other marketing decisions of the firm.
- *Secondly*, a forecast of the wholesalers' reactions is necessary. The short-term reaction of wholesalers is focused on a change in the buying pattern because of a change in the policy regarding stocks and a change in the price to retailers.
- In the *third* place it is necessary to forecast the reactions of retailers to the price changes by wholesalers. The retailers could also change their stock levels (and purchases).
- *Fourthly*, the eventual success of a price change depends on how final consumers react to changes in the retail price. It is this reaction which the firm usually tries to forecast (compare the price elasticity of demand).
- In the *fifth* place it is necessary to forecast how competitors will react to a price change. They can decide to charge the same or a higher or a lower price; they can ignore the price change by the firm; or they can react by taking a decision other than price, ie they can take competitive action by making a product, distribution or marketing communications decision.

In the following section the reaction of the marketer to **price changes by competitors** is discussed.

16.11.5 Reaction to price changes by competitors

It is not possible to indicate exactly how the marketer has to react to the price changes of his competitors. Only a few guidelines are provided. The enterprise has to consider:

- Why the competitor changed his selling prices. A change can be aimed at the utilisation of excess capacity, the adjustment to a changed cost structure, or to promote a price change by the industry.
- Whether the price change by the competitor is of a temporary or permanent nature. A temporary price change will probably be ignored, but the same does not apply to a permanent price change.
- What will happen to the market share and net profit of the firm if the competitor's price change is ignored over the long term.
- Whether other enterprises in the industry will react to or ignore the price change by the competitor.
- What the reaction of the competitor and the other enterprises will be to each possible counter-measure by the marketer.

The appropriate course of action requires an analysis of the particular circumstances underlying the preceding considerations. The firm threatened by competition must consider inter alia:

- the stage of the product in the product life cycle;
- the importance of the product to the sales of the firm; and
- the intentions and abilities of the competitor.

Such an analysis is not always possible. Another alternative is to decide in advance on a plan of action indicating how to react to competitors' price changes. An example of such planned decisions is given in Figure 16.9.

FIGURE 16.9   Planned course of action to deal with a competitor's price reduction

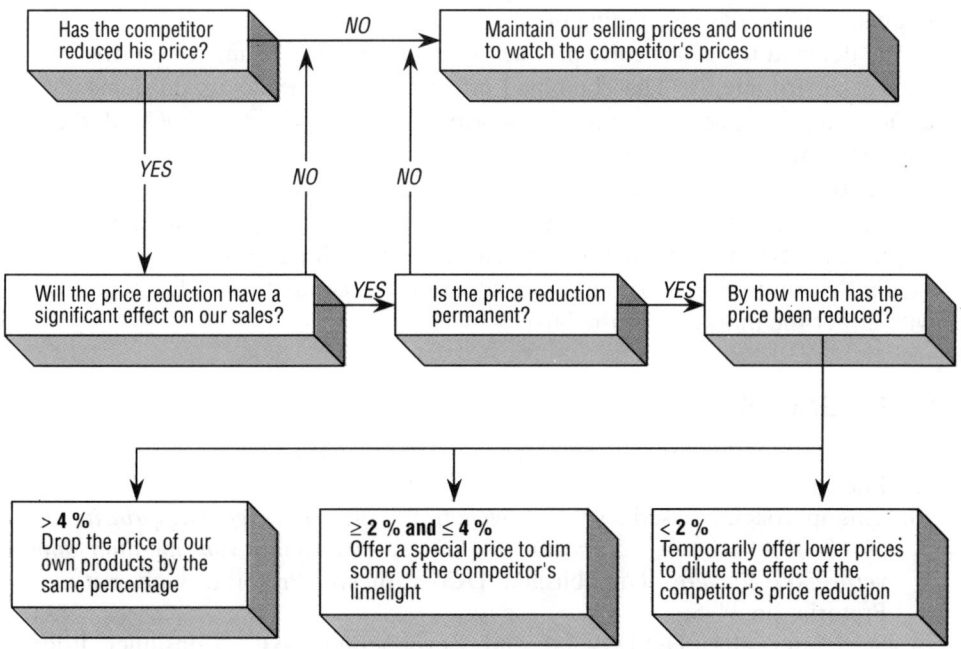

16.12 SUMMARY

The pricing decisions of a firm are important because they have a direct influence on profitability. In practice not all marketers actually make pricing decisions. Some firms are mainly price-takers. For various reasons these firms have very little influence on the selling prices of their products. Some examples are small firms, where the product is subject to price control, where resale price maintenance is legal, and where price leadership occurs.

The pricing decisions of the firm must relate to and support the objectives of the firm. The objectives of the firm can be summarised in three phases and they must also be aimed at in the order mentioned — the firm must ensure its **continuity**, and only then can it **earn** and **divide**. The role of prices during the process of earning should thus be aimed at a particular profitability objective.

According to economic price theory three factors determine the price of a product, namely the **supply** (costs) of the product, the **demand** for the product, and the degree and extent of **competition**. This approach was also followed in this chapter. Theoretical pricing has, because of the illogical assumptions which apply in the analysis, limited practical applications for the marketer. It nevertheless offers useful guidelines regarding prices.

The use of total cost as a basis for pricing is exceptionally complicated when fixed costs have to be allocated to more than one type of product. Although absorption cost as a basis for pricing has serious limitations, it is nevertheless a popular method of determining prices.

The demand for a particular product is determined by the micro-, macro- and market environments. The combined effect of all these factors on demand is difficult to describe and only a few aspects of the effect of each of these environments on demand were discussed.

The third factor which determines prices, namely competition, is very subjective and qualitative. In any competitive situation the marketer and the buyer can enter into negotiations to determine the selling price. It goes without saying that in a particular marketing situation the competitive advantage rests with either the marketer or the buyer.

REFERENCES

1. Notice No 801, *Government Gazette* 10211 of 2 May 1986.
2. Loc cit.
3. This approach is based on Van Aswegen, PJ. 1975. *Prysbepalingsprinsipes in die Suid-Afrikaanse sakesektor by die vervaardiging van nie-duursame verbruikersgoedere.* Unpublished DCom thesis. Pretoria: University of Pretoria, pp 44–5.
4. See, inter alia, Dekker, HJ and Zevenbergen, AP. 'Consumer Price Sensitivity and Retail Pricing Policy' in *Journal of Dietetics and Home Economics,* vol 15, no 2, 1987, pp 45–7.
   Gabor, A. 1977. *Pricing, Principles and Practices.* London: Heinemann Educational Books, chapter 12.
   Leavitt, HJ. 'A Note on Some Experimental Findings about the Meaning of Price' in *Journal of Business,* vol 27, July 1954, p 207.
   McConnell, JD. 'The Price–Quality Relationship in an Experimental Setting'. *Journal of Marketing Research,* vol 5, August 1968, pp 300–3.
   Tull, DS, Bosing, RA and Gonsior, MH. 'The Relationship of Price and Imputed Quality' in Taylor, B and Wills, G. 1969. *Pricing Strategy.* London: Staples, pp 44–9.

5. Based on Shapiro, BP. 'The Psychology of Pricing' in Rachman, DJ (ed). 1970. *Retail Management Strategy, Selected Readings.* Englewood Cliffs, New Jersey: Prentice-Hall Inc, pp 229–34.

6. See Harper, DV. 1966. *Price Policy and Procedure.* New York: Harcourt, Brace and World Inc, pp 82–3.

7. Winkler, J. 1975. *Company Survival during Inflation.* Epping, Essex: Gower Press, p 135.

8. This section is based on Gabor op cit, chapter 12.

9. Oxenfeldt, AR. 1975. *Pricing Strategies.* New York: Amacom, p 189 and Gabor, A op cit, p 223.

CHAPTER 17

THE FINAL SELLING PRICE AND OTHER ASPECTS REGARDING PRICING DECISIONS

17.1 INTRODUCTION

In Chapter 16 the influence of costs, demand and competition on the price of a product was discussed. The emphasis fell on guidelines as to how these three factors individually influence the pricing decision. Once the price of a product is determined, it does not automatically follow that the product will be marketed at that price. The purpose of this chapter is to explain deviations from the basic price which was calculated according to the principles of costs, demand and competition.

Three factors can cause the calculated price often to be changed. These factors are discounts which are usually granted; deviations attributable to the geographical location of buyers; and some psychological aspects of the consumer's attitude towards prices. A discussion of these factors will be followed by a consideration of skim-the-cream and market penetration pricing decisions. When a new product is introduced breakeven analysis is done to determine the price at which the product should be sold.

ORGANISATION OF THE CHAPTER

Discounts: Trade or functional discounts, quantity discounts, cash discounts, seasonal discounts, discounts for special price offers, discounts for co-operative advertising

Geographical price diffentials: Free-on-rail price, freight-absorption price, uniform regional price, base-point price.

> **Pricing decisions based on the consumer's attitude towards prices:** Odd-number prices, price lines, traditional prices.
>
> **Skim-the-cream and market penetration pricing decisions.**
>
> **Breakeven analysis.**

17.2 DISCOUNTS

Trade or functional discounts, quantity discounts, cash discounts and diverse other discounts are identified and discussed briefly.

17.2.1 Trade or functional discounts

In order to illustrate the principles involved in determining prices, the role of middlemen was excluded in Chapter 16. Trade or functional discounts are discounts granted to middlemen and are usually calculated on the retail price (the price the consumer pays). Assume the retail price on an invoice issued by the producer to the wholesaler is R300 and trade discounts of 30 per cent and 10 per cent are granted.

The two percentages quoted indicate that the manufacturer utilises the services of a wholesaler and a retailer in the marketing of his products. The retailer usually performs more marketing activities than the wholesaler and therefore the higher trade discount is applicable to the retailer. The trade discounts are calculated on the selling prices of the various middlemen.

Calculation of retail and wholesale trade discounts

In the example above the retailer sells the product to the consumer at R300. The retailer bought the product at R210 from the wholesaler {R300 − 0,3(R300)}. The wholesaler sold the product at R210 to the retailer and must pay the manufacturer R189 {R210 − 0,1(R210)}.

Besides the exchange activities of buying and selling the middlemen perform other marketing activities:

- They buy in bulk and sell in smaller quantities.
- They buy products from a variety of suppliers (a wide assortment). The middlemen then make up those assortments of products which will best satisfy the needs of consumers.
- They often deliver the products.
- They grant credit.

The purpose of the trade discount is to compensate the middlemen for the activities they perform in the distribution channel so that they:

- earn a satisfactory net profit after deduction of their costs; and
- are encouraged to continue stocking the product.

It should be clear that the trade discount granted to the middleman is the difference between his (the middleman's) selling price of the product and his cost price thereof. A uniform trade or functional discount granted to middlemen in an industry is out of the question because such a situation will probably amount to an infringement of the prohibition of 2 May 1986 (see Chapter 16, section 16.4.2).

Nevertheless, the difference between the selling price and the cost price is also the gross profit, which means that the trade discount and the gross profit are related concepts. As mentioned earlier, the trade discount is calculated on the selling prices of the various middlemen, while the gross profit is usually calculated as a percentage of the purchasing price (cost price). The mark-up on the cost price and the mark-up on the selling price are, however, entirely different entities. The following serves as an illustration:

Calculating the mark-up

Calculate the mark-up on the selling price if the mark-up on the cost price is 25 per cent.

The mark-up is calculated on the cost price and therefore the cost price is assumed to be 100 (it can be R100 or 100 cents, et cetera). If the cost price is 100, and the mark-up on cost 25 per cent, the selling price must be 125. The mark-up expressed as a percentage of the selling price is thus:

$$\frac{25}{125} \times \frac{100}{1} = 20 \text{ per cent}$$

Calculate the mark-up on the cost price if the mark-up on the selling price is 20 per cent.

The mark-up is calculated on the selling price and therefore the selling price is assumed to be 100 (it can be R100 or 100 cents, et cetera). If the selling price is 100, and the mark-up on the selling price 20 per cent, the cost price must be 80. The mark-up expressed as a percentage of the cost price is thus:

$$\frac{20}{80} \times \frac{100}{1} = 25 \text{ per cent}$$

It goes without saying that only those firms which suggest retail prices to the middlemen can grant trade discounts. In these cases the basic price of the manufacturer makes provision for the trade discounts granted to middlemen. In those cases where the manufacturer does not suggest prices to the middlemen, the latter themselves determine the basic selling price of the products they bought from the manufacturer along more or less the same lines as set out in Chapter 16. In these cases the middlemen thus themselves determine their mark-up (gross profit), being the difference between their cost price (the selling price of the manufacturer) and their eventual net selling price (the basic selling price minus or plus any deviations).

In the following discussion of trade discounts it will be assumed that the manufacturer suggests the retail price to the middleman. It is necessary briefly to consider the factors to be borne in mind when determining the extent of the trade discount because it is not a fixed percentage of the suggested retail price which is the same for all products and all middlemen. The following factors, inter alia, have to be considered in determining the size of the trade discount:

- Traditional trade discounts often exist for some products and a manufacturer who drastically deviates from this will probably not obtain the middlemen's co-operation.
- Middelmen often expect different trade discounts for the products in a product line.
- The trade discount must relate to the services rendered by the middleman.
- The operating costs of the middlemen.
- The costs of marketing to the middlemen.
- The trade discounts granted by competitors to the middlemen.
- The intensity of distribution.
- The turnover of the middlemen.
- The negotiation abilities and persuasiveness of the producer and the middleman.

Some of the above factors are naturally not readily quantifiable.

17.2.2 Quantity discounts

Two types of quantity discount are identified, namely cumulative quantity discounts and non-cumulative quantity discounts.

Cumulative quantity discounts

Cumulative quantity discounts are discounts which are granted on the basis of the amount of products bought over a certain period of time from the marketer.

The purpose is not quite to promote large orders at a time, but rather to establish a long-term relationship with the buyer and, as it were, to bind him to the marketer. The cumulative quantity discount is not calculated per order, but on the total purchases after, and on expiry of a certain period.

The long-term nature of cumulative trade discounts means that the marketer can plan more effectively. Thus the marketer is able to forecast possible demand more accurately, which facilitates smoother production runs. The buyer enjoys the benefits of lower inventory costs, especially in the case of perishable products.

Non-cumulative quantity discounts

The aim of non-cumulative quantity discounts is to encourage large orders per transaction. Quantity discounts usually increase progressively with order size.

Example of non-cumulative quantity discounts		
Order size		Percentage discount
	R 100	0%
> R 100	⩽ R 250	2%
> R 250	⩽ R 500	4%
> R 500	⩽ R1 000	5%
> R1 000	⩽ R5 000	6%
> R5 000		$7\frac{1}{2}$%

The benefits of large orders for the marketer are inter alia lower administrative costs owing to need for fewer packaging personnel and clerks, and lower inventory costs compared to the inventory costs if small orders are placed.

Large orders, however, mean higher inventory costs for the buyer. The quantity discount therefore has to be determined in such a way that the lower prices do not eliminate the benefit of large orders for the marketer and yet motivate the buyer to hold inventories.[1]

17.2.3 Cash discounts

Cash discounts are granted by the marketer to the buyer should the latter settle his account within a certain period. The cash discount is usually indicated on the invoice and a typical notation, for example, is 2/10, net 30. This notation means that 2 per cent discount will be allowed on the net amount of the invoice (trade discounts are usually already subtracted from the gross amount) should the account be settled within 10 days from date. The account has to be settled within 30 days of date in any case.

Example of a cash discount

Suppose that the net figure on the invoice is R100. Should the buyer settle within 10 days, he is allowed R2 discount, or 2% discount, and pays only R98. As the buyer would have settled within 30 days, he earns R2 on an investment of R98 for 20 days. The effective interest rate of the 2% discount is thus:

$$\frac{2}{98} \times \frac{360}{20} \times \frac{100}{1} = 36{,}73 \text{ per cent per annum.}$$

The following reasons can be advanced for granting cash discounts:

- To encourage the prompt settlement of accounts. The prompt settlement of accounts effects an improvement in the seller's liquidity position and a decrease in the debtor administration and collection costs.
- To reduce the costs of bad debts.
- To comply with discount traditions in a particular industry.

The manner in which the cash discount is granted is important. Research indicates that consumers prefer positive alternatives to negative alternatives.[2] The consumer regards a choice between negative alternatives as no choice at all.

Suppose the cash discount and credit terms of a firm appear as follows on an invoice of R100:

Terms: 2/10 net 30. A service charge of 10 per cent is levied on accounts outstanding for more than 30 days.

The consumer must:

- pay R98 within 10 days; or
- pay R100 between the eleventh and thirtieth days; or
- pay R110 after the thirtieth day.

The consumer is offered a reward (positive alternative) for the prompt settlement of the account but is also threatened by a penalty clause (negative alternative) should he postpone payment of the account.

Suppose the invoice is for R110, but the consumer is offered a reward of R12 should he pay within 10 days and a reward of R10 should he pay between the eleventh and thirtieth day. The consumer now has a choice between two positive alternatives.

17.2.4 Seasonal discounts

Seasonal discounts are granted if the product is bought during a particular season or month or week or day or time of the day. In South Africa fertiliser firms offer a seasonal discount on fertiliser purchases. The earlier the fertiliser purchases are made before the planting season, the bigger the percentage discount on the cost price. A positive reaction to such a discount usually has a favourable influence on the firm's liquidity position, inventory costs and utilisation of production capacity. The last-mentioned objective is aimed at especially by firms in the tourist industry when granting seasonal discounts.

17.2.5 Discounts for special price offers

These discounts are granted by the marketer to the middleman when the marketer is eager to make his products available to the final consumer at a lower price than usual. As the middleman can perhaps make his shelf-space available for more profitable products, it is logical that he will expect special discounts from a marketer offering special prices to the final consumer.

17.2.6 Discounts for co-operative advertising

These are granted by the marketer when the middleman incurs advertising costs on his behalf for a particular product. These discounts are not the same as functional discounts.

17.3 THE GEOGRAPHICAL LOCATION OF THE BUYER

The geographical location of the buyer as against the location of the marketer means that decisions have to be taken as to who should be responsible for which transport costs. The following geographical price differences or price differentials are identified, namely free-on-rail pricing, freight-absorption pricing, uniform regional pricing and base-point pricing.

17.3.1 Free-on-rail pricing

According to free-on-rail pricing (for or fob — free on board) the marketer quotes prices for delivery at his location. The marketer therefore receives the same price for similar products regardless of the buyer's location. The buyer pays the full railage costs on the products from the marketer's location. This geographical pricing decision means that the marketer, all other factors being equal, has a price disadvantage when compared to marketers located nearer the buyer, as the buyer has to pay lower railage costs.

17.3.2 Freight-absorption pricing

A disadvantage of free-on-rail pricing is that special monopolies can be created. To obviate this disadvantage some firms follow freight-absorption pricing. In this case the marketer quotes uniform prices irrespective of the buyer's location. The total transport costs are usually budgeted for and an average transport cost per order is built into the cost price of the product. Freight-absorption pricing is also known as postage stamp pricing.

17.3.3 Uniform regional pricing

Uniform regional pricing is a combination of a free-on-rail pricing approach and freight-absorption pricing. According to this uniform prices are found within each particular region, while the prices vary from region to region because of transport costs (free-on-rail pricing). A typical example in South Africa of uniform regional pricing is the price of petroleum products.

17.3.4 Base-point pricing

A base-point price to some extent corresponds with a free-on-rail price, except that the seller quotes prices that include the transport costs from a certain place (base point). More than one point is often used and these base points can be located at the same places as the factories, although not necessarily so. Base-point pricing can be applied by an individual firm or by an industry. Base-point pricing is illustrated in Figure 17.1. Some advantages which the participants gain from an industry base-point price are that price competition based on differences in transport costs is eliminated, and the geographical extent of the market is not limited by transport costs.

Possible disadvantages are that the elimination of price competition can result in higher and rigid prices, and consumer resistance can develop if the consumer discovers that he pays transport costs from a place other than the place of origin.

It is important to note that an industry base-point pricing system implies that collusion exists among the members of the industry. The only industry in South Africa which applies a variation of the base-point system is the cement industry. This industry received exemption from the prohibition of 2 May 1986 (see Chapter 16, section 16.4.2).

It is sometimes alleged that the consumer is greatly influenced by odd-number prices, traditional prices and price lines. The consumer's attitude towards prices is important to the marketer because it eventually determines the demand for his products. The aspects to be discussed are odd-number prices, price lines, and traditional prices.

17.4 PRICING DECISIONS BASED ON THE CONSUMER'S ATTITUDE TOWARDS PRICES

17.4.1 Odd-number prices

Odd-number prices refer to prices ending with an odd number, such as one, three, five, seven or nine. Usually, however, the term refers to prices ending just under round figures, such as 99 cents; R4,99; R990 and R39 900. Supporters of odd-number prices are convinced that:

- The consumer regards a price of R4,99 as being significantly lower than R5,00; and
- a price of R4,99 sounds like a bargain, but a price of R4,80 does not.

FIGURE 17.1   Base-point pricing

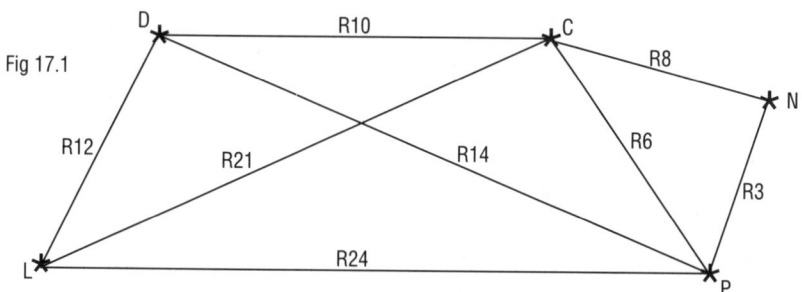

Fig 17.1

Base point: C, P
Production points: D, C, P
Price per unit: R40 ex-factory

Transaction	Price (R)	Real freight (R)	Buyer pays (R)	Sales (R)	Freight absorbed by producer (R)	Phantom freight (R)
C to C	40	0	40	40	0	0
C to P	40	6	40	34	6	0
C to N	40	8	43	35	5	0
D to D	40	0	50	50	0	10
D to L	40	12	61	49	0	9
P to N	40	3	43	40	0	0
P to D	40	14	50	36	4	0
P to L	40	24	61	37	3	0

Source: Stanton, WJ. 1971. *Fundamentals of Marketing.* 3rd edition. New York: McGraw-Hill Book Company, p 461.

The demand curve for odd-number prices is given in Figure 17.2.

Figure 17.2 shows that quantity OQ is demanded at an odd-number price of OP. According to the law of supply and demand a price lower than OP should give rise to sales higher than OQ. The demand curve for odd-number prices, however, shows that at a price of OP_1 (lower than OP) only OQ_1 units (smaller than OQ) are demanded. The consumers thus buy more of a product whenever it has an odd-number price.

The benefits of odd-number prices to the firm have not been proven to date. Conspicuous, however, is the great number of products which have odd-number prices — a cursory glance at prices at any supermarket will confirm this statement.

The popularity of odd-number figures probably emanates from the retail trade. Odd-numbered prices probably forced the salesperson to ring the amount on the

FIGURE 17.2   The demand curve for odd-number prices

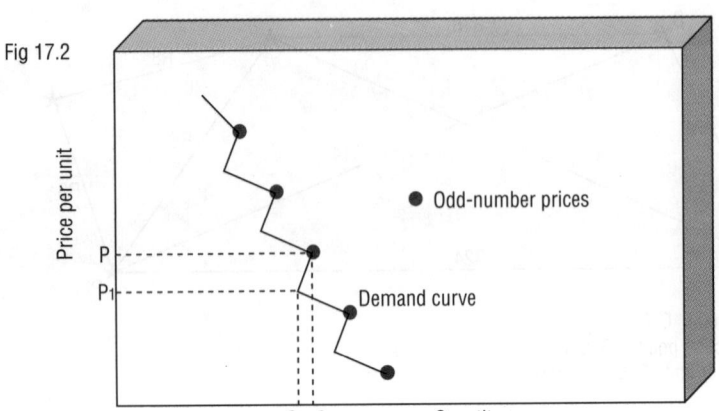

cash register in order to give change to the consumer. The introduction of general sales tax (GST) apparently did not play a role regarding consumers influenced by odd-number prices.

17.4.2 Price lines

Price lines occur in those cases where the retailer has a limited number of prices in each of his product lines. Three prices are usually found in a particular product line — the so-called good, better and best product approach. The prices have to differ in such a way that they impart the relevant quality differences, for example shirts at R54,99; R69,99 and R74,99.

The demand curve for price lines is shown in Figure 17.3.

Figure 17.3 shows that consumers will buy OQ units of the product even if the price thereof varies between OP and OP_1 each. The consumer accepts that prices between OP and OP_1 for the product are more or less the same. Any price decrease between OP and OP_1 will make no difference to the quantity demanded — the price difference must thus be more than PP_1.

An advantage of price lines to the consumer is that he can exercise his right of choice somewhat more easily. It is usually easier to choose between three alternative prices for a similar product than ten.

17.4.3 Traditional prices

Traditional prices refer to the practice of maintaining the retail price of a product at the same level over long periods. Cost increases are not recovered in the price but are met in other ways, such as lowering the quality of the product, lessening the amount of product in the package and lower packaging costs. Supporters of

FIGURE 17.3   The demand curve for price lines

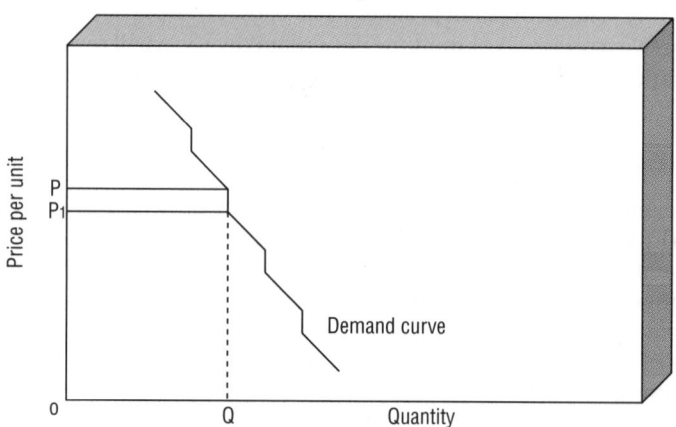

traditional prices allege that the consumer has become so accustomed to certain prices that a higher price will not be acceptable to him.

Traditional prices were to be found once, such as confectionary and ice-cream selling at 5 and 10 cents. It is doubtful whether any products with traditional prices are being marketed in South Africa at present. Double-figure inflation rates and the influence of general sales tax over the past number of years make traditional prices virtually impossible.

17.5 SKIMMING-THE-CREAM AND PENETRATION PRICING DECISIONS

The skimming-the-cream and penetration pricing decisions are two extremes which can be found in the introductory phase of a new product.

A skimming-the-cream decision is followed when a **relatively high price** is charged, and this is possible if:

- The demand for the product is price inelastic or relatively price inelastic.
- Few potential competitors exist.
- Prices are used to segment the market.
- The costs and demand are unknown. Should the price be set too high it can always be reduced at a later stage.
- The consumer knows little about the new product.
- A speedy recovery of the investment is required.

A penetration pricing decision is followed when a **relatively low price** is charged and this is possible if:

- The price elasticity of the demand is relatively high.
- Savings in production costs are possible with a higher production volume.
- A market exists which will not or cannot accept high prices.
- A strong possibility of potential competition exists.

The skimming-the-cream and penetration pricing decisions are two extremes which probably seldom occur in practice. The choice of a particular price often lies between these extremes. A skimming-the-cream decision will result in lower sales and penetration pricing decision in higher sales, all other factors being equal.

17.6 BREAKEVEN ANALYSIS

The breakeven point of an enterprise is the extent of activities (marketing and production) where the total cost (the total fixed and total variable cost) is equal to total revenue. It is thus the extent of activities where the enterprise does not make a profit or a loss but stands at the threshold of doing so. Breakeven analysis is therefore also known as threshold analysis. The threshold is reached when the production of one more unit will mean a profit.

If for example the total fixed cost to produce and market between 10 000 and 12 500 units is R10 000 and the selling price per product is R5 and the variable cost R4 per product, then the profit or loss position of the enterprise at different production levels is as follows:

Item	Units produced and marketed		
	9 999	10 000	10 001
Total revenue (units X R5)	R49 995	R50 000	R50 005
Less:: Total fixed cost	R10 000	R10 000	R10 000
Total variable cost (units X4)	R39 996	R40 000	R40 004
Total cost	R49 996	R50 000	R50 004
Profit (loss)	R (1)	R0	R1

From the above it is clear the enterprise at a capacity of 10 000 units will neither make a profit nor a loss (the profit threshold of the enterprise is 10 000 if it is accepted that it is possible to sell all the units produced). The enterprise is now on the threshold of making a profit — which will happen if one more product is produced and marketed. When 10 001 units are sold a profit of R1 will be made. The enterprise is also on the threshold of making a loss. This will happen if one unit less than the threshold volume is produced and marketed. This will happen when 9 999 units are produced. The loss will be R1.

The profit of R1 made when 10 001 units are produced is equal to the selling price (R5) *less* the variable cost (4). This difference between the selling price and variable cost is known as marginal revenue. The selling price of the first unit manufactured and marketed brings about a marginal revenue of R1. The selling price of R5 covers the variable cost thereof (R4) and the difference (R1) is a contribution to cover the fixed cost of R10 000. Therefore the marginal revenue is regarded as a contribution towards the total fixed cost. If the enterprise produces and markets 10 000 units each one will contribute R1 to the total fixed cost — R10 000. When the total fixed cost is covered, marginal revenue will be equal to profit.

To summarise

(i) Beneath the breakeven point the marginal income will contribute to total fixed cost.

(ii) Above the breakeven point the marginal income will be equal to profit.

The following formula is used to determine the breakeven point in units (BEU). (The foregoing example is used to illustrate the use of the formula):

$$\text{BEU} = \frac{\text{Total fixed cost}}{\text{Price per unit (p)} - \text{Variable cost per unit (vc)}}$$

$$= \frac{10\ 000}{5 - 4}$$

$$= 10\ 000 \text{ units.}$$

The breakeven point is shown in the following figure:

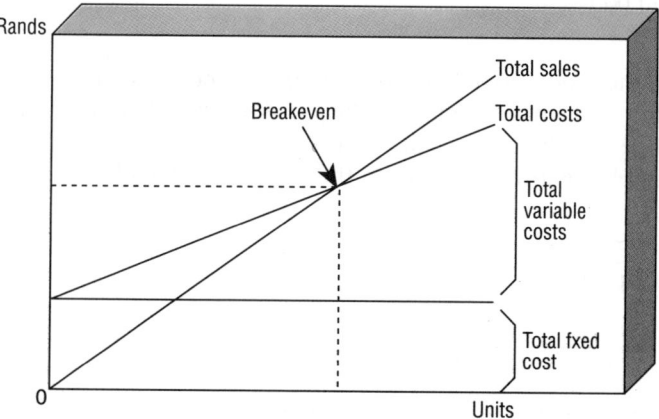

17.6.1 The profit/volume ratio

The profit/volume ratio indicates the relationship between marginal revenue and the selling price per unit. In the above example this equation is:

$$\frac{\text{Marginal revenue}}{\text{Selling price}}$$

$$= \frac{1}{5}$$

$$= 0,2.$$

The breakeven in rands (BER) is calculated as follows:

$$\text{BER} = \frac{\text{Total fixed cost}}{\text{Profit/volume ratio (pv)}}$$

$$= \frac{10\ 000}{5 - 4/5 \text{ (or 0,2)}}$$

$$= \text{R50 000.}$$

OR

$$BER = \frac{\text{Total fixed cost}}{\dfrac{\text{Price} - \text{Variable cost}}{\text{Price}}}$$

$$= \frac{\text{Total fixed cost}}{1 - \dfrac{\text{Variable cost}}{\text{Price}}}$$

$$= \frac{10\ 000}{1 - (4/5)}$$

$$= \frac{10\ 000}{0,2}$$

$$= R50\ 000.$$

The profit/volume ratio (pv) defined as the marginal income (price (p) — variable cost (vc) divided by the price per unit). The pv is thus the relationship between the marginal income and the price of the product.

A high pv implies a low rc relative to the price, for example:

$$pv = \frac{P - vk}{p}$$

$$0,7 = \frac{1 - 0,3}{1.}$$

A low pv implies a high vc relative to the price, for example:

$$pv = \frac{P - vk}{p}$$

$$0,3 = \frac{1 - 0,7}{1.}$$

A high pv means that the BEU and BER are sooner reached in comparison with a lower pv. In the following example, in which the fixed cost of both enterprises is equal to R10 000, the pv for enterprise A is 0,7 and that for enterprise B is 0,03.

	Enterprise	
	A	B
BER	10 000 0,7	10 000 0,3
=	R14 285,71	R33 333,33

A high pv means that the breakeven point is reached sooner and a quicker increase in profit after the breakeven point has been reached. An increase in turnover of R1 000 results in a profit of R700 for enterprise A but the same increase in turnover results in a profit of only R300 for enterprise B.

The profit of an enterprise can therefore be calculated as follows:

Enteprise A

$$\begin{aligned} \text{Profit} &= (\text{Total sales} \times \text{pv}) - \text{total fixed cost} \\ &= (15\ 285{,}71 \times 0{,}7) - 10\ 000 \\ &= \text{R700} \end{aligned}$$

Enteprise B

$$\begin{aligned} \text{Profit} &= (\text{Total sales} \times \text{pv}) - \text{total fixed cost} \\ &= (34\ 333 \times 0{,}3) - 10\ 000 \\ &= \text{R300} \end{aligned}$$

17.6.2 Guidelines for breakeven analysis

17.6.2.1 *An increase in the total fixed cost influences the breakeven point*

Consider the case where the total fixed cost increases from R10 000 to R15 000. Determine the breakeven point in rands if the profit/volume ratio is 0,2.

$$\begin{aligned} \text{BER} &= \frac{\text{Total fixed cost}}{\text{pv}} \\ &= \frac{15\ 000}{0{,}2} \\ &= \text{R75 000.} \end{aligned}$$

The previous breakeven point was at R50 000. In the example the total fixed cost increases with only R5 000 but sales must increase with R25 000 for the profit threshold to be maintained.

17.6.2.2 *A change in price influences the breakeven point*

Consider the case where the price increases from R5 to R6. Now determine the breakeven point in rands if the total fixed cost is R10 000 and the variable cost per unit is R4.

$$\begin{aligned} \text{BER} &= \frac{\text{Total fixed cost}}{\text{pv}} \\ &= \frac{10\ 000}{(6-4)/6} \\ &= \text{R30 000} \end{aligned}$$

The previous breakeven point was at R50 000. If the price (as in the example) increases with only R1 sales can decrease with R20 000 for the profit threshold to be maintained.

17.6.2.3 *A change in the variable cost per unit influences the profit threshold*

Consider the case where the variable cost per unit increases from R4 to R4,50. Determine the profit threshold in rands if the selling price per unit is R5 and the total cost R10 000.

$$\text{BER} = \frac{\text{Total fixed cost}}{\text{pv}}$$

$$= \frac{10\ 000}{(5-4,50)/5}$$

$$= \text{R100 000}$$

The previous breakeven point was at R50 000. If the variable cost per unit in the example increases with 50 cents sales must increase by 100 per cent (from R50 000 to R100 000 in order for the profit threshold to be maintained.

17.6.2.4 *A change in the price or the variable cost influences the profit/ volume ratio*

The profit/volume ratio is equal to the marginal income divided by the selling price. The marginal income is equal to the selling price minus the variable cost per unit. If the selling price or the variable cost per unit changes the profit/volume ratio will change.

17.6.2.5 *Products with the same profit threshold earn profits or sustain losses in terms of the profit/volume ratio*

The following example shows that products with the same profit threshold earn profits or sustain losses in terms of the profit/volume ratio:

	Product	
Item	A	B
Total fixed cost	10 000	20 000
Price (R) Variable cost per unit (R)	5 4	25 15
Breakeven in rand	50 000	50 000
Profit/volume ratio	0,2	0,4

If sales of products A and B are R50 001 each the profit earned by A and B will be:

$$\text{Profit} = \text{Total sales} \times \text{pv} - \text{total fixed cost}$$

Therefore for product A the profit is:

$$(\text{R50 001} \times 0,2) - 10\ 000 = 20c\ (\text{of } 0,2 \text{ of R1});$$

and for product B the profit is:

$$(\text{R50 001} \times 0,4) - 20\ 000 = 40c\ (\text{of } 0,4 \text{ of R1}).$$

17.6.3 The breakeven analysis in multiproduct enterprises

The breakeven analysis as explained is usually not applicable to multiproduct enterprises. The reason for this is the differences between the marginal income and the profit/volume ratios of the different products in the enterprise's product range. A multiproduct enterprise uses the weighted marginal income relationship. The profit/volume ratio of the different products in the product range is weighted with the percentage of the turnover attributed to the products.

Consider the case where an enterprise with total fixed cost of R120 500 manufactures and markets products A, B and C.

The details are as follows:

Item	Basis	Product A	B	C
Selling price per unit	R	18	20	25
Variable cost per unit	R	12	15	20
Marginal income per unit	R	6	5	5
Marginal income relationship		0,33	0,25	0,20
Expected percentage of turnover	%	20	30	50
Weighted marginal income		0,066[a]	0,075[b]	0,10[c]
Total wieghted marginal income relationship			0,241[d]	

(a) $0,33 \times 0,2$ (20 per cent of expected turnover)

(b) $0,25 \times 0,3$ (30 per cent of expected turnover)

(c) $0,20 \times 0,5$ (50 per cent of expected turnover)

(d) $0,066 + 0,075 + 0,10$

Now determine
    (i) The profit threshold in rands
    (ii) The profit if sales are R3 million

Calculation:

$$\text{(i)} \quad \text{BER} = \frac{\text{Total fixed cost}}{\text{pv}}$$

$$= \frac{120\ 500}{0,241}$$

$$= \text{R500 000}$$

$$\text{(ii)} \quad \text{Profit} = (\text{Total sales} \times \text{pv}) - \text{total fixed cost}$$

$$= (3\ 000\ 000 \times 0,24) - 120\ 500$$

$$= \text{R599 500}$$

17.7 SUMMARY

The marketer cannot take it for granted that he will sell the product at the calculated selling price. The most important factors which could lead to this deviation are the various types of discount granted by the marketer, the geographical location of the buyer, and aspects of the consumer's attitude towards prices. The chapter was concluded by a short discussion of the two divergent pricing decisions in the introductory phase of the product life cycle and breakdown analyis. Refer also to the pricing decisions during the product life cycle as discussed in Chapter 18.

REFERENCES

1. See Crowther, JF. 'Rationale for Quantity Discounts'. *Harvard Business Review*, No 42, March/April 1964, pp 121–37 for a practical example of the determination of the optimal non-cumulative quantity discount.
2. See Jellison, JM and Harvey, JH. 'Determinants of Perceived Choice and the Relationship between Perceived Choice and Perceived Competence', *Journal of Personality and Social Psychology*, No 28, 1973, pp 376–82; and Jellison, JM & Harvey, JH 'Why we like Hard, Positive Choices', *Psychology Today*, No 9, March 1976, pp 47–9.
3. Partly based on Tucker, SA. 1966. *Pricing for Higher Profit*. New York: McGraw Hill, Chapter 10.

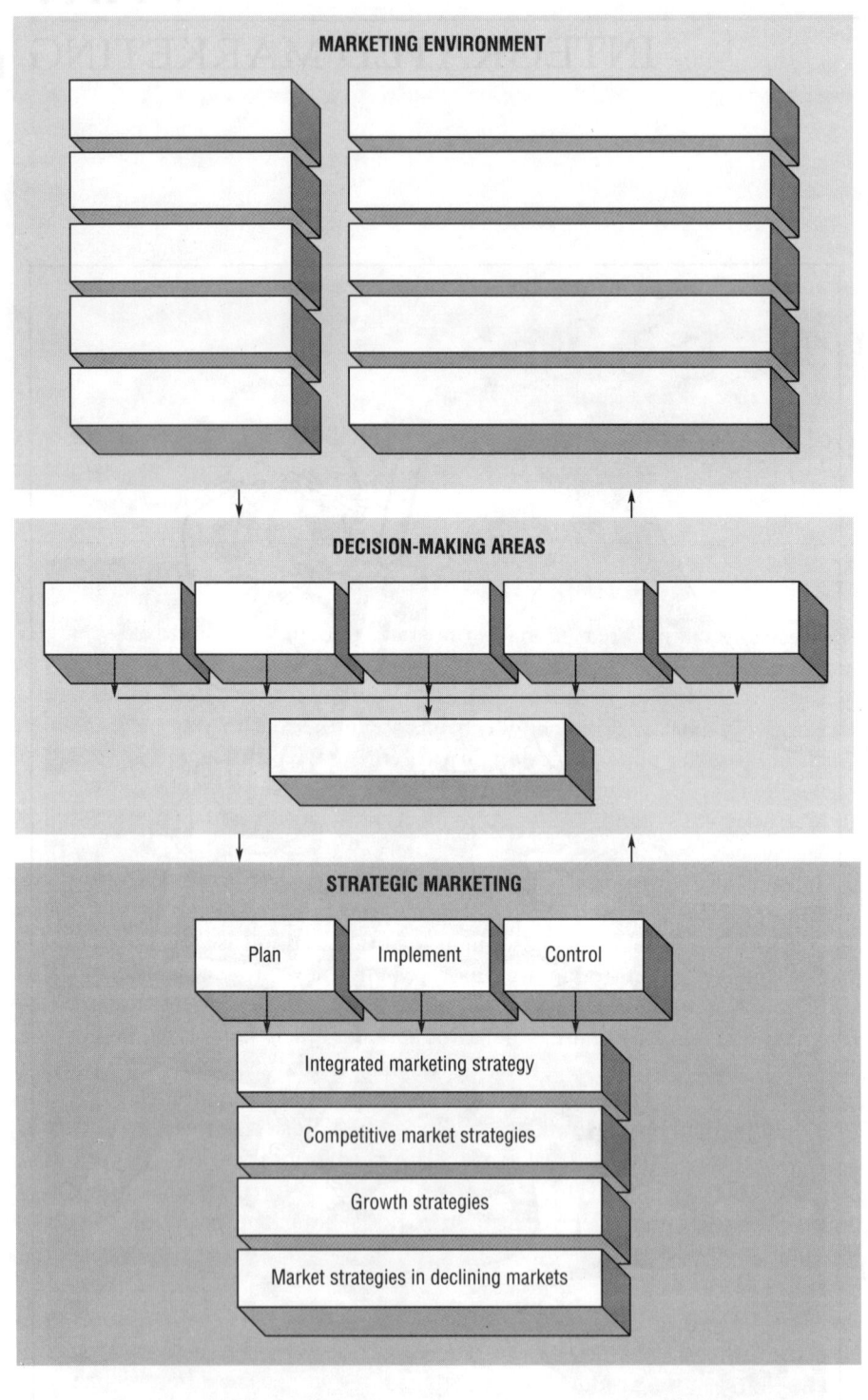

MARKETING ENVIRONMENT

DECISION-MAKING AREAS

STRATEGIC MARKETING

Plan   Implement   Control

Integrated marketing strategy

Competitive market strategies

Growth strategies

Market strategies in declining markets

CHAPTER 18

THE PRODUCT LIFE CYCLE

18.1 INTRODUCTION

The decision making areas in marketing management were discussed separately and in detail in the previous eleven chapters. Attention was paid to product decisions, distribution decisions, marketing communication decisions and price decisions. As already explained, decisions about the four marketing instruments which fall directly under marketing management are combined in an integrated marketing strategy, earmarked for a specific target market. This chapter is the first of three in which a number of different facets of the integrated marketing strategy are discussed.

The aim of this chapter is to explain the general characteristics of a typical consumer product life cycle. Shakespeare wrote about the 'seven ages of man' — the product also has several phases in its life cycle. In this case there are only four phases, namely the introductory phase (when a new product is offered on the market for the first time), the growth phase (during which product sales gradually increase), the maturity phase (when product sales reach their peak), and then the declining phase (when, unavoidably, stagnation and decreasing sales set in). Because the competitive situation and consumer behaviour patterns, too, change with time the marketing strategy often has to be adjusted during the product life cycle. Mention is also made of warfare during the phases in the life cycle when marketing management is threatened by competitors, forcing it to change or adapt the marketing strategy, depending on whether an attack or a strategic withdrawal is planned.

ORGANISATION OF THE CHAPTER

The course of the product life cycle: The different phases, different kinds of product life cycles, product life cycle of a fad and a trend, product life cycle of a product class, form and brand, the life cycle of a product mix.

> **Characteristics of the phases in the product life cycle:** Introductory phase, growth phase, maturity phase, declining phase.
>
> **Integrated marketing strategies during the product life cycle:** The meaning of 'strategy', integrated marketing strategy and warfare during the introductory phase, integrated marketing strategy and warfare during the growth phase, integrated marketing strategy and warfare during the maturity phase, integrated marketing strategy and warfare during the declining phase.

18.2 THE COURSE OF THE PRODUCT LIFE CYCLE

18.2.1 The different phases in the product life cycle

Products, just like biological beings, have specific life cycles. They are developed (prenatal phase), placed on the market for the first time (born), compete in the market and reach maturity (maturity phase), and are eventually withdrawn from the market (die). Product development ends with commercialisation. This is where the successfully developed and tested product is introduced to the target market on a large scale for the first time. The steps in new product development have already been discussed in Chapter 8. In this chapter the further life course of the product is sketched.

During the product life cycle, ie from its first introduction to its eventual withdrawal, the product time and time again finds itself in different competitive market environments, necessitating changes to the marketing strategy. Depending on the extent of, as well as the relative growth rate in product sales (which, measured over time, usually has an S-shaped development), an introductory, growth, maturity and declining phase can usually be identified in the life of the product in the target market.

The duration of the product life cycle varies from product to product. Fashion articles and accessories, for instance, have a very short life span of approximately one to three months, whereas other products, such as coal stoves and bicycles could have a very long life span. In general, however, it appears that the life cycles of products are tending to decrease. Bennett & Cooper[1] are of the opinion that too many enterprises allow their products to reach the maturity and declining phases without developing new products to replace them. Yesterday's market leaders with their highly successful products are thus not the market leaders of tomorrow because their enterprises' emphases have shifted from research and development to a non-product phase. All attention is thus focused on the marketing communications instruments as well as the price and distribution instruments, at the cost of long-term product leadership. (This aspect is discussed in greater detail in Chapter 19.) The four phases of the product life cycle are now examined in more depth. Noticeably, the four life cycle phases are closely related to the diffusion process discussed in Chapter 8.

Phase 1: Introductory phase. The introductory phase begins after preparations for entering the target market have been completed and the product is offered for sale. The initial sales are usually relatively small. However, after it has been approved of by the first adopters, purchases by early adopters follow. Satisfaction, reinforced by promotion, leads to repurchasing and as soon as sales increase further, the product exits this phase.

Phase 2: Growth phase. The growth phase is characterised by a strong growth in sales in the target market, especially because of the increase in repurchasing and purchases across a wide spectrum by the early majority of consumers. Competitors enter the target market with similar products (if they can) and the impact of their promotions gives further momentum to the demand for the product.

Phase 3: Maturity phase. As soon as the maturity phase is entered, sales growth and the demand for the product in the target market level off. The late majority are also already buying the product and relatively few non-consumers remain in the target market. Few, if any, additional competitors enter the market with similar products. Improved products that satisfy the same needs are launched, attracting the first and early adopters. A stage of **market saturation** is eventually reached — sales of the product level off and start to decline. The laggards now start buying the product.

Phase 4: Declining phase. The declining phase is characterised by a rapid decline in sales in the target market. New uses for and consumers of the 'old' product are totally lacking and all the new competing (and substitute) products enjoy increasing acceptance in the target market.

Figure 18.1 shows the four phases in the product life cycle together with the sales and profit curves.

The sales curve increases during the introductory and growth phases and reaches its peak in the maturity phase. During the declining phase the sales curve starts declining. The profit curve has the same course, but starts to increase later in the introductory phase. The reason for this is the high costs of product development that have to be recovered before a profit is shown. The profit curve also starts to show a decline sooner than the sales curve. This results from intense competitive conditions, causing the price of the product and thus also its profit to drop. Together with the drop in price and profit, the costs of the product rise because of the need for increased marketing communication to stimulate demand for the product. The marketing manager should always strive to keep the product in the profitable phases of the product life cycle as long as possible.

If the product does reach the declining phase, management should consider withdrawing it. Alternatively, the product should be adapted physically and/or psychologically so that a new life cycle can be created for it, before the profit curve starts showing its declining tendency. As soon as profit starts decreasing, the growing profit of a new model should make up for it.

Neidell[2] emphasises the fact that for strategic planning purposes it is necessary to take the investment recovery curve and the sales curve into account.

FIGURE 18.1 Phases in the product life cycle

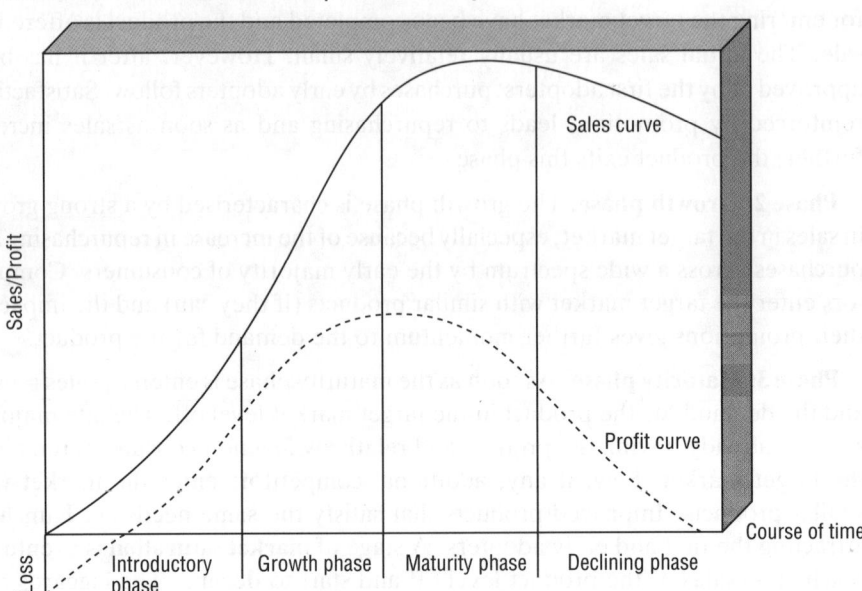

Figure 18.2 indicates the relationship between the product life cycle curve and the investment recovery curve. A new product penetrates the market as soon as sales of the 'old' product start declining.

18.2.2 Different kinds of product life cycles

The sales and profit curves in Figures 18.1 and 18.2 show the traditional life cycle of a product. Note that not all products have this kind of life cycle. Product life cycles sometimes differ vastly regarding the period as well as the course of the curve.[3] Figure 18.3 shows a few product life cycles.

The **traditional** product life cycle curve entails the clearly distinguishable periods of introduction, growth, maturity and declining. The **classic** product life cycle curve describes the surging sales growth and the reaching of a plateau phase where sales volumes stagnate as a result of a lack of new consumers or outlets. The **fashion fad** is a product which gains and loses popularity with the same rapidity. Examples of such products are pet rocks and the rugby jerseys of all the nations that participated in the 1991 World Rugby Cup sold in certain department stores. The **extended fashion fad's** course is similar, except that sales stabilise at a lower level after the initial success. An example of such a product is aerobic exercise classes; after an initial strong growth it fell back, but is still popular. The **seasonal** or **fashion curve** results when a product sells well in successive periods. Examples of such products are school clothes of which sales are good at the beginning of the year and then decline, and subsequently show a sturdy growth again at the beginning of the winter season. The **revival** curve shows a product that was regarded as old-fashioned and then suddenly revived, gaining popularity again.

An example is the mini-skirt, which first gained popularity in the early sixties and which makes a reappearance from time to time. It is at present very fashionable again. The **fiasco** curve occurs where the product was a failure right from the outset. In the eighties Brooke Bond, for example, launched a product called 'Snackpot', marketing it as an instant pasta dish in plastic packaging. Although the idea was good, consumers showed no interest in it.

FIGURE 18.2   Product life cycle and investment recovery curve

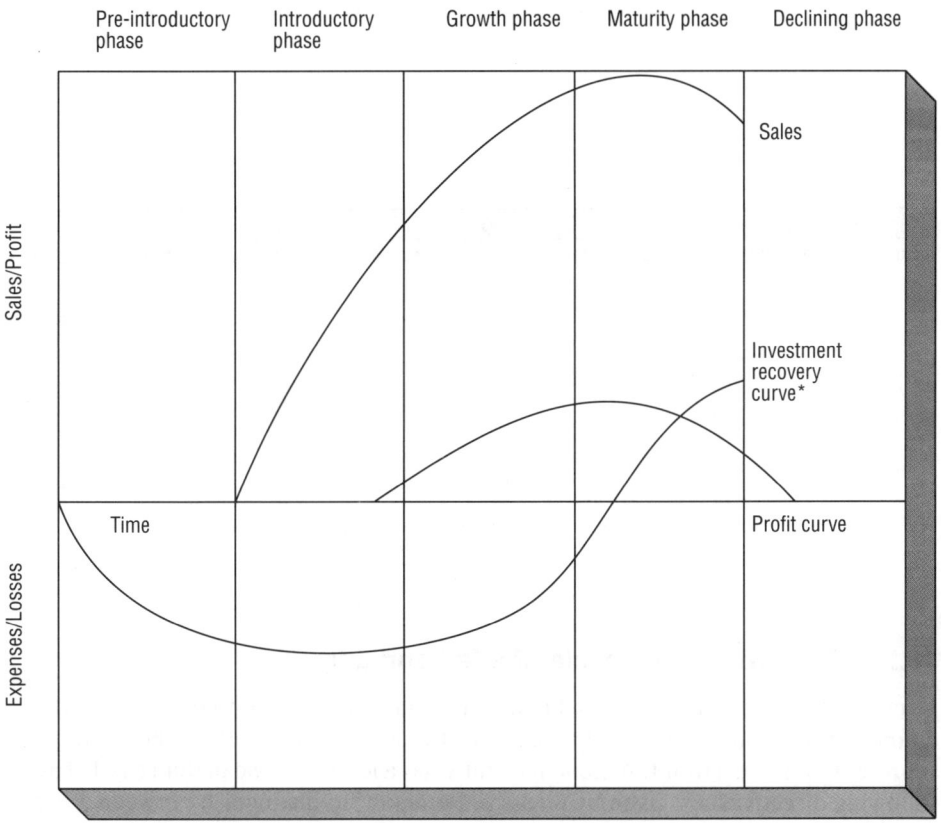

* Where investment recovery = Sales income – expenditure incurred

Source: Adapted from Neidell, LA. 'Don't Forget the Product Life Cycle for Strategic Planning'. *Business,* April–June 1983, p 31.

FIGURE 18.3   Different product life cycle patterns

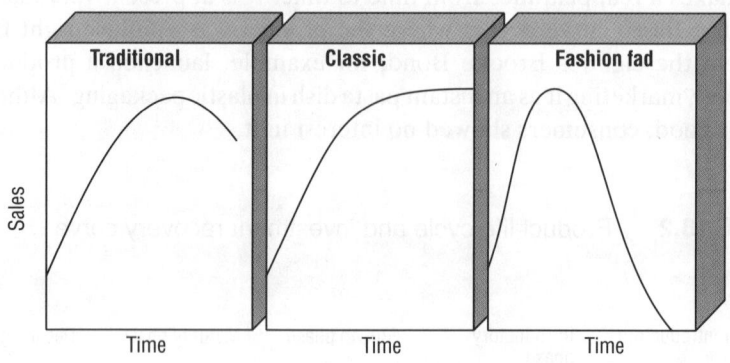

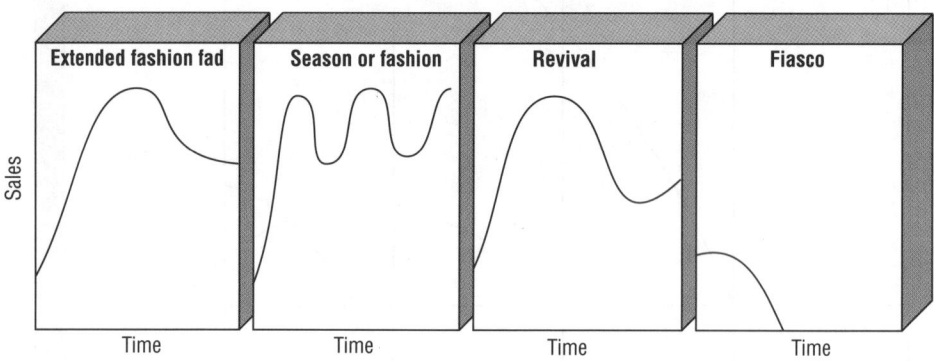

18.2.3 The product life cycle of a fad and a trend

Gross & Peterson[4] emphasise that marketing management has to think about the course of a product timeously and has to determine whether the product represents a fad or a trend. A trend naturally has a longer life-span than a fad. The following directives are given by Gross & Peterson[5] to distinguish between a fad and a trend:

- The new product has to fit into the changes in life style and values to be identified as a trend. The drastic increase in the sales of instant food is a trend which can be attributed to the change in the woman's life style, who has become both a housewife and a breadwinner working full time.

- The sources and the kind of information associated with the product show its importance. The increased consumption of margarine is, for instance, associated with reliable information regarding health, thriftiness, diet, and looking after family interests. The popularity of margarine is thus a trend rather than a fad.

- A new product's chance of survival improves tremendously if it is used in different ways by different people. The application possibilities of a product that is regarded as a fad are relatively limited. Not many adults will be convinced to acquire a punk hairstyle. This shows that this hairstyle is a youth fad of a passing nature.

- If prominent personalities are identified as early adopters of the new product, the chances are good that the trend will be established. Holiday timeshare is an example of a scheme where people of standing were first appealed to.

- Basic themes have a longer life span than specific incidents. Physical fitness is regarded as a trend, while rollerskating and BMX-racing can be seen as fads.

- A new development will more easily become a trend if it is linked to similar trends. Non-smoking is a trend because it is supported by trends related to fitness, general health and the combatting of stress.

18.2.4 The product life cycle of a product class, product form and brand

Up to this stage the product life cycle has been discussed in terms of a single dimension, namely as a basic product or service offered to the consumer. As already discussed in Chapters 7–9, it appears that there are still other product dimensions related to the product life cycle. The three dimensions according to which a product life cycle can be distinguished are the following:

- The life cycle of the **product class** (for instance, cigarettes).

- The life cycle of the **product form** (for example, ordinary filter cigarettes).

- The life cycle of each **brand** (for example, Lexington, Chesterfield and Philip Morris cigarettes).

In a classic article the relationship between the three life cycles regarding the cigarette market (for the cigarette industry) in the United States of America is illustrated (Figure 18.4).

From Figure 18.4 it is clear that the life cycle of the product class is longer than that of a particular product form and definitely longer than that of a specific brand.

The sales of most of the product classes will probably remain in the maturity phase for an indefinite period, especially because it is related inter alia to population size and growth. The life cycles of product forms usually reflect the typical life courses of products more reliably than product classes. Product forms, such as the gramophone, horse-cart, the power-paraffin-driven tractor and parquet floors, certainly went through an introductory, a growth, a maturity and a declining phase. The sales of individual brands are often subject to great

FIGURE 18.4 The three life cycles involved in the cigarette market in the United States of America

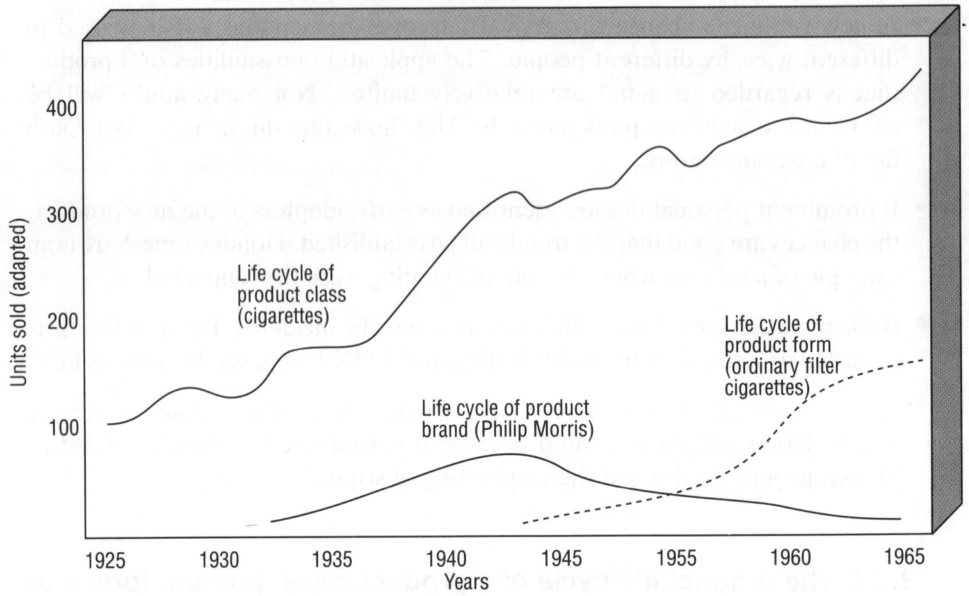

Note: Units sold indicate the number of cigarettes per $100 sold (at constant prices)

Source: Taken from Polli, R & Cook, V. 'Validity of the Product Life Cycle' in *Journal of Business,* vol 42: no 4, October 1969, p 385. (Own title and captions.)

fluctuations, especially because of changing competitive strategies. The life cycle of a specific brand does thus not always necessarily show the traditional smooth S-shaped development, and a brand in the maturity phase can, for instance, suddenly experience a sharp increase in growth for some or other reason.

18.2.5 The life cycle of the product mix

The product life cycle concept is especially useful for marketing management because it gives a broad framework in which effective marketing strategies can be formulated and decisions taken for each life cycle phase of individual product items in the product mix.

Most manufacturing enterprises manufacture different kinds of product items with varying ages and sales volumes. The product life cycle concept is an especially useful aid in considering the ideal product mix, i e the product mix which the enterprise has to have all the time in order to attain its objective, expressed in expected sales growth, market share and profitability. The survival, growth and profitability of the enterprise is thus determined by a combination of individual product items which are in different life cycle phases in the various target markets. Figure 18.5 illustrates this statement.

FIGURE 18.5   Sales of the enterprise and sales of individual product items in the product mix

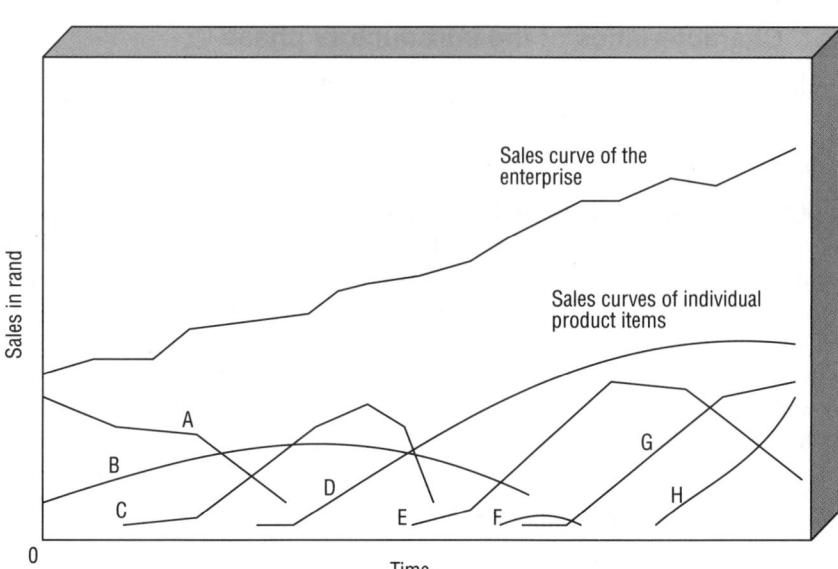

Source: Adapted from Luck, DJ. 1972. *Product Policy and Strategy*. Englewood Cliffs, New Jersey: Prentice-Hall Inc, p 14.

From Figure 18.5 it appears that, as the sales of some products drop, the turnover of other products in the product mix must show powerful growth if the enterprise wants to maintain increasing sales. The integrated marketing strategy during each product's life cycle phases is aimed at ensuring this increasing trend. (This aspect is discussed further in Chapter 19.)

The characteristics of the four phases in the product life cycle are discussed with reference to the traditional life cycle curve of a specific product item (although the characteristics also, to a lesser or greater degree, apply to the phases of the product life cycle of a product class, a product form and even the product mix).

The marketing decisions regarding the product life cycle can probably best be described if they are linked to the characteristics of each phase of this life cycle. In actual fact, the characteristics and marketing decisions involved in the introductory, growth, maturity and declining phases of the product life cycle of each product are inseparable. An attempt is none the less made to concentrate first on the characteristics before the integrated marketing strategies are considered.

18.3 CHARACTERISTICS OF THE PHASES OF THE PRODUCT LIFE CYCLE[6]

18.3.1 Characteristics of the introductory phase

Only the most important characteristics of the introductory phase are indicated.

Consumer resistance

One of the most serious risks in the market development of new products is the non-acceptance of the product by the target market. The introductory phase is especially characterised by consumer resistance to change existing buying and consumption patterns in favour of new substitute products. Steps must thus be taken to stimulate awareness, interest, trial purchases and repurchases of the product by the target market. During this phase usually only innovators and the early adopters buy the product, later to be followed by the majority during the growth phase, if the product is satisfactory.

Production problems and minor product modifications

Various delays in the establishment of the necessary production capacities and technical difficulties in manufacturing the product in large quantities, usually develop during this phase. In addition, new products are usually not completely free of technical defects. During the product development phase all shortcomings should be identified and rectified. But even with the most comprehensive quality control and testing techniques, design and technical mistakes still occur during the introductory phase. For this reason minor product modifications are not unusual during this phase.

Several hold-ups, such as stock shortages, delays in containerisation, the administrative handling of incoming orders, initially relatively small orders, and the geographical dispersion of outlets can lead to considerable delays and bottlenecks in the physical distribution of the new product. As with consumers, retail outlets also initially show a degree of resistance to new products. This resistance is partly responsible for limited distribution and hampers the acquisition of the necessary display accommodation and shelf-space.

Slow growth in sales

Consumer resistance, bottlenecks in production and in physical distribution and limited distribution, together with the insufficient display accommodation and shelf-space, cause a relatively slow growth in the sales of the new product during the introductory phase.

Little direct competition

If a product is introduced by one manufacturer exclusively, direct competition is, of course, out of the question, because similar products do not exist. Indirect competition between the new product and those product classes that satisfied consumer needs up to that stage does, however, take place. In this way the first microwave oven had no direct competition, yet, indirectly, it competed against existing electric stoves. As long as the electric stove continued to meet consumer needs, many potential buyers of microwave ovens probably preferred spending their money on something else. (Today there are many competing microwave ovens available and competition takes place directly between brands.)

High production costs and limited number of models

Owing to the uncertainty about the possible success of the new product, attempts are usually made at this stage to manufacture the product by means of discontinuous piece-work processes using existing multi-purpose equipment and tools. If this is impossible, large capital investments in special production equipment and tools are normally required for the effective production of the new product. The depreciation of this equipment, together with relatively short production runs as a result of limited demand, the initial lack of the necessary know-how and skills of workers (the learning curve), the idle time of machines, material wastage and several bottlenecks in production planning lead to a relatively high production cost per product unit and a limitation on the number of models of the product produced during the introductory phase.

High marketing costs

If marketing management wishes to counteract resistance against the new product and change the existing buying and consumption patterns, aggressive personal and non-personal persuasive communication with middlemen and the market are especially important (see Chapters 12–15). Consumers have to be informed about the new product, and persuaded to make trial purchases, and retailers have to be encouraged to stock the product. This persuasion process is usually costly and, together with low turnover, a relatively high marketing cost per product unit sold is incurred.

Lack of profit

The contribution each product has to make to the redemption of its development costs, together with the high production and marketing costs per unit, and the relatively low sales volumes (even if selling prices are set exceptionally high), result in the new product not actually being able to contribute to the profit of the enterprise during the introductory phase.

18.3.2 Characteristics of the growth phase

Only the most important characteristics of the growth phase are indicated.

Rapid growth in sales

If the new product satisfies the needs of the target market, its sales rise rapidly because the innovators make repurchases and the early adopters and the early majority procure the product for the first time. Furthermore, these fast-growing sales are also partly attributable to the other characteristics of this phase.

Increase in the number of direct competitors

As soon as it is clear that the new product is a success and has good sales and profit prospects, new competitors usually enter the target market. This entry occurs throughout the entire phase and reaches its peak by the end of the phase. Larger enterprises can accomplish a more rapid entry into the market by inter alia taking over some of the smaller firms, normally at relatively high prices.

Significant product improvements

During this phase the various competitors make definite attempts to make their products more reliable and especially to improve them technically. Slight product differentiation, with a view to effective competition and the exploitation of new target markets, also occurs during this phase.

Rationalisation of production methods

This phase is usually characterised by changes in and improvements to production methods. The increasing rise in sales and the prospect of further increases in future encourage the enterprise to move away from discontinuous piece-work to continuous production processes. Furthermore, under these circumstances management is usually prepared to invest further in specially developed single-purpose manufacturing equipment for mass production. The production cost per product unit then usually decreases as a result of the more effective production methods and the increased production size.

Downward trend in prices

The selling prices of new products usually tend to drop somewhat during the growth phase. The following factors are inter alia responsible for this: the early adopters, but especially the early and late majority, are usually from the middle and lower income groups and are thus relatively price sensitive; higher sales lead to a better utilisation of the marketing capacities with a consequent lower marketing cost per unit; more effective production methods and increased size usually result in a lower production cost per unit; and the increased number of competitors holds the possibility of price reduction and even price wars.

Big profit

The rapid increase in sales and the relatively big drop in production and marketing costs per product unit, together with stable or even lower selling prices, lead to a considerable increase in the total profit of the new product. In fact, the new product earns the largest possible profit per unit during this phase compared with profits during the other phases in its life cycle.

Scramble for outlets

The increasing number of competitors of more or less the same product, but with a variety of brands, scramble to market their product through the existing distribution channels. Usually no bottlenecks are experienced during this phase because the rapid increase in profitable sales for the entire industry encourages outlets to stock this variety of brands of the same product class.

18.3.3 Characteristics of the maturity phase

In the maturity phase two stages of maturity are clearly distinguishable

First, a period of **maturing** is distinguished. The total sales of the product grow relatively slowly because the early and late majority have already entered the market. *Secondly*, a **market saturation** period is identified where sales remain at more or less the same level and consist mainly of replacement demand and little or no growth approximately in accordance with population growth in the target market.

The most general characteristics of the maturity phase are the following

Decline in sales growth rate

The first sign that a product is entering the maturity phase is a decline in the rate at which sales grow. The product is now generally accepted in the target market. In time, replacement purchases dominate, i e the product is mainly purchased by those who have already bought the product in the past. The sales growth more or less corresponds to the population growth.

Management challenges

Management challenges increase in the maturity phase, especially in the case of durable products. This is because the new product has already been on the market for some time when it reaches the maturity phase. Trade-ins, service, and the stocking of spare parts now become particularly important and complicated management challenges. For example, the large variety of existing and new products (especially durables) and the continual changing of existing ones demand special service departments and large quantities of different spare parts for efficient maintenance and repairs. Trade-in, service and spare parts policies of retailers, in particular, become more complicated if they stock competitive products. Stocking and labour costs, together with the accompanying challenges to management to handle a large variety of parts and service situations, often result in the costs of maintenance and spares services exceeding the income.

Product differentiation and product range expansion

Psychological and technical differentiation and product range expansion with a view to more effective competition and the drawing of all kinds of consumers into the target market are among the most important characteristics of the maturity phase. Even with durable consumer products, such as cars, electrical equipment and furniture, new models are launched annually, placing the emphasis on technical improvements and styling.

Profit and profit margins of retailers decrease

The profit and profit margins of retailers tend to decrease as a result of certain income-lowering and cost-increasing factors. For example, growing price competition between new models of durable products in particular, greater pressure for trade-in concessions, and the transfer of the present year's models at reduced prices to the following year often compel retailers to reduce their profit margins which can, at more or less constant turnovers, lead to a decline in profit.

We have already seen that certain costs, such as service and inventory costs, tend to increase in the maturity phase. These income-lowering and cost-increasing factors, which have initially a small and eventually no increase in sales, often lead to lower profit and profit margins for the retailer. To reduce this pressure on their profits, the outlets try to rationalise the service and inventory positions of especially durable products. They usually do it by eliminating 'problem products' and those that perform relatively poorly. This usually causes a distribution problem for the specific manufacturer.

More intense competition

The general decline in sales growth causes a degree of superfluous capacity in the industry. This, in turn, leads to increased competition in an attempt to obtain larger market shares.

Competitors make numerous attempts to expand their market share, including price reductions, price wars, special prices and other attractive conditions of sale to middlemen. Furthermore, relatively large amounts are spent on marketing communications, research, and product development in order to increase sales and expand market shares. These attempts do not always succeed and the result is capital drainage, profit erosion and the eventual elimination of weaker competitors.

Entering the target market is especially difficult during the maturity phase. Established enterprises are usually large and financially strong with big sales volumes and market shares, considerable capacity savings, low costs per product unit, strong brand preferences by consumers, established and loyal distribution channels, and extensive functional skills and expertise. In these circumstances entry is particularly difficult for a relatively small enterprise, which is by nature not financially very strong. Just think what it would entail for a new manufacturer to enter South Africa's beer market today!

18.3.4 Characteristics of the declining phase

It is said that when the laggards start showing interest in the product, the declining phase has arrived. The innovators and the early adopters are now no longer interested in the product. Other characteristics of the declining phase are the following.

Permanent drop in sales

An absolute and permanent drop in sales of the product takes place, except where marketing management succeeds in creating a 'second' life cycle for it.

Elimination of product

As consumers increasingly start switching to a new substitute product, consumer demand for the product starts decreasing drastically. The product then of sheer necessity has to be eliminated.

Reduction in marketing costs

As it becomes clear that the decreasing sales are an accomplished fact, manufacturers reduce the money spent on marketing the product. Thus there is a shift away from the mass advertising media to the more selective media, which reach only the target markets still buying the product. Certain distribution channels and outlets are also eliminated, and only those that still reach the remaining target markets are concentrated on.

Prices initially drop, stabilise for a time and can then even show an upwards tendency

As soon as a product enters the declining phase manufacturers usually try to stimulate sales through price reductions. The time comes, however, when even drastic price reductions are insufficient to encourage sales of the product. The demand for the product thus becomes reasonably inelastic and prices stabilise for a while. The dwindling market in time, however, becomes so insensitive to price changes that the price can even be increased somewhat without influencing the demand much.

Drastic decline in the number of competitors

As the industry sales of the product form drop, more and more enterprises stop producing and marketing the old product, applying their production factors in more profitable directions. It is possible that all manufacturers will stop production and that in due course the product will thus not be available any more. However, it often happens that sufficient demand remains, making it possible for a small number of enterprises or even one enterprise profitably to continue with its activities. There are, for instance, still a few small enterprises that make horse-carts for people taking part in gymkhanas or who practise horse-cart driving as a hobby. These enterprises are usually relatively small and specialised because the remaining market is not big enough for the larger enterprise.

During the course of the product life cycle the competitive position and consumer preferences often change, necessitating adjustments to the integrated marketing strategy. Marketing management has constantly to make decisions about product adjustments, distribution channels and methods, and marketing communications and prices. Attention is focused on these aspects in the following sections.

18.4 INTEGRATED MARKETING STRATEGY DURING THE PRODUCT LIFE CYCLE

18.4.1 The meaning of strategy

Marketing strategy has often been referred to earlier on in this chapter as well as in other chapters in the book. Nowhere, however, has it been shown how the marketing strategy is formulated although it is already clear that the strategy consists of a combination of product, distribution, marketing communications and price decisions. The word 'strategy' points to a general statement of the way in which the enterprise plans to reach objectives. The plan or strategy entails a combination of specific tactics required to carry out the plan or strategy. 'Strategy' is defined as 'the art of war or the art of planning and directing larger military movements . . . or war' (*Oxford English Dictionary*).

It thus has a definite military connotation. Army commanders make tactical decisions, combine them in a strategy and then implement the strategy in order to outwit and overcome the enemy. In the world of business these concepts have proved to be popular, especially in a dynamic and competitive situation where marketing management continually has to formulate strategies in order to ensure its own survival and profitable existence.

Marketing strategy refers to marketing management's (and thus the entire enterprise's) plan to achieve specific objectives. The main objective is naturally, as mentioned earlier, the maximisation of profitability in the long term. The plan consists of a set of tactical actions which are integrated as a unit and are in line with the main objective. Product, distribution, marketing communication and price decisions can be seen as specific tactics to execute the plan. Jointly, and as an integrated unit, these techniques form the marketing strategy. Usually, but not always, the threat from competitors is the impetus for the action plan (or, then, the marketing strategy). The marketing strategy thus, to an increasing degree, attains an aggressive character. Indeed, the latest textbooks commonly refer to marketing 'warfare'.

In this part of the chapter the way in which the four marketing instruments can be combined are discussed. For the first time, the integrated unit, with which indeed a 'war' can be waged, comes into consideration.

Please note that according to the approach followed in this book, the concept 'strategy' is used only if the possibility of a combination of decisions exists. It is thus not advisable to refer to 'product strategy' or 'price strategy' but rather to product decisions and price decisions.

Various strategies for marketing warfare are also discussed in this section. Strategies can be offensive or defensive. In each phase of the product life cycle different strategies can be planned against the enemy (the competitors) and carried out. It has to be stressed again that marketing strategies are nothing but a skilful combination of the marketing instruments. The only weapons used in this warfare are the ways in which the marketing instruments are combined as an integrated unit.

18.4.2 Integrated marketing strategy during the introductory phase

18.4.2.1 *Decisions regarding the four marketing instruments*

Product decisions

In addition to minor product modifications which may be required, the product remains the same as when it was introduced to the market for the first time.

Distribution decisions

Distribution decisions are very important during this phase. The ability of the manufacturer to ensure optimal distribution can lead to the success or failure of the new product introduction. Distribution channel decisions, and especially the choice of distribution channels, link the enterprise with specific middlemen for a relatively long time. The number and kind of middlemen, as well as the use of an own sales force, especially affect the price and marketing communications decisions about the new product directly since these decisions are taken with the path the product is going to follow, from the manufacturer to the consumer, in view. If exclusive distribution, for instance, is preferred the possibility exists that only a relatively small portion of the target market will be reached, while selective and intensive distribution will by their very nature make the product available to a larger portion of the target market.

Generalisations about the most suitable middlemen and market coverage for new products are not really possible. The intensity of market coverage is inter alia determined by the nature of the product, the nature and geographical dispersion of the market, the nature of the existing and available middlemen and the extent to which the manufacturer himself will undertake the distribution of the product. However, it appears that new products usually have a reasonably limited distribution during the introductory phase, seen from both a geographical and a market coverage viewpoint.

Price and marketing communication decisions

Given the product and effective distribution, the enterprise can especially use price and marketing communications to create a primary demand for the new product. Proceeding from the price level and the extent of the marketing communication for the new product, price and marketing communication can be combined in at least four ways.

First, the product can be introduced at a high price, supported by an aggressive marketing communication campaign. Gross & Peterson[7] describe this as a **high-profile combination.** A high price is asked to earn the largest possible gross profit per unit. At the same time, large sums of money are inter alia spent on advertising and personal selling in order to convince the market of the advantages of the product. High expenditure on communication is an attempt to increase the rate of market penetration. This combination can also be used if a large section of the potential market is unaware of the product, if those that are aware of it are keen to obtain it at a relatively high price, if the manufacturer expects competition, and if he wants to promote brand preference for his product.

Secondly, the product can be launched at a high price, combined with a low expenditure on marketing communications. Gross & Peterson[8] refer to this as **selective penetration**. The aim with the high price is once again the greatest possible gross profit per unit while the marketing costs are kept as low as possible with moderate marketing communication expenditure. This combination is typical skimming strategy by which an attempt is made, already in the introductory phase, to make a profit on the product. This skimming strategy is significant if the product is an innovation.

In the third place the product can be marketed at a low price together with a high expenditure on marketing communication. Gross & Peterson[9] describe this as **preventative penetration**. This combination usually gives the manufacturer the most rapid market penetration rate and the largest market share. Market penetration can especially be followed if the market is very large, if the market is reasonably unaware of the product, if most consumers are price sensitive, if strong potential competition exists, and if manufacturing costs per unit product decrease considerably with an increase in production size.

Lastly, the product can be brought on to the market at a low price and low expenditure on marketing communication. Gross & Peterson[10] call this a **low-profile combination**. The low price should encourage the rapid acceptance of the product, whereas marketing communications costs are kept low in order to realise a larger profit. With this combination the assumption is valid that the demand is very price elastic. This strategy is acceptable if the market is large, the consumers already know the product, the market is price-sensitive, and a reasonable measure of competition already exists.

The above price and marketing communication decisions are summarised in Figure 18.6.

FIGURE 18.6   Price and communication decisions during the introductory phase

MARKETING COMMUNICATION

	High	Low
Price — High	High profile	Selective penetration
Low	Preventative penetration	Low profile

Source: Adapted from Gross, CW & Peterson, RT. 1987. *Marketing: Concepts and Decision Making.* New York: West Publishing, p 215.

18.4.3 Marketing warfare during the introductory phase

Durö & Sandström[11] regard the introductory phase as the phase during which a product's future success can be determined on the business battlefield especially. Durö[12] is of the opinion that the enterprise must establish a bridgehead at this phase for future offensive attacks. In the introductory phase there are few direct competitors, but the danger of potential competitors if the product is a success is always there.

According to Durö & Sandström[13] and Kotler, Fahey & Jatusripitak[14] the following alternative strategies can be followed.

Flank attack

This is an indirect strategy where the weaknesses of competitors are concentrated on. The enterprise identifies a profitable niche and sees to it that it is successfully defended at all costs. A South African example is the success obtained by Pep Store in selling low-cost clothing to the lower-income population. In time Pep has consolidated its presence in this niche and is at present preparing itself for a frontal attack on clothing competitors serving the middle-income group.

Guerrilla strategy

The core of this strategy is surprise attacks launched at competitors' weaknesses. The competitor has to try to defend on several fronts simultaneously and is thus kept off balance while a frontal (direct) attack is being planned. A good example is Tony Factor's discount operation, which for the past year has made one-week forays into the Pretoria market selling clothing at discount prices. This retailer does not have permanent retail facilities in Pretoria, but uses the Pretoria Showground as temporary retailing outlet.

Frontal attack

Marketing management tackles competitors on their strengths. Such a strategy assumes that the enterprise has the required capital and expertise, otherwise it can lose the battle. Toyota's heavy vehicles (trucks) are busy with a frontal attack on the market leaders of the heavy-vehicle market, namely Mercedes Benz (SA).

Avoidance strategy

In this case a strong competitor is avoided by occupying niches in alternative target markets. North Star sneakers, which are renowned as low-cost casual wear, are following an avoidance strategy by not competing directly with established names like Adidas, Reebok and Nike, which are competing for the higher-income segment.

18.4.4 Integrated marketing strategy during the growth phase

18.4.4.1 Decisions regarding the four marketing instruments

Product decisions

Product decisions are still relatively unimportant in the formulation of a marketing strategy during the growth phase. Only moderate differences exist between competitive products, and the individual manufacturer also offers only a small variety of models for the new product. Because the basic models sell so well, expensive product differentiation is not required and the emphasis is rather on the ability to produce the new product in sufficient quantities and to make it available to a fast-growing market at the right place and the right time.

As the competitive products differ only slightly, service strategy becomes very important during this phase. If the new product demands regular after-sales service, a convenient, swift, reliable and expert service is important for capturing a significant market share. Take, for instance, how important after-sales service was and still is, in the marketing of television sets in South Africa. After-sales service is thus one area where strong competition occurs during the growth phase.

Distribution decisions

Fast-growing sales and tougher competition force the individual manufacturer to expand and intensify his market coverage. Depending on the kind of product, the nature and geographical dispersion of the market, and the nature of the existing distribution channels, the individual manufacturer has to make definite attempts to make the new product available at the outlets where it will have maximum exposure to the target market, while maintaining its profitability. This attempt was referred to earlier as the **scramble for outlets.**

Physical distribution demands special attention during this phase. Delays with delivery of the new product can result in some outlets' stocks being exhausted. This, together with the fact that competitive products do not differ much and that a large demand exists for the product class or form, results in outlets and consumers switching from one brand to another relatively easily. The producer having problems with physical distribution can thus as a result suffer serious damage to his competitive position.

Price decisions

In general, selling prices show a declining tendency during the growth phase. The extent of this decline is largely determined by the price level during the introductory phase, the cost advantages per product unit, and the intensity of competition during the growth phase. If the market is entered with a relatively low selling price (market penetration pricing), the profit margin is also usually relatively small. Marketing management is then limited to slight price reductions during the growth phase, even if sales were to increase rapidly and many competitors were to enter the market.

Relatively high selling prices during the introductory phase (market skimming pricing) are, however, usually followed by drastic price reductions in the growth phase.

Consider, for example, the selling price of microcomputers in South Africa. This has dropped since 1980, in spite of a high inflation rate. This price reduction is probably attributable to the cost advantages of large-scale production and marketing and intensive competition.

Marketing communication decisions

During the introductory phase the potential market is usually informed about the existence, advantages and uses of the new product class or form (this is also known as creating primary demand). During the growth phase, however, a shift in emphasis occurs and secondary demand creation becomes very important. Manufacturers now make definite attempts to inform potential consumers about their own product, to remind them of it, and to convince them to buy it.

The expenditure on marketing communication, expressed as a percentage of sales, also drops considerably during this period as a result of the rapid increase in turnover.

This declining ratio of communication expenditure to sales is an important cause for the big profit made during this phase. As larger and more intensive market coverage occurs, the media such as the radio, television and national magazines and newspapers can be used effectively to advertise the new product. Point-of-purchase advertising at retail outlets is particularly important during this phase.

18.4.4.2 *Marketing warfare during the growth phase*

Durö & Sandström[15] are of the opinion that in this phase attention should be paid to marketing communications, staff training and the expansion of the distribution network. Durö[16] is of the opinion that this is the ideal stage to occupy the market leadership position. At this stage the market intelligence system must be fully operational to keep track of activities of competitors and market trends. It is also the phase in which marketing management should be especially creative in respect of new product development and the take-over of competitive enterprises as well as those that market complementary products. According to Durö and Sandström[17] the following marketing strategies apply during the growth phase.

Frontal attack

The competitor is directly confronted and taken on on his strengths. The manufacturer acts aggressively in the same target market as the competitor. It should, however, be emphasised that the aggressor must have a definite competitive advantage (for example, financial security), otherwise he could lose the battle.

Encircling

In this case the competitor is encircled and attacks are launched in various fields. Products are set up against those of competitors, target markets served by the competitor are also identified as target markets, the same distribution outlets are used and the marketing communications campaigns copied. The purpose of the strategy is to divide the competitor's power, thus capturing market share.

Furthermore, flank attacks can be launched, as in the introductory phase (see above), by constantly hammering at the weaknesses of the competitor.

18.4.5 Integrated marketing strategy during the maturity phase

18.4.5.1 *Approach to the maturity phase*

Marketing management can follow at least three marketing strategies for a product which is in the maturity phase of its life cycle.

First, the marketing manager can decide to **maintain the status quo,** ie the existing marketing strategy is retained in order to maintain the existing sales and market share.

Secondly, the present product can be retained and the other marketing instruments **revised.** Here, there are also three possibilities:

- Existing consumers can be encouraged to use the existing product more regularly. Light consumers can be persuaded to become medium consumers and the latter to become heavy consumers — two cars per family instead of one and five men's suits instead of three. This strategy demands adjustments in the price, distribution, and/or marketing communications decisions.

- New consumers can be canvassed for the existing product. Someone who, for instance, does not have a microwave oven or does not really want one is persuaded to buy one. Here, market development crops up and especially marketing communications decisions, and possibly also price and distribution decisions, have to receive special attention.

- Attempts can be made to encourage different uses of the existing product among existing and new consumers. Johnsons Baby Shampoo can, for instance, be used by babies and adults. This strategy is competition-oriented and usually forms the basis for marketing communications, price and distribution decisions that can be followed during the maturity phase.

In the *third* place the existing product and the other marketing instruments can be changed by inter alia entering new markets and market segments with the development of new products from the old ones. Nylon, for example, was initially used for parachutes, thread and rope, later for hosiery and lingerie, and then for clothing, carpets and tyres. This strategy demands adjustments in the product, distribution, marketing communications and price decision. Psychological and technical product differentiation and product range expansions feature very prominently here.

The three basic strategies are now discussed in more detail.

18.4.5.2 *Different marketing strategies*

Retain the existing marketing strategy

A manufacturer can retain the present marketing strategy, making no changes, during the maturity phase if he believes that his market share will remain the same in spite of possible intensive competition in the form of inter alia price reductions, aggressive advertising campaigns, product differentiation, better profit margins to middlemen, and lower net profits. Under these circumstances a successful static marketing strategy is possible only if brand loyalty is particularly strong and the sales and market share are consequently insensitive to price differences, product differentiation, and aggressive marketing communications efforts. Even for a product with an apparently quasi-monopolistic position in the market such a static marketing strategy could have serious consequences, should the competitor's marketing strategy be underrated.

A static marketing strategy during the maturity phase is possible if:

- All the enterprises in the industry work informally together and do not opt for an intensive competitive strategy to expand their market share at the cost of others.

- A degree of competitive stability exists in the industry which is dominated by a single manufacturer who does not really have the desire to extend his domination.

- Population and especially income growth take place fast enough to ensure sufficiently rapid growth for all the manufacturers.

- The enterprise rather devotes the additional funds and attempts required to maintain the product's competitive position to the development of more profitable new products. All other things being equal, the available funds should be directed at those fields where the highest rate of return can be earned in the long term.

Retain the current product and revise the other marketing instruments

If the market for a specific product has sufficient vitality, the present market share and sales can be maintained and even increased at the cost of competitive products by retaining the product base but amending one or more of the other marketing instruments. Under these circumstances an attempt is thus made to increase the demand for the present product by inter alia encouraging consumers to use more and/or find new uses and/or consumers for the product.

Here, the marketing strategy can be changed in at least four different ways:

- **Changing price**
  Prices can be reduced drastically, either permanently or temporarily, in order to involve new market segments or to attract consumers of competing products. The influence of a price reduction on the profitability of a product is naturally important and this strategy should be followed only if the demand for the product is characterised by a relatively high price elasticity.

- **Changing marketing communication**
  Marketing communications attempts and, especially, advertising and personal selling campaigns with a special impact, can be launched to persuade present consumers to make bigger repurchases and potential consumers to make first purchases. A high communications elasticity of the demand, ie when the market reacts particularly favourably to advertising and personal selling, is naturally a prerequisite for the strategy to succeed.

- **Changing distribution**
  Marketing management can adjust the distribution channel with a view to more effective market coverage and a stronger thrust in the channel, by reviewing agreements with existing middlemen and/or eliminating certain distribution channels and/or adding new ones.

- **Changing price, marketing communications and distribution**
  Usually more than one marketing instrument at a time is adjusted, but the adjustment can entail a combination of price, marketing communications and distribution adjustments. This is illustrated in Figure 18.7.

FIGURE 18.7   Marketing decision adjustments for a product in its maturity phase

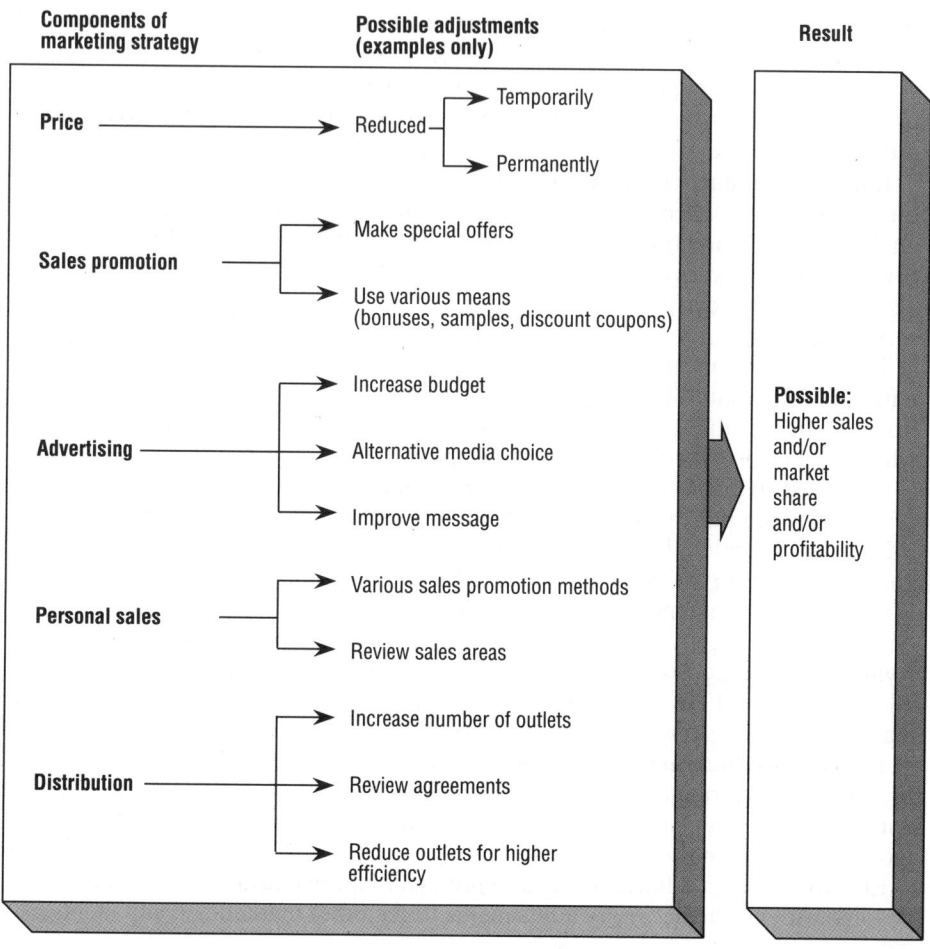

Source: Adapted from Mason, RS. 'Product Maturity and Marketing Strategy', *European Journal of Marketing*, vol 10, 1976, p 41.

Change all the marketing instruments

Marketing management can increase the sales of the existing product in the maturity phase through product differentiation and product range extension, which will attract consumers from new target markets and other market segments and/or make existing consumers increase their consumption. Product differentiation in the form of improved quality, product characteristics and styling, as well as product range extensions, are particularly important here.

Improved quality is usually aimed at the improvement of the functional efficiency of the product in respect of its durability, reliability, speed, performance, or any other functional characteristic. The enterprise following this strategy accepts that the differential advantage flowing from the improved quality is bigger than the costs involved.

The strategy is effective if the product is susceptible to quality improvements, the consumers believe the claim based on the grounds of the improved quality, and a significant portion of consumers in fact react to the quality improvement.

Versatility, safety, packaging, size, colour, mass and comfortable handling are usually the most important product characteristics which can be improved during the maturity phase.

Improved product characteristics can be very beneficial to the enterprise. It is one of the most effective ways of giving the enterprise an image of product leadership. Additionally, it is an excellent, adjustable, competitive instrument, as certain characteristics can be added or removed immediately. Furthermore, it can also develop a special product class preference in the target market. Finally, it can serve as motivation for the sales force and the middlemen handling the product.

The development of improved product characteristics is usually costly and can naturally be imitated by competitors, to a lesser or greater degree. The guiding principle here is that the improved product characteristics have to be worth their while, ie the costs involved must not be greater than the returns.

Improved styling or efforts to improve the appearance of the product by means of changing the packaging, colour, form, material and other product characteristics, is an exceptionally important competitive strategy especially with consumer goods and fashion articles. Improved styling is a form of product differentiation. If marketing management uses it purposefully and effectively a unique image can be created among style-conscious and fashion-conscious consumers. Improved styling is used extensively in the automobile industry where models such as the Nissan Sentra and Toyota Corrola are improved by the introduction of a new grill, leather seat covers and rear-view mirrors.

Through **product range extensions** an enterprise can also increase the sales of its present product ranges. New target markets and other market segments are entered in this way, and the present target market can also be encouraged to buy more of the existing products.

Effective product differentiation and product range extensions are, of course, not possible without the necessary adjustments to the other marketing components.

18.4.5.3 *Marketing warfare during the maturity phase*

According to Durö & Sandström,[18] fixed lines of defence must be avoided. This implies that the manufacturer must identify and utilise new opportunities and constantly be aware of threats. A facade of superiority must be maintained to frighten competitors. Increased cost effectiveness, achievement of scale benefits, reduction of price variations and the moving away from products that perform poorly (product rationalization), can improve the profit margin and offer the enterprise a competitive advantage. Internal marketing (to the staff of the enterprise) to keep the morale high is of vital importance.

Durö & Sandström[19] and Kotler, Fahey & Jatusripitak[20] recommend the following marketing strategies during the maturity phase. Because competition in this phase is the toughest and the dangers of decreasing sales are imminent, no stone must be left unturned to win the 'war'.

FIGURE 18.8   Defence strategies during the maturity and declining phase

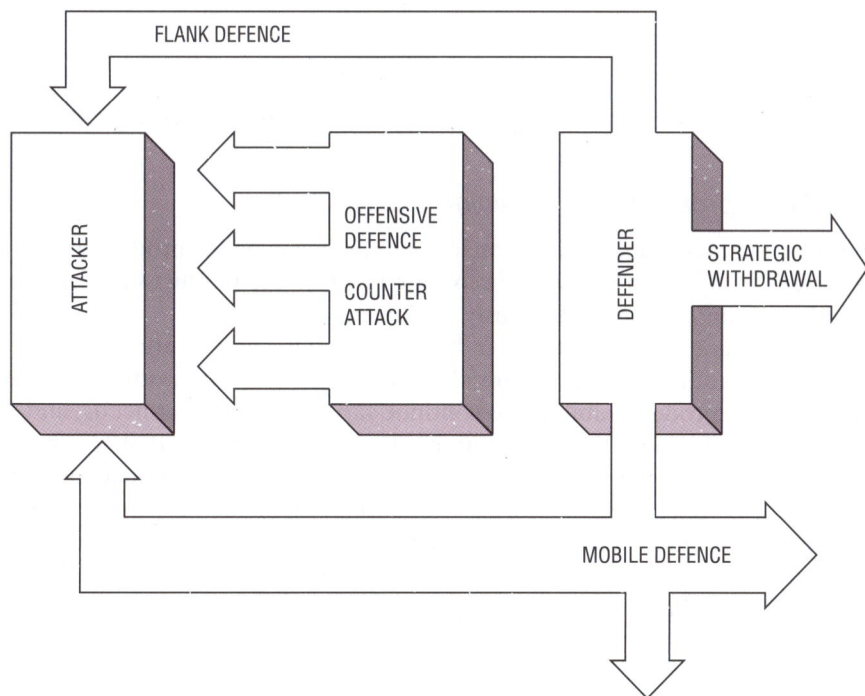

Source: Adapted from Kotler, P., & Singh, R., 'Marketing Warfare in the 1980s'. *Journal of Business Strategy,* vol 2, no 3, 1981, p 38.

- **Mobile defence:** This strategy implies a movement away from existing products/services, a broadening of the business horizons and an avoidance of marketing myopia.[21]

- **Offensive defence:** The principle applicable with this strategy is that attack is the best defence. The broad spectrum of attack strategies (already discussed) is at the disposal of the enterprise, for example frontal attack, flank attack, guerrilla attack and encircling.

- **Counterattack:** When the enterprise is attacked by competitors, a counter-attack can be launched. The competitor's attack is analysed and the weakness in the strategy is established. In this way for example poor services rendered in certain distribution channels may be exploited by hammering at the current level of poor service. Effective distribution networks and outlets can help to overwhelm the competitor and reclaim the market share. Remember that attack and defence are two sides of the same coin. If a competitor decides to attack, the enterprise must react by either going on the defence or going on the offence.

- **Flank defence:** Flank defence implies that the enterprise must protect its own flanks against attacks by competitors. Strengths and weaknesses within the enterprise must be identified timeously in order to reinforce them and to retain market share.

These defence mechanisms are shown in Figure 18.8.

18.4.6 Integrated marketing strategy during the declining phase

18.4.6.1 *Approach to the declining phase*

An important task of marketing management in managing the product during its life cycle is to lay down measures according to which the product's performance and achievement can be continuously evaluated.

The significant indicators that can be used for this purpose are the trends in sales, prices, profit and market share; the nature and extent of substitute products that occur; the product's abilities to continue satisfying consumer needs; and the amount of management time taken up by the product. Section 18.4.5.2 showed that three possible approaches can be followed after the product has been evaluated according to these norms: to continue with the marketing strategy unchanged; to keep the product as it is, revising the other marketing instruments; and to review the entire existing marketing strategy, including the current product. These three alternative approaches also apply to a product in the declining phase of its product life cycle. A fourth approach is, however, added, namely abandoning of the product. These strategies are now discussed within the context of the declining phase of the product life cycle.

18.4.6.2 *Different marketing strategies*

Continue with the existing marketing strategy

Not all manufacturers of a product class or form in the declining phase abandon it simultaneously. The enterprises that decide to continue with the product in spite of declining industry sales can experience an increase in sales in the short term if the rate at which the demand decreases is more rapid than the rate at which sales decrease. Some enterprises will react aggressivley during this phase by buying out competitive firms in order to close their production facilities and to limit the supply of the product. It is also very important not to start a price war during this stage if you want to extend the declining phase.[22]

Enterprises that continue marketing the product in the declining phase can do so by maintaining the existing marketing strategy. The same target market, price, distribution and marketing communications instruments can be used until the product is eventually removed from the product mix. Such an inflexible marketing strategy, however, cannot be followed indefinitely without serious profit erosion for the product. If sales drop, production cost per production unit can increase as a result of smaller production runs and idle machine time, and overhead costs per unit can rise because management spends relatively more time on the poor product. The marketing costs (such as advertising, personal selling and physical distribution costs) per product unit can also rise because the total marketing costs of the product can now be distributed over a smaller sales volume. As soon as the turnover of the product drops below the break-even point, and especially if it no longer provides a marginal income, either the marketing strategy has to be drastically adjusted or the product has to be abandoned.

Revise the existing marketing strategy partly or entirely

The enterprise can continue marketing the product in its declining phase simply by directing its marketing strategy only at the most profitable target market. This implies that especially the distribution of the product and marketing communications in the weaker target markets have to be terminated.

Marketing management can also decide drastically to cut back on the marketing costs of the product, with the knowledge that the product will fizzle out sooner but hoping that a larger profit will be earned in the declining phase. It can happen that a group of loyal consumers with a strong class loyalty remains, making profitable marketing of the product possible, with relatively little marketing communication and even at higher prices. If necessary, the product range can be reduced further and expensive packaging practices discarded.

Withdraw the product from all markets

As soon as marketing management decides to abandon the product in the light of its sales, price and profit trends, its ability to satisfy consumer needs and other indicators, the method and timetable for withdrawal have to be considered. First, the product can be eliminated **gradually** in order to have sufficient time for making the necessary adjustments to production, personnel, marketing, inventory and other activities which may be involved, with the least inconvenience for the parties concerned. Secondly, the product can be abandoned **immediately and finally** before any resistance develops and the decision is possibly reversed. Finally, marketing management also has to decide on the supply of spare parts and the provision of after-sales service after the manufacturing and marketing of the product have been terminated.

18.4.6.3 *Marketing warfare during the declining phase*

Durö & Sandström[23] are of the opinion that competitors should be kept in the dark about marketing management's plans with a dwindling product. If withdrawal is decided on, it should take place in an orderly fashion and not look like 'fleeing', thus damaging staff morale.

According to Durö & Sandström[24] the other strategies discussed in the previous life cycles can be applied again, depending on the situation and the resources at the enterprise's disposal. A further strategy identified is strategic withdrawal. Study Figure 18.8, which shows strategic withdrawal as a defence mechanism. The strategy implies that the enterprise withdraws from certain target markets, concentrating on more profitable target markets. The impression should not be left that the battle is lost, but rather that forces have been mobilised to launch an attack in another area.

18.5 SUMMARY

In this chapter the product life cycle has been examined. It has also been shown that the life cycle consists of four definite identified phases, namely the introductory phase, the growth phase, the maturity phase and the declining phase. As the contemporary enterprise functions in intense competitive conditions, mention has been made of marketing warfare against competitors during the different phases of the product life cycle.

In Chapter 19 further attention is paid to the integrated marketing strategy. The modern large enterprise, which manufactures and markets a product mix consisting of numerous product items and lines, is especially focused on. In addition to management tasks, strategies concerning the composition and management of the enterprise's product portfolio are discussed.

REFERENCES

1. Bennett, RC and Cooper, RG. 'The Product Life Cycle Trap'. *Business Horizons*. September–October 1984, pp 8–9.
2. Neidell, LA. 'Don't Forget the Product Life Cycle for Strategic Planning'. *Business*. April–June 1983, pp 30–4.
3. Based on Lucas, GHG (ed). 1983. *The Task of Marketing Management*. Pretoria: Van Schaik, pp 273–83.
4. Gross, CW and Peterson, RT. 1987. *Marketing: Concepts and Decision Making*. New York: West Publishing, p 214.
5. Ibid pp 214–17.
6. Based on Marx, S and Dekker, H. 1986. *Marketing Management: Principles and Decisions*. Pretoria: HAUM, pp 437–48.
7. Gross and Peterson op cit, p 215.
8. Ibid p 217.
9. Ibid p 216.
10. Ibid p 217.
11. Durö, R and Sandström, B. 1987. *The Basic Principles of Marketing Warfare*. Chichester: John Wiley and Sons, p 143.
12. Durö, R. 1989. *Winning the Marketing War: A Practical Guide to Competitive Advantage*. Chichester: Wiley, p 147.
13. Durö and Sandström op cit, p 147.
14. Kotler, P, Fahey, L and Jatusripitak, S. 1985. *The New Competition*. Englewood Cliffs, New Jersey: Prentice-Hall Inc, p 234.
15. Durö and Sandström op cit, p 144.
16. Durö op cit, p 41.
17. Durö and Sandström op cit, p 144.
18. Ibid, p 145.
19. Ibid, p 147.
20. Kotler, Fahey and Jatusripitak op cit, pp 145–9.
21. Levitt, T. 'Marketing myopia' in Kotler, P and Cox, KK. 1984. *Marketing Management and Strategy: A Reader* (3rd edition). Englewood Cliffs: New Jersey: Prentice-Hall Inc, pp 3–20.

22. Harrigan, KR. 'Will you be "the last iceman"?' *Sales and Marketing Management.* January 1990, p 62–7.
23. Durö and Sandström op cit, p 146.
24. Ibid p 147.

CASE STUDY

REVIVAL OF THE BEETLE LEGEND

Birth of the Beetle[1]

The first Volkswagen Beetles were produced just before the Second World War as Hitlers' 'people's car'. During the war the production facility was changed to produce Volkswagen based military vehicles and was repeatedly bombed until production was finally stopped in 1944.

When the war ended in 1945, Wolfsburg fell under British military rule. A few jobless German workers then began to manufacture the first post-war Beetle. Heinz Nordhoff, once an executive at a rival motor manufacture, took the job of heading the Volkswagen factory after the war. One of his prime objectives was to find export markets for the Beetle and so Nordhoff came to South Africa.

In August 1951 the first Beetle to be assembled in South Africa came of the South African Motor Assemblers and Distributors (SAMAD) plant in Uitenhage. In 1956 the controlling interest of SAMAD was taken over by Volkswagenwerk of Wolfsburg and by 1960 over 16 000 Volkswagen Beetles were sold. At this stage the product range included the Volkswagen 1200 and 1500 Beetle, the Volkswagen Kombi and the Volkswagen 1600 TL Fastback Sedan. On 17 November 1966 the company's name was changed from SAMAD to Volkswagen of South Africa Limited.

A milestone was reached on 17 February 1972 when the Beetle became the most produced vehicle in the history of the motor industry — it had by then surpassed the 15 007 000 mark of the Model T Ford that was set in 1929. In 1973 the Beetle remained the best selling model in South Africa for the 16th consecutive year. In 1974 a further milestone was reached when the first watercooled, front engined Volkswagen — the Passat — was marketed in South Africa and when the 250 000th locally produced Beetle was completed.

At this stage limited versions of the Beetle, such as the Fun Bug and the Lux Bug were introduced and the Super Bug was also brought out. At this stage a limit was reached in the technological upgrading of the Beetle and the time was ripe for the introduction of a new high technology 'people's car'.

The last of the South African Beetles rolled off the production-line plant in 1981. So ended a product which had created a legend of toughness and dependability in its time. One of the unique features of the Beetle was the fact that it defied the pitfalls and limitations of class-consciousness — the Beetle was driven by people of all classes. A key feature of the Beetle's success was the fact that it had a life cycle of more than 30 years, which is by any automobile standard a very long time indeed.

The years after the Beetle

Volkswagen South Africa introduced the Golf I as the substitute for the Beetle.

During the period 1978-1984 Volkswagen South Africa encountered problems with the quality of their cars and consequently Volkswagen's market share fluctuated. The years 1982 to 1984 saw a decline in Volkswagen's market share which by the end of 1984 pitched at a low of 10,6 per cent.[2] According to Clive Warrilow[3] the problem was largely due to the fact that Volkswagen was chasing volumes in a growing market and neglecting quality in the attempt to capture market share. The result was that Volkswagen's main competitor, Toyota, made inroads into their market share. Although the Golf I was a success with its low petrol consumption at a time when the petrol price was increasing, quality problems encountered led to a decline in market share.

The Jumbo Golf was launched in October 1984. The new generation Golf made it difficult for Volkswagen to compete on price against the aggressive trading of its competitors in the fast growing small car sector of the South African market.

The birth of the Citi Golf

Volkswagen's answer to this problem was the introduction of the Citi Golf, based on the Golf I, earlier in 1984. The initial Citi Golf was only available in a 1300 4-speed model and was aimed primarily at younger, new car buyers with a strong metropolitan bias. In terms of psychographics these were people who were fashion conscious, outgoing, fun-loving and unconventional. A total of 3 921 Citi Golfs were sold during 1984 resulting in a 1,5 per cent market share of the total South African passenger market and a 3,2 per cent share of the small car market. The Citi Sport, a 1600 5-speed model, was introduced in 1985, strengthening the Citi Golf's male owner profile. Sales for 1985 were 3 383 in a declining car market resulting in a 1,6 per cent share of the passenger market and a 2,8 per cent share of the small car market. The year 1986 saw a meteoric rise in the sales of the Citi Golf. A total of 5 588 were sold in a still depressed automobile market, resulting in a 3,2 per cent market share of the passenger market and a 5,1 per cent share of the small car market. The strong growth in the sales of the Citi Golf continued in 1987 with a 3,8 per cent share of the passenger market and a 5,8 per cent share of the small car market.

Emergence of the Fox

The third quarter of 1987 saw the launch of the Fox, a clone of the old Jetta. It was launched in three different models, the Fox 1.3 — 4-speed, the Fox 1.6 automatic and the Fox 1.6 — 5-speed. Sales of the Fox for the last two quarters of 1987 were outstanding at 2 258 units which gave it a 1,1 per cent share of the total passenger market and a 1,7 per cent share of the small car market.

REASONS FOR THE SUCCESS OF THE CITI GOLF AND FOX?

The reasons for success are the following:

- The general economic situation declined — the average car price has increased three-fold during the past decade while the consumer's discretionary income has lagged behind. According to Pretorius[4] the cost of buying a new car consisted 65% of a white household yearly income in 1981 and that this figure for 1991 is now 90%. The result has been a 'trading down' for the average consumer leading to the greater interest in lower priced cars, especially the Citi Golf and Fox ranges.

- An elaborate promotional campaign created the incentive for first-time buyers and particularly the young buyer to purchase these cars. The campaign emphasised low prices, value for money and quality assurance.

- A dramatic change took place in Volkswagen South Africa. Management realised that the perception of quality was foremost in the minds of the consumer. Volkswagen embarked on a drive to improve the quality of its cars. The 'Towards Excellence Programme', which outlines the drive to convey the principles of excellence to all employees of Volkswagen South Africa,[5] was introduced. This programme resulted in a dramatic increase in the level of productivity at Volkswagen's Uitenhage plant and resulted in Volkswagen receiving the National Productivity Institute Award for outstanding achievements in productivity in 1987.

- Together with the general improvements in productivity at Volkswagen cost savings that resulted from the 'Towards Excellence Programme' made an impact on the final price of the whole range of Volkswagens produced by the Uitenhage plant.

- Another cost-related reason for the success of the Citi Golf and Fox ranges is the fact that the presses and moulds necessary for the production of these cars were already paid for. The original Golf was introduced in South Africa in 1978 and production ended in 1984. At that stage all expenses with respect to moulds and presses had been written off. With the successful reintroduction of the Citi Golf these presses and moulds were again utilised without the additional costs that are part of the introduction of a new model. Further economies of scale were realised because the Volkswagen pick-up truck uses the same production line as the Citi Golf and the Fox. The engine, gearbox and suspension are similar to the Jumbo Golf which makes further economies of scale possible.[6] All these factors resulted in yet another unique feature for the Citi Golf and Fox, namely that these cars have the highest local content (80 per cent) of all cars manufactured in South Africa.

CITI GOLF AND FOX — FOLLOWING IN THE FOOTSTEPS OF THE BEETLE

In keeping with the Beetle philosophy the Citi Golf and Fox were amongst the least expensive vehicles on the market. Although they are the entry models in Volkswagen's passenger car range, there is certainly nothing lacking about these car's specifications, quality or appearance.

Like the Beetle before them the Citi Golf and Fox have managed to develop a charismatic personality and character that is both inimitable and unique. While the initial target market was clearly young, first-time buyers, customer research has shown that the appeal of Citi Golf and Fox is not limited by age or monetary considerations. In this respect they have become, like the Beetle before them, a range of 'classless' and 'classic' cars.

BIBLIOGRAPHY

1. Public Relations Department of Volkswagen of South Africa, *A History of Volkswagen of South Africa*, 1976.
2. Von Keyserlingk, C. *Finansies en Tegniek,* volume 39, number 37, 18 September 1987: 12.
3. *Loc. cit.*
4. SA motorbedryf moet marknisse kry. *Beeld* 22 November 1991: S4.
5. VW makes historic recovery — a doubled market share in three years, *Marketing Mix.* Volume 5, number 11. November/December 1987: 54.
6. Von Kayserlingk, C op cit: 13.
7. Reprinted with permission of Van der Walt, A (ed). 1989. *Marketing success stories.* Johannesburg: Southern, pp 228-234.

QUESTIONS

1. Identify the attack and defence warfare strategies of Volkswagen South Africa after the decline experienced in the period 1978 to 1984.

2. From 1984 onwards Volkswagen South Africa lost its number one position as the top automobile seller and it has been mentioned that Toyota made inroads into its market share. What was the reason for this decline and what is the link with the demise of the Beetle?

3. Analyse the present situation in the automobile market and try to identify the stage in the life-cycle of the Citi Golf and the Fox.

4. Are the Volkswagen ranges in direct competition with one another (e.g. are the Citi Golf and Fox ranges in competition with the Golf II and the Jetta ranges)? Motivate your answer.

5. When did the Beetle enter the decline phase of its life-cycle in South Africa?

6. With the introduction of the Fiat Uno, the Citi Golf and Fox automobiles lost their position as the cheapest cars in the market. Explain the current marketing warfare position at the lower end of the market.

7. What are the most important reasons for the cost savings on the Citi Golf and Fox ranges?

8. Why are the Citi Golf and Fox ranges classless? Does this imply that the life-cycle of these two ranges will follow the same road as the Beetle?

9. Evaluate the product mix of Volkswagen South Africa at the present moment. Use figure 18.5 to draw the individual life-cycles of the product items in the Volkswagen range.

10. Are the life-cycles of the Beetle, Citi Golf and Fox ranges following the classic pattern of an S curve? Motivate you answer.

CHAPTER 19

STRATEGIC MARKETING

19.1 INTRODUCTION

The objective of this chapter is to consider the planning, implementation and evaluation of marketing and market strategies. This process begins with the analysis of the internal and external environments within which the enterprise has to perform its marketing task. The environment can be regarded as the background against which strategic marketing is carried out. Planning entails the setting of objectives and spelling out the activities necessary to achieve these objectives. The marketing manager or director is the head of the marketing department and he directs the marketing strategy. Although it is essentially a middle management post, it is important for the marketing manager or director to have status at top management level as well. This applies especially to multi-product enterprises where a number of strategic business units (SBUs) have a degree of independence yet have to work together to achieve the overall business objective. In such an enterprise there is a number of different possible market strategies in respect of all the products in the product portfolio. The market strategy forms the primary basis for the corporate (or business) strategy. A consumer-oriented enterprise acts in a market-directed way because it has accepted the marketing concept as its basic point of departure. With competitive market strategies attempts are made to establish barriers against competitors' assaults. This refers to the creation of sustained competitive advantages which are the core of the competitive market strategy. With growth strategy attempts are made to maintain and expand the market position. Withdrawal strategy is considered when a product that is no longer profitable is withdrawn from the market and the funds thus generated are invested in another product.

It is important that marketing decisions and strategies be regularly revised and evaluated. Evaluation techniques are used to monitor and control marketing results. Corrective action can then be timeously planned and taken.

Strategic marketing entails the decisions of the marketing department with a view to long-term growth and survival in a competitive environment. All the management tasks of planning, co-ordination, leading and controlling are thus taken into consideration in the discussion of the planning, implementation and evaluation model, depicted in figure 19.1.

ORGANISATION OF THE CHAPTER

The meaning of strategic marketing: Components of the process, strategic marketing in multi-product enterprises.

Planning: The planning process, environmental scanning, the enterprise's mission, objectives, planning models, planning the organisation structure.

Implementation: Marketing strategy and market strategy, competitive market strategies, growth strategies, market strategies in declining markets.

Evaluation: The meaning of evaluation/control, steps in the evaluation process, evaluation techniques, control and evaluation.

19.2 THE MEANING OF STRATEGIC MARKETING

19.2.1 Components of the process

It has already been pointed out in Chapter 1 (section 1.4.1) that the latest development in the field of marketing involves a strategic approach to marketing management. This development can be attributed to the fast-changing marketing environment and the realisation that marketing management can deliver important inputs to the corporate strategy.

Strategic marketing is a continuous process that mainly (but not exclusively) takes place at top management level. Marketing decisions and strategies at this level are necessarily influenced by the decisions and strategies that apply in other functional areas, and vice versa. The process is so intervowen that it is sometimes almost impossible to distinguish between functional marketing (at middle management level) and strategic marketing (at top management level). It is furthermore also difficult to describe strategic marketing step by step, and the dividing lines between specific concepts become quite vague. It is, for instance, impossible to establish where planning starts and where it ends. These problems are probably the reason for the confusing use of terminology in various books, where the terms 'strategic planning', 'strategic marketing planning', 'strategic marketing' and even 'strategic market management' are used for more or less the same concept.[1] In this book the point of departure is that strategic marketing is the task of marketing management at middle and top management levels and that this task, seen broadly, consists of planning, implementation and evaluation of marketing and market strategies. These three distinguishable components are also contained in Figure 1.10 (Chapter 1), which is the model on which the book is based.

Figure 19.1 also shows the three main components and the aspects of the strategic marketing process which receive attention in this chapter.

FIGURE 19.1   Planning, implementation, and evaluation model

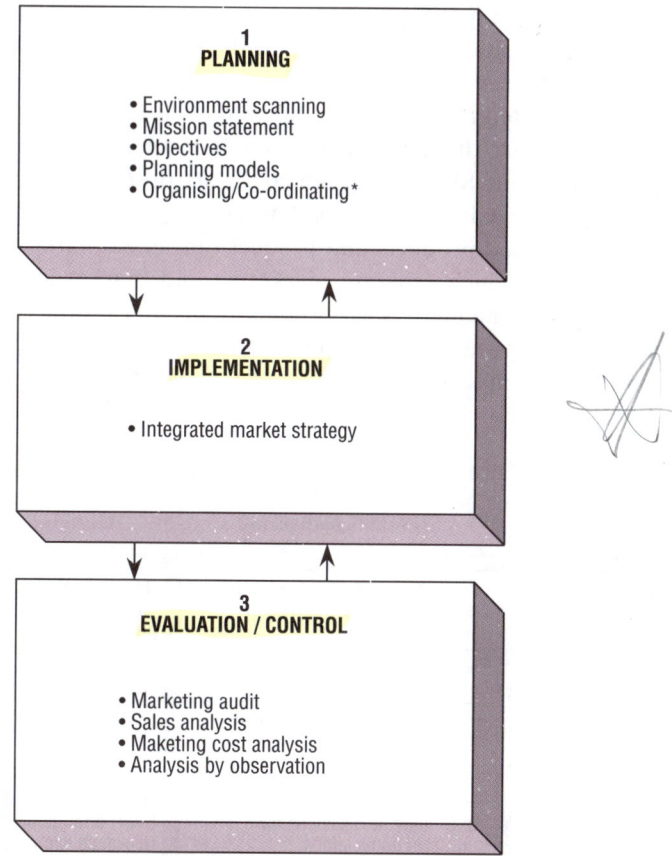

1
PLANNING

• Environment scanning
• Mission statement
• Objectives
• Planning models
• Organising/Co-ordinating*

2
IMPLEMENTATION

• Integrated market strategy

3
EVALUATION / CONTROL

• Marketing audit
• Sales analysis
• Maketing cost analysis
• Analysis by observation

*See the explanation for including organising/co-ordinating in
planning, section 19.3.6.1.

Block 1 shows the planning process, which consists of the gathering of information on the enterprise, the market and the product, and decision making regarding the marketing of the enterprise's products. **Block 2** shows that the decisions taken during planning culminate in the execution of specific strategies, depending naturally on the circumstances that led to the decisions. Suppose that analysis of the environment shows that the enterprise has under-utilised resources at its disposal and that promising gaps exist in the market, enabling the enterprise to position a market offering. Then a decision to expand can be realised in a growth strategy. In the same way competitive strategies will be implemented if the enterprise faces tough competition, as is often the case in the growth phase of the product life cycle. **Block 3** shows the evaluation process and the techniques used to exercise control over marketing activities

19.2.2 Strategic marketing in multi-product enterprises

In large multi-product enterprises which market a variety of products and product ranges, strategic marketing takes place through the establishment of independent divisions called strategic business units. **A strategic business unit (SBU) directs its product offering at a specific market and manages the production, distribution and marketing communications function with a degree of independence.**[2] The marketing strategies of the SBUs vary but complement each other, and are usually co-ordinated by the parent company. It is clear that individual SBUs all have to contribute to the success of the parent company. The parent company may regard the different SBUs as 'products' in its product porfolio. Furthermore, individual SBUs usually do not market only one product item. There is more likely a number of related products and product ranges earmarked for certain target markets and for which separate marketing and market strategies have to be planned and implemented. Such product items and product ranges are usually combined in the product portfolio unique to the individual SBU. The relative differences between strategic marketing and marketing management are given in figure 19.2.

FIGURE19.2   Strategic marketing and marketing management

POINT OF DIFFERENCE	STRATEGIC MARKETING	MARKETING MANAGEMENT
• Need for information	Information regarding the future is needed from a great variety of sources	Decisions are taken based on information from marketing research projects
• Details	Plans are spelled out broadly in general terms	Plans are spelled out in detail
• Relationship with financial function (and other functions of the enterprise)	A close relationship is maintained throughout	Relationship is less clear
• Timeframe	Long-range, ie decisions have long-term implications	Short term, ie decisions have relevance within a given financial year
• Decision process	Primarily bottom-up	Mainly top-down
• Opportunity sensitivity	Ongoing to seek new opportunities	Ad hoc search for a new opportunity
• Organisational behaviour	Constantly strives to achieve synergy between different departments	Pursue interests of the marketing departments
• Nature of job	Requires high degree of creativity and originality	Requires maturity, experience and control orientation
• Leadership style	Requires proactive perspective	Requires reactive perspective
• Mission	Deals with the activities of the SBU's	Deals with running the marketing of a specific SBU

Source: Adapted from Jain, SC. 1990 *Marketing Planning and Strategy*. Cincinnati: South Western Publishing, p 34 and Weitz, BA & Wensley, R. 1984. *Strategic Marketing: Planning, Implementation and Control*. Boston: Kent Publishing Co, pp 2–5.

The points of difference serve to emphasise the importance of a strategic approach to the marketing task. It is inconceivable that a multi-product enterprise with different, more or less independent SBUs could survive in the long term if marketing management is not strategically oriented.

It is now also not as easy to distinguish the planning, organising, co-ordinating, leading and controlling management tasks from each other, as was the case in Chapter 1. The management tasks are regrouped as in Figure 19.1, and planning is discussed first.

19.3 PLANNING

19.3.1 The planning process

Planning as a management task was touched on in Chapter 1. In section 1.5 (Chapter 1) the process was identified as a management task and briefly defined. The viewpoint was reasonably simple and direct and described planning at a functional level. The planning task in strategic marketing, where a multi- product enteprise has a number of independent SBUs and markets many different products, is much more complicated, as will be seen in the following discussion.

Planning always starts with the gathering of information. When strategies are planned at any level whatsoever, information is gathered from the internal and external environments, interpreted and constantly monitored.

19.3.2 Environmental scanning

Environmental scanning was discussed in depth in Chapters 2 and 3. Management is constantly weighing up the internal strengths and weaknesses against external opportunities and threats in order to formulate a strategy that will lead to the achievement of business objectives. The internal variables in respect of resources, abilities and skills were discussed in Chapter 2, which also focused on the macro-variables which leave the enterprise no choice but to adapt. The market variables, namely consumers and competitors, were discussed in Chapter 3. The way in which information on these variables are systematised and kept up to date in a marketing information system, making them conveniently available for planning purposes and market forecasting, was discussed in Chapters 5 and 6.

Marketing planning is by its very nature a future-directed activity. Comprehensive information about all applicable environmental variables is necessary in order to make an approximate estimate of what the future holds in store. Strategic decisions taken today can be implemented only at a later stage. Marketing planning usually occurs in the short, medium and long term. In the short term (usually one year) it is reasonably easy to make forecasts. In the medium term (three to five years) it is more difficult. Long-term forecasts (five years and longer) are increasingly risky and uncertain. Planning for all three terms begins with a mission statement which indicates the direction in which the enterprise wishes to move.

19.3.3 The mission of the enterprise

Figure 19.1 shows that stating the mission is the second step in the planning process. Already while scanning the environment the mission of the enterprise is of vital importance because it determines which environmental variables have to be monitored. **The mission statement describes the nature of the enterprise's activities.**[3] It is naturally difficult, especially for large enterprises, to reflect the nature of their activities in a single statement. It is none the less important to describe these as accurately as possible, as the mission serves as a direction indicator. It should be possible to derive the following answers from the mission statement:

- What is the nature of the business undertaken by the enterprise?
- Who are the consumers?
- What are the consumers' needs?
- What is the nature of the internal resources and abilities at the enterprise's disposal?
- How can the enterprise satisfy consumer needs?
- What environmental factors have to be taken into consideration?

From these questions it appears that the mission statement has more to do with the market, and especially the consumers, than with production processes and problems. This indicates that the marketing philosophy, as contained in the marketing concept, is the basis of the mission statement.

Shell Oil's mission

'Meet the energy needs of customers world-wide.'

Source: Busch, PS and Houston, MJ. 1985. *Marketing Strategic Foundations*. Homewood, Illinois: Richard D Irwin, p 47.

Setting objectives can be seen as the third important step in the planning process. As repeatedly mentioned earlier, the marketing objectives must contribute to the achievement of the overall main objective of the enterprise. The mission points the way in which this main objective will be realised, while other supplementary objectives are set more specifically, giving a precise indication of what is to be achieved, be it an expansion of the market share, an increase in sales figures, or a decrease in marketing costs.

19.3.4 Objectives

19.3.4.1 *Requirements for objectives*

The general requirements for objectives are the following:[4]

- Objectives must be set in **order of priority**. Because objectives are often set at different levels for different products, an order of priority is required to prevent conflict and waste of resources. Objectives achieved in a preset order can contribute more to the overall objective than when pursued haphazardly. Planning thus entails careful consideration of the order of priority.
- Objectives must, where possible, be set in **quantitative terms**. Where the overall objective of the enterprise somewhat vaguely refers to the 'maximisation of profitability' the marketing objective usually indicates exactly what must be achieved, for example: to increase the market share by five per cent or to realise a rate of return of 30 per cent.
- Objectives should be **consistent** and appropriate — this means that objectives should support and reinforce each other. A marketing objective to reinforce the image of the retailer can, for instance, be supported by a striving for better service by the sales personnel.
- Objectives must be **reasonable**. Far-fetched and impossible objectives discourage personnel and dampen enthusiasm.
- Objectives must be set for a **specific period**. Naturally, the short- and medium-term objectives must eventually lead to the achievement of objectives set for the longer term.

Objectives must be measurable, realistic and must be set for a specific period in written form.

19.3.4.2 *The hierarchy of objectives*

In strategic marketing, different objectives are set to facilitate the marketing task. These objectives must be realistic, as far as possible be set out in measurable terms and have a bearing on one another. Objectives are set for all products in all phases of the product life cycle and for all four marketing instruments. Objectives regarding research, new product development, price, advertising, sales and distribution are strived for. Most of these objectives were discussed in the preceding chapters.

The overall objective of the enterprise applies to the entire enterprise, all its product market units (PMUs) and its strategic business units. All marketing objectives are deduced from this objective. Specific marketing objectives are set for specific PMUs and/or SBUs. At the functional level objectives are set for each of the four marketing instruments.

Figure 19.3 shows the hierarchy of objectives.

FIGURE 19.3   Hierarchy of objectives

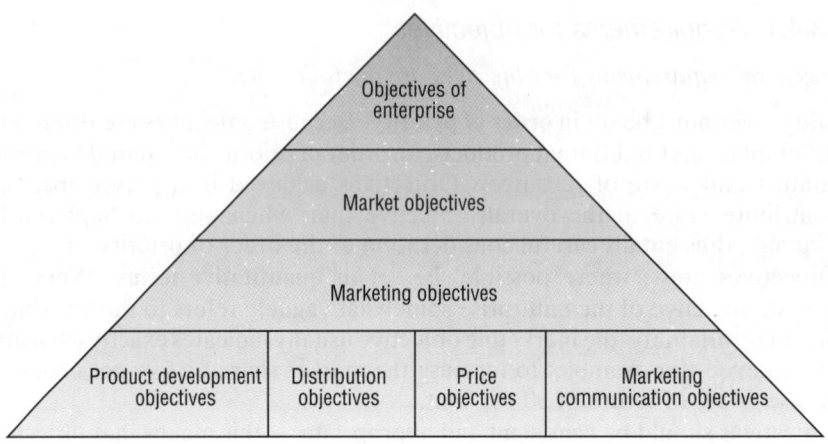

19.3.4.3 *Market and marketing objectives*

Mainly four secondary objectives are pursued in strategic marketing, namely a high rate of return on investment, an increase in sales, an increase in market share and continued growth.

A high rate of return on investment

This objective corresponds with the overall business objective and originates in the marketing department of each individual PMU and SBU. In the composition of the product portfolio the highest possible rate of return on investment is strived for. Each separate product in the portfolio must make a contribution to a high rate of return. When this happens the profitability objective of the enterprise is achieved.

Marketing management must continually develop new products on which a high rate of return can be realised. With the same objective in mind, non-profit-making products must be withdrawn and the funds re-invested in more promising opportunities.

An increase in sales

To maintain sales growth it is important that a product portfolio should preferably consist of a variety of products in different life cycle phases and with different sales volumes. Success is thus not determined by the sales of a specific product but rather by the sales of a variety of products in different life cycle phases.

A high and ever-increasing sales volume will not necessarily lead to a high rate of return. Costs incurred to maintain the sales volume can be detrimental to the rate of return. This objective can thus only be strived for in combination with the other objectives.

Increase in relative market share

Research has undoubtedly proved that relative market share has a decisive influence on the profitability of an enterprise.[5] Figure 19.4 shows that the rate of return on investment increases with a increase in market share.

In Figure 19.4 enterprises with a relative market share above 40 per cent have a rate of return of more than three times that of enterprises with less than 10 per cent. The rate of return increases because a large market share in relation to those of competitors brings about a higher sales volume and a lower unit cost.

Continued growth

In a balanced product portfolio the different elements of the portfolio are combined in such a way that the growth objective is attained. Because the environment changes often and drastically, new products have to be developed constantly, non-profit-making ones withdrawn, new competitve market strategies considered and marketing decisions implemented. In the discussion on planning models which follows, it is shown how a product portfolio is compiled to ensure continued growth. It was not without reason that nearly 30 years ago Drucker[6] had already referred to 'tomorrow's breadwinners', 'today's breadwinners', 'yesterday's breadwinners', 'dropouts' and 'failures'. It is also evident from the latest planning models that products which could be breadwinners of the future are necessary to create opportunities for growth and to compensate for dropouts and failures.

FIGURE 19.4   Relationship between rate of return on investment and relative market share

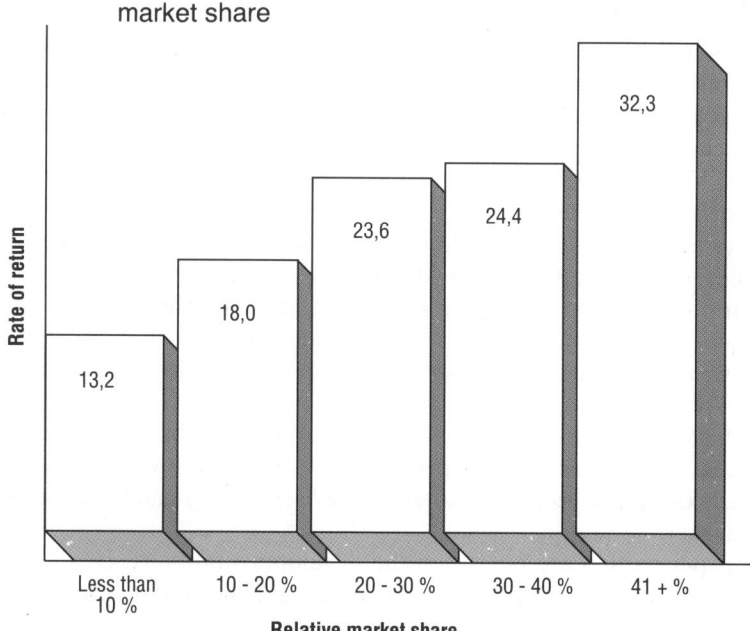

Source: Based on Buzzel, RD and Wiersema, FD. 'Successful Share-Building Strategies'. *Harvard Business Review*. January 1981, p 137.

19.3.5 Planning models

19.3.5.1 *Planning of the product portfolio*

Two different planning models, the **market growth/market share matrix** (also called the Boston Consulting Group (BCG) Matrix)[7] and the **market attractiveness/enterprise strength model**,[8] both based on an analysis of the product portfolio, are now discussed.

19.3.5.2 *Market growth/market share matrix*

According to the Boston Consulting Group, which compiled the matrix in 1960, products of a multi-product enterprise can be categorised in a matrix classification. A broad interpretation is attached to the term 'products'. Products are not necessarily only physical objects; they can also be services, while departments or branches of a large enterprise, or enterprises which operate as independent strategic business units, are often regarded as 'products' of the larger parent enterprise.

The matrix is defined by the market growth rate and the product's relative market share. Four different product classes with very descriptive names are distinguished and represented in the matrix:

- **Stars** are relatively new products in the market growth phase of their life cycle. Each star has attained a relatively large market share and has growth potential. However, they need cash to maintain their position because of the many competitors entering the target market under such satisfactory circumstances. Traditionally the stars use more cash than they generate. The growth rate will necessarily dwindle with time and stars will either become cash cows or lose their position in the market.
- **Cash cows** are the successful stars of the preceding period. They are well established in respect of market share, but few prospects for further market growth exist. They are probably in the maturity phase and do not require much cash to keep them in this profitable position. These products generate cash.
- **Problem children** (also called wildcats) have a relatively small market share and require a continued marketing effort just to retain their market share. The problem child is often a new product which can become a star if it develops successfully. Much cash is, however, required to develop the problem child to its full potential.
- **Dogs** have a low market share and market growth possibilities are limited (or do not exist at all). Because prospects are so poor cash flow to these products is limited. Dogs can be sold to other enterprises or they can be withdrawn from the market.
- **New products** that are not yet in the developmental phase by rights have no place in the market growth/market share classification of products because it is not sure if growth possibilities exist for them. The success of the enterprise nevertheless depends on the quality of new products than can be manufactured.

Figure 19.5 shows the market growth/market share matrix.

FIGURE 19.5   Market growth/market share matrix

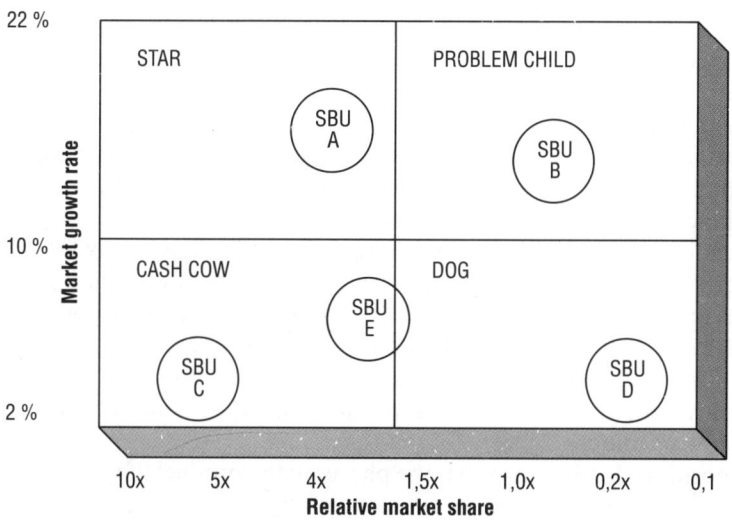

Figure 19.6 shows a number of SBUs in an imaginary enterprise's market growth/market share categorisation.

FIGURE 19.6   SBUs in a product portfolio

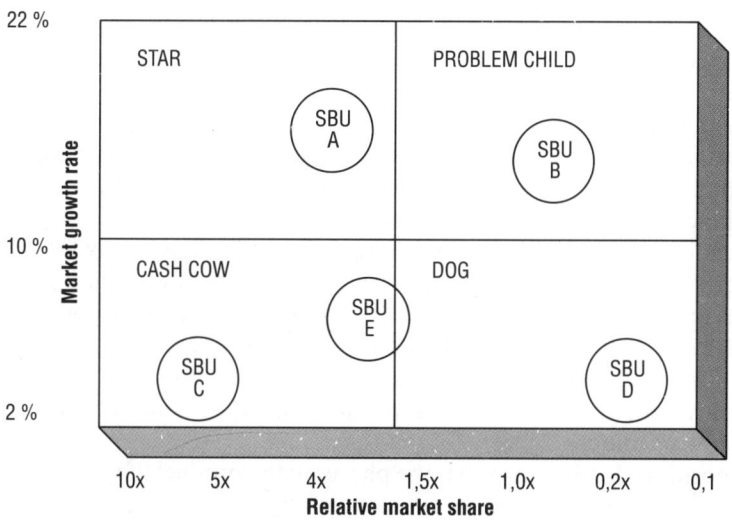

Source: Adapted from Busch, PS and Houston, MJ. 1985. *Marketing Strategic Foundations.* Homewood, Illinois: Richard D Irwin, p 57.

The relative growth rate on the vertical axis is the annual growth in sales in the market in which a product competes. In Figure 19.5 it is described as High and Low and in Figure 19.6 the low quadrant indicates a growth rate of 2–10 per cent. Relative market share shows the SBU position relative to the most important competitor. In Figure 19.6 the cut-off point between High and Low, 1,5×, is shown on a logarithm scale. This means that SBUs that have a relative market share of 5× have a market share five times larger than that of their nearest competitors. In refining such a classification further the diameters of circles representing SBUs can also give an indication of the relative contribution to the profitability of the parent company.

The dimensions of the matrix and the division between High and Low are usually decided arbitrarily by management, using information regarding the market and the competitive position. Products, product ranges, services and strategic business units can be divided into the matrix categories. The parent company's product portfolio consists of a combination of SBUs whereas the SBU's product portfolio consists of products in its product mix. The product assortment in a departmental store can, for example, be categorised according to the matrix, as can the services of a financial institution or the different products in the product range manufactured by a small businessman in his factory, when relative market share and growth rate are known.

In an optimal product portfolio the product composition is balanced. On the face of it, the product portfolio in Figure 19.6 seems unbalanced because there is only one problem child which could possibly become a star in future. There is also a dog that will probably be withdrawn shortly, while there is another one (SBU E) that will attain dog status soon.

In a well-balanced product portfolio there are several stars which have further growth possibilities and can contribute greatly to the rate of return. There is also a number of cash cows in respect of which a harvest strategy can be followed (this is also referred to as the 'milking strategy'). The cash generated by the cash cows is used to stimulate further growth possibilities for stars and problem children. Dogs are usually withdrawn from the market when they can no longer produce any more cash. Obviously a balanced product portfolio has few dogs.

In a balanced product portfolio the **success progression** is from new product to problem child, star, and cash cow — where the product should stay for as long as possible until it inevitably later attains dog status. In highly exceptional cases it sometimes happens that a dog is revived and returns to a cash cow position before it is withdrawn. A holding strategy is followed in respect of such dogs.

The **failure progression** occurs when a promising problem child (or new product) moves directly to the dog position and thus never holds the profitable star and cash cow positions.

This exposition clearly shows that the phases in the product life cycle are closely related to the products in the product portfolio. The new product is in the development phase, the problem child in the introductory phase, the star in the growth phase, the cash cow in the maturity phase and the dog in the declining phase (see Chapter 18 in this regard).

19.3.5.3 *Market attractiveness/enterprise strength model*

This model was developed by McKinsey, a marketing consultant for General Electric.[9] The model consists of a market grid and is based on the rate of return (and not the cash flow position as in the matrix). The market grid is bounded by two variables, namely market attractiveness on the horizontal axis and enterprise strength on the vertical axis. Management evaluates different products or SBUs and places them in a low, an average or a high position in the grid as indicated in Figure 19.7.

The **market attractiveness** position is a compound index and consists of the following variables:

- **Market segment.** Large market segments are more attractive than small market segments.
- **Market growth rate.** Markets with high growth rates are more attractive than markets with low growth rates.
- **Profit margin.** Markets with higher profit margins are more attractive than markets with low profit margins.

FIGURE 19.7 Market attractiveness/enterprise strength model

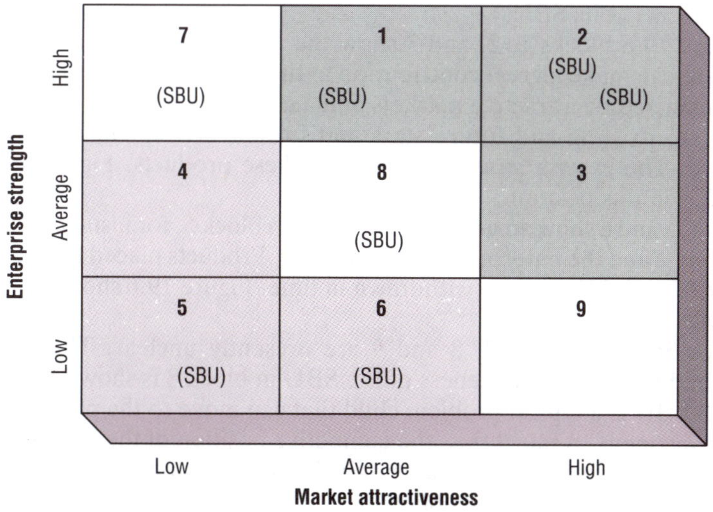

Source: Adapted from Cravens, DW. 1982. *Strategic Marketing*. Homewood, Illinois: Richard D Irwin, p 73.

- **Competitors.** Markets with few or no competitors are more attractive than markets with a number of strong competitors.
- **Economic conditions.** Markets that are strongly influenced by a change in economic conditions are less attractive.
- **Technological changes.** Markets that are strongly influenced by technological changes are less attractive.

Socio-cultural changes. Markets that are strongly influenced by socio-cultural changes are less attractive.

Action by authorities. Markets that are strongly influenced by action by the authorities are less attractive.

The **enterprise strength** shows how strong the enterprise is compared with its competitors. The following variables are evaluated and combined in an index:

- **Market share.** The bigger the market share, the stronger the enterprise's competitive position.
- **Profitability.** A low cost structure makes price competitiveness possible and increases the rate of return.
- **Technology.** Access to the latest technology increases the enterprise's competitive position.
- **Product quality.** The ability to manufacture and market high-quality products strengthens the corporate image and its competitive position.
- **Resources.** Availability of adequate resources strengthens the enterprise's competitive position.
- **Knowledge of the market.** Thorough knowledge of the market reinforces competitive abilities.

The enterprise itself determines which variables are applicable in the evaluation of its products (or its SBUs).

In Figure 19.6 blocks 1, 2, and 3 show the attractive zone. Products (SBUs) placed here can make a great contribution to the rate of return because the zones are characterised by attractive markets and a strong competitive position. These products are existing and future stars and further investment in them can be considered. The growth strategy applies to these products. Figure 19.6 shows three SBUs in this position.

Blocks 4, 5 and 6 show an unattractive zone. In block 5, for instance, the market attractiveness and the enterprise strength is low. Products placed here are current and future dogs which will be withdrawn in time. Figure 19.6 shows two SBUs in this position.

The positions in blocks 7, 8 and 9 are presently unclear. The competitive position and market attractiveness of the SBU in block 8 is shown as an average only. This SBU is a typical problem child that can move to the positive side with further investment. Against this, the competive position of the SBU in block 7 is strong but the market attractiveness is low. This is probably a cash cow in respect of which the holding strategy applies.

It is clear that the two planning models discussed complement each other. Both the market share/market growth matrix and the market attractiveness/enterprise strength model can be used in the planning and implementation of market strategies. A specific organisational structure should be created in order to be able to implement the market strategies. Organisation is discussed in the following section.

19.3.6 Planning the organisation structure

19.3.6.1 *The organising process*

Organising has already been shown to be a separate management task in Chapter 1. In the planning, implementation, and evaluation model (figure 19.1) this aspect is indicated as a planning step in strategic marketing. This means that much thought must be given to the creation of an internal organisational structure in order to make the implementation of the market and marketing strategies possible. The organisational structure determines the flow of information and authority in the enterprise and thus the marketing department as well. Information flow is necessary for the development of a strategy while lines of authority determine who is responsible for what during implementation.

Organising can be described as a process that consists of:

- an analysis of the activities involved and necessary to achieve the marketing and, ultimately, the business objectives;
- the grouping of activities in rational and more or less homogeneous groups;
- the allocation of these groups of activities to specific departments, such as marketing research, advertising, product development, distribution and sales;
- the allocation of authority and responsibility to carry out specific activities;
- the establishing of lines of authority and communication and the co-ordination between different departments and individual posts.[10]

Before the merits of the different types of organisational structure can be discussed, the position of the marketing department within the enterprise is considered.

19.3.6.2 *The position of the marketing department*

The place of the marketing department in an enterprise with a functional organisational structure is indicated in Figure 19.8.

FIGURE 19.8   The position of the marketing department

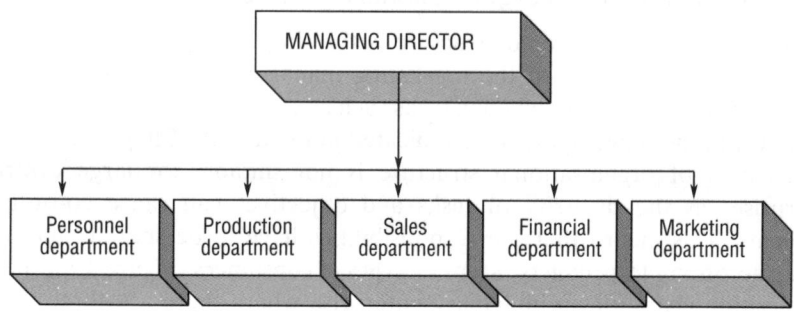

Figure 19.8 is a simple organisation chart and shows five functional departments in an imaginary enterprise. The marketing manager (director) heads the marketing department and manages the enterprise together with the other departmental heads. These managers are responsible for the planning, implementation and evaluation of the business strategy, based on the separate strategies of the departments, among others financial strategy, purchasing strategy and marketing strategy. (See also Chapter 1, section 1.3 and Figure 1.4 where these aspects are touched on as well.)

The market strategies discussed later in this chapter are not the marketing department's responsibility only, but should rather be seen as a joint effort by the various departments. The market strategy is market-directed and it has to do with the enterprise's approach to consumers and competitors in a rapidly changing environment.

The market strategy embraces the marketing strategy and also contains elements of other departmental strategies. External as well as internal aspects exist in the environment; these receive pertinent attention in the business strategy, but are not contained in the market strategy. Aspects such as money and capital markets, manpower provision, raw material supplies (all external factors), and productivity, technology, labour issues, and computerisation (internal factors) are elements that are not necessarily included in the market strategy, but which will indeed be echoed in the business strategy.

Once again, it is found that these concepts are not clearly described in textbooks and that they are sometimes confused. For the purposes of this book **business strategy** is regarded as the combination of the strategies of all the different departments (shown in the organisation chart); **market strategy** refers to the enterprise's (or the SBUs') activity in the market; and **marketing strategy** to the combination of the four marketing instruments directed at a specific target market. The marketing department is responsible for the marketing strategy and gives important inputs to the business strategy. (These aspects are discussed in more detail in section 19.4.)

19.3.6.3 *The functional organisational structure*

The functional organisational structure is the simplest and most general kind. According to this structure the marketing manager has line authority over a number of subdivisions involved in tasks such as advertising, marketing research, and new product development, as indicated in Figure 1.8 (Chapter 1).

This kind of organisational structure is not suitable for large centralised enterprises as the diversity of tasks and objectives can cause co-ordination problems. This means that the responsibilities have to be shared, and usually occurs according to **products**, **areas** or **types of consumers**. Figure 19.9 shows an organisation chart for an imaginary enterprise where there are three different consumer groups (A, B and C) and marketing departments have been created for each type.

FIGURE 19.9   Organising according to consumer group

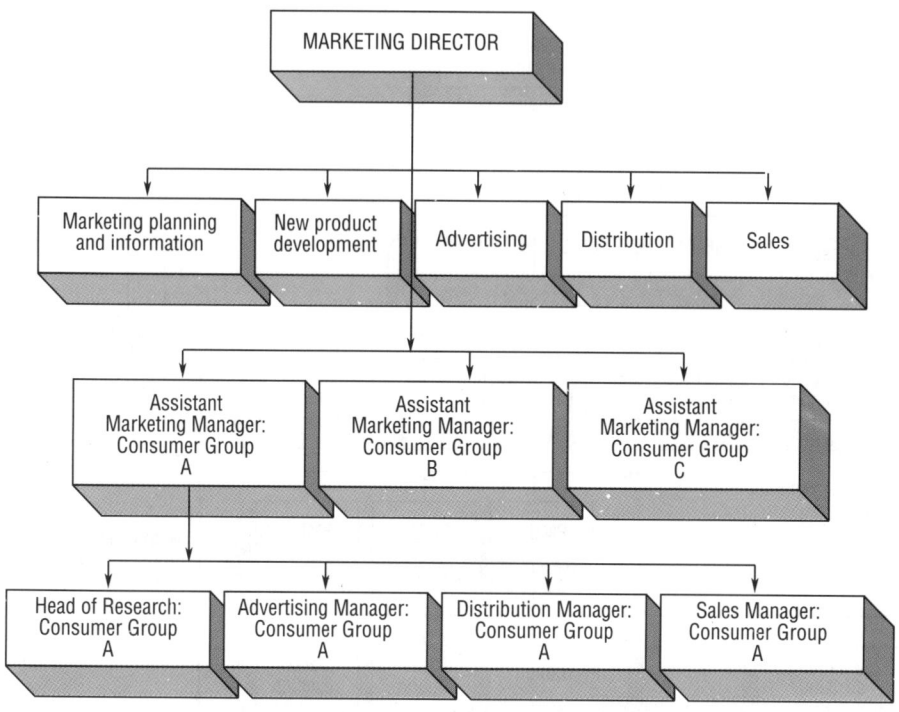

Source: Adapted from Pride, WME & Ferrell, OC. 1985. *Marketing: Basic Concepts and Decisions.*
Boston: Houghton Mifflin, p 587.

In Figure 19.9 the marketing director has line authority over the marketing planning, new product development, advertising, distribution and sales departments, as well as the assistant marketing managers for consumers groups A, B and C and the subdivisions resorting under each one. In the same way an organisation chart can be compiled to include assistant marketing managers for products A, B and C or areas A, B and C.

The marketing planning and information, new product development, advertising, distribution and sales departments do not have direct line authority over the divisions which are the responsibility of the assistant marketing managers. They are, however, involved in advising and the planning of the various activities.

19.3.6.4 *Organisational structure of a multi-product enterprise*

The organisational structure becomes even more complicated if the parent company has a number of SBUs each responsible for the marketing of its products. Figure 19.10 illustrates such a situation.

This enterprise form has been developed to solve the strategy formulation and implementation problems that arise in large enterprises. Accordingly the enterprise is divided into a number of strategic business units, which in turn can consist of a number of product/market units.

FIGURE 19.10   Hierarchical levels in a multi-product enterprise

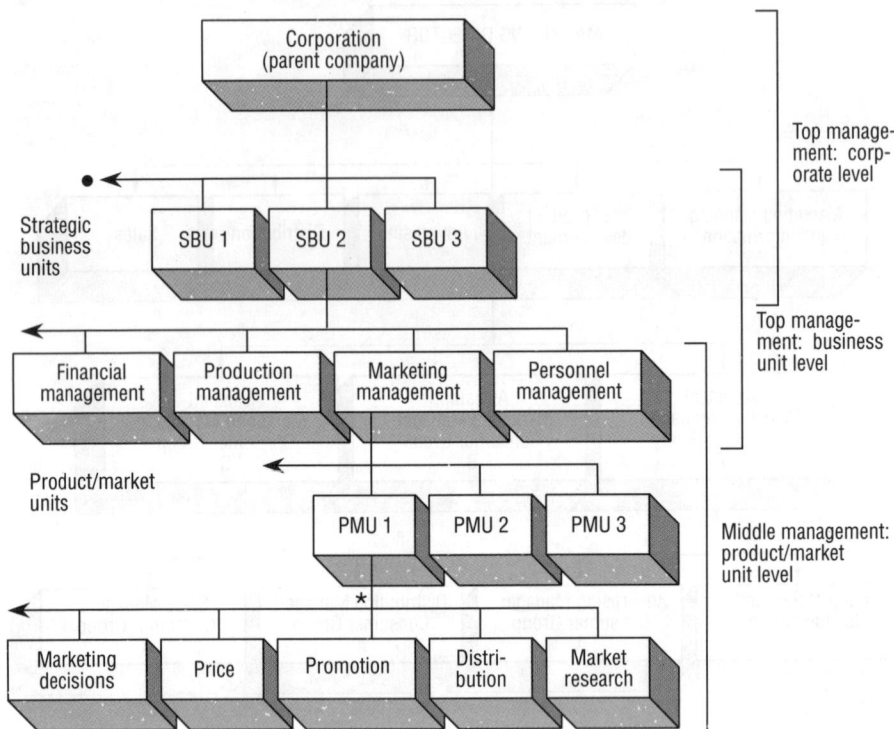

● The arrow at the SBU level implies that more can exist than the three shown. The same principle applies to the three other levels where arrows are shown.

★ Each PMU manager is linked to the marketing function managers because the latter assist the PMU managers in the development of their specific market offerings.

Furthermore, the strategic business unit can also be organised according to the traditional functional method (product management, financial management, marketing management, etc.)

The marketing department now consists of a marketing manager or director, a number of product or market managers (each in control of a product/market unit) and a number of function managers, such as promotion, market research, distribution and sales managers who perform specialised marketing activities, in conjunction with the specific product or market manager for each product/market unit. In overall command is a planning or controlling body, known as the parent company or corporate headquarters. Together with the SBU level, this level is usually known as top management. Naturally not all enterprises are organised on this basis, and numerous different combinations and variations occur in practice.

19.3.6.5 *A matrix organisational structure*

The matrix organisational structure is an attempt to help solve the co-ordination problems encountered in other kinds of organisational structure. An additional management level, namely project management, is added between departments and functional management. The organisation chart resembles a matrix, as illustrated in Figure 19.11.

FIGURE 19.11   The matrix organisational structure

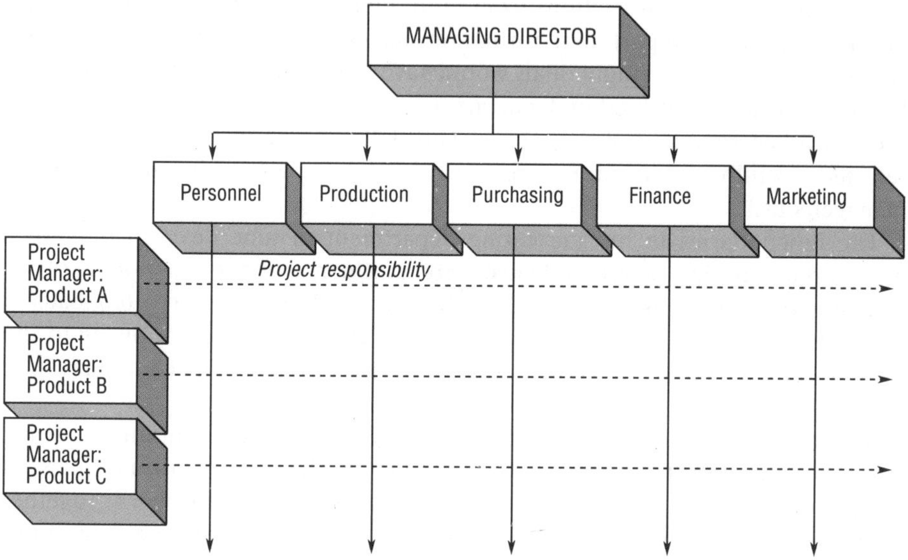

The project manager is responsible for the managing of a small group of products or brands. His responsibility includes personnel, production, purchasing, finance and marketing.[11] In such a structure the project manager does not have line authority. This means that he has to work closely with managers who do have line authority over the various functional departments. General Electric and IBM use this kind of organisational structure and call the product departments profit centres.[12]

An organisational structure usually develops as the enterprise develops. When the enterprise expands, the structure inevitably changes. The structure is also often revised. The saying 'Structure before strategy' points to the importance of an organisational structure being created for the implementation of strategy because nothing will happen until tasks and responsibilities are allocated to specific people.

It is also necessary constantly to motivate the people who have to perform these tasks. It could thus be said that the motivation of functionaries is part of the design of an organisational structure for a marketing department.

19.3.6.6 *Organising and motivating*

Motivation could be described as all attempts (including the organising of the marketing department) made by marketing management to encourage marketing personnel voluntarily to give their best performance to achieve marketing objectives. Motivation aims at fostering a positive attitude amongst marketing personnel toward the enterprise.[13]

The design of the marketing organisation structure influences the motivation of the marketing staff. Thus a functional organisational structure could lead to individuals receiving instructions from more than one head. This could cause a negative attitude. Department formation according to geographic dispersion could mean that certain individuals would have to work in areas they do not like. People could also be placed in departments and posts for which they do not have the desired personality traits, expertise and skills. Marketing personnel must be selected carefully and encouraged regularly to perform well. This is the marketing manager's task.

The functionaries in the marketing department in time develop their own mutual relationships. This could have a great influence on the functioning of the formal marketing organisation. In fact, this informal organisation often leads to the formal organisation functioning differently than was planned, owing to the fact that individuals have their own ways of working together and communicating informally.

Marketing management should see the informal organisation as being complementary to the formal organisation. In this way informal lines of communication reinforce formal ones, allowing people to work together effectively and creating a team spirit that spans numerous departments. Groups and individuals can motivate one another to give their best performance to the enterprise. Purposeful attempts at achieving co-ordination at formal and informal levels help motivate people to perform at their best.

19.3.6.7 *Co-ordinating of activities*

Co-ordinating of activities plays a very important role in organising.[14] Co-ordinating in the marketing department entails obtaining co-operation between individuals and groups inside and outside the marketing department and the enterprise in order to act as tightly knit units striving to achieve the business objectives in general and the marketing objectives in particular.

Marketing management should thus design the marketing organisation in such a way that effective co-operation is achieved with top management, other departments in the enterprise outside the marketing department, between individuals and divisions inside the marketing department, and with outside institutions.

This type of co-ordination is established by effective communication, leadership, and the diplomatic handling of conflict.

Communication to achieve co-ordination

Communication paths as well as communication aids are especially important in the design of a marketing organisation. Provision should be made for at least three communication paths, namely:

- **Vertical communication paths**, where communication flows downwards and upwards from and to top management.
- **Horizontal communication paths**, where communication takes place between people of the same rank and in the same department, and are usually used for the purpose of advising and conveying information between people at the same level in the marketing department.
- **Cross-communication paths**, where communication concerning specific activities which directly affect most departments takes place between subordinates in the marketing department and the personnel of other departments in equal, lower or higher ranks, often at informal level.

The communication methods are mainly verbal and written. Written communication is usually in the form of instructions, reports, guidelines, budgets, circulars, sales reports and newsletters.

Exercising authority

Like communication, leadership is required to ensure that the marketing organisation runs smoothly. The marketing manager is the leader who has to exercise authority and see to it that the marketing task is performed. By authority is meant:

- The right and power given to a person in a management position to carry out certain actions and to take certain decisions required to perform his task.
- The right to give instructions to subordinates and others regarding the performance of certain tasks.
- The right to demand obedience.
- The right to take punitive measures if specific instructions are not carried out.

The marketing manager has **line authority** over the subordinate functionaries in the marketing department (just as he himself falls under the line authority of the general manager). The marketing manager also has **functional authority** over functionaries in other departments regarding important matters affecting the performance of the marketing function. Furthermore, the marketing manager is also in an **advisory position** in respect of some other functions of the enterprise. He, for example, liaises with the financial department about the availability of funds and with the purchasing department about the stock position.

In all these authority relationships a good leader will place co-operation and the attainment of objectives foremost and avoid or reduce conflict as far as possible.

Handling conflict

In the marketing department conflict is avoided by creating a culture of co-operation and effective motivation. Conflict with other divisions and departments is almost unavoidable. The reason for this is that different functional departments strive for different objectives. The financial department, for example, demands strong motivating of expenditure and adherence to inflexible budgets, while the marketing department often reacts to intuitive feelings about market factors, expecting budgets to be adjusted to changing circumstances. The marketing manager must have good insight into the activities and circumstances of all functional departments, and he must have the ability to solve problems through effective communication. The ability to negotiate and to compromise is also an essential characteristic of a good manager.

19.4 IMPLEMENTATION

19.4.1 The integrated marketing strategy

The integrated marketing strategy, which was discussed in detail in Chapter 18, changes continually over the life cycle of a product, and adjustments made to one marketing instrument invariably influence decisions that have to be taken about other marketing instruments and their combination in a marketing strategy.

Implementation thus entails the execution of the plans made and the decisions taken. As already frequently mentioned, planning and implementation are ongoing processes. One could thus not say that planning ends where implementation begins. In carrying out plans new plans are made every time an environmental variable necessitates some or other adjustment to the original plan. The implication of this reasoning is obvious when studying Figure 19.12, which represents the critical path analysis in the introduction of a new product. With each circle a critical expiry date is given so that everything can be ready for the introduction of the product at a specific date. The critical path can thus be regarded as an action plan. When the plan is implemented and the unforeseen occurs, for example during the selection and training of sales representatives, negotiations with channel members and the introduction of the product are delayed. When executing the plan new plans have to be made to adapt to unforeseen events, and in such a way that the introduction of the product is not adversely affected.

The critical path thus shows the sequence of the implementation activities.

The integrated marketing strategy forms a particularly large component of the market strategy. The **market strategy** refers to the **unique combination of the four marketing instruments**, the **positioning of the market offering** in respect of external environmental factors and the **timeous availability of internal resources**.[15] The market strategy is the enterprise's 'total onslaught' on the market and is thus market-directed. Three different kinds of market strategies are now discussed, namely competitive market strategies, growth strategies, and market strategies in dwindling markets.

FIGURE 19.12   Critical path analysis for the introduction of a new product

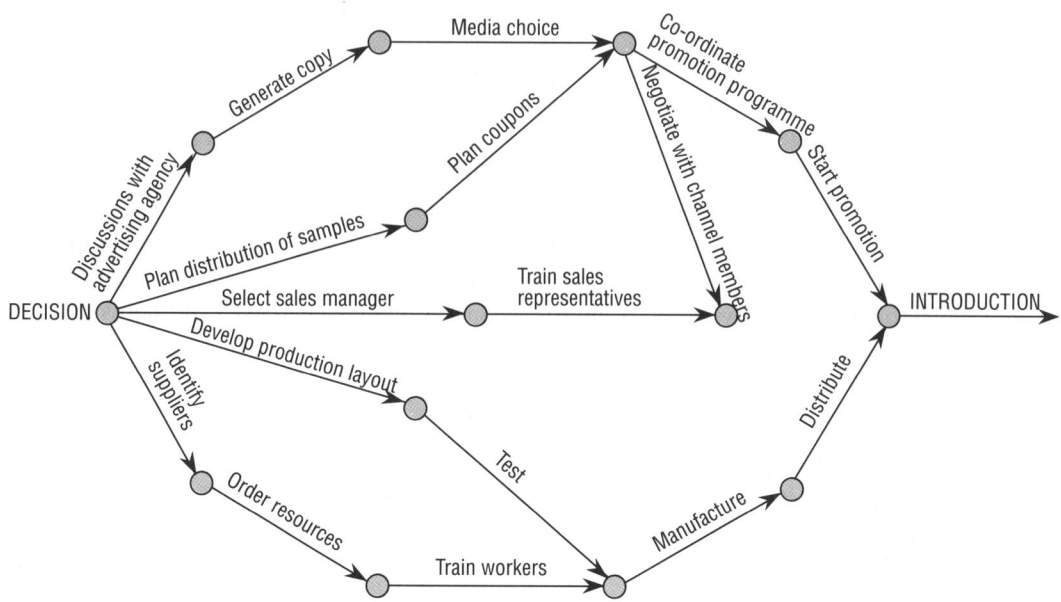

Source: Urban, GL and Hauser, J. 1980. *Design and Marketing of New Products*. Englewood Cliffs, New Jersey: Prentice-Hall Inc, p 469.

19.4.2 Competitive market strategies

19.4.2.1 *The creation of sustainable competitive advantages*

The main objective of competitive market strategies is to create and establish competitive advantages over competitors.

With competitive market strategies the availability of internal resources and the positioning of the enterprise in respect of competitors are of the utmost importance. The competitive situation and positioning regarding competitors was referred to in Chapters 3 and 4. Warfare against competitors during the product life cycle received attention in Chapter 18. It was shown how the four marketing instruments can be used to launch attacks against competitors. It is, however, obvious that attacks on competitors will lead to counter-attacks. The enterprise must be prepared for this, since it would be foolish to launch any attacks before reinforcing and protecting its own position. When the enterprise has done this, it can dare to become involved in warfare. By creating **sustainable competitive advantages**, the so-called SCAs, barricades can be established, making penetration by competitors difficult. All functional departments must actively contribute to the development of SCAs.

In order to maintain a sustainable competitive advantage, the enterprise must develop strengths in one or more of the following fields:

- the ability to innovate;
- the ability to manufacture a high-quality product;
- the ability to manufacture and market a product at a relatively low cost;
- skilled management;
- marketing orientation by top management;
- a large market share.

From this list it is once again obvious that the inputs of marketing management in the creation of SCAs are crucial. The marketing department often initiates the development of innovations; it guards against a quality decrease (and helps to create a quality image of the product); it contributes to the decrease in marketing costs; it works closely with a skilled marketing-oriented top management team; and constantly strives for a larger market share.

Different competitive marketing strategies are now discussed, namely the differentiation, low-cost and focus strategies. All these strategies aim at creating sustainable competitive advantages which will protect the competitive position of the enterprise.

19.4.2.2 *Differentiation strategy*

Various differentiation methods can be used to distinguish essentially identical products in such a way that they will be regarded and accepted as separate products by the target market. When differentiation succeeds the enterprise has created a sustainable competitive advantage for itself. Such an enterprise often claims that there are no substitutes, but only cheap imitations. Methods to differentiate products are the following:

Differentiation on the basis of product/service quality

Product quality goes hand in hand with performance, durability and reliability. Usually the consumer cannot judge these characteristics in making a choice and thus he concentrates only on the finish. If the finish is good, he accepts that the quality is also good. This is a kind of 'halo effect'. It is even more difficult for a consumer to evaluate the quality of services. The politeness, helpfulness and friendliness of the staff of a service organisation all serve as a measure to evaluate the quality of services. It has been found that there is a direct relationship between a reputation for high-quality products and size of market share. High quality is thus one of the most important methods to create a sustainable competitive advantage.

Differentiation by brand

Brands distinguish competitive products from one another, but also give them specific symbolic value, creating an image or personality for the product. (Refer also to Chapter 9.)

Differentiation by unique product characteristics

Unique product characteristics, which make a product just somewhat better or different, initially create a competitive advantage. The unique characteristic can be protected against imitators by patent rights, but unfortunately it is also possible to circumvent patent rights. Unique product characteristics can thus serve as a competitive advantage but it is difficult to keep on differentiating products in this way. The 'me-too' policies of competitive enterprises quickly wipe out the initial differential advantages created by introducing unique product characteristics.

Differentiation by distribution

New and unusual distribution channels not only create new market possibilities but can also serve to differentiate products. Tupperware, for example, differentiated its products by using agents who arrange parties to introduce and sell the product.

Differentiation by marketing communication

Promotional methods and messages are an ideal way of distinguishing a product from those of competitors. Unfortunately the effect is relatively short term, especially in cases where marketing management is constantly amending its advertising theme. A jingle or a slogan helps to create a unified theme, especially if it is often repeated.

Price differentiation

Products can also be differentiated by unusually high or low prices. A high price creates a quality association, whereas a low price can easily create a 'cheap image'. With a high price other product characteristics have to support the quality image and this causes a cost increase. A low price has to be supported by low manufacturing and marketing costs, otherwise losses can be sustained.

Differentiation based on consumer orientation

Nearly all large enterprises these days project an image of being consumer-orientated and thus true to the principles of the marketing concept. This is often only a half-truth. It is also general knowledge that consumers in South Africa are treated shabbily, so much so that almost every newspaper has a column in which consumers can object to exploitation. The Consumer Council is inundated with complaints. Mention has been made of legislation to protect consumers against undesirable business practitioners.

An enterprise which intentionally strives to meet consumer needs, demands and preferences has already laid the basis for a very strong and sustainable competitive advantage. Loyal consumers are an inalienable asset because they do not even consider buying the products of competing enterprises.

19.4.2.3 *Low-cost strategy*

An enterprise which successfully adopts a low-cost strategy can quote lower prices than its competitors and thus create a sustainable competitive advantage for the product. Cost savings can be achieved in various areas but it is first of all important to establish a low-cost culture in the enterprise. Staff will then constantly be on the lookout for the wasting of resources and attempt to keep costs low. It is not easy to establish a low-cost structure because staff members have to be convinced that cost savings are to their benefit. A good example is the public service departments which cannot reward staff for cost savings and therefore find it difficult to establish a low-cost culture. Forced savings merely create conflict and seldom work. Lower prices than those of competitors are not the only advantage of a low-cost strategy. Higher profit and the availability of funds to expand the market share, utilise new opportunities and develop new products stem from preventing squandering.

19.4.2.4 *Focus strategy*

The focus strategy creates a sustainable competitive advantage when the enterprise decides to occupy only one specific niche in the market with a limited product range. This happens if the enterprise's resources and abilities are insufficient to tackle a full-scale battle in the mass market. The big competitors do not usually pay any attention to small fry and thus leave them be. A geographically based focus strategy gives the enterprise the opportunity first to satisfy the needs of a limited market segment before further geographical expansion takes place.

> Some of the large chain stores started off as small corner-shops. As soon as they expand, they create new opportunities for other small entrepreneurs. The development of the large supermarkets and hypermarkets has now been taken so far that new opportunities exist for the smaller speciality grocery stores offering specialised services to consumers.

Focus strategy can succeed only if a profitable target market is selected, if consumers are totally satisfied with the market offering, and if management is involved in and enthusiastic about being successful.

19.4.3 **Growth strategies**

19.4.3.1 *The meaning of growth*

One of the important secondary objectives of the enterprise (and thus also of marketing management) is to promote continued growth. The growth strategies which are now discussed are all directed at this objective. The development of sustainable competitive advantages is naturally also directed at growth. Unique product characteristics and advantages — that 'something' which a product has that its competitors do not have — inevitably draws new consumers and enlarges the market share.

Methods of stimulating growth were discussed in Chapter 18 (during the growth and maturity phases of the product life cycle). Growth strategy is thus essentially an extension as well as a summary of what has already been touched on in Chapter 18. (Once again, the importance of marketing management's inputs becomes very clear.)

19.4.3.2 *Growth in existing markets*

Growth can be achieved by encouraging existing users of a product to buy and use more of the product or to test new uses for the existing product. Reminder advertising, a special discount, giant-sized packaging, and wider openings in toothpaste tubes are examples of methods to stimulate demand and encourage consumption.

Buy more, consume more

- The South African Dried Fruit Board uses home economists to compile recipes using dried fruit.
- The television advertisement for Aromat, encourages children to sprinkle it on a variety of foods.
- SAA's business class passenger service offers a special bonus ticket to regular passengers.

19.4.3.3 *Growth through product development*

Growth can also be achieved by making small changes and improvements to existing products, for example a sunroof option for an existing car model. The product range can also be enlarged to offer consumers an even greater degree of satisfaction. Furthermore, a new product can be developed for an already existing market. Sunlight, for example, developed a fabric softener for the existing loyal Sunlight soap and detergent powder market.

19.4.3.4 *Growth through expansion of the market*

Geographical and even international expansion is a growth possibility that can make very big demands on an enterprise in terms of resources and expertise. Many of the large international enterprises started off as small local enterprises which later achieved phenomenal success through gradual expansion programmes. Often, when an expansion programme is considered, new product, distribution, marketing and pricing decisions have to be taken. New competitive market strategies also have to be planned and implemented because the environment in which the marketing task has to be carried out differs from place to place.

19.4.3.5 *Integration*

Growth can take place through:

- Vertical integration (the manufacturer buys or creates his own retail outlets, for example Edworks).
- Backwards integration (the retailer buys or creates his own manufacturer, for instance Edgars, which has control over a manufacturing enterprise, Celrose).
- Horizontal integration (the enterprise takes over a competitor and thus reinforces its position).

When integration has to be considered, the advantages and costs must be weighed up to determine if it will be economically viable. Integration increases risks when entering a new field and also implies a loss in flexibility (Edworks, for instance, is forced to supply to its own shops).

The advantages of integration are higher profits through cost savings. Control over a source (backward integration) or an outlet (vertical integration) brings about a greater degree of security.

19.4.3.6 *Diversification*

Diversification means **expansion to related markets** with existing or related products, or **expansion to unrelated fields**. Expansion in existing markets adds up to integration and has already been discussed. A closer look is now taken at unrelated diversification. It is the most risky method of expansion because the enterprise finds itself in a totally strange field and can thus easily fail. It cannot lean on loyal consumers, existing distribution channels or a familiar brand name. Successful diversification, however, offers the possibility of big profits. Unrelated diversification usually takes place through take-overs or mergers.

The reasons for diversification are, among others, the following:

- The enterprise experiences a high cash inflow which has to be invested at a profit.
- An unexpected bargain crops up.
- There is a need to spread the risk over a number of products and markets.
- Utilisation of tax benefits.
- Encouraging management enthusiasm.
- The striving for a higher rate of return.

There are many examples of unrelated diversification which failed and in the process damaged the parent company itself. The appraisal of take-overs and mergers is thus very important and should be undertaken with great circumspection by experts.

Peter Drucker states that successful diversification demands

'. . . a common core or unity represented by common markets, technology, or production processes'.[16]

The greater the risk, however, the greater the profit possibilities. Most large and successful enterprises are characterised by diversified interests.

Guidelines for the decision to diversify are the following:

- Diversify with the long-term objective in mind.
- Diversify in markets in which the enterprise already has a measure of experience.
- Utilise special knowledge and resources which exist.
- Utilise opportunities which interest management because enthusiasm is a motivating factor.

19.4.4 Market strategies in declining markets

If, in the last phases of the product life cycle, profits decrease drastically and sales figures stagnate and start to drop, it is still necessary to plan and implement market strategies in order to ensure the survival of the enterprise. In addition to take-overs by competitors and attempts to revitalise declining markets through renewed investment (through the development of unique new product characteristics and intensive advertising campaigns), the enterprise can implement a holding strategy, a harvest strategy, or a withdrawal strategy. Each of these strategies aims at preventing serious financial losses and even the ruin of the enterprise.

Holding strategy

With this strategy just sufficient funds to retain production facilities, product quality and consumer loyalty are spent judiciously. The image of the enterprise must be protected until new growth possibilities occur. This is especially so in the case of a cash cow which is still generating sufficient cash flow. The danger of a holding strategy is that the enterprise can continue for too long with it, missing promising opportunities, while funds are wasted in trying to maintain the holding strategy.

Harvest strategy

In this situation the objective is to bring in cash as quickly as possible. All further investment in the product is stopped and costs are cut to the bone. The cash is invested elsewhere and the product is allowed to die a slow death. This is especially the ideal strategy if there is still a strong demand for the product in smaller market segments and if a degree of consumer loyalty exists. This strategy has a dampening effect on management's self-confidence, morale and enthusiasm. Competition can intensify during a harvest strategy that carries on too long, forcing the product to withdraw prematurely.

Withdrawal strategy

A withdrawal strategy is recommended if cash flow dries up and the enterprise starts showing losses, especially if there is a dominant competitor forcing prices down and few loyal consumers remain.

It is often difficult to take withdrawal decisions. The following obstacles could hinder withdrawal decisions:

- production facilities and equipment being so specialised that they cannot be used for anything else;
- long-term contracts that are difficult to break (for example labour contracts);
- the fact that the withdrawal decision can damage the enterprise's reputation;
- the fact that management's pride and the enterprise's image are affected and will be damaged by the 'failure';
- the fact that the product has emotional meaning for the enterprise or a small group of consumers that still show loyalty towards the product.

19.5 EVALUATION/CONTROL

19.5.1 The meaning of evaluation

Evaluation is a continuous process through which management exercises control, and by which actual activities are measured against those that were planned. It has to be established whether the objectives set in the marketing department were in actual fact achieved and, if so, to what extent. During planning certain standards are laid down; during evaluation it is established whether it was possible to meet those standards or not. It is clear that evaluation should take place on an ongoing basis and that corrective steps be taken as soon as required. Evaluation thus offers the opportunity for recovery and prevention. Evaluation implies measurement and the timeous identification of looming problems and failures. Evaluation takes place before and after an activity is completed, but during it as well.

In Chapter 1 the gap between planned objectives and actual performance is referred to. Evaluation attempts to bridge the gap and make it as small as possible. Evaluation and control are synonymous concepts. They entail three distinguishable steps, which are apparent from the following description:

Evaluation (control) is a systematic attempt to bring standards in line with the marketing objectives, to compare actual achievements observed with standards, and to take corrective steps to ensure that all the enterprise resources are applied as effectively as possible to achieve the marketing and enterprise objectives.[17]

19.5.2 Steps in the evaluation/control process

19.5.2.1 *Determine performance standards*

During the planning process certain performance standards regarding desired achievement are determined. The business and marketing objectives are examples of such performance standards. In section 19.3.4.1 it was indicated that performance standards must inter alia be measurable, placed in priority order, and achievable. Performance standards meeting these requirements facilitate the evaluation process considerably. Vague, generalised and unrealistic performance standards make evaluation impossible.

Standards, as achievable objectives, can be determined for various marketing activities and are especially useful with routine activities, such as the number of visits and demonstrations per day by the sales force. Standards can naturally also be laid down for once-off marketing projects, for example activities involved in a specific advertising campaign.

Furthermore, standards can be set in quantitative and qualitative terms for the different marketing activities. Quantitative standards are emphasised in this section and consist of **input**, **output** and **efficiency standards**.[18]

Input standards

Input standards are specified norms and are usually quantified in money value and/or manpower application.

Input standards quantified in money value usually appear in the budget. *A budget is a plan expressed in money indicating the marketing activities for a specific future period.* Different budgets, such as term, project, year, advertising and cash budgets, and in which the marketing activities are incorporated, can be compiled.

Manpower application is also an important input in the marketing effort. A manpower budget, consisting of an estimate of the number of people (manhours) allocated during a specific budget period, is inter alia required for the allocation of sales areas to representatives.

Output standards

Output standards are norms used in the evaluation of the marketing results. Sales, measured in income or physical units, is probably the most important marketing output. Other marketing results, such as the size of the market share, contribution to the gross profit and net profit, and contribution to the enterprise's growth and profitability, are directly derived from the sales volumes of the enterprise.

Three output standards can be derived from sales as the most important marketing output:

- A **sales forecast**, the estimated sales of the enterprise's products in all its target markets, expressed in rand value and/or physical units, can be made for a specific future period. (See Chapter 6 in this regard.)
- **Sales quotas**, consisting of quantitative targets which have to be reached in a specific period, can be established by regional offices, branch offices, sales departments and individual sales representatives to direct the sales activities of these units.
- The **sales budget** is an output standard with which the marketing results can be compared. A sales budget consists of a forecast of possible sales in rands and/or

physical units and a forecast of the sales costs incurred to realise these sales within a specific future period.

Marketing outputs not directly related to sales are naturally also possible. Outputs, such as brand recognition, brand preference and brand insistence; the speed at which orders are dealt with and delivered; the number of advertisements placed in a specific time; the utilised shelf-space at retailers; and the number of visits paid and demonstrations held by sales representatives can serve as important output standards to evaluate specific marketing activities.

Efficiency standards

Efficiency standards are determined by expressing closely and rationally associated inputs and outputs as a relationship. These relationships or ratios indicate the relative efficiency with which certain tasks are performed. Efficiency standards especially useful in evaluation are, inter alia, the turnover of stock, the turnover per m^2 of sales space; the turnover per rand rent paid; the turnover per rand reimbursement of the sales staff; the average cost per visit of sales representatives; and the number of visits per day by sales representatives.

19.5.2.2 *Measurement and noting of the actual performance*

Strategic control points are established and overseen by persons who have the required authority to exercise control. The product manager, the advertising manager, and the sales manager, inter alia, are responsible for measuring and noting actual performance against the preset standards in their departments.

It has already been mentioned that evaluation is appropriate before the actual activity takes place, while it takes place and after it has been completed. The ideal is to evaluate before or at least while things are happening, so that deviations from the standard can be spotted in time and changes made before large sums of money or time are wasted. This is, however, not always possible, and marketing control is often required after the event has occurred. Then it is a matter of **recovery management**. The purpose of recovery management is to establish a basis for future planning and to prevent a repetition of the deviation in future — this points to **prevention management**.

In large enterprises it is often difficult for management to exercise effective control. Strategic control points are thus delegated to the lower levels, while only exceptional differences and deviations from the standards are reported to management. This is referred to as **control by exception**.

Where deviations occur the nature and extent thereof and the reasons therefor have to be determined before corrective steps can be taken.

19.5.2.3 *Corrective action*

Where actual performance is below the standards set, measures can be taken to improve performance. If sales in the first quarter are lower than the norm set in the sales budget, then corrective measures can possibly entail an intensive marketing campaign.

Where the deviation can be attributed to uncontrollable environmental factors (such as an economic depression), standards have to be lowered as they were initially set too high. In favourable circumstances it is also possible that actual performance can exceed the standards laid down. Once again, standards will have to be adjusted. If sales in the first quarter are much higher than the norm set in the sales budget, an adjustment will have to be made to avoid stock problems in the second quarter.

Information on deviations, the reasons for deviations, and the nature of corrective action are used in the forecasting process in order to be able to set better planning standards for future periods.

Evaluation techniques include the marketing audit, sales analysis, cost analysis, efficiency analysis and qualitative observations. These techniques are now discussed.

19.5.3 Evaluation/control techniques

19.5.3.1 *The marketing audit*

A marketing audit can be described as a periodic, comprehensive, systematic and independent investigation into the enterprise's marketing environment and specific marketing activities, with the aim of identifying opportunities and challenges and to recommend action plans in order to increase the enterprise's overall marketing efficiency. Four aspects in this description of a marketing audit merit special attention:[19]

- It is a **periodic** investigation. The marketing audit should be carried out on a regular basis, usually annually, and not only when there are problems.
- It must be **comprehensive**. The marketing audit must involve the entire marketing function and not only be directed at one or a few marketing problems.
- It must be carried out **systematically**. The investigation must be carried out in an analytical, critical, systematic and scientific way. Furthermore, the investigation report should contain short- as well as long-term suggestions to increase marketing efficiency.
- It is an **independent** investigation. The marketing audit should be carried out by independent persons in order to ensure the necessary objectivity and top management's trust. Expert and independent management consultants can be used for this purpose.

These persons submit a research report to top management based on the results of a comprehensive audit investigation. Figure 19.13 shows the dimensions of a marketing audit. The consultants summarise the diagnosis, the prognosis and the recommendation to top management.

From Figure 19.13 it is apparent that the marketing audit consists of four major dimensions. Each one has a number of pertinent questions and thus offers a complete picture of the marketing activities.

FIGURE 19.13   Framework for the marketing audit

Dimension	Diagnosis	Prognosis	Recommendations
Objectives Hierarchy Secondary objectives Market activity objectives			
External environment Macro-variables Competitive environment Consumers			
Internal environment Organisational structure Resources Abilities and skills Motivation and attitude			
Marketing strategy Products Prices Channels Marketing communications			

Source: Adapted from Murphy, PE and Enis, BM. 1985. *Marketing.* Glenview, Illinois: Scott, Foresman, p 555.

19.5.3.2 *Sales analyses*

Sales analyses entail a careful and comprehensive investigation into the composition of the enterprise's sales as it appears in the income statement.[20] This is an important method of control and is done to determine whether actual sales correspond with planned sales.

Different bases can be used for sales analysis, such as sales per area, product range, consumers, distribution channel and size of order. These analyses can be made in physical units and/or rand values. It is important to note that the gathering and processing of sales information for control purposes is meaningful only if standards are set beforehand.

Table 19.1 shows the difference (variance) in sales and planned sales in 1987 for products A, B, and C of an imaginary enterprise.

TABLE 19.1   Sales analysis for products A, B, C

Product	1987 Actual sales (R mil)	1987 Sales forecast (R mil)	Variance (R mil)
A	14,0	15,6	– 1,6
B	14,2	14,1	+ 0,1
C	14,6	14,6	+ 0,0

Source: Adapted from Busch, PS and Houston, MJ. 1985. *Marketing Strategic Foundations.* Homewood, Illinois: Richard D Irwin, p 787.

From the table it is clear that product A has not achieved the set standard whereas product B has slightly over-achieved and the forecast for product C was accurate. Variance for sales per region can also be calculated to determine in which region product A performed poorer than was expected. It is now easier to determine the reason for the variance (possibly a poor sales representative?). The problem with sales analyses is that costs of sales are not taken into consideration.

19.5.3.3 *Marketing costs analysis*

A marketing costs analysis entails a comprehensive investigation into the enterprise's total marketing cost structure, as it appears in the income statement. It is a useful method of determining whether the current marketing activities must be continued along the same lines, expanded, reduced or eliminated.

Marketing costs analyses have three dimensions:[21]

- It begins with the income statement which contains the actual cost centres, such as salaries, travelling and subsistence costs, and rent.
- These actual cost centres are then allocated to specific marketing activities, such as sales, advertising, and marketing research. Thus a marketing cost statement is arrived at which indicates the total costs of each marketing activity.
- In the third place, the total costs of each marketing activity must be allocated to individual sales areas, products, customer groups, distribution channels or any meaningful decision making centre for which standards are set.

The information in the income statement of the enterprise forms the basis for the analysis of marketing costs. A simplified income statement of an imaginary enterprise, XYZ (Pty) Ltd, indicating budgeted and real amounts for certain cost centres, appears in Table 19.2. The difference between the budgeted amounts and the actual costs included is also shown.

The analysis and comparison of the costs in the income statement are reasonably simple and easily understood by marketing management. This method is, however, not sufficiently analytical and accurate to create clear guidelines for improved marketing performance. The most important shortcoming of the costs in the income statement is that they are mainly classified according to the nature of the costs rather than the specific purpose for which they are incurred. For effective control the cost data in the income statement should thus be allocated to the various marketing activities necessary to achieve the marketing objectives as well as to the various products.

If necessary, the table can also be extended to include the previous year's actual and budgeted costs and the industry average. Table 19.3 shows a number of direct cost centres and the allocation thereof to products A, B and C. This table can also be expanded to include budgeted costs and the previous year's performance.

TABLE 19.2 XYZ (Property) Limited. Simplified income statement for the year ending 28 February 19........

CENTRE	Budget (B)		Current year (A)		Difference R (A) – (B)
	R	% of sales	R	% of sales	
Sales	100 000	100,0	110 000	100,0	+10 000
Minus: Cost of sales	66 920	66,9	70 000	63,6	+3 080
Gross profit	33 080	33,1	40 000	36,4	+6 920
Cost					
Salaries and wages:					
Administrative staff	8 000	8,0	8 000	7,3	—
Sales representatives	9 730	9,7	9 000	8,2	−730
Advertising	3 130	3,1	3 000	2,7	−130
Travelling and subsistence costs	2 180	2,2	2 002	1,8	−178
Telephone fees and postage	720	0,7	670	0,6	−50
Representatives' commission	654	0,7	700	0,6	+46
Unrecoverable debts	80	0,1	44	0,1	−36
Assessment rates	900	0,9	900	0,8	—
Rent	2 820	2,8	2 820	2,8	—
Total expenditure	28 214	28,2	27 136	24,7	−1 078
Net profit	4 866	4,9	12 864	11,7	+7 998

Source: Marx, S and Dekker, HJ. 1982. *Marketing Management: Principles and Decisions*. Pretoria: HAUM, p 503.

TABLE 19.3   Allocation of marketing costs to products A, B and C

Cost centre*	Product A R	Product B R	Product C R	Total R
Advertising	14 000	8 000	7 500	29 000
Personal selling	18 000	10 000	12 000	40 000
Transport	5 000	2 000	2 000	9 000
Storage costs	1 800	2 000	3 000	6 800
Market research		1 000	1 000	2 000

*Only a limited number of direct costs have been included in the table

In the same way cost allocation can also be done per geographical area or consumer group. With this kind of detail it is easier for management to exercise control over costs.

With the allocation of costs to products (per geographical region and consumer group) an allocation problem in respect of indirect costs arises. Certain cost centres can be directly allocated to specific marketing activities (such as salaries of sales representatives, which are directly linked to sales). Other indirect cost items must, however, be allocated to the various marketing activities in some or other way. Thus rent and assessment rates can, for example, be allocated on the basis of floor surface area taken up by each marketing department. The allocation of indirect costs is often arbitrary because they cannot be calculated accurately.

19.5.3.4 *Efficiency analysis*

Efficiency standards are established by expressing closely and rationally associated inputs and outputs as a relationship. The relationship figures which thus arise give an indication of the efficiency with which marketing activities are performed.

In addition to the familiar financial ratios, the following ratios can be used to evaluate the efficiency of marketing activities:

- Efficiency of sales representatives:
- Average costs per visit
- Sales per m² sales space
- Number of lost clients per time period.
- Advertising effectiveness.
- Delivery costs per order.
- Handling costs as percentage of sales.

These ratios must be compared with the standard ratios if they are available. An enterprise can compile its own standards list from historical information in order to make comparisons possible. Standard deviations can also be investigated. A shortcoming of the method is its episodical nature. No ratio exists which reflects the enterprise's overall marketing efficiency.

The setting of standards and the application of evaluation techniques involve various experts and departments in the enterprise. The marketing, financial, and especially the administrative departments are usually very closely involved in these activities. The administrative department has at least to compile the necessary information and support marketing management in its usage. Once again, the importance of co-operation and co-ordination between people and departments in the enterprise is highlighted.

The evaluation techniques discussed so far are mainly of a quantitative nature. The performance standards mostly have to do with figures and relationships. Qualitative performance standards, however, also have to be evaluated through observation.

19.5.3.5 *Evaluation by observation*

Observation as a qualitative method of control[22] makes it possible for the marketing manager or the sales manager to monitor marketing activities during execution thereof, for example, by accompanying sales representatives on their visits; visiting middlemen who handle the enterprise's products and evaluating their wares presentation.

Observation is an especially useful method of control for the retailer. A systematic, conscious and determined observation tour through the store by the retail manager enables him to observe aspects such as the sales habits of clients, the wares presentation, the neatness of the store, and the actions of the sales personnel. The mere presence of the manager is in itself a control technique, because people are aware of his presence and know that they are being observed and judged. All kinds of equipment, such as mirrors and closed-circuit television to observe people and electronic devises to reduce shop lifting, is especially used in the retail business.

19.5.4 **Control and evaluation**

Control was identified as a management task in Chapter 1. In this chapter it is shown that **evaluation**, a component of the strategic marketing model, in actual fact has more or less the same meaning as control.[23] The evaluation techniques discussed in section 19.5.3, for example, are in essence control measures introduced to establish whether functionaries are doing what they are supposed to be doing. Because the control concept has a negative connotation for most people, the term 'evaluation' is preferred. Control implies that people cannot be trusted and that they have no freedom to show initiative. Most people associate control with punishment instead of reward and are therefore negative regarding all forms of control. Whereas control is mostly enforced from the top down to subordinates, evaluation is a process that can take place from the bottom upwards. Each functionary can to a certain extent evaluate his own performance and task, himself accept the responsibility for it, and report to his superiors. In this way co-operation and enthusiasm are fostered, facilitating the control process. The importance of voluntary co-operation is frequently stressed in this chapter on strategic marketing. Where people co-operate enthusiastically the cost of control can thus be kept low. The unwritten rule of control remains that it should not be so comprehensive and complicated that the cost exceeds the advantages.

19.6 SUMMARY

The three components of strategic marketing, namely planning, implementation and evaluation, direct the marketing task in the enterprise. Marketing and market strategies are planned by marketing management, taking the internal strengths and weaknesses as well as the external opportunities and threats into consideration. The strategies are market-directed, and consumer needs, demands and preferences and the competitive position of the enterprise are considered. The main objective of the enterprise, namely maximisation of profitability, can be realised only through aggressive marketing efforts, the creation of an effective organisational structure, the judicious application of resources and the establishment of an evaluation system through which performance standards are set and activities controlled. In the following chapter it becomes evident that strategic marketing is applied to the marketing of agricultural and industrial products, in non-profit organisations and retailing. This chapter is an appropriate conclusion and a summary of tasks and responsibilities of marketing management at middle and top management levels.

REFERENCES

1. See for example:
   Cravens, DW. 1982. *Strategic Marketing*. Homewood, Illinois: Richard D Irwin; Aaker, DA. 1988. *Strategic Market Management*. New York: John Wiley & Sons; Busch, PS and Houston, MJ. 1985. *Marketing Strategic Foundations*. Homewood, Illinois: Richard D Irwin, pp 40–69; Pride, WM and Ferrell, OC. 1985. *Marketing: Basic Concepts and Decisions*. Boston: Houghton Mifflin Co, pp 592–605.
2. Busch and Houston op cit, p 56.
3. The section on the mission is based on Aaker op cit, pp 39–49.
4. Busch and Houston op cit, pp 47–9.
5. Buzzell, RD et al. 'Market Share — Key to Profitability'. *Harvard Business Review,* January 1975, pp 96–100.
6. Drucker, P. 'Managing for Business Effectiveness'. *Harvard Business Review,* May 1963, p 59.
7. The section on the market growth/market share matrix is based on the discussion in Allen, GB et al. 1975. *A Note on the Boston Consulting Group Concept of Competitive Analysis and Corporate Strategy*. Boston: Intercollegiate Case Clearing House. See also Abell, DF and Hammond, JS. 1979. *Strategic Market Planning*. Englewood Cliffs, New Jersey: Prentice-Hall Inc, pp 214, 374–375.

8. The section on the market attractiveness/enterprise strengths model is based on the discussion in Cravens op cit, pp 72–9.
9. Cravens op cit, p 72.
10. Marx, S and Dekker, HJ. 1982. *Marketing Management: Principles and Decisions*. Pretoria: HAUM, pp 462–3.
11. Murphy, PE and Enis, BM. 1985. *Marketing*. Glenview, Illinois: Scott, Foresman, p 521.
12. Lucas, GHG (ed). 1983. *The Task of Marketing Management*. Pretoria: Van Schaik, p 282.
13. Marx and Dekker op cit, p 473.
14. This section is based on Marx and Dekker op cit, pp 470–2.
15. The section on the different market strategies is based on Aaker op cit, pp 17–19, 201–15, 219–23, 235–49, 264–9, 280–5.
16. Aaker op cit, p 269.
17. Lucas op cit, p 652.
18. The standards are discussed in more detail in Marx and Dekker op cit, pp 487–9.
19. Lucas op cit, p 673.
20. Marx and Dekker op cit, p 501.
21. Ibid p 496.
22. Ibid p 499.
23. Well-known writers do not distinguish clearly between evaluation and control. See for example Assael, H. 1985. *Marketing Management Strategy and Action*. Boston: Kent, p 623 and Busch and Houston op cit, p 55. In both books these concepts are used interchangably.

CASE STUDIES

1 MILESTONES IN MARKETING

In 1987 Kotler[1] identified the most important milestones in marketing in the past four decades. These milestones illustrate the development of marketing thought, which can be summarised as follows:

THE CONCEPTS OF THE 50s

- *The marketing mix.* The combination of marketing instruments is utilised in the marketing of consumer products.
- *The product life-cycle.* The phases in the life-cycle, from introduction and growth through the maturity and decline phases, are identified and further refined throughout the next decades.
- *The brand image.* The image of a branded product as perceived by consumers was first introduced in 1955.
- *Market segmentation.* The idea that the market can be subdivided in significant segments and marketing programmes can be directed at specific target markets is born.
- The *marketing concept.* Marketing management begins to realise that consumers' needs and preferences should receive attention.
- The *marketing audit.* The marketing strategy must be monitored throughout to ensure its successful adaptation to changing circumstances.

THE SOARING 60s

- *The four Ps.* The most important instruments of the marketing mix, namely product, price, promotion and place, are identified.
- *Marketing myopia.* Companies fail when they focus on the product and not the consumer and define their products too narrowly.
- *Life style.* The psychographic attributes of target markets are recognised and marketing communication is formulated with these attributes in mind.
- *The broadening of marketing.* Management realises that not only products and services, but also companies, persons, places and ideas can be marketed more or less in the same way as consumer products and services.

THE TURBULENT 70s

- *Social marketing.* Social and welfare programmes can also be marketed.
- *Positioning.* Increasing competition compels marketers to position their brands against competitors.
- *Strategic marketing.* A distinction is made between tactical marketing, which includes the usual marketing activities, and strategic marketing at top management level. Marketing management is responsible for important inputs to strategic corporate planning, especially in a turbulent environment. The Boston Consulting Group formulates the market growth/market share matrix.

- *Social responsibility.* Companies accept their responsibilities to the society in which profits are made. The long-term welfare of society increases in importance.
- *Macromarketing.* The gap between marketing and public relations becomes narrower. All company activities are directed at ensuring consumer satisfaction and the welfare of society.
- *Services marketing.* The marketing of services increases in importance. Medical services, consultancy services and financial services are also marketed. The theory of services marketing is refined.

THE UNCERTAIN 80s

- *Marketing warfare.* Increasing competition and the proliferation of products and services cause strife between competitors, which confront each other directly like Coca-Cola/Pepsi-Cola, Butter/Margarine, BMW/Mercedes-Benz.
- *Internal marketing.* A marketing culture in a company ensures close co-operation between all departments. All activities should be directed at successful marketing of the enterprise's products and services.
- *Global marketing.* Domination of world markets results in economics of scale. Large enterprises in industrialised countries has already succeeded in achieving the success in global markets.
- *Local marketing.* Consumers in certain areas have distinctive needs and preferences which can only be satisfied by products specifically developed for them. In such cases local marketing is important. Cosmetics are advertised as 'suitable for the drier climate in South Africa' and automobiles are adapted to suit local conditions and consumer demands.
- *Direct marketing.* There is a sharp increase in door-to-door marketing, mail advertising, telephone marketing and home marketing of products advertised on television or by means of Beltel.
- *Relationship marketing.*[2] Maintaining enduring relationships between the enterprise and its internal and external markets is the basis for long-term success. Two other Ps are added to the marketing mix, namely people and processes. All the Ps are directed at providing consumer satisfaction.
- *Megamarketing.* Close cooperation between marketing and public relations is imperative to overcome barriers to successful marketing. A further P is thus 'public relations' or alternatively 'perception'[3] because successful marketing is soundly based on consumers' perception of products, services, companies, persons and ideas.

THE 90s AND FURTHER

- *Unprecedented growth in public relations activities.* This is the prediction of large public relations agencies.[4]
- *Technological developments.*
- *World-wide communications networks.*
- *Mistrust in the effectiveness of advertising messages because of more or less similar products being marketed.* Warsop[5] maintains that 80 per cent of all advertising messages go unnoticed in what he calls a barrage of print and

electronic media. Marketers therefore must use public relations as part of their 'mix of tactics'.[6]
- *An increase in activism and consumerism.*[7]

QUESTIONS

1. 'The marketing theory currently being studied in South Africa is outdated.' Do you agree with this statement? Motivate your answer.

2. Is public relations an independent managerial function or is it a subsection of marketing? Give your opinion.

3. Give examples of South African enterprises in which relationship marketing and internal marketing are practised.

4. Why is it necessary for marketing management to build enduring relationships with the following?
   — Consumers/customers
   — Suppliers
   — The general public
   — Employee markets
   — Influencers (financial institutions, the government and trade unions)
   — Internal markets (own employees)

   Give your opinion and motivate your answer.

REFERENCES

1. Marketing Milestones of Four Decades. *Marketing News,* 31 July 1987.
2. Christopher, M, Payne, A and Balantine, D. 1991. *Relationship marketing.* Oxford: Heineman, p 8.
3. Harris, T L. 1991. *The marketer's guide to public relations: How today's top companies are using the new PR to gain a competitive edge.* New York: Wiley, pp 280-281.
4. Harris, op cit, p 283.
5. The Art of the Mix. *Adweek's Marketing Week,* 18 September 1989.
6. Zoio, V. *Finance Week,* 9-15 April 1992, p 23.
7. Harris, op cit, p 284.

2 ENGEN CAREFUL WITH ITS MARKETING STRATEGY

The marketing team of Engen is confronted by several challenges in its attempt to establish the new name of Mobil and to prevent customers from switching to competitive brands.

Mobil advertising is continuing for the time being.

A new marketing organisation, known as Engen Marketing, has recently been substituted for the old Mobil marketing. Its main task is to develop a new marketing plan.

All this follows Mobil Oil's decision to withdraw from the South African market in 1989 and the subsequent change of the name to South African Energy Company. The latter's name changed to Engen in May 1992.

The Mobil and Engen brands will both be marketed for a year after which Mobil marketing will be gradually phased out, according to Mr Barry Jordan, marketing manager of Engen.

After 97 years Mobil has become a well-known name in South Africa and as such Mobil marketing will be able to give Engen a good start.

The Mobil name is connected to international advanced technology and everything possible will be done to ensure that Mobil's good reputation will gradually be carried over to Engen.

This will mean that consumers will have to be informed about the change of name, which must take place before June 1994 according to the agreement with Gencor, the controlling company of Engen.

'Consumers will have to be convinced that the technology of Engen, as a South African company, will be as advanced or better than that of Mobil. In the past Mobil SA was compelled to use the technology of the Mobil Corporation, but now as an independent company Engen is free to purchase the best technology available or even to develop its own specialty for the conditions in the South African market,' says Mr Jordan.

It is generally accepted that consumers resist change and Engen Marketing will have to do everything in its power to convince customers to accept the change of name.

In contrast to Mobil the dividends of Engen will be reinvested in South Africa and it is to be expected that patriotic South Africans will prefer to support a South African company, as is the case with Sasol.

According to Mr Jordan the name Engen has been thoroughly researched and there has been no negative reaction with language groups. Both Engen and the Engen Corporation will be marketed simultaneously thereby gaining the benefits of rationalisation.

The first corporate advertisements are planned for the middle of 1992. The exact date is kept a secret in an attempt to pre-empt competitors who may decide to launch their new marketing plans simultaneously. Marketing Engen products will only commence after the first fourteen test service stations are in full operation and the name Engen is well established.

It will cost between R100 000 and R130 000 to display the new name at service stations. Each service station will be allowed to formulate its own marketing plan. Engen itself will spend between R110 million and R130 million (almost one third of the company's profit for 1991) on the total marketing action and aims to convert about eight service stations per week as soon as the marketing programme is in full progress.

An example of an Engen service station is being built behind high walls in Krugersdorp. Several designer concepts are being tested. The decision to keep the white, red and blue colours and also the red e (which stands for energy and Energen), similar to the red O in Mobil, are all attempts to retain the colour link and the relationship with Mobil.

At the top of the petrol pumps there will be large billboards which will display specific South African themes, like the flowers of Namaqualand.

The stores at many of the Engen service stations will be converted to small supermarkets where bread, newspapers, milk and fast foods will be sold. In the past these stores sold only Mobil products and spare parts.

'All the Mobil 1-Stops on the main highways will be changed to Engen 1-Stops. Currently there are four Mobil 1-Stops and one in process. Within three years Engen hopes to have at least twelve Engen 1-Stops. The ten independent Mobil Truck Stops will also be changed to Engen Truck Stops. More is planned,' says Mr Jordan.

The Mobil Foundation has now been substituted by the Energos Foundation which, like its predecesor, will make R8 million available for social responsibility programmes.

The involvement of Engen as sponsor for the Volkswagen and Audi racing cars is merely to test Energen products in practical situations and to promote it to the general public. Engen does not have international marketing aims as Sasol perhaps has.

Source: Johan Coetzee, translated and reprinted with permission of *Finansies & Tegniek,* 22 May 1992, p 26 (slight changes).

QUESTIONS

1. Imagine that you are the marketing manager of Engen. Write a report suggesting budget allocations for Engen's social responsibility programme. Explain at length why you have decided on the chosen projects. Discuss the advantages that your company can expect from these projects.

2. Suggest a marketing communications programme to introduce the new name to the South African public.

3. Describe how you would conduct a research project to choose a suitable name for a product like petrol.

CHAPTER 20

APPLICATION AREAS OF MARKETING

20.1 INTRODUCTION

Up to this point in this book, the focus has been on the marketing of goods and services from the point of view of the producer who markets consumer products/ services to the final consumer. The majority of the information provided has been universal in nature and can thus also be applied to the marketing of other products and services, such as industrial products, agricultural products, services and non-profit organisations. Each of the above-mentioned does, however, possess its own unique characteristics which present unique challenges to the marketer thereof. The aim of this chapter is to discuss the most important differences in the marketing of industrial products, services, agricultural products, and non-profit organisations.

ORGANISATION OF THE CHAPTER

Marketing of industrial products: Definition and classification of industrial products, characteristics of industrial products, and the purchasing behaviour of the industrial buyer.

Marketing of services: Definition and description of services, and the characteristics of services.

Marketing of agricultural products: Factors influencing the marketing of agricultural products, the controlled marketing of agricultural products, the Marketing Act, marketing schemes, and uncontrolled marketing.

Marketing in non-profit organisations: Definition of non-profit organisation, characteristics of non-profit organisations, and marketing decisions of these organisations.

20.2 MARKETING OF INDUSTRIAL PRODUCTS

20.2.1 Introduction

The industrial market is comprised of organisations and institutions which purchase products and services with the aim of either using them to produce other products and services, or for their own use. Industrial products are therefore differentiated from consumer products with regard to the aim of their final usage. Industrial products are products that are applied/utilised for the manufacturing of other products and/or for the running of the business. It is also possible to market a product as both an industrial and a consumer product. For example, a personal computer that is marketed for use by a business enterprise is marketed as an industrial product, but the same personal computer can be marketed to a consumer for personal use. Industrial marketing refers to the marketing of industrial products to industrial consumers.

Industrial products are purchased by industrial, institutional and intermediary buyers. Industrial buyers, such as manufacturers, purchase products and services for production and commercial use, while institutional buyers, such as the central government, purchase products and services in order to provide services to the community (for example education, medical, roads, etc). Intermediary buyers, such as wholesalers and retailers, buy products and services with the aim of commercial reselling to the industrial and/or final consumer markets.[1]

Because the industrial market is a relatively unknown quantity, its importance and the extent thereof is not always realised. Approximately 50 per cent of all manufactured products, for example, are marketed in the industrial market. As far as the extent thereof is concerned, an indication can be obtained by considering the main categories according to which industries are classified:

- Agriculture, forestry and fishing.
- Mining and quarrying.
- Manufacturing (see Figure 20.1 for the distribution thereof according to industry).
- Electricity, gas and water.
- Construction.
- Wholesalers and retailers, catering and accommodation.
- Finance, insurance, real estate and business services.
- Community, social and personal services.
- General government.[2]

In this section emphasis will be placed on the marketing of industrial products purchased by manufacturers. Attention will be focused on the classification of industrial products, characteristics of industrial products, the purchasing behaviour of the industrial buyer, and several marketing implications.

FIGURE 20.1   Division of manufacturing enterprises per section, RSA 1987

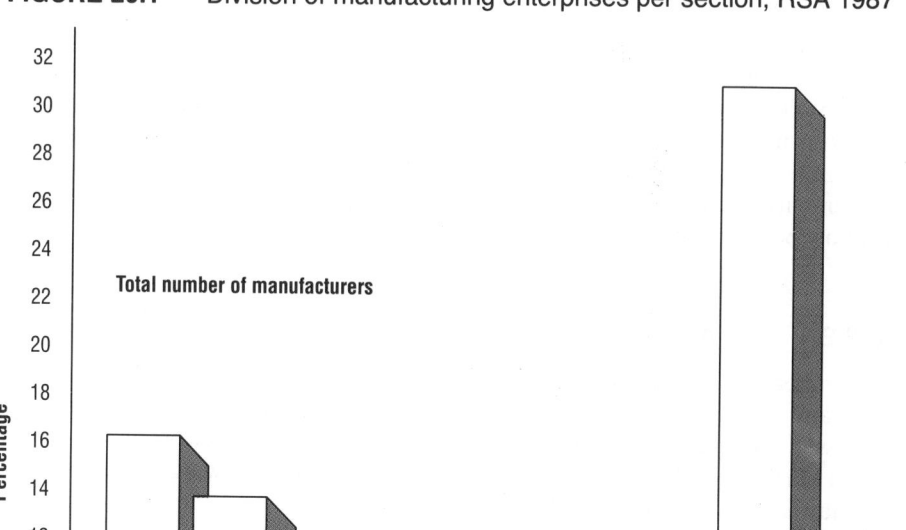

1. Food and nutritional products
    Tobacco products

2. Textiles
    Clothing
    Leather and leather substitutes
    Footwear

3. Wood and cork products
    Furniture and furniture products

4. Paper and paper products
    Printing and publishing industry

5. Industrial chemicals
    Other chemicals
    Petroleum refineries
    Petroleum and coal products
    Rubber products
    Plastic products

6. Earthenware and porcelain
    Glass and glass products
    Other non-metal mineral products

7. Basic iron and steel industries
    Basic non-metal industries

8. Manufactured metal products
    Machinery
    Motor vehicles and parts
    Transport equipment
    Scientific equipment

9. Other

Source: Van Zyl, JH. 1987. *Die Houding van Bemarkingsbestuur van Vervaardigingsondernemings in die RSA rakende Faktore wat Bemarkingsproduktiwiteit beïnvloed.* Unpublished thesis, University of the Orange Free State, p 39.

20.2.2 Classification of industrial products[3]

The large variety of industrial products can be classified into five categories, namely raw materials, part-processed materials and components, installations, accessory equipment, and operating supplies. Each of these groups of products possesses unique characteristics which create unique marketing challenges. The most important characteristics and marketing considerations of each of the abovementioned product categories are summarised in Table 20.1. Each category will now be discussed.

20.2.2.1 *Raw materials*

Raw materials, such as crude oil, iron ore, diamonds and coal, originate in the earth and are extracted from the earth. These products have usually not been processed and are finally utilised in the manufacturing of other products.

The marketing of raw materials is influenced by the following characteristics peculiar to this type of product:

- The supply is often limited and cannot be increased.
- A small number of producers is involved.
- Products are often bulky in nature and need to be transported over long distances.
- Products are not standardised and need to be graded.

The abovementioned characteristics have distribution implications for marketing. Distribution channels are usually simple in nature, but problems regarding physical distribution, especially transport and storage, arise. Raw materials are directly marketed by producers to industrial consumers by means of long-term contracts which ensure the user of sufficient supplies. Advertising, branding, packaging and product differentiation are irrelevant in the marketing process of raw materials. Competition occurs as regards price and the assurance that the specified products can be provided.

20.2.2.2 *Part-processed materials and components*

Products in this category are industrial products which will eventually constitute part of a final product. Part-processed materials have been partially processed, but still need to undergo further processing by the buyer. Examples include pig iron used for the production of steel, yarn used for weaving and flour used for the baking of bread. Components are usually used in the final product without undergoing any further changes, for example spark plugs, batteries, fan belts and oil filters.

Part-processed materials and components are usually purchased in large quantities via long-term contracting. The result is that most of these products are sold directly to the buyer by the producer. Middlemen are used only where there are many buyers and smaller but regular orders are placed. Branding, packaging and advertising are unimportant. The purchasing decision is predominantly based

TABLE 20.1 A utilitarian classification of industrial products, the product branding and certain production considerations of each

Product characteristics and marketing considerations	Industrial products classified according to nature of usage				
	Raw materials	Fabricating minerals and parts	Installation	Necessary equipment	Operating supplies
Price characteristics:					
1. Price per unit	Very low	Low	Very high	Average, between high and low	Low
2. Life cycle	Very short	Depends on final product	Very long	Long	Short
3. Quantities purchased	Large	Large	Very small	Small	Small
4. How often are purchases made	Long-term pruchase contract; regular delivery	Irregular purchases but regular delivery	Very irregular	Average, between regular and irregular	Often
5. Degree of standardization of competitive products	Very high grading is important	Very high	Very low	Low	High
6. Supply	Limited; cannot be, or can only be increased slowly	Usually freely available	Usually not a bottleneck	Usually not a bottleneck	Usually not a bottleneck
Marketing considerations:					
1. Length of the distribution channel	Short, if there are any middlemen, they are usually agents	Short; only middlemen where small quantities are purchased	Short	Longer distribution channel	Longer distribution channel
2. Negotiating period	Difficult to generalise	Average, between short and long	Long	Average, between short and long	Short
3. Price competitiveness	Important	Important	Not the most important aspect	Not the most important aspect	Important
4. Pre- and after-sales service	Not important	Not important	Very important	Important	Not important
5. Stimulation of demand	Little	Average	Sales representative Very important	Important	Not so important
6. Brand preference	None	Usually unimportant, although some marketers try to create preference.	High	High	Low

Source: Marx, S & Dekker, H. 1982. *Bemarkingsbestuur: Beginsels en Besluite*. Pretoria: HAUM, p 531.

on price considerations and the ability of the seller to carry out orders according to specifications on a regular and timely basis. However, manufacturers of components sometimes direct their marketing efforts towards the final consumer, *first* with the aim of developing brand preference in the replacement market, and, *secondly*, in the hope that the final consumer will develop a preference for products with specific parts or components.

20.2.2.3 *Installations*

Installations are completely manufactured products such as buildings, machinery and heavy equipment that have a direct influence on the production process. Installations usually have a long life time, are relatively expensive, and directly determine the capacity of the industry. Installations can be divided into two main groups:

- Land and buildings.
- Capital equipment such as graders, mining machinery, rock drills, earth-moving equipment, production and packaging machinery, ie products that are directly used for or contribute to the main manufacturing activities of the industry.

The marketing of installations take place directly between buyers and sellers. Because large amounts of money are involved in the buying and selling of installations and because they have a direct influence on the manufacturing process, it is essential that the purchasing process is carefully planned and executed after thorough negotiations. The purchasing decision is based on the ability and characteristics of the product, the reputation of the producer and the pre-sales and after-sales services that are provided.

The marketer of installations must therefore pay careful attention to the following:

- The composition and quality of the sales force. A specific sales approach is often necessary. A sales force of this type is composed of individuals with specific skills (for example a product engineer, a maintenance engineer and a sales manager) who make proposals to potential buyer(s) and then participate in negotiations with them.
- Services that are provided. Attention needs to be paid to services such as product guarantees, technical advice, installations, maintenance, demonstration, training of buyer's employees, availability of credit and hire-purchase facilities, and the execution of feasibility studies.

20.2.2.4 *Accessory equipment*

Accessory equipment consists of industrial products used as facilitating mediums in the production process, but which do not have a notable influence on production capacity. Examples of accessory equipment are smaller tools, computers, forklifts, etc. These products do not form part of the final product, their life time is usually shorter and the installation thereof is usually cheaper.

Accessory equipment is usually standardised equipment that can be marketed in several industries. The products are largely marketed via middlemen, competition is intense, and prices are an important consideration in the purchasing decision.

20.2.2.5 *Operating supplies*

Operating supplies are products that have been manufactured, such as cleaning equipment, polish, stationery, oil and petroleum. These products are relatively cheap, have a short life time and are purchased without any effort. These products are so to say the convenience goods of the industrial market.

These products are predominantly distributed via middlemen, but it can happen that producers of these supplies serve a few 'bulk purchasers' on a personal basis. The products are standardised and it is price rather than brand preference which influences the purchasing decision.

20.2.3 **Characteristics of industrial products**

The marketing of industrial products is influenced by a number of unique characteristics of each of the industrial products. The most important of these characteristics and the influence thereof are discussed below.

20.2.3.1 *The demand for industrial products is a derived demand*

The demand for industrial products is a derived demand, as it is derived from the demand for the final products in which the industrial product is used. For example, a demand for leather will result because there is a need for shoes, purses, handbags and other products manufactured from leather. If the demand for these products increases, then the demand for leather and thus also for skins and hides will also increase, while the opposite situation is also true.

The implication of the derived demand is dual in nature:

* *First*, marketers of industrial products find it difficult to increase the direct demand for their products by aiming their marketing actions at the direct consumers/customers of their products. As a result some manufacturers direct their marketing efforts at increasing the demand for final products that require the use of their industrial products in the manufacturing process. An example of such a marketing effort would be to increase the demand for clothing that is manufactured from wool and cotton by making use of an advertising campaign that will reveal the intrinsic advantages of products manufactured from these raw materials.
* *Secondly*, derived demand creates exceptional challenges as regards marketing research and sales forecasting because of the fact that manufacturers need to keep track of the final consumers' preferences, needs and purchasing habits and

behaviour (ie the derived demand). These are markets with which manufacturers of industrial products are not well acquainted.

20.2.3.2 *The demand for industrial products is inelastic*

The demand for industrial products is not strongly influenced by price changes. Manufacturers of shoes will not buy considerably more leather if the price thereof should decrease — nor will they purchase notably less leather should the price of leather increase. The above is especially true in cases where the products constitute a minor percentage of the composition of the final product. The demand for an individual manufacturer's product can, however, be price sensitive; in other words, if a specific manufacturer increases the price of its products considerably, it can happen that the demand will move to brands whose price has not increased.

20.2.3.3 *The market consists of knowledgeable purchasers*

Industrial products are purchased by well-trained and informed purchasers according to planned and structured purchasing procedures. The purchaser is not only well informed as regards the firm's own specific needs, but also completes a thorough analysis of all possible manufacturers of the product. Usually more than one person is involved in making the purchasing decision. The purchasing decision of industrial products is primarily based on rational considerations, while that of consumer goods is often primarily based on considerations such as the satisfying of psychological and social needs. The following are the most important criteria on which the choice of suppliers is based:

- Reliability of delivery.
- Adaptability.
- Price.
- Technical specifications.
- Technical services.
- Usefulness.
- Reliable information.
- After-sales service.[4]

20.2.3.4 *A relatively small number of buyers geographically concentrated*

The market for industrial products is composed of a relatively small number of buyers who mostly purchase in large quantities. These businesses are usually concentrated in the Pretoria-Witwatersrand-Vereeniging, Durban-Pinetown, Port-Elizabeth-Uitenhage, and Cape Peninsula areas. More than 80 per cent of all South African businesses are established in these four metropolitan areas.

This characteristic of the industrial market makes it possible for marketers in industrial markets to serve potential clients on a more direct manner via sales representatives.

An investigation conducted amongst 54 South African organisations which purchase high-technology laboratory equipment revealed the following concerning the number of persons involved in the final choice of suppliers:

One	:	7%
Two	:	41%
Three	:	33%
Four	:	7%
More than four	:	11%

The criteria according to which the selection of supplies takes place include the following in order of priority:

- Technical services provided.
- Product reliability.
- After-sales service.
- Supplier's reputation.
- Ease of maintenance.
- Ease of operation.
- Price.
- Confidence in the sales representative.
- Product flexibility.

The most important sources of information about products include the following:

- Sales representatives.
- Trade shows.
- Conferences.
- Direct-mail advertising.
- Advertisements in specialised journals.
- Word-of-mouth.

Source: Abratt, R. 1987. *Marketing Management: SA Cases and Readings.* Durban: Butterworths, pp 91–3.

20.2.4 Purchasing behaviour of industrial buyers[5]

As discussed earlier, the purchasing decision of individual buyers is largely determined by rational considerations. This is in contrast to final consumers who purchase consumer goods primarily according to their own personal preferences, likes and dislikes. The various factors that have an influence on the purchasing behaviour of the buyer can be divided into four main categories, namely environmental, business, interpersonal and individual factors.

Environmental factors

The purchasing behaviour of the industrial buyer is first determined by external factors such as physical, technological, economic, political, legal and cultural environmental influences. All these factors can have a significant influence on the purchasing process. Environmental factors can, for example, influence the availability of goods and services, create the general business climate in which transactions take place, and influence the norms and value systems of people.

Business factors

Each business has its own mission, objectives, procedures, organisational structure and systems which have an unquestionable influence on the purchasing process. Business factors that may influence the purchasing decision making process are:

- The business's mission and objectives.
- The business's approach — is it technical-, product-, sales- or marketing-orientated?
- The status of the purchaser in the business.
- The freedom the buyer possesses to make decisions regarding purchasing.
- The degree of co-operation/friction that exists between various departments in the business.
- The size of the business.
- The degree to which the purchasing function is centralised or decentralised.

Interpersonal factors

A variety of people usually takes part in making decisions regarding purchases. These individuals, however, differ in terms of the amount of authority they possess, the status of their positions, their ability to be convincing and their degree of empathy. These factors can be grouped in the following categories:

- **Users** of the product or service. This category includes those persons that usually initiate the act of purchasing and play an important role in defining the various purchasing specifications. Users can influence buyers' actions negatively (by, for example, refusing to use a particular supplier's product) or positively (by, for example, using a new product that is more cost-saving).
- **Influencers**, ie all persons who have a direct or indirect influence on the purchasing decision, for example engineers involved in the design of product specifications or the evaluation of alternatives.
- **Buyers** who have the authority to select suppliers and sign contracts.
- **Decision makers** concerned with the approval of transactions. In the case of routine purchases the buyer usually makes the decision but in the case of unique and important purchases, senior management usually approves the transaction.

- **Gatekeepers**, ie those individuals in the business who control the flow of information from one person/department to another person/department, for example the restricting of salesmen from making direct contact with users or influencers.

The question as to whether purchasing decision making is executed individually or as a group activity is influenced by the **risk** involved in the case of an incorrect decision. The greater the risk, the greater the probability of the purchasing decision being a group activity.

The **type of buying situation**, in other words a straight rebuy, a modified rebuy or a new task purchasing decision, also influences the decision. A straight rebuy takes place where a repetitive or continuous need is satisfied on a routine basis. These purchases are usually automatically executed by the purchasing department. A new task purchasing decision arises when there is a new need to be satisfied, ie a need that has not been identified before. The purchasing decision will usually be influenced and made by a group of persons in this case. Modified rebuying situations develop from new purchases or direct rebuying. The purchasing alternatives are known, but additional information is required before the purchasing decision can be taken. In such a case the purchasing decision can be taken individually or in group context.

Where **time pressure** is involved, ie if the decision to purchase must be taken within a short period of time, it will normally be delegated to one or only a few individuals. Another factor is the **size of the business** — the larger the business, the larger the number of individuals involved in influencing the purchasing decision making process. The greater the degree of **centralisation of authority**, the more autonomous the purchasing decision.[6]

Individual factors

The purchaser (buyer) as an individual is central to the decision making process. Just as the final consumer is influenced, so the buyer is influenced by his own motives, personality, attitudes and convictions, previous experiences, self-image, perceptions, etc. For example, a purchaser who is conservative by nature will not easily change from one product or supplier to another. In the execution of his task as buyer, the buyer experiences both task and non-task motives. Task motives originate from the buyer's job description. The more personal, non-task orientated motives include motives such as the buyer's striving for success, achievement and avoidance of risk. The result is that a buyer will limit those purchasing decisions that will have a negative influence on himself or the business to a minimum.

The unique characteristics of industrial products influence the product, distribution, marketing communication and price decisions. The product life cycle concept and strategic marketing are also applicable to industrial goods, as in the case of consumer goods.

20.3 MARKETING OF SERVICES

20.3.1 Nature of services

In almost all products a product component and a service component are apparent. The marketing of services becomes a major concern in cases where the service component is more important than the physical or product component — in other words, all those cases where a supplier of these 'products' considers himself a marketer of services rather than a marketer of products. Although similarity exists between the marketing of products and services, there are also significant differences. The aim of this section is to define the concept of service, identify the distinguishing characteristics of services, and reveal the differences in the marketing decisions concerning services.

20.3.2 Definition and classification of services

From Figure 20.2 it is evident that a service is not easily defined. In summary it can be said that services include all intangible advantages obtained independent of tangible products offered in the satisfying of consumer needs.

FIGURE 20.2   Definitions of the concept 'service'

> Kotler[7] defines a service as any activity or benefit that one party can offer to another that is essentially intangible and does not result in the ownership of anything. Its production may or may not be tied to a physical product.
>
> According to Marx & Dekker[8] services can be considered as intangible utilities applied for the need-satisfaction of consumers.
>
> Stanton[9] states: 'Services are those separately identifiable essentially intangible activities that provide want-satisfaction and that are not necessarily tied to the sale of a product or another service.'
>
> Reibstein[10] describes a service as follows: 'Services are not objects. They are products in the form of performances, deeds or acts.'

In cases where a tangible product or facility is included in the provision of a service (for example, the hotel or hotel room in the case of hotel services), there is no transfer of ownership as far as the tangible product is concerned. Services that are marketed as part of a tangible product, for example delivery, installation and credit, are excluded from this definition.

In order to gain a clearer understanding of exactly which 'products' are considered to be services, services can be classified as follows:

* **Housing:** rental of flats, houses, farms, hotel accommodation and other forms of accommodation.

- **Household services:** repair and maintenance of buildings and household equipment, household cleaning, landscaping and garden services.
- **Recreation and entertainment activities:** sports clubs, recreation facilities, holiday resorts, bioscopes, theatres, amusement centres and travel agencies.
- **Personal care:** laundries, dry cleaners, hairdressers, beauty salons and health services.
- **Medical and other health care:** all medical services, both private and public.
- **Professional services:** legal, accounting, management consulting, computer services, marketing research practitioners, advice regarding insurance and investments.
- **Financial services:** banking, insurance, investment and loan services.
- **Transport and communications:** private as well as public services provided.[11]

See also the classification of products and services in Chapter 7.

There are several ways in which services can be classified. Figure 20.3 reveals some of the criteria according to which services can be classified.

FIGURE 20.3   Classification of services

According to object

Services offered to the person:

- Primarily intellectual (education, theatre, entertainment).
- Primarily physical (medical, personal care, haircut).

Services to the customer's property:

- Tangible assets (dry cleaning, garden services).
- Intangible assets (banks, stockbrokers).

According to degree of customer/provider relationship

- Client has a formal ongoing relationship with the provider of the service (telephone, bank account, insurance).
- Each transaction between the customer and the service provider is a discrete event (hotel accommodation, repairs, entertainment).

According to the role played by physical facilities

- A customer consumes a non-durable product in a physical facility (restaurant, bar).
- A customer acquires the right to use (hire) a durable product or facility for a defined period of time (hotel room, motor vehicle, a flat/apartment, video).

- Services that require the presence of certain physical facilities. The quality of the physical facilities have a direct influence on the quality of the service provided (transport, medical).
- A customer takes the physical appearance of the physical facilities for granted (sports events, education, postal services).

According to the extent of personal services

- Personally delivered service is the primary component (music lessons, psychological therapy).
- Personal service is one of several elements in the service package, but is more important than the other elements (medical service, legal service, personal care).
- Personal service forms part of the service package offered, but is of secondary importance (restaurant, bank, education).
- Minimal or no personal service is apparent (dry cleaning, laundromat, slot machines).

According to the duration of benefits

- Benefits received primarily during the delivery of the service (theatre, hotel, restaurant).
- Benefits received during a short period of time following service delivery (personal care, dry cleaning, garden services).
- Benefits received during a relatively long period of time after the service delivery (income tax consultation, pest control).
- Long-term benefits received after the service (insurance).

Source: Reibstein, DJ. 1985. *Marketing: Concepts, Strategies and Decisions.* New York: Prentice-Hall Inc, pp 607–8.

20.3.3 Characteristics of services

Services possess unique characteristics which create unique marketing challenges and opportunities. The most important of these characteristics will now be discussed.

Intangibility

Most services are both physical and conceptually intangible to consumers. Services cannot be tasted, seen, felt, heard or used (physically intangible). The consumer also finds it difficult to visualise the advantages the service provides (intellectually intangible). It is, for example, difficult for a buyer of an insurance policy to visualise what the real value of the policy will be after twenty years.

The fact that services are intangible creates exceptional challenges for the marketing of services. The marketing of services must be concerned especially with the establishment of confidence and trust in the service and the supplier of the service. The confidence of the consumer can be gained in the following ways:

- The advantages of the service rather than the nature thereof must be emphasised. The emphasis in the marketing of an insurance policy would thus fall on the assurance that the consumer will, at the time of his/her retirement, enjoy security or the luxuries that he/she will purchase, for example, an overseas trip, a yacht or a home near the sea.
- The intangibility of a service is represented in a tangible manner, for example, the yellow umbrella of Santam, the golden slice of the Natal Building Society, the facilities of a hotel or the testimony of a satisfied client.
- A trade mark is attached to the service.

Inseparability

In many cases the service provided cannot be separated from the person or institution which provides and markets it. These services are simultaneously provided and marketed, for example entertainment, medical services, education and personal care. This inseparability creates problems, particularly for product development, the use of middlemen (distribution channels), and capacity. Direct distribution is often the only method of distribution, while growth may be restricted because each service supplier's capacity is restricted. An example is a hairdresser who can cope with only a certain number of clients per hour.

Heterogeneous quality

It is impossible for a supplier of services to standardise its quality of service inputs. The quality of one particular service unit is not necessarily the same as that of the next unit. Thus the final product will vary from one hairdresser to another, just as the final product of the same hairdresser will not necessarily always be the same. This is especially true in cases where services are labour-intensive. The problem of quality control indicates that it is necessary that special attention be paid to the product planning stages of the marketing programme in order to ensure that a constant quality of service is provided. The result will be an image of quality service.

The most general dimensions of service quality are:

- Tangibles — physical facilities, equipment, the appearance of personnel.
- Reliability — the ability to perform the service properly the first time.
- Responsiveness — a willingness to help customers and to provide prompt service.
- Competence — knowledge and skill of employees and their ability to create confidence.
- Credibility/trustworthiness — believability and honesty of employees.
- Empathy — provision of care and individualised attention to customers.
- Courtesy — friendliness and courteousness towards customers.
- Communication — informing customers and listening to them.

Marketers are increasingly using service quality as a way to differentiate their services and to attain competitive advantage. The key to the success of such a strategy is the ability to meet or exceed "target customer" expectations of service quality. If there is a gap between the customer's expectations and the level of service quality he receives, the customer feels unsatisfied and perceives the quality of service as poor.

Parasuraman, Zeithamel and Berry developed the so-called Gaps Model of service quality.[12] This model explains the factors that determine a customer's expectations and perceptions concerning service quality as well as the five gaps that can cause unsatisfactory service delivery. The Gaps Model is presented in Figure 20.4.

The following gaps can be identified:

Gap 1: Arises between the marketer's perceptions of the customer's expectations. This gap arises because managers do not always have an accurate understanding of what customers want.

Gap 2: Arises between the marketer's perceptions and service quality specifications. Management could have a clear understanding of what customers want but that understanding might not get translated into effective quality specifications.

Gap 3: Arises between service quality specifications and service delivery.

Gap 4: Arises between service delivery and external communications. The quality of service experienced by the customer does not correspond with the promises in advertisements or those made by salesmen.

Gap 5: Arises between perceived service and expected service. It is this gap that really leads to customer dissatisfaction. Gap 5 results when management fails to close one or more of the other four gaps. Gap 5 will disappear automatically if management eliminates the other four gaps.

The following actions could be supplemented by marketers in order to close the gaps:

Gap 1: Market research and evaluation of customer complaints.

Gap 2: Communication and implementation of policies concerning customer service to all employees.

Gap 3: Training of employees concerning customer service, control of performance and reward of good service.

Gap 4: The creation of realistic expectations by means of true marketing communication.

FIGURE 20.4   Service quality Gaps Model

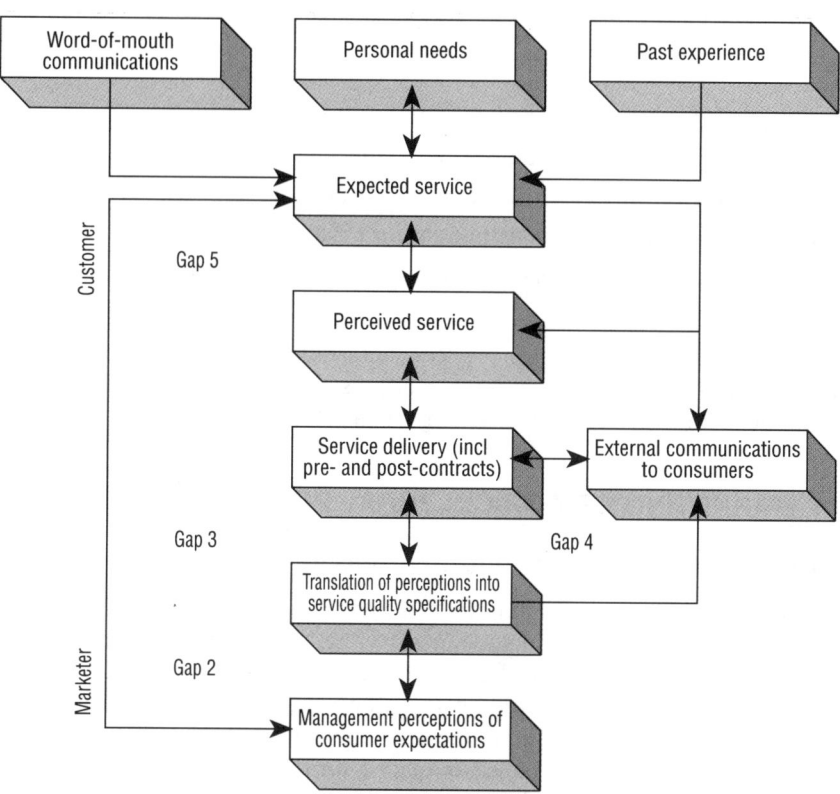

Source: Adopted from Parasuraman, A, Zeithaml, VA and Berry, LL. 1985. "A conceptual model of service quality and its implications for future research" *Journal of Marketing*, Fall, p 44.

Perishability

Services are perishable and cannot be stored. Empty seats in a cinema, an empty hotel room, an unutilised hairdresser, are examples of lost services. They cannot be provided at a later stage. This characteristic of perishability results in considerable fluctuations in the demand for services, because services not used during quiet periods cannot be used during peak periods.

Marketers can attempt to equalise the demand for and supply of services.

The demand side can be influenced by:

• developing the market during low periods, for example Holiday Inn's Weekenders and Southern Sun's Sun Scapes;
• providing complementary services in order to decrease the demand for the original service, for example Standard Bank's Auto Card that allows for depositing as well as withdrawal of money outside of normal banking hours;

- quoting lower prices during low periods and higher prices during peak times, for example the rates for long-distance telephone calls which are cheaper between 18:00 and 21:00 during week days and even cheaper from 21:00 to 07:00 as well as during weekends.

The supply of services can be influenced by:

- the appointment of part-time personnel during peak periods;
- the providing of only essential services during peak periods;
- implementing consumer participation, for example self-service in a restaurant;
- utilising existing facilities simultaneously, for example Saswitch and Multinet Systems.[13]

The unique characteristics of services determine the product, distribution, marketing communications and price decisions. The product life cycle concept is also applicable to services while strategic marketing can also be applied.

20.4 MARKETING OF AGRICULTURAL PRODUCTS

20.4.1 The nature of agricultural products

Agricultural products are raw materials that have their origin in the soil as as result of the actions of man. They include forestry, agronomy and stock breeding.[14]

The marketing of agricultural products is, in comparison to that of manufactured products, a relatively complicated process. The marketing of agricultural products differs from that of manufactured consumer products in two important ways. In the first place, emphasis is placed on the collection and distribution functions, because agricultural products are seasonal in nature and there is a large number of small producers. All the small producers' products need to be collected before they can be distributed. In contrast to this, the emphasis is primarily placed on the distribution function in the marketing of consumer products. Secondly, a pull process takes place in the marketing of agricultural products. In other words, consumers need to go to a great deal of trouble in order to obtain the product and pull it through the distribution channel. In contrast to agricultural products, the marketing of consumer products requires both a pull and push process.

The factors influencing the marketing of agricultural products stem from the production, product and consumer characteristics of the products. These characteristics and their influence on the marketing process will next be discussed.

20.4.2 Factors influencing the marketing of agricultural products

20.4.2.1 *Production characteristics of agricultural products*

In the *first* place the agricultural sector is characterised by a **large number** of production units which predominantly exercise **small-scale production** and are geographically scattered. The result is:

- The producer (farmer) concentrates on the production function because he neither has the time, the knowledge nor the ability to perform the marketing function himself.

- The individual producer, alone, is not able to influence the demand and supply for his product.

- The collection function becomes an important marketing function.

Secondly, the **seasonal nature** of agricultural production further complicates the marketing process. Although the consumption of most agricultural products is evenly distributed throughout the year, they are normally only available during certain seasons. In spite of the advancements made in storage, refrigeration, transport and financial facilities, peak periods still exist. This creates marketing problems which are generally not experienced in the marketing of manufactured products.

Thirdly, as a result of the relatively long production cycle of agricultural products, the supply of these products is relatively **inelastic**. Thus, the supply of agricultural products cannot be considerably increased or decreased over a short period of time. For example, it is not possible, in the short term, to adapt the supply of slaughter stock in accordance with price increases. Similarly, it is not possible to withhold supply during times of price drops in order to stabilise the price.

20.4.2.2 *Product characteristics of agricultural products*

Several factors influencing the marketing of agricultural products are related to the physical characteristics of the product.

First, agricultural products are characterised by a **disadvantageous volume-value relationship**. This means that the mass and volume thereof is large in comparison to the monetary value thereof. The result is that the costs of transport, reassortment and storage of agricultural products are relatively high.

Secondly, there are several agricultural products, for example fruit, vegetables, meat and milk, which are extremely perishable. This necessitates the need for effective and efficient refrigeration and transporting facilities so as to maintain the quality of the products.

In the *third* place, the quality of specific agricultural products can vary from region to region, farmer to farmer and from one season to the next. It is therefore possible for a farmer to produce different qualities in one harvest. The result is that the marketing functions of standardisation and grading of agricultural products are of cardinal importance.[16]

20.4.2.3 *Consumer characteristics of agricultural products*

The demand for most agricultural products is relatively inelastic as regards income and price. Food in the form of agricultural products provides for many essential needs and the rate of consumption per person cannot be arbitrarily changed. A decrease or increase in the price of agricultural products or a decrease or increase in the income of the consumer does not have a significant influence on the quantity of products purchased by the consumer over the long term.

20.4.2.4 *Price fluctuations*

The marketing of agricultural products is made more complex because of considerable fluctuations in price. The prices of these products can vary from year to year, month to month or even from one day to the next. Under circumstances where true competition occurs, price determination is effected through the working of the market mechanism which results in fluctuations in accordance with demand and supply. This means that if the demand exceeds the supply, the prices will decrease. The demand for agricultural products is relatively inelastic as regards price. If the price changes, the demand will still remain more or less constant. The abovementioned happens often when the supply of agricultural products is erratic because of climatic conditions. A sharp decrease in the supply can normally result in a sharp increase in the price. A sharp increase in the supply is usually coupled with a sharp drop in the price because of the fact that demand is price inelastic. In general, it can be assumed that supply has a greater influence on prices than demand.

In view of the above problems which complicate the marketing of agricultural products, it is necessary to realise that the producer of agricultural products experiences an inherent handicap as far as the marketing of products is concerned, because products are subject to extreme price fluctuations, whereas in the free competitive market economy prices react in accordance with demand and supply. In the light of these basic inherent problems faced by marketers of agricultural products the South African producers and authorities attempted to create greater stability and improve the marketing of agricultural products.[17]

20.4.3 The controlled marketing of agricultural products

20.4.3.1 *Marketing Act (Act 59 of 1968)*

It is a world-wide phenomenon that countries producing their own food endeavour to be self-sufficient. This urge can result in a surplus in production during good seasons and a shortage during poor seasons. In these circumstances the prices of agricultural products will fluctuate considerably from season to season. These fluctuations in the price of agricultural products will in turn have a direct effect on the supply as well as production. The instability in prices and production resulting from these fluctuations creates considerable problems for the maintenance of economically sound agricultural industries. As a result of the necessity for self-sufficiency in the production of food (as far as a country's natural resources will allow it) and the importance of the agricultural sector in the economy, the concept of government intervention in the marketing of agricultural products was accepted more than fifty years ago.

Originally the proposal was to enforce compulsory co-operative marketing of agricultural products in order to encourage more orderliness in the marketing process and thus greater price stability in the particular agricultural industries. Co-operatives could only market their members' products and, because many producers were not members of co-operatives, these bodies could not succeed in effective marketing and influencing market prices.

It became evident in 1934 that co-operatives could not fulfil all the requirements of price control. Thus, in terms of special legislation, provision was made for the controlled marketing of several agricultural products, amongst others, dairy products, slaughter stock, wheat and maize. This system was, however, also ineffective. Between 1930 and 1935 legislation had to be adapted and approved in order to make provision for major legislative powers and to adjust control so as to make provision for development of particular industries and marketing processes. The result was the passing of the Marketing Act in 1937. This Act has been changed over the years and was finally consolidated and replaced by the Marketing Act of 1968 (Act 59 of 1968).

20.4.3.2 *Aims of the Marketing Act*

The Marketing Act has three aims, namely price stability, reduction of marketing costs, and increasing productivity and effectiveness in the agricultural sector.

The *first* aim of the Act is **price stability**. Earlier it was indicated that the demand and supply of agricultural products is relatively price inelastic and that products are subject to a considerable degree of price fluctuations. Price fluctuations result in economic instability for the producer and have a negative effect on the effectiveness of the agricultural industry. The price fixing that is executed by agricultural control boards results in greater stability for the producers and assures them of reasonable prices for their products. Price fixing also eliminates speculation — something that is disadvantageous for the producer and may only be an advantage for speculators.

A *second* aim of the Marketing Act is the **reduction in marketing costs**. The purpose of this is to keep the gap between the price received by the producer and the price paid by the consumer as small as possible. It is the task of marketing control boards to reduce marketing costs by more effective marketing and processing of agricultural products.

The *third* aim is to **increase the productivity and effectiveness** of the industry. With a view to effective agricultural production farming practices should, by considering demand and the needs of the consumer, be adjusted to suit the characteristics of the particular region in which they function.

In conclusion, the main objectives of the Marketing Act can be summarised as follows: on the one hand it helps to ensure stabilisation of the prices of agricultural products, and on the other hand it helps to bridge the gap between producers and consumer prices by means of co-ordination and co-operation. In the attempt to achieve the abovementioned, productivity and effectiveness in agricultural production is increased.[18]

20.4.3.3 *Marketing schemes*[19]

The Marketing Act also makes provision for the implementation of marketing schemes that are officiated by various agricultural control boards, with the aim of regulating the marketing of agricultural products.

> Since the passing of the Marketing Act (Act 59 of 1968) twenty-three marketing schemes have already been implemented. Approximately 65% of the total agricultural production in 1985 (gross value) was marketed through the control boards in terms of marketing schemes. About 12% was marketed under other laws, while no control was executed over 21% of the agricultural production.
>
> Source: *Annual Report*, Department of Agricultural Economics and Marketing, 1986, p 29.

The characteristics of the various types of schemes will now be discussed. The grouping of these schemes is represented in Figure 20.5.

Single-channel fixed price schemes

Maize, winter grains and industrial milk (including butter, cheese and cream) fall into this category. These schemes are characterised by extensive control measures over the marketing of products from the producer to the final consumer.

The essential characteristics of this scheme are:

- The products concerned may only be sold to or sold by the particular control boards.
- Fixed prices, according to grade and class, are paid to producers, while selling prices for the interior tertiary and secondary sectors are primarily fixed too.
- Losses resulting from the exporting of surplusses are recovered from the stabilisation funds of the control boards.
- Prices are periodically determined by the Minister of Agriculture based on recommendations made by the particular boards of control.

Single-channel pool scheme

The single-channel pool scheme is applicable to the following agricultural products: dried fruit, lucerne, oil seeds, buck wheat, bananas, rooibos tea, deciduous fruit for export, chicory, citrus fruit, fresh milk in controlled areas, mohair, wool and tobacco. The extent of the control measures is usually less than in the case of the single-channel fixed-price schemes, especially as regards the distribution channel used.

FIGURE 20.5   The South African Agricultural Control Board System according to type of scheme*

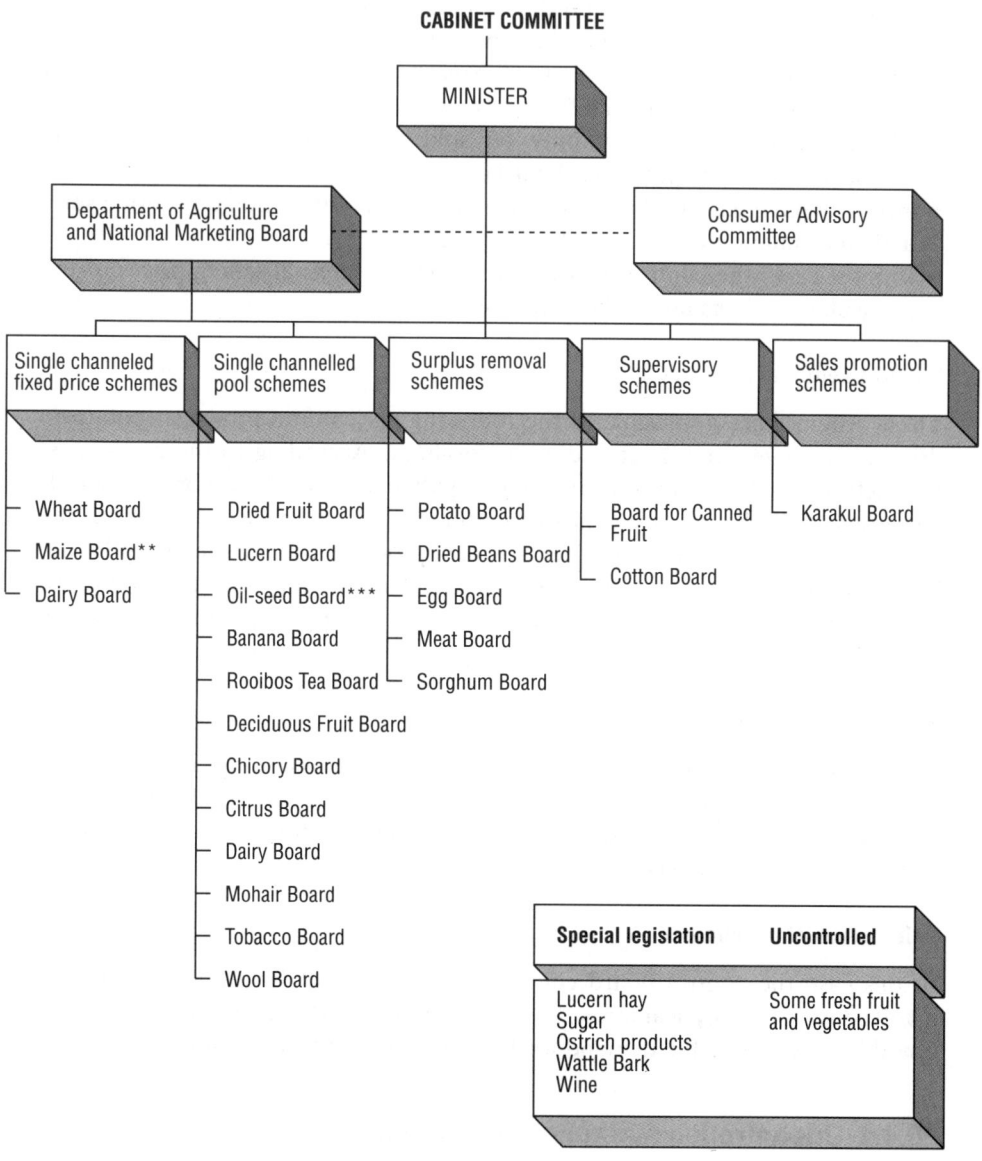

*   Updated as on 1 January 1987
**.   Including buck wheat (pool scheme)
***   Including soy beans (surplus removal scheme)

Source: Willemse, BJ. 1981. *Die Beheerraadstelsel.* Pretoria. Document 41/81 of the South African Agricultural Union.

The most important characteristics of single-channel pool schemes are:

- Producers are not paid a fixed price for their products, but receive an advance payment on delivery of their products, a middle and/or final payment after the entire harvest has been sold and the pool account has been closed off.
- The extent of control exercised over the marketing channels is far less than that exercised over single-channel fixed-price schemes.
- The primary product may only be sold to or in accordance with the arrangements of the particular board of control.
- Advance payments are based on the expected net realisation of internal sales and an estimation of the export realisation.
- In most cases the control boards determine the internal selling prices of the particular products under their control.

Surplus removal schemes

These schemes are applicable to the following agricultural products: potatoes, dried beans, eggs, red meat and grain sorghum. According to these schemes, products are sold by producers on the public market. The control boards concerned will then apply control measures when necessary, by supporting market prices or announcing prices at which products will be bought up by the boards in cases where prices drop below those announced by the control boards. The supplies that are bought up by the boards to support price can either be exported or sold later.

Supervisory schemes

These schemes for canned fruit and cotton make provision for price protection, thorough grading and payment for quality. The control boards involved do not participate in the physical marketing of products but ensure orderliness in the marketing of the products.

Sales promotion schemes

In this case the control board concerned, the Karakul Board, is not directly involved with the physical marketing of the product. The main objective of this board is to stimulate the demand for the products by means of advertising.

20.4.4 Uncontrolled marketing of agricultural products[20]

Uncontrolled marketing is a relatively vague concept which is not clearly defined or described in the literature. There is only the general viewpoint that uncontrolled marketing refers to the marketing of agricultural products which is not affected by the regulations of the Marketing Act. If it is borne in mind that the main objective of the Marketing Act is price stability, then it can be inferred that 'uncontrolled marketing' is applicable to all products and transactions where price stability measures are not relevant. Controlled marketing is very clearly defined in terms of the Marketing Act and all products not classified in this category fall into the category of uncontrolled marketing.

In the literature and official agricultural statistics the term 'uncontrolled' is used especially in the marketing of fresh fruit and vegetables and livestock. In the RSA an institutional structure has been developed for the marketing of uncontrolled agricultural products. The structure for the marketing of fresh fruit and vegetables predominantly consists of the municipal market system, marketing agents, wholesalers and retailers, and direct marketing.

In the case of livestock, the statutory power of the Meat Board is limited to the so-called controlled markets. The uncontrolled institutional structure for the marketing of livestock is predominantly constituted of direct marketing (to feedlots, speculators and private abattoirs) and the stock auction marketing system.

One of the major differences between controlled and uncontrolled marketing is the fact that producers of a product that is subject to controlled marketing must bear the objectives and policies of the controlled marketing system in mind when they execute their planning. The producers of products in uncontrolled marketing systems, on the other hand, need to formulate their own marketing philosophy, do their own planning, distribution, price determination and promotion.

20.5 MARKETING IN NON-PROFIT ORGANISATIONS

20.5.1 Definition of a non-profit organisation

Fundamentally there is no difference between the marketing concepts of businesses in the profit and non-profit sectors. Organisations in both sectors are concerned with the provision of a market offering which is central to the marketing of a product or service which will satisfy the needs of a particular market segment. There are, however, differences in the implementation of marketing and the attitude of management towards marketing.

The primary difference between marketing in profit and non-profit organisations is that the ultimate aim of marketing in non-profit organisations is not the realisation of profit. The objective of most non-profit organisations in marketing is the provision of goods or services to the general public. Theoretically both profit and non-profit organisations strive towards the satisfaction of a community's needs. In non-profit organisations this is an aim in itself, while in profit organisations it is merely a stepping-stone or medium to assist the organisation to achieve its ultimate goal, namely the realisation of profit over the long term. Non-profit organisations thus implement marketing for reasons other than the realisation of profit, market share, sales or return on investments. Although there is a large variety of non-profit organisations, these organisations can be classified as follows:

- charitable organisations, such as Child Welfare, SANCA, Red Cross;
- educational institutions, such as private schools, universities and colleges;
- cultural organisations, for example museums, art galleries, dramatic societies;

- religious organisations, such as church denominations;
- sport and recreational organisations, for example sport clubs, amusement centres;
- institutions concerned with social concerns, such as family planning, alcohol and drug abuse and child welfare;
- institutions concerned with health care, for example, the Heart Foundation of Southern Africa and the National Cancer Association;
- political parties;
- institutions that promote certain ideas, for example don't-drink-and-drive, road safety, littering and free enterprise;
- project-orientated institutions, such as the Urban Foundation and Operation Hunger;
- social, professional and membership societies such as associations of ex-students, housewives leagues, Sabee, Afrikaanse Handelsinstituut;
- local governments marketing tourist attractions, industrial premises and their towns.

The abovementioned categories of non-profit activites can be privately and/or government owned, financed and/or managed. A social club or professional society can be privately managed while the state could launch a family planning campaign and a university can be funded by government subsidies, but privately marketed with respect to the services it offers.

20.5.2 Characteristics of non-profit organisations

The most important characteristics of non-profit organisations differentiating them from profit organisations are discussed.

- **Nature of products:** The vast majority of non-profit organisations offer services and social benefits, rather than tangible products. Thus the principles discussed in the marketing of services are applicable to the marketing of non-profit organisations.
- **Multi-interest groups are served:** Non-profit organisations usually have at least two interest groups with whom they maintain good relations: the clients they serve, and their donors or funders. There are also several other groups who need to be considered and who influence the organisation.

A university can for example serve the following interest groups, each requiring a different marketing effort:

- prospective students and their parents
- present students and their parents
- ex-students
- lecturers
- business enterprises

- potential donors
- the government/state
- the general public

- **Non-financial objectives:** The objectives of non-profit organisations are normally not profit-orientated and focus primarily on a variety of social objectives.
- **The public eye:** Non-profit organisations are carefully scrutinised by the general public because many of these organisations and institutions are subsidised by the government, are exempt from income tax, and serve a social concern. These non-market factors place extra pressures on this type of organisation which would not be experienced in the profit organisation.
- **Exchange relationship:** The exchange relationship of profit organisations is a simple two-way exchange between buyer(s) and seller(s). The buyer pays a price to the seller and receives a product or service in exchange for the price paid. Both the buyer and the seller thus gain direct advantages from the exchange relationship. In the case of non-profit organisations there are three parties involved in the exchange relationship: the donor, the beneficiaries and the society. The donor provides the funds, support and voluntary assistance. The beneficiaries receive some or other advantage after the donors' contributions have been transformed into goods, services or ideas while the general society will benefit indirectly over the long term. The donors do not normally have any control over the expenditure of their donations and are not normally direct beneficiaries. An indirect benefit, for example publicity, is gained by the donors.
- **Attitude towards marketing:** Non-profit organisations have gradually begun to apply business principles in the management of their organisations. However, the implementation of marketing principles and the thorough planning of marketing attempts are scarce and lethargic. Management is inclined to limit marketing efforts to marketing communications attempts, such as advertising and personal selling. The approach of equating marketing communications to marketing has several dangers. *First*, an aggressive advertising campaign may result in a negative reaction from interest groups because these groups consider it to be unethical. *Secondly*, it could create an impression that the institution is experiencing problems as regards the support it receives. *Thirdly*, supporters who are not required may be attracted because thorough market segmentation has not yet been applied. *Fourthly*, it can be an indication that the institution is largely product- or sales-orientated, rather than market-orientated. The dilemma facing non-profit organisations is quite clear: on the one hand there is a negative and even an unethical attitude towards marketing, and on the other hand the organisation has a need for an effective marketing programme in order to generate funds and to market its product or service or idea to the target markets.

20.5.3 Phases in the implementation of marketing[21]

Non-profit organisations can implement marketing in six phases:

- A marketing committee can be formed that will handle the organisation's marketing actions. This committee should pay attention to the identification of marketing opportunities and threats and the planning of marketing actions.
- Task groups can be formed in order to provide more members the opportunity of taking part in the abovementioned activities.
- The services of specialised firms such as advertising agencies, market researchers and direct marketing organisations can be acquired to assist the institution with its marketing efforts. These organisations will not only provide specialist services but at the same time they will introduce marketing thought and skill in the organisation.
- A further step could be the obtaining of the services of a consultant who will execute a complete marketing audit in order to identify marketing opportunities and threats.
- Finally, a full-time marketing manager or official could be appointed. Amongst other things, such an individual will also have to accept responsibility for the functions of public relations, market analysis, development of new services, marketing strategy formulation, execution of action plans, control over marketing actions, etc.

20.5.4 Market offering

Finally, attention will be focused on the market offering of non-profit organisations.

Product decisions

The products offered by non-profit organisations cover a wide spectrum from products, services, and facilities, to places, ideas, and donations. These products are usually intangible, and those that are tangible are usually linked to the delivery of a service (for example, food and clothing provided to disaster victims is considered a service offered by the Red Cross).

The products offered by non-profit organisations are influenced by the aims and objectives of the organisation and the target markets served. For example, the 'products' offered by the University of South Africa (UNISA) are different to those offered by a residential university, while those offered by a technikon differ from those 'products' offered by a university, merely because their missions and objectives vary.

Pricing decisions

As far as price formulation is concerned, non-profit organisations can be divided into two broad categories: those that can attach a monetary value to their services, and those that cannot attach a monetary value to their services. The first-mentioned category of firms will thus determine a price, expressed in monetary value, for their services, usually following a cost-based approach. Thus, clubs and societies require a membership fee, a museum an entrance fee and universities charge class fees. Some of these organisations set their prices in such a way that they cover their costs, while others cover only a portion of their costs. With the exception of exclusive and elite organisations, demand factors are completely ignored in the price determination process. Certain price differentials, such as multiple pricing, quantity discounts, seasonal discounts and cash discounts, can be applied in non-profit organisations.

The second group of organisations includes all those organisations which do not attach a price to their services. The primary objective of these organisations is to provide a service to the community and more specifically to the underprivileged. These services are normally provided free of charge and the service costs are usually financed from donations received. Some clients of non-profit organisations do, however, make non-monetary sacrifices, such as inconvenient changes in behaviour, sacrifices made by acting in a certain way, the opportunity cost in terms of time spent at the institution, or the humiliation experienced.

Distribution decisions

The distribution decisions of non-profit organisations involve two aspects: the choice of the distribution channel, and the physical distribution of their services to clients.

The distributional channels used are short and direct, without the services of middlemen. Middlemen are, however, used in the form of persons or groups who raise funds or provide services. For example, the Child Welfare Society can make use of the services of volunteers to sell tickets for a competition or show in order to raise funds to care for or accommodate (house) children.

Because non-profit organisations seldom handle inventories, physical distribution decisions are primarily concerned with choice of location. The choice of location is important for the following reasons:

- The **situation** must be convenient for prospective donors. The result is that certain fund-raising campaigns will be launched at places such as large shopping centres where a large number of potential donors will be concentrated. For example, the liaison bureau of the University of the Orange Free State has opened an office in Johannesburg, primarily with the aim of serving potential donors concentrated in the Witwatersrand area.
- The **office** of the non-profit organisation will also indicate the organisation's involvement in a certain area and will thus increase the credibility of the organisation.
- The location will also make the organisation more accessible to its **target markets**. For example, the Child Welfare Society will establish a nursery school in an underprivileged suburb, while mobile clinics for the provision of medical services will be used on farms and in residential areas.

Marketing communication decisions

As observed earlier, marketing communication is the element of marketing which is applied to a considerable extent by non-profit organisations. This is done with the aid of advertisements, direct mail, personal contact sales promotion, and public relations. Marketing actions are directed at both clients and donors of funds of the organisation. In the case of donors and potential donors, marketing actions are directed at persons or institutions who will be convinced to make funds available to organisations so that they can realise their objectives.

In the case of clients, marketing actions can be directed at the following:

- convincing clients to do something (to seek help, avoid drugs, not to drink and drive);
- changing clients' attitudes and behaviour (family planning);
- introducing new services or actions (a new course at a university);
- elimination of bad habits (drug and alcohol abuse);
- making information about services available;
- creating awareness (road safety or free-enterprise systems).

Advertisements directed at donors as well as clients are placed in mass media (newspapers, magazines, radio and television) while direct mail is an effective means of reaching selected persons. Personal contact with donors as well as clients is unavoidably part of the marketing efforts of non-profit organisations.

20.6 SUMMARY

In this chapter several unique applications of universal marketing principles were discussed. First the nature of industrial products and the purchasing behaviour of industrial buyers was discussed, and their influence on marketing decisions was indicated. Secondly, the marketing of services was discussed, and thirdly the factors differentiating the marketing of agricultural products from that of consumer products. Attention was also given to the controlled marketing of agricultural products. The marketing decisions of non-profit organisations were also considered.

REFERENCES

1. Marx, S and Dekker, H. 1982. *Marketing Management: Principles and Decisions*. Pretoria: HAUM, p 529.
2. Lucas, GHG (ed). 1983. *Die Taak van Bemarkingsbestuur*. Pretoria: Van Schaik, pp 164–5.
3. Predominantly based on Marx and Dekker op cit, pp 530–3 and Stanton, WG. 1981. *Fundamentals of Marketing*. New York: McGraw-Hill, p 441.
4. Lehmann, DR and O'Shaughnessy, J. 'Difference in Attribute Importance for Different Industrial Products'. *Journal of Marketing*, April 1974, p 39.
5. Predominantly based on Jooste, CJ. 'Die Aankoopgedrag van die Aankoper: 'n Gedragswetenskaplike Benadering'. *Purchasing South Africa*. May 1981, pp 3–4.
6. Marx and Dekker op cit, pp 536–8.

7. Kotler, P. 1986. *Principles of Marketing*. Englewood Cliffs, New Jersey: Prentice-Hall Inc, p 681.
8. Marx and Dekker op cit, p 525.
9. Stanton op cit, p 441.
10. Reibstein, DJ. 1985. *Marketing: Concepts, Strategies and Decisions*. Englewood Cliffs, New Jersey: Prentice-Hall Inc, p 607.
11. Stanton op cit, p 442.
12. Parasuraman, A, Zeithaml, VA and Berry, LL. 1985. A conceptual model of service quality and its implications for future research'. *Journal of Marketing*, Fall, p 44.
13. Marx and Dekker op cit, pp 527–8.
14. Ibid p 545.
15. Lucas, et al. 1979. *The Task of Marketing Management*. Pretoria: Van Schaik, p 735.
16. Marx and Dekker op cit, p 546.
17. Lucas et al op cit, pp 736–7.
18. Ibid pp 738–740.
19. This section is primarily based on Van Vuuren, JP. 1985. *'n Bedryfsekonomiese Ondersoek na die Bemarking van Rooivleis in die Beheerde Gebiede van die RSA met Spesifieke Verwysing na die Rol van Produsente en Vleishandelaars*. Unpublished dissertation. Bloemfontein: University of the Orange Free State; and Van Zyl, PA. 1988. *'n Bedryfsekonomiese Ondersoek na die Funksionering van die Veeveilingbemarkingstelsel*. Unpublished thesis. Bloemfontein: University of the Orange Free State.
20. Van Zyl op cit, pp 41–3.
21. Based on Kotler, P. 'Strategies for Introducing Marketing into Non-profit Organizations'. *Journal of Marketing*, January 1979, pp 37–44.

ASSIGNMENTS

1. Explain fully how the buyer behaviour of a buyer who purchases a hundred personal computers for a company manufacturing and marketing pharmaceuticals differs from that of a consumer purchasing for the first time a personal computer for his own personal use.

2. Draw up a questionnaire for a commercial bank with the aid of which customer service to current customers can be measured. Ensure that your questionnaire measures all the dimensions of customer services.

3. There is a popular demand for a greater degree of deregulation of marketing of agricultural products.

   (a) Discuss the role of the control boards critically.

   (b) What implication will deregulation have on the producer (farmer) in terms of the marketing of his products?

   (c) Will deregulation be to the advantage of final consumers or not?

4. Evaluate the marketing strategies and programmes of the university, or technikon or college where you are studying. Which recommendations can you make with regard to future marketing strategies?

CHAPTER 21

RETAIL MARKETING

21.1 INTRODUCTION

Retail marketing plays an important role in the development of a country or region in respect of bridging the gap between the producer and final consumer. The retailer is regarded as the last link in the distribution chain connecting the producer with the consumer. In this process, the retailer supplies the products and services required by the consumer at the right time and place and in the right quantities.

The retail infrastructure of a country reflects its level of economic development. South Africa is in the unique position of comprising a developed First World, particularly in the urban areas, and an underdeveloped Third World, particularly in the rural areas. Development in retailing reflects this dualism and creates accompanying opportunities and threats. The opportunities and threats occur in the external environment and the retailer must scan this environment to take advantage of the opportunities and ward off the threats.

This chapter defines retailing and classifies the different types of retailers into those who trade from stores and those who do not. The South African retail environment is scanned and the manner in which a retailer — especially the small businessman — manages his operation is described. The location of a retail store receives attention and, since a retail store is in reality a marketing institution, marketing decisions and strategic marketing are discussed in depth.

ORGANISATION OF THE CHAPTER

The nature of retail marketing: Definition, classification, retail development, the retail environment, retail management.

Locational factors: Types of enterprises, trade areas, store image, utilisation of space in the store, small business retailing, entrepreneurship.

> **Marketing strategy:** Decisions with regard to product, distribution, marketing communication, price.
>
> **Strategic marketing:** The marketing concept, market positioning, strategic planning, the retail life cycle, market strategies, control.

21.2 THE NATURE OF RETAIL MARKETING

21.2.1 The retail sector in South Africa

The South African retail sector is regarded as the leader in its field in Africa. There are approximately 60 000 retailers, who in 1988 were responsible for a turnover exceeding R30,6 billion. These retailers provided 30 million consumers with products and services and more than 328 000 people with employment. Although the retail industry plays a dominant role in the South African economy, it must be emphasised that it does not function in isolation and that external factors exert a great influence on it. These factors are discussed later in the chapter (and in Chapter 2). First, however, retailing must be defined and a classification system developed for the different types of retailers in South Africa.

21.2.2 Definition of retailing

Retailing can generally be regarded as the business activity by means of which products and services are made available to consumers. The Central Statistical Service[1] defines retailing as follows:

"The resale (sale without transformation) of new and used goods to the general public, for personal or household consumption or utilization, by shops, department stores, stalls, mail-order houses, petrol filling stations, retail motor vehicle dealers, hawkers and pedlars, consumer co-operatives, etc. Also included are establishments engaged in selling to the general public, from displayed merchandise, products such as typewriters, stationary, lumber or petrol, or undertaking repair for the general public, are classified as retailers, though these sales or repairs may not be for personal or household consumption or use. However, establishments which sell such merchandise primarily to institutional or industrial users are classified as wholesalers."

The general definition implies three subordinate concepts:

- The purpose of retailing
- The variety of retailing
- The size of retailing

As far as the **purpose** of retailing is concerned, it is generally accepted that retailers strive towards economic objectives, i.e. the maximisation of profitability on investment in the long term within the constraints set by the resources of the trader.

Variety refers to the fact that retailers can be found in the primary, secondary and tertiary sectors. In the primary sector the retailer can supply raw materials to a manufacturer. According to the Central Statistical Service, such an enterprise can be classified as a retailer if 50 % of the sales are to the general public for private or for household consumption or use.

Regarding the **size** of retailing, much attention is at present being given to the difference between a large and small business. Small business retailing is discussed in section 21.4.4.

21.2.3 Classification of retailing

Kotler and Armstrong[2] distinguish between two basic types of retailers: those who operate from stores and those who do not.

Retail stores

Attention has already been given in Chapter 10 to the different types of retailers. Table 21.1 summarises the methods according to which the different types of retail stores can be classified.

TABLE 21.1   Methods of classifying retail stores

Scope of services rendered	Range of products offered	Relative price	Control	Location
Self-service	Speciality store	Discount store	Corporate chain	Central business district
Limited service	Supermarket	Catalogue sales	Cooperative	Secondary business district
Full service	Departmental store		Franchise agreement	Shopping centre
	Hypermarket		Conglomerate	
	Service enterprise			

Nonstore retailing

There are three types of nonstore retailers:

- **Direct marketing.** Postal advertising by means of pamphlets and telephone marketing are examples of direct marketing. Consumers can also choose from catalogues supplied to specially selected customers. A new method of direct marketing is electronic marketing whereby orders are placed by means of electronic media such as Beltel and delivered to the consumer. Television is at present also used to demonstrate products. Here the consumer dials a toll-free number to order a product. Direct marketing is advantageous to the retailer because of the low costs involved.

- **Direct sales.** Examples are door-to-door sales, sales by means of the so-called party plan and street hawkers.
- **Coin-operated machines.** These are used to make convenience products available to consumers at a large variety of places. Examples of such products are cool drinks, sweets and cigarettes.

21.2.4 Retail origin and development in South Africa

The history of South African retailing shows that the majority of perishable foodstuffs produced in South Africa at the turn of the century was supplied either direct or by a general dealer to the final consumer. According to Coetzee,[3] nonfoodstuff products (fabric, tools, etc.) were imported mostly by importers based on the coast at import harbours (principally Cape Town and Durban). These products were taken into the interior by hawkers and speculators, who traded in these products with the inhabitants.

Independent retailers established themselves in these coastal towns and supplied the local population with imported wares. As the interior developed, a gradual need arose for wholesalers at places such as Kimberley, Johannesburg and Pretoria to supply the retailers.

The discovery of gold on the Witwatersrand and the subsequent population growth caused the existing distribution system to become inadequate in meeting the needs of the rapidly-growing market.

Regarding industrial products, the mining companies such as De Beers began importing industrial equipment and machinery direct and can, according to Gray,[4] be regarded as the first direct competitors of the import houses.

Following the establishment of the Witwatersrand gold mines, secondary industries developed in the area to meet the immediate needs of the inhabitants, specially after the Second World War. Technical innovations such as improved transport and communication also contributed to the establishment of the rural wholesale trade and development of a sophisticated distribution system. Countrywide markets developed and were further stimulated by the use of advertising media such as national newspapers and the radio.

Accompanying the development of the rural wholesale trade was that of local retailing, to such an extent that it had become a full link in the South African distribution chain by midcentury. Close liaison with the wholesaler provided the retailer with a guaranteed supplier of products and helped to shift the storage function from the dealer back to the wholesaler. The general dealer gradually developed and opened branches, which in turn led to the origin of chain store groups in South Africa. These diversified further and developed into departmental discount and supermarket chain stores.

The supermarket in South Africa finally gained acceptance in 1947 with the opening of the first self-service store. These stores were concentrated in the urban areas and were particularly popular as grocery stores. As a result of innovations in cooling and storage facilities, it became possible to make perishable products such as meat, fish and vegetables available direct to the public. The self-service trend was justified exclusively on economic grounds, since the profit margins on groceries and foodstuffs were low and came under great pressure with the increase in labour costs. The obvious solution was to switch to self-service, which decreased labour costs, and, because of changed consumer perceptions, led to a higher turnover and a resultant higher net profit.

"Supermarket and Retailer"[5] points out that the market research group A C Nielsen found in a survey conducted in 1970 that, in respect of the sales of groceries, toiletries and cleaning agents, the 1 950 self-service stores operating at that time formed only 7 % of the total number of retail institutions (which numbered 29 000) but realised 42 % of the total sales of these products. In a subsequent survey conducted in 1980, Nielsen[6] found that self-service stores had increased by 1 218 and that their share in the sales in the above products had increased to 64,7 %.

The increasing trend in urbanisation resulted in the urban distribution system having to be adapted to accommodate the increasing number of consumers. This led to the establishment of suburban shopping centres. These centres were initially modest in scope and comprised a grocery or food outlet as the point of attraction (also known as a magnet or anchor) and a few speciality stores grouped round it.

Additional facilities such as restaurants, speciality stores and banks were established in these shopping centres, which made it unnecessary for the suburban consumer to go to the central business district.

South African retail infrastructure is the most modern in Africa and compares favourably with the majority of European and North American countries. The average South African shopping centre compares well with its American counterpart.[7]

The development of retailing and the continuous innovation in this field are the result of the intensive competition, which compels a retailer to find methods of differentiating his enterprise from others.

Lusch and Dunne[8] maintain that "the Wheel of retailing" explains development in retailing. According to this theory, retailers enter the market as entrepreneurs with low profit margins, prices and status. This gives them a differential advantage and enables them to draw customers from established retailers. If these low-status entrepreneurs are successful, they expand their facilities and a higher profit margin and higher prices result, thereby creating a gap for other, small, low-status stores to enter the market with the same recipe.

"The retail accordion" is another theory attempting to explain changes in retailing. According to this theory, a store initially offers a wide assortment of products, then gradually begins to specialise in specific areas and product ranges and later, as the situation requires, expands its assortment of products again. General dealers in the rural areas, for example, used to offer a very wide product assortment from pencils to bicycles to tobacco, bread and mealie meal. The rise of speciality stores limited the assortment. Now it is hypermarkets that offer a very wide product assortment, but the trend is turning again towards stores specialising in specific areas.

21.2.5 Retail management

Ferrell and Hirt[9] define management as the process of coordination of an enterprise's human, physical and financial sources to attain the enterprise's objectives. The definition emphasises the fact that management involves the systematic application of an enterprise's resources to reach the set objectives. The management tasks of planning, organising, coordinating, leading and controlling discussed in Chapter 1 also apply to retail management. Amer[10] defines retailing by referring to the following responsibilities of a retail manager:

- Creating the physical facility, which comprises the store, whether rented or owned, and the equipment.
- Purchasing, which is essential in the acquisition of inventory.
- Management of inventory, which forms part of purchases.
- Management of expenditure, which can mean the difference between survival and ruin.
- Marketing (the subject of this chapter).
- Management of manpower, it being essential that this be done as effectively as possible since retailing depends on its personnel. This includes liaison with trade unions, which have been making greater demands on retailing over the past few years.
- General management, which involves planning, organising, leading and controlling.

Davidson, Sweeney and Stampfl[11] refer to the functions of retail management as the acquisition of stock, and exchange of stock for money with a view to the realisation of a satisfactory profit for the dealer, in a highly competitive environment. It would therefore appear that retail management forms the foundation for success in retailing.

In addition to the lack of expertise experience by many South African retail managers is the problems caused by the highly competitive and rapidly changing retail environment.

21.3 THE RETAIL ENVIRONMENT IN SOUTH AFRICA

21.3.1 The importance of environmental scanning[12]

Retailing is not a self-sufficient entity but depends for its continued existence on the environment in which it operates. The environment influences retailing and retailing influences the environment. Mutual dependence thus exists between retailing and the environment.

Uncontrollable variables such as technological renewal (innovation), economic and political events, a lack of natural resources and social change in the community contribute to this relationship becoming increasingly complex. Survival in retailing therefore depends on staying one step ahead of change in the retail environment. Change may involve positive and/or negative consequences for retailing and it is essential that these opportunities and/or threats be identified in time.

A good example of opportunities in the retail environment identified in time is food retail outlets such as supermarkets realising that a change is taking place in the composition of the central business district's consumer market. It is being increasingly experienced that it is the lower and middle income groups that are now buying in that area. It is therefore not the extent of the buying power in the central business district that is changing, but the target market, which means the retailers' product mix has to be adapted. A greater volume of transactions is being carried out in the city centre but the monetary value per transaction is smaller than in the past. The changing profile of the consumer market in the city has also created new opportunities for retail outlets such as restaurants and speciality stores to provide for the needs of this new consumer. The shift in the buying power of the higher income group to suburban shopping centres has similarly created opportunities there: new shopping centres that are situated conveniently near this income group are being erected. The product mix is also being adapted to meet the requirements of this particular target market.

21.3.2 The internal environment

Particulars of an enterprise's internal environment are discussed in Chapter 2. These also apply to retailing.

21.3.3 The market environment

21.3.3.1 *The consumer market*

The consumer market is discussed in Chapter 3. Consumer behaviour and consumerism also apply to retailing.

Some aspects that directly concern the retail market environment are elucidated below, particularly with regard to suppliers and competitors.

21.3.3.2 *Suppliers in the retailer's market environment*

One of the greatest problems in retailing is increasing concentration in various branches of manufacturing. Forward vertical integration is being found more and more, which means the supplier is attempting to secure reliable distributors for his products and services. The majority of suppliers have also gradually diversified and are today involved in more than one branch of manufacturing.

21.3.3.3 *Competitors in the retailer's market environment*

Tough competition prevails in the South African retail environment, which is intensified during recessionary times, as is the case at present. Oligopolistic competitive situations exist in the majority of industries. The large food retail industry can be taken as an example of this: The three largest food retail groups (Checkers, OK Bazaars and Pick 'n Pay) handled about 63 % of all food sales in 1987 with 2,7 % of the 23 370 food retailers. In contrast, the four largest food retailers in America handle only 17 % of food sales.

Davidson et al[13] distinguish three levels of competition in retailing:

- *Source market competition*

This means there is competition for sources available to retailing. The availability of certain sources leads to potential competition among retailers:

— Location
— Money and capital market
— Labour market
— Produce market
— Technology
— Facilitating market

With regard to **location**, the retailer competes for a specific property or suitable premises within a shopping centre.

Large retailers compete in the **money and capital market** for funds from investors. The three large food retailers are listed on the Johannesburg Stock Exchange, where funds may be obtained relatively easily. Especially Pick 'n Pay and, to a lesser degree, OK Bazaars and Checkers (Tradegro) are popular shares traded regularly on the stock exchange because of regular increases in annual turnover and net distributable profits. It has even been speculated that Pick 'n Pay in particular performs the function of a bank, since it maintains an average stock turnover rate of twelve times a year. This means stock is sold within 30 days; creditors are paid over 60 to 90 days. The money due to the creditors, for the period that it is under the control of Pick 'n Pay, is invested and earns interest — which can be a sizable amount at the high interest rates and with a turnover of R3,869 thousand million for 1989.[14]

Intensive competition also exists on the **labour market**, specially among the large food retailers. In a country where skilled workers and management expertise are available only at a premium, retailers generally find it difficult to recruit and retain suitable personnel. Particularly the remuneration package offered by food retailing is not sufficiently competitive to draw and retain top-quality personnel.

The **produce market** also entails intensive competition for the South African retailer. It is essential, for example, that the product assortment of the food retailer meet the requirements of consumers. The large food retailers therefore have to compete with one another to procure products. It is for this reason that dealer brands are gaining such wide acceptance in South Africa. If the food retailer obtains control over the supply of a product, he is assured of a regular supply of that product. Competition is further intensified because of the regular out-of-stock situations that arise at the large food retailers' outlets. "Supermarket and Retailer"[15] reports that the first four months of 1990 were characterised by a shortage of supplies in supermarkets and hypermarkets and gives the following reasons for this situation:

- Strikes and unrest.
- A lack of investment in manufacturing equipment.
- The use of new stock control systems (just-in-time orders).
- Poor planning by the manufacturer, who closes factories for December and then takes four months to catch up on his backlog.

The shortage of supplies thus increases competition in the produce market for the products that are available.

There is tough rivalry among the large food retailers to implement **new technology** that can lead to greater consumer satisfaction. Here electronic funds transfer systems (EFTPOS) can be quoted as example. Checkers and First National Bank joined forces to implement such a system and, in so doing, gained a financial edge over their competitors. Checkers had the advantage of increasing consumer satisfaction by enabling its customers to pay with a credit card where the transaction is offset immediately, which eliminates finance charges and enables a customer to know exactly what his balance is. First National had the advantage in that its joint venture with Checkers persuaded a number of consumers to acquire credit cards from First National, which meant more client accounts.

In the **facilitating market** the retailer competes for the goodwill of the local authorities and government institutions concerned by complying with the prescribed requirements, regulations and legislation. At the municipal level, the retailer must obey certain regulations such as health requirements and the zoning of areas.

At **government level**, the retailer competes for more favourable legislation, a case in point being the Competition Board's inquiry into unfair practices by the large food retailers. In this inquiry[16] the large food retailers had to compete for the goodwill of the authorities by arguing against the institution of restrictive legislation (which would have restricted their powers of negotiation).

The retailer has to hold his own in all these markets to attain any measure of success, since any changes within these resource markets directly affect his competitive position.

- *Distribution market competition*

The type of competition, which is experienced by the retailer in the distribution market, largely determines the nature of competition in the source and consumer markets. Within this market, retailers compete **in the first place** directly with other retailers who essentially sell similar products and run the same type of business (such as a Pick 'n Pay supermarket in Pretoria East that competes directly with a

Checkers supermarket in the same area). This is regarded as the traditional type of retail competition on the horizontal level and is known as intratype competition. Lusch et al[17] defines this as two similar competitors vying for the consumer's money. The three large food retailers compete with one another in this traditional way: OK Bazaars owns supermarkets and hypermarkets, while Checkers also owns supermarkets and multi-markets (its version of hypermarkets), and Pick 'n Pay owns supermarkets, hypermarkets and super stores. The three groups thus sell similar product assortments in similar stores in the same areas.

A **second** type of competition that occurs is intertype competition, which means retailers competing with other retailers who do not sell similar products and do not run the same type of business. Lusch et al[18] defines this as different types of retailers selling similar products and competing for the same funds. An example of this type of competition is found throughout South Africa, where supermarkets compete with department stores, discount stores and cafés. OK Bazaars' supermarkets in Pretoria, for example, compete with Garlicks, Woolworths, Dions and the local café.

A **third** type of competition is vertical system competition, which entails a broader definition of competition than intra and intertypes of competition. This refers to the competition that exists among different vertical systems. An example is to be found in South African food retailing where OK Bazaars, Pick 'n Pay and Checkers represent a different vertical system in contractual agreements to the Spar retail system. Even among the three large food retailers themselves there are differences that distinguish them from one another as vertical systems. The backward vertical integration undertaken by Pick 'n Pay with the opening of the Price Club cash-and-carry wholesale group serves to illustrate this point. Vertical system competition will in future play an increasingly large role in changing and renewing the existing retail environment.

The **last** form of distribution market competition is free-form competition, which will also play a larger role in the future. This entails the formation of retail conglomerates or multi-concept enterprises. Conglomerates are formed when retail enterprises move away from the narrowly structured single form of business towards a wider, multi-business form, in other words a conglomerate. Leiboldt and Van Tonder[19] are of the opinion that the increasing formation of retail conglomerates can lead to tougher competition in retailing. The reason for the formation of retail conglomerates lies in the fact that the levelling off in economic growth is limiting profitability. The solution, according to the authors, is diversification into other (not necessarily related) industries. This, in turn, places existing enterprises in the industry under pressure to increase their profitability through diversification as well. The trend towards the formation of conglomerates can lead to intense competition and a shortage of retail facilities. Leiboldt and Van Tonder[20] define retail conglomerates as "multi-line product enterprises under central ownership in which various retail forms are combined to bring about a certain measure of management and distribution integration".

Examples of retail conglomerates in the South African retail environment are given in Table 21.2.

TABLE 21.2   Retail conglomerates in South Africa

Edgars Stores	Pep Stores	Foschini Ltd	Scott Stores	Woolworths/ Truworths
Ackermans	Pep	American Swiss	Dresstown	Woolworths
Edgars	Half-Price	Foschini	Jills	Truworths
Jet	Hyperette	Markhams	Scotts	Topics
Sales House	Shoprite	Pages		Top Centre

The retail conglomerates given in Table 21.2 refer to the situation in 1985. Some of the conglomerates have changed in the meantime (Pep Stores, for example, now own Ackermans and Checkers) but the situation still reflects the formation of conglomerates now occurring in South African retailing.

● *Consumer market competition*

This can be classified into four subdivisions. The **first** market that has been identified is the individual consumer and household market, which are regarded as the largest component of the consumer market. The most important aspects of this market are discussed in Chapter 3. In addition to the tough competition that exists for the goodwill of the consumer, the retailer also has other forms of competition to contend with. One of these is the alternative institutions in South Africa that meet the same consumer requirements. Examples of these are wholesalers such as Metro and Macro where the public can buy in bulk. This form of buying, which is popular for various reasons, is in direct competition with that offered by the ordinary retailer. It is precisely this form of competition that necessitated a large food retailer such as Pick 'n Pay to undertake backward vertical integration with the opening of its own wholesale section. Increasing competition from these alternative stores will result in further changes in retailing in the future.

The **second** market that has been identified is the institutional market, which in South Africa is still in its infancy. This market will, however, grow with the increasing pressure being exercised on the government to privatise more public institutions. Certain institutions are already competing in the retail market. Examples are South African universities, which now have the power to negotiate in the retail environment. They can, for instance, liaise directly with food manufacturers to supply groceries to residences and cafeterias and, in so doing, eliminate the middleman and negotiate better prices.

The **third** market that has been identified is the business market. This has been making rapid progress in South Africa. Examples are large businesses initiating car purchase schemes for their personnel because they have the financial clout to negotiate special discounts in the retail market. Another example is clothing schemes administered by enterprises on behalf of their personnel. There are also cases where business enterprises negotiate benefits on food for their employees, while other business enterprises supply their workers with subsidised food.

The **last** market that has been identified is the government market. This market forms a substantial part of South African retail sales. A good example of the influence it exercises is the pharmaceutical industry, where manufacturers of pharmaceutical products can supply medicine at a lower rate to government institutions, which have great purchasing power, than to the ordinary pharmacist. A further example of competition by this market is food purchases made by the Department of Defence, which buys food for the army.

The discussion above makes it clear that the competitive position of the South African retailer is much more complicated than would seem initially. The retailer should therefore see competition in a broader sense and not simply in the light of enterprises with similar stores and product assortments. Any institution that can lure customers away from the retailer should thus be regarded as a competitor. It is precisely these severe competitive circumstances that in the past have contributed to renewal taking place in South African retailing.

21.3.4 Macroenvironmental variables

The macroenvironmental variables which influence South African enterprises are discussed in Chapter 2. In this section only brief references are made to those which influence the retail trade directly, besides those discussed in Chapter 2.

Technological variables

Technological innovation like electronic scanning offers new opportunities for retailers. Virtually all large supermarkets in South Africa already use these time and labour-saving innovations, which facilitate pricing, merchandising, transactions and payment of accounts by means of the EFTPOS system. New products and services are continually being developed. Consider the marketing implications of the following technological innovations:[21]

- Cancer cures
- Chemical control of mental health
- Desalination of sea water
- Electronic pain killers
- Tiny but powerful computers
- Household robots
- Nonfattening, tasty, nutritious foods
- Electric cars
- Voice and gesture-controlled computers

Social variables

Certain demographic tendencies like changes in the population composition and urbanisation have special implications for the retail sector. High unemployment (about six million are unemployed[22]) has led to the growth of the informal sector where at least 28 % of the urban black population is working (as determined in 1988). Activities include the sale of food and liquor, making and selling clothing, hairdressing and taxi services. The development of spaza stores was the direct result of these activities taking place in the informal sector. These stores operate in the black townships from residences and sell basic products like bread, milk, eggs, toiletries and detergents virtually all in the smallest units.[23] These stores have become a competitive force which must be taken into account by traditional retailers. Convenience is probably the main reason for the popularity of the spaza store. Table 21.3 shows which stores were visited by black buyers in the month before the date of the survey:[24]

TABLE 21.3   Stores visited by black buyers in townships

General dealer		**41 %**
Spaza		**38 %**
Supermarket	**OK Bazaars**	**33 %**
	Checkers	**17 %**
	Pick 'n Pay	**9 %**

Many spaza stores are moving closer to the formal sector because they have succeeded in obtaining a hawker's licence, they pay taxes and they purchase from wholesalers. These stores maintain low overheads and use taxis to perform physical distribution activities.

Hawkers sell fruit, vegetables, flowers, fast foods, manufactured articles and liquor from street pavements, entrances to shopping complexes and stalls wherever there is a concentration of potential customers. There are 150 000 hawkers registered at ACHIB (the African Council of Hawkers and Informal Business) but there are certainly also many other nonregistered hawkers.

Physical variables

The retailer also has a social responsibility to the physical environment in which he conducts his business. An ecological protest against pollution and the destruction of the environment which directly involves the retailer is the use of CFCs (chloro-fluoro carbons) in aerosols, air conditioners and refrigeration systems. This chemical agent destroys the ozone layer in the atmosphere and there are calls for its banning worldwide. Responsible retailers consequently refuse to stock these harmful products — even if the alternatives are currently more expensive.

21.4 LOCATIONAL FACTORS IN RETAILING

21.4.1 The locational decision

A prospective retailer must decide where to locate his business enterprise as his decision will have a decisive influence on its success in the market. Before this a decision must be taken on the most suitable form of enterprise that will best fit the circumstances. It is also important to create a specific store image and to utilise selling space fully. The inherent abilities of the entrepreneur must also be taken into account as these have an influence on success in the market as well as further growth and survival. Human inability can lead to failure even if all the other factors are favourable.

21.4.2 Forms of enterprises in retailing

In South Africa retail enterprises mostly assume the form of sole proprietorships, partnerships, companies, close corporations or co-operatives. (Co-operatives, which may be established in terms of the Co-operative Act[25] in South Africa, are distinctive organisations with limited possibilities of utilisation. Co-operatives try to achieve certain economic advantages for their members through joint action. In South Africa co-operatives are found mostly in the rural farming communities in the form of marketing and/or supply organisations for products/goods and services. As a result of its distinctive characteristics a co-operative is not usually an alternative for the other forms of enterprise referred to, and therefore it will receive no further attention in the following discussion.)

In the choice of a form of enterprise the following considerations should apply:[26]

- The legal personality of the enterprise, that is whether, from a legal point of view, the enterprise can exist independently and as such disposes of its own assets and liabilities.
- The **liability of the owner(s)** for the outstanding debts of and claims against the enterprise.
- The degree to which the proprietor(s) has/have direct **control and authority** over the activities of the enterprise, and over the utilisation of its assets and the distribution of its profits.
- The possibilities for the enterprise of acquiring capital on its initial establishment and with further expansion. Here factors such as the permitted number of owners and their liabilities and authority in management play a role.
- The possibilities of a change in ownership or, in other words, the ease with which an owner can transfer his interest in the enterprise to someone else.
- The **legal requirements** regarding the establishment, management and dissolution of the enterprise and the **tax liability** of the enterprise and its owner(s).
- The most important characteristics of a sole proprietorship, partnership, company and close corporation will now be discussed in the light of the above.[27]

The sole proprietorship

A sole proprietorship concerns only one individual owner and has no **independent legal personality.** Consequently it cannot exist independently of the owner. The assets of the enterprise belong to the owner himself, and he is also personally liable for all the debts of and claims against the enterprise. In the case of a sole proprietorship it is therefore possible that the proprietor may lose all his personal possessions if the enterprise cannot meet its obligations.

The owner has direct **control and authority** over the activities of the enterprise and he receives all the profits of the enterprise.

Usually he acts as manager of the enterprise and he can freely make decisions regarding its running. As a result the enterprise can easily adjust to changes. On the other hand, a sole proprietorship may, according to circumstances, make exceptionally high demands on the management skills and personal freedom of the owner.

The partnership

A partnership corresponds in many respects with a sole proprietorship, and many of the disadvantages of the sole proprietorship are therefore also applicable to the partnership. A partnership can be defined as a contractual relationship between two or more persons (known as partners), but usually not more than twenty, who practice a lawful business to which every partner has to contribute something with the objective of making a profit to be distributed among them.

Partnerships are found in the form of **ordinary** and **extraordinary partnerships.** We emphasise the former, since it is the more common.

A partnership does not have a legal personality and all transactions, contracts or agreements are entered into by the partners in their personal capacities and not by the partnership. The partners are jointly and severally liable for claims against the partnership, irrespective of which partner is responsible for them. The personal belongings of the partners are therefore not safe-guarded at all.

Unless the partners decide differently beforehand, they have joint **control and authority** over the enterprise. Obviously this can, in the case of disagreements, cause problems, and in this respect the partnership is less adaptable to changing circumstances than the sole proprietorship. The fact that more people have a say in management may improve management, because the knowledge, experience and skills of more people can be drawn upon. At the same time this presents an opportunity for the division of labour and specialisation with the additional advantage that the individual partners are subjected to less personal stress than is the case with the owner in a sole proprietorship.

The *possibilities* of acquiring capital are usually better for a partnership than for a sole proprietorship — there are more people available to make contributions and to provide security for credit.

Transfer of ownership is generally more difficult in the case of a partnership than with a sole proprietorship — once again because more people are involved, and the provisions of the partnership contract (if this exists) have to be complied with. On the other hand, it may be easier for a partner to sell his share in a partnership than it is to sell a sole proprietorship. The reason for this is to be found in the advantages of a partnership over a sole proprietorship, namely better possibilities of acquiring capital, better management abilities, the possibilities of the division of labour and specialisation, and less personal stress. The most common ways in which an existing partnership can be dissolved are through

- a mutual agreement between the partners
- the retirement or death of one of the partners
- the joining of a new partner
- a declaration of insolvency (or other declaration of contractual incompetence) of a partner or the declaration of insolvency of the partnership, in which case the individual partners are of course also declared insolvent.

The company

The company (which functions under the Companies Act 61 of 1973, as amended) may be regarded as a more advanced form of ownership in which the disadvantages of the sole proprietorship and the partnership, especially in so far as these concern unlimited liability and the ability to acquire capital are eliminated.

In South Africa two forms of companies can be distinguished, namely the private company and the **public** company. The main differences between these are briefly:

- The number of members (shareholders) of the private company varies from one to fifty persons. The public company must have at least seven members, but there is no maximum, so long as the authorised number of shares is not exceeded.
- The private company must have at least one director, and a public company at least two.
- The general public cannot apply for shares in a private company, while they can in a public company.
- The transferability of shares in a private company is limited and usually occurs only with the approval of the board of directors. Shares in a public company are freely transferable.
- The name of a private company has to end with the words (Pty) Ltd or Proprietary (Limited), while that of a public company has to end with Ltd or Limited.
- Both private and public companies are subject so a number of legal requirements and limitations, but the private company less so than the public company.

A company has a legal personality, and its assets and liabilities are therefore divorced from those of the owners (shareholders). The personal assets of the shareholders are consequently not involved where claims are made against a company. The liability of the shareholders is limited to the amount paid by them for their share capital — if this share capital has not been paid up in full, the shareholders may, in the case of a claim against the company, be expected to pay up their shares in full — this is, however, their maximum liability.

The **control and authority** over the activities and assets of a company reside essentially in two bodies, namely a board of directors and a general meeting of members. The operational management of a company is usually entrusted by the articles of the company to the board of directors, while the general meeting of members is authorised to amend the articles and is consequently able to bring about a redistribution of powers between itself and the board of directors.

The company has definite advantages over the sole proprietorship and the partnership regarding the **possibilities of acquiring** capital, and this applies particularly to the public company. This is so because the general public are invited to invest capital in such a company, and members of the public are usually prepared to do this because of the legal personality the company has, the limited liability entailed by this, and the strict legal requirements the company has to adhere to. For the same reasons financial institutions are more willing to invest funds in a company than in a sole proprietorship. The possibilities of obtaining capital can be increased if shareholders, and particularly the directors, are prepared to provide, in their personal capacities, additional security for loans. This often happens in practice.

The **transfer of ownership** in a public company occurs by the unlimited and free transfer of shares.

A company is subject to many more legal **requirements** than a sole proprietorship or partnership. **Firstly**, with the establishment and registration of a company the requirements of the Companies Act have to be complied with, for example the registration of the memorandum and articles of association as well as the payment of registration fees. **Secondly**, requirements regarding accounting practices, financial reports, auditing minutes, membership register, and so on, have to be complied with. **Thirdly**, the Companies Act contains requirements regarding the rights, powers and duties of directors and other office-bearers, in which respect the relevant provisions of the articles of association also have to be adhered to. **Fourthly**, there are legal requirements concerning the dissolution or liquidation of a company. **Finally**, there is the taxation of the company and its shareholders. The company pays a fixed percentage of its pre-tax profits (usually not less than 40 %) as income tax, while shareholders have to add part of their profit from the company (company dividends based on their shareholdings) to their taxable incomes — hence the so-called double taxation on company profits.

The close corporation

A **close corporation**, which is a relatively new form of enterprise in South Africa, functions in terms of the Close Corporation Act. A close corporation is free of many of the formal requirements that govern companies and offers an attractive alternative to entrepreneurs, who would otherwise have been obliged to make use of a partnership or private company or even a sole proprietorship to do business. The abbreviation CC has to appear after the name of a close corporation.

A close corporation has an **independent legal personality**, and its members are therefore in general **not liable** for its debts or other claims against it. The close corporation has the same legal capacity as a natural person (individual) in respect of matters such as entering into agreements and the registration of fixed property in its name. Membership of a close corporation may vary from one to ten and is limited to natural persons or trustees of natural persons.

The close corporation is "closed" in the sense that there is no **divided responsibility** between **control and ownership**. The interest of a member in a close corporation is expressed as a percentage, and the total membership interest must always be 100 %. Where a close corporation consists of two or more members, it is desirable, although not legally obligatory, to enter into an association agreement between members. Consequently certain internal arrangements can be stipulated in the agreement — for example that all members may actively take part in the management of the corporation, and that authority is based on the percentages of membership interest in the corporation.

A member of a close corporation is in a fiduciary relationship with the corporation and is therefore expected to fulfil his duties honestly and "in good faith", and he may not overstep his authority.

Unlike in the case of companies, close corporations are not expected to employ auditors, but an accountant has to be appointed.

The profits of a close corporation are taxed at a fixed rate, which is the same as the rate applicable to companies. Distributed profits (dividends) are however, unlike in the case of companies, not taxable in the hands of members.

In the beginning a retail enterprise is often a sole proprietorship. Later when it extends its operations it can choose to become a close corporation or a company, whichever is more advantageous at that stage of development.

21.4.3 Trading areas

A small business retailer often locates his store in the area where he lives. But in deciding about the location of a shopping centre, computer models and statistical calculations are used to select the best location. Estate agents, city planners, trade associations and municipalities are sources of information that can be consulted by retailers or developers when planning to locate a store or a shopping centre.

A potential retailer can consider different areas for the location of his outlet. The **Central Business District** (CBD) in earlier times was an advantageous location much in demand but in recent times the popularity of the central business district has declined because of the following reasons:

- The high rent and taxes
- The old and unattractive buildings
- The lack of parking space
- The tendency of the less affluent to set up residence in old buildings in the city
- The high incidence of crime
- The popularity of the shopping complex where everything can be bought under one roof

Efforts to revitalise the central business district have been made by municipalities in large cities. Neglected buildings have been renovated, streets are being turned into shopping malls and closed to traffic, and flea market stalls are encouraged.

The Tremshed in Pretoria City has been restored and changed into an attractive shopping complex with many speciality stores, restaurants and theatres.

Secondary business districts away from the city core house smaller retailers and banks and are much in demand because of lower rents and taxes. Most suburbs also have a neighbourhood shopping street where hairdressers, dry-cleaners and the convenient little corner store are located.

Shopping complexes are found in many large cities. Well-known ones are Menlyn in Pretoria, Cavendish Square in Claremont and East Gate and Rosebank Mall on the Rand. The shopping complex usually reflects the economic status of its immediate environment. The shopping complex therefore in an affluent neighbourhood will present a more exclusive image than one in less well-to-do areas. The décor in the complex and the product assortment in the stores reflect an exclusive image. A shopping complex usually has a logo and a specific colour scheme. The rentals are high, the prices are "up market" and the complex itself is well promoted.

The developers of a shopping complex usually conduct intensive research on the ideal location and the best mix of stores in the complex. A large and well-known supermarket and/or discount store serves as an anchor store to draw adequate traffic to the shopping complex. An anchor store usually advertises intensively and widely to attract customers from far and wide. Many bargain hunters and customers of discount stores, however, do not ensure a brisk customer flow to the speciality stores in the complex. The more affluent customers who patronise these stores with their higher prices tend to avoid very busy shopping complexes.

All retailers should carefully consider the possible customer base that they can attract to their stores in terms of the high rent that they must pay.

21.4.4 Considerations regarding store location

Convenience

Reilly's Law of Retail Gravitation,[28] which was formulated in 1920, used to be applied to determine the best and most profitable location for a retail store. This law is based on two variables, namely population and distance. Therefore the larger the population that is conveniently close, the better the location under consideration. Modern and improved public transport and increased car ownership have made convenience and distance less important considerations. Today the development and success of spaza-type stores in the townships, however, suggest that less-privileged consumers still prefer the convenience of shopping near their places of residence.

The neighbourhood

The neighbourhood also influences the locational decision. The other stores nearby, the availability of parking, local rules and regulations, the rent, the possibility of extending the store and the attractiveness of the neighbourhood are important considerations in the selection of a site.

Economic considerations

The sales potential is probably the most important consideration. Without customers the enterprise loses its reason for existence. The index of retail saturation (IRS)[29] is similar to the formula for the market measurement and is used to determine the potential sales per square metre which can be realised by a store on a specific site.

The formula is as follows:

$$IRS = \frac{(P_A)\,(A\,E)}{S_A}$$

IRS = Index of retail saturation

P_A = The number of persons in the area who will probably be customers for the specific types of products

AE = Average per capita expenditure on these products

S_A = Total space devoted to sales of these products in all stores in the area A

The calculation is simple but the problem is to obtain correct and reliable information regarding the population, per capita expenditure and total space offered by all stores in the area. If this information is available the formula will give the sales per square metre. The retailer then knows what to expect and how the answer compares with target sales that will enable him to achieve his profit goal.

Only few retailers take the trouble to do these basic calculations. They react according to intuition and the availability of sites.

INDEX OF RETAIL SATURATION

There are, say, 100 000 consumers in area A. They are spending on average R30,50 per week in a food supermarket. There are 20 supermarkets in the area serving area A and a total of 20 000 m^2 of selling space. The calculation is as follows:

$$IRS = \frac{100\ 000 \times R30,50}{20\ 000}$$

$$= \frac{3\ 050\ 000}{20\ 000}$$

$$= R152,50$$

If the prospective retail store consists of 980 m^2 the retailer can expect R152,50 × 980 = R149 450 per week from sales. The question is whether this will be enough to cover costs and to make a profit. How does this compare with sales in other areas?

Personal considerations

The retailer has personal preferences. He wants to maintain or even improve his quality of living and will be unwilling to locate his store in an area where he will feel unwelcome even if the profit potential is promising. Level of education, political attitudes, social class and even age are factors that can influence quality of living. The presence of recreational facilities, parks, schools and theatres and the climate are personal considerations in a retailer's locational decision.

21.4.5 The store image

Store construction and layout

In planning the building, the retail store is regarded as a machine "designed to display, house and sell merchandise".[30] The building's external appearance and the internal space are important in planning as these two factors combine to create a store image. Large stores are planned by architects, interior decorators, shop fitters and engineers. The small business retailers must often obtain information before he attempts to do this on this own. Books, magazines and trade associations are sources that can be consulted. The following aspects of construction and layout must receive attention:

- The store front is an advertisement which should entice passersby and give information on the type of store and the store's image.
- The store name and logo in distinctive lettering and colours are usually placed above the entrance or on the windows.
- The display window creates the first impression, as do the products offered for sale. Professional window dressers should be employed for this purpose. Consumers often use the window display as a source of information in consumer decision making.
- The entrance to the store must preferably be impressive, like a solid wooden door with brass handles at the entrance to an exclusive boutique. Unfortunately practical considerations often make an impressive entrance impossible. In a supermarket there are usually trollies standing around.

Functional and aesthetic considerations influence store layout, which should maximise efficiency and minimise cost. The free-form or grid layout (Figure 21.1) is used in self-service stores. The typical gondolas near store shelves create the impression that the products they contain are cheaper than those placed neatly on the shelves. Ethical considerations prevent the retailer from creating false impressions and misleading his customers. Gondolas are therefore merely used to attract attention to specific products (so-called specials). The store interior creates an opportunity for marketing communication (point of purchase communication) by means of demonstrations and billboards. The flooring, colour scheme and lights help to create a specific image. Branches of chain stores usually all have the same distinctive décor.

Space utilisation

Retailers do not always realise the importance of utilising interior space to its fullest extent. The cost of space is calculated as follows:

$$\text{Cost} = \frac{\text{Rent paid}}{\text{Square metres}}$$

Between 70 % and 80 % of total space must be allocated to sales activities. Space taken up by nonproductive, nonsales activities must be limited to the absolute minimum. It is only logical to devote more space to departments with higher sales. Space utilisation is often expressed as R-sales per square metre. This figure enables the retailer (retail management) to identify less profitable departments. It is also important to realise that narrow aisles and merchandise stacked high on the shelves create a cheap store image and are possibly only suitable for hypermarkets and discount stores where a low price image is desirable. In many exclusive stores only a few expensive items are displayed.

In 1989 Edgars' sales per square metre were R3 130 and those of Pep R2 222.

Source: *Finansies & Tegniek*, 30 June 1989, p 53.

FIGURE 21.1   Store layout

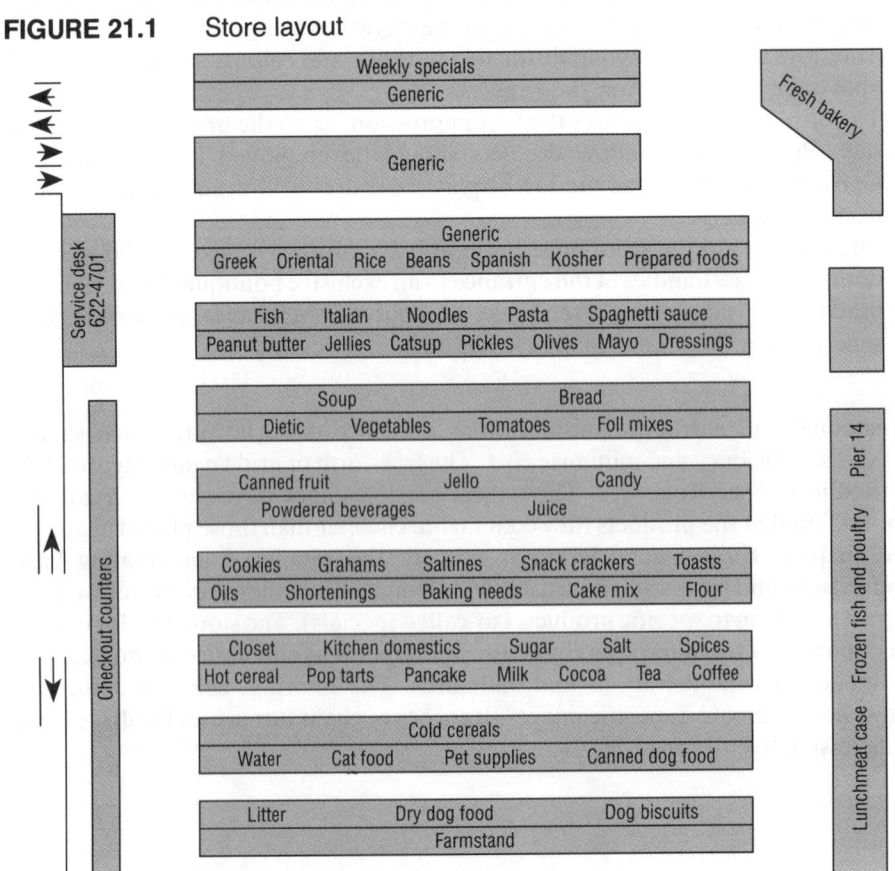

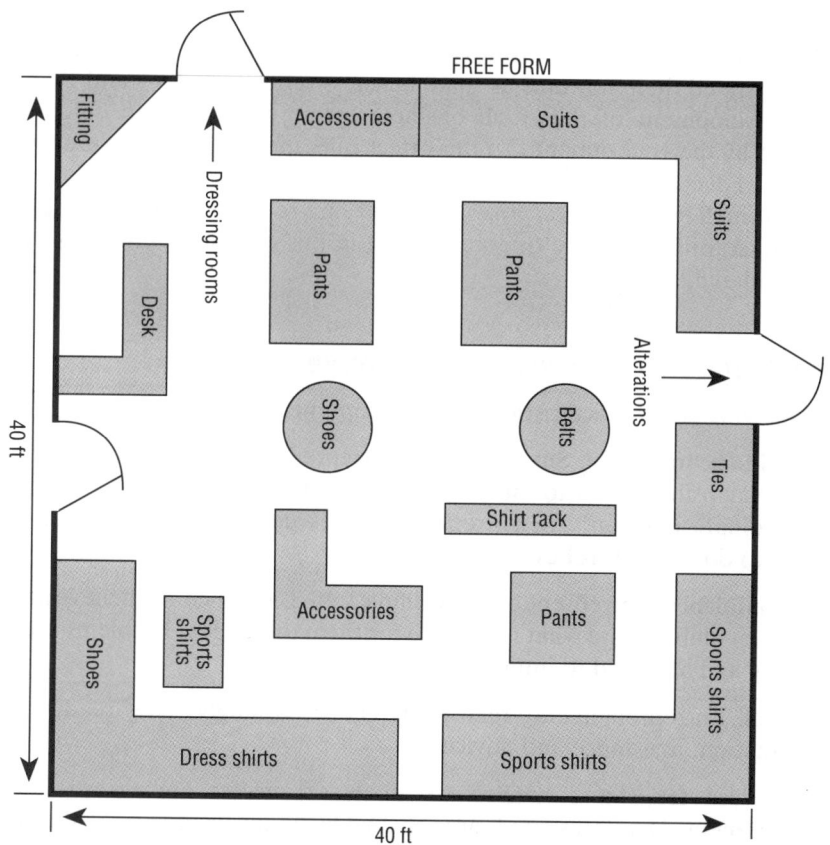

Source: Mason, J.B. Mayer, M.L. & Ezell, H.F. 1988 *Retailing* Plano Texas: Business Publications. pp 416-417.

21.4.6 The entrepreneur in small business retailing

21.4.6.1 *The development of small business retailing*

For a small retailer to be classified as a small business enterprise the following requirements[31] must be complied with:

- The enterprise must be owned by the owner.
- The enterprise must operate independently.
- The total turnover per year may not be more than R2 000 000 (as determined in 1987).
- Total assets may not be more than R1 000 000.
- Not more than 100 persons may be employed by the enterprise.
- There may not be more than five units (for example branches).

As a result of the current economic climate in South Africa, the high unemployment figure and the slow development in the Third World component of the population, small business enterprises flourish. The many spaza stores, the pavement hawkers and flea market stalls prove this statement. Today Pick 'n Pay and Pep Stores are not small business enterprises any longer. Both entrepreneurs, however, stated their ventures as small business retailers in 1967 and 1953.

The development of the small business sector is actively encouraged and promoted by the government. To this effect rules and regulations were changed and control decreased.

Not all small business enterprises, however, are retailers. Many consist mainly of manufacturing or service operations, but in this chapter attention is focused only on retailing.

21.4.6.2 *The characteristics of the entrepreneur*

The following are characteristics of the entrepreneur:[32]

- **A need to be in control.** Small business entrepreneurs need to have freedom to take responsibility and to initiate new ideas. They do not want to work in a sub-ordinate position. An entrepreneur does not delegate tasks easily and wants to do and control everything himself.

- **Self-confidence.** Entrepreneurs have ample self-confidence and believe implicitly in their abilities and what is possible for them to achieve. Problems are faced directly and attended to immediately.

- **Realism**. Entrepreneurs are realistic and act accordingly. They readily accept information, assistance and advice.

- **Little need for status symbols.** Symbols of success are external to the entrepreneur. His status needs are satisfied by his achievements — thus rather the success of his enterprise than the car that he owns.

- **Objectivity.** The entrepeneur avoids emotions and interpersonal involvement. He judges his employees objectively in terms of what they can do. He is often regarded as insensitive. He is emotionally stable and is not easily discouraged.

- **A need for challenges.** The risks inherent in developing a business enterprise are carefully determined and considered and regarded as challenges to be met. Too high a degree of risk is avoided.

- **Drive**. The successful entrepreneur wants to be actively involved and inactivity makes him impatient. He does not tire easily and he enjoys good health. He strives to realise the objectives he has set for himself.

The entrepreneur's ability to generate cash and to exercise good control over funds is one of the critical success factors in small business management.[33] It is therefore to be expected that small business enterprises that base their main activities on cash sales have a greater chance of success than those that are less interested in money matters.

The questionnaire in the example below indicates the typical questions that can be put to a person to determine if his personal characteristics will enable him to become a promising entrepreneur.

QUESTIONNAIRE FOR POTENTIAL ENTREPRENEURS

Under each question, check the answer that says what you feel or comes closest to it. Be honest with yourself.

Are you a self-starter?
- ☐ I do things on my own. Nobody has to tell me to get going.
- ☐ If someone gets me started, I keep going all right.
- ☐ Easy does it. I don't put myself out until I have to.

How do you feel about other people?
- ☐ I like people. I can get along with just about anybody.
- ☐ I have plenty of friends — I don't need anyone else.
- ☐ Most people irritate me.

Can you lead others?
- ☐ I can get most people to go along when I start something.
- ☐ I can give the orders if someone tells me what we should do.
- ☐ I let someone else get things moving. Then I go along if I feel like it.

Can you take responsibility?
- ☐ I like to take charge of things and see them through.
- ☐ I'll take over if I have to, but I'd rather let someone else be responsible.
- ☐ There's always some eager beavers around waiting to show how smart they are. I say, let them.

How good an organiser are you?
- ☐ I like to have a plan before I start. I'm usually the one to get things lined up when the group wants to do something.
- ☐ I do all right unless things get too confused. Then I quit.
- ☐ You get all set and then something comes along and presents too many problems. So I just take things as they come.

How good a worker are you?
- ☐ I can keep going as long as I need to. I don't mind working hard for something I want.
- ☐ I'll work hard for a while, but when I've had enough, that's it.
- ☐ I can't see that hard work gets you anywhere.

Can you make decisions?
- ☐ I can make up my mind in a hurry if I have to. It usually turn out OK, too.
- ☐ I can if I have plenty of time. If I have to make up my mind fast, later I think I should have decide the other way.
- ☐ I don't like to be the one who has to decide things.

Can people trust what you say?
- ☐ You bet they can. I don't say things I don't mean.
- ☐ I try to be on the level most of the time, but sometimes I just say what's easiest.
- ☐ Why bother if the other fellow doesn't know the difference?

Can you stick with it?
- ☐ If I make up my mind to do something, I don't let *anything* stop me.
- ☐ I usually finish what I start — if it goes well.
- ☐ If it doesn't go right, I quit. Why beat your brains out?

How good is your health?
- ☐ I am *never* run down!
- ☐ I have enough energy for most things I want to do.
- ☐ I run out of energy sooner than most of my friends seem to.

Now count the checks you made.

How many checks are there beside the *first* answer to each question?
How many checks are there beside the *second* answer to each question?
How many checks are there beside the *third* answer to each question?

If most of your checks are beside the first answers, you probably have what it takes to run a business. If not, you're likely to have more trouble than you can handle by yourself. Better find a partner who is strong on the points you're weak on. If many checks are beside the third answer, not even a good partner will be able to shore you up.

Source: Ibid pp 210-211.

21.5 THE RETAILER'S MARKETING STRATEGY

As is the case when any consumer product is marketed, the retailer's marketing strategy consists of four marketing instruments used in a specific environment with a view to reaching a specific market. The four areas of marketing where decisions are taken are discussed in Part 3 of this book in Chapters 7 to 17. These chapters are referred to in the brief discussion below on those aspects applicable specifically to retailing.

21.5.1 Product decisions of the retailer

Since the retailer is not involved in the physical production process and since consumer needs are satisfied through the right products being made available at the right price and the right time, not all the decisions regarding products that are discussed in Chapters 7, 8 and 9 apply to retail marketing. Only some aspects are therefore dealt with here.

The product concept

Formal products in retailing consist of various types of products and brands. **Core products** are those that meet specific consumer requirements (such as medicine sold by pharmacists). The **total product concept** refers not only to the physical objects themselves but also the salesperson's advice, the after-sales, the guarantee, the credit facilities and even the wrapping of gifts. The **product image**, together with other image-creating variables such as decor and service rendered by sales staff, contributes to the overall store image. The product mix that is stocked is reflected directly in the store image.

The product mix

Product mix refers to all the series, lines and items of products that are for sale. The retailer has to decide whether he wants to stock a narrow, wide, shallow, deep or combined product mix.[34]

- A narrow and deep product mix consists of limited product ranges in numerous sizes and colours.
- A wide and shallow product mix consists of numerous product ranges in a limited range of designs.
- A combination product mix consists of some product ranges with a narrow and deep level and some with wide and shallow level.

The ideal product mix has to satisfy both the retailer's profit objectives and the customers. The retailer is restricted in the composition of his product mix by his financial resources and the space available in his store. He is further restricted in that some products have a higher profit margin than others. The ideal for a retailer would be to stock only products with a high profit margin but this would be at the expense of stock turnover and the risk of losing customers.

Brand decisions

The advantages of brands for retailers have already been addressed in depth in Chapter 9, as have the differences in dealer brands, producer brands, generic brands, and individual and family brands.

The importance of loyalty cannot be overemphasised. Store loyalty is achieved when consumers prefer a specific store to others and buy there regularly. There are various reasons for store loyalty:[35]

- Convient location.
- Sufficient parking.
- A wide product mix.
- Low prices.
- High-quality products.
- A friendly sales force.
- Good after-sales service.
- The satisfaction of social needs (contact with other people).

If these are catered for, a pleasant shopping atmosphere is created and consumers are encouraged to return to the store time and again. Some stores attempt to win store loyalty through extending credit facilities but as a result frequently lose cash buyers, who are in such a case often neglected and even perhaps made to feel unwelcome. Too little attention is generally given to store loyalty, which may explain why South Africa ranks second on the list of poorest service rendered. Bad service in stores is often attributable to disinterested and/or untrained sales staff who do not care whether customers are loyal or not.

Packaging decisions of retailers

Decisions regarding packaging are generally taken by the manufacturer and very little repackaging is done in the modern retail outlet. Packaging material prominently displaying the store's name is usually supplied to customers by the retailer himself. This practice, which is adhered to throughout South Africa, leads to waste and pollution. In Europe and the United States customers are supplied with a few carry bags that they have to pay for. They bring their own bags or baskets for their purchases. The South African practice is so deeply rooted, however, that is would be difficult to change it. Some exclusive stores such as jewellers and boutiques supply customers with specially designed packaging material for products bought from them.

Large retailers set very strict requirements to manufacturers where packaging size, colour and material are concerned. If the retailer is the channel leader, he can enforce his requirements. Packaging material damaged in the store or during transport is generally for the manufacturer's account. This frequently results in large-scale waste, since a few dented cans in a pack can lead to the entire pack being rejected and sent back to the manufacturer.

The manufacturer has to prove to the large retailer that his packaging deserves a place on the store shelves because packaging takes up valuable sales space. Retailers give preference to manufacturers who are creative in the packaging of their products. Small packets of soap powder illustrate this point. With this new type of packaging the manufacturer creates a pull effect to draw customers to the store. The same goes for kaleidoscope packaging, which contains collector's items such as cards, teaspoons or even small diamonds, or which advertises competitions on the labels. Decisions regarding packaging are discussed in detail in Chapter 9.

21.5.2 Distribution decisions of the retailer

Distribution as a marketing instrument has already been discussed in Chapters 10 and 11. The majority of aspects discussed also apply to retailing, although seen from a different perspective. Aspects that are particularly important here are achieving cooperation in the distribution channel, dealing with conflict, channel leadership and the various types of retail stores.

An aspect that deserves attention but has not yet been addressed is the distribution decision regarding the acquisition of inventory. Bolen[36] describes this process schematically in Figure 21.2.

FIGURE 21.2   The management of inventory

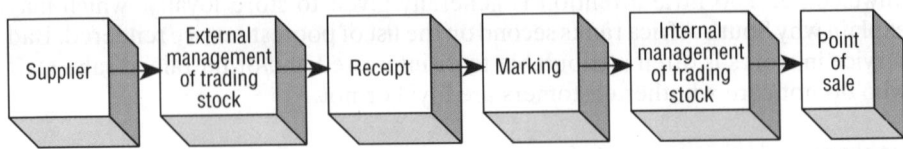

Supplier → External management of trading stock → Receipt → Marking → Internal management of trading stock → Point of sale

The external management of inventory involves the management of stock from the time it is purchased to the time it reaches the retailer. The aim is to get the right product at the right place at the lowest price. Important aspects here are the right quantity of the right quality. Other aspects that apply are the most economic order quantity and just-in-time (JIT) merchandising.

On receipt, stock has to be secured and then properly stored so that it can be identified and controlled. The control process involves ensuring that the documentation corresponds with what has been received and that the products are in good condition. The stock is then marked and recorded in a stock register. After this it is sent on to the point of sale. Special care is taken during this process to prevent theft, both internally (by personnel, for example) and externally.

21.5.3 Pricing decisions of the retailer

21.5.3.1 *The need for information*

All decisions must be based on some type of information, as the decision can never be better than the information on which it is based. The better the applicability and quality of the information, the better the quality of the pricing decision will be. As far as price determination is concerned, information is needed on cost, demand and competition. Cost can be taken into consideration especially in order to determine a target price which will be able to satisfy the objectives of the retailer. Demand and competition can be taken into consideration in order to determine what the market can bear and will accept. The retailer cannot take just one of these aspects into consideration and neglect the others. He must find some compromise between these different factors.

Cost

Cost is a collective noun for many types of cost. Total fixed and direct variable costs play important roles in price determination and must be explained:

Total fixed costs are those costs which remain unchanged in total over a period and with a given capacity irrespective of the sales volume of the retailer. An increase in the sales volume within a certain capacity brings about a smaller fixed cost per unit. In retail terms the fixed costs can for example include the monthly rental of the store, electricity and water bills and the salaries of permanent personnel.

Direct variable costs represent costs which vary directly with the sales volume. This direct variable cost includes the price paid for the product by the retailer and all other costs directly attributed to the product until it is placed on the shelf for sale.

The cost price refers to the total cost of the product (including fixed and variable costs). This cost price can be seen as the minimum price at which a product can be sold in the long term. This is also the basis for the calculation of the ultimate selling price of the product. Breakeven analysis (see Chapter 17) is an important aid for a new retailer considering to open a store.

Demand

In deciding on a price structure, the retailer must take the ability and willingness of the consumer to pay a certain price into consideration.

In economic theory price is determined by demand and supply. The lower the price is, the higher the demand. In reality, however, the consumer often uses the price of a product as an indicator of the quality, especially in the absence of other reliable indicators by which the consumer can judge quality. Perfume is usually quoted as a good example here. The consumer also tends to use price as an indicator of product quality in cases where the product is quite expensive and the consumer is afraid of making the wrong decision. The consumer can therefore decide to choose the higher-price product (for example a radio) to reduce his risk of making the wrong choice.

The price band is the limit (price gap) that the consumer perceives as appropriate or acceptable for a specific product. By carefully researching the consumer market the retailer is able to determine the price limits and the sum of money that the consumer will be prepared to pay for certain products, and also how many consumers will be willing to purchase at different prices.

Competition

Competition does not necessarily mean that the selling prices for similar products must be the same at competitive retailers. Many factors can be used to differentiate the product offering of a retailer from those of the competitors. Differentiation can give the retailer much more freedom in deciding on prices. The product offering can be differentiated by means of services offered, the prestige and image of the store, location, the use of dealer brands, convenience such as parking and store hours, and product assortment. Other aspects such as vertical integration, low overhead costs and special agreements with suppliers can also give the retailer a leading edge over the competition.

The retailer must decide on a price level compared to the average market price offered by the competitors. The retailer can either decide on a price level equal to the market price, above the market price or below the market price. Only when products are successfully differentiated can the retailer charge prices higher or lower than the market price.

In terms of cost, demand and competition specific factors influence the overall price level:

- The location of the store is not only linked to the rental to be paid, but also to the convenience of the consumer.
- The store hours can also increase the convenience for the consumer and he will, for example, be willing to pay more for milk late at night at a cafe or superette than at the dairy or supermarket.
- The services offered by the retailer can also increase the convenience of the consumer and may also be reflected in the price level. The retailer can, for example, offer delivery, installation, credit facilities and a trade-in service.

- The store image can be important for consumers who do not necessarily look for low prices. There may be prestige attached to shop at certain stores or own a product bought from an up-market store. Certain consumers may also prefer to shop at a store with an up-market image created by atmosphere, decor, air conditioning, space and exclusive products. The prestigious image of a store must necessarily be reflected in the price levels.

Dealer and generic brands are respectively brands which are exclusively used by the retailer and the no-name brand of the store. Producer brands usually cost more than dealer or no-name brands because of the extensive advertising and other marketing expenses borne by the manufacturers. Retailers can consequently sell the dealer and no-name brands for less than other brands while building store loyalty.

The cost of the merchandise obviously has an influence on the price level at which the store will be able to sell the product. A large retail chain can buy in bigger quantities than a small superette, hardware store or toy store, enabling it to make use of its bargaining power to obtain lower prices.

21.5.3.2 *Determining the retail selling price*

The retail price is usually calculated by adding a markup to the cost of the product.

Cost + Markup = Retail price

In order to be able to calculate the retail price it is in other words necessary to determine the cost of the product and to decide on the markup percentage to add to the cost.

Determine the cost of the product

The first step in determining the retail price of a product is to determine the cost of the product. The cost of the product includes the following:

Cost of product = Supplier's price − Discount (like cash or quantity discount) + Transportation costs.

This cost of the product is the basis or point of departure for the calculation of the retail price.

Determining the markup percentage

The markup is the difference between the retail price and the cost of the product. The markup must make adequate provision for covering the retailer's overheads and also provide an adequate profit.[37] The target rate of return is reflected in the markup percentage, for example, 25 percent on cost.

Many retailers will consider markup as a percentage of cost based on the following formula:

$$\text{Markup percentage on cost} = \frac{\text{Markup amount (R)}}{\text{Cost (R)}} \times \frac{100}{1}$$

Most retailers, especially the progressive retailers, express markup as a percentage of retail price. This allows the retailer to relate markup to store operations. Another major reason for doing this is the common practice of reporting such expenses as advertising and salaries as percentages based on selling prices.[38] The following formula is applicable here:

$$\text{Markup percentage on retail price} = \frac{\text{Markup amount (R)}}{\text{Retail selling price}} \times \frac{100}{1}$$

When you do these calculations you will notice that the markup based on retail price resulted in a lower percentage than that based on cost because the retail price is higher than cost and the fraction is therefore smaller. It is very easy to calculate the retail price of the markup based on cost, but not so easy to do the same for a markup on retail price. When the cost and the desired markup percentage on retail is available, the retail price can be calculated as follows:[39]

$$\text{Retail selling price} = \frac{\text{Cost (R)}}{100\ \% - \text{markup}\ \%}$$

Sometimes retailers use different markups for different categories of merchandise. Products with a high turnover rate (frequently purchased products like fast moving consumer products) will usually have a lower markup than many shopping and speciality products with high prices.

Determining a markdown

A reduction in the retail selling price is known as a markdown. Few retailers are able to operate without finding it necessary to mark down merchandise to new lower prices. The majority of the markdown can be traced to one or more of the following reasons:[40]

- Errors in buying
- Errors in pricing
- Promotional reasons
- End of season
- Late deliveries from suppliers
- Dated merchandise
- Odds and ends
- Damaged or soiled products
- Returned products
- Deliberate overbuying
- Clearance of inventory.

Retailers generally view markdowns as a strategic tool for selling.

The markdown can be expressed as a percentage of the old retail price or of the new selling price:

$$\text{Markdown percentage} = \frac{\text{Markdown amount}}{\text{Old selling price}} \times 100$$

$$\text{Markdown percentage} = \frac{\text{Markdown amount}}{\text{New selling price}} \times 100$$

The retail price as calculated above may from time to time be adjusted for different reasons. The final selling price paid by the consumer can be the result of the application of different adjustments to the selling price.

21.5.3.3 *Adjustments to the selling price*

Price lines

Price lines occur in those cases where the retailer has a limited number of prices in each of his product lines. Price lines were discussed in Chapter 17.

Leader pricing

Leader prices are usually a temporary reduction in the price of a product (usually a well-known product) to a price lower than the usual retail price. This pricing decision is mainly used by retailers by way of special offers with the purpose of enticing consumers into the store and hoping that they will buy other products as well. Sometimes the price of a leader product is reduced to a level below the cost price, in which case it is referred to as a loss leader.

The ideal leader price product is the following:

- It is a well-known and popular brand.
- The price should be so low that it will encourage many people to buy it and not only a few.
- The price reduction should be large enough to generate interest.
- It should preferably not be a product that the consumer could buy and store in bulk.

Unfortunately this decision also has some disadvantages:

- It could start a destructive price war because it could be counteracted very swiftly, which could neutralise the effect to a great extent.
- Many consumers might buy the leader product only (called cherry picking).
- Sometimes a manufacturer is against the use of his product as a leader thinking that it could have an adverse effect on the prestige image of the product.

Bait pricing

Bait prices are temporarily reduced prices, as in the case of leader prices, with the purpose of luring people into the shop. The differences are:

- The retailer does not really want to sell the bait price product. Sometimes he has only a few of these items or even nothing at all. In other cases he tries his utmost to discourage the consumer from buying the product.
- The retailer usually tries to sell similar products at much higher prices when the customer is lured into the store.

Bait pricing is unethical, directly opposes the marketing concept, could lead to consumer resistance and have a negative effect on the image of the store. Bait pricing is usually strongly condemned by the general public and the consumer protection authorities.

Discounts

Discounts are reductions in price by the retailer and were discussed in Chapter 17.

One price versus variable prices

One-price means that all customers pay the same price for the same product. Customers benefit from a one-price decision by the assurance that all shoppers in the store pay the same price. Thus, they have no fear that they will be cheated.

A variable price enables customers to bargain over prices. Contrary to the attitude of most consumers who prefer a set price, some shoppers enjoy the challenge of haggling with retailers. Because sales transactions involving bargaining require additional time and attention, they cost more. Consequently variable pricing is generally restricted to high-ticket merchandise such as cars and furniture. Only experienced and trusted sales people can be allowed to change prices at their own discretion.

Unit pricing

Many supermarkets have adopted unit pricing in order to aid consumers in making comparisons and buying decisions. It is frequently difficult for consumers to compare the prices of different products when they are not of equal size, mass or content. One bottle may for example contain 350 ml of sauce, another 500 ml and another 400 ml with different prices attached. To compare the prices of these products, the consumer must convert the prices to price per ml. In unit pricing this calculation can be indicated on the shelf or on the product itself.

Odd-even prices

In the case of odd (uneven) prices amounts such as R0,29, R4,95 and R99 are used instead of R1,00 or R100,00 to create the illusion of low prices. It could be used to make the basic price seem lower in cases where the basic price is higher than the market price. There are other less convincing reasons given for the use of uneven prices. Another reason is also pure habit.

Prestige prices

Prestige prices are high prices used to indicate quality. Many manufacturers may even be strongly opposed to low prices or the granting of discounts on their products because it may, in their opinion, ruin the quality image of the product. The retailer must identify products whose prices may be closely associated with quality for example certain brands of perfumes, cameras, hi-fis, clothing and knives. The retailer may also want to display an image of prestige and quality in which a certain high price level may play a part.

21.5.4 The retailer's marketing communication decisions

21.5.4.1 *Definition*

Marketing communication can be defined as an integrated programme of communication where the ability of a product (in this case a store) to satisfy the needs of potential consumers is presented with a view to ensuring the long-term profit objectives of the enterprise.[41] Marketing communication has already been discussed in depth in Chapters 12, 13, 14 and 15. The theory in these chapters also applies to marketing communication in retailing. Some aspects of marketing communication decisions as they affect retailers are emphasised in this section.

21.5.4.2 *Objectives of the retailer's marketing communication programme*

The following marketing communication objectives are set by retailers:[42]

- To draw buyers to the store
- To build sales volume
- To enhance the image of the store
- To promote loyalty to the store
- To differentiate the store from others
- To ensure regular purchases
- To establish the reputation of the store

These objectives should be derived from the primary objective, they should be quantifiable and measurable and they should be valid for only a specific period.

21.5.4.3 *Marketing communication strategy*

In order to realise his objectives, the retailer uses a specific combination of elements in his marketing communication strategy, as depicted in Figure 21.3.

FIGURE 21.3   Marketing communication strategy

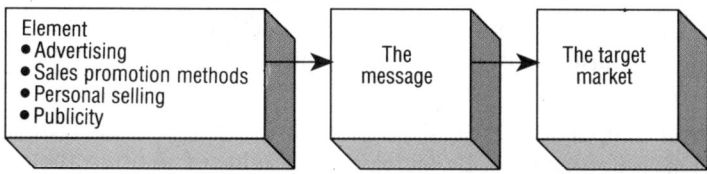

Research is done to determine what the composition of the four marketing communication elements should be in order for the retailer to reach his objectives. A marketing communication budget is then drawn up and funds are allocated to the various elements. The retailer spends what he can afford or uses the objective and task method to draw up his budget. The cost of the various marketing communication elements determines which elements can be used to carry out the task (such as persuading the consumer or creating a store image). A separate budget is drawn up for each of the marketing communication elements, as is indicated in figure 21.3.

ADVERTISING BUDGET PERCENTAGES

Pick 'n Pay

Outdoor advertising	1%
Television	8%
Radio	1%
Cinema	1%
Newspapers	89%

OK Bazaars

Television	15%
Radio	3%
Outdoor advertising	2%
Magazines	1%
Newspapers	79%

Source: *Marketing Mix*, April 1985, pp 21–23.

A small retailer with a limited marketing communication budget has to be creative to convey his marketing message at the lowest possible cost. Publicity can be used to good effect and relatively inexpensive sales-orientated methods can be used instead of expensive advertising campaigns. The excerpt from "Marketing Mix" shows the importance of sales-orientated methods (or below-the-line advertising), particularly for retail.

Slipping below the line . . . into a world of opportunity

Sales promotion techniques are being used more and more widely in diverse industries such as groceries, consumer durables, publishing, cosmetics, records, clothing and fast foods. Even among industrial companies it is making its presence felt.

Sales promotion campaigns are usually used as a response to short-term opportunities. This is unfortunate. By increasing the value of an offer, they provide an additional reason, over a tactical period of time, for buying the product. It should therefore fit into the overall strategy, and should contribute to business success.

Advertising is used to position a brand with continuity and consistency. Sales promotion can contribute strongly to this image building, but only when it is integrated with the strategy. If this is done it will have long-term benefits, no matter what its tactical duration. As in mass markets around the world, sales promotion here has grown to be one of the most important marketing tools. The South African market is an especially complex one, with a dire shortage of skilled manpower, tight margins, discerning customers, and a retail environment where the big chains are relentlessly increasing their dominance. More than ever, marketers need results from their budgets.

Sales promotion has boomed for the following reasons:

- With its range of techniques, it has proved its ability to achieve every major marketing objective.
- Campaigns can be tailored to suit the biggest or the smallest budgets.
- Sales promotion often have virtually immediate effect on sales.
- The value of the sales promotion as a communication medium has been recognised and exploited. Marketers are spending more than ever on advertising that promotes the promotion.
- The balance of power has shifted from the manufacturer to the retailer, and it is on his turf that the action is taking place.

The role of sales promotion is, in one way or another, to motivate the consumer. In this way the marketer can achieve a wide variety of goals: stimulating trial, encouraging repeat purchases (building brand loyalty), broadening purchases across the entire range, highlighting product features and benefits, increasing distribution, supporting new product launches . . . the list goes on and on. Marketers often miss the opportunity of capitalising on their efforts. All too often we see below-the-line campaigns that bear no resemblance to the advertising, so that the consumer is presented with two different identities for the same band.

It also happens that a company will spend thousands sponsoring a public event, yet will make no effort to carry this through to the point of sale, whereby converting into revenue all the publicity and goodwill generated. There are few marketing tools that can match sales promotion for cost effectiveness, versatility and potency.

Source: O'Hagan, B. Slipping below the line . . . into a world of opportunity. *Marketing Mix*, January 1985: 33-34. (Slightly adapted).

The article does not say so explicit, but sales promotion and personal selling are also interrelated. Sales personnel can be motivated to promote sales by a variety of incentive schemes, while the support of sales personnel is also necessary to coordinate sales promotion campaigns. In the following section some of the more commonly used sales promotion techniques are dealt with.

Panasonic advertises a competition in which the largest prize ever can be won — that of R8 000 000. Advertising appears in the press and on the radio and television (July 1992).

It is especially important for the retailer to ensure that the marketing communication messages conveyed by the marketing communication elements support and reinforce one another. Contradictory information will confuse the consumer and will be unconvincing. Poorly trained sales personnel in particular can convey a message that is conflicting with that conveyed by image-creating advertising.

21.5.4.4 *Personal sales in retailing*

Personal sales are frequently underestimated in retailing. Poorly trained and remunerated people are often used to make sales despite the fact that the power of persuasion lies in direct, face-to-face communication.

> Nothing happens in retailing before someone has sold something.

Personal sales are discussed in detail in Chapter 14. The principles propounded in that chapter also, with certain exceptions such as determining sales areas, applies to retailing.

Sales personnel in retailing should be recruited, selected and trained not only to carry out the task of sales (tidying shelves) and transactions but also to carry out the important task of marketing. The retailer should therefore manage his sales personnel well and would, in so doing, create a favourable corporate culture. Personnel would then be encouraged to render as good a service as possible. If a corporate culture is negative, the sales personnel will be disinterested and even rude in their dealings with customers. Good sales personnel in retailing are an indisputable competitive advantage.[43] Well-trained sales personnel who promote store loyalty in customers will:

- be enthusiastic in helping to draw customers to the store and will in this way help with prospecting
- take the trouble to become acquainted with the features and technical details of the products they are selling
- cultivate the ability to sum up customers correctly
- approach customers in the desired way (not in a too familiar or hearty manner)
- quickly determine customers' requirements
- be able to deal with complaints and solve problems diplomatically
- encourage customers to buy more than they intended
- deal with transactions efficiently
- take the trouble of allaying cognitive dissonance (which always occurs when someone spends a large sum of money)
- provide after-sales service as determined by the retailer's policy
- help other personnel to render a good service
- recognise regular customers and address them by name
- take an interest in the plans, successes and advertising campaigns of the retailer.

21.6 STRATEGIC MARKETING IN RETAILING

21.6.1 The nature of strategic marketing

This section is based on Chapter 19 in which strategic marketing has been discussed. Other aspects closely related to strategic marketing (which take place on top management level) are the **marketing concept** as the basic philosophy for all retailing activities and the **positioning** decisions of retailers in a competitive environment. The theoretical bases for these two topics are to be found in Chapters 1 and 4.

Strategic marketing takes place in large retail companies where a corporate organisational structure with several strategic business units (SBUs) has evolved. All the activities of the different SBUs must eventually contribute to achieving the primary objective of the parent company. Branches of a retail chain can be regarded as SBUs if they maintain a degree of independence. The parent company manages these SBUs as if they are products in a product mix. Some SBUs in advantageous circumstances are allowed to grow and to develop by means of investment funds allocated to them by the parent company. Other SBUs where little further growth is envisaged but which are still well supported receive less investment funds and must provide cash for more promising SBUs. Those which are no longer profitable can be eliminated. Branches in a retail chain can therefore be classified in a portfolio matrix in order to facilitate managerial decisions. Large and very successful retailers often have very complicated organisation structures and diversified interests as indicated by the example of PEPKOR.

In order to be considered an SBU, it must meet with the following requirements:

- An SBU has its own mission.
- It has a clearly definable set of competitors.
- It is able to plan independently from other SBUs.
- It can manage its own resources.
- It is large enough to justify top management's attention.
- It must be responsible for achieving its own profitability and other objectives.

The objectives of an SBU set performance standards and bench-marks against which they can be measured and evaluated in a given time period. In Figure 21.4 performance criteria and possible measures are indicated.

21.6.2 SWOT analysis

In strategic marketing planning in retailing SWOT analysis is of crucial importance. The whole strategy revolves round environmental changes.

Figure 21.5 contains typical questions in a SWOT analysis for a retailer.

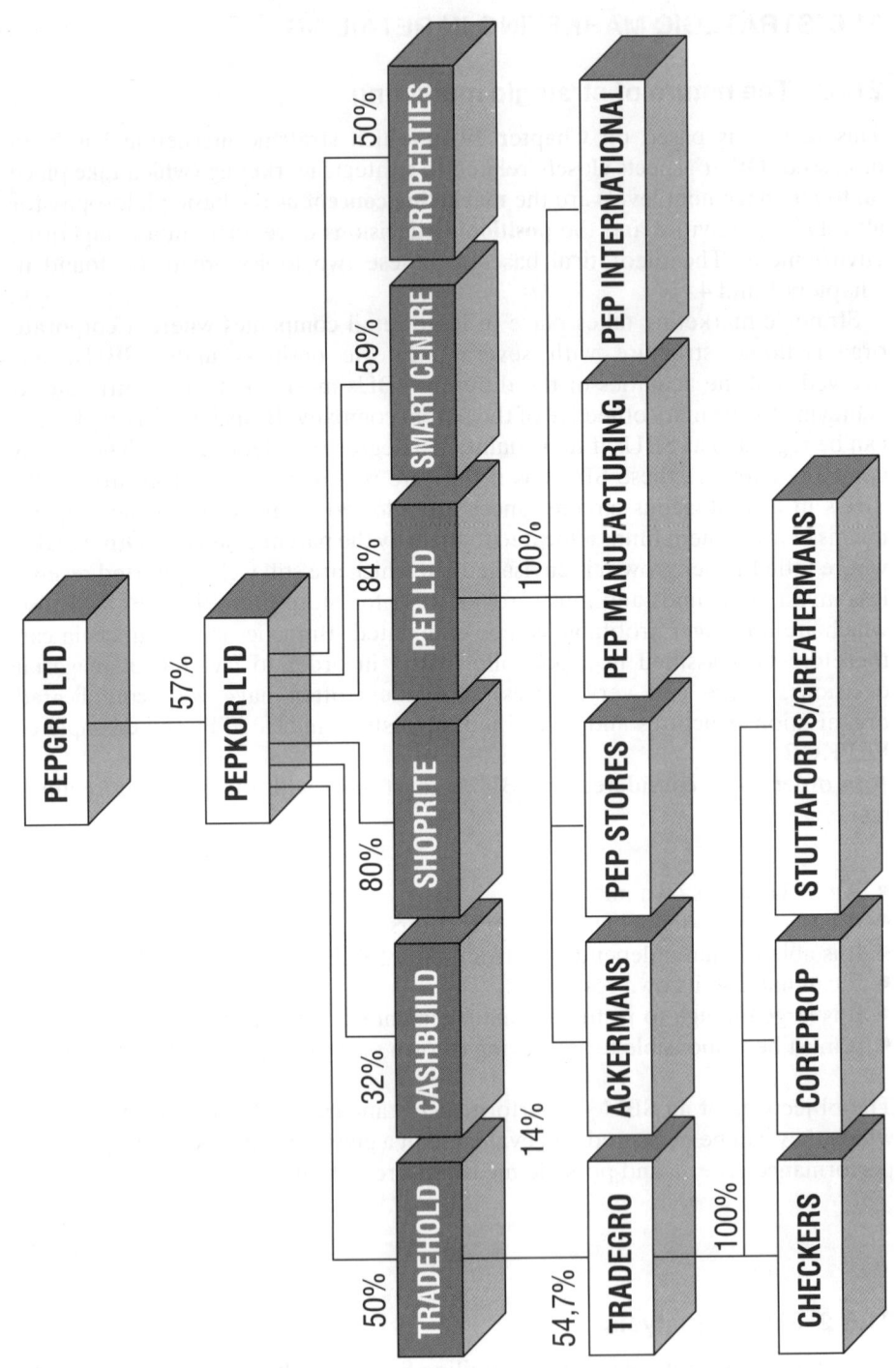

FIGURE 21.4   Performance criteria

PERFORMANCE CRITERIA	POSSIBLE MEASURES
• Growth	• R sales • Unit sales • Percent change in sales
• Competitive strength	• Market share • Brand loyalty
• Innovativeness	• R sales from new products • Percent cost savings from new processes
• Profitability	• R profits • Profit as percent of sales • Contribution margin • Return on investment (ROI)
• Utilisation of resources	• Sales per m² • Sales per salesman
• Contribution to customers	• Price relative to competitors • Product quality • Customer satisfaction
• Contribution to employees	• Wage rates, benefits

Source: Adapted from Boyd, H P and Walker Jr, O C. 1990. *Marketing management: A strategic approach.* Homewood: Irwin, p 52.

FIGURE 21.5   SWOT analysis

INTERNAL EVALUATION		EXTERNAL EVALUATION	
Strengths	Weaknesses	Opportunities	Threats
What is the current position?	What is the current position?	In which areas is success probable?	In which areas can weak performance be expected?
What are the unique strengths?	What are the retailer's problems?	Which are favourable environmental conditions?	Which unfavourable environmental conditions exist?
What are the retailer's resources and abilities?	What is the retailer unable to do? What are the main inadequacies?	How do the markets develop? Where are the gaps in the market?	What are competitors doing and what are the developments in competitive conditions?

Source: Adapted from Mason, J B and Mayer, M L. 1990. *Modern retailing: Theory and practice.* Homewood: Irwin, p 63.

Answers to the questions posed in Figure 21.5 indicate the position of the retailer. They can only be obtained by intensive marketing research, not only on strengths and weaknesses internally but also on those of competitors. Environmental scanning, consumer research, supplier investigations and market measurement and forecasting by using secondary sources of information as well as primary research are necessary before answers can be obtained.

21.6.3 Strategic marketing process

In Figure 21.6 the strategic marketing process is explained in the form of a model. This model should be read together with the planning implementation and control model in Chapter 19.

21.6.4 The business philosophy of the retailer

The philosophy that the implementation of all business activities should centre on the satisfaction of customer needs ensures the realisation of corporate objectives and the creation of a competitive advantage for the retailer.

The essence of this philosophy is included in the marketing concept which is discussed in Chapter 1. According to the marketing concept consumers will purchase and use only those products that provide need satisfaction. This simple but critical logic is the basis of business success.

It is especially the principle of social responsibility that has a long-term dimension. Its aim is to ensure the well-being of society in the long-term and not only to concentrate on the satisfaction of customers' current needs. Retailers often do not realise the importance of this principle of the marketing concept.

21.6.5 Positioning in retailing

A retailer segments the consumer market and directs his strategies at selected target markets. An exclusive fashion store identifies, for example, a very narrow target market consisting of well-to-do persons in the highest social classes: people who are able to choose and afford designer items. Other stores direct strategies at different segments. Edgars, for example, stocks imported designer infant clothing as well as more reasonably priced good quality local garments. The same holds for cosmetics. Ranges intended for the mass market as well as more specialised and expensive ranges are offered by retailers.

Positioning of the retailer against competitors is a strategic decision usually taken by top management. Positioning determines the reason for existence of the parent company and its SBUs. The retailer can decide to occupy a niche in the market — a niche where there is little or no direct competition or one where competitors are confronted directly, a decision that will undoubtedly cause a marketing war. These decisions can only be taken after careful consideration of the resources and skills of the retail company.

FIGURE 21.6 Strategic retail marketing

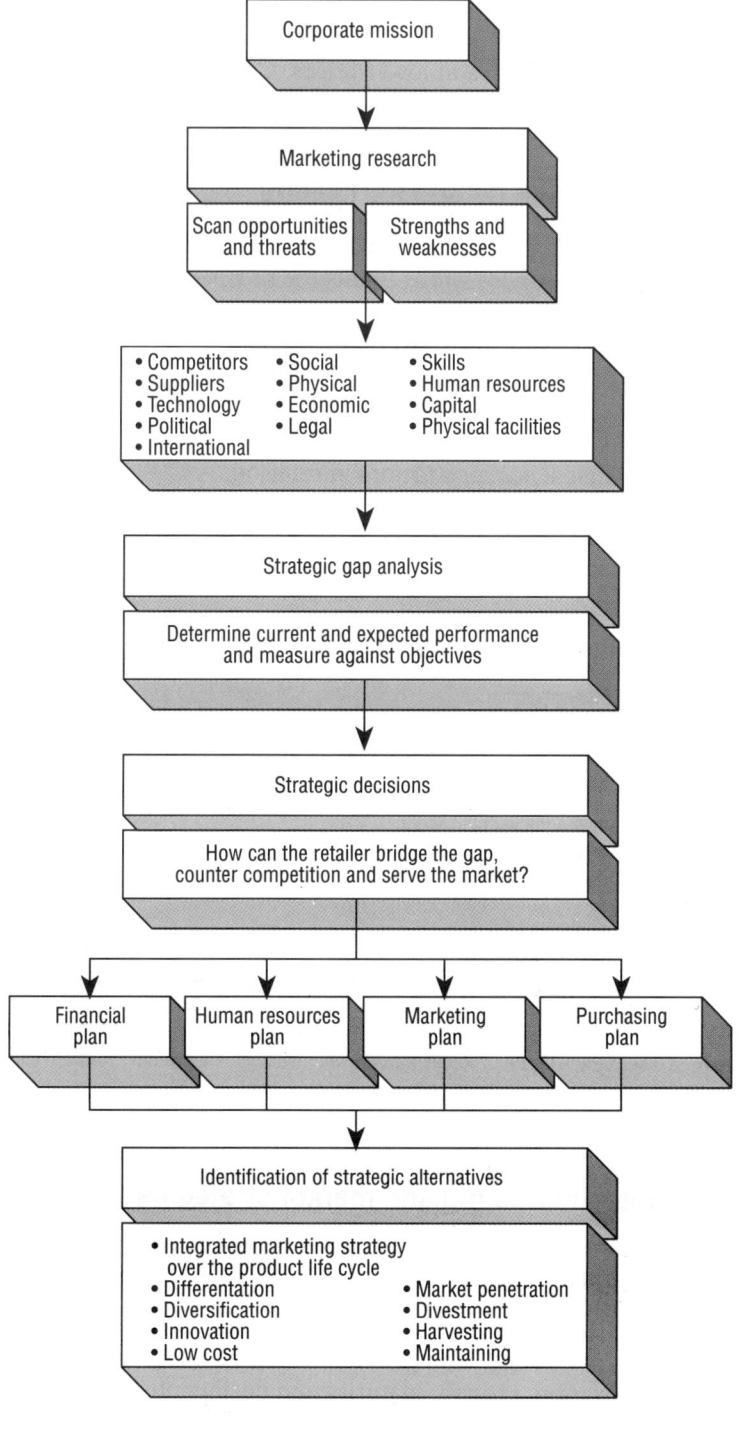

The positioning decision can be taken with the aid of a positioning map. The variables on this map can for example be a high-service level against a low-service level and a high pricing structure against a low pricing structure. A speciality store, for example, maintains a high service level and a high pricing structure while a discount store offers less service at lower prices. Other positioning variables are also possible and must be determined by the retail store.

21.6.6 Critical success factors in retailing

Figure 21.7 gives a list of strengths which are also regarded as the critical success factors. If the retailer has these strong points the prospects are good. The critical success factors also serve to differentiate the retail enterprise from competitors.

The critical success factors form part of the marketing and market strategies of a retailer, who must, in a competitive environment, struggle to survive and to grow.

FIGURE 21.7   Critical success factors in retailing

- Efficiency at low cost
- Customer service
- A long-term relationship with customers
- A long-term relationship with suppliers
- Goodwill towards the retail enterprise by the general public
- An ethical code of conduct and integrity
- Sufficient capital
- Control over sources of raw material (inventory sources)
- A good reputation and store image
- Customer loyalty
- Effective marketing communication
- A high turnover of inventory
- Innvoation
- Skilled purchasing
- A large market share
- Good sales staff
- Good management

Source: Adapted from Jain, S C. 1990. *Retail planning and strategy*. Cincinnati: South-Western, pp 199 and 204.

21.6.7 Integrated marketing and market strategies

21.6.7.1 *The retail life cycle*

The retail life cycle has four phases similar to the product life cycle (see Chapter 18). An integrated marketing strategy is implemented in each of the four phases. These are the innovation, growth, maturity and decline phases.

In the **innovation phase** the entrepreneur opens a store on what he perceives as a competitive advantage — usually it is pricing. In the **growth phase** there is competition from other similar stores. Geographic expansion takes place and branches are established. There is competition for available sites. Profits begin to decline. Intensive advertising campaigns are launched and point of purchase marketing communication intensifies. In the **maturity phase** profits decline even further especially if expansion has taken place too quickly, management is weak or a new type of competitor has appeared with a new kind of store, giving rise to warfare (see Chapter 18) between competitors. In the **decline phase** the retailer struggles to survive but does not always succeed.

An example of this is supermarkets which have entered the decline phase. It is of course possible for a store in the decline phase suddenly to revive and make a new beginning — but it is usually with a new strategy and in a new format.

In Figure 21.8 an example is given of enterprises in different phases of the retail life cycle.

FIGURE 21.8   The retail life cycle

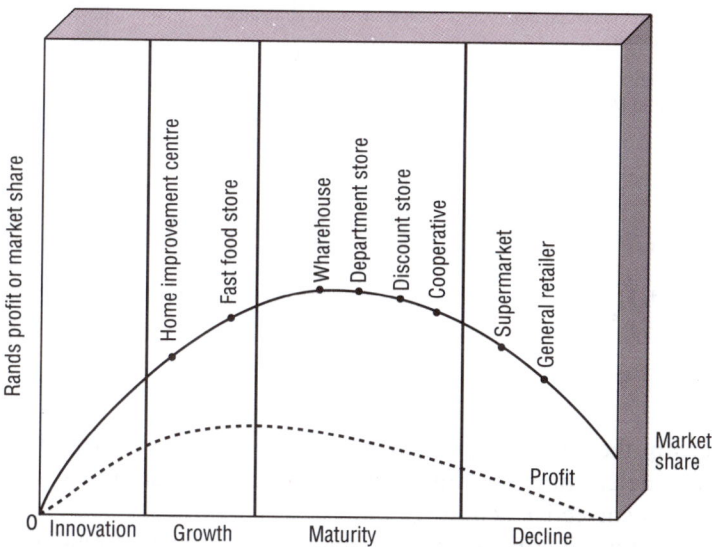

Source: Berkowitz, E N, Kevin, R A and Rudelius, W. 1989. *Marketing*. Homewood: Irwin, p 426.

21.6.7.2 *Competitive market strategies*

The competitive market strategies are discussed in Chapter 19. The retailer implements these strategies in competitive situations taking into account the store's unique strengths and weaknesses. The competitive market strategies are the following:

- Differentiation strategy
- Low-cost strategy
- Focus strategy

21.6.7.3 *Growth strategies*

These strategies are discussed in Chapter 19.

Figure 21.9 shows a summary of all the alternative growth strategies that can be considered by a retailer in situations where **new markets** must be entered with new or current products as well as the strategies to penetrate more deeply into **current markets** with new or current products.

FIGURE 21.9   Alternative growth strategies

	Current products	New products
Current markets	Market penetration strategies • Increase market share by improved marketing	Product development strategies • Extend product lines • Offer different or new product mixes • Innovation

New markets	Market development strategies
	
	• Geographic expansion into new areas
		Diversification strategies
		
		• Vertical integration
		  Forward integration
		  Backward integration
		  Horizontal integration
		• Diversification into unrealted businesses

Source: Adapted from Boyd, H P and Walker Jr, O C. 1990. *Marketing management: A strategic approach*. Homewood: Irwin, p 53.

21.6.8 Control

In retailing the steps in the control process are the same as those indicated in Chapter 19, namely determining performance standards, measuring actual performance and taking corrective action.

Control methods used in retailing are the strategic audit, efficiency analysis, budgets and observation. The last-mentioned method can be carried out by the retailer himself or by a so-called mystery shopper, an independent person observing the actions of sales staff during a sale. The "mystery shopper" then reports to the retailer.

In a **strategic audit** an independent researcher looks for answers to questions on seven different topics:

● The relationship between the strategy employed and environmental conditions
● Customer and competitor analysis
● The best strategy for the life cycle phase in which the store finds itself
● Internal variables with regard to the management and philosophy of the retailer
● Resources in terms of capital, manpower and inventory

- Risks involved in different strategy decisions
- Alternative plans if the strategy fails or if conditions change

In **efficiency analysis** relationships which can give an indication of the efficiency with which tasks are performed are determined.

In figure 21.4 a number of performance criteria used in efficiency analysis are mentioned. These relationships enable the retailer to make comparisons with historic figures or even with figures of other enterprises.

Budgets are generally used as instruments to plan and to control. Deviations from budget allocations can timeously be identified and corrected.

The control process supplies information for a new planning phase and the implementation of revised strategies.

21.7 CONCLUSION

This chapter indicates that strategic marketing is of utmost importance for large retail companies that must manage several branches and must make strategic long-term plans in a turbulent business environment.

Intensive competition and even warfare make survival difficult and growth problematic. Even so the retail enterprise must either grow or go into decline. Stagnation is invariably impossible in the long-term.

This chapter is complicated and has many interfaces with virtually all the other chapters in the book. To avoid repetition only the unique characteristics of retail marketing have been included. The student will be compelled to refer back to the basic theoretical principles in earlier chapters to form a comprehensive understanding of the fascinating field of retail marketing.

REFERENCES

1. Central Statistical Services. 1981. *Standard industrial classification of all economic activities (SIC)*. 3rd edition. Pretoria: Government Printer, p 77.
2. Kotler, P and Armstrong, G. 1990. *Marketing — An introduction*. Englewood Cliffs: Prentice Hall, pp 352–3.
3. Coetzee, J G. 1974. *The retail patterns of greater Johannesburg with particular reference to the maintenance of large-scale retailing*. Stellenbosch: Unpublished D Phil thesis, p 2.
4. Gray, C E A. 1980. *An investigation into methods of evaluating the performance of retail chain stores*. Cape Town: Unpublished MBA dissertation, p 9.
5. *Supermarket and Retailer*. April 1971, p 12.
6. *Supermarket and Retailer*. September 1980, p 20.
7. *Business Times*. 28 July 1985, p 5.
8. Lusch, R F and Dunne, P M. 1990. *Retail management*. Cincinatti: South-Western, pp 183–9.

9. Ferrel, O C and Hirt, G. 1989. *Business*. Boston: Houghton Mifflin, p 177.

10. Amer, P J. 1970. *Retail management*. London: International, pp 6–8.

11. Davidson, W R, Sweeney, D J and Stampfl, R W. 1988. *Retailing management*. 6th edition. New York: Wiley, p 21.

12. Strydom, J W. 1991. *Innovasie in die Suid-Afrikaanse groot voedselkleinhandel*. Pretoria: Unpublished D Com thesis, pp 38–50.

13. Davidson, et al op cit, p 20.

14. Strydom, op cit, pp 42–5.

15. *Business Day*. 6 June 1990, p 1.

16. *Supermarket and Retailer*. March/April 1990, pp 3–4.

17. Lusch, R F, Dunne, P M and Gable, M. 1990. *Retail management*. Cincinatti: South-Western, p 180.

18. Ibid.

19. Leibolt, M and Van Tonder, C J. 1985. Multiple-concept management — The challenge to retail conglomerates. *South African Journal of Business Management*. Vol 16 no 1, p 12.

20. Ibid.

21. Kotler, P and Armstrong, G. 1990. *Marketing: An introduction*. 2nd edition. Englewood Cliffs: Prentice Hall, p 126.

22. *Sunday Times*. 7 June 1992, p 6.

23. Cooke, T D. 1990. *Third World meets first world — How people power has changed the face of the economy of Southern Africa*. Unpublished paper. Conference on changes in socio-cultural structure and their implications for marketing, p 58.

24. Ibid.

25. Act 91 of 1981.

26. Marx, F W and Van Aswegen, P J (eds). 1983. *Die bedryfsekonomie: 'n Kort oorsig*. Pretoria: HAUM, p 39.

27. Cronjé, G J de J et al (eds). 1990. *Inleiding tot die bestuurswese*. 2nd edition. Johannesburg: Southern Book Publishers, pp 36–41.

28. Burstiner, I. 1986. *Basic retailing*. Homewood: Irwin, p 251.

29. Burstiner, op cit, p 259.

30. Burstiner, op cit, p 268.

31. Central Statistical Services. 1981. *Standard industrial classification of all economic activities (SIC)*. 3rd edition. Pretoria: Government Printer.

32. Welsch, J A & White, J F. 1986. *The enterpreneur's master planning guide. How to launch a successful business*. New York: Prentice Hall, pp 41–46.

33. Welsch and White, op cit, p 47.

34. Beisel, J L. 1987. *Contemporary retailing*. New York: MacMillan, p 313.

35. Pride, W M and Ferrel, O C. 1989. *Marketing: Concepts and strategies*. Boston: Houghton Mifflin, pp 130–1.

36. Bolen, W H. 1988. *Contemporary retailing*. 3rd edition. Englewood Cliffs: Prentice Hall, p 138

37. Morgenstein, M and Strongin, H. 1987. *Modern retailing: Management principles and practices*. New York: Wiley, p 300.

38. Ibid, p 301.

39. Davidson, et al op cit, p 451.
40. Beisel, op cit, p 442.
41. Burnett, J J. 1984. *Promotion management: A strategic approach*. St Paul ?, p 15.
42. Bustiner, op cit, p 534.
43. Roux, J. 1985. *Take your marketing medicine. Successful salesmanship*. Vol 19 no 8, August, p 16.
44. Jain, S C. 1990. *Retail planning and strategy*. Cincinnati: South-Western, p 17.

CASE STUDY

CONFLICT BETWEEN RETAILERS AND DEVELOPERS

Retailers and developers are constantly in conflict not only over rent but also over the requirements set by developers for window displays.

It is especially the smaller retailers with less negotiating power who are negatively affected and who tend to take up less space in shopping centres because of increasing rent.

Wholesalers and retailers contend that shopping complexes are developed even before it is really justified by demand. Most large retail groups are very conservative in taking investment decisions leading to an early death for shopping complexes, on the drawing board, if they are not regarded as viable opportunities.

There are complaints that the opinions of retailers are not taken into account before locational decisions are taken. Mitchells Plain's Westgate and Kagiso Malls are examples of this. Here taxi stands were built but never used.

The greatest complaint, however, is the exclusive shopping complexes being located in middle-class suburbs. Examples are N1 City in Goodwood, Cape Town, which is a luxury shopping complex in a middle-income area. N1 City must therefore draw its customers from higher-income areas such as Durbanville, which is already served by its own shopping centres, Tygervalley and The Link. The luxuriousness of many shopping complexes irritates retailers. The marble, the many escalators and fountains increase cost and accordingly the rent. If developers are more pragmatic there would be less risk for smaller retailers locating their stores in shopping complexes.

According to Mr Mike Lewin, group real estate manager of Edgars, fashion stores need to be located in a shopping complex. In this market references are made to the comparative shopper, who likes to compare clothes in several stores before buying. This person will prefer to shop at a shopping complex where there are many stores under one roof.

The larger fashion stores are also increasing their floor space in shopping complexes and Edgars has had success in locating product corners such as for On Track sporting equipment, perfume, curtaining and bed linen.

The larger chains wish to increase their customer base by opening new stores but often the new store will only succeed in cannibalising customers from nearby stores. Edgars is therefore very careful in locating a second store near an existing one.

The customer in the A-income group does not really want to come into contact with D-income group people and therefore the mix of stores in a shopping complex must be carefully planned by the developer.

A successful solution to this problem has been achieved in Golden Walk in Germiston where luxury stores are located in the western side of the shopping complex and stores for the lower-income groups on the eastern side near the station entrance.

Smaller retail groups tend not to prefer trading in shopping areas because of requirements set by developers and the high rental. If they locate in shopping complexes they reduce floor space and fewer products can then be properly displayed. This is directly reflected in the lower rate of return, according to Mr Dawie Scholtz, the real estate and development manager of Pep Stores.

Even if developers prefer a turnover clause for rent the smaller stores are still reluctant. It is said that the developer is eager to share in good times with the turnover clause for rent in the rental contract but when the situation worsens he still insists on his basic rent.

Stores for the lower-income groups have even more problems with the developers of luxury complexes. Dealers are for example expected to conform to window display standards, not to play loud music and not to approach prospective customers outside their stores.

Mr Ferdi Lamprecht, director of development of Lewis Stores, said that smaller retail groups are not allowed to advertise their names on the outside of the shopping complex either.

The developers show a lack of insight in customer characteristics. A typical example is the higher-class Westgate in Mitchells Plain, which is located in a lower-income group area.

Pep Stores is located in smaller shopping centres where rental is lower, according to Mr Scholtz. The most popular design is the horseshoe-type, which facilitates entry.

All the retail groups use market research to make projections of intended investment in shopping complexes. The results are not always very accurate and experienced investment managers rely on intuition and guesswork based on experience and often succeed in hitting the nail on the head.

Source: Johan Coetzee, *Finansies & Tegniek,* 8 May 1992.

QUESTIONS

1. Are developers responsible for marketing a shopping complex properly? Give your opinion.

2. What is meant by a comparative shopper?

3. 'If a shopping complex in a high-income area attracts many shoppers from lower-income areas the image of the shopping complex will suffer.' Discuss this statement critically.

4. What is in your view an ideal mix of stores in a shopping complex? Give reasons for your answer.

INDEX

WORLD CLASS! STRATEGIES FOR WINNING WITH YOUR CUSTOMER
by Tony Manning

As South Africa re-enters the mainstream of world business, local businessmen face an unprecedented stream of new threats and opportunities. Whether they choose to export or trade in this market, they'll be up against aggressive world-class competitors. To survive and thrive in the '90s they'll have to radically rethink and reshape their strategies and rebuild their business systems. This book is a 'must-read' for this new age of competition. It's the only South African book with a global focus, and the only one that addresses the all-important issue of customer satisfaction.

THE RACE TO LEARN
by Tony Manning

The only way to get ahead and stay there in the race for customers is by changing and improving faster than your competitors. In this book guidelines are given as to how successful organisations continually reinvent themselves by learning at incredible speed what works and what doesn't. It packs a huge amount of business wisdom into a pocket-sized package. All the latest theories are here, in a down-to-earth way that lets you turn them into action ... FAST.

ACCOUNTING FOR MANAGERS
by E Uliana & D Marcus

Accounting is littered with jargon. This book aims to explain the terminology and main principles of financial and management accounting to non-accountants. The book is not intended to be an exhaustive reference to all aspects of financial and management accounting, but is designed to promote an understanding of the key principles and to serve as a foundation to further study of the aspects discussed.

CORPORATE REPORTING
by Geoff Everingham

Disclosure requirements for South African companies have multiplied in recent years, mainly due to the increasing pace at which statements of generally accepted accounting practice have been issued. This work summarises these various requirements in a usable fashion. The book includes specimen financial statements for public and private companies and close corporations, and a checklist of discloseable items.

GENERALLY ACCEPTED ACCOUNTING PRACTICE - A SOUTH AFRICAN VIEWPOINT
by Geoff Everingham & Brian Hopkins

A loose-leaf publication indispensable to anyone involved in the preparation or analysis of financial statements. Existing statements and exposure drafts are carefully analysed and alternative approaches to problems are evaluated. Where appropriate, reference is made to accepted practices in other parts of the world. The manual is regularly updated by means of revision services incorporating new statements and exposure drafts.

MANAGEMENT

ON THE EDGE - HOW SOUTH AFRICAN COMPANIES COPE WITH CHANGE
by Piet Human & Frank Horwitz

Change is a prerequisite for survival. South African companies face an uncertain future and many managers feel themselves to be precariously balanced at the edge of a dark, yawning abyss. They are aware that the comfortable habits of the past, if persisted in, will destroy them in a rapidly changing business environment. Through a detailed study of of the views and attitudes of some six hundred managers, the authors of this book have developed a unique model of the South African company coping successfully with change.

MANAGEMENT PRINCIPLES - A CONTEMPORARY SOUTH AFRICAN EDITION
by P J Smit & G J de J Cronjé

This book was written with the objective of contributing towards much needed management education in South Africa. It is a book which, like many foreign texts on general management principles, deals with the things managers do, or should do, to improve the performance of their companies and, ultimately, to create wealth. Unlike the foreign texts, it was written by a team of South African academics who know the realities of South Africa and the educational needs of the South and southern African student. The discussion of concepts and principles is richly illustrated with examples from the South African environment.

LEADERSHIP - THE HUMAN RACE
by Guy Charlton

The successful organisation has one attribute that sets it apart from that which is unsuccessful; dynamic and effective leadership. This incisive work deals with the development of leadership. It highlights methods for the identification of specific competencies and provides a tried and tested model of strategic leadership development.

THE MARKETING DECISION-MAKER
by Leyland F Pitt & Derek Bromfield

The organisation, management, and control of information is a prerequisite for business success. These processes are fundamental to marketing. Effective marketers and customer-oriented organisations require not only information, but information that is timely, organised, useful, and in a form that can be understood and manipulated so that decisions can be made. Information technology has revolutionised the handling of information. This book focuses on the harnessing of technological developments to enable marketers to gather, and use, information to retain competitive superiority.

SOUTH AFRICAN MARKETING - CASES FOR DECISION-MAKERS
by Leyland F Pitt, Derek Bromfield & Deon Nel
This casebook utilises the experiences of well-known but diverse South African companies. Emphasis is placed on areas where there is a need for learning and tremendous opportunities for debate are offered. The work is enhanced by the availability of detailed teaching aids containing overhead transparencies, audio-visual material containing interviews with the managers concerned, company visual material or tapes of radio advertisements. Spreadsheets are supplied to enable PC analysis, and additional role plays, games and exercises ensure that this title is the most detailed marketing casebook yet to be published in South Africa.

EDUCATING & DEVELOPING MANAGERS FOR A CHANGING SOUTH AFRICA
edited by Linda Human
At a time when the development of managers for all sectors of the South African economy has become a crucial issue, many organisations and individuals are dissatisfied with their progress. This book provides an understanding of why our thinking in relation to management education and development has to change. It questions, and often rejects, traditional values, attitudes and practices relating to the development of people and puts forward exciting, new ideas.

AFFIRMATIVE ACTION IN A DEMOCRATIC SOUTH AFRICA
edited by Charl Adams
South Africa has been a late starter in the modern world of technological and human resource development, due in no small measure to past political paradigms and the discriminatory practices that flowed from these. This book is intended to help businessmen and women correct the imbalances and disparities that have become germane to South African businesses. In it past procedures are challenged and questioned, outdated modes of thinking are rejected and, most importantly, suggestions are made on how to democratise the workplace so that all may prosper.

SOUTH AFRICA: PROSPECTS FOR SUCCESSFUL TRANSITION
edited by Bob Tucker & Bruce R Scott
South Africa's prospects for a successful transition to democracy are analysed in this, the printed version of the Nedcor/Old Mutual scenarios. This work summarises the findings and conclusions of a diverse team of twenty-three people who worked together over a six-month period to analyse South Africa's past and present and to consider its alternative paths into the future.